ART PAST ART PRESENT

ART PAST ART PRESENT

DAVID G. WILKINS
BERNARD SCHULTZ

HARRY N. ABRAMS, INC., PUBLISHERS, NEW YORK

For our Students

Project Director: SHEILA FRANKLIN LIEBER
Editor: JOANNE GREENSPUN
Art Direction: DIRK LUYKX
Designers: LYDIA GERSHEY, YONAH SCHURINK
Photo Research: BARBARA LYONS, JENNIFER BRIGHT

Library of Congress Cataloging-in-Publication Data

Wilkins, David G.
       Art past/art present / David G. Wilkins, Bernard Schultz.
              p.   cm.
       Bibliography: p.
       Includes index.
       ISBN 0–8109–1749–1
       1. Art—History. I. Schultz, Bernard, 1948–   II. Title.
N5300. W64 1990
709—dc20   89-35747
                                                   CIP

Text copyright © 1990 Prentice-Hall, Inc.
Illustrations copyright © 1990 Harry N. Abrams, Inc.

Published in 1990 by Harry N. Abrams, Incorporated, New York
All rights reserved. No part of the contents of this book may be
reproduced without the written permission of the publisher

A Times Mirror Company

Printed and bound in Japan

Pages 12–13:   Louise Nevelson. *Sky Cathedral* (detail of fig. 548)
Pages 260–61: Elevation of St. Peter's (detail of fig. 294)
Pages 304–5:   Rembrandt. *A Man Rowing a Boat on the Bullewyk*
                        (detail of fig. 353)
Page 348:   Johann Balthasar Neumann. Kaisersaal, Episcopal
                        Palace (detail of fig. 383)
Pages 366–67: John A. Roebling. Brooklyn Bridge (detail of
                        fig. 428)
Pages 432–33: Jackson Pollock (detail of fig. 539)

CONTENTS

PREFACE AND ACKNOWLEDGMENTS

We have written this book especially for the person with a general interest in understanding art and art history, and for the one-semester introductory course in art history or art appreciation. Our goal has been to present a clear, concise treatment of a limited number of artistic monuments. We have chosen to emphasize the historical and cultural context which helps explain these works by placing them within a strict chronological framework. In thumbing through the book, you will note that the bold dates in the upper corner of the right-hand pages form a chronological sequence. This organization allows us to present the developments of art as they happened.

In condensing the history of art into a limited space, we have had to omit many interesting works of art; this is especially true both for the twentieth century, where some significant movements are represented by a single work, and for non-Western and non-traditional developments, which are represented by only a few monuments. At the same time, however, we have given the individual works selected a more complete treatment than is found in many survey books. Clear information about the techniques and processes of art is included because this can be crucial for understanding the work of art. We have quoted contemporary documents and comment when appropriate, believing that the words of those who lived when the art was created have a particular force and authority.

In the text that follows there are several kinds of distinct units. A section introducing art opens the text; it discusses general concepts and defines some of the terms important for understanding the material in the rest of the book. A chronological development follows, which includes introductions to major styles and periods (e.g., Egyptian, Roman Imperial, eighteenth century) and double-page units discussing works of that style or period (e.g., the pyramids, the Pantheon, eighteenth-century portraiture). Sections within the introductions discuss the status and role of the artist in each culture or period. Approximately one hundred and fifty double-page units form the basis of our text; each focuses on a key work or works and is complete in itself. Interspersed with these are boxed units on technical and other important issues (e.g., post-and-lintel construction, etching). The units on technique are positioned within the chronological sequence at the point when a new development had an impact on the evolution of art. Our dating of works of art may sometimes seem unorthodox, but we have tried to reflect new discoveries and most recent scholarship. The captions for the illustrations often include significant historical and factual information, and are best read in tandem with the main text. The maps which precede many of the sections include place names relevant to that particular section.

A word is necessary about titles, for only in the relatively recent days of inventories, reproductions, art books, and museums has it been considered necessary to give each work of art a specific, short title for identification purposes. A Renaissance artist, asked for the "title" of his or her work, would most likely have replied not with a brief phrase, but with a discussion of the meaning of the specific interpretation of the subject represented. If asked to "identify" fig. 295, it is unlikely that Michelangelo would have replied, "The Creation of Adam." Where works are known by later, popular titles which can be misleading, such as the "Great Sphinx," the "Mona Lisa," and "The Night Watch," these titles are given in quotation marks.

The Glossary lists and defines terms and gives references to illustrations or passages in the text where the term is further explained and/or illustrated in a diagram or work of art. Seeing terms within their historical context and in relation to illustrations clarifies their meaning.

A text of this breadth requires the generous efforts and insights of many people, especially colleagues at the University of Pittsburgh and West Virginia University who willingly shared their expertise: Robert Anderson, Kahren Arbitman, William Arnett, Vange Beldecos, Urban Couch, Ann Sutherland Harris, Fil Hearn, Margaret Rajam, Patricia Rice, Matthew Roper, John Super, Thomas Tavella C.S.P., Frank Toker, H. Anne Weis, John Whitty, and John Williams all lent their authoritative understanding to different parts of the text. Graduate students at the University of Pittsburgh who offered good advice were Mark Brown and Roger Crum. Belinda Brooks, Carol Naatz, Michael Porcaro, and Lorena Sehgal gave perceptive analyses from a student's perspective, while reviewers for Prentice-Hall, Inc., and Harry N. Abrams, Inc., offered many helpful suggestions.

We extend a particular recognition in our gratitude to our colleague and friend, Katheryn M. Linduff, Associate Dean for Academic Affairs and Professor of Fine Arts and Anthropology at the University of Pittsburgh, who authored the sections on Chinese, Japanese, African, Mesoamerican, American Indian, Islamic, and Indian art for this book. As we reviewed many introductory art-history texts, it became apparent that the rich artistic traditions of cultures and civilizations outside Western developments were too often given a merely descriptive treatment. Kathy has contributed substance and understanding for the reader, while adding immeasurably to our knowledge. She has been a generous partner to many aspects of our efforts.

We were fortunate that our families embraced this project with personal and professional support. Ann Thomas Wilkins added to our understanding of classical civilizations, and Rebecca Wilkins read and critiqued the manuscript at several stages. Mary Louise Soldo Schultz "field tested" the manuscript with her students and advanced discerning editorial comments.

We owe a special debt of gratitude to the personnel at Prentice-Hall, Inc., and Harry N. Abrams, Inc. Norwell "Bud" Therien, Jr., at Prentice-Hall supported this text from its inception, and his continuing encouragement and judicious counsel eased our task. At Harry N. Abrams we were encouraged and inspired by the professional assistance shared with us by Sheila Franklin Lieber, Joanne Greenspun, Dirk Luykx, Lydia Gershey, Yonah Schurink, Barbara Lyons, and Jennifer Bright. Some of the new drawings, made to our specifications, were created by Marlene Boyle.

David G. Wilkins
Bernard Schultz
July 1989

World Map

I

INTRODUCTION

Experiencing Art

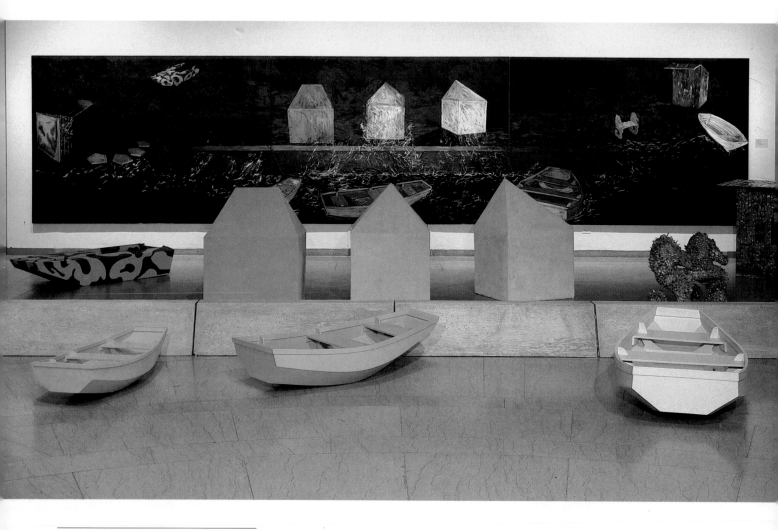

1. JENNIFER BARTLETT
Sea Wall. 1985. Mixed-media installation, as seen at the Brooklyn Museum

In creating *Sea Wall* (fig. 1), Jennifer Bartlett has fashioned an arrangement that includes brilliantly colored boats, a concrete-and-shell bench with supports shaped like sea horses, brightly painted three-dimensional objects that resemble cabanas or beach houses, and an expansive, panoramic painting. This is a mixed-media work, composed of a variety of different materials encompassing painting, sculpture, and sculptural forms that suggest architecture. The objects have been positioned on the museum walls and floor so that our attention is drawn as much to the composition of the ensemble as to any individual part. The installation was especially arranged by the artist for this location. The warm, luminous colors of the three-dimensional objects attract our attention, and a sense of intrigue develops as we begin to perceive the complex ways in which these objects interrelate with each other and with the painting behind.

The large painting, composed of three horizontal sections, depicts an evocative nocturnal setting with a sea wall and beach. Three row-boats, attached by lines to the sea wall, seem to ride the surging waves; water splashing over the wall reinforces our perception of the sea's rhythmic motion. In the painting, a concrete sea-horse bench, other boats, and beach houses are positioned like solitary sentinels on the sand.

As we study the painted scene, the artist draws us into an illusion. The objects represented suggest real objects within actual space. It is easy to be drawn into this imaginary and expressive world, despite the fact that her interpretation of the scene is not detailed. In fact, Bartlett's painting has an energy and life that a more photographic view could not have. Although the beach is empty, the scene seems animated. This effect is produced by the manner in which the artist has handled the paint, using loose, free movements of the brush to apply bold, thick lines and patches of color. Such a lively application of paint blurs the edges of objects, contributing to a dense yet vigorous atmospheric effect. Near the bottom of the painting, the brushstrokes create passages that evoke the rhythmic surge and sound of the water lapping on the sea wall and boats.

In contrast to the illusion of objects in space offered by the painting, Bartlett's three-dimensional objects share the real space in which we move and live. Although they exist outside the painted scene, these objects are openly identified with the painting. The colors of these objects, which in form are similar to the boats, beach houses, sea wall, and bench, are the same as those which distinguish the related objects in the painting. And in this particular installation, the artist has created a spatial arrangement that approximates the position and relationships she gave them within the illusory space of the painting.

By inviting us to explore and discover the relationships between these sculptural forms and their counterparts in the painting behind,

Bartlett poses a series of visual and intellectual questions. Within the context of the painting, the representations of boats and other objects have a certain integrity; we can easily understand the scene. The sculptural forms affect us in quite another way, for they are unconvincing as boats and beach houses: reduced in size, they lose reference to practical function, and even the sea wall seems diminished. The bright, even colors applied to the simplified forms encourage us to appreciate the forms not as common objects in our real world, but as abstract sculpture. As a result, Bartlett leads us to consider the nature of our perception and the issue of how we recognize "everyday" objects in our environment. What are the visual clues, for example, that lead us to recognize an object as a boat or a beach house?

Other, more complex observations begin to draw our attention. The colors of the beach houses in the painting are not quite the same as those on the sculptural forms. The variations of color in the beach houses in the painting and the dramatic activity of the brush enliven their surfaces. The forms in the painting seem more "alive," less static, than do the objects on the museum floor. The camouflage boat most closely matches a sculptural form to the painted image, yet it too is distinct: this type of camouflage works within the illusionistic painting but not on the museum floor.

Bartlett's use of different media to create a complex ensemble is not a modern invention. In the past, an artist or group of artists have often joined elements of varied media to create a single composition. *Sea Wall* emphasizes the visual properties of the work of art, setting Bartlett's installation work within our recent, modern experience of art. Also modern is the manner in which Bartlett's work can evoke a personal reaction based on the experiences of the viewer. She encourages each of us to react to this tableau as an individual with a storehouse of memories.

In this installation work, Bartlett's transformation of objects from the illusory space of the painting to three-dimensional, abstract sculptural forms challenges not only our perception of our environment, but our conception of art. In many ways, the objects in the painting seem more real and comfortable than do the abstract representations of the beach houses and boats which exist in our own real space. We begin to question the differences between illusion and reality and to contemplate the relationships that can be postulated between art and the world.

Jennifer Bartlett's *Sea Wall* installation is an intriguingly intricate work of art. The specific questions that *Sea Wall* poses express the interaction and communication which we can share with art. One way to open this communication is to ask general questions that can help lead us to an understanding of each work of art as a unique visual expression and as an historical experience. The following list of questions is not meant to be comprehensive, and not all questions will apply to every work of art. The terms used are part of a specialized vocabulary that is useful in sharing ideas and information concerning works of art.

Questions to ask about a work of art:

Does it communicate certain emotions and feelings? What is its expressive content?

Does it belong to a clearly recognizable artistic tradition? Is it related to a particular historical style?

Who was the artist (or artists), and did the artist's individual personality play a role in the creation of the work? Does the work demonstrate individual style?

What can a visual examination and analysis of the work tell us? How can a formal analysis be useful?

How are the various visual elements of the work arranged? What is its composition?

What materials is it made of? What is the medium?

How have the artist or artists used these materials? What techniques were employed to make the work?

Did someone ask the artist or artists to create the work and did they also pay for it? Who were the patrons?

Why was it made? What purpose did it fulfill? What was its function when it was first created?

Was it created for a specific location, and did the artist adjust the composition for that location? Has the artist used collocation?

What is its subject matter? What does it represent? What is its iconography and iconology?

What can it tell us about the ideas, beliefs, or attitudes current in the period when it was created? What is its historical significance and its historical context?

VIEWING ART

2. *King Menkure and His Queen.* c. 2470 B.C. Schist, height 56". Museum of Fine Arts, Boston. Found at Menkure's temple complex, next to his pyramid at Giza (figs. 40, 41).

Art's communicative value, which at first may seem foreign and difficult, demands an understanding of a work's visual and expressive qualities and of its relationship to its historical period. The task of art history is to ease and advance our understanding of the communication between works of art from past cultures and ourselves.

To give order to the art that has been created in the past, as well as that being created now, the modern study of art history has developed a system of classification which relies on the concept of style. Our word style is derived from the Latin *stylus*. Originally the word referred to a writing instrument, but in time the meaning changed to include the manner, or art, of writing. Each of us writes differently, and our style of writing has a personal quality related both to our individual training and to the context of our education and experience, that is, the historical period in which we live. Documents from past centuries easily demonstrate how writing styles have changed over time. Historical style describes how the visual appearance of a work of art is tied to the period during which the work was created. Works of art from the same historical period and culture often share similar visual characteristics. In art history, specific historical periods and cultures are examined within a chronology, and we view the evolution of the history of art as a succession of period styles. Thus, for example, we speak of Egyptian style and Baroque style.

Style, however, can also have a more intimate meaning, referring to the particular manner of expression used by an individual artist. This style can change as the artist's personality matures and develops. Relationships may also be discerned between the personal style of an artist and the period style of the time in which he or she lived.

Our discussion of how to approach a work of art, how to become receptive to its communication, opens with a consideration of the styles of two sculptures (figs. 2, 3). *King Menkure and His Queen* was carved in ancient Egypt about 4500 years ago; Bernini's *Apollo and Daphne* was created in Italy less than 400 years ago. The sculpture of King Menkure and his queen proclaims both stability and rigidity; the poses of the Egyptian pharaoh and his queen are confined within a rectangular composition, and there is no suggestion of movement. There is a slight hint of portraiture in their faces, but their bodies are idealized, abstracted to conform to a standard of perfection, dictated in this case by Egyptian cultural preferences. Bernini's sculpture of the mythological story of Apollo and Daphne is dramatic and dynamic. The figures express a transient moment, forever caught in time. The Baroque sculpture is also naturalistic, for the figures, drapery, landscape, and tree segments all reproduce the appearance of these forms in nature. (The term realism, which is sometimes confused with naturalism, refers to subject matter drawn from actual life.)

These values of stability and dramatic movement characterize the stylistic differences between ancient Egyptian and Baroque art. They find expression in other media from these historical periods. Egyptian painting and architecture stress an enduring permanence. Baroque painting and architecture emphasize visual, dynamic flux.

The study of style assists us in classifying a work of art within the visual traits of a particular historical period. Formal analysis examines how the integral parts of a work of art are united to produce its historical and individual style. Our interpretation of *Menkure and His Queen* as both stable and rigid is based on a number of particular observations. The axis, an imaginary center line passing through each figure, conforms to a vertical line. The vertical or horizontal components are visually stable and appear to be balanced and in equilibrium. The vertical axes, then, combine with the rectangular composition to communicate a contained, balanced stability. The vertical axis also contributes to the stiff posture of the figures, producing a rigidity reinforced by the compact outlines of the sculpture, which is a monolithic, rectangular solid.

Bernini's sculpture is composed primarily on a strong diagonal axis. Diagonal components, which break the equilibrium of the vertical and horizontal, communicate movement. If *Menkure and His Queen* appears closed and self-contained in space, *Apollo and Daphne* seems open and expansive. This openness is due to the extension of the figures' limbs and drapery out into the immediate space; here the surrounding space is energized by the sculptural form.

Formal analysis reveals how these sculptures attain different visual expressions, and why each makes a distinct impact on us. These different expressions are also related to the materials (media) and techniques employed in each work. *King Menkure and His Queen* and Bernini's *Apollo and Daphne* are both executed in the bold medium of stone, but Bernini's work is made of Italian marble, which is soft and rather easily carved, while the Egyptian work, carved by an anonymous artist or workshop of artists, is made of schist, a dense, hard, and brittle stone.

The examination of subject matter is expressed on two levels: the subject matter must be identified and its meaning must be assessed with regard to the work's historical context. The term iconography (from the Greek *eikon,* image, and *graphein,* to describe or to write) is used to designate the art-historical study of the specific subject matter of the work of art, while iconology (Greek for image discourse) interprets the meaning of the subject matter as it can be understood within the historical period and culture that produced it.

Menkure and his queen ruled in ancient Egypt, and the iconography of the sculpture is their representation as royal personages. Although the figures of Apollo and Daphne greet us with a greater naturalism, they are actually legendary figures from Greek mythology. Apollo, the god, desires the lovely Daphne, daughter of a river-god. He chases her but when he catches her, Daphne, who has prayed to be delivered from Apollo's unwanted advances, is magically transformed into a laurel tree. In Bernini's sculpture, Daphne's left side metamorphizes into a trunk, while her fingers and hair become branches and leaves. The expression Bernini puts on Apollo's face is complex: it is a mixture of joy, at the attainment of his goal, and wonder, as the hand with which he reaches to embrace Daphne touches not flesh but bark.

The theme of Bernini's sculpture is drawn from a specific literary source from ancient Rome, Ovid's *Metamorphoses* (I, 545–59), written in the early first century A.D.:

> So ran the god and [Daphne], one swift in hope,
> The other in terror, but he ran more swiftly,
> Borne on the wings of love, gave her no rest,
> Shadowed her shoulder, breathed on her streaming hair.
> Her strength was gone, worn out by the long effort
> Of the long flight; she was deathly pale, and seeing
> The river of her father, cried, "O help me,
> If there is any power in the rivers,
> Change and destroy the body which has given
> Too much delight!" And hardly had she finished,
> When her limbs grew numb and heavy, her soft breasts
> Were closed with delicate bark, her hair was leaves,
> Her arms were branches, and her speedy feet
> Rooted and held, and her head became a tree top,
> Everything gone except her grace, her shining.

As we investigate the iconology of our sculptures, we more fully enter the realm of historical significance and historical context, for religious, political, social, economic, scientific, and philosophical

3. GIANLORENZO BERNINI
Apollo and Daphne. 1622–25. Marble, height 96". Borghese Gallery, Rome

values can all come to bear on the interpretation of a work's meaning and function. *Menkure and His Queen* is one of several sculptures intended to provide a home for the souls of the pharaoh and his queen throughout eternity (see pp. 49–53); this is its function. Its original location was within a funerary precinct, close to the pharaoh's tomb. The stable, rigid form of the sculpture conveys its expressive content, a majestic presence. More importantly, the form also affords protection from breakage over time, thus safeguarding the home of the soul in the afterlife. This enduring strength is reinforced by the use of schist as a medium. Bernini's sculpture communicates both general and particular aspects of Italian Baroque culture: it demonstrates the predilection for classical antiquity which existed in seventeenth-century Italy and, as Ovid was a popular source for learning Latin, the tale of Apollo and Daphne would have been known to all educated persons. *Apollo and Daphne* served to delight visitors and display the intellectual and artistic taste of its patron, Cardinal Scipione Borghese, an important member of the Roman aristocracy and an official of the hierarchy of the Catholic church. Discerning style, formal analysis, iconography, iconology, function, and historical context are ways in which we begin to understand the meaning of a work of art. Works of art are far from being mute, but to hear them speak, we must be open to the expression and content of their language.

ANALYZING PAINTING

4. PIETRO PERUGINO
Christ Giving the Keys to St. Peter. 1482.
Fresco, 11 x 18'. Sistine Chapel,
Vatican, Rome

5. PIET MONDRIAN
*Diamond Painting in Red, Yellow, and
Blue*. 1921–25. Oil on canvas on fiber-
board, 56 1/4 x 56". National Gallery
of Art, Washington, D.C. (Gift of
Herbert and Nannette Rothschild,
1971)

In Perugino's *Christ Giving the Keys to St. Peter* (fig. 4), we recognize figures, landscape, and architecture from the real world. Perugino's painting is illusionistic, for the objects represented seem to be tangible and weighty and appear to exist within actual space. Mondrian's painting (fig. 5) does not have forms that resemble those in the visual world. It is non-objective or non-representational.

Traditionally, a painting can be defined as a planar, two-dimensional surface to which liquid colors have been applied. Flatness, the most distinctive attribute of paintings, is a useful starting point in their analysis. The flat surface is known as the picture plane, and in Mondrian's painting the colors and shapes are two-dimensional and they reinforce the flatness of this plane. In illusionistic paintings, like Perugino's, the picture plane seems transparent, like a large window.

Both paintings are made up of forms. Mondrian's are limited to black lines and squares or rectangles of a single color. Perugino's forms are naturalistic objects: figures, trees, a public square, and a building. In both paintings forms are organized into a composition. Perugino's composition is arranged to emphasize the figures of Christ and St. Peter in the middle. A row of apostles to either side frames them, and the Renaissance structure in the background helps draw attention to them. The receding lines of the square converge at a central point. Perugino's composition is balanced, symmetrical, and centralized. The composition of Mondrian's painting is neither centralized nor symmetrical, but it is balanced. Although Mondrian's square format is placed diagonally, his black lines are horizontal and vertical, and they meet the edges of the painting at forty-five-degree angles. We are drawn to the contours of the composition by these angles and by the red, yellow, and blue found in these areas. These colors are placed so that they balance each other, with no single color dominating. Mondrian's composition might be described as decentralized, for it leads us to the periphery without concentrating our attention on any single area or element. His painting seems simple, but he has developed such a perfect balance that any change in color or composition would destroy the work's equilibrium.

Mondrian's composition is easier to analyze than Perugino's, for it exists completely in two dimensions. Perugino's composition must be analyzed both in terms of the patterns on the two-dimensional surface and as an illusion of three-dimensional reality. Note, for example, that when we analyze the painting as a two-dimensional object, the lines of the pavement of the square converge toward a central point, but in actual space, these lines would be parallel to each other. This controlled spatial effect is a system of creating depth (perspective) known as scientific perspective (see pp. 232–33). Other devices used by Perugino to help create his illusion are atmospheric perspective (the sky shades from blue toward white at the horizon, and the forms near the horizon are blurry and softened in color), diminution (forms in the distance are smaller), and overlapping (forms are placed in front of other forms).

Perugino's medium was fresco; Mondrian's was oil on canvas (see pp. 123 and 240). Both artists used a technique of smooth, regular brushstrokes. Because most of the forms in both paintings are sharply defined, with precisely delineated edges, they can be termed linear (the opposite effect, in which broad, free brushstrokes are used to define form, is termed painterly; for an example see fig. 310).

Perugino's colors are naturalistic, that is, taken from nature, which enhances his illusionism. Mondrian's selection of colors is restricted to red, blue, and yellow. Perugino changed the value and intensity of his colors to suggest the changes in value and intensity that result when light hits a form and creates highlights and shading; these changes are called modeling. Mondrian used pure colors, which are colors at their maximum or full intensity.

Perugino's painting was created during the Renaissance in Italy; it is one of a series of paintings of the lives of Moses and Christ which decorate the side walls of the Sistine Chapel in Rome. *Christ Giving the Keys to St. Peter* reveals the abilities of a Renaissance artist to reproduce natural effects within a harmonious and clear composition. Mondrian's painting, on the other hand, is related to his personal philosophy and to the principles of the De Stijl movement (see p. 474). While searching for a truly "universal means of expression," Mondrian wrote that beauty and harmony could only be expressed by "abstraction of form and color, that is to say, in the straight line and the clearly defined primary color." His search for pictorial balance must be related to the search for universal peace in the years following World War I. Despite their pronounced differences, these two paintings share a surprisingly similar expressive content: they are orderly, serene, and, ultimately, calming. Both artists achieve visual harmony and balance.

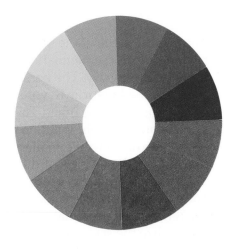

6. Color wheel. In the technical terminology used to discuss light and color, black and white are not considered to be colors. When color is seen in terms of light, black is understood as the absence of all color and white as the mixture of all colors. On the color wheel red, yellow, and blue are known as the primary colors because all other colors are made of a combination of these three hues (hue is the property which gives a color its name). Other properties that a color can demonstrate are value (relative darkness or lightness of the color) and intensity (the level of richness or saturation of the color).

ANALYZING SCULPTURE

The bronze statue of the Minuteman at Concord was commissioned to celebrate the centennial of the famous Revolutionary War battle fought there (fig. 7). The heroically scaled statue depicts the citizen soldier of the American Revolution, poised with a plough in one hand and a musket in the other. The figure stands alert and determined. The sculpture is representational, and although the medium is bronze, we can readily perceive, in the manner in which the artist has finished the surface, the illusion of different textures: the flesh suggests the anatomical structure beneath, the folds of the clothing respond to the body, and these textures contrast with the cold metallic handle of the plough. Such representational qualities help us recognize the forms and realize the sculpture's commemorative, historical purpose.

David Smith's *Cubi XIX* (fig. 8) is very different. It is a non-objective work of art, for it does not imitate actual figures or objects. In Smith's sculpture, the medium is stainless steel. Smith has brushed the surface of the steel, which gives a textural unity. The brushed steel surfaces reflect, in a diffused way, the atmospheric light around them. The appearance of the sculpture, then, changes in response to atmospheric conditions; it might appear dull gray-blue on an overcast day, or reflect a slight golden glow on a sunny day.

Both the *Minuteman* and *Cubi XIX* are examples of sculpture in the round, that is, sculpture which is fully three-dimensional and finished on all sides. Sculpture exists in real space, and space is an integral element in analyzing sculpture. Depending on the composition of the sculpture, the surrounding space can play a role in the effect and communication of the work. Although they are very different, French's *Minuteman* and Smith's *Cubi XIX* share similar compositions and a similar spatial involvement. Both sculptures have forms which develop from a vertical axis—the arms and right leg of the *Minuteman* and the rectangular and rounded steel forms of *Cubi XIX*. Both sculptures are set on bases. The large granite base of the *Minuteman* contributes to our recognition of the statue as a commemorative work; *Cubi XIX*'s base primarily offers support, but its design is in keeping with the non-objective composition. The composition of each work is also animated by a suggested movement. With the *Minuteman*, this is created by the contrast of the vertical axis of the figure with the forward diagonal of the right leg and musket. *Cubi XIX* offers an interplay of vertical, horizontal, and diagonal forms.

The compositions of French's *Minuteman* and Smith's *Cubi XIX* urge us to consider the sculptures from different viewpoints. The diagonal of the Minuteman's musket, which is reinforced by the implied movement of the right leg, creates an oblique motion which invites us to walk around the sculpture. In a similar way, diagonal elements break the planarity, or two-dimensional, view of Smith's work, drawing us around the sculpture to consider how the composition changes from varying points of view. Both sculptures make full use of the three-dimensional space in which they, like ourselves, exist.

7. DANIEL CHESTER FRENCH
Minuteman. 1873–75. Bronze with granite base, height 84". Old North Bridge, Concord, Massachusetts

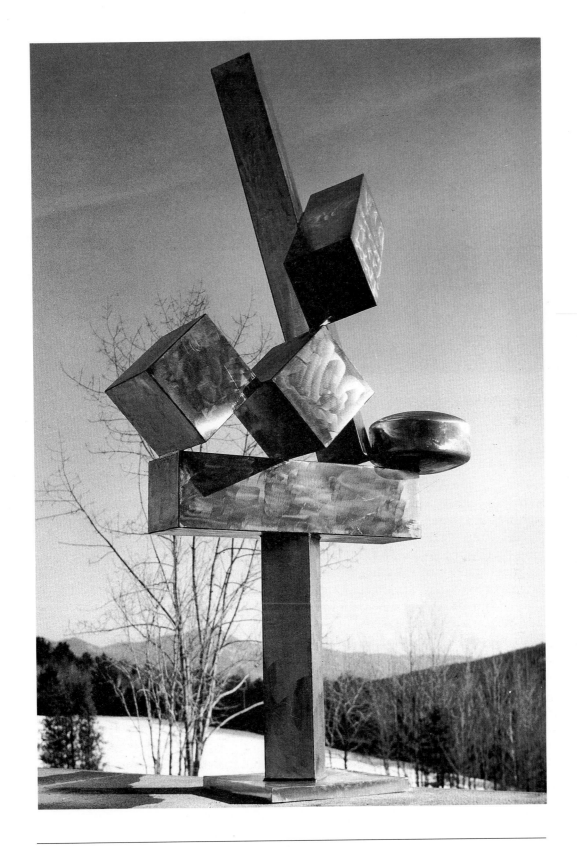

8. DAVID SMITH
Cubi XIX. 1964. Stainless steel, height 9' 5 1/8". The Tate Gallery, London. The abstract title of this sculpture reinforces its non-objective content. It is number nineteen in a series of sculptures by Smith which present variations on compositions of rectangular and cylindrical stainless-steel forms.

ANALYZING ARCHITECTURE

9. ANDREA PALLADIO
Villa Rotonda (also known as the Villa Capra), Vicenza, Italy. c. 1567–70

10. ANDREA PALLADIO
Plan, Villa Rotonda

Both the sixteenth-century Villa Rotonda and the twentieth-century Fallingwater (figs. 9, 11) were designed as country homes for private patrons: the Villa Rotonda for a retired official of the Catholic church, who used the villa for receptions and entertaining, and Fallingwater for the Kaufmann family of Pittsburgh, who used the home as a country retreat. Each structure communicates a distinct architectural effect and each relates to its site (setting) in a different manner. Situated at the crest of a hill and backed by a wooded area, the Villa Rotonda is an impressive and commanding structure. Its four bold, columned porches, set at right angles to each other and extending from a central domed mass, dominate the site. These porches serve a practical as well as aesthetic function, for they afford the guests varied views of the surrounding countryside and, since each is partially enclosed on the sides, the possibility of always being able to find a shady spot away from the hot Italian sun.

The most striking feature of Fallingwater is the way the structure cooperates with the site. This is characteristic of many of Wright's designs. The architect once commented: "A good building is one that makes the landscape more beautiful than it was before." In creating Fallingwater, he integrated the design with the natural environment, while at the same time establishing in the landscape a forceful abstract arrangement of rectangular forms. The large terraces allowed the Kaufmanns and their guests to enjoy the sun and views into the surrounding forest.

The ledges of rock which form the falls at the site create a horizontal pattern. This is echoed in the thrusting, horizontal terraces above,

11, 12. FRANK LLOYD WRIGHT
Above left and right: Exterior and interior, Fallingwater, Bear Run, Pennsylvania. 1936. Bear Run is in the Allegheny Mountains of western Pennsylvania.

which project out from a massive vertical core faced with natural stone quarried near the site. Nature's design has been reinterpreted and reinforced by the abstract architectural forms integrated within it.

The exterior design of the Villa Rotonda expresses a stable harmony. Symmetry governs the arrangement of the architectural forms, and vertical and horizontal elements are carefully balanced. The visual equilibrium revealed on the exterior also governs the interior design. The plan (fig. 10) is composed of proportional geometric shapes; a central, circular space is circumscribed by a square plan. From the central space, halls radiate to each porch. The symmetry and harmonic proportions which govern the exterior also control the plan and the interior scale of the rooms.

In contrast, the exterior design of Fallingwater is asymmetrical. A unified composition, however, is achieved by balancing the horizontal thrust of the terraces against the vertical massing of the central core. Another unifying feature is the adherence to rectangular forms throughout. The asymmetrical balance of Wright's exterior concept also characterizes the plan and interior (figs. 12, 13). Rooms and hallways repeat the rectangular forms of the exterior. Wright extends the rooms of the house into the space of the environment, while in Palladio's design the distinction between the building and its environment is firmly stated.

The principles of construction used to build the Villa Rotonda have a long tradition in architectural history. They include the use of walls, the post-and-lintel system (see p. 62), and the arch (see p. 126). The expressive drama of Fallingwater is bound to the design of the main terraces thrust over the waterfall. This adventurous architectural achievement was accomplished by the use of modern construction materials which have a high tensile strength, meaning that they strongly resist the strain of the architectural load and the pull of gravity. In Fallingwater, the terraces are made of concrete reinforced with steel rods. The availability of these materials gave Wright the possibility of using the cantilever (see p. 459).

13. FRANK LLOYD WRIGHT
Plan, Fallingwater

ART AND ARTISTS IN HISTORY

Throughout most of Western history, definitions of art were different from our modern view. The word art is derived from the Latin *ars*, meaning either manual skill or professional activity. Art had a broad definition, encompassing what we would now think of as the sciences, as well as many practical handicrafts and occupations. An artist, for example, might practice the art of painting, while a physician would practice the art of medicine.

In the classical world of ancient Greece and Rome, the making of art was generally viewed as a manual profession, taught in workshops, and it was not related to the more esteemed liberal arts, which were distinguished by intellectual, speculative thinking. Our Greek vase painting illustrates this workshop tradition (fig. 14). Apprentice vase painters, some of them female, are working side-by-side with the master of the shop. Women must have been given the lesser positions within the workshop, for no Greek vases signed by women are known.

14. LENINGRAD PAINTER
Greek Potters at Work (detail). c. 450 B.C.
Greek vase. Torno Collection, Milan

15. JOHANN ZOFFANY
The Life Drawing Class at the Royal Academy. 1772. Oil on canvas, 40 x 58". Collection Her Majesty the Queen, Windsor Castle. Zoffany's painting shows all the members of the Royal Academy except for Angelica Kauffmann and Mary Moser, who, as women within this restrictive academic climate, were not permitted to attend the life drawing class because of the nude male models. Zoffany ingeniously included them by painting their portraits hanging on the back wall. The sculpted figure with a raised right arm, just below the lamp, is an *écorché,* a sculpture of a flayed anatomical figure used to study surface muscles.

The Middle Ages continued to identify art as a manual profession. Artists formed guilds—legal organizations rather like trade unions—which, while assuring professional standards of accomplishment, also reinforced the distinction between the mechanical, or manual, arts, which included the production of works of art, and the so-called liberal arts, which during the Middle Ages encompassed arithmetic, geometry, astronomy, music theory, grammar, rhetoric, and logic.

The traditional classification of the visual arts as mechanical arts was first transformed during the Renaissance. Both artists and writers began to emphasize the scientific and intellectual aspects of art, often applying the program of the liberal arts to the education of the artist. It was argued, for example, that arithmetic was needed by the artist for the study of proportion, and that geometry figured in the proper calculation of perspective. The artist was beginning to be seen as an educated professional versed in both the practice and theory of art. The new attitude that the artist was a skilled and educated individual was accompanied by a new social status. Artists became the companions of intellectuals, princes, and emperors.

This remarkable evolution also affected the classification of the visual arts. By the sixteenth century, painting, sculpture, and architecture were grouped together as the arts of *disegno* (an Italian word that refers both to the making of drawings and to the concept of design), and were elevated to a status higher than other utilitarian arts. Discussion of art theory had become commonplace among intellectuals, and treatises were written to define art and to discuss its developing history. By the later sixteenth century, art academies began to replace the workshop tradition; artists were now educated in both the practical and theoretical aspects of art. Zoffany's painting depicts the male members of London's Royal Academy attending a class with live models (fig. 15). Plaster casts of the great works of classical sculpture, which were thought to exemplify the highest ideals of art, line the walls. The members of the academy are involved in rational discourse on the subject of life drawing.

The association of the arts of *disegno* with the intellectualism of the liberal arts was one of the mainstays of the new academic education given to artists. By the eighteenth century, art academies had proliferated throughout Europe. From this academic wellspring, a definition of the fine arts (*les beaux arts*) developed which included painting, sculpture, poetry, music, and dance on the basis that these are the arts that delight us. Arts which primarily served a utilitarian purpose continued to be termed mechanical arts, while architecture, which was considered to combine usefulness with beauty, occupied a third, independent category.

Although our understanding of art's role within the interpretation of the fine arts is of late historical vintage, developments since the nineteenth century have already begun to question these academic definitions of art. Early in the nineteenth century, when dramatically changing economic and social conditions were transforming Western cultural values, the concept of the artist as a member of the *avant-garde* (French for vanguard) was born. Attacking the conservativism of academic training and public taste, many artists assumed roles as prophets, leading society toward a modern, often utopian, vision of life. In our time the parameters within which visual artists work have changed. Happenings and Performance Art have blurred the distinctions between the traditional media of the visual arts and other art forms, including speech, music, dance, film, and video.

In non-Western cultures, China nurtured the oldest continuous painting tradition in the world. Its historical isolation, imperial patronage, art academies (begun as early as the eighth century), and a bureaucratic elite of Confucian scholar-officials contributed to a unique tradition in the fine arts. Most Chinese artists were not only painters. Many were also poets, calligraphers, statesmen, officials, antiquarians, scholars, collectors, connoisseurs, and mystics. They were part of the cultured elite, the *wen-jen* or literati, who were the main participants in the Chinese classical tradition.

Chinese painting derived from the art of writing and is, therefore, a linear art. Its brushwork is imbued with calligraphic formulas. The highest aesthetic aim of the literati painters was to capture the spirit of what was depicted, rather than merely its appearance (see fig. 16). For these literati painters, the creative process embodied the *Dao*, or Way of Nature, with its holistic vision of organic and metaphysical

产于荆巽寄于云林青白其眼金玉其音十日画水五日石
高安排蕭露三步回頭五步坐而消磨寸隙捎漆園野馬之
塵埃向怙射神人之冰雪執玉弗揮于以觀其葳蕤詳雅豐
手不帆昌足論其葳漆童之摩詰神文海岳達生傲睨玩世
諸諢人將此之愛佩茱羅裳之謝玄吾獨以為起出金畫門
之方朔也句典外史張雨贊

properties. In many Chinese paintings, idea and technique are one; the act of painting and the picture itself both carry meaning. Interestingly, these literati artists did not create sculpture or architecture, which were the work of highly skilled artisans.

In other traditions the position of artists varies. In Africa, for example, the sculptor of ritual objects is a highly regarded member of society (sometimes a holy man) believed to be invested with special creative (spiritual) abilities. There, too, both the craft of making and the final object are collectively considered as a work of art.

In India, religion is the major force which stimulates art and architecture. Most systems of Indic thought consider the phenomenal world to be illusory, perceived and interpreted by the senses. These perceptions yield information of a personal rather than a universal nature. The challenge for the Indic artist is, therefore, to express concepts beyond the limits of the phenomenal world. The artist creates symbolic devices, or *murtis* (images, icons, or sculptures), which refer to the ultimate Truth and render the abstract, transcendent realm more approachable and comprehensible. Communication of universal religious ideals, not egoistic expression, is the goal of the Indic sculptor. As a result, variations on traditional artistic canons are limited, and few names of ancient artists are known. However, the task of the artist is an extremely important one, for the devotee can gain spiritual power by viewing an image or by being in the presence of a great person. Such a belief, therefore, gives the visual arts an especially important role in Indic culture.

16. Chinese. *Portrait of Ni Tsan.* c. 1370 (Ming dynasty). Scroll, ink on paper. National Palace Museum, Taibei, Taiwan, R.O.C. Chinese literati painters worked alone, seated at desks in their studios. Paintings were executed on the flat surface of the table with natural bristle brushes in watercolor and ink on silk or paper. All necessary brushes, paints, and inks were close at hand.

NORWAY

SWEDEN

SCOTLAND

North Sea

IRELAND

DENMARK

*Atlantic
Ocean*

ENGLAND

Thames R.

Stonehenge •

•Neanderthal

NETHERLANDS

GERMANY

Seine R.

CZECHOSLOVAKIA

Danube R.

•Carnac

Willendorf

FRANCE

Dordogne R.

SWITZERLAND

AUSTRIA

•Lascaux

Altamira •

•Pech-
Merle

•La Madeleine

Pyrenees

Rhone R.

ITALY

Adriatic Sea

PORTUGAL

SPAIN

M e d i t e r r a n e a n

A F R I C A

Boundaries of the Ice Age

PREHISTORIC ART

Baltic Sea

POLAND

U. S. S. R.

HUNGARY

Caspian Sea

ROMANIA

Black Sea

TURKEY

0   300 miles

•Catal Hüyük

GREECE

SYRIA

Sea

PALESTINE

•Jericho

EGYPT

INTRODUCTION

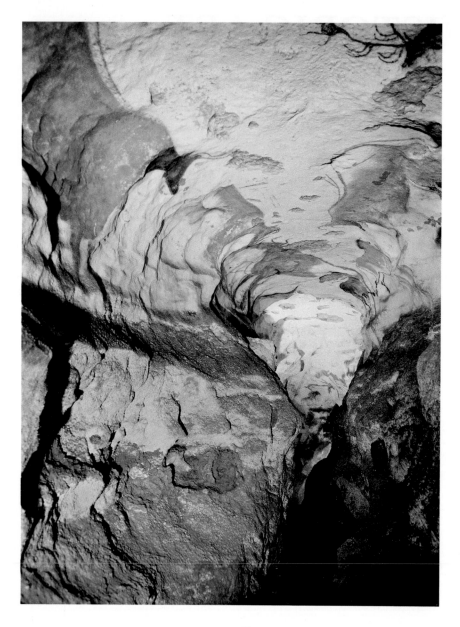

17. Axial gallery, Lascaux cave, Dordogne, France. c. 15,000–13,000 B.C. Cave painting; animals are about lifesize

In a cave at Lascaux, painted animals—cattle, horses, bison, and deer—seem to roam across walls and ceilings (see figs. 17, 18, and 22). The naturalism of these images is striking, for the sensitively observed animals are represented by means of a subtle and lively application of line and color. In some areas the natural undulation of the cave's surface supports the animals' anatomical presence, and their animation would have been enhanced by the quivering flames of the lamps or torches used for illumination. These images, created in the period known as prehistory, before the development of writing, present many mysteries; specialists are still speculating on their function and meaning.

THE DISCOVERY OF PREHISTORIC PAINTING

During the summer of 1879, a Spanish archaeologist was digging near the entrance of a cave near Altamira. He was hoping to find artifacts, like the prehistoric tools with images of animals that had been unearthed in France since 1840. His young daughter wandered into the cave, and soon cries were heard. When her anxious father entered, he found her excitedly pointing to bison—animals which had disappeared from Spain more than twelve thousand years before—painted on the ceiling. Cave art had been discovered, but the paintings at Altamira would not be accepted as genuine until 1902; only after similar discoveries elsewhere would archaeologists accept the fact that such imagery and style could have been achieved by prehistoric people. Lascaux, the most impressive of these sites, was not discovered until 1940.

HISTORY: THE PALEOLITHIC ERA

The origins of image-making date at least as early as the Paleolithic (c. 35,000–8000 B.C.), a period which is characterized by the use of refined stone tools (the term Paleolithic, Old Stone Age, derives from the Greek words *palaios*, old, and *lithos*, stone). At this time, during the last Ice Age, glacial ice extended to areas in southern Europe, but during the warmer months, when temperatures reached 60° Fahrenheit, people probably lived in tents covered with animal skins. As cold weather approached, they sought protection in rock shelters or in mouths of caves.

Paleolithic people were nomadic hunter-gatherers. They journeyed in bands of probably twenty to thirty members. Their contact with other nomadic groups may explain similarities in Paleolithic art over vast geographic areas. As they followed the migrations of animal herds, men hunted while women, in addition to bearing and caring for children, gathered mainstay dietary staples—plants, fruits, nuts, and shellfish.

18. Plan of the cave at Lascaux. Like most cave paintings, those at Lascaux are not near the entrance and are rather difficult to reach, supporting the theory that they are ritualistic rather than decorative.

THE "IMAGE BY CHANCE"

Painted or sculpted images of animals often make use of natural protrusions in the cave wall or floor. The human imagination was evidently inspired by areas of natural relief which suggested the forms of a particular animal; by adding paint or by carving, representational images were created. The theory that art originated in the "image by chance" was first stated by the fifteenth-century artist and theoretician Leon Battista Alberti. In his book *On Sculpture*, Alberti writes about the birth of sculpture: "I believe that the arts of those who attempt to create images and likenesses . . . originated in the

19. *Skull,* found at Jericho. c. 7000 B.C. Human skull with plaster and seashells. Archaeological Museum, Amman, Jordan

following way. They probably observed in a tree-trunk or clod of earth and other similar inanimate objects certain outlines in which, with slight alterations, something very similar to . . . Nature was represented. They began . . . [to] take away or otherwise supply whatever seemed lacking to effect and complete the true likeness." Alberti had not seen 'cave art, but recent archaeological discoveries have lent credibility to his theory.

HISTORY: THE NEOLITHIC ERA

The Ice Age, which had dominated the experience of Paleolithic culture, began to give way to a more moderate climate about 10,000 B.C. in Europe. The warming trend increased the available food supply for the hunter-gatherers. During the Mesolithic period (Middle Stone Age), techniques of gathering food became more efficient, and the cultivation of plants is likely. These developments led to the Neolithic period (New Stone Age) in about 8000 B.C. in the Near East and Asia and about 5000 B.C. in Europe, when the domestication of plants and animals and a sedentary life-style developed. The bands of hunter-gatherers began to settle into larger communities, probably as a result of several factors, including defense (scenes of human conflict are found in Mesolithic rock painting), economy, religion, and, perhaps, an increased birthrate related to greater food production. Architecture of stone, mud bricks, and timber provided more permanent homes, and the development of pottery for storing and protecting food also contributed to a stabilized environment. In western Europe, Neolithic peoples raised large stone monuments, as at Stonehenge (see fig. 54).

JERICHO AND ÇATAL HÜYÜK

Important remains of sophisticated Neolithic communities have been excavated at Jericho and Çatal Hüyük. The community at Jericho flourished from about 7500 B.C. It is perhaps the oldest surviving town in the Middle East. Jericho, built around a freshwater spring, a life-giving necessity in an arid region, was a settlement of homes of mud brick surrounded by massive walls for protection. Among the artifacts unearthed are human skulls covered with plaster and painted; seashells are inlaid in the eye sockets (see fig. 19). The heads were found in rooms of private homes, placed above bodies buried below. The purpose served by these Jericho skulls eludes us, but the preservation of individual remains and the almost portrait quality of some of the skulls suggest new attitudes about the worth of the individual. Perhaps these skulls were believed to house the spirit of the deceased in an ancestral worship practice.

The settlement of about ten thousand people at Çatal Hüyük, still only partially excavated, prospered from about 6700 to about 5700 B.C. Besides agriculture and animal breeding, Çatal Hüyük was also an important center for trade. A shrine excavated at the Neolithic community of Çatal Hüyük contains a painting of a red bull surrounded by miniature human figures (fig. 20). Unlike Paleolithic cave paintings, which were executed directly on walls or ceilings, here a surface of white plaster was carefully prepared. If a new painting was required, another layer of plaster was laid over the previous painting to avoid the superimposition seen in some Paleolithic painting. The bull probably relates to a religious ritual, for it was most likely a symbol of the male deity, embodying strength and fertility; skulls and horns were found in some shrines. The bull at Çatal Hüyük lacks the naturalism and vitality of its Paleolithic predecessors. It is less descriptive of a particular animal and more a diagrammatic symbol. This transformation might be the result of a different function for the image of the bull, or it might also reflect an abstraction brought about by sequential repetitions of an earlier painting of a bull. This more schematic rendering of the animal and the increase in the number of human figures portrayed are characteristic of Mesolithic and Neolithic painting.

20. *Animal Hunt,* restoration of Shrine A III. 1, Çatal Hüyük, Turkey. c. 6000 B.C.

POTTERY

A modest clay pot is evidence of one of the most consequential transitions in the development of humanity (fig. 21). Its simple design reveals both its function, as a container for food, and, with the twisted cord impressions, the artist's desire to make the object look pleasing. (These designs were also an aid in firing.) The use of pottery was important to a stabilized living environment, where fired clay vessels were created for cooking, transporting, and storing food. Pottery also assisted economic developments, for the making of clay vessels became a specialized activity of artists, who could trade their wares for other goods within their own community; later, pottery became one of the commodities traded from one community to another.

The origins of pottery vessels are uncertain, but we now know that pots, first fashioned in the Mesolithic period, became a standardized production in the Neolithic. Early clay pots may have been molded over a round stone or hand built by coiling (building up the walls of the vessel by successively adding long ropes of clay and then smoothing the joints). The pots were usually fired in open pits over fires of wood or dung, but soon special furnaces called kilns were developed for the firing of clay objects. The patterns on some early vessels may be adapted from weaving patterns. Perhaps wet clay was used to strengthen and waterproof woven baskets, and clay vessels were then made in imitation of the clay-impregnated baskets. By approximately 3000 B.C., the potter's wheel (a small revolving platform on which clay vessels are formed), which greatly increased productivity and encouraged the development of new modes of decoration, was in use throughout the Middle East.

21. Clay pot, found in the Thames River near Hedsor, Buckinghamshire. c. 3100–2500 B.C. Terra-cotta, height 5". British Museum, London

PALEOLITHIC CAVE PAINTING AND SCULPTURE

22. *Bulls.* Rotunda, Lascaux cave, Dordogne, France.
c. 15,000–13,000 B.C. Cave painting

These bulls (fig. 22) are painted in the rotunda of the cave complex at Lascaux (see also figs. 17 and 18). The smaller bull, the first to be painted, is represented in a quiet pose, as if grazing; its shape is created by a solid area of color. Painted over this at some later date is the outline that defines the large bull; he seems to be ambling to the left. Only a few details, such as the eye and shoulder vein (a target for the hunter?), are drawn within the contour lines. Both images were created by artists sensitive to the anatomy and liveliness of the animals.

Sometimes Paleolithic artists drew directly on the wall with chunks of red, yellow, brown, or black minerals or earth, but more often they created liquid pigments by grinding minerals and mixing them with animal fat, vegetable oil, or bone marrow. They could apply these paints to the wall using a brush made of animal hair or a frayed stick, while dots of color could be pressed onto the wall with fingers dipped into the paint. Broader areas of color could be applied by blowing paint through a hollow reed or bone. Whatever technique was employed, the skill was remarkable, not only in the fluid execution of the painting, but also in the exacting observation and memory of the artist, who reproduced these naturalistic animal forms —some seemingly in movement—by lamp or torchlight.

Some animal images are shown pierced with spears or arrows, possibly as a practical demonstration to younger hunters..But the location of the paintings and the overpainting of images on successive occasions, perhaps hundreds or even thousands of years apart, suggest that they may have served a ritualis-

tic purpose. Perhaps in making these paintings the Paleolithic artist also acted as a shaman, a person believed to have power to affect the spiritual world. The ritual of re-creating the animals through representation may have been an attempt to capture their life spirits and to thus insure a successful hunt. Whatever their function, the images had to be both lively and identifiable by species. The relatively rare occurrence of the human figure in Paleolithic art ranges from the representational to the schematic. The majority are sticklike figures. Perhaps it was feared that too naturalistic a representation would capture the life spirit of the figure portrayed.

Our ancestors left a record of their presence in hand prints made by placing a hand against the wall and blowing pigment around it through a reed or hollow bone (see fig. 23). These prints may be "signatures" left by the artists or by those who were present during a particular ritual. Some record hands with missing fingers. Perhaps the fingers were lost due to frostbite or hunting accidents, or they may have been doubled under to form hand signals, symbols of silent communication used by the hunters to indicate the presence of game. Or possibly the hands were purposely mutilated for some ritualistic reason, such as

12,000 B.C.: The dog is domesticated and used for hunting
10,000 B.C.: Human population of earth is about 3 million
8000 B.C.: Human population of earth is about 5.3 million
7000 B.C.: Wheat is domesticated

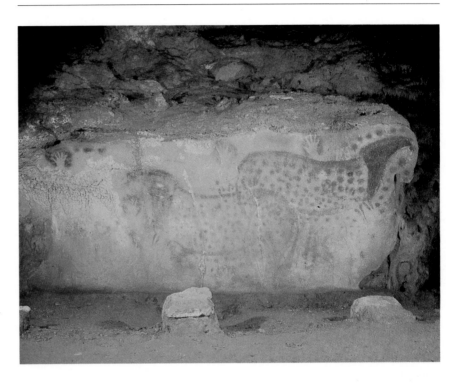

an initiation ceremony or to pacify spirits.

One group of about one hundred fifty sculptures poses unique problems of interpretation (see fig. 24). Barely a few inches in height, these represent female figures with a pronounced emphasis on breasts, abdomen, hips, and thighs. Traditionally they have been viewed as images of fertility, perhaps for use in a ritual dealing with childbearing, and the exaggeration of those parts of the body related to procreation are often assumed to be conscious abstractions by the artist. Scholars have also suggested that these figures might represent the "ideal" Ice Age woman, with the fat accumulation desirable to conceive and bear healthy children during periods of food scarcity. Other explanations propose that these figures functioned as guardian figures or as dolls. Recent scholarship has demonstrated that as a group, they display various stages in a woman's life, from youth, maturity, and pregnancy to old age. Some archaeological evidence suggests that they were made and used by women. Our uncertainty about the function of these sculptures is directly related to the limited evidence we have about Paleolithic life and culture. Our understanding of prehistoric art is itself still evolving.

23. *Spotted Horses and Negative Hand Imprints.* Pech-Merle cave, Lot, France. c. 15,000–13,000 B.C. Cave painting, length approx. 11'. The spots of the horses are created with dots of color pressed onto the wall using fingers dipped in paint.

24. *Statuette of a Woman,* found at Willendorf, Austria. c. 25,000–20,000 B.C. Stone, height 4 3/8". Museum of Natural History, Vienna. Statuettes such as this one have been traditionally, but improperly, known as Venuses. Other similar figures are carved of mammoth ivory or modeled of clay. The navel of this figure is a natural indentation in the stone.

Atlantic Ocean

ENGLAND
Stonehenge · London

GERMANY

Rhine R.

Elbe R.

· Carnac

Seine R.

· Paris

Loire R.

FRANCE

Danube R.

Lake Geneva

Vienna

AUSTRIA

Dordogne R.

Alps

Po R. Venice

Pyrenees

Nîmes ·

Apennines

Florence ·

Adriatic Sea

YUGOSLAVIA

Arno R. **ITALY**

Split

SPAIN

Prima Porta
· Rome

Tiber R.

· Praeneste

Ostia ·

Naples · · Boscoreale

Mt. Vesuvius

Macedonia

Salonika

· Pompeii

Herculaneum · Paestum

Mt. Olympus ▲

Tyrrhenian Sea

Corfu

GREECE

Cape Artemisio

Mt. Parnassus ▲

Delphi

Palermo ·

Olympia ·

Mediterranean

Sicily

Corinth

Sparta

Carthage ·

Timgad ·

North Africa

Leptis Magna ·

0   300 miles

ANCIENT ART

ROMANIA

Black Sea

A n a t o l i a

TURKEY

Caspian Sea

Samothrace
Contantinople•

•Teheran

•Troy

•Pergamon

•Dur Sharrukin
•Nineveh
•Nimrud

Marathon
•Athens   *Chios*
•Ephesus   *Asia Minor*   Assur• ASSYRIA
Samos   MESOPOTAMIA
Anavysos   •Issus   LURISTAN
Cyclades •Halicarnassus   Antioch *Euphrates R.* Tell Asmar
Knidos   Side•   Dura Europos•   •Baghdad   •Susa
Epidaurus   *Rhodes*   SYRIA   AKKAD   ELAM   •Persepolis
                                 Babylon• SUMER
Crete   •Baalbek   BABYLONIA •Uruk
S e a   Al'Ubaid• •Ur

PERSIA

Tigris R.

PHOENICIA   *Persian Gulf*

Jerusalem• •Jericho
PALESTINE   JORDAN
         Bethlehem•

Alexandria•   A R A B I A

Cairo•
Giza•
Saqqara•
The Faiyum
Lower Egypt

•Beni Hasan
•Tell el-Amarna

Nile R. Karnak
Deir-el-Bahari• •Thebes
Hierakonpolis• Luxor

Upper Egypt •Aswan

Abu Simbel•

Red Sea

INTRODUCTION

25. Chinese. *Fang ding* (ceremonial food vessel). c. 1150 B.C. (Shang dynasty). Bronze, height 24 1/2". Excavated from tomb 1004, Houziazhuang, Anyang (Henan province), China. Academia Sinica, Taibei, Taiwan, R.O.C.

Chinese bronze vessels, like this *fang ding,* immediately attract our attention because of their powerful, simple shapes and extravagant, abstract patterning (fig. 25). Careful examination reveals that what at first seems to be abstract patterning is based on the forms of animals, parts of animals, or combinations of parts of beasts and/or birds. In this case the main motif is the most famous pattern used on ancient Chinese bronzes, the *taotie,* or monster mask. Each mask is arranged in a symmetrical fashion with each part repeated exactly across the central axis; eyes, ears, an open jaw, and feet are parts of all *taotie.* Sometimes the ears resemble those of oxen or cows; other times they appear to be closer to deer, moose, or elk. Why references to certain animals were made is not known, but the image is always powerful and presumably also shows considerable respect for the animal kingdom.

This vessel (and the *guang* seen in fig. 27) were created to hold sacrificial offerings of food and wine during ancient Chinese ceremonies dedicated to the veneration of ancestors. Sets of these containers were placed on family altars, but they were also buried in tombs of members of the ruling and aristocratic classes. These early bronze vessels sometimes had inscribed dedications to the deceased; later inscriptions referred to historic events and legal transactions and are an important source of information about ancient Chinese life from

26. Etruscan. *Engraved Back of a Mirror.* c. 400 B.C. Bronze, diameter 6". Vatican Museums, Rome. The highly polished bronze surface of the reverse would have functioned as a mirror; the handle is lost.

about 1000 B.C. onward. The tombs where such vessels were found also contained bronze weapons, sometimes inlaid with semi-precious stones, ceramic vessels, and objects carved from jade and other stones. These luxurious art objects were intended to confirm the political, military, and spiritual power of their patrons.

The particular piece-mold process of casting used for the production of these vessels was quite distinctive of early China. Anyang, where the *fang ding* was excavated, was the last capital of the Shang dynasty (c. 1766–1122 B.C.), and the vessel's decoration referred to the royal clan that ruled China during this period. The *taotie* on all four sides of the *fang ding,* for example, is thought to be the particular emblem of the Shang. The animal forms that create the vessel's patterns are believed to represent mediums through which communications were transmitted from earthly beings to the spirits of the ancestors. This idea is related to shamanistic religious practices in which communication with the spirit world was aided by animals who were thought to have special powers of transcendence. A priest or holy person, often wearing a mask or costume made up of animal parts (horns, feathers, skins), was understood to change not only appearance, but also his or her state of being, to transcend this world to that of the spirits (see also p. 456). Sometimes the very shape of the vessel mimicked an animal form, as in the *guang* (fig. 27).

Like many objects that survive from the world's ancient cultures, the Etruscan mirror served both a practical and a religious purpose (fig. 26). Used not only for personal grooming, these elegant, decorated mirrors were also frequently placed in or near tombs for use in the afterlife. The engraved design on the back of the mirror is drawn from the traditions of Greek mythology, which were popular with the Etruscans. It depicts Calchas, a diviner, who is shown "reading" the spots on the liver of a sacrificed animal in order to foretell the future. The naturalism evident in the figure of the winged Calchas, the surrounding grapevine, the table, and the vase represents an approach more often found in the ancient Western civilizations of Greece, Etruria, and Rome than in China or India. But the subject matter seen here—the practice of interpreting natural occurrences and objects as omens—was widespread throughout the ancient world. It is but one revelation of the complex intertwining of religious doctrine with everyday life common to these early peoples.

The Etruscans, whose civilization paralleled that of Greece in time, created a loosely bound federation of city-states in central Italy. They were a vigorous and religious people, and our knowledge of them largely derives from the evidence of the complex burial practices that grew from their belief in the afterlife. The deceased were apparently accompanied with virtually all the goods they might need after death.

HISTORY

As those factors which distinguished Neolithic culture, including husbandry and communal living, continued, certain areas gradually underwent a development toward a more complex, urban existence. In fertile river valleys—the Tigris and Euphrates in Mesopotamia, the Nile in Egypt, the Indus and Ganges in India, and the Huang Ho and Yangtze in China—where abundant food was available, new, large urban civilizations developed.

The first cities became administrative and/or religious centers for the surrounding territory. As these cities and their territories grew in size and population, production became specialized and a division of labor developed, often reinforcing class distinctions. In some cultures, the administrative authority of the political/military and religious classes, which often existed in a symbiotic relationship, was supported by a system of taxation or tribute. In many ancient cultures, monumental works of public architecture were symbolic of the new central governing authority.

Another key to the development of ancient civilization was the growth of systems of writing and mathematics that evolved in response to the needs of the new urban centers. The promulgation of laws and the keeping of accounts and records helped to provide order and continuity within the new complexity of urban life. Writing and mathematics contributed to the goal of an orderly society within the complicated structure of the urban environment, but they also made possible the advent of literature and science.

These aspects of a more complex and interrelated urban life-style, or civilization, were present in different measures in societies beginning about 4000 B.C., but the development is not uniform. In Sumer and Egypt, such developments were present beginning about 4000 B.C., while in India they date to about 2200 B.C. and in China to 2000 B.C. In the Americas, settled life was known in the first millennium B.C. In western Europe, civilization emerged noticeably late, as is indicated in this text by the placement of the important Neolithic monument of Stonehenge (fig. 54) after the discussion of the developments in Sumer and Egypt. By the end of the ancient period, however, developments in Greece, Etruria, Rome, India, and China established advances in art and architecture that mark the foundation for civilization. These civilizations were characterized by a sense of self-reflection and concern for fellow human behavior as opposed to a primary preoccupation with gathering food supplies.

ANCIENT ART

What we know about ancient civilizations most frequently comes from the analyses of archaeological remains and the examination of artifacts produced by skilled artisans. Another source can be the study of literature written by ancient authors. Literary remains are virtually non-existent for some ancient cultures, however, and the fact that most of the artifacts that we study are the result of archaeological investigations also means that we must work with a very limited sample of evidence. But all early peoples produced materials which, when investigated today, can help us in our attempts to understand their most cherished beliefs about spiritual as well as political, social, and economic matters. The monumental architecture and public works (temples, baths, and granaries, for example) known in the Indus Valley and the Roman republic and empire, tell us that the parent societies cared about issues of public as well as spiritual health. In ancient Mesopotamia, Egypt, and at Teotihuacán, large-scale architectural and sculptural monuments—ziggurats, pyramids—are known to have been dedicated to the display of both political and spiritual ideals. In China, spiritual and political power was more often expressed in ritual vessels and burial practices than by architecture. In ancient societies, sculptures and paintings often represented deities and leaders, but some examples also record everyday activities. Works of ancient art and architecture were made from a wide variety of media, from common limestone to the most precious metals and gems. One can expect to find some sort of visual arts in all ancient societies, but the "perishable" arts, such as literature and music, are

27. Chinese. *Guang* (ceremonial food vessel). 12th century B.C. (Shang dynasty). Bronze, length 12 1/4". Excavated from a royal tomb at Anyang (Henan province), China. Freer Gallery of Art, Smithsonian Institution, Washington, D.C.

largely lost to us. They often must have been as significant as their more permanent visual counterparts. Study of all remains can begin to provide clues to the discovery of common and distinctive traits of human behavior worldwide.

THE ANCIENT ARTIST

In most ancient civilizations, artists—the men and women who created what we now deem to be works of art—were counted among the ranks of laborers, and their products were seen as the result of manual effort. Apprentices in workshops learned the traditional artistic forms and techniques that ensured a continuity of artistic and iconographic formulas. Most works of art were the product of a group of trained artists working together in a workshop which took advantage of a distribution of labor.

While at times rulers took pride in employing artists of significant talent, these instances did not contribute significantly to the social or economic prestige of the artist. In ancient Egypt the architect Imhotep (see fig. 44) was a member of the pharaoh's court and later he was even deified, but this seems to have been a unique development within ancient world cultures.

In Greece, the personality and individual style of a number of artists is documented. These artists gained fame, yet despite the fact that they were personally admired, their profession was still viewed as lacking the philosophical and educational values of the liberal arts. Later Roman patrons valued Greek works of art as well as Greek artists, but the Roman artist was confined to anonymity.

In China and India, embellished objects such as cast bronzes and stone carvings were designed by specialists who usually worked together as part of a team of craftspeople involved in the creation of a work. The designers, the metallurgists and casters, and the miners and carvers of jade and stone each possessed specialized knowledge of patterns, designs, and techniques which must have conferred on them a special status in their communities. Certainly teams of architectural designers/builders were similarly considered in ancient India, Mesoamerica, and elsewhere. The creation and construction of the many vast ancient religious and urban complexes was a task that required cooperation, specialization, and overall coordination—prerequisites for ancient civilization.

THE LADY FROM DAI

In China, new types of art objects began to be produced from about the sixth century B.C. onward. Sometimes these new objects also reveal new approaches to representation as well. The painted silk banner from the tomb of the Lady from Dai (fig. 28) comes from south China, near Changsha in Hunan province. It was found draped over the innermost part of four coffins. Its iconography is descriptive and its presentation representational rather than emblematic and geometricized, as was the decor of the ritual bronzes (figs. 25, 27). What is depicted on the banner is the path of the souls after death—the underworld, the earthly realm, and the Land of the Immortals. The underworld, or watery realm, is represented by fishes and deities of that world of darkness. The soul is called back to earth, where it rejoins the other soul and is feasted by the family of the deceased. The detail here portrays the Lady from Dai as she returns to the earth. The top of the banner describes the Land of the Immortals where creation tales are told. A preoccupation with immortality and with its attainment characterize most funerary art of the later period in ancient China and reflects the patrons' interest in Daoism (see p. 30).

Banners of this type were described in literary accounts; they were probably carried in funerary processions before being buried with the deceased. This is the first such banner discovered, and it is an early example of polychrome silk painting in China. Naturalistic depictions of human beings such as we see here were rare in China before the rise of Confucian humanism in the sixth century B.C. The new philosophical and moral attitudes of Confucius, with their self-reflective attitudes toward human life, clearly had a direct impact on painting. In the ancient world, the arts were a sensitive barometer of changes in social and intellectual order.

28. Chinese. *Lady from Dai with Attendants* (detail of a painted silk banner). c. 180 B.C. (Han dynasty). Silk T-shaped banner, 80 3/4" tall; 36" wide at the top. Formerly Historical Museum, Beijing

Introduction to Egyptian Art

29. *The Pharaoh Khafre.* c. 2500 B.C. Diorite, height, 66"; over-lifesize. Egyptian Museum, Cairo. This is one of a number of similar sculptures found in the valley temple at Giza, site of the three great pyramids from the Old Kingdom (see figs. 40, 41). The temple is located along the causeway which connects Khafre's pyramid with the *Colossal Statue of Khafre as the God Hu.*

30. *Queen Hatshepsut.* c. 1495 B.C. Limestone, height 78". The Metropolitan Museum of Art, New York (Rogers Fund and contribution from Edward S. Harkness, 1929)

The over-lifesize figure of Khafre is shown majestically seated on his throne (fig. 29). It expresses the absolute authority of the Egyptian ruler, who was known as the pharaoh. The idealized body is as architectonically rigid as the throne. There may be a hint of portraiture in the face, but the effect of the figure is grand and intimidating. Khafre's head is embraced by the wings of the Egyptian sky god Horus, represented as a falcon, to symbolize the god's divine protection.

The statue, carved from an extremely hard stone and compactly composed, gives the appearance of being able to last forever. The Egyptians believed that the *Ka*, the part of the human spirit that defined a person's individuality and that would survive on earth after death, needed a physical dwelling place. The corpse of Khafre was mummified to provide this home, but if it should decay or be destroyed, one or more sculptures of the deceased pharaoh could provide a home for the *Ka*. The solid and rigid character of this sculpture was the artist's way of meeting an extraordinary demand—that of creating a sculpture that to serve its purpose had to endure for eternity.

HISTORY

Egyptian civilization was nurtured by the Nile River as it flows northward into the Mediterranean Sea. Egypt was the "gift of the

31. *Akhenaten with Nefertiti and Their Children.* c. 1370–1353 B.C. Limestone relief, 13 x 15". Staatliche Museen, East Berlin

32. Rock Temple of Ramesses II, Abu Simbel. c. 1257 B.C. Height of sculpture about 67'. In 1968 these gigantic figures of sandstone were raised about six hundred feet to save them from being flooded by the lake created by the Aswan Dam.

river," wrote the Greek historian Herodotus. The nine hundred miles of the Nile that flow through ancient Egypt sustained life in an otherwise arid desert region. Every summer the Nile, swollen by torrential rains, would flood its banks, depositing fertile silt to support Egypt's agricultural development. Neolithic settlements along the Nile date from as early as 7000 B.C. Agriculture was sustained by the annual flood and, later, by irrigation, while the flanking desert offered protection from foreign invaders. The economy gradually prospered, and later crop production included flax for the making of linen and papyrus for paper and rope. By the fifth millennium B.C., the settlements coalesced into distinct cultural areas. The northern area was known as Lower Egypt because of the flow of the Nile from south to north; Upper Egypt was to the south. Around 3168 B.C., a legendary king (now identified with Narmer; see pp. 54–55) forcibly united Upper with Lower Egypt, establishing a political state that endured almost continuously for over two thousand years.

This vast expanse of Egyptian history is subdivided into three major periods of political stability and cultural and economic growth known as the Old, Middle, and New Kingdoms. The Old Kingdom (c. 2686–2182 B.C.) was characterized by an expansion of the central authority of the pharaoh, who ruled over Egypt's local administrative provinces. Its economic prosperity is evident in the funerary precinct at Giza, which includes the three largest pyramids (see fig. 40). Political unrest led to the end of the Old Kingdom when an economic depression, perhaps caused in part by lavish expenditures, was compounded by a famine, and local governors of the provinces broke the central authority of the pharaoh.

The Middle Kingdom (c. 2050–1786 B.C.) saw a reunified Egypt. The pharaoh Sesostris III strengthened the central government, and new trade routes were established, stimulating the economy. The Middle Kingdom ended when a group of foreign settlers, the Hyksos, took advantage of a weakened government and of a new weapon—the horse-drawn chariot—to establish a separate kingdom.

Within a century, however, the Hyksos were expelled and Egypt entered a final period of cultural and economic prosperity, the New Kingdom (c. 1576–1085 B.C.). The architectural remains of the New Kingdom reveal a vigorous economy, political stability, and the assured power of the pharaoh. This latter quality is reflected in the statue of Queen Hatshepsut (fig. 30), Western history's first recorded female monarch, who governed Egypt from about 1501 to 1482 B.C.

There was an important, if short-lived, disruption in Egypt during the New Kingdom. The reign of the pharaoh Akhenaten (c. 1365 B.C.), known as the Amarna period because his capital was located near present-day Tel el-Amarna, witnessed the disruption of many traditional cultural and artistic values. The relief of Akhenaten with Nefertiti and their children (fig. 31) retains some of the usual conventions of Egyptian art, such as the simultaneous combination of frontal and profile views (see p. 55). But the artist has imparted a new fluid naturalism to the figures. Unlike the earlier geometric treatment of the figure, the bodies of Akhenaten and his family are given sensuous curving forms which contribute to the relaxed intimacy of the scene. The fact that Akhenaten's queen is seen on the same scale as the pharaoh himself reveals the revolutionary equality that characterized the Amarna period. In other Egyptian periods women are

33. *Throne of Tutankhamen.* c. 1350 B.C. Gold, silver, colored glass paste, glazed ceramic, and inlaid calcite, height 45". Egyptian Museum, Cairo. Tutankhamen, whom we popularly know as King Tut, was a pharaoh of relatively minor importance in Egyptian history. He succeeded to the throne following the rule of Akhenaten's son and died at an early age. Tutankhamen's fame is primarily due to the fact that his tomb furnishings were largely intact when discovered by the British archaeologist Howard Carter in 1922.

shown as notably smaller in scale (see fig. 52). Following this period, the rigid conventions of older ways returned as the pharaohs established an authoritative continuity with their predecessors. The statues of Ramesses II that flank the entrance to his mortuary temple at Abu Simbel (fig. 32) recall the formal rigidity of the Old Kingdom statue of Khafre. But the colossal size of these sculptures, about sixty-seven feet high and carved from the actual cliffs of the site, reveal the grandeur typical of the New Kingdom. The Ramesses dynasty (ended 1085 B.C.) was the last significant dynastic family of the New Kingdom. During the following centuries the power and splendor of the empire abated, and in 332 B.C. Egypt was conquered by Alexander the Great.

RELIGION

Egyptian religion was a complex faith which included polytheism, magic, politics, and a steadfast belief in an afterlife. As was also true of Neolithic agricultural communities, wonder at the forces of nature and the spirit of animals led to the development of polytheism, with local gods or goddesses being affirmed in different communities. Early depictions of these deities include representations as animals, such as Horus (the sky god as a falcon), or as animal-headed humans, like Anubis (a jackal-headed god associated with mummification).

For the Egyptians, whom Herodotus described as "religious to excess," magic was as much a part of their religion as was attending the great religious festivals. Believing that the spiritual world governed all aspects of life, the Egyptians even accompanied the commonplace practice of taking medicine with ritualistic incantations. Religion was also bound to politics. The pharaoh was viewed as a god who ruled with absolute authority in secular and religious matters. Often a god or goddess worshipped by a particular pharaoh would become the center of the state religion and be imposed over local religious practices.

Much religious ritual accompanied the belief in an afterlife. Although this belief remained constant, rituals changed as a result of the complex developments in Egyptian religious practice. The most important entity of the human soul to be served in the afterlife was the *Ka*. After death the *Ka* required an earthly abode, and the body of the deceased was preserved through mummification (mummy is from the Arabic *mumiya*, meaning bitumen—a petroleum substance mistakenly believed to have been used in mummification). The process of mummification, strictly governed by religious ritual, took seventy days. The lungs, stomach, liver, and intestines were removed to separate containers called canopic jars, while the body was treated with chemical solutions to draw out moisture before being wrapped in as many as twenty layers of linen. A song inscribed on a predynastic tomb reveals the reward for the *Ka*: "The span of earthly things is a dream, but a fair welcome is given him who has reached the West." (The world of the afterlife was associated with the sunset and was therefore thought to be in the west.)

EGYPTIAN ART

Providing service to the *Ka* was a mainstay of artistic production in Egypt. Tomb walls were painted with everyday scenes (see figs. 51, 52) to re-create a pleasant environment, and small servant figures, usually carved from wood and painted to appear lifelike, performed a host of common duties. Woodworkers constructed a series of coffins which were decorated by artists. Some were carved from stone (these are called sarcophagi, from the Greek *sarkophagos*, flesh-eating stone).

In addition to the artistic preparations made especially for the use of the *Ka* in the afterlife, such precious objects as jewelry and items of personal use were placed in the tomb. The throne of the pharaoh Tutankhamen (fig. 33) displays the exquisite artistry and conspicuous wealth of the New Kingdom, while the relaxed figurative poses demonstrate influence from the Amarna period.

Although much of preserved Egyptian art relates to funerary practices, the Egyptians as a people were not concerned only with the afterlife. Tomb paintings record the labor of the lower classes and such festive occasions for the nobility as banquets with music and dancing. But even commonplace scenes often adhere to time-honored conventions of artistic practice. The visually unnatural formula used in Egyptian art to depict pharaohs and aristocrats is a combination of frontal with profile views that creates a static figure typical of Egyptian art (see fig. 53).

34. *Bust of Ankhaf.* c. 2500 B.C. Painted limestone, height 22". Museum of Fine Arts, Boston

The relatively unchanging nature of Egyptian artistic practices reveals the stability of its civilization, yet artists were not slaves to formulas. Akhenaten caused a religious, political, and artistic revolution, but even before him, other currents brought degrees of diversity and vitality to Egyptian art, as is seen in the portrait bust of Ankhaf (fig. 34). The portrait bust as a type was related to funerary practices, probably as an additional home for the *Ka*. Ankhaf, a court official to Khafre, was buried in the necropolis at Giza. The painted image, found in the chapel of his tomb, displays a subtle surface anatomy: the deep-set eyes, swelling of the cheeks, and the diagonal lines from the nose to the corners of the mouth reveal an attentive sense of life akin to the naturalism observed in some tomb paintings. This bust contrasts with the authoritative power of royal portraiture.

THE EGYPTIAN ARTIST

In Egypt, as throughout most of the ancient and medieval periods, no distinction was drawn between the artists who designed sculptures and paintings and the numerous skilled laborers in workshops who brought their concepts into being. Artists labored as members of the lower classes. The exception was the architect, who enjoyed the status of a court official. Imhotep, the first recorded artist of Western history, designed Zoser's Old Kingdom funerary complex at Saqqara (fig. 44). His fame was so great that by the New Kingdom he was deified as the god of learning and medicine.

VOTIVE PALETTE OF KING NARMER

In the past, important historical developments often led to the creation of significant works of art that interpreted or commemorated an event. It seems no accident that the first great work of Egyptian art, the *Votive Palette of King Narmer,* marks the establishment of the unified nation of Egypt. Narmer, who has been indentified with Menes, first king of the first Egyptian dynasty, appears three times. As the largest figure on side A (fig. 35), he wears the crown of Upper Egypt and brings under his control a figure who probably represents Lower Egypt. The nearby human-headed figure with six papyrus blossoms being held captive by the god Horus (shown as a falcon) almost certainly represents, in a symbolic manner, the submission of Lower Egypt to Upper Egypt. This use of symbols to represent complex ideas is an important new development in art, and one which hints at the later development of Egyptian hieroglyphs, in which figures or pictures signify words or sounds. At the bottom of side B (fig. 36), Narmer himself appears as a symbol—a horned bull,

35. Left: *Votive Palette of King Narmer* (side A). c. 3168 B.C. Slate, height 25". Egyptian Museum, Cairo. The shieldlike shape and shallow indentation reveal that this is an enlarged, ceremonial version of an everyday object, a palette used for the grinding of pigments for eye shadow. This palette was found at Hierakonpolis, a sacred city of prehistoric Egypt.

36. Right: *Votive Palette of King Narmer* (side B)

Votive Palette of King Narmer: **c. 3168** B.C.

4236 B.C.: Earliest date in the traditional Egyptian calendar
4000 B.C.: Earth's population reaches about 85 million
3760 B.C.: Earliest date in the traditional Jewish calendar
3500–3000 B.C.: Wheeled vehicles in use
3000 B.C.: Earth's population nears 100 million
c. 3000 B.C.: Bronze is first produced

victorious over an enemy and the enemy's fortified city. At the bottom of side A are two more defeated antagonists and small symbols of a fortified city and a gazelle trap that suggest victories in the city and countryside. Near the top of side B, Narmer, wearing the crown of Lower Egypt and accompanied by a processional retinue, views the decapitated corpses of enemies. The central symbol at the top of both sides represents Narmer's name and his palace. It is flanked by horned animals representing the sky-mother (Hathor), in whose shrine the palette was probably dedicated. In addition to Narmer's assumption of the two crowns, union is also suggested by the joining of two fantastic, long-necked lionesses on side B, their serpentine necks intertwined to form the shallow indentation that refers to the function of the object.

A number of the most important surviving works of art from predynastic Egypt are similar palettes or fragments of palettes. The decoration is usually political in nature. Apparently the larger versions of these palettes were displayed as votives (gifts made to a god or goddess), and they may also have been used to grind and mix the pigments that adorned the eyes of the cult statue of the deity. The *Votive Palette of King Narmer* probably had several functions: as a decorative object to be used in a religious ritual; as a votive offering to the god or goddess (most likely Hathor); and as a commemoration of the military and territorial victories of Narmer. Such a union of political statement with religious ritual is typical of Egyptian art and culture.

Narmer is, in every case, represented as unnaturally larger than his subordinates and enemies, a means of visually conveying importance called hierarchical (or, less correctly, hieratic) scale common in religious and political art. This emphasis and the lucid presentation make the meaning more easily comprehensible. The human figures on the palette present the human body in a design which clarifies the parts and their interrelationships—legs, head, and arms are seen in strict profile, while the torso and the eye are seen directly from the front. These demonstrate the same clarity seen in the three-dimensional figure of Khafre (fig. 29), but here they are united and suppressed into what is essentially a two-dimensional medium, low relief (see below). As unrealistic as this pattern is, it is easily read and it emphasizes strength. It would continue in Egyptian art for more than three thousand years.

RELIEF SCULPTURE

The technique of sculpting figures or forms which are part of (or, less commonly, attached to) a background is known as relief sculpture. Because the figures are very flattened, the style of carving in the *Narmer Palette* is known as low or bas-relief. There is no differentiation in color, but light hitting the delicately varied levels of relief allows us to read the forms. This technique, difficult to master, was also practiced by later artists. The Egyptians also excelled at an unusual type of low relief known as sunken relief, in which the figures are recessed into the surface (visible in fig. 31). High relief is relief sculpture with forms that project substantially from their background (see fig. 94). During the Renaissance, sculptors perfected a pictorial relief that conveyed an illusion of depth by using a subtle transition from high to progressively lower relief (see fig. 236). In Egypt, as well as in later cultures, relief sculpture often has color added to support its design (see fig. 53).

THE ANCIENT NEAR EAST: THE ART OF THE SUMERIANS

Civilization began in Egypt and Mesopotamia at about the same time, between 4000 and 3000 B.C. Unlike the relatively stable government of Egypt, ancient Mesopotamia saw a succession of cultures, including those of the Assyrians and Persians, which will be discussed later (see p. 68).

The Sumerian civilization began to flourish about 3000 B.C., as the Sumerians brought the Tigris and Euphrates rivers under control for irrigation. A flourishing agricultural economy developed, along with trade, commercial enterprise, and technological innovation (the Sumerians are credited with the invention of the wheel). The Sumerians controlled southern Mesopotamia until about 2350, when they were conquered by another people. They regained control about 2150 B.C. and remained rulers until 2030 B.C. The Sumerians invented writing when the system of pictographic signs which they had developed for record-keeping evolved into a phonetically based system known as cuneiform. In *History Begins at Sumer,* S. N. Kramer lists thirty-nine "firsts" that can be attributed to the Sumerians, including the first schools, the first historian, the first love song, and the first library catalogue. Among the Sumerians' heritage for later generations were important developments in ethics, education, and written law. Humanity's first great poem, written during the Akkadian period in Sumer, was based on an old Sumerian tale. This is *The Epic of Gilgamesh,* a tragic poem that tells of a Sumerian king's

37. *Worshippers and Deities.* c. 2750 B.C. Gypsum, height of tallest figure approx. 30". The Iraq Museum, Baghdad, and The Oriental Institute, University of Chicago. These figures were found at the Temple of Abu at Tell Asmar, Iraq.

38. *The Storm God and Two Stags.* Lintel from a temple at Al'Ubaid, Iraq. c. 2500 B.C. Copper sheets over wooden core, length 94". British Museum, London

quest for glory and immortality and ends when he discovers that even the bravest heroes must face death. At its height the Sumerian civilization included more than a dozen loosely unified city-states. Each had a population of between ten and fifty thousand inhabitants. The cities were fortified with broad walls, gates, and towers, and their dominating feature was a towering religious shrine known as a ziggurat.

Sumerian religion was polytheistic, with more than three thousand gods and goddesses. It was also animistic, encompassing virtually all aspects of nature. The divine, which was manifested in nature, was present in every object. Each city had a patron deity. Among the significant surviving Sumerian objects are simple standing figures, found in groups within a shrine, that are identified by inscriptions as representations of deities, priests, and individuals (see fig. 37). They probably do not include the cult statue of the main god or goddess, which most likely assumed a more abstract form. These figures, conical and cylindrical, are shown with their hands rigidly clasped and with enormous eyes inlaid with semi-precious blue lapis lazuli (imported from Afghanistan) or with shell. All wear the typical Sumerian costume, a simple skirt-like apron. The gods in the group are distinguished from the individuals by hierarchical scale and by the enlarged size of their eyes. The statuettes of the individuals were placed as votive offerings in temples and served, in an animistic sense, to present the life spirit of the donor in an attitude of continuous and vigilant prayer. Each was a permanent and ever-alert substitute for the donor, who may not have been allowed to enter the sacred shrine.

A potent Sumerian object is the large high-relief sculpture that presumably surmounted the entrance of a small temple (fig. 38). The central figure—a magnificent and threatening lioness-headed eagle with wings spread—is Imdugud, the force that exists within a storm cloud. This frontal deity is framed by

39. Ziggurat, Ur. c. 2100 B.C. Fired brick over mud brick core, 210 x 150' at base; original height approx. 70'

two symmetrical stags, which surely represent other natural forces, to create a simple composition that is both commanding and awesome.

The most impressive structure of a Sumerian city—and of ancient Near Eastern cities in general—was the ziggurat (from the Akkadian, pinnacle or mountain-top), a high, terraced structure. The ziggurat at Ur (the Sumerian city thought to be the childhood home of the Old Testament figure Abraham) survives in the best state of preservation (fig. 39). It was built on the ruins of earlier ziggurats by several Sumerian kings, including Ur-Nammu, who wrote one of the earliest code of laws. Approximately as tall as a six- or seven-story building, it had two temples—one at the foot of the ziggurat and, on the summit, a second built entirely of blue enameled bricks. This ziggurat was dedicated to Ur's patron, the moon god Nanna-Sin. On the New Year

festival, processions would ascend the three staircases and proceed through a ceremonial gateway to the brilliantly decorated temple with its cult statue and sacrificial altar at the top. Herodotus, the Greek historian, wrote about a ziggurat when he described the "Tower of Babel": it was three hundred feet tall with, at its apex, a temple with a large couch and table of gold for use by the god when he came down to earth. The Sumerian mother goddess was Ninhursag, the lady of the mountain, and the mountains were the source for the water that nourished their country. As a humanly made sacred mountain, the ziggurat offered the king and priests the possibility of ascending during rituals to visit the residence of the gods and to ask for divine guidance in political and religious affairs. An early Mesopotamian text refers to a ziggurat as the "bond between heaven and earth."

THE PYRAMIDS

40. Pyramids of Menkure (c. 2470 B.C.; see fig. 2), Khafre (c. 2500 B.C.), and Khufu (c. 2530 B.C.), Giza. Original height of the Pyramid of Khufu, 480'; length of each side at base 755'. The three great pyramids at Giza, built of limestone and granite, were viewed as architectural wonders even in the ancient world. Constructed as royal tombs, they are the best known of more than eighty pyramids built in ancient Egypt.

Associating the transition to the afterlife with the sunset, the great pyramids—burial places of the pharaohs—were located on the western side of the Nile River (fig. 40). Today the desert area around the pyramids reveals little of the complex of funerary temples and other grave sites which once formed this great necropolis (city of the dead); the "*Sphinx*" is part of the funerary precinct of Khafre (fig. 41). The face of the "*Sphinx*" bears the features of the pharaoh Khafre,

41. *Colossal Statue of Khafre as the God Hu,* later known as the "*Great Sphinx,*" with pyramids at Giza in the background. c. 2500 B.C. Sandstone probably as Hu, the reincarnation of the sun-god Re. (The name sphinx, meaning stranger or mysterious person, by which we know the monument today, was first used by the ancient Greeks.)

Grave sites in predynastic Egypt were usually shallow pits marked with mounds of sand near the edge of the desert. By about 2900 B.C., nobles were buried in underground chambers marked by mud-brick structures called mastabas (from the Arabic *mastabah*, bench) with battered (sloped) walls (fig. 43). Mastabas contained offerings to the *Ka* and chambers for a statue of the deceased.

About 2750 B.C., during the Old Kingdom, the pharaoh Zoser commissioned Imhotep to design and construct a funerary complex at Saqqara (fig. 44). The architectural climax was a large step pyramid. This solid structure suggests the superimposition of progressively smaller mastabas.

It is not completely clear why the pyramidal form was used in this funerary context. One theory suggests that it derives from the cult image of the sun god Re, a small pyramidal stone that symbolized the rays of the sun descending to earth. A widely accepted view is that the pyramid fulfilled both spiritual and practical needs by offering a monumental and secure abode for the *Ka* and assisting the pharaoh's spirit in its ascent to heaven. A text found inside a pyramid states: "I have trodden these rays as ramps under my feet where I mount up to my mother Uraeus on the brow of Re."

Each of the great pyramids took over twenty years to build. Labor was probably supplied by the people, who gave their time during the three months of the summer flood when their land was under water. The high waters of the Nile facilitated the transport of limestone and granite, quarried miles away.

Building the pyramids was a laborious and exacting process. Surveyors would determine the cardinal directions by observing a star in the northern sky and would orient the square base with each wall facing a cardinal direction. The limestone blocks were transported, probably on a type of sled, up inclined ramps. A polished granite or gilded capstone would catch the first and last of the sun's rays. False passages were constructed to discourage grave robbers, but almost all Egyptian royal tombs were plundered in ancient times.

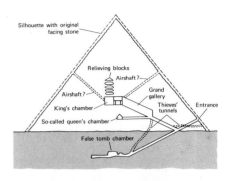

42. Section of Pyramid of Khufu. The pyramid of Khafre is the only one that preserves any of its outer dressed stone exterior. Many stones were taken from the site to build medieval and modern Cairo.

43. Mastabas. Reconstruction with section

44. IMHOTEP (architect)
Funerary District of King Zoser, Saqqara. Reconstruction model. c. 2750 B.C. Height of stepped pyramid about 200'

THE EGYPTIAN TEMPLE

45. Courtyard built by Pharaoh Amenhotep III, Temple of Amun-Mut-Khonsu, Luxor. Begun c. 1390 B.C. View of hypostyle hall from courtyard. The temple is dedicated to Amun, the sun god, his consort Mut, and Khonsu, the moon god.

The enormous New Kingdom temples at Karnak and Luxor (see figs. 45, 46, 49, 50), which are among the largest religious structures ever built, played an important role in Egyptian religion and politics, especially the annual festival of Opet, a twenty-four-day celebration of the New Year when the Nile was at full flood. At this time the pharaoh and his family would come to Karnak to participate in a procession accompanying the golden statue of Amun, the chief Egyptian deity, to the shrine of his wife (the goddess Mut) and son (Khonsu, the moon god) at Luxor. The pharaoh, identified with Amun, emerged from the pylon at dawn as the sun rose behind, framed by the pylon's flanking towers.

As is most often the case with religious architecture, the design of an Egyptian temple is based on its ritual use. Beginning with the long rows of sphinxes flanking the avenue to the entrance, the organization is axial, relating to the progress of the pharaoh's procession, and is characterized by bilateral symmetry (the forms are identical on either side of the central axis). As the pharaoh proceeded, he passed through a clear sequence of architectural spaces, beginning with the open road, flanked by sphinxes, and moving through the pylon, an entrance gate (see fig. 47) with broad battered towers and flag-poles flanking the doorway, into the sacred precinct. He then proceeded into one or more colonnaded courtyards open to the sky and framed on two or three sides by rows of columns (later pharaohs would often add additional courtyards, as at Luxor, fig. 49, where the latest open courtyard, added by Ramesses

II, is out of alignment with the earlier structures). Next he would enter a large room filled with columns known as the hypostyle hall (see fig. 46). The only light in this area would be that which filtered down from the raised roof area along the central axis, where there are long vertical openings (such a raised area with windows is known as a clerestory; for later examples see figs. 145, 200). The final sequence of rooms, all fully enclosed, became progressively smaller, lower, and darker until the priest and/or the pharaoh would enter the most sacred chamber, with the cult statue. (The Temple at Luxor was exceptional, for there were two sacred chambers; the one at the back, which was entered directly from the exterior wall, was where the sacred boat of Amun was placed after carrying the pharaoh over the Nile from

Karnak.) The hierarchical and exclusive quality of Egyptian society is expressed in these temples, for only a select few could follow the pharaoh into the courtyard, fewer yet into the hypostyle hall. The enormous walls of the sacred enclosure (more than a mile long at Karnak) served to exclude the multitude and remind them of their inferior social, political, and religious status, as did the overwhelming scale of the structures themselves.

The architecture stressed stability, weight, monumentality, and durability. These temples were meant to endure, and Amenhotep III described a temple he had built at Thebes as "an eternal, everlasting fortress of fine white sandstone, wrought with gold throughout; it is made very wide and large, and established forever." The massive stone walls were solid, without windows, and weight and stability were further expressed by the heavy cornices and battered walls of the pylon. Virtually all surfaces were covered with low or sunken relief carvings that emphasize the mass and weight of the stone. The hypostyle hall was a veritable forest of huge fat columns (at Karnak the largest were sixty-nine feet tall and twelve feet in diameter, with a circumference of almost thirty-three feet), and the effect was claustrophobic and intimidating. The solidity and austerity of these Egyptian temples seem to be direct reflections of the stable and controlled civilization that created them.

46. Hypostyle hall, Temple of Amun, Karnak. Reconstruction model of central section. 1350–1205 B.C. The Metropolitan Museum of Art, New York (Levi Hale Willard Bequest, 1890)

47. Typical pylon gate, showing the rising sun and the pharaoh emerging from the central doorway

POST-AND-LINTEL CONSTRUCTION

lintel / entablature

post

48. Diagram of post-and-lintel construction

The type of construction used for Egyptian colonnaded courtyards and hypostyle halls (see p. 60) is known as post and lintel, the post being the vertical supporting member, usually a cylindrical column, and the lintel being the horizontal member, often known as the entablature (fig. 48). The only simpler types of construction are the wall and the mound. The engineering dynamics of post and lintel are straightforward—the weight of the entablature presses downward on the column, which must be strong enough to support the entablature's weight (see p. 81). If the entablature is too long or lacks sufficient tensile strength (longitudinal strength sufficient to support itself without breaking), it may collapse in the middle or shear and break where it meets the column. In post-and-lintel architecture the columns are usually decorated, especially at the top, or capital. In Egypt the column and capital may resemble greatly enlarged papyrus, date palms, or bundled reeds (such forms may derive from the use of actual bundled reeds in early Egyptian wall architecture). Although the post-and-lintel system is simple, the rhythmic placement of the columns and the relationship of vertical to horizontal allow many architectural and aesthetic variations.

The Egyptian builder was restricted by the available materials, which included vast amounts of stone but virtually no wood. The dense and brittle nature of the local stone kept the lintels short and the columns heavy and close together. The hypostyle hall was virtually the only large enclosed space that could be constructed.

HOW TO READ ARCHITECTURAL DIAGRAMS

hypostyle hall

49. Plan, Temple of Amun-Mut-Khonsu, Luxor. Statistics for a similar temple precinct at Karnak reveal the tremendous scale of these projects; Karnak is 1220' long, and the sacred enclosure encompasses 62,000 acres.

50. Temple of Khonsu, Karnak. c. 1080 B.C. Isometric projection with plan and longitudinal section

The drawings of architecture in this book are meant to aid in your understanding of principles of design and construction. Some of these diagrams reveal how a building would look if it were sliced through, as in a plan (or ground plan; fig. 49), which shows the building as if truncated by a horizontal plane approximately one foot above the floor level (solid lines are structure, with openings indicating doors and windows; lighter lines indicate floor patterns; dotted or light lines indicate the patterns of the ceiling; see fig. 198). A cross section shows the building sliced by a vertical plane from side to side (see fig. 83), while a longitudinal section slices the building from front to back (for an example see fig. 50). An elevation shows the exterior surfaces and their decoration diagramatically, not as the human eye would see them (see fig. 294). A relatively recent kind of diagram is the isometric projection, which includes both a ground plan and a view of the exterior and/or interior from a specific point of view (see fig. 50). The axonometric projection (fig. 101) is slightly less realistic than the isometric projection. Because of the artificial and two-dimensional nature of most of these diagrams, an understanding of any building requires an examination of several diagrams.

Today buildings are erected using architect's diagrams similar to those discussed above, but we still do not know much about the use of drawings by architects, engineers, and construction crews in the past. The earliest surviving examples date from the Gothic period. In some early periods architects and engineers apparently laid out the building full scale on the ground, using pegs and string or vines to mark the contours.

EGYPTIAN PAINTING AND PAINTED RELIEFS

51. *Pond in a Garden.* Fragment of a painting from the Tomb of Nebamun, Thebes. c. 1390 B.C. Paint on plaster wall, 24 x 28". British Museum, London

52. *Hunting Scene.* Fragment from the Tomb of Nebamun, Thebes. c. 1400 B.C. Paint on plaster wall. British Museum, London

The vast numbers of Egyptian paintings that survive—preserved by the arid desert climate—are tomb paintings on plaster and, because of the demand that tomb decoration preserve the pleasant everyday life of the Egyptians so that the *Ka* could enjoy these pleasures throughout eternity, these paintings have a broad human interest and appeal. They tell us a great deal about ancient Egyptian life and customs. When analyzed, they reveal Egyptian patterns of thinking and organizing ideas. *Pond in a Garden* (fig. 51) provides a view of a rectangular pool, with ducks, fish, lotus blossoms, and flowering and fruit-bearing trees. Completeness and clarity were demanded

of the Egyptian painter, for anything not clearly included in the tomb painting would not be available to the *Ka* in the afterlife. This explains why each object has to be shown in its most easily recognized view—the pond is represented as if seen from above, while everything else is in profile. The relationships among the objects in reality are also made clear in the representation: fish, ducks, and lotus are seen as within the pool, and trees surround it. The trees are seen right side up and sideways, but not upside down—those at the bottom side of the pool are upright. The Egyptian artist worked within the strict limitations imposed by the function of the work. This approach,

which is not naturalistic, uses only frontal and profile viewpoints, the characteristic points of view in Egyptian art.

The *Hunting Scene* from the Tomb of Nebamun (fig. 52) offers similar organizational and decorative principles. The marsh weeds and the water are shown in section, as if cut away and seen from the side, while all the other elements are represented in their clearest silhouette. Nebamun, accompanied by his wife and daughter (both shown much smaller in scale), holds aloft his throw stick and grasps three birds. He is portrayed simultaneously hunting and holding aloft his trophies. His cat or mongoose, trained to retrieve, is shown in midair capturing three

53. *Ti Watching a Hippopotamus Hunt.* c. 2400 B.C. Painted limestone relief, height approx. 46". Tomb of Ti, Saqqara

birds at once. While the bounty of game is surely exaggerated, the migration of birds and fish to the marshes of the Faiyum in winter was an annual event, and hunting, sacred to the marsh goddess, was both recreational and religious.

The hippopotamus hunt from the Old Kingdom Tomb of Ti is a painted relief which combines the naturalistic color of painting with the durability of relief (fig. 53). The parallel lines that create a foil for the organic shapes of the figures and animals indicate a setting deep in the marsh, for these are the stems of the reeds that burst into leaf and blossom near the top of the relief. In this upper area predators stalk birds, creating strikingly naturalistic patterns against the geometric stalks as well as a metaphor for the hunt taking place below.

FIGURE-GROUND

The distinct contrast that can be noted between forms and background in most works of art is called the figure-ground relationship. In our *Hunting Scene*, for example, we read the humans and the cat, birds, fish, foliage, and boat as "positive" elements—figures—isolated against a "negative" white plane—the ground—behind them. A similar effect can be noted when works of sculpture and architecture are isolated and stand out against or within their surroundings. In analyzing works of art, the positive-negative, figure-ground relationship is always an important component. In some modern works, artists have achieved visual ambiguity by allowing the positive and negative forms to assume virtually equal importance in the composition.

NEOLITHIC MEGALITHS

While the Egyptian civilization was prospering during the Old Kingdom, western Europe was experiencing the transformations of the Neolithic period. The potent testimony of prehistoric monuments in France and England is best evoked by the remains of Stonehenge (fig. 54), where an outermost ring of smaller stones set flush to the ground surrounds an inner ring, a cromlech, composed of large stones known as megaliths (from the Greek *megas*, large, and *lithos*,

stone). The innermost megaliths form a horseshoe which defines an axis within the circular plan. The axis at Stonehenge is oriented toward the point on the eastern horizon where the sun rises on the dawn of the summer solstice. Other stones were apparently aligned to the setting sun on the winter solstice and various phases of the moonrise.

The alignment of the megaliths suggests that rituals of worship were related to celestial events, while the emphasis on

54. Stonehenge. c. 2750–1300 B.C. Megaliths and earth markings, diameter of circle 97'; height approx. 13' 6". Salisbury Plain, Wiltshire, England. Stonehenge was constructed in four stages between c. 2750 B.C. and 1300 B.C. Some of the megaliths were transported as far as one hundred ninety miles, probably by being dragged on sleds. They may have been raised using a series of levers. Earthen ramps were constructed to place the lintel stones.

Stonehenge: c. 2750–1300 B.C.
c. 1728 B.C.: Hammurabi's Code of Laws

55. Stone alignment, Carnac, France. c. 3000 B.C. Megaliths, height 6' to 15'

the summer solstice implies that it was the major festival. This union of religion with celestial events is frequent in early belief systems. An understanding of the regular cycles of the seasons based on celestial observation is intimately related to the cultivation of crops, and both ritualistic and practical needs may have been served by Stonehenge.

At other Neolithic sites, from Europe, across Central to East and Southeast Asia, large upright boulders were used as individual markers or in combinations to form geometric patterns over a large land area. Near Carnac, rows of upright megaliths called menhirs (large stones) run for almost two miles across the countryside (fig. 55). Sections of eleven, ten, and thirteen lines were probably erected over different periods but may have been made to adjoin one another. The sections organize space and direct our attention toward circles which contain grave sites.

LATER DEVELOPMENTS IN THE NEAR EAST: ASSYRIAN AND EARLY PERSIAN ART

The *Lamassu* (fig. 56) seems to have been intended to intimidate the visitor—and especially foreign ambassadors—before they entered into the presence of the Assyrian king. The threatening content is supported by the treatment of the material, for the high polish of the stone emphasizes its density, while the patterns and fine detail of the beard and wings stress the massive scale and powerful forms. The figure is given five legs to offer a convincing solidity and physicality from both the front view, on approach, and the side, in passing.

The Assyrians and Persians successively controlled Mesopotamia. The Assyrians established a powerful kingdom in northern Mesopotamia from the ninth through the seventh centuries B.C., while the early or Achaemenid Persians were centered in southern Mesopotamia during the sixth and fifth centuries B.C. Both cultures were known for their powerful kings, who tried to conquer and control vast territories. The Assyrians in particular were feared for their atrocities during war, but the Persians, who for a brief period even conquered Egypt, tried to establish a reputation for benevolent rule and had greater success in creating a huge empire.

Assyrian and early Persian palaces were similarly decorated, with low reliefs lining the palace rooms and passages. In Assyrian palaces the themes were ritualistic, honorific, militaristic, or any subject that would impress the visitor with the unquestionable power and undeniable majesty of the royal personage. The Assyrian palace at Khorsabad

56. Assyrian. *Human-Headed Winged Bull (Lamassu)*, from the gateway, Palace of Sargon II, Dur Sharrukin (Khorsabad, Iraq). c. 720 B.C. Limestone, height 14'. The Louvre, Paris

Human-Headed Winged Bull: **c. 720** B.C.
776 B.C.: First Olympic Games in Greece
1000–960 B.C.: David rules as king of Israel

58. Early Persian. Portion of Royal Audience Hall (Apadana) and Stairway of the Palace of Darius, Persepolis, Iran. c. 500 B.C.

covered more than twenty-five acres and had more than two hundred courtyards and rooms. Here and at Nimrud and Nineveh, continuous low reliefs depicted Assyrian military victories and the subsequent pillage and carnage. The reliefs emphasized the Assyrian king's strength in battle or in sport. In one series he is shown engaged in a hunt in which lions and lionesses were released from cages. The king is represented victorious in his chariot, surrounded by dead and dying animals. In the detail pictured (fig. 57), a lioness is shown in her death throes, dragging her paralyzed legs behind her and uttering a cry or moan of death. The artist's sensitivity to the suffering of the animals is unforgettable.

The Palace of Darius at Persepolis (fig. 58) had grand staircases decorated with reliefs of seemingly endless processions and large scenes in which, following an old Near Eastern tradition, a fierce beast is represented attacking a domesticated animal. Such scenes are open to a number of levels of interpretation. On one level they probably symbolize Persian power and victory, but they may also refer to political and even to cosmic conflict. These stairs led to a sequence of magnificent square throne rooms and ceremonial chambers filled with large columns. The largest was two hundred fifty feet square with columns at least forty feet high. In form the capitals are unusual and uniquely Persian, with gigantic figures of paired bulls (see fig. 59). Stylistically, the debt of the Persians to Assyrian art is evident in the contrast between bold simple masses and fine, abstract detail, but the Persian compositions have an increased refinement and elegance.

59. Early Persian. Bull Capital from the Apadana, Persepolis. Width 12'3". The Louvre, Paris

Introduction to Greek Art

60. Severe style. *Apollo and the Battle of the Lapiths and the Centaurs,* detail from the west pediment, Temple of Zeus at Olympia. 468–460 B.C. Marble, over-lifesize. Museum, Olympia

In the midst of a chaotic combat (fig. 60), the god Apollo majestically restores order. He occupies the axis of the composition, just below the apex of the temple roof. Apollo's calm yet commanding presence contrasts with the outburst of the surrounding activity.

The sculptures on the pediment of the Temple of Zeus at Olympia were completed during a period of transition. They originally decorated the triangular end (pediment; see figs. 84, 86) of the gable roof of the temple, approximately fifty feet above ground level. The composition is clear, the movement is bold and direct, and the details of anatomy and drapery are easily read by the viewer below. The sculptures illustrate a mythological subject. Among the guests at a wedding feast were drunken centaurs (creatures who are half-human, half-horse) who attempted to abduct and rape the women. This theme had an immediate significance for the Greeks at this time. Their recent victory over the Persians (479 B.C.) was symbolically expressed in the victory over the centaurs. On a more profound level, the calm presence of Apollo represents the mastery of reasoned order over brute force. The scene had a special meaning because of its location at Olympia, for during the famous games there, a truce was observed among the Greek city-states. The ideals exemplified by the myth and its representation at Olympia promote attitudes which distinguish the Greeks from their neighbors in the ancient world.

HISTORY

About 1100 B.C., a tribe called the Dorians entered the Greek peninsula from the north. The Dorians overwhelmed the Mycenaeans, who had ruled this area for the preceding five hundred years, and gradually a new culture, historically known as the ancient Greek civilization, evolved. By the eighth century B.C., the two great Homeric poems, *The Iliad* and *The Odyssey,* had been composed, and Greece had evolved into a grouping of independent city-states. Each city-state *(polis)* commanded the loyalty of its citizens, especially in religious, military, and economic matters. Their fierce independence prevented the political unification of Greece. In 776 B.C. the first Olympic Games were held. Called once every four years, they were held in honor of Zeus, ruler of the gods. Winners gained personal fame, and achievement in sports was celebrated in such works of art as the victory vase (fig. 61), whose runners move across the surface with rhythmic energy.

During the eighth century B.C., developing commerce among the city-states led to a prosperous economy. One of the major products was pottery, and the Geometric style *Vase* (fig. 62), with its bands of severe patterns, demonstrates the artistic beginnings of the Greeks. The animals on the neck of the vase and the human figures occupying the central band conform to repeated geometric shapes and rhythms. The highly abstract human shapes represent female mourners pulling their hair at a funeral; the deceased lies on his bier. The scene relates to the purpose of the vase, which marked a grave site. Such vessels played an important role in honoring the dead. Oil, poured into them to commemorate the deceased, would flow through the open bottom and into the ground.

During the Archaic period, from the seventh century to the early fifth century B.C., trade routes expanded, and the Greeks began to colonize areas of southern Italy and Asia Minor. At this time the Greeks began to produce lifesize figurative sculpture and to construct marble temples.

The early fifth century B.C. was a time of significant artistic and political changes. In both sculpture and painting, we witness a more naturalistic rendering of the human figure. In architecture, temples

61. Archaic style. *Panathenaic Amphora with Runners.* c. 520 B.C. Painted terracotta, height 24 1/2". The Metropolitan Museum of Art, New York (Rogers Fund, 1914). The Panathenaic amphora was a special, large vessel given as a prize in the Olympic Games. It was filled with oil made from olives grown on special trees.

62. Geometric style. *Vase with Mourners Around a Bier.* c. 750 B.C. Terra-cotta, height 61". National Archaeological Museum, Athens. The decorated pottery vessels of the Greeks are traditionally known as vases. Vases such as this one are sometimes referred to as Dipylon vases because they were found at the Dipylon Cemetery in Athens.

undergo a process of visual refinement, giving the buildings a new sense of elegance.

In 490 B.C. the Persians invaded Greece. The city-states formed a defensive alliance and defeated the invasion force at Marathon, about twenty-six miles northeast of Athens. (After the battle, a courier ran to Athens bringing news of the victory; he fell dead of exhaustion after exclaiming, "Rejoice, we conquer." His run is commemorated in today's marathon races.) Ten years later the Persians captured Athens and sacked the Acropolis, but in 479 B.C. the Greeks defeated the Persians at the naval battle of Salamis. No peace treaty was signed until 449 B.C., and during the thirty years following the second Persian defeat, Athens, which had agreed to supply the navy for the Greek military alliance, continued to collect taxes from the other city-states. During this period Athens became the preeminent political and economic center, but only at the cost of jealousy from the other city-states.

The mid-fifth century B.C. is known as the Classical period of art and culture. Its center was Athens, where a popular politician named Pericles was continuously reelected chief general of the city from 460 to 430 B.C. The Athenian government was the first major democracy in the Western world, although only free men were allowed to vote.

Pericles used the wealth of Athens and the taxes collected from the other city-states to embark on an ambitious campaign of renewal, which included rebuilding the temples on the Acropolis destroyed by the Persians. The Acropolis (from the Greek *akros,* highest, and *polis,* city) is an outcropping of rock which dominates the center of Athens (see fig. 64). To the Greeks it was the sacred location where Poseidon and Athena had contested for control of the city below. Poseidon, god of the sea, caused salt water to flow from a spring on the Acropolis, but Athena's gift of an olive tree was deemed more beneficial to the people. Thus, tradition held, Athens took its name from the Greek goddess of wisdom. As late as the second century A.D., a saltwater spring and an olive tree could still be found on the Acropolis.

Pericles knew the value of providing an intellectual, physically healthy, and aesthetically pleasing environment for the citizens of Athens. Later, when war had broken out in Greece, he offered a funeral oration for Athenian soldiers: "Our constitution is called a democracy because power is not in the hands of a few, but of the people. Our laws secure equal justice for all in their private disputes, and our public opinion welcomes and honors talent in every brace of achievement; what counts is not membership in a particular class, but the actual ability a man possesses.

"Yet ours is no mere work-a-day city. No other provides so much recreation for the spirit—contests and sacrifices all the year round, and beauty in our public buildings to cheer the heart and delight the eye day by day.

"We are lovers of the beautiful without being extravagant, and lovers of wisdom without being soft. We regard wealth as something to be used properly, rather than as something to boast about. . . . We decide and debate, carefully, and in person, all matters of policy, for we do not think there is an incompatibility between words and deeds.

"Our city is an education to Greece."

63. Theater, Epidaurus. c. 350 B.C.
Diameter of the projected circle, 378'

64. Acropolis, Athens. Reconstruction
model. Royal Ontario Museum,
Toronto, and J. Walter Graham

As the political dominance of Athens grew, so did the resentment of the other city-states. The Peloponnesian wars erupted in 431 B.C., plunging Greece into war. When the war ended in 404 B.C., the power of Athens was broken, and Sparta and Corinth assumed a more prominent role in the political affairs of Greece. By the later fourth century B.C., however, a new force from the north would command attention, and the final chapter of Greek history is written by two Macedonian kings, Philip and Alexander (see pp. 95–97).

A GREEK VIEW OF THE WORLD

Although beset by internal political conflicts, the Greeks, who called themselves Hellenes, shared a common language and culture.

Greeks divided the world into two types of people, those whose native language was Greek and others, who were called *barbaroi* (barbarians). The derogatory association that we have with the term barbarian developed slowly, but as a result of the Persian wars, the Greeks continued to define how their culture was different from that of the barbarians.

INTELLECTUAL AND SCIENTIFIC ACTIVITIES

The love of wisdom of which Pericles spoke found expression in philosophy and science as well as art. From the mid-fifth through the fourth century B.C., philosophy developed from the speculative questioning of Socrates and the ideal forms of Plato to the natural observations by Aristotle. The Hippocratic medical writings, by several different authors, represent a diverse body of literature on healing practices and were the foundation of ancient medical study. The Greek pursuit of reason and speculative thought led to many practical inventions.

At the heart of this world view was the belief that human reason could define the rational order of the universe, an order which was revealed through an understanding of mathematics. In the sixth century B.C., Pythagoras wrote of the relationship between mathematics and musical harmony, noting that a stretched string, when plucked, produces a certain note by its vibration. When the string is measured and plucked at points which correspond to exact divisions by whole numbers—1/2, 1/3, etc.—the vibrations will produce a harmonious chord. If the string is plucked at any other interval, the sound will seem discordant.

To the Greeks, this discovery had a powerful impact. If the sounds of nature were governed by the order of mathematics, then the universe itself must obey the harmony of mathematical concurrences. This notion of a universal harmony that could be perceived by human reason came to govern the rules of art and architecture during the Classical period.

RELIGION

The Greeks worshipped numerous gods and goddesses who ruled over all aspects of life and death. Leader among the gods was Zeus (see fig. 75), who established the rule of the deities by overthrowing his father. Hera, wife of Zeus, was queen of the gods and protectress of women. Along with other deities, Zeus and Hera were believed to reside on Mount Olympus. Although some Egyptian gods had been represented in human form, it was the Greeks who fully anthropomorphized their deities, giving them both human form and attributes. Numerous mythological tales speak of the exploits of gods and goddesses, who often deemed it necessary to alter human affairs.

Sacrifices to the gods were joined with great festivals which might include athletic games, such as the Olympic Games, and theatrical productions. Greek theater developed from the rituals honoring Dionysus, an important, popular god and patron of drama and song. The Greek playwrights Æschylus, Sophocles, Euripides, and Aristophanes wrote plays to be performed during an annual Athenian festival honoring Dionysus.

Greek theaters were open-air arenas. Theaters such as the one at Epidaurus (fig. 63) have semicircular rows of marble seats built into the hillside. The circular area below was the stage. The Greek theater combined practical function with harmonious design.

GREEK ART

Greek art was distinguished by a dramatic evolution over a relatively short five-hundred-year period. The abstract features of Archaic period sculptures (figs. 68, 69) were transformed into the Severe style (see figs. 60, 70, 75, 76) and then into the idealized representations of the Classical period (figs. 78, 85–87), which sought to equate the perfection of art with the harmonies of the natural order. By the time of Alexander the Great, realistic and emotionally dramatic representations were common (figs. 90, 93, 94). In painting, flat shapes (fig. 62) gave way to elements of illusionism (fig. 92), and in architecture proportions and decorative elements underwent a progressive transformation toward a more refined ideal (figs. 72, 82). The process of revision in Greek art is one manifestation of the questioning Greek mind.

THE GREEK ARTIST

The Greeks valued both intellectual and physical achievements, and it is not surprising that they would begin to praise the artist as an individual with unique talents. An exceptional development in the seventh century B.C., with virtually no precedent in earlier cultures, occurred when artists began with regularity to sign their works. Such signatures are clearly an indication of personal pride. In addition, they might also be an early form of advertising. Literary sources from both ancient Greece and Rome offer descriptions and criticisms of works of art which were deemed famous. By the fourth century B.C., such references begin to include comments on the personalities of specific artists and anecdotes about their lives. An ancient discussion of Apelles, recorded by Pliny, reveals the respect enjoyed by a successful artist: "Nevertheless the painter who surpassed all those who were born before him and all those who came later was Apelles. . . . He produced volumes, which contain his doctrine. . . . He . . .was also gifted with a courteous nature and . . . was on quite good terms with Alexander the Great."

GREEK VASE PAINTING

65. EXEKIAS (painter and potter)
Achilles and Ajax Playing Draughts (detail). c. 530 B.C. Painted terra-cotta amphora, height 24". Vatican Museums, Rome. The stories represented on Archaic vases, which usually told of Greek mythological or historical events, were at first illustrated with black figures on a red background. Works in this style are known as black-figure vases.

During the Archaic period, the decorative bands prevalent on earlier Geometric vases (see fig. 62) were relegated to the base and neck, and increased surface area was given to figurative narration. This vase (fig. 65) depicts the Greek warriors Achilles and Ajax playing draughts (an ancient game related to our game of checkers) during a lull in the Trojan War. The signature "Exekias painted me and made me" indicates an artist talented in both pottery and painting. This was rare in ancient Greece, for usually a division of labor was practiced in the production of vases. The composition, with its strong symmetry, and the manner in which scene and decoration are related to the shape of the vase reveal the Greek search for balance and harmony.

The various shapes of Greek vases developed according to both purpose and the Greek interest in aesthetic forms. By the Archaic period, specialized forms had become associated with specific functions as indicated in the diagram of shapes (fig. 66). After the vase was formed but before it was fired, the painter, using slip (a mixture of clay particles in water, sometimes combined with wood ash), painted the black figures in silhouette. As the vase was being fired in the kiln, the air vents were closed, causing the entire vase to turn black for a period as the red iron oxide of the terra-cotta was converted into black and magnetic iron oxides. When the air vents were again opened, the iron in the clay body returned to its red-orange color except in those areas covered by slip. In the firing, the slip had formed a glazed surface coating, sealing these areas from the air. They remained black, creating the black figures and decoration on the vase. Details of the decoration and of the figures' anatomy, drapery, and armor were then added by incising lines into the surface of the glaze. Working with a sharp pointed tool known as a burin, the artist engraved lines through the black glaze, exposing the terra-cotta color beneath. On Archaic vases the artist delighted in decorative geometric patterns that asserted the two-dimensional quality of the figures.

Around 530 B.C. a new technique which reversed the figure-ground colors was introduced, perhaps by a student of Exekias sometimes identified as the Andokides Painter. Known as the red-figure style, this technique offers figures and objects silhouetted against the painted black background. Details of anatomy and costume are painted on, rather than incised into, the surface of the vase.

The vase with the *Death of Sarpedon,* signed by Euxitheos and Euphronios, was created shortly after the introduction of this new red-figure technique (fig. 67). It depicts the slain body of Sarpedon, a fallen Trojan hero killed by Patroclus, being carried from the battlefield by personifications of Sleep and Death. Hermes, who will lead Sarpedon's soul to Hades, stands behind (*The Iliad*, XVI, 426 ff.). The figures convey a physical and emotional presence that is new to Greek vase painting. Somber facial expressions betray the tragic loss. We sense the physical strain required to lift the body, while diagonal patterns of limbs and flowing blood pull the composition downward. Details of anatomy and drapery are more naturalistically rendered, and the manner in which some parts of the body are shown as if seen in sharp recession is an early example of foreshortening (see also p. 249). The greater naturalism is also made possible by use of the brush, in contrast to the incising tool employed by the black-figure painter.

The level of artistry reached in these vases testifies to a refined understanding of both functional and visual values. The black-figured amphora has two handles for carrying and an opening large enough to admit a ladle. The broad opening of the red-figured calyx krater made possible the mixing of water and wine. In each of our examples the painter has adapted the composition to the form of the vase. The arched backs of Achilles and Ajax echo the inward curvature of the amphora, while the composition on the calyx krater, with the horizontal body of Sarpedon balanced by the vertical pose of the attendants and the parenthetical effect of Sleep and Death, emphasizes the inverted trapezoidal form of the vase. It was this ability to join form, function, and decoration which made Greek vases valued objects throughout the ancient world.

EXEKIAS, *Achilles and Ajax Playing Draughts:* **c. 530** B.C.
580 B.C.: Nebuchadnezzar begins building the Hanging Gardens of Babylon

amphora   Panathenaic   calyx krater   volute krater   kylix   lekythos
            amphora

66. Typical Greek vase shapes. The amphora and Panathenaic amphora are containers to store wine, olive oil, honey or water. The calyx krater and volute krater are bowls for mixing wine with water, which was the Greek custom. The kylix is a drinking cup and the lekythos is a container for olive oil.

67. EUPHRONIOS (painter) AND EUXITHEOS (potter)
Death of Sarpedon During the Trojan War. c. 515 B.C. Painted terra-cotta calyx krater, height 18". The Metropolitan Museum of Art, New York (Bequest of Joseph H. Durkee, gift of Darius Ogden Mills, and gift of C. Ruxton Love, by exchange, 1972). Red-figure vases feature red figures against a black ground.

SCULPTURE: ARCHAIC STYLE AND SEVERE STYLE

68. Archaic style. *Kouros,* from the Tomb of Kroisos, Anavysos, Greece. c. 520 B.C. Marble with red paint on the hair, headband, and pupils of the eyes, height 72". National Archaeological Museum, Athens. The inscription on the base reads: "Stop and grieve at the tomb of the dead Kroisos, slain by wild Ares in the front rank of battle."

The earliest large-scale Greek sculptures (c. 600 B.C.) are indebted to Egyptian prototypes that were certainly known to the Greeks, who had a trading station in Egypt as early as the mid-seventh century B.C. But by about 520 B.C., when the *Kouros* (youth) from Anavysos was created (fig. 68), the new direction Greek art would take was already evident. The Greek figure represents an athletic ideal and a new understanding of the organic nature of the human body. And, while the Greek figure maintains a stance derived from Egyptian models (see fig. 2), with one leg advanced and hands clenched at the sides, the stone passages, which in Egyptian figures connect the forward to the rear leg and the arms to the torso, have been carved away. The Greek figure is tense and prepared to take action, not frozen for all eternity. In contrast to Egyptian sculptures, most Greek male figures are nude. While Greek athletes competed nude at the games held during religious festivals, the nudity also demonstrates new Greek attitudes concerning the beauty and integrity of the human body. The slight smile, which suggests a confident assurance consistent with the buoyant energy of the body, recognizes the psychological and emotional aspect of human life in a manner foreign to most Egyptian art. Nude male sculptures were set up as votive offerings at shrines and were used as grave monuments. That these youthful figures were sometimes used to mark the tombs of older men suggests that they represented a philosophical and visual ideal, not a specific individual.

The style of Greek sculpture from about 650 to 480 B.C. is usually referred to as Archaic, while figures from the first half of the fifth century B.C., which in retrospect are moving toward the Classical style of the second half of the century, are now usually designated Severe style (or Early Classical style or Transitional style; c. 480–450 B.C.). The contemporary Archaic sculptures of female figures—the *Kore* (maidens)—were used almost exclusively as votive figures, and they are always dressed (the female nude does not become common in Greek art until the fourth century; fig. 69). The gentle swelling of the body beneath the drapery suggests an interest in the organic qualities of the human figure, while rich visual patterns are offered by the subtle and varied textures of pleated drapery and plaited hair. This particular example preserves much of the color which was painted on the marble to enhance both its beauty and the lifelikeness of the sculpted figure.

The *Kouros* known as the *Kritian Boy,* because it is similar to works attributed to Kritios, represents the figure in a position that combines flexed and relaxed muscles (fig. 70). Although his feet are lost, enough of the figure survives to reveal that he was represented in the relaxed and

69. Archaic style. *Kore,* from Chios (?). c. 510 B.C. Marble fragment with red, blue, and violet paint, height approx. 22". Acropolis Museum, Athens. Such Archaic sculptures of female figures are much rarer than their male counterparts.

realistic position known since the Renaissance as *contrapposto.* The weight of the body is borne on one leg while the other is relaxed. *Contrapposto* (from the Latin *contrapositio,* counterpositioning) is related to a natural, relaxed stance. It has its basis in real life. *Contrapposto* affects the entire body, for the counterpositioning juxtaposes the forward, relaxed leg to the opposite shoulder, which also moves forward. The resulting figure seems to stand freely. Imaginary lines drawn across the body through knees, pelvis, and shoulders will rotate about the figure's axis. More importantly, *contrapposto* suggests the potential for movement, making possible figures that offer a new momentary quality. In addition, a sculpted figure standing in *contrapposto* becomes freestanding, a sculpture in the round, intended to be seen from many viewpoints. *Contrapposto* creates a unified figure standing in space, banishing the static Egyptian views (frontal, left profile, right profile) that had conditioned Greek sculpture at its origins.

To understand the revolutionary quality of this *Kouros,* we must try to view it as would a Greek of the period. The pose, which must have seemed startlingly new and amazingly naturalistic, is enhanced by a softness and organic unity in the articulation of the muscles. The sculptor appears to have breathed life into the stone itself. Sculpture would never be the same.

70. Severe style. *Kouros* (also known as the *Kritian Boy*). c. 480 B.C. Marble fragment, originally with inlaid eyes, height 36". Acropolis Museum, Athens

THE CLASSICAL ORDERS

Doric

Ionic

Corinthian

1 cornice
2 frieze
3 architrave
4 capital
5 column
6 entablature

71. Diagram of Doric, Ionic, and Corinthian orders

An order gives aesthetic definition and decoration to the post-and-lintel system (see p. 62). Between the seventh and fifth centuries B.C., the Greeks developed three architectural orders—the Doric, Ionic, and Corinthian—which have been in virtually continuous use up to the present day. The Greeks' invention and development of these orders (fig. 71) reveal their philosophical and analytical approach to architecture. An order establishes the specific architectural elements, which are designed to integrate with each other and with the building as a whole, and dictates the proportional scheme governing the interrelationships of the parts. The elements of an order include the column, with its capital, and the entablature, composed of architrave, frieze, and cornice. A column is often decorated with vertical lines known as flutes, which accentuate its cylindrical and vertical quality.

The classical orders, including the later Composite and Tuscan orders, became the most basic design element for architecture. They were used not only as supports, but as decoration on buildings that were not post and lintel in construction (for example, the Roman Colosseum; fig. 121). In later periods half-round decorative columns were often attached to a supporting or enclosing wall. These are known as half or engaged columns. When they are flattened they are called pilasters. When an order is used, however, it offers more than merely articulation and decoration, for it also carries the cultural significance of its origins in ancient Greece, and it can impart to a building the dignity, harmony, and sense of philosophical reason that is part of our reassuring heritage from the Greek world. The orders are generally regular and predictable, and when the harmonious relationships and proportions are ignored, there is a strong sense of violation.

The Doric order, well established by 600 B.C., is vigorous and austere: its fluted columns are strong in appearance and stand directly on the stylobate (stepped platform), without a decorated base. The Doric echinus appears to be a resilient cushion tucked between the column and the square abacus, suggesting in a clear, visual manner the nature and even the idea of support. Together echinus and abacus provide a simple and muscular transition from the vertical column to the horizontal superstructure. The Doric architrave is broad and simple, and the frieze area is decorated with triglyphs which alternate with metopes (originally metopes seem to have been painted panels of terra-cotta; later they were sculpted). The ancient Roman architect Vitruvius argued that the Doric order was originally derived from wooden architecture and that the tapering of the column was based on the use of tree trunks for early columns.

The Ionic order, which was first used in the sixth century, is lighter in proportion and more elegant in detail than the Doric. Columns have richly decorated bases, and the Ionic capital is characterized by a scroll-like motif called a volute. Ionic temples often feature a continuous frieze in place of the triglyphs and metopes. The planar, frontal Ionic volutes created a problem at corners that was solved by the development, during the fifth century, of the Corinthian order, which employs a cylindrical capital decorated with acanthus leaves. The increasing elegance of the Greek orders is revealed by the constantly changing proportions of the column. In the Doric the relationship of height to diameter is usually 4:1 to 6:1 or even 7:1. For Ionic it is 7:1 to 8:1; Corinthian can be 8:1 to 9:1.

The Composite order combines the Corinthian with some Ionic features, including very small volutes, while the Tuscan order is a variant of Doric developed by the Etruscans and popularized by the Romans. The latter is unusual in its preference for a smooth column, without fluting.

DORIC ARCHITECTURE: THE SECOND TEMPLE OF HERA AT PAESTUM

72. Second Temple of Hera (at right), Paestum, Italy. c. 460 B.C. Southern Italy and Sicily were first colonized by the Greeks in the seventh century B.C. The temples constructed in these colonies during the sixth and fifth centuries B.C. are among the best preserved examples of Greek architecture. The temple at the left is the Temple of Athena. c. 530–520 B.C.

A Doric temple (see figs. 72, 73) is an imposing structure, an autonomous object complete within itself. The architectural forms are vigorous and assertive. The vertical fluting of the columns, reinforced by the triglyphs in the frieze above, produces an upward thrust which is held in balance by the horizontal articulation of the entablature and gable roof. The visual forces are in equilibrium (see fig. 74), yet the temple is not static. Its massive forms communicate an almost muscular vitality.

The walled inner sanctuary, or *naos* (from the Greek, to dwell), would have contained the cult statue (see fig. 83). On the exterior, the perimeter of the temple is surrounded by a colonnade, or continuous row of columns, called a peristyle (from *peri*, around, and *style*, column); such temples are termed peripteral. Only priests or priestesses and attendants were allowed inside the temple, and most rituals occurred outside, at an altar in front of the temple.

A post-and-lintel system forms the peristyle, while walls enclose the *naos*. Columns support the entablature and roof. The pediments at either end of the gable roof are in some temples filled with sculpted figures. The roof was made of wooden rafters covered with terra-cotta tiles.

The earliest Greek temples were small shrines containing a cult statue. During the eighth and early seventh centuries B.C., large wooden temples with peristyles were built. By the later seventh century B.C., stone construction began to replace wood,

73. Plan, Second Temple of Hera

74. Diagram of the evolution of Doric proportions. The changing scale and proportions of the Doric order, seen here in the evolution of the proportion of and relationship among column, capital, and entablature, reflect the search for an aesthetic harmony that was integral to Greek art.

partially as a practical response to the problem of supporting the heavy terra-cotta roof tiles. Stone construction, which coincides with the advent of monumental stone sculpture, reflects a confident new spirit of permanence and achievement.

Once the design for a temple was approved, stonecutters began to cut marble at the quarries. The blocks of stone, formed to specifications to reduce transportation weight, were moved to the construction site in specially designed carts pulled by teams of animals. After the temple's foundation had been built to the stylobate, the peristyle was set up. Columns were constructed of unfluted cylindrical units called drums held in place by wooden centering pins. The drums for the columns and the blocks of stone for the walls of the *naos* were lifted into place with pulleys and cranes. No mortar was used to hold the stones in place. The blocks of the *naos* walls were secured by iron clamps encased in lead to prevent rusting. The roof was constructed of wooden beams and rafters. A beam supported the apex of the gable roof, while additional support for the roof was provided by columns inside the *naos*. Finally, as the temple neared completion, the columns were fluted. The fluting disguised the joints of the drums and, by creating patterns of shadows, reinforced the three-dimensionality of the columns.

GREEK BRONZE SCULPTURE: SEVERE STYLE

75. *Zeus.* c. 460 B.C. Bronze with inlaid eyebrows, lips, and nipples, height 82". National Archaeological Museum, Athens. Lost in an ancient shipwreck at about the time of Christ, this sculpture was found in the sea near Cape Artemision in 1926–28. It is sometimes identified as representing Poseidon, god of the sea. The eyes were originally inlaid.

76. *Charioteer*, from a votive quadriga dedicated in the Sanctuary of Apollo at Delphi. c. 477 B.C. Bronze with inlaid stone and glass eyes, height 71". Museum, Delphi. This figure and its quadriga were buried after they were damaged, perhaps in an earthquake. Of the horses and chariot only fragments survive.

This larger-than-lifesize figure of Zeus originally held a lightning bolt, the god's symbol, in his right hand (fig. 75). His energetic movement is communicated by the tensed muscles of torso and abdomen, the distended veins, the buoyant position of the feet, and by the arms, which are outstretched for balance and to focus on the victim. The left foot is supported only on the heel and outside edge, the right touches only with the ball and toes. Three prongs in the soles held the figure in position on its base. His pose expresses the perfect physical development of the god and his complete physical control, while his severe facial expression complements the aggressive action.

Such a position would be impossible in marble, for marble's lack of tensile strength would not allow the outstretched arms, while the pose of feet and legs would not support the weight of the upper body. Because of its greater possibilities for both naturalistic effects and convincing movement, bronze was the favored sculptural medium of the Greeks after the Archaic period. But few ancient Greek bronzes have survived, since they can so easily be melted down and the bronze reused for weapons or other purposes. In this figure the color of the bronze suggests a naturally suntanned, oiled body (the Greeks oiled their bodies when exercising), and the inlaid eyes and teeth, fringed sheet bronze eyelashes, and inlaid colored nipples reinforce the naturalistic impact.

The *Charioteer* (fig. 76) was originally part of a large votive monument that included a chariot and four horses (a quadriga). The patron was a tyrant from Sicily who commissioned the work as an offering to Apollo

and a commemoration of the victory of his team and charioteer in the Delphic Games. The subtle and delicate pose evolves from a slight twist of the upper part of the body. The figure wears the appropriate racing garment, and the artist has delighted in representing the patterns of a delicate material caught and

pleated by a belt and ribbons or straps. The head represents the ideal Greek type, with a strong nose which continues the line of the forehead, large eyes and ears, full jawline, broad cheeks, and prominent lips. The expression is alert and self-confident, with a hint of the pride appropriate to a winner.

LOST-WAX BRONZE CASTING

The earliest-known bronze monumental sculptures in Greece date from the late sixth century B.C., but these were preceded by the casting of bronze body armor, which may have suggested and supported the development of bronze sculpture. Ancient Greek bronzes are hollow-cast of an alloy of copper and tin by what is known as the lost-wax method (fig. 77). A sculptor begins by forming a mass of clay (or some other malleable material) into the rough shape of the planned sculpture, but slightly smaller. This is covered with a layer of wax of the thickness desired for the finished bronze and approximating the surface finish of the planned sculpture. This wax coating is then encased in another layer of clay. When it has dried, the wax is melted away, leaving a hollow mold between core and exterior (supports hold the two in place). Molten bronze is poured into the mold. After it cools and hardens, the mold is broken or cut away, leaving bronze which has assumed the form first created in wax.

It is difficult to cast large figures in bronze, for the bronze can cool before it has reached the full extent of the mold. The ancient Greek bronzes discussed here were cast in several sections. The *Charioteer* is composed of seven pieces and, as is common, pieces of different textures were cast individually. The *Charioteer*'s right arm, for example, was cast separately and is fitted into the opening left in the sleeve when the drapery was cast. Actual cloth, impregnated with wax, may have been used to help form the draped patterns of the costume, and it has also been suggested that the ancient Greek sculptors may have created body parts using molds made from living human figures.

inner core of clay

wax, later replaced with bronze

outer mold of clay

metal pins that hold inner core in place when wax is melted out

77. Lost-wax bronze casting. Conjectural reconstruction of technique for right arm of fig. 76.

After casting, the bronze would be tooled and polished (worked with tools and an abrasive) to achieve the finished surface. Lips, nipples, and eyebrows were sometimes highlighted and given a realistic reddish cast by being overlaid with copper or with bronze of a high copper content. Fringed sheet bronze eyelashes, inlaid stone and glass eyes, and teeth of silver, marble, or ivory were applied after the polishing of the bronze was complete. These additional colors and materials enhanced the beauty of the work, impressed the observer with the skill of the artists, and, most importantly, played a vital role in achieving the verisimilitude desired by the Greeks. They made these beautiful and ideal figures seem even more real.

CLASSICAL STYLE SCULPTURE: THE *DORYPHOROS* BY POLYKLEITOS

"Beauty . . . arises . . . in the commensurability [proportion] of the parts, such as that of finger to finger, and all of the forearm to the upper arm, and . . . of everything to everything else, just as it is written in the *Canon* of Polykleitos. For having taught us in that book all the proportions of the body, Polykleitos supported his treatise with a work; he made a statue according to the tenets of his treatise, and called the statue, like his book, the *Canon*" (Galen, a Greek physician, writing in the second century A.D. on Greek aesthetic theory).

The firm muscular structure of the *Doryphoros*, (spear carrier; originally the figure carried a spear in his left hand) is enlivened by the *contrapposto* stance (fig. 78). The specific subject of this sculpture, which probably depicts an ideal Olympic athlete, was less important than the fact that it demonstrated a system of perfect proportions. Polykleitos' text, called the *Canon* (from the Greek *kanon*, rule), established a set of ideal proportions for the human figure, and the *Doryphoros*, created to illustrate the measurements revealed in the text, is sometimes also called the *Canon* of Polykleitos. The written text is lost, but numerous copies of the statue verify its significance in the classical world.

The *Doryphoros* was considered to be an ideal figure because its proportions adhered to common fractions (exact divisions by whole numbers) of the figure's height. Since both Polykleitos'

78. POLYKLEITOS
Doryphoros. Roman copy after a bronze original of c. 450 B.C. Marble, height 84". National Museum, Naples. This copy is generally considered to be the best version of Polykleitos' lost figure, but the spear that it once carried is missing, and the bronze original would not have had the tree trunk supporting the right leg and the marble bar supporting the right arm.

original figure and text are lost, the precise measurements of his canon remain undetermined, but the later Roman writer Vitruvius advocated a rule whereby the head (from the crown of the hair to the chin) was one-eighth of the total height, the width of the shoulders one-quarter the height, and so on, until every anatomical feature and the proportions among them are woven into a system of mathematical measurements.

A century before the *Doryphoros* was created, Pythagoras had presented mathematical proportion as the basis of musical harmony. Polykleitos' proportional system was more than a set of abstract principles, for it is

related to the Greek belief in the agreement between natural and mathematical harmony, a belief that brought a new vitality to the human figure in sculpture and to the visual arts in general.

Vitruvius reported that the proportions which governed the human figure in art also determined the proportions of Greek temples: "Further, it was from the members of the body that [the Greeks] derived the fundamental ideas of measures." Vitruvius defines proportion in a manner similar to our understanding of the Polykleitian

Canon as "a correspondence among the measure of an entire work, and of the whole to a certain part selected as a standard." Just as the Greeks gave human characteristics to their gods, they also humanized their architecture. The relative proportions, the capital as the head of the column, and the slight muscular swelling of a Doric column (*entasis,* see p. 89), all contribute to an empathetic understanding between us and the temple. This empathy was an extension of the Greeks' rational definition of their world.

THE GOLDEN SECTION

The proportion which governs the design of the Parthenon and may also have been the basis of the Polykleitian *Canon* is 5:8, a relationship adapted by Greek artists in the fifth century as the key to visual harmony. This ratio was used to govern the relationship among the parts of a design and of each part to the whole. To the Greeks, this was known as "the division of a line in extreme and mean proportions." Since the early nineteenth century it has been called the golden section (fig. 79).

The rule of the golden section is that the size of the smaller part relates to the greater part as the greater part relates to the whole. This is stated by the algebraic equation E:F = F:A. In the diagram, the ratio of the short side of the rectangle (D) to the long side (A) is the same as the ratio of the long side (A) to the sum of the long and short sides (D+A). It follows that the proportions among the parts determine the proportions of the whole, and the resulting golden rectangle is more visually pleasing than a square or a rectangle in which the proportions of the short to the long side are 1:2. The golden section is related to certain patterns and proportional changes observable in nature, especially in botanical specimens and in such seashells as the chambered nautilus. The actual golden number is irrational, an unending decimal, but artists use 0.625 or 5:8 as a working ratio.

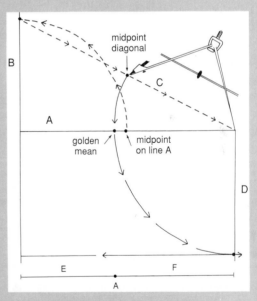

79. Diagram of the golden section and rectangle. Constructing the golden section and rectangle. The given measurement is the length of line A. Draw lines B and D perpendicular to the ends of line A. Find the midpoint on line A and with compass extend to line B. At point of intersection on line B extend a diagonal to the opposite end of line A. Find the midpoint of the newly constructed diagonal. With compass at midpoint on diagonal, extend through line A to line D. From the point of intersection extend perpendicular line back to line B. The rectangle formed is the golden rectangle.

DORIC ARCHITECTURE: THE PARTHENON, ATHENS

In the history of human accomplishment, the Parthenon on the Acropolis in Athens stands as one of the most famous monuments (figs. 80–83). Its significance is not due to its basic form, which continues the Doric temple type developed more than a century earlier (see p. 82). Rather, it is the exquisite harmony and grace of its proportions that make the Parthenon great. Its fame derives from its beauty.

The Parthenon functioned as a home for the goddess, and in its grandeur was a monument to the wealth, power, taste, and piety of Athens. The interior includes two chambers, a smaller one where the goddess's and city's treasure was stored, and the *naos*, where the colossal ivory and gold cult statue of Athena in military dress was enshrined (see fig. 83). Although all could look in from the door, only a few were allowed to enter these chambers. The rituals in honor of Athena were held outside, at a sacrificial altar to which the Parthenon was the backdrop.

The grace and beauty of the Parthenon are the culmination

80. KALLIKRATES AND IKTINOS (architects)
Parthenon, Athens. Reconstruction model. 447–438 B.C.; sculpture completed by 432 B.C. Pentelic marble, 111 x 237' at base. The Metropolitan Museum of Art, New York (Levi Hale Willard Bequest, 1890). The temple to Athena, goddess of wisdom and fierce protectress of Athens, was built after the Persian wars, when Athens was controlled by Pericles, who insisted that the Athenians rebuild the temples after the Persians had destroyed the earlier ones. The name Parthenon means maiden, and the temple was dedicated to Athena, the maiden (parthenon was the name given to the room in a home where unmarried, virginal daughters lived). The Parthenon was the preeminent religious structure in Athens and later served as a Christian church dedicated to Mary and in the later Middle Ages as a cathedral church. After the conquest of Athens by the Turks, it served as a mosque. It was severely damaged in 1687, during a war between the Venetians and the Turks.

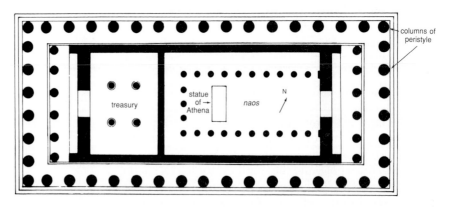

81. Plan, Parthenon

of a long development within the Greek search for the ideal temple. The simple dynamics of the post-and-lintel system were a vehicle which encouraged Greek architects to examine and achieve the most satisfying equipose. Compared to the Second

82. Exterior of Parthenon today

5   0   25 m

83. Section of the *naos*, Parthenon, with the ivory and gold statue of Athena by Phidias. The forty-foot statue was supported by a ship's mast; the flesh was composed of carved pieces of ivory, the dress and armor were of sheets of gold. The section shows the gable roof construction and the superimposed columns of the *naos*.

Temple of Hera at Paestum (fig. 72), the Parthenon offers a new grace and elegance.

There are a number of remarkable visual refinements in the Parthenon. All the horizontal lines—steps, stylobate, entablature—are raised slightly in the middle, ostensibly to correct the sag that the human eye imparts to a long horizontal (such a procedure also has a practical application, for it helps the rain to run off). Like the other optical refinements of the Parthenon, the lifting of the middle of the horizontals gives the building elasticity and a sense of life. Such adjustments made the structure more difficult to engineer and construct, for each block of marble would have to be cut to fit its exact place. Other refinements include the tilting inward of the three columns at the corners, to enhance the effect of stability and compactness, and their placement closer together, to compensate for the dissolving effect of light at the corners. The entire stylobate is tilted upward at the southwest corner to make the building more impressive both from the city below and from the entrance to the Acropolis. Perhaps the single most revealing refinement is the *entasis* of the columns, which do not taper in a straight line but bulge outward about one-third of the way up from the base. This creates an effect of muscular elasticity which assists in giving the Parthenon a human, organic quality. Later copies and variations often seem rigid and cold because they lack these refinements. The Parthenon is a monument that reveals the analytical quality of the human mind and the human search for the harmonious, the ideal, and the beautiful.

CLASSICAL STYLE SCULPTURE: THE SCULPTURE OF THE PARTHENON

84. Diagram of the Parthenon sculpture in situ. The sculpture is attributed to Phidias and his workshop.

85. PHIDIAS AND WORKSHOP
Three Goddesses on Mount Olympus, from the east pediment of the Parthenon, Athens. c. 438–432 B.C. Marble, height of center figure 60"; the figures are slightly over-lifesize. British Museum, London. These three figures have been identified as Hestia, Diove, and Aphrodite. The Parthenon pediments were over ninety feet long and at the center they rose to a height of over eleven feet. The platform on which the figures were placed was about three feet deep.

The Parthenon's architectural beauty and richness were enhanced by the sculpture that was integrated into the Doric design (see fig. 84). The pediments at both ends were filled with over-lifesize figures; there were ninety-two metopes sculpted in high relief; and a continuous low-relief frieze 550 feet long encircled the outside of the *naos* wall. Like the edifice they adorn, these sculptures display complete mastery of form and technique. That they were all completed in about twelve years reveals that there must have been a large workshop of sculptors and assistants, but a general consistency of design suggests that a single sculptor was in charge, most probably Phidias, who also designed the ivory and gold statue of Athena that stood in the

naos (fig. 83). The consistency of the sculptural conception suggests that Phidias provided drawings—perhaps on the stone itself—to guide the sculptors.

The iconographic themes are related to the dedication of the Parthenon to Athena, to the victories of the Greek over their barbarians, and to Athens's political leadership among the city-states in Greece. The east pediment presented *The Birth of Athena* (fig. 86), the west *The Contest Between Athena and Poseidon.* The metopes featured a series of battle scenes, including a battle of centaurs with men. The continuous frieze represented the procession of the Great Panathenaea, a special celebration that was held every four years, with musicians, elders, horsemen, chariots, and sacrificial

cattle and sheep. It culminates in the votive offering, in the presence of the gods and goddesses on Mount Olympus, of a new robe for a venerated olive wood statue of Athena kept on the Acropolis. Such offerings were undertaken to please the goddess, so that she would favor and protect her city.

On the east pediment the dramatic birth of Athena—who sprang full grown, wearing armor, from the head of her father Zeus—is conveyed by figures who move outward from the central episode. There is a coherent unity of time and place similar to that which developed in contemporary Greek drama. The magnificent group of seated and reclining goddesses, for example (fig. 85), turn as they become aware of the birth. To

86. East pediment of the Parthenon. Reconstruction showing *The Birth of Athena* by Phidias and his workshop. The darkened figures show the original location of the *Three Goddesses* (fig. 85). The dark lines indicate surviving fragments, the light lines are conjectural figures.

87. Horsemen, from the frieze of the Parthenon. Marble low relief, height approx. 43". British Museum, London

compose within the sloping pedimental shape was a challenge for the Greek artist, but these goddesses fit within the pediment; shown in graceful, natural poses, and beautifully unified as a group, they do not seem forced into the increasingly constricted space of the pediment. The voluptuous bodies are clothed in clinging drapery that is gathered and folded into patterns which emphasize the sculptural presence of the figures. The clarity of the poses is remarkable, as is the graceful and flowing role they play within the triangular composition. Filling the outermost corners of the pediment are, on the left, the sun-god's rising chariot to signify dawn and, on the right, the horses of the moon's chariot. These forms are cut off by the pediment to suggest that the realm of the gods continues beyond the restricted space of the pediment.

The Parthenon frieze is a tour de force of low-relief carving which offers the illusion of as many as six figures and horses overlapping within a relief that is no more than three inches deep (see fig. 87). The relief is carved more deeply near the top as a concession to the placement of the frieze. By thus giving the work greater readability, the Greek sculptor makes it clear that this frieze is for the enjoyment and enlightenment of the human spectator and is not merely a decoration added to the temple in honor of the goddess.

All the Parthenon's sculptures had additions made of metal, some perhaps gilded, to represent armor, straps, and other refinements, and many of the details of the figures were heightened by paint, although there is still controversy over the actual colors used. A bright blue has been proposed as the background for the pedimental figures, a red background for metopes and frieze. Color would have enhanced the beauty of the marble figures and clarified the compositions. The hair of the figures may have been gilded; the drapery hems were probably decorated with textile patterns.

SCULPTURE AND PAINTING OF THE FOURTH CENTURY B.C.

88. Copy after **PRAXITELES** *Hermes with the Child Dionysus.* 1st-century B.C. copy after 4th-century B.C. original. Marble, height 80". Museum, Olympia. The lower left leg and foot of the figure have been restored.

Hermes with the Child Dionysus (fig. 88) depicts Hermes, messenger of the gods, holding the infant Dionysus, a god and patron of drama and song. The child reaches forward, probably to grasp a bunch of grapes that Hermes held in his right hand. The articulation of muscles contrasts with that of the *Doryphoros* (fig. 78). While the *Doryphoros'* muscles are clearly marked and distinguished, those of Hermes have a softer, more natural appearance. The stance of *Hermes* reinforces this new organic unity, and the axis of the figure follows a shallow *S*-curve which adds to the sense of relaxation. What we can determine from this copy after Praxiteles, who was one of the dominant artists of the fourth century B.C., indicates a continued evolution toward naturalism and a new, refined elegance of the figure.

Praxiteles also sculpted a statue of Aphrodite (fig. 89), the goddess of love and beauty, for a temple of Venus on the island of Knidos. This is one of the first life-size figures in Greek art to depict the female nude. Her nudity is explained by the vase and drapery under her left hand: she is represented entering or leaving her bath. Lucian, a Greek rhetorician who saw the statue, observed: "So strongly has the artist's art prevailed, that the recalcitrant and solid nature of the stone has been transformed in each limb." The temple on Knidos had a back door specifically for those who wished to view the sculpture from behind, and Lucian reports, "[As we viewed the figure from behind], unforeseen amazement at the goddess' beauty seized us." The *Aphrodite*, like the *Hermes*, is freestanding and composed as sculpture in the round (see p. 24). The diagonal movement of the right arm and hand and the slightly lifted left leg create an impelling motion across and, by implication, around the body. Unlike

399 B.C.: Socrates is condemned to death
333 B.C.: Alexander defeats Darius
323 B.C.: Death of Alexander

89. Copy after **PRAXITELES**
Aphrodite of Knidos. Roman copy
after 4th-century B.C. original.
Marble, height 80". Vatican
Museums, Rome

earlier Greek sculpture, which primarily has a frontal orientation, these works invite us to observe them from different viewpoints.

We know from literary sources that the sense of drama and spatial involvement which characterized fourth-century sculpture was paralleled by advances in painting, but unfortunately no certain examples of fourth-century painting survive. Ancient literary sources offer an account of accomplishments in perspective and illusionism which astonished viewers. One ancient author reports, for example, on a contest between two artists: "[Parrhasios] entered a contest with Zeuxis, and when the latter depicted some grapes with such success that birds flew up to the [painting], Parrhasios then depicted a linen curtain with such verisimilitude that Zeuxis, puffed up with pride by the verdict of the birds, eventually requested that the curtain be removed and Parrhasios' picture shown . . . when Zeuxis understood his error, [he] conceded defeat with sincere modesty, because he himself had only deceived birds, but Parrhasios had deceived him, an artist. It is said that afterward Zeuxis painted a picture of a boy carry- ing grapes, and when the birds flew up to them, he approached the work and, in irritation with it, said, 'I have painted the grapes better than the boy, for if I had rendered him perfectly, the birds would have been afraid'" (Pliny, *Natural History,* XXV).

The ability of painters to ren- der the naturalism of appearance paralleled the subtle anatomical features, spontaneous attitudes, and increased spatial involve- ment of contemporary sculpture. These trends would develop as the influence of Greek culture spread throughout the eastern Mediterranean region.

Introduction to Hellenistic Art

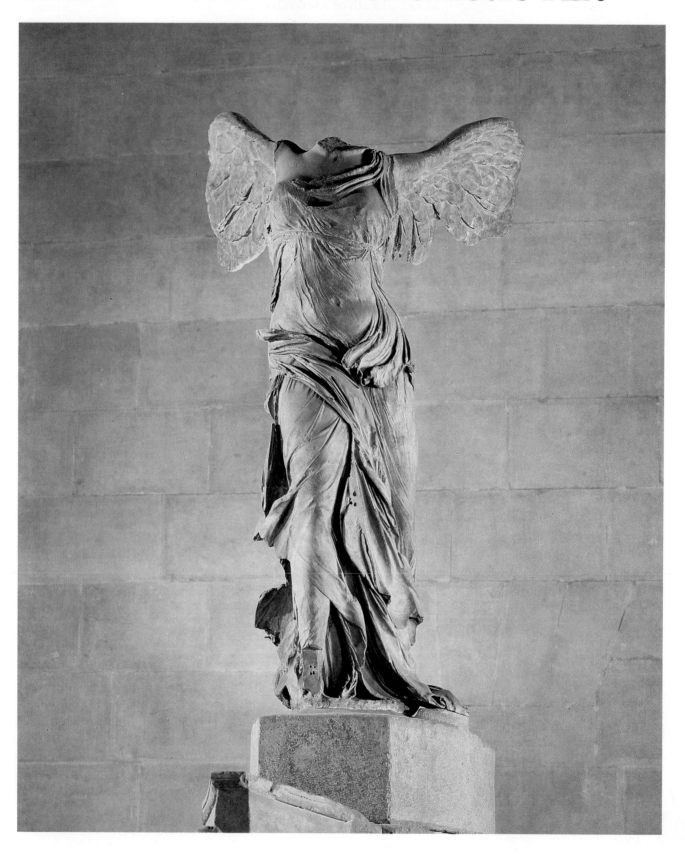

Despite the loss of head and arms, the *Winged Victory of Samothrace* expresses heroic triumph (fig. 90). The diagonal forward thrust of the body creates a dynamic effect of forward movement. The posture is strengthened by the complex and subtle patterns of drapery which envelop the figure and the contrasting position of the unfurled wings. Effects of wind are felt as the drapery both presses against the body's surface and unfurls in vigorous forms which billow into space, echoing the movement of the wings. The dramatic spatial involvement and dynamic movement displayed by the *Winged Victory* are typical of Hellenistic art.

HISTORY

In the late fourth century B.C., while the Greek city-states maintained a tenuous political stability, the hereditary kings of Macedonia, a kingdom to the north of Greece, strengthened their political power. Philip II, king of Macedonia, proposed a plan for the unification of Greece under his rule. In 338 B.C., while the Greeks debated his proposal, Philip defeated them. Philip's union of Greece with Macedonia was the initial step in a grand design to establish an empire which would include Persia. After Philip II was killed by an assassin in 336 B.C., his son Alexander, nineteen years old, ascended the throne. Following the vision of his father, he led a military campaign against Persia, defeating King Darius in 333 B.C. (see figs. 92, 318). Later conquests extended the boundaries of his vast empire south through Egypt and east to the borders of India before the still youthful Alexander died in 323 B.C.

Alexander had been educated by Greek standards, and his tutor was Aristotle, the great philosopher and natural scientist. The young conqueror envisioned a unity between the Greeks and the Persians based on the cultural values of Hellenism. After his death, Alexander's dream of unity was fractured by the reality of political conflict among his own generals. Soon his empire was divided into smaller independent powers. Common to these diverse regions, however, was the unifying influence of Greek culture.

Alexandria, founded by Alexander in Egypt in 332 B.C., became a famous center of learning. The great library there may have contained as many as five hundred thousand volumes; its holdings represented the accumulated wealth of knowledge of the ancient world. The library was part of a complex known as the museum (from the Greek *mouseios*, of the muses, referring to the ancient Greek goddesses of art and music). The major centers of art production, which were founded outside the Greek mainland, included Alexandria, the island of Rhodes, and Pergamon in Asia Minor (see p. 98).

90. *Winged Victory of Samothrace.* c. 180–160 B.C. Marble, height 96". The Louvre, Paris. This figure celebrates a naval victory, perhaps a victory of Rhodes at Side in 190 B.C. At Samothrace the statue was erected on a darker gray marble base in the form of the prow of a ship and, to give the effect of a ship coming into harbor, statue and base were set in two pools, one with a rippled marble bottom and a second with huge boulders.

91. *Portrait of Alexander the Great*, from Pergamon. 2nd century B.C. Marble, height 16 1/8". Archaeological Museum, Istanbul

DEVELOPMENTS IN ART

The developing naturalism which characterized Greek fourth-century sculpture and painting continued through the Hellenistic period (c. 400–100 B.C.). The appreciation of art was no longer restricted to the educated citizens of the city-states; the new empathetic naturalism of art appealed to a wider audience. Displays of human emotion and drama paralleled the melodramatic staging of contemporary Greek theater.

The Hellenistic flair for visually recording the details of life is exemplified by changes in the portrait bust. In the portrait of Alexander, we sense the mental and physical alertness of the young warrior (fig. 91). His muscular neck, set on a diagonal, imparts strength and movement and suggests spontaneous action. The deeply set, searching eyes, complemented by the furrowed brow, reveal a psychic energy and a mood of inspiration, while the open mouth adds to the uninhibited naturalism.

The Hellenistic emphasis on naturalism can be related to a changed philosophical outlook epitomized in the teachings of Aristotle. Aristotle's teacher, Plato, had viewed material objects as mere imperfect reflections of ideal forms. Aristotle, in contrast, stressed the roles of natural observation and experience in understanding reality. He sought to comprehend nature by perceiving its particular manifestations in the biological and earth sciences. The direction of Aristotle's philosophy, based on a penetrating observation of nature, parallels the realism of fourth-century and Hellenistic art.

PAINTING

As with Hellenistic sculpture, much of our knowledge of specific works is based on literary sources and/or Roman copies in mosaic or fresco. The *Battle of Alexander and Darius* is thought to preserve the composition of a Hellenistic painting (fig. 92). The successful representation of vivid and energetic activity demonstrated in the mosaic testifies to the continuing advances in illusionism in Hellenistic painting. Alexander rides into the battle from the left, raising his spear; Darius anxiously looks back toward his pursuer. The foreshortening of the central horse and the frantic activity of the team pulling Darius's chariot add complexity to the tumult of the battle. Within the turbulent scene, the Hellenistic painter added a detail to demonstrate virtuosity: reflected in a Greek shield below Darius's chariot is the anguished face of a young Persian about to be crushed by the wheels of the chariot. The representation of death was a challenge to the Hellenistic artist (see fig. 93), and here the horror reflected on the Persian's face dramatically communicates the personal reality of battle.

92. *Battle of Alexander the Great and King Darius of Persia.* Roman copy of Hellenistic painting of c. 300 B.C. Stone and glass mosaic, height 10' 6". National Museum, Naples. Found in the House of the Dancing Faun at Pompeii, this impressive mosaic used more than a million small *tesserae* to create the illusion of the battle. The Hellenistic original may have been by Philoxenos or Helena of Alexandria.

HELLENISTIC SCULPTURE IN PERGAMON

93. *Dying Trumpeter.* Roman copy after a bronze original of c. 230–220 B.C. from Pergamon. Marble, lifesize. Capitoline Museum, Rome

The *Dying Trumpeter* (fig. 93), one of a group of defeated Gauls from a large monument at Pergamon, displays the psychological and physical naturalism that characterizes Hellenistic art. Clearly distinguished as a Gaul by his matted, greasy hair, his moustache, and the torque around his neck, this soldier is shown pierced in the side with blood spewing from the wound. His face mirrors defeat, and his last moments of life are as tenuous as his upraised torso on the uncertain, trembling arm. Even in the marble copy, a keen observation of surface anatomy complements the psychological drama of impending death; both body and soul are rendered with unsparing reality.

During the mid-third century B.C., the Hellenistic kingdom of Pergamon, in Asia Minor, became a major political power and art center. In 263 Pergamon split from Syria to form an independent kingdom. In 230 King Attalus I of Pergamon defeated an invasion by the Gauls, who had entered Asia Minor following their invasion of Greece in 279 B.C. In defeating the foreign invaders, Attalus I was able to establish his kingdom as the principal poli-

Dying Trumpeter: **copy after original of c. 230–220 B.C.**
225 B.C.: Romans defeat the Celts
215 B.C.: Romans defeat Hannibal at Nola

tical force in the Near East.

During the Hellenistic period, art no longer exclusively served the worship of the gods or the embellishment of the city-states; it could extol the exploits of a political leader and so act to capture public support. This was the motivation in constructing the great Altar of Zeus and Athena at Pergamon (fig. 94). The balance between theme and form demonstrated in the earlier *Dying Trumpeter,* however, gives way by the second century to an emphasis on drama which approaches the melodramatic.

The altar was raised on a platform about twenty feet high. Approaching the steps that lead to the altar, we view a dramatic frieze in such high relief that the sculpted figures seem to kneel and fall onto the steps on which we are walking. The frieze depicts the Gigantomachy—a mythological battle between the giants and the Greek gods. At Pergamon the overt display of emotion and the convulsive interlacing diagonals of the figural composition combine to create an overwhelmingly dramatic presentation.

94. Altar of Zeus and Athena from Pergamon. c. 181–159 B.C. Marble, 120 x 113' at base; the frieze is 7' 6" high; the figures are well over-lifesize. Pergamon Museum, East Berlin

EARLY BUDDHIST ART: THE GREAT STUPA AT SANCHI

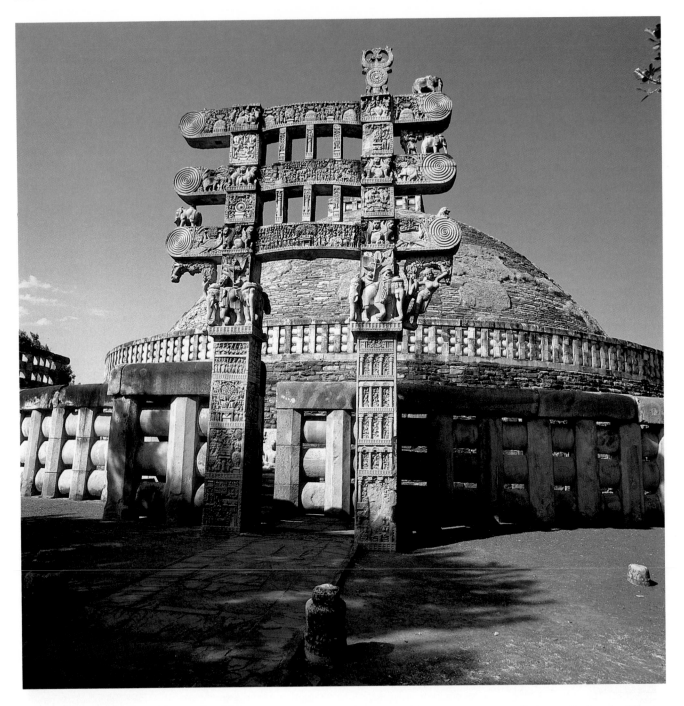

95. The Great Stupa, Sanchi, India. Begun 3rd century B.C., with later additions. Brick and rubble originally faced with painted and gilded stucco, rails of white stone. It may be assumed that *stupas* were the first sacred Buddhist buildings and that the Great Stupa at Sanchi is the earliest surviving example. The core of the structure probably originated in the third century B.C. Here, as in many Indian *stupas*, the original building was encased in a mass of earth and stone before it was enlarged, for it was considered a sacrilege to destroy any of the original monument.

96. The *Boh* tree, sculptural detail on the south pillar of the east gate to the Great Stupa, Sanchi

The Great Stupa at Sanchi stands on a hill rising out of the plain not far from Bhopal in central India (fig. 95). A *stupa* is a burial mound; its form dates back to prehistoric times. This monumental form, as used for the burial of princes, had the shape of a large hemisphere. At an early date, this kind of tomb developed into a commemorative monument and was adopted by Buddhists as one of their main symbols and as the center of their religious compounds. The *stupa* could be an actual tomb, placed over the remains of Buddha or other holy persons, or it could act as a symbol to commemorate a sacred place, such as a site where an important event took place in Buddha's mortal life. The *stupa* played a crucial role in Buddhist beliefs for it is the very symbol of *nirvana,* or final enlightenment, the goal of every Buddhist.

All such monuments follow a similar plan (see fig. 97). They are mounds of rubble and brick faced with stone, covered with white stucco partly gilded and surmounted by a three- (or more) part umbrella symbolizing the three most basic aspects of Buddhism—the Buddha himself, Buddha's law, and the monastic order. The rail around the umbrella shaft is thought to reflect the ancient concept of marking off a precinct around a sacred tree, symbolic of vitality and fertility. On the base around the hemispherical dome is a narrow path along which processions moved. A second path is at ground level, where pilgrims could circumambulate clockwise, symbolic of walking the Path of Life around the World Mountain, following an ancient

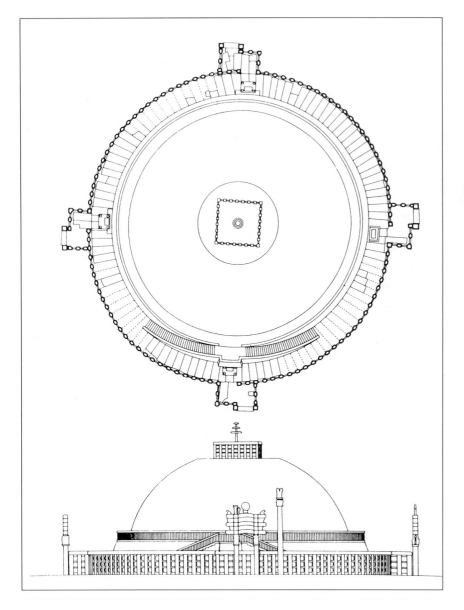

97. Plan and elevation, Great Stupa

ral form—a kind of symbolism called aniconic, or without image. His presence is suggested by symbols such as a wheel, footprints, a throne, or the *Boh* tree (fig. 96), all important emblems of his life. It was thought to be impossible to represent Buddha in human form since he had already passed into *nirvana*, an otherworldly state of being.

A richly decorated structure such as the Great Stupa took decades to complete. We can no longer see these monuments in their former splendor, with smooth white or gaily colored plaster exteriors and sculpted decoration with polychrome painting. The sculpture depicted stories quite like folk tales and brought the life of Buddha to visitors in familiar terms.

The massive domes frequently contain a system of concentric or radial supporting walls arranged by symbolic, rather than technical, considerations. They face the points of the compass and represent rays leading out from the center, a plan in the form of a *mandala,* or diagram of the cosmos. This was not visible from the exterior, but was of crucial importance for the sacred substance of the monument. Its profound importance in Buddhist belief and practice is attested by its long use and survival into the present day.

These early constructions celebrate the life of the historic Buddha, a man called Siddhartha

Indian rite of retracing the path of the sun while making offerings and ritual performances. The path is enclosed within a tall stone railing which isolates this sanctuary from the outside world. Access to it is gained through four monumental gateways some thirty-two feet in height and set at the cardinal directions. The uprights and crossbars are lavishly carved with stories from the life of

Buddha; with *jataka* tales, edifying legends in which Buddha is shown as pious and wise; and with large guardian figures called *yakshas* and *yakshis*, ancient gods and goddesses of fertility. These lively sculpted panels contrast dramatically with the massive character of the *stupa* and railing, emphasizing their presence and narrative content.

It is significant that Buddha himself is not represented in figu-

Gautama. He was born about 560 B.C. of a noble family living in the foothills of the Himalayas. He gave up his princely life of fine robes and jewels in order to seek out the cause of suffering, disease, and misery which he saw all around him. India of the sixth century B.C. was undergoing rapid and violent political and social change. As had many of his contemporaries, Prince Gautama renounced his former life and, as an ascetic, contemplated and discussed the sorrows of the world with other learned recluses on the outskirts of villages. At age thirty-five he sat under a large pipal tree in the town of Gaya and resolved not to leave his seat until the riddle of suffering was solved.

After hosts of temptations, he sank deeper and deeper into meditation and at dawn on the forty-ninth day he knew the truth, the secret of sorrow, and knew what to do to overcome it—release the mortal soul from the cycle of rebirth. He had reached *nirvana*. He remained seated under the Tree of Wisdom (the *Boh* tree) meditating on the truths he had found. He then journeyed to Deer Park (modern Sarnath) and preached his first sermon—in Buddhist phraseology, he "set the Wheel of the Law in motion." Soon he had a band of sixty ascetics who became his followers as he went on preaching the Buddhist *dharma* (doctrine). For eight months of the year they wandered from place to place, but in the rainy season they stopped to live in huts at one of the parks given by wealthy lay followers. These were the first of the great Buddhist monasteries of later times.

Buddha's quest was a personal one. He sought *nirvana*, a refined stage of enlightenment accepted by adherents of various religions of the time. *Nirvana* marked an end to the cycle of rebirth and was thought to be a state of enduring permanent bliss, called the Supreme Truth or Reality. Buddhist *dharma* claims that there is no existence without suffering, that the cause of suffering is egocentric desire, and that the elimination of desire will end suffering.

After Buddha's death at age eighty in about 480 B.C., the religion grew and changed along with the political institutions of India. The third leader of the first great Indian empire, called the Mauryan dynasty (322–183 B.C.), was named Asoka (269–232 B.C.). He expanded Mauryan political influence over much of the Indian subcontinent. According to tradition, Asoka was moved to remorse and pity by the horrors of war and came to the conclusion that true power was realized through religion, not force. Thus he became an active patron of Buddhism and supported the communities of monks. The political might of the Mauryans, as well as their patronage, brought the full institutionalization of Buddhism. A set of Buddhist religious offices (services) was created; numbers of monks occupied monasteries which acquired property; the canon was expanded, diversified, and refined. Asoka himself is said to have erected eighty-four thousand *stupas* over the relics of Buddha throughout the empire. Thus the search for personal salvation by one man, Buddha, became an institution involving millions of people supported by one of the world's greatest ancient empires.

The *stupas* became the center of life in the monasteries, which included buildings used as lecture halls, kitchens, and hostels. Their locations and the lifeways of the monks were guided by recollections of Buddha's life. These *chaityas* (sacred locations) were to a remarkable degree coincident with trade routes of the day, as the initial spread of religion under the state patronage of Asoka was linked to commerce. Since Buddhists enjoyed the protection of the state, traders associating with them came under the same protective umbrella. Monasteries were safe havens which received the financial support of their visitors. The symbiosis between monks and traders was ultimately the agency that took this religion out of India and into China, Japan, and Southeast Asia.

Introduction to Roman Republican Art

98. *Husband and Wife*. Grave relief from the Via Statilia, Rome. 1st century B.C. Marble, height 72". Capitoline Museum, Rome

99. *A Roman Patrician with Portrait Heads of His Ancestors.* c. A.D. 15. Marble, lifesize figure. Capitoline Museum, Rome. The head of the main figure is removable, perhaps because it was used in family ritual.

This high relief (fig. 98) exhibits the Roman continuation of the Mediterranean practice of marking graves with images of the deceased, but the stern man and his dignified wife communicate the austere values and virtues of the Romans of the republic, as they were defined by ancient writers: he seems sober and determined, hard and severe, demanding and uncompromising, while his wife appears dutiful and obedient, consistent with the proscribed role of women during the republic. The Romans of the early republic were self-disciplined, devout, conservative, and supporters of traditional values. They admired military valor and prized family, heritage, and the state. They respected law and legal obligations. Their language, Latin, is remarkable for its lucid order and rigid rules.

The Romans of the Republican period showed little interest in art and even later, under the Roman Empire, never indulged in the philosophical discussions about the nature of art that had been so important for the Greeks. But a Roman strength that persisted into the empire was their ability to absorb whatever was useful or good from other traditions, and in art the Romans owed a rich debt to the Etruscans (see p. 44), the pre-Roman people who had inhabited the Italian peninsula, and the Hellenistic Greeks (see p. 95). Only in a few areas did the Romans of the republic make significant new contributions, most notably in architecture and engineering, and especially in the use of concrete and the arch and vault (see pp. 126–27).

THE PORTRAIT

The Roman interest in and devotion to the family explains the development of the individualized portrait bust. It was Roman tradition and ritual practice for patrician families to preserve wax, terra-cotta, or marble portrait heads of their male ancestors, like those held by the figure in the Capitoline Museum (fig. 99). These were kept in "the most conspicuous position in the house, enclosed in a wooden shrine" and "when any distinguished member of the family dies they take them to the funeral" (Polybius, *The Histories).* These portraits often emphasize the peculiarities of the man (moles, wrinkles, large ears) in order to capture the uniqueness of the specific person. This respect for the individual—although limited, as in most early cultures, to the male—can be related to Roman republicanism, for a system of government that encourages individual responsibility seems to lead to the development of veristic portraiture in art (for later examples see seventeenth-century Holland, p. 326, and early America, p. 360).

HISTORY

By 269 B.C., the Romans, who in the eighth century B.C. were one of several groups of people living in villages along the Tiber River, were

100. Temple of Portunus (formerly called Temple of Fortuna Virilis), Rome. Late 2nd century B.C.

already governing a unified state that encompassed the entire Italian peninsula. In the subsequent two centuries they defeated Carthage in North Africa and annexed Greece, Spain, Asia Minor, and the south of France. The government developed as a republic (c. 510–31 B.C.), with rule by two consuls, a hierarchy of public officials, and a senate. The early Romans had not defined a policy of expansion, but their interest in commerce led them into contact with many of their neighbors. Eventually the Romans were forced to protect their borders and guarantee their peace after attacks from the outside. In about 390 B.C. the Gauls sacked Rome and later Carthage led Rome into war. The rapid growth of the city of Rome, which by 250 B.C. housed almost one hundred thousand people, required a vast territory to support it. The Romans were generally benevolent conquerors, who absorbed rather than suppressed, offering citizenship to the conquered and acknowledging the significance of local traditions. Personal ambitions and the difficulties of governing vast territories and the huge city of Rome led to administrative difficulties and eventually to civil wars and attempts by military figures to seize control; the republic came to an end in 31 B.C. when Octavian, who later became the emperor Augustus, assumed power.

A REPUBLICAN TEMPLE

The Temple of Portunus in Rome (fig. 100) demonstrates the derivative nature of republican religious architecture. The high podium, restriction of steps to the front, and deep porch are related to temples created by the Etruscans, while the suggestion of a peripteral colonnade is Greek. Note, however, that only the porch columns are freestanding; those of the sides and back are merely sculpted portions of the wall structure—engaged or half columns. The temple is, therefore, not peripteral but pseudo-peripteral. This emphasis on the interior space is directly related to the Roman practice of entering the temple to worship. The columns provide a graceful rhythm and announce that this structure is a temple, but the pseudo-peripteral design reveals the Romans' lack of interest in the aesthetic unity and logic characteristic of its Greek source.

101. Sanctuary and Temple of Fortuna Primigenia, Praeneste (Palestrina), Italy. c. 80 B.C. Axonometric projection

SANCTUARY AND TEMPLE AT PRAENESTE

The innovative architecture of the Roman republic centered around great public buildings and engineering projects for which new techniques and materials were evolved which would be further developed during the empire. The arch and vault were combined with the new use of concrete (see pp. 126–27) to make possible the relatively rapid construction of such impressive complexes as the Sanctuary and Temple of Fortuna Primigenia at Praeneste (fig. 101). The design is based on the development of a sequence of public and sacred spaces along the axis followed by visitors as they moved through the sanctuary. This molding of space and control of the observer's experience will also be an important feature of Roman imperial architecture. The sacred shrine at Praeneste occupied a hillside, and Roman engineers and architects systematized the site, giving the shrine order, regularity, and clearly identified punctuation marks—the small temple facades at midpoint, the circular temple at the apex—within the aesthetic and religious experience. The semicircular steps that lead up to the final circular temple are a foil for its shape and, in addition, provide a theater for the enactment of sacred drama.

THE ROMAN HOUSE AND VILLA

102. Isometric projection with plan and longitudinal section, House of Pansa, Pompeii, Italy. 2nd century B.C. There are shops to either side of the entrance. The women who died in this house during the Vesuvius disaster were wearing gold ear pendants, necklaces, and rings. When the eruption began, a sculpture of Bacchus was placed for safety in a copper kettle in the garden.

Most of our knowledge of Roman life is the result of materials preserved by the eruption of the volcano Vesuvius in A.D. 79. The volcanic ash and mud lava buried the seaside town of Pompeii, preserving shops, temples, houses, drainage and sewage systems, furnishings, food, and even the anguished positions of a number of the victims.

A letter by Pliny the Younger described the disaster: "The buildings were now shaking with violent shocks . . . Outside . . . there was the danger of falling pumice-stones. . . . As a protection against falling objects [the people] put pillows on their heads . . . they were still in dark-ness, blacker and denser than any ordinary night. . . . We also saw the sea sucked away and apparently forced back by the earthquake . . . a fearful black cloud was rent by forked and quivering bursts of flame, and parted to reveal great tongues of fire, like flashes of lightning magnified in size. . . . People bewailed their own fate or that of their relatives, and there were some who prayed for death in their terror of dying. Many besought the aid of the gods, but still more imagined there were no gods left, and that the universe was plunged into eternal darkness for evermore."

The houses and villas of mid-

103. Atrium, House of Menander, Pompeii. c. 70 A.D. The atrium is a feature well suited to the Mediterranean climate. The outer walls of the house were usually windowless, and the atrium allowed light and fresh air to enter, as well as rainwater, which was gathered in a central pool to flow into a cistern. The atrium functioned as a sitting room, and it usually contained the shrine for the household gods; to either side were small chambers for dining and sleeping.

dle- and upper-class Romans followed a regular plan with rooms arranged along a longitudinal axis from entrance to garden (fig. 102). The plan is dominated by the atrium (open court). The rooms were decorated with

House of Pansa, Pompeii: 2nd century B.C.
214 B.C.: Construction begins on China's Great Wall
191 B.C.: Gaul (France) becomes a Roman province
101 B.C.: Chinese ships reach India

104. *The Unswept Floor.* Roman copy by Heraclitus of a Hellenistic mosaic by Sosos. A.D. 2nd century. Mosaic fragment; the forms are lifesize. Vatican Museums, Rome

richly patterned ceilings and wall paintings (fig. 105), but actual furnishings were minimal. Couches, used for resting, sleeping, studying, and dining while reclining in the Greek fashion, were usually the most elaborate pieces of furniture. Virtually all houses in Pompeii had water pipes with taps, as well as pipes leading to a sewer or trench.

The floors in the main rooms were made of mosaic—small pieces of marble and stone—arranged in decorative patterns. The richest homes had floors which copied famous Hellenistic paintings or patterns. One copy of a Hellenistic mosaic featured *The Unswept Floor* (fig. 104) , a realistic depiction of the debris one might find underfoot after a banquet, complete with shadows to make it more realistic—pity the poor servant who had to clean such a design after a night of Roman revelry. A mosaiced vestibule might have a chained dog and the words "Beware of the Dog," or a human skeleton and "Enjoy life while you have it."

The variation in design of the wall paintings at Pompeii reveals how fashions of decorating changed. Executed in a durable *fresco secco* technique (see p. 123), these works were intended to transform the rooms into an elegant ambience for living and entertaining. The paintings are illusionistic. The simplest seem to be walls paneled in fine marbles. In some the wall is painted away by a suggestion of continuous space. The subjects include realistic or fantastic views of architecture, landscapes, still lifes, portraits, and themes from Greek and Roman mythology and theater. The still lifes usually represent food—game, fruit, eggs—and may refer to the Roman custom of giving such food as gifts (fig. 120).

105. Frescoed room from the House of the Vettii, Pompeii. A.D. 63–79

Introduction to Roman Imperial Art

Remember thou, O Roman, to rule the nations with thy sway—
these shall be thine arts—to crown peace with law,
to spare the humbled, and to tame the proud in war
(Virgil, *Aeneid*, VI, 851–53).

The over-lifesize statue of the Roman emperor Augustus (fig. 106) commands our attention by the extended arm, suggesting an oratorical announcement, and the serious expression. Augustus wears parade armor decorated with reliefs of the Earth Mother with a cornucopia—symbolic of abundance—and of a Parthian, a Roman enemy, surrendering a battle standard in the presence of divinities, which refers to a major diplomatic coup. These triumphs were also celebrated in poetry: "Your age, Augustus, permitted the fields to bear rich harvests once more, and returned to the skies the battle standards, wrenched from the proud barbarians" (Horace, *Carmina*,

106. *Emperor Augustus.* c. A.D. 15. Marble, with traces of paint and perhaps also gilding, height 84". Vatican Museums, Rome. This work, discovered at the villa of Augustus's wife Livia at Prima Porta (see fig. 119), nine miles south of Rome, is sometimes known as the *Augustus Prima Porta.* As the back is not complete, the statue must have been intended for placement in a niche. It may have been a cult statue, for after his death Livia was made the priestess in charge of the cult of the deified Augustus. Fragments of paint, such as reddish circles for the irises of the eyes, reveal that details were once painted.

IV, 15, 4–7). The sculpture probably dates after Augustus's death, for it represents the emperor without boots, suggesting that he has been deified. The *putto* (male baby angel) and dolphin by his right leg provide additional support for the sculpted figure and, as attributes of Venus, they refer to Augustus's divine lineage, for he was said to be a descendant of Aeneas, son of Venus. The facial features identify the figure as Augustus, but they also represent an ideal, for Augustus was always shown in his early maturity, as here, although he was seventy-six when he died in A.D. 14. In pose the model was the Greek *Doryphorus* (fig. 78), which the Romans thought was a representation of the hero Achilles. A complimentary comparison between Augustus and Achilles is almost certainly intended. This sculpture, then, is an idealized portrait of a specific emperor; although based on classical Greek prototypes, its iconography and scale are specifically Roman, for they exalt the emperor and the empire.

HISTORY

In 31 B.C., Octavian, nephew and adopted son of Julius Caesar, became the sole ruler of Rome and all its territories; in 27 B.C. the senate named him Augustus ("noble, honored, consecrated one") and after his death they declared him a god. Brilliant and resourceful, Augustus, who wrote that he "found Rome a city of brick and left it a city of marble," became the first emperor and ruled the empire

107. *Altar of Peace (Ara Pacis)*, Rome. Reconstruction. 13–9 B.C. Marble, approx. 39 x 35'

longer than any who followed him. He continued the expansion of the Roman state, as did his successors, and by the death of Trajan in A.D. 117, Rome's population was about seven hundred fifty thousand and the Mediterranean had become a "Roman lake." The difficulties of governing this enormous area and its diverse population made the Romans masters of efficiency and organization. They had little time for, or interest in, the philosophical speculations that had formed Greek art and culture. Their most significant contributions are in world government and order, encompassing such diverse issues as legal codes and city planning.

The Romans had a strong sense of their historical importance and their contributions to world history: Julius Caesar wrote an account of the Gallic Wars; the emperor Claudius wrote two lost historical works; and Augustus made a list of his accomplishments known as the *Res Gestae*. Roman attitudes toward history and art are expressed in the *Altar of Peace* (*Ara Pacis*; fig. 107) in Rome, which commemorated a particular concept, the *pax romana* (Roman peace) that had been declared by the Roman senate in 13 B.C. to express and commemorate the peace brought by Augustus to Italy and to the Roman state. They could not know that never again would peace prevail for so many years over so vast an area. The senate's declaration and the richly decorated altar were intended to bring recognition to this historic fact and to establish it as a Roman accomplishment and ideal. Augustus, accompanied by his family and friends, appears in the procession representing the altar's dedication. Although the stylistic sources for the reliefs lie in such Greek models as the Parthenon frieze (see fig. 87), Greek idealism is ignored in favor of documenting a specific historic moment and distinctive individuals. Their presence at this sacrifice reveals their piety and concord; the more important figures are in higher relief for emphasis and focus. Even the decorative motifs glorify the empire and allude to its peace-giving role, for the garlands below refer to the abundance made possible by peace.

THE CITY OF ROME

Rome, which at its largest had a population of nearly a million, was in many ways similar to a modern city. It had impressive public spaces with state buildings and religious structures, as well as shopping areas, apartment buildings of five or six stories, and rooming houses. Most of the population lived in rental housing; a fourth-century A.D. document lists 46,602 apartment and rooming houses in the city and only 1,797 private homes. The apartment houses at Ostia (fig. 108), the port of Rome, were three or four stories high with an inner garden court and balconies, similar to late-twentieth-century apartment blocks.

The emperors kept the urban populace happy by providing food, facilities, and entertainment. Elaborate programs of building in the imperial forums (fig. 109) impressed the public with the power and magnificence of the specific emperor and of the state. Theaters and amphitheaters provided places of entertainment for tens of thousands, and the public baths offered facilities for communal bathing and exercise, as well as for social and intellectual gatherings.

ROMAN IMPERIAL ART

The scale and diversity of the empire (31 B.C.–c. A.D. 400) meant that Roman imperial art encompassed a variety of types and styles, especially as local traditions were incorporated into the works of art. Here we have chosen to limit our discussion almost exclusively to works of art created within the city of Rome and for its inhabitants. The majority of the artists employed by the Romans were of Greek ancestry. Greek artists were imported as early as 500 B.C., during the republic, and works of art were also ordered from artists active in Greece. The demand for Greek works, new and old, accelerated after the Romans sacked Corinth in 146 B.C. and brought a number of important Greek works to Italy.

Among the most impressive and characteristic monuments of Roman art are those which honor the empire and emperor. These are often on an enormous scale to communicate the size, power, and authority of the empire. Huge buildings and interrelated groups of buildings that express the grandiose aspirations of the empire were made possible by the new techniques of construction that had been developed during the Roman republic. The empire's use of the arch, the vault, and concrete—devices which made feasible not only the huge and magnificent monuments of ancient Rome, but also the powerful molding of space so important in Roman architecture—are among the most significant of all Roman accomplishments (see pp. 126–27).

The creation of works of art honoring and commemorating an emperor's deeds and victories was a constant challenge to artists in the service of the empire. Emperors and generals were sometimes honored with equestrian monuments; the only surviving example is the *Marcus Aurelius* (fig. 110). He has the same commanding gesture

110. Left: *Equestrian Monument of the Emperor Marcus Aurelius.* c. A.D. 161–80. Bronze, over-lifesize. Piazza del Campidoglio, Rome. Originally there was probably a figure of a defeated enemy crouching under the horse's upraised hoof. Marcus Aurelius, who wrote the *Meditations,* has the longish hair and full beard that characterized the "poetic" emperor. The military type of emperor was clean-shaven with short hair. The bronze is an impressive technical accomplishment, but its preservation results from the incorrect medieval interpretation that the statue represented Constantine, the later emperor who accepted Christianity.

111. Right: Arch of Titus, Rome. c. A.D. 81. Marble over concrete core

as Augustus (fig. 106), but here his power is emphasized by the control he demonstrates over the lively and nervous horse.

Another commemorative monument is the triumphal arch. While its origins can be traced to republican days, the first to be called *arcus triumphalis* were the large and permanent triumphal arches erected during the reign of Augustus. Eventually there were more than fifty in Rome. The Arch of Titus (figs. 111, 112) memorializes Titus's suppression of a Jewish revolt and his capture of Jerusalem in A.D. 70–71. The arch itself is simple and handsome, with a compact and tightly knit composition of horizontal and vertical members enframing the tunnel vault. There are two types of columns, both variations on the Composite order, and the juxtapositions between fluted and plain shafts and elaborate and simple capitals gives a variety and liveliness to this monument which would have been unthinkable in a Greek monument. The simple basic form, an arch enclosed within a rectangle, is also enlivened by the stepped frieze, and originally the whole was surmounted by a huge bronze quadriga with the emperor's portrait. The reliefs under the arch represent the triumph of Titus and the parading of the treasures of the Temple in Jerusalem through the streets of Rome (fig. 112). The deified Titus, who died shortly before the monument was completed, is shown in the center of the vault being carried to heaven on the back of an eagle.

Commemorating the emperor Trajan's early-second-century vic-

112. *The Spoils of the Temple at Jerusalem Exhibited in Rome.* Marble relief from the Arch of Titus. Height 79"

tories over the Dacians in eastern Europe is a huge freestanding column (fig. 113), as tall as a twelve-story building, which was originally topped with a monumental gilded bronze statue of the emperor (now replaced with a statue of St. Peter). The column is carved with a spiraling relief that tells in detail the episodes of Trajan's campaigns and victories. The style is lively and direct, but it was not necessary that every detail of every scene be visible. The scale of the column and the length of the relief convey the extent and complexity of Trajan's exploits. Some of the upper scenes could have been read by people standing on the balconies of the courtyard of Trajan's library, which surrounded the column. Column and library were only part of Trajan's contributions to the imperial forums. Emperors embellished the imperial forums as a way of asserting their presence and impressing the people with their magnificence.

THE CONCEPT OF CLASSICAL ART

We have already learned that the term Classical period was used to designate a time within the development of ancient Greece (see p. 75). The Classical period was so named because it was seen in the nineteenth century as the summit of Greek art and culture. With the rise of art academies in Europe, beginning in the later sixteenth century, the most important monuments of ancient Greek and Roman art were viewed as manifesting the order, harmony, and clarity of the classical aesthetic. From the seventeenth century onward, the art of both of these ancient, or antique, cultures was viewed as exemplary,

113. Left: Column of Trajan, Rome. A.D. 113. Marble, height originally 128'; length of frieze, approx. 625'

114. Right: **HAGESANDROS, ATHENODOROS, AND POLYDOROS**

Laocoön and His Sons. Early 1st century B.C.(?). Marble, height 96". Vatican Museums, Rome. This sculptural group was carved by three Greek sculptors from the island of Rhodes.

and the term classical art began to be used for these periods. Today, this broader use of the term classical encompasses the art and the civilizations of both ancient Greece and Rome.

THE ROMAN ARTIST

In ancient Greece, artists had been famous and respected, but during both the republic and the empire the artists in the service of the Roman state became anonymous laborers once again. Few artists are known by name; not a single painting bears a signature and only a few are documented as the work of a particular artist. In most cases the large and elaborate programs of Roman art seem to have been accomplished by groups of artists working together, probably in well-organized workshops, and submerging their individuality in the concept of a unified project.

The few names of artists that are recorded are Greek, and these are names of sculptors. Even during the republic it was recognized that Greek sculptors represented a long-standing tradition of excellence. The famous *Laocoön and His Sons* (fig. 114), once thought to be a work of the Greek Hellenistic period imported to Rome, is now believed to be a Roman work created by Greek sculptors working in a revival of the Hellenistic style for a Roman patron.

TECHNOLOGY AND ENGINEERING

To run a large empire, to communicate and move supplies, and to feed the masses gathered in growing cities demanded important new developments in technology and organization that ultimately affected the production and style of works of art. The Romans are famous for their roads and aqueducts, which were engineered to solve the particular problems of a specific area or terrain. Some ancient aqueducts, roads, and bridges are still in use. The arch, the vault, and concrete solved engineering and construction problems on a large scale (pp. 126–27).

The Roman interest in order, efficiency, and organization is revealed by the Roman town plan (fig. 115), which developed from Egyptian, Greek, and Hellenistic prototypes to spread throughout the Roman world, from London to North Africa. The streets are laid out in a grid pattern within fortified walls, and the center of the town is marked by the intersection of the two main thoroughfares, the *cardo*, running north-south, and the *decumanus*, running east-west. Nearby is the forum—the social, political, and commercial heart of the city. The intersecting *cardo* and *decumanus* divide the city into quarters, each of which is further subdivided by streets meeting at right angles; only irregular or large buildings such as theaters or public baths disrupted this regular plan. The Roman solution to urban design is evident in major cities of the Western world, where avenues cross streets in grid patterns.

RELIGION; MYSTERY RELIGIONS

The more important official Roman deities were derived from the gods and goddesses of the Greeks, but their names were changed: Zeus became Jupiter, Aphrodite became Venus, and Dionysus became Bacchus, for example. But the number of Roman deities continually expanded, for when the Romans conquered and annexed a new area, the local deities were usually added to the Roman hierarchy of gods. At the Pantheon in Rome (see fig. 127), there was even an altar dedicated to those gods whom the Romans had not yet discovered.

During the later empire, the religious life of many Romans was dominated by participation in mystery religions, cults which centered on a savior who promised some kind of life after death. Their widespread popularity has been seen as a reaction to the materialism and spiritual emptiness of ancient Roman life. The Greek religion had one such deity in Dionysus (the Roman Bacchus), who represented the irrational and irrepressible elements in human nature. His cult at the city of Pompeii led to the creation of one of the greatest Roman paintings, the frescoes at the Villa of the Mysteries (see fig. 117). Other mystery religions centered around the worship of Isis, an Egyptian goddess whose temple at Pompeii included a shrine with a reservoir of holy water from the Nile, and Cybele, the Great Mother (Magna Mater). An ancient Roman temple to Mithras, a militant god-hero who represented the victorious forces of light over darkness, was discovered in London, in excavations after the bombings of World War II. Mithraism, an especially important late Roman cult, was widespread throughout the empire as a result of its popularity with members of the army.

THE END OF ROME'S EMPIRE

Political, religious, and spiritual turmoil and threats from Northern barbarians characterize the later empire. Diocletian (ruled 284–305) consolidated imperial rule, but he also banned and persecuted the Christians. Constantine lifted the ban on Christianity in 313 and later may have converted to the religion himself. But Rome lost much of its importance when Constantine shifted the imperial capital to Constantinople, which he had founded at a site on the Bosphorus named Byzantium (present-day Istanbul). In 395, at the time of the death of the emperor Theodosius I, the empire was divided in half. But while the eastern empire centered around Constantinople enjoyed political stability, the western empire was beset with uprising from Germanic tribes. One of those tribes, the Visigoths, captured and sacked Rome in 410.

LATE ROMAN SCULPTURE

Constantine's sculpted head (fig. 116) has a dramatic and intimidating impact, not just because of its enormous size, but also as a result of the powerfully abstract facial features. Portraiture has moved away from the highly realistic busts of republican and early imperial Roman art, and although Constantine's head retains certain specific physical traits, such as the thick, muscular neck and the Roman nose known from his other portraits, these realistic features are joined with abstract patterns in the perfectly coiffured hair over the forehead and the huge, staring eyes. The latter suggest Constantine's authoritarian power, his deified presence, and his ability to penetrate the world of the divine. There are indications from contemporary literary sources that the late Roman emperors, who were viewed as gods while they were living, were adorned like statues of gods and behaved in a manner which encouraged belief in their deified status.

It is difficult to determine why the new abstract patterning occurs during the late Roman Empire, a period sometimes referred to as late antiquity. It cannot be dismissed as a lack of technical ability on the part of the artist, for its use seems intentional, to promote such abstract concepts as imperial authority or divine power.

New, spiritual attitudes entered late antiquity with the mystery

115. Plan, Thamugadis (Timgad), Algeria. Founded c. A.D. 100

116. *Head of Constantine.* A.D. early 4th century. Marble fragments, height of head 8' 6". Palazzo dei Conservatori, Rome. These fragments are part of a colossal statue, originally about thirty feet tall, of the enthroned emperor Constantine initially placed in the apse of the Basilica of Constantine (fig. 126). The head and limbs were carved from marble while the torso was fashioned of a brick core covered with wood and overlaid with bronze. The head once had a metal diadem.

cults and early Christianity. The most eloquent spokesperson for these values was Plotinus, a third-century philosopher. One of his pupils, Porphyry, wrote a life of Plotinus in which he noted the difficulty of artists who wanted to create a portrait of the philosopher: "Plotinus . . . gave the impression of being ashamed that he dwelt in a body [and] he deemed it so degrading to submit himself to being a subject for a painter or sculptor that he said to Amelius, who asked him to permit his portrait to be made: 'It is not sufficient just to carry around that image which nature has imposed on us, without making concessions to it by deciding to leave behind a more lasting image of the image, as if it were one of those things which is particularly worth seeing.'" The antiphysical attitude of Plotinus is in sharp contrast to the historical and naturalistic values which had been so prized in Roman figurative art. As in the colossal head of Constantine, inner spiritual life is deemed more significant than an exact portrait representation. We will see that such an approach is consistent with the development of Early Christian art.

ROMAN FRESCOES AND ILLUSIONISM

117. *The Bacchic Mysteries.* Villa of the Mysteries, Pompeii, Italy. c. 30 B.C. Fresco, size of room approx. 29 x 19'; height of figures approx. 60". Whether these paintings, which are superb in quality, are copies of a lost Hellenistic painting from Pergamon or original Roman works is still debated by experts.

118. Corner of the room in the Villa of the Mysteries, with a flagellation scene. Whipping in this context may be a ritual meant to ensure fertility.

119. *Garden.* Wall painting from the Villa of Livia, wife of the emperor Augustus, at Prima Porta near Rome. Late 1st century B.C. Fresco, height of wall 10'. Museo delle Terme, Rome. Fig. 106 was also discovered at Livia's villa.

This room of frescoes (fig. 117) representing Bacchic (or Dionysiac) mysteries is exceptional in quality and subject, as well as in scale, for nearly lifesize figures such as these are rare in Roman painting. In addition, these frescoes are one of the first great examples of mural painting (painted wall decoration that is integrated with the physical space and architecture).

The secret rites depicted here have not yet been fully explained, but this painting reveals the importance of the cult of Bacchus, god of wine and fertility, in Roman life. It has been proposed that the sequence of scenes, which seems to read from left to right, represents either the initiation of a new member into the cult or the transitions in the life of a young woman when she marries and becomes a Roman matron.

The central figures, badly damaged, represent the enthroned Ariadne, to whom Bacchus gave immortality, with the god reclining on her bosom. The initiate, or bride, would be the figure entering on the far left. She is enthroned as a matron on the far right (not visible in this view). In the interim she encounters various trials and experiences. Among the dramatic episodes is the imminent unveiling

120. *Still Life with Eggs and Thrushes,* from the House (or Villa) of Julia Felix, Pompeii. Before A.D. 79. Fresco, 35 x 48". National Museum, Naples. The house where this fresco was found during excavations in 1755–57 is the largest yet discovered at Pompeii. The fresco shown here is one of a sequence of still-life paintings of food.

of a large phallus to the right of the central figures of Ariadne and Bacchus. The regular, architectural rhythm of the paneling behind the figures sets off their poses, while the strong red background adds an element of drama appropriate for the subject.

The most dramatic episodes are represented at the two corners, where the artist took advantage of the walls meeting at ninety-degree angles to represent interacting figures. At one corner a fierce Silenus, who may be reading the young woman's fortune in the residue left in a wine cup, looks back at her as she flees in terror. At the other corner a winged figure in a spiraling

movement flogs the initiate or bride, who reclines on the lap of another woman (see fig. 118).

One of the most beautiful of all Roman fresco decorations is the painting that covered the four walls of a room in the Villa of Livia at Prima Porta (fig. 119). It represents a garden with fruit trees, flowers, and songbird set off by a background of sky. The fresco has all the freshness of nature's colors: the rich greens of the garden; the varied shades of fruit, flowers, and plumage; and a wonderful blue sky. All are executed with a light touch of the brush, as if the wind were just beginning to stir this idyllic environment.

ROMAN FRESCO TECHNIQUE

Fresco painting (fresco is Italian for fresh), which involves painting directly on the plaster wall, was used by the Egyptians, Greeks, Romans, and later civilizations as well. When properly executed it is durable, and when it is subtly related to the particular architectural setting, as in the cycle at Pompeii, it can be both decorative and dramatic. Generally fresco painters have to cover large expanses of wall, and they often work quickly; the sketchy and suggestive quality of most Roman and later frescoes creates a lively and vivacious effect.

The Roman fresco painter began by applying two or three layers of fine plaster to the wall surface to be decorated. The background would be painted on the top layer of plaster—sometimes while it was still moist—and left to dry. Figures, ornaments, and architecture were usually added later. The natural pigments, which were made from earth, minerals, or animal or vegetable sources, were mixed with limewater. Glue and wax were sometimes added to create a hard and shiny surface. Painting onto wet plaster is called *buon fresco* (Italian for good or true fresco) and painting on the already hardened dry plaster is known as *fresco secco* (Italian, meaning dry fresco).

ILLUSIONISM

Livia's garden room (fig. 119) is more delightful and seductive than a framed painting of a garden, for it creates the illusion that we are in a natural setting. Such illusionism also played a role in the *Still Life with Eggs* (fig. 120), for in both works the artists want to fool us into believing, albeit momentarily, that we are looking out into a real garden or at a real dish full of actual eggs. This type of illusionism, which is also known by the French phrase *trompe l'oeil* (fool the eye), is a pleasant bit of trickery. Such paintings are meant to amuse and delight us, as was already recognized by the Roman author Philostratus the Younger, writing about A.D. 300: "To confront objects which do not exist as though they existed and . . . to believe that they do exist, is not this, since no harm can come of it, a suitable and irreproachable means of providing entertainment?" The illusionism of Roman painting is inherited from an earlier tradition that developed in Greece. The sense of pleasure in experiencing illusionism is not unique to the Greeks and Romans, as is revealed by the popularity of *trompe l'oeil* in later societies and even today.

There are several criteria for a successful illusionistic or *trompe l'oeil* painting. The objects in the painting should be represented in their natural scale in a clearly structured space, as is the case with both Livia's *Garden* and the *Still Life*. In the *Garden* the artist has carefully developed the space in overlapping levels within the pictorial space. Cast shadows define the placement of the object within the illusionistic space, as is especially evident in the *Still Life*, and the objects are naturalistically modeled with transitions from light to dark that indicate both the three-dimensionality of the objects and the source of the light (later, at the time of the Italian Renaissance, this will become known as *chiaroscuro*, from the Italian words for light and dark). Naturalistic lighting effects suggest the textures of the objects: note the different textures of the eggs and the metal vessels in the *Still Life*. Often painters will introduce an object in the immediate foreground that establishes the frontal plane of the illusionistic space; this form, known as a *repoussoir* (French, meaning to push back), can be noted in the low, openwork fence in the foreground of Livia's *Garden*. The use of the *repoussoir* in the *Still Life* is especially interesting, for the bowl of eggs seems to extend over the frontal plane of the base—the *repoussoir*—to jut out into our space. To make the illusion convincing, the subject matter is usually everyday objects that need no interpretation or explanation. The goals of such art are obvious, for the purpose, beyond Philostratus's "entertainment," is to impress us with the technical skill of the artist.

THE FLAVIAN AMPHITHEATER (COLOSSEUM), ROME

121. Exterior, Flavian Amphitheater (Colosseum), Rome. Begun A.D. 72; dedicated A.D. 80; construction completed A.D. 96. Approx. 615 x 510'. The building was damaged in later centuries, when much of the dressed stone of the outer surface was taken away to be used in the construction of other buildings.

122. Flavian Amphitheater. Reconstruction model. Museum of Roman Civilization, Rome

Through the ages, the Flavian Amphitheater has conveyed the scale and strength of the Roman Empire (fig. 121). Begun by Vespasian, an honored military leader and first emperor of the Flavian dynasty, it was built in part to reassure the Roman citizenry that the cruelty and self-indulgence of the reign of Nero, the last Julio-Claudian emperor, had ended; Vespasian destroyed the lake and pleasure garden of Nero's Golden House, with its ostentatious gardens, to establish a site for the amphitheater. It was dedicated by Vespasian's son Titus with gladiatorial games that lasted over one hundred days and featured a thousand gladiators and the deaths of thousands of animals.

The Roman amphitheater or arena was so well conceived that it has become the prototype for

Flavian Amphitheater, Rome: begun A.D. 72

A.D. 43: Roman London (Londinium) is founded
A.D. 70: Titus destroys Jerusalem
c. A.D. 70: Writing of the Gospel of St. Matthew
A.D. 73: Fall of Masada

123. Flavian Amphitheater.
Isometric projection, with section

the modern sports stadium. The oval plan seems to have developed from the idea of facing and enclosing two theaters (amphitheater derives from the Greek *amphi*, around, and *theatron*, theater). The Flavian Amphitheater, the largest amphitheater of the ancient Roman world, could hold about fifty thousand spectators. They were sheltered from sun and rain by an awning rigged by sailors and supported by horizontal poles anchored in the top level. Eighty arched passageways on the ground floor allowed entrance to a double row of annular tunnel vaults (see figs. 122, 123) encircling the arena which led to interior stairs leading to vaulted passages on the upper levels. Such a plan permitted easy access and exit by a crowd of spectators.

Construction materials in-

cluded concrete, brick, and tufa (see p. 127). When finished, the exterior was faced with blocks of local travertine stone held in place by iron clamps. The exterior design was unified by the repetition of arches flanked by half columns. The capitals on the three arched stories change from Doric below to Ionic and Corinthian for the second and third floors; Corinthian pilasters articulate the fourth level.

The amphitheater was an arena for displays of combat: gladiators battled other gladiators and animals, while animals, especially lions and tigers brought from Africa, were pitted against one another. Women gladiators participated until A.D. 200. The fight was usually to the death, a practice which may have evolved from an earlier Etruscan ritual in which a deceased relative was honored by a fight to the death between slaves. The floor of the Flavian Amphitheater was landscaped with trees and large rocks. Animals were raised by lifts from underground chambers, now visible after excavations. The amphitheater could be artifically flooded for contests mimicking naval battles. Although a few Romans denounced these games as bloody spectacles, most viewed them as displays of courage and virtue.

To the ruling families of Rome, the games also served a political purpose. At times, the unemployment rate reached approximately fifteen percent and, in addition to religious festivals, approximately one hundred and fifty days each year were celebrated as holidays. Providing spectacular games became a political scheme to keep an often idle population entertained and content.

During the Early Christian era some martyrdoms may have occurred here, but most public persecutions were held in the Roman circuses (arenas especially designed for chariot races). After Christianity was legally recognized by the emperor Constantine in A.D. 313, growing numbers of Christians argued against the brutality of the games. Gladiatorial contests were banned in the early fifth century, but the animal games continued into the sixth century.

Until at least the mid-fourth century, a colossal (almost one hundred feet tall) bronze statue of Nero as the Sun God stood next to the Flavian Amphitheater. In the eighth century, a popular guidebook to Rome applied the term colosseum, taken from the colossal sculpture, to the amphitheater itself, and ever since we have known it by this name.

THE ARCH, THE VAULT, AND CONCRETE

124. Diagrams of a round arch; a tunnel vault; a cross vault; and a dome on a drum. The arrows indicate outward thrusts.

Although the arch was known earlier, it was the Romans who recognized its utility for engineering projects and its potential for spanning large spaces to create huge public buildings. An arch (fig. 124) is a means of construction by which an opening—usually semicircular—is spanned by elements (stone or bricks) smaller than the opening itself; these elements are most often wedge-shaped blocks known as voussoirs. The central voussoir is called the keystone. The arch is the

basis for all the vaults discussed below. Arches and vaults are usually constructed upon a wooden support known as centering that can be reused. The point at which the arch or vault begins to curve inward and upward is known as the springing; the blocks immediately below the springing may jut out to support the centering. The dynamics of an arch or vault create outward diagonal thrusts that must be counteracted by buttressing (providing a masonry support that counteracts

the thrust; for a later example, see figs. 200, 202).

A vault is a structural system that is based on the arch. The simplest type of vault is a tunnel (or barrel) vault, a deep, continuous arch. Although light can enter at either end, the continuous buttressing required to contain the outward thrust prohibits large openings along the sides. For a bridge and aqueduct such as the Pont du Gard (fig. 125), however, the tunnel vault is the perfect solution. The lowest row supports

125. Pont du Gard (bridge and aqueduct), near Nîmes, France. Late 1st century B.C. Length 900'; height 162'. Aqueducts (Latin for conduits of water) transported water from the hills into Roman cities using the force of gravity.

126. Interior, Basilica of Constantine, Rome. Reconstruction with section. c. A.D. 306–313. This basilica was begun by the emperor Maxentius and is also known as the Basilica of Maxentius and Constantine (see fig. 116).

the road and protects the foundation against the force of the spring floods. A second row provides the extra height needed for the aqueduct at the top, which is raised on smaller arches. When tunnel vaults and arches are placed in rows, each neutralizes the outward thrust of the adjacent member, but those on the ends must be well buttressed, a function here performed by the riverbanks to either side.

The square vaults that spanned the central area of the Basilica of Constantine (fig. 126) were formed by the intersection at right angles of two tunnel vaults; these are called cross (or groin) vaults. The outward thrusts of a cross vault are concentrated at the corners, and buttressing is only required at these points; the vertical members that support a tunnel or cross vault are known as piers. The area between piers, covered by either a cross or barrel vault, is known as a bay. When placed in a row, as here, or in groups, cross vaults can span vast areas and still permit large windows.

A dome is a semi-spherical structural system that can be understood as an arch rotated one hundred eighty degrees on its axis. It must, therefore, be buttressed on all sides. The problem of light can be solved by opening the top of the dome with an oculus, as in the Pantheon (fig. 127), by piercing the edges of the dome with small windows, or by raising the dome on arches or tunnel vaults.

In many of the finest Roman buildings the material was dressed stone (that is, each piece was cut for its specific position) and no mortar was employed. Repeated arches, such as those of the Pont du Gard, meant that stones of regularized shape could be cut, and the structure could be fabricated of stones marked at the quarry to indicate their specific placement.

The most revolutionary Roman innovations in arches and vaulting occur in combination with the development of *opus caementicium*—concrete (fast-drying, hardening volcanic sand). The sand was combined with mortar (mud or clay), lime, broken bits of stone and/or brick, and water to provide a building material that hardened quickly into a solid mass. Concrete was cheap, readily available, flexible, and fire-resistant. For the finished surface of their buildings, the Romans were usually not satisfied with concrete, which they would cover with stucco and paint or with marble or other stones.

The arch, vaults, and concrete were developed precisely because they responded to the Roman demands for enormous scale, for efficiency and economy, and for flexibility. They helped to create and to convey the power and majesty of the Roman Empire.

THE PANTHEON, ROME

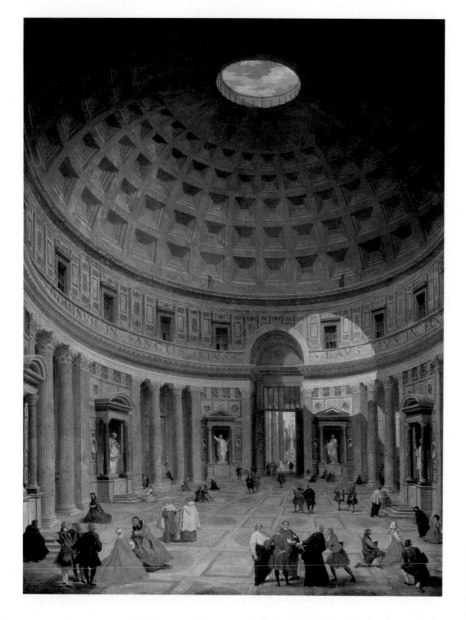

127. Interior, Pantheon. A.D. 117–125. As seen in an eighteenth-century painting by Giovanni Panini in the National Gallery of Art, Washington, D.C. (Kress Collection). Height of interior 144'. The Roman Pantheon was dedicated to all the gods of the Roman religion; its name derives from the Greek *pan* (every) and *theos* (god). The inscription on the exterior pediment ("Marcus Agrippa . . . built this") is misleading, for it refers to an earlier temple built on this site in 27 B.C. The current structure was erected by the emperor Hadrian, who, with characteristic modesty, copied the inscription from the earlier temple.

The Pantheon was regarded in ancient times as one of Rome's most distinguished temples. It joins two disparate architectural designs, a Corinthian portico and a domed rotunda (see figs. 127–29). Viewing the building from today's significantly raised street levels, the modern visitor is aware of the cylindrical walls and dome, but these were not visible in antiquity. A colonnaded forecourt and the portico, which was raised atop a flight of steps, masked these elements. The impressive entrance, with towering monolithic marble columns and huge bronze doors, gave no hint of the cylindrical walls of the rotunda. The concrete dome, the largest built in Europe prior to the twentieth century, is perfectly hemispherical, and the distance from the floor to the top of the dome is the same as the diameter of the rotunda. The interior proportions, then, are governed by the geometrical purity of a sphere (fig. 128).

A series of transverse barrel vaults hidden within the more than twenty-foot-thick walls concentrate the weight of the dome on eight massive piers. The concrete of the dome must have been poured in sections over a huge mold supported by a centering structure so complex it

128. Section of the Pantheon, showing the stepped buttressing that contains the outward thrust

129. Conjectural reconstruction of the exterior of the Pantheon and its forecourt in ancient Roman times. Model. Museum of Roman Civilization, Rome

would have made the interior look like a dense forest of hewn lumber. The weight of the dome is relieved by a series of coffers (the recessed panels—here square—that decorate the interior surface of a vault), which also add geometrical articulation to the hemisphere. The thickness of the dome decreases from twenty feet at the springing, where it is reinforced with stepped buttressing, to only six feet at the oculus, the circular opening thirty feet in diameter at the apex of the dome. The oculus allows adequate light, and

the rain which enters is drained off by small, inconspicuous openings in the floor.

The Roman gods were represented by sculptures along the walls, while the dome assumed the symbolic significance of the heavens. Perhaps the most dramatic effect of the Pantheon is the harmony it demonstrates with the natural world. As the sun passes through the sky, a natural spotlight is cast into the rotunda, progressively illuminating the interior. To the Romans, the sun symbolized the eye of Jupiter, and its penetrating pres-

ence inside the temple seemed to make the deity manifest.

The Pantheon expresses the vision of the Roman Empire. It is a technological wonder of construction—like the vast network of highways built to communicate with the corners of the empire—and materials used in its construction and decoration were transported from lands as distant as Tunisia and Egypt. The engineering achievement exhibited by the building makes possible an edifice which relates the order of Roman rule to their reverence for a universal order.

ROMAN PUBLIC ARCHITECTURE

130. Central hall, Baths of Caracalla, Rome. 211–217. As seen in a restoration drawing by G. Abel Blonet

The Roman taste for grand architecture also found expression in two secular building types, the bath and the basilica. To a Roman, visiting the bath, which was built at state expense and entered for a nominal fee, was a ritual of daily life. The baths offered services which fostered both intellectual and social life. There were many baths throughout the empire, but the most elaborate were those in Rome, built by the emperor Caracalla.

The Baths of Caracalla complex covered fifty acres, and approximately sixteen hundred people could be accommodated. Initially mixed bathing was permitted, but later the sexes were segregated, with women and men bathing at different times. The plan was organized along a central axis; the *tepidarium* (warm-water pool), *calidarium* (hot-water pool, usually circular in shape), and *frigidarium* (cold-water pool) were all located on the axis (see figs. 130, 131). Gymnasia flanked the pools, and gardens, barber and hairdresser shops, libraries, and meeting rooms completed the complex. Water, transported by aqueducts from outside the city and heated by fires in basements, was passed to the pools in clay or lead pipes.

A visit to the bath usually began with physical exercise followed by a stay in the steam room. In the *calidarium* oil was used to cleanse the body. After cooling down in the *tepidarium* and *frigidarium*, a visitor would receive a massage, which completed the bath. The visitor might then take a walk in the gardens, study in the library, or attend lectures.

Lavish marble, stucco, and painted decoration embellished the interior surfaces. By the first century A.D., the Roman statesman and author Seneca, recalling the austere values of the Roman republic in *Moral Epistles*, complained that new bath structures were too ornate: "We think ourselves poor and mean if our walls are not resplendent with large and costly mirrors; if our marbles from Alexandria are not set off by mosaics . . . if our vaulted ceilings are not buried in glass; if our swimming pools are not lined with Thasian marble, once a rare and wonderful sight in any temple. . . . What a vast number of statues, of columns that support nothing, but are

131. Plan, Baths of Caracalla

132. Plans, Roman and Imperial Forums, Rome, with the Basilica Ulpia. Compare to the reconstruction in fig. 109.

built for decoration, merely in order to spend money!" Most Romans would not have agreed with Seneca, for they viewed the ritual of bathing and socializing within an opulent architectural environment as one of the joys of civilized life.

Another dramatic public space created by the Romans was the basilica, which usually adjoined the forum, the public square which was the center of commercial and social activity. The Roman Forum was developed beginning in the sixth century B.C. Later, imperial forums were built by different emperors; they are unified along a longitudinal axis (see figs. 109, 132). At the northwestern end of this axis is the Forum of Trajan, with the Basilica Ulpia (in Roman architecture a basilica, from the Greek *basilike* [royal court], is a large building, often with an interior colonnade, used for public administration; Ulpius was Trajan's family name). Derived from earlier Greek buildings with colonnades, it was entered on its longitudinal side. The interior was divided into three areas, two side areas known as aisles or side aisles that flanked a large central axial hall called the nave (from the Latin *navis*, ship, due to its resemblance to the upturned hold of a ship). Both ends of the nave terminated with an apse, a large niche composed of a half cylinder surmounted by a half dome.

Given the enormous size of the building (the Basilica Ulpia is more than four hundred feet long), the Roman architect was confronted with the problem of how to light the vast interior space. To solve this problem, the wooden gable roof of the nave was raised above the aisles to permit clerestory windows. The basilica served a variety of secular purposes for the Romans; business and administrative offices were located there and law courts met there. Often the apses contained shrines to deities. The Basilica Ulpia adjoined libraries which flanked the Column of Trajan (see fig. 113).

The Roman baths, forums, and basilicas gave the Western world a heritage of architecture and ideas. Our spas and community centers reflect the public baths on a more modest scale, while the forum survives in Italian piazzas and in our own public squares. The basilica served as the prototype for Christian churches in western Europe.

ART IN THE AMERICAS: TEOTIHUACÁN

133. Aerial view of Teotihuacán, with Pyramids of the Sun and Moon, central Mexico. c. 100 B.C.–A.D. 650. The complex covers thirteen square miles.

The name of the city Teotihuacán means birthplace of the gods. Myth tells us that after the sun "died" (the sun was equivalent to an era) the gods gathered there to create a new city. Monumental architecture appeared at the site in the first century A.D. with one of the most ambitious undertakings in all of Mesoamerica—the Pyramid of the Sun (fig. 133). Built over a cave held sacred since more ancient times, the pyramid retains the stepped outline of earlier examples but here is built on a gigantic scale. The ground plan reveals a square base which

is 738 feet across. The total height, including a temple that once stood on the upper platform, is about 246 feet. Dating somewhat later in the same period is the Pyramid of the Moon. The structure is more sharply delineated on its surface and is of more modest size than its counterpart. The placement of the smaller pyramid in the northern part of the valley, on gradually rising terrain, brings the upper platform to roughly the same altitude as that of the Pyramid of the Sun.

These two edifices with their severe contours set against the

mountainous landscape on the horizon dictated the features of the city's growth. For example, the Pyramid of the Sun is oriented precisely at the point on the horizon where the sun sets over Teotihuacán the day it reaches its zenith at the summer solstice. Furthermore, the Avenue of the Dead, the city's mainline of a slightly later date, runs strictly parallel to the main facade of the Pyramid of the Sun and is perfectly aligned with the axis of the Plaza of the Moon and that of the Pyramid of the Moon. With these pyramids completed,

134. Pyramid of Quetzalcóatl (detail of the facade with heads of Quetzalcóatl and Tlaloc)

Teotihuacán: c. 100 B.C.–A.D. 650
320: Gupta dynasty begins to unify India
325: Council at Nicea, first ecumenical council of the Christian church
410: City of Rome is sacked

135. Representation of Tlaloc (god of rain). Fresco. Palace wall of Zacuala, Teotihuacán

a gigantic urban plan began to emerge that reflected current ideas about astronomy and the desire to identify with the semi-arid and serene landscape of this central Mexican plateau.

Some fundamentals of these complexes were set in Meso-america by earlier peoples. The use of truncated pyramids as a temple base, the careful place-ment of terraces, platforms, and temples to form plazas, the skill at handling open spaces using fixed axes (probably set accord-ing to symbolic considerations) were constant from earlier peri-ods. Such monuments are not strictly architectural since they do not function as enclosures of space; rather, they work as sculp-ture, with exterior space acting as a constructed, environmental art form.

Teotihuacán was an urban center which at its peak in the second and third centuries A.D.

attained a maximum population of about two hundred thousand. Teotihuacán was the civic, reli-gious, political, and economic center for all the surrounding valleys. Also in the city were foreign enclaves, thousands of artisans in the marketplaces, and a ritual center of immense, monumental proportions. Dur-ing religious festivals the city population would swell even more with pilgrims.

A second stage of building at Teotihuacán began between the second and third centuries A.D. and reflected an abrupt spurt in urban growth. The Avenue of the Dead was laid out then, and around it arose a number of cere-monial complexes. Residential sectors which were once mainly to the northwest of the two great pyramids then began to grow in all directions—outward from the Avenue of the Dead and from the broad East and West avenues

perpendicular to it. During this period an important architec-tural refinement was initiated, the *tablero,* a heavy, projected, rectangular molding outlined by a thick frame. This detail ap-peared on all religious structures whether a simple altar, ceremo-nial platform, small temple, or majestic pyramid.

Perhaps the most splendid example of the *tablero* is on the Pyramid of Quetzalcóatl, the plumed serpent (fig. 134). The enormous heads of Quetzalcóatl emerge from the *tableros* and al-ternate with heads of Tlaloc, the deity associated with water and rain whose cult apparently flour-ished in semi-arid Teotihuacán. Polychromed reliefs of undulat-ing plumed serpents and sea-shells added to the ornamental richness of the structure. The plumed serpent, here associated with marine symbols and with the god Tlaloc, also must have been a central deity. Aside from the symbolic and aesthetic ap-peal of the Pyramid of Quet-zalcóatl, its structure is based on technological advances. For ex-ample, the entire nucleus of the pyramid is reinforced with a skeleton of limestone. The colos-sal heads are deeply anchored into the core of the *tableros* and show an incredible sophistication in the joining of stone, since use of hard metal tools was not known to these builders.

The plan of the entire city is noteworthy for its regularity of city blocks and the density of residential sectors. Apparent is the rechanneling of rivers, the existence of large reservoirs, steam baths, specialized workshops, open-air markets, administrative buildings, theaters, and areas set aside for ball games and other public functions. The layout of the city was regular and based on a module of 187 feet, which formed the standard blocks in residential areas. Multiples of the module apparently formed other compounds in the city as well and divided it into a grid which suggests the existence of rather rigorous city planning as well as a centralized ruling group, both spiritual and temporal. The Palace of Zacuala—an excellent example of what must have been the luxurious residence of a rich Teotihuacán merchant or high functionary—included a chapel decorated with brightly colored mural paintings depicting Tlaloc (fig. 135). The opulence and spaciousness of the palace attest to the existence of a powerful upper class and to the importance of spiritual devotion in connection with that wealth.

Teotihuacán was apparently the most highly urbanized center of its time in the New World. The life-span of the center was roughly from 500 B.C. to A.D. 650. This period left a spectacular mark on Mesoamerica, with high points reached at Teotihuacán as well as at Monte Albán in Oaxaca and in the Maya region. Each had a planned urban center with astronomical orientation for streets and buildings, monumental architecture, and intellectual achievements such as the perfection of the calendar, mathematics, writing, and astronomy (the latter especially among the Maya). This was a splendid age of the arts and architecture which was reflected in the pyramid-temples at Teotihuacán and Tikal, in mural painting, ceramics, and mosaics. Professional people and artisans were organized into guilds. Traders were also well organized, and in large and efficient markets goods from many regions were exchanged. Merchants carried such items as feathers of exotic tropical birds, cotton, cacao, jade, and turquoise into Teotihuacán. The society was sharply stratified, militaristic, and theocratic. The predominance of religious representations in Teotihuacán as well as the presence of altars in the central courtyards of each house testify to the importance of religion in this community. Religious, civic, and secular activities were joined in the centers, which supported priest-chieftains, nobles, merchants, poets, musicians, actors (who were highly respected and took part in religious and secular ceremonies), artists, laborers, farmers, servants, and slaves.

MEDIEVAL ART

•Vladimir

• Moscow

U. S. S. R.

arsaw

• Kiev

• Rostov

Sea of Azov

Caspian Sea

MOLDAVIA
Carpathians

Bucharest •
ROMANIA

Black Sea

BULGARIA

Constantinople •

•Teheran

Salonika •

• Ankara

MACEDONIA
GREECE
aphni • • Athens

T U R K E Y

P E R S I A

I R A N

MESOPOTAMIA

• Antioch

•Dura
Europos

• Samarra

• Baghdad
IRAQ

Zagros Mts.

SYRIA

LEBANON •Damascus

• Kufa

S e a

Jerusalem
•
ISRAEL   **JORDAN**

Cairo •

▲ *Mt. Sinai*

EGYPT

• Medina

Red Sea

• Mecca

INTRODUCTION

In its gigantic public scale and complex subject matter, the Hindu relief at Mahamallapuram (fig. 136) can exemplify the religious art that was produced in many centers throughout the world in the period between the third and fifteenth centuries. During this period, which in Europe is known as the Middle Ages or medieval period, religions such as Buddhism, Christianity, Hinduism, and Islam expanded far beyond their places of origin to find tremendous increases in numbers of followers. New centers with significant monuments were dedicated to serve the needs of religious practitioners, including priests and other members of religious hierarchies and the common people.

The site of Mahamallapuram, in south India on the shores of the Indian Ocean, was a pilgrimage center for Hindu believers. On gigantic natural outcroppings of granite, sculptors carved shrines and reliefs of immense proportions. The *Descent of the Ganges* is carved on the face of a cliff above which is a natural pool. During the rainy season, the overflow cascades down the natural cleft to be collected in a pool at the base. Over millennia this cleft has been smoothed by the flowing action of the water.

The natural phenomenon of the cleft may have inspired the Hindus, who sculpted the cliff with the creation story. Although the iconography of specific details is still much debated, all action focuses attention on the cleft near the center. This water is usually identified with the river Ganges, one of the three sacred rivers of India and thought to have life-giving powers. Representatives of all the living beings of the world—deities of the river, elephants, lions, gods, human beings, and even a cat and mice—are assembled on this great carving. The god Siva, one of the major manifestations of the godhead in the Hindu religion, appears several times to symbolize the destructive and creative conduct of nature.

In contrast to the Hindu relief is a small Christian object shaped like a church (fig. 137). The Christian content is evident in the iconography of the reliefs, which feature Old Testament prophets, Christ, and the apostles, as well as scenes from the life of Christ, including the crucifixion. This object functioned as a reliquary—a container for the bones of a holy person or for objects associated with that person (see also fig. 178). Reliquaries were displayed to the faithful, who hoped to benefit from the proximity to holy things.

HISTORY: GROWTH OF A WORLD CULTURE

The growth of powerful proselytizing religions was only one manifestation of worldwide change during this long period. A number of

136. Indian. *Descent of the Ganges,* Mahamallapuram, India. c. 625–74 (Middle Pallava period). Carved on a granite cliff, height 20'

important political entities flourished at this time, including the Gupta rule in India; the successive Han, Sung, and Tang dynasties in China; the Maya and Aztecs in the Americas; and the Carolingian, Ottonian, Romanesque, and Gothic cultures in Europe. There was commercial, intellectual, cultural, scientific, and religious exchange on a large scale. This period saw the silk routes of commerce flourish between east and west. Marco Polo, the Venetian who visited the court of Kubla Khan in China, is only one of the many examples of contact between vastly different cultures that characterizes the period. Islam preserved much of ancient Greek and Roman literature and philosophy and then reintroduced them into European culture at the end of the Middle Ages. Islamic science, mathematics, and medicine became well known in Europe at the same time. Scientific advances included astronomical investigations in India and Mesoamerica and the invention of gunpowder in China. Other inventions were the wheelbarrow, the compass, paper, and the spinning wheel. Practical, labor-saving inventions meant that there was less need for the slave labor that had characterized much of the ancient world. As large and powerful cultures and religious traditions developed, there was also contact through wars, including the religious and commercial wars known as the Crusades. An increased awareness of divergent cultures was a hallmark of this period.

The term Middle Ages was invented during the Italian Renaissance to designate for European culture the interim period between the "new" Renaissance age and the ancient civilizations of the Greeks and Romans. The Middle Ages were then thought to be an interval of darkness and cultural inactivity. Historians today recognize the vitality of the Middle Ages or medieval period, which is considered to extend from the second century A.D. (when Christian art was first produced) until the fourteenth or early fifteenth century in Italy, and even later in northern Europe. (This term has also been used by Western scholars, perhaps inappropriately, to describe certain contemporary phases of Indian and Chinese art.)

WORLD RELIGIONS

The spiritual content of Christianity, which played a crucial role in forming the life and culture of the Middle Ages in Europe, is difficult to summarize, in part because of the many different interpretations of Christian belief that have developed. Christianity, a religion of salvation, emphasizes the inner, spiritual life, offering the promise of life after death for the soul in Paradise. Medieval Christianity emphasized belief in a single God understood as a Trinity, an indivisible unity of three persons: God the Father, the creator; Jesus Christ, his son, who assumed human form in the Incarnation; and the Holy Spirit, who is believed to be continuously active in the world. Jesus Christ is held to be the son of God, who was born to a pious woman known as the Virgin Mary. He died by crucifixion after being charged with blasphemy. Medieval Christian art often depicted the Last Judgment (see figs. 185, 186, 213), when Christ would come at the end of time to judge humanity.

The Hindu religion developed a complex set of stories to explain the workings of nature, and especially fertility and procreation. The traditions emphasize a single godhead which is capable of an infinite number of manifestations, assuming male, female, animal, and mixed animal and human forms. In personal terms the most important aspect of Hinduism is the belief in reincarnation—every individual will return to life as another living creature. Good behavior in one life will lead to a higher state of existence in the next. The religion is thought to have combined ancient beliefs about fertility with ideas derived from social customs such as hierarchy and caste. The highest order of gods is a trinity: Brahmin the creator, Vishnu the preserver, and Siva the destroyer. Images of these deities and many others and their multitudinous activities were thought of as aids in contemplation and as a focus for identification. The southern Hindu tradition, as at Mahamallapuram, and its art forms were passed along the trade routes across the seas to Cambodia and Indonesia.

Buddhism is based on the life and teachings of Siddhartha Gautama, who became an ascetic and emphasized that his followers should eliminate desire in order to achieve *nirvana* (see p. 103). Islam is a monotheistic religion based on a book of holy writings, the Koran, compiled by the prophet Mohammed in the sixth century A.D.; the practitioners of this religion are known as Muslims. God is known as Allah, and among the prophets whose writings and/or lives are included in the Koran and other Islamic writings are Abraham, Moses, Christ's mother Mary, Christ, and Mohammed.

EUROPEAN MEDIEVAL ART

Although a unified style cannot be defined for all European medieval art, many medieval works offer a stylistic treatment that emphasizes Christian spiritual values accompanied by an intentional denial of the ancient classical traditions of naturalism, individualism, and illusionism. This is a broad generalization that offers some unity to the art produced in the diverse styles of the medieval period in Europe. In addition, the great majority of surviving European medieval works of art are directly related to and created for the rituals and practices of the Christian church.

THE MEDIEVAL ARTIST

In Europe there are few signed works of art during the medieval period before the last, or Gothic, period. The individuality of the artist

137. Left: German. *Reliquary in the Shape of a Church.* Probably made by a workshop in Cologne, Germany. c. 1170. Gilt cast bronze, enamel, and walrus ivory reliefs on a wooden core, height 21 1/2". Victoria and Albert Museum, London. This reliquary was originally in the convent of Hochelten in the Lower Rhine region.

138. Right: **MASTER OF ST. GILES** *The Mass of St. Giles.* c. 1500. Oil on wood, 24 1/4 x 18". National Gallery, London. A late-fifteenth-century painter here represents a ninth-century miracle taking place at an altar at the Church of St. Denis, near Paris.

139. TAKAYOSHI (attributed)
First illustration to the "Azumaya" chapter of *The Tale of Genji*. 12th century (Late Heian period). Hand scroll, ink and color on paper, height 8 1/2". Tokugawa Art Museum, Nagoya, Japan. The first novel, written in Japan by Lady Murasaki, is called *The Tale of Genji*. It recounts the amorous adventures and intrigues of the young prince Genji at the court. This illustration shows a group of court women and their attendants. Naka no Kimi is having her hair combed after washing, while her half-sister, Ukifume, faces her and looks at picture scrolls and an attendant reads the accompanying text. That there had been an attempt to seduce Ukifume only hours before is not explicitly illustrated, for the painter describes a scene of refined activity.

was not an issue during a period in which individuality generally was denigrated; many of the most important medieval works were, in fact, produced by groups of artists and artisans working together. The artists of the Middle Ages included an important new class of artist: monks and nuns who, living within monastic communities, joined artistic productivity with the religious life. In Europe the crafting of manuscripts and other liturgical objects was such an important activity that abbots of monasteries and even bishops would continue to be active as artists after they had risen in the ecclesiastical hierarchy. But there were also many lay artists, who lived in the cities and were not connected to any religious order. By the tenth century we have evidence that lay artists were organizing themselves into professional organizations, rather like trade unions, called guilds.

In non-European cultures during this period, the artists worked in groups, and the large endeavors required by religious practices were produced by workshops of artists and laborers. There are isolated instances of signed works, but these are not common. The main exception to this attitude toward the artist is in China, where the status of the artist as a scholar-intellectual working within the court means that the majority of works are signed (see p. 171).

ART AND THE CHRISTIAN CHURCH

In Europe the dominant medieval institution—culturally, educationally, spiritually, and often politically—was the Christian church. In both east and west, some Christians withdrew from the world into monasteries and nunneries to follow a life of work and prayer. The church developed a ruling hierarchy headed by the pope (the bishop of Rome, the first of whom had been St. Peter) and local bishops, and which included the heads of monasteries and nunneries. The expanding institutions and hierarchy of the church created a great demand for works of art.

Christianity developed a series of rites and services known as the liturgy. The central Christian rite was the mass or eucharist, a service at which the Last Supper was reenacted and salvation for repentant believers was promised. By the early fourth century this service was usually held in a church at an altar, which became the focus for the ritual and for works of Christian art. Our painting (fig. 138) demonstrates the rich decoration at a medieval altar. The priest, dressed in elaborately decorated vestments, stands at an altar with a bejeweled cross, a gold altarpiece, and a brocaded altar frontal. He raises the host, a consecrated piece of bread that stands for the body of Christ. (Missing from this representation is a chalice, the vessel which held the wine standing for Christ's blood; see fig. 193.)

THE SCROLL AND BOOK

In the painting depicting the mass, an open book is prominent on the altar. The hand-lettered, decorated manuscript played an important role in Christianity and Christian art during the European Middle Ages. The Bible, the holy book of Christianity, was held to be a compendium of divine proclamations and a record of God's actions in history. It has two sections: the Old Testament, which encompasses the books of the Jewish faith, and the New Testament, composed of four versions of the life of Christ (the Gospels, written by the Evangelists—Matthew, Mark, Luke, and John) and other writings. Throughout the Middle Ages, Bibles, service books, and private prayer books were written by hand—usually on treated animal skins (vellum or parchment)—and, because they represented the word of God, they were richly adorned with fine materials and were illustrated.

Illustrated and decorated manuscripts were also an important part of religious and secular traditions in other parts of the world. Islam avoided the representation of the human figure, but copies of the Koran were decorated with spectacular calligraphic decorative patterns. In the Far East, novels and religious tracts were written on hand scrolls, which unrolled from right to left. Readers held the scrolls in both hands; only a small portion of the scroll was visible at any one time. The manner in which Takayoshi painted the scene illustrated here (fig. 139) is a calculatedly decorative one, using the screens, walls, and sliding panels typical of an aristocratic Japanese house to break up the composition. Such angular placement of shapes and the use of colors both bright and subtle create an agitated mood perhaps reflecting the earlier events of the day. This style of painting was called *yamato-e* (Japanese picture). The metered control with which pictures such as this were designed and executed led to a highly refined and yet vital painting style identified by the Japanese as a native style of art.

JEWISH ART: THE SYNAGOGUE AT DURA EUROPOS

140. West wall, with the Torah niche, Synagogue, Dura Europos. Erected 244/245. Tempera on plaster, length of wall approx. 40'. Reconstruction in the National Museum, Damascus. The Roman frontier city of Dura Europos in Mesopotamia was a crossroads and minor trading center which has provided rich archaeological information, especially in its several places of worship, including a synagogue, a Christian site with a baptistery with frescoes, and temples to Bel, Zeus, and Mithras.

Discovered in 1932, this synagogue (fig. 140) astonished archaeologists and scholars, for its capacious house of assembly had, quite unexpectedly, figurative decoration: a complicated sequence of paintings of Old Testament scenes in bands around all four walls and a ceiling of tiles decorated with personifications, astrological subjects, animals, flowers, and other themes. Both scripture (the second of the Ten Commandments: "You shall not make for yourself a graven image [idol], or any likeness of anything that is in heaven above, or that is in the earth below, or that is in the water

under the earth") and historical writings seem to imply that it is unlawful for Jews to make or have images. That this prohibition was not followed by all Jews is revealed by archaeological excavations at Dura and elsewhere and by Jewish books from the Middle Ages, such as the many beautifully illustrated Passover *Haggadah*s. The cycle at the Dura synagogue includes such scenes as Solomon receiving the Queen of Sheba, David as King of Israel, Moses receiving the Law, the Consecration of the Temple, Moses leading the chosen people out of Egypt, Mordecai and Esther, Moses and the

Burning Bush, Exodus and the Crossing of the Red Sea, and even a cityscape with a representation of Jerusalem and the Temple of Solomon.

In terms of art, Dura Europos was an unimportant provincial city, and the conventions of the figures and the use of iconographic stereotypes well known from other sites suggest that the Dura cycle was derived from a pattern book—a book of images, prepared as an artist's tool, which preserved a tradition of illustrated scenes, in this case from the Old Testament. In *Moses Giving Water to the Tribes* (fig. 141), Moses stands in a relaxed

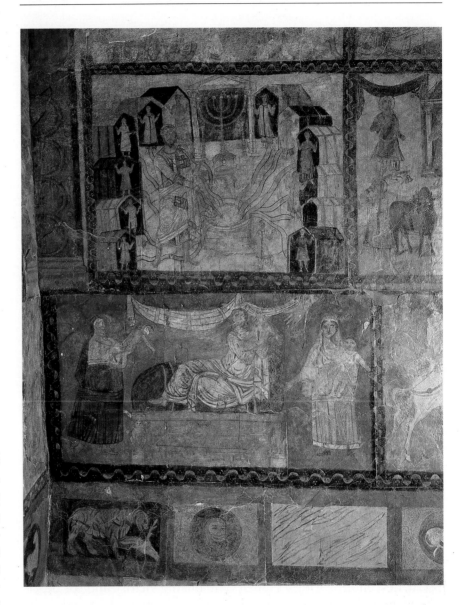

141. *Moses Giving Water to the Tribes* and *Elijah Receives the Widow's Child* (detail of fig. 140). The figures are smaller than lifesize.

contrapposto position derived from ancient Greek and Roman art, but the schematic nature of the composition, with smaller figures representing the tribes of Israel placed evenly around the edge of the scene, and the unrealistic manner in which streams of water reach out to each tent are consistent with developments in Early Christian art. The Jews, a small minority at Dura, created an impressively decorated synagogue which expresses their piety and the dignity of their traditions.

Introduction to Early Christian Art

The Three Hebrew Children in the Fiery Furnace from a Christian cemetery (fig. 142) represents the Old Testament story of righteous Hebrew children who were saved by God after being thrown in a furnace for refusing to worship pagan idols. Three frontal figures, their arms raised in a position of prayer, stand amid flames. Their pleas for deliverance are answered, and a dove, symbolic of the Holy Spirit, descends bearing a branch symbolizing victory and/or peace. The message of the painting is direct: faith brings salvation.

Catacombs, underground burial complexes used by both Christians and pagans, were originally known by the Greek *coemeteria* (places of rest, from which we derive our word cemetery); later, the term *catacomba*, which initially referred to a specific cemetery in Rome, came into general use. The walls of the narrow, labyrinthine passages in the catacombs, cut from soft rock, had horizontal niches to hold the bodies of the deceased. Larger chambers, also underground, were used for funerary rites. Catacombs were not secret

142. *The Three Hebrew Children in the Fiery Furnace.* Early 3rd century. Fresco, approx. 20 x 30". Catacomb of Priscilla, Rome

143. *Good Shepherd*. Late 3rd century. Marble (restored), height 39". Vatican Museums, Rome

burial places, as legend has it, although they may have been used as hiding places during times of Christian persecution.

The painting of *The Three Hebrew Children* expresses the faith of the early Christians by promising divine salvation in time of need and suffering. The Old Testament story was perceived as a precedent for New Testament teachings. Christians understood Christ as the Messiah who fulfilled the prophecies of the Old Testament, and theologians and artists often associated the two religious traditions. The style of the painting is suggestive and animated, continuing a Roman manner of painting using loose paint and flowing brushstrokes. Some modeling is used, but the strong outlines flatten and dematerialize the figures, and the emphasis on their large eyes enhances the spiritual intent.

HISTORY

A few years after Christ's death and resurrection, Paul (originally named Saul), a Jew who had persecuted Christians, was converted to the new faith (see fig. 335). He zealously preached the message of

Christ, converting many to Christianity. By about A.D. 40, the term Christian was first used to designate these followers of Christ's teachings, and about A.D. 70–80, when the Gospels of the New Testament were being written, Christianity broke decisively with Judaism.

By the early second century, an internal structure and hierarchy were being formed within the church, and liturgical rites for worship were developed. Although subject to periodic and often vicious persecution, the new religion, with its emphasis on spiritual values, spread rapidly. In a letter written to the Roman emperor Trajan in 110, Pliny the Younger warned of this "extreme superstition. . . . Many of all ages, of all ranks, of both sexes, are being brought into danger, and will continue to be brought. The blight of this superstition has not been confined to towns and villages; it has even spread to the country."

EARLY CHRISTIAN ART

Early Christian art (c. A.D. 150–400) developed gradually, in part because of intermittent persecution. Stylistically the new art was initially dependent on Roman and Hellenistic sources. In many cases only the Christian subject matter indicates its religious function. Early Christian artists worked in a diverse range of media. Painters not only decorated church and catacomb walls but also created book illustrations. Sculptors made marble sarcophagi and ivory carvings. A favored medium for church decoration was mosaic.

One house at Dura Europos was converted for Christian services in 231. It included a baptistery with an image of the Good Shepherd (from the parable in Luke 15:3–7) above a scene of Adam and Eve in the garden. Here Old and New Testaments are intellectually related—the Good Shepherd becomes a reference to Christian redemption, overcoming the sin of Adam and Eve. The Good Shepherd image appears often on Early Christian sarcophagi and reliefs, and even as single figures (see fig. 143), but it is uncertain whether these beardless youths represent Christ as the Good Shepherd or the more general concept of God caring for his flock. In any case, the humble modesty of the figure is consistent with the spirit of early Christianity.

THE EARLY CHRISTIAN ARTIST

Early Christian artists were challenged to express the promises and mysteries of their new faith. As in ancient Roman art and in most later medieval art, artists were laborers who worked in a communal situation, and their works are anonymous. They created the means to communicate the ideals of Christianity as it changed and became more public. These anonymous artists, at once conventional and innovative, helped effect a transition from the ancient to the medieval world.

144. *Sarcophagus of Archbishop Theodore.* 7th century. Marble, length approx. 72". Sant'Apollinare in Classe, Ravenna. This Byzantine work continues the tradition of symbolism of the Early Christian period.

CHRISTIANITY AND SYMBOLISM

From Judaism, Christianity inherited a disposition against representing the divinity, an attitude which was also supported by Christian criticism of the pagan practice of worshipping idols. As questions arose about the appropriateness of figurative art in the early church, a vocabulary of symbols was developed to express abstractly the tenets of the new faith. For example, the anchor, referred to in Paul's letter to the Hebrews (6:19), became a symbol of resolution and hope, while the first two letters of the Greek word for Christ, *X* and *P*, were combined to form a monogram of Christ [�֎]. The fish became a symbol for Christ because the first letter of each word in the phrase "Jesus Christ, Son of God, Savior" forms the Greek *ichthus*, fish.

Christian symbols alluding to salvation were especially prominent on funerary art, as seen in the *Sarcophagus of Archbishop Theodore* (fig. 144). Ancient legend held that the flesh of the peacock was immune to decay and that its feathers contained the complete spectrum of colors; thus the peacocks flanking the �֎ monogram symbolize eternity. The A, alpha, and Ω, omega—first and last letters of the Greek alphabet—are placed like ornaments hanging from the ✖ monogram and crosses because Christ said, "I am Alpha and Omega, the beginning and the end" (Revelation 1:8). The curving vine and grapes refer both to God's relationship with his people ("I am the vine, you are the branches"; John 15:5) and to the wine used in the mass to represent the blood of Christ. The wreaths on the lid, an ancient Greek and Roman motif that refers to victory, enclose Christian symbols, suggesting the soul's desire to triumph over death.

EARLY CHRISTIAN ARCHITECTURE

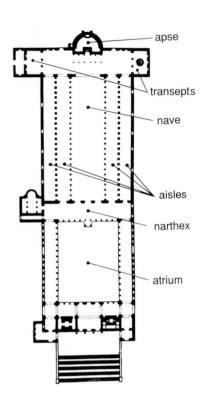

145. Nave, Old St. Peter's Basilica, Rome. Reconstruction. c. 333–390. Interior approx. 368' in length. This original basilica was demolished in the sixteenth century, when today's imposing edifice (figs. 290–94, 345) was begun. The earlier church then became known as Old St. Peter's.

146. Plan, Old St. Peter's Basilica

Old St. Peter's Basilica served as a prototype for developments in Christian architecture (figs. 145, 146). The plan was initially adapted from the Roman basilica (see fig. 126), which was usually entered on its long side, but the Christian church was entered through an atrium and narthex (entrance hall) on its short side. This narthex is usually on the west, and the altar was toward the east, an orientation followed in most later medieval churches.

The interior division of space, with a nave flanked by side aisles, is similar to certain Roman basilicas. Old St. Peter's has transepts (from the middle Latin *transseptum,* meaning transverse enclosure), a feature that will become traditional in Christian churches. These architectural spaces, extensions to the north

and south, meet the nave at the crossing. Transepts create a cross shape; the term cruciform (cross-like) basilica designates Early Christian churches with transepts. At St. Peter's, as in many Roman basilicas, wooden trusses supported a gable roof, and clerestory windows allowed light to illuminate the nave. The columns used at Old St. Peter's were taken from earlier Roman buildings; materials thus reused are known as *spolia* (Latin for spoils).

The size of Old St. Peter's mirrors the triumphant attitude of Christianity following the Edict of Milan in 313, which granted religious freedom to the Christians. Constantine realized the unifying strength that the newly recognized religion could bring to his reign. Many privileges, including tax exemptions

and donations of land and money, were granted the church. Constantine personally contributed to the construction of St. John Lateran in Rome (begun 313), which marks the first use of the basilica plan for Christian architecture. Constantine's support was further evidenced by his decision to build Old St. Peter's, which was both a *martyrium* (built over the grave site of St. Peter, it marked and commemorated his martyrdom) and a basilica used for worship. It is believed that the development of the transept at St. Peter's derived from the need for additional space for worshippers and pilgrims around the shrine and a desire to separate Peter's grave from other tombs in the nave.

Old St. Peter's had a plain brick exterior, but the interior

Old St. Peter's Basilica, Rome: c. 333–390
312: Constantine, after having a vision of the cross, defeats Maxentius
410: Goths sack Rome

147. Plan, Santa Costanza

148. Interior, Santa Costanza, Rome. c. 354

was adorned with precious materials, including marble Roman columns, mosaics, and frescoes. The decorated interior contrasted with the exterior, reminding the visitor that the beauty of the inner spirit was more important than external, physical adornment. From the entrance, one's attention was focused on the high altar, set below an enormous arch on which a mosaic depicted Christ, St. Peter, and the emperor Constantine with the inscription: "Because under Your guidance the world rose triumphant to the skies, Constantine, himself a victor, built You this hall."

In the apse, where in a Roman basilica a statue of the emperor might be located, another mosaic displayed an enthroned Christ flanked by Sts. Peter and Paul. A reference to Christ as the supreme judge is thus found at a point where, in a Roman basilica, law had been dispensed. (In some churches the *cathedra*, or throne, of the bishop was set in the apse. These churches, the residences of bishops, are called cathedrals.) With the support of Constantine, who probably converted to Christianity near the time of his death, the flourishing Christian faith adapted the architectural forms and imperial symbolism of ancient Rome.

Another type of design adapted by the early Christians was the centrally planned structure, in which all parts of a building radiate from a central point. It was used for baptisteries and mausoleums. Santa Costanza exemplifies the centrally planned structure (figs. 147, 148). Built about 354 as a mausoleum for Constantia, daughter of Constantine, it features a central altar within a ring of paired columns that support the dome and clerestory and create a circular corridor between the domed space of the altar and the exterior walls. This passage, which at Santa Costanza was barrel-vaulted and decorated with mosaics, is called the ambulatory (*ambulare*, to walk). Four large niches in the walls define the shape of a Greek cross (a cross with four equal arms). The cross circumscribed by the circular plan symbolized salvation and eternal life for the Christian and was thus an appropriate design for a Christian tomb.

Introduction to Byzantine Art

149. *The Transfiguration of Christ.*
c. 560. Apse mosaic. Monastery of St.
Catherine, Mount Sinai, Egypt. The
Monastery of St. Catherine is at the
foot of Mount Sinai where, the Old
Testament reports, God gave the Ten
Commandments to Moses. Isolated
in the Sinai Desert, the monastery,
which has been in continuous use
since the sixth century, is a repository
of early manuscripts and other works
of art.

The Transfiguration occurred when three apostles accompanied
Christ to the top of a mountain. While they prayed, Christ was lifted
up into the sky, surrounded by an aura of heavenly light, and
appeared flanked by the Old Testament prophets Moses and Elijah
(Matthew 17:1–13). The voice of God the Father was heard from a
cloud, "This is my beloved Son: hear him." Christ is represented on
the axis surrounded by a mandorla (almond-shaped halo) of blue
light which emphasizes his resplendent white robes (fig. 149). Moses
and Elijah symmetrically flank Christ, while the apostles below
gesture with wondrous exclamation.

At Mount Sinai the divinity of Christ is demonstrated in a scene
that has a spiritual emphasis which removes it from our physical
world. No geographic details are given, and the event is bathed in a
golden light symbolic of the spiritual enlightenment of God. Although modeling is used, the shadows are linear patterns, denying
the figures the illusion of weight or mass.

HISTORY

In 323 Constantine decided to move the capital of the Roman Empire
from Rome to the eastern part of the empire, to an historic trading

150. *The Prayer of Isaiah,* from the *Paris Psalter.* c. 900. Manuscript painting on vellum, 14 x 10 1/4". Bibliothèque Nationale, Paris

center on the Bosphorus called Byzantium (from which we derive the name for the Byzantine civilization). The eastern provinces of the empire, already strongly Christianized, had become increasingly more important, and the new capital was far from the political instability of Rome and the threats of barbarian invaders. The new capital, dedicated in 330, was named Constantinople.

Constantine's decision was a wise one. A port located at the center of regional trade routes and surrounded by rich timbered forests and agricultural fields, Constantinople developed rapidly as an economic and cultural center. This growth led to an increased military capability, and, during the reign of Justinian in the sixth century, areas of the empire that had been lost—Italy, southern Spain, and North Africa—were again brought under the emperor 's rule. Under Justinian, an intelligent and efficient emperor, Byzantine civilization prospered. His wife, Theodora, a former circus performer, gave resolute counsel in assisting to govern the empire. Justinian and Theodora shared a vision of reviving the grandeur of the Roman Empire while advancing the Christian faith.

But Justinian's military gains proved costly and short-lived. Later the empire was reduced through uprisings in western Europe and, beginning in the seventh century, through the rapid advance of the Islamic religion, which with prophetic zeal spread the ideals of the prophet Mohammed to Arabia, Persia, North Africa, and into Spain. Gradually the influence of Roman culture in Constantinople was supplanted with Greek taste and values, and Greek replaced Latin as the official language at court. In 1204 Constantinople was captured and sacked by the Crusaders, who ruled the area for approximately fifty years. Cultural and political stability was restored for a while, but in 1453 Constantinople surrendered to the Ottoman Turks and was later renamed Istanbul.

BYZANTINE ART

Many aspects of ancient Greek art and culture were preserved in the eastern, Byzantine empire. This influence is exemplified by a manuscript painting from the *Paris Psalter* (a book of Psalms) in which Isaiah's prayers are met by a ray of light which extends from the hand of God (fig. 150). The figures on either side of Isaiah are classical personifications: Night is a female *contrapposto* figure wearing a Greek costume and with a veil of stars over her head, while Dawn is a boy with a lighted torch. The gold background is still dominant, as it was four centuries earlier in *The Transfiguration* at Mount Sinai, but elements of landscape recalling Hellenistic and early Roman painting have been retained. The classicizing influence is more strongly stated here than in comparable manuscript illuminations from western Europe.

THE BYZANTINE ARTIST

Byzantine artists, like their Roman predecessors, were trained and practiced in a workshop system. While they constructed and decorated public buildings and churches, the collective efforts of these artists in different media were coordinated by an official overseer. As is true of much of the Middle Ages, artists worked in anonymity.

Specialized workshops produced a variety of media, including mosaics, mural and icon paintings, manuscript illustrations, and small sculpture. Large-scale figurative sculpture, one of the cornerstones of Greek and Roman art, was seldom produced during the Byzantine era, perhaps out of fear that such works would have the connotations of pagan idols. Byzantine carvers produced sarcophagi reliefs and small, exquisitely refined ivories to adorn religious and secular objects.

THE ICON AND ICONOCLASM

One unique form of painting which developed in orthodox Christianity was the icon (Greek for image). Used during religious services and to decorate churches, an icon displayed a holy person or event and was viewed as a vehicle to communicate with the spiritual world. Some icons were believed to date from the time of Christ, and the most famous were thought to be of divine origin. The *Virgin En-*

151. *Virgin Enthroned with Sts. Theodore and George and Angels.* 6th century. Encaustic on wood, 27 x 19 3/8". Monastery of St. Catherine, Mount Sinai

throned with Sts. Theodore and George (fig. 151) is a rare surviving example of a sixth-century icon. The drapery patterns tend to flatten the figures, but the modeling and the attempted *contrapposto* postures seen in the saints continue the classical interest in naturalism. Above the Virgin two angels look sharply upward to God, whose hand descends into the pictorial space, emitting a strong ray of light. The static composition of the Virgin and saints, with their intense staring eyes, is characteristic of icon paintings. The medium is encaustic (from the Greek *enkaiein,* to burn in). It involves mixing dry pigments with hot wax, a technique which creates a translucent and brilliant effect.

By the later sixth century, the faithful attributed miraculous powers to certain icons. Conservative factions, called iconoclasts (image-destroyers), feared that icons had become objects of worship, which would be heretical; the divine nature of Christ, they argued, should not be represented, and to do so would be idolatrous. They were countered by the iconodules (image-venerators), who argued that as Christ had become human (the doctrine of the Incarnation), it was permissible to depict him in his human form. The dispute erupted into open and at times bloody conflict between 726 and 843, a period in Byzantine history known as the iconoclastic controversy. During this period, icons and other religious images were damaged or destroyed, accounting for tremendous losses of works of Early Christian and Byzantine art. A final victory for the iconodules occurred in 843; even today one Sunday in the Orthodox Christian church calendar celebrates the restoration of images.

HAGIA SOPHIA, CONSTANTINOPLE

152. ANTHEMIUS OF TRALLES AND ISIDORUS OF MILETUS (architects)
Interior, Hagia Sophia (Holy Wisdom), Istanbul (Constantinople), Turkey.
532–37. The plan of Hagia Sophia, 270 feet in length, covers almost one and a
half acres, and the great central dome, 108 feet in diameter, crowns at a height
of over 185 feet. After the Ottoman Turks captured Constantinople in 1453,
Hagia Sophia was converted to an Islamic mosque. Towering minarets, from
which the faithful were called to prayer, were added to the exterior, while on
the interior the Christian mosaics were covered and eight huge discs with
sayings from the Koran were added. Hagia Sophia influenced later developments in Islamic mosque architecture. Today the former imperial church and
mosque is a state museum.

The interior of Hagia Sophia (fig.
152) offers a dramatic interplay
of two crucial architectural elements: space and light. On entering, the visitor is astonished by
the enormous interior space.
Flanked by semi-domes on two
sides, the central dome rests like a
colossal canopy on four gigantic
piers. The windows at the base
of the dome create rays of light
which dematerialize these supports. The high dome appears
suspended, hovering in space
above us.

Just as the drama of light at the
Pantheon in Rome (fig. 127) represents a metaphysical joining of
the physical and spiritual worlds,
so too was the amplitude of light
within Hagia Sophia bound to
the religious purpose of the
building. Originally, the light was
even more intense, for the windows were successively decreased when the dome was
rebuilt three times due to structural damages from earthquakes
in 558, 989, and 1346. Light was
an integral part of Hagia Sophia's
effect, for when combined with
the immense interior space and
mosaics, the building created a
powerful physical and spiritual
experience, as recorded by Pro-
copius, the court historian to
Justinian, writing shortly after
the church was decorated: "The
sun's light and its shining rays
fill the temple. One would say
that the space is not lit by the sun
without, but that the source of
light is to be found within, such
is the abundance of light. . . . So
light is the construction, the dome
seems not to rest on a solid structure, but to cover the space with
a sphere of gold suspended in
the sky. . . . The scintillations of
the light forbid the spectator's

gaze to linger on the details; each one attracts the eye and leads it on to the next. The circular motion of one's gaze reproduces itself to infinity. . . . The spirit rises toward God and floats in the air, certain that He is not far away, but loves to stay close to those whom He has chosen."

This remarkable synthesis of light and architectural form was conceived by Anthemius of Tralles, an artist and scientist, and Isidorus of Miletus, an architect and engineer. During a brief six-week period, they evolved a new architectural plan that combined the longitudinal orientation of the basilica with the central plan (figs. 153, 154). Unlike Roman architects, who preferred to support a dome on a drum, Anthemius and Isidorus raised the central dome on penden-

tives, curving triangular segments which provide the transition from the square plan of the piers to the circular base of the dome (see fig. 124), and flanked it with semi- or half domes. The huge piers reduced the load-bearing function of the walls, allowing for large amounts of window space (such non-supporting walls are known as

screen walls). That Hagia Sophia was completed in just five years demonstrates the importance of the building in Justinian's plans. It is reported that at its dedication in 537, the emperor compared his accomplishment to that of Solomon, builder of the Temple in Jerusalem, when he proclaimed, "Solomon, I have outdone thee!"

SAN VITALE, RAVENNA

155. Opposite: Interior, San Vitale, Ravenna, Italy. 526–47. Ravenna had been the capital city of the Ostrogoths, a German tribe which conquered Italy by 493, but in 540 the city, taken by Justinian's army, became a regional Italian capital and the local religious center of the Byzantine empire.

The centrally planned church of San Vitale has the plain brick exterior which characterized much Early Christian and Byzantine architecture, but inside a comprehensive mosaic program synthesizes Christian iconography with imperial Byzantine politics (fig. 155). It is a complex ideological program which joins Old and New Testament scenes, symbols, decorative patterns, and imperial portraiture. The unity of the mosaic program is defined by the axial placement of a number of images and symbols of Christ on, for example, the apex of the arch and at the center of the groin vault, where a lamb symbolizes Christ and his sacrifice. The monogram ✸

leads to the most important of these references, the youthful Christ seated on the blue sphere of the universe in the apse. These align with the altar, where Christ's sacrifice is reenacted during the mass, reinforcing this programmatic unity.

The offering of bread and wine at the altar is prefigured by scenes from the Old Testament. In the semicircular area enclosed by the arch (this area is termed a lunette) to the left of the altar, Abraham is depicted feeding three angels symbolic of the Trinity. To the right Abraham is shown about to sacrifice his son Isaac, a narrative prophetic of Christ's sacrifice.

On the left wall of the apse, a

rectangular mosaic depicts Justinian with ecclesiastical personnel on his left, including Maximianus, bishop of Ravenna, and civil and military personnel on his right (fig. 156). Justinian carries the vessel that held the bread for the mass; on the soldier's shield at the left border, a ✸ monogram indicates the political importance Christianity had assumed within the empire. Although the figures are frontal, their isocephalic arrangement suggests a procession. Justinian never visited San Vitale, but his significance in this, his western capital, is implied by the mosaic.

Justinian's placement, flanked by ecclesiastical and civil representatives, communicates his

San Vitale, Ravenna

156. Right: Mosaics, San Vitale

157. Below: *Theodora and Attendants.* c. 547. Apse mosaic, San Vitale position as head of both church and state (in the Byzantine empire, the emperor appointed the patriarch of Constantinople). Individualized portraits are restricted to Justinian and his close associates. Although the figures overlap one another and some modeling is suggested, the scene, with its gold background, denies the illusion of real space. It is as if the earthly court of Justinian has been transfigured into a spiritual realm. As emperor, Justinian wears a jeweled crown, while as the earthly representative of God, he is shown with a halo. A decorative, rainbow-like mosaic band rises vertically above his head to descend to the opposite mosaic of the empress Theodora, shown bringing the chalice of wine to the altar, and her attendants (fig. 157).

In the semi-dome of the apse, the beardless Christ hands a crown to the Early Christian martyr St. Vitalis, for whom the church was named. To Christ's left, Bishop Ecclesius, who laid the plans for the church, presents a model of the church. The complex ideological interrelationship of the mosaics is typical of Byzantine art, in which each figurative or decorative element is part of a comprehensive architectural and thematic unity.

MOSAIC TECHNIQUE

The technique of mosaic seems to have developed from an earlier technique of pressing small, natural pebbles into plaster to form a durable and decorative floor covering which was common in the classical world. By the late fifth century B.C., Greek artists began arranging the pebbles into abstract and figurative designs. Soon, natural stones were replaced by *tesserae* (singular: *tessera*, from the Greek *tesseres*, a square), cut pieces of colored stone, especially marble (*tesserae* is also the word used for the pieces of stone and glass used for wall mosaics, as at Ravenna). At first, Roman mosaic was used primarily on the floors of private homes (see fig. 104), but occasionally it also decorated walls. Roman wall mosaics began to use glass *tesserae* in many colors, as well as gold *tesserae*, formed by sandwiching gold leaf between two layers of glass. The early Christians used mosaics to embellish the walls of their churches, but it was during the Byzantine era that the most splendid effects were achieved, as walls and vaults were covered with glass and marble mosaics enhanced by the predominant gold background.

In creating a mosaic, the image is first outlined on the floor, wall, or vault. Successive areas of this surface are covered with fresh cement or plaster, and *tesserae* are placed into it, following the established design. As the cement or plaster hardens, the *tesserae* are held firmly in place. When *tesserae* were set into walls and vaults, care was taken to adjust each so that its surface was at a slight angle to that of the neighboring *tesserae*. As the ever-changing light from the windows strikes the polished or glass *tesserae*, the changing angles of refraction create a shimmering and ethereal effect, a vision particularly suited to the mystical values of Christianity.

The figure of the Pantocrator at Daphni (fig. 188) is an impressive example of fully mature Byzantine mosaic technique. The *tesserae* are arranged to reinforce the definition of an edge or surface; note, for example, how the curved patterns on Christ's forehead create a sense of plastic form while strengthening the vigorous facial expression. Except for the gold background, large areas of a single color are avoided. At Daphni the highlighted area of Christ's brown robe contains gold and red *tesserae* to make it seem not merely lit, but radiant.

ANGLO-SAXON METALWORK

158. *The Sutton Hoo Purse Cover.* c. 620. Gold with Indian garnets and cloisonné enamels, originally on an ivory or bone background (now lost), length 8". British Museum, London. Found in 1939 in a ship-burial mound at Sutton Hoo, England, as part of the treasure of a king who probably died between 625 and 640, this purse lid of precious materials and masterful technical proficiency once adorned a cloth or leather pouch. It would have been attached to the owner's belt by hinges. When placed in the burial mound it contained gold coins and ingots. The huge ship, approximately eighty-nine feet in length, in which the treasure was buried, would have demanded thirty-eight oarsmen, and the richness of the treasure, which included a helmet, shield, spears and a sword, bowls, drinking horns, remains of a musical instrument, and twenty-six pieces of gold jewelry, revealed the important status of the deceased, who is still not identified with certainty. With the spread of Christianity, the pagan tradition of ship burial, which provided the soul with a vehicle in which to travel to the next world, gradually declined, but there are suggestions that the Sutton Hoo king may have been a convert to Christianity.

Sutton Hoo Purse Cover: **c. 620**

609: Pantheon in Rome is reconsecrated as Santa Maria Rotonda
625: Mohammed begins to dictate the Koran
638: Muslims capture Jerusalem

The abstract, heavily patterned style of the *Sutton Hoo Purse Cover* is distinctive (fig. 158). In its use of valuable materials and in its emphasis on minute, fine craftsmanship, it continues the interest, typical of earlier nomadic tribes, in art that is valuable, portable, and a part of personal adornment. The most characteristic motif of Anglo-Saxon and Irish metalwork is the interlace, a complex pattern composed of a single line which intertwines and overlaps, filling completely the available space. This common motif can be found in small works made in pre-Roman Gaul (France) and in ancient Roman and Early Christian works as patterns of intertwining vines and plants. Here it has a strongly two-dimensional effect. In Anglo-Saxon art the interlaced line is often given an animal head, the mouth of which bites down on its own tail. The legs and snouts of the four beasts at the top center of the *Sutton Hoo Purse Cover* also participate in the interlace pattern.

The discoveries at Sutton Hoo confirmed the reports of rich possessions and similar burial practices found in the somewhat later Anglo-Saxon poem *Beowulf:*

And there they brought the
  beloved body
Of their ring-giving lord,
  and laid him near
The mast. Next to that noble
  corpse
They heaped up treasures,
  jeweled helmets,
Hooked swords and coats
  of mail, armor
Carried from the ends of
  the earth; no ship
Had ever sailed so brightly
  fitted,
No king sent forth more
  deeply mourned. . . .
Take these treasures, earth,
  now that no one
Living can enjoy them.

The Sutton Hoo treasury offers valuable evidence for a civilization about which we have little information. There are few written records and only limited monuments and archaeological remains. Many documented works were melted down, destroyed by fire, or lost during attacks and invasions. The Anglo-Saxons descended from Germanic tribes which emigrated to England in the fifth century. Christianity was strengthened in England in 597 when Augustine of Canterbury landed with forty missionaries and converted Ethelbert, king of Kent, and his court. Christianity and paganism existed side-by-side for a period; as late as the seventh century, an Anglo-Saxon king dedicated one altar to heathen gods and another to Christ.

The few fragments of Anglo-Saxon poetry and documentation that have survived reveal an aesthetic that delighted in luminous materials (especially gold) and in the color red. The interest in filling every available space with pattern or design seems to be related to their Germanic origin and traditions. The artists included monks, nuns, and lay people. By the end of the Anglo-Saxon period there is some evidence that craft guilds—medieval organizations of lay artists—were beginning to develop in England. When artists are mentioned, special attention is always given to the worker in precious metals, and it is on pieces of fine metalwork that we find the few artists' signatures of this period.

HIBERNO-SAXON MANUSCRIPT ILLUMINATION

The integration of interlace motifs into a Christian context occurred most dramatically in a series of manuscripts produced in Anglo-Saxon (English) and Irish monasteries between 600 and 800. Similarities in style and other interrelationships make it difficult to distinguish their production, which is perhaps best called Hiberno-Saxon (Hibernia was the ancient Latin name for Ireland). In some of these manuscripts, whole pages are devoted to abstract designs. These are called carpet pages because of their resemblance to Oriental carpet patterns. In this example from the *Lindisfarne Gospels* (fig. 159), geometric panels are set within a surging sea of blue and red interlace. In the middle of each side are the confronted heads of a dog and a bird of prey. If we follow the patterns we discover that the lines forming the outer borders of the decoration are their much elongated bodies and that these lead to the corners, where their legs are intertwined with those of a beast from the adjacent side.

The techniques used by the Hiberno-Saxon monks who made these manuscripts are difficult to reconstruct, and exactly how they accomplished such minuscule regular patterns without the aid of a magnifying glass is unknown. In one of the *Lindisfarne* carpet pages, the geometric pattern was first drawn on the back of the page using a ruler and compass, and the most important points of the design were pricked through the vellum to provide a guide for the

159. *Carpet Page,* from the *Lindisfarne Gospels.* Painted by Bishop Eadfrith. c. 698. Manuscript painting on vellum, 13 1/2 x 9 3/4". British Library, London. The *Lindisfarne Gospels* contains a dedication to God and local saints which also identifies the artists involved: "Eadfrith, bishop of the church at Lindisfarne, originally wrote [lettered] this book for God and St. Cuthbert—jointly—for all the saints whose relics are in the island. And Ethelwald, bishop of the Lindisfarne islanders . . . covered [bound] it . . . and Billfrith, the anchorite, . . . adorned it with gold and with gems . . . and Aldred, unworthy and most miserable priest, glossed [translated] it in English between the lines. . . . [They] made or, as the case may be, embellished this Gospel Book for God and Cuthbert." Eadfrith (bishop from 698 until his death in 721) was both scribe and decorator, a combination not atypical at this time. Another inscription reveals a typical medieval rationale for artistic creation: "Thou living God, be thou mindful of Eadfrith, Ethelwald, Billfrith, and Aldred a sinner; these four have, with God's help, been engaged upon this book."

painter. The isolation of different types of decoration into geometric areas sets up maximum contrast between the widely varied patterns: fine and broad interlace, with and without zoomorphic additions, and swelling, swirling shapes. As a result, the interrelationship of the patterns as positive and negative forms and their placement in depth (which patterns are in front of or behind others) are tantalizingly difficult to decipher. The intensive, onerous, and time-consuming nature of the design and execution is related to the austere and isolated nature of life in a Hiberno-Saxon monastery.

Monasticism flourished in Ireland earlier than in England, and Irish monastic *scriptoria* (halls where manuscripts were written and decorated) were producing important volumes by the middle of the sixth century. In England the monastic tradition was established in the early seventh century, when King Oswald founded the monastery at Lindisfarne.

The earliest surviving Hiberno-Saxon manuscripts reveal an interest in decorating the lettering in the Gospel books, a not surprising development when we remember that the words are believed to be proclamations of God. This tendency reaches its peak in the *Book of Kells* (see fig. 160). When the text in the Gospel of St. Matthew (1:22) reaches the crucial point where the Incarnation of Christ is mentioned, the letters burst out in joyful, exuberant patterns. A whole page is devoted to the three words *Christi autem generatio* (the birth of Christ), with most of the page devoted to the first three letters of *Christi* (*X R I*). The

Carpet Page, **from the** *Lindisfarne Gospels:* **c. 698**
687: First Doge of Venice
711: Moors invade the Iberian peninsula

160. *Incarnation Page,* from the *Book of Kells.* c. 800(?). Manuscript painting on vellum, 13 x 9 1/2". Trinity College Library, Dublin

X is the dominant form, and it surges outward in bold and varied curves to embrace Hiberno-Saxon whorl patterns. Free-form interlace fills other areas, and simple colored frames set off the large initials amid the consuming excitement. The human head that forms the end of the *P* also dots the *I*. Near the lower left base of the *X* a small vignette shows cats watching while two mice fight over a round wafer similar to those used in the mass—a scene surely of symbolic intent, even if the exact meaning is lost to us today.

The pulsating vitality of the

word of God and the exciting news of the impending birth of his son, Jesus Christ, is thus visually demonstrated. A twelfth-century writer who was shown a precious manuscript in Ireland—perhaps the *Book of Kells* itself—wrote: "Look more keenly at it and you will penetrate to the very shrine of art. You will make out intricacies so delicate and subtle, so exact and compact, so full of knots and links, with colors so fresh and vivid, that you might say that all this was the work of an angel and not of a man."

THE JAPANESE HORYU-JI TEMPLE AT NARA

161. Horyu-ji complex, near Nara, Japan. 7th century (Asuka period). Stone, wood, plaster, and tile

162. Plan, Horyu-ji complex

Horyu-ji is the oldest Buddhist temple in all of East Asia of which main parts have survived (figs. 161, 162). It was founded in 607 and is a treasure house of immense value as an example of this early phase of art. One enters the temple-monastery complex through the *chumon*, the gate on the south face of the encircling cloister, and finds to the left (west) a *pagoda* and to the right (east) the Golden Hall (*kondo*). Both are equidistant from the *chumon* and are simultaneously visible to the worshipper as he or she enters. Instead of proceeding into the depths of the compound through a succession of buildings, as was the custom in China, the pilgrim makes a lateral turn. This eschewing of lin-

Sea of
Japan

JAPAN

Ikaruga • Nara

Pacific Ocean

0   400
     miles

Horyu-ji Temple, Nara: 7th century
7th century: Rise of the Japanese feudal nobility
612: Monastery of St. Gall is founded
613: Mohammed begins preaching openly
632: Mohammed dies

ear penetration in favor of lateral movement is repeatedly met in Japanese spatial conceptions through history (see fig. 139). The individual buildings of Horyu-ji are, however, typically continental (Chinese) in style. They stand on raised stone bases and are built on a bay system, with post-and-lintel construction, tile roofs, and elaborate *tou-kung* bracketing designed to transmit the thrust and weight of the heavy tile roof down through the wooden members into the principal columns that support the structure. The *kondo* is oriented to the four cardinal directions with a stairway on each side leading to a double door.

The interior of the hall is almost completely taken up by the platform and its cult statues, frequently numerous and of very great size. The main function of the temple hall is to enclose them, forming a shrine rather than an assembly hall for a community. A special hall on the north end outside the cloister was set aside for sermons and disputations. In the *kondo* are the images of the main cult statue of Buddha in a triad. This group is the spiritual center of a temple complex and is therefore most lavishly embellished: the pillars and beams are painted and gilded; the ceiling, in the form of a canopy, represents Paradise or heaven. On each wall are paintings (damaged by fire in 1949) which represent Buddha and paradises of the cardinal directions. This program of statues and paintings in the *kondo* makes the temple a terrestrial representation of Buddha's blissful realm. The sight of the gilded statues radiating the light of Buddha's wisdom and mercy is intended to inspire the believer. All the figures combine in a *mandala*, the center of which—the center and axis of the cosmos—is occupied by Buddha seated on his lotus throne. In that way the temple is similar to a *stupa* (see p. 101). Such buildings were part of a faith which had grown and changed from its beginnings in the sixth century B.C.

Buddhism was the first world religion known to history. From its main center of origin in northeastern India, it spread across vast areas of Asia, radiating outward in all directions—except toward the west—bringing its universal doctrine of salvation for all human and other living creatures, its philosophy and ethics, its learning and art. It bridged the differences among the rich and creative cultures of India, China, Japan, and Southeast Asia. In the course of the first millennium A.D., Buddhism led to the rise of a great spiritual and cultural community with far-ranging and profound inner unity of spiritual consciousness, manifest in remarkable similarity in patterns of life and thought, and not the least in art.

The faith grew to a national religion in India under King Asoka (269–232 B.C.) and by the second century A.D., missionaries had carried the tradition to northwest India and the provincial Greco-Roman world in Gandhara (Afghanistan). There new schools developed, called Mahayana, which taught that salvation was open to all people through faith and good works. Buddha in their view ceased to be primarily an earthly teacher, but was thought of as pure abstraction, as the "universal principle," the godhead, from whom truth radiates with a blinding light across the universe. The Buddha reached far beyond the grasp of mortal beings, but there were approachable deities in this newer Buddhism, the *bodhisattvas*, ones destined for enlightenment who had earned the right to enter *nirvana* but postponed it in order to administer to the needy.

Buddhism reached Japan in the middle of the sixth century from Korea after centuries of development in China. The introduction of Buddhism exerted a far-reaching effect on many aspects of Japanese life. The *kami* (spirits) of the native, nature religion of Japan were intensely important but had no specified forms or attributes. In contrast, principles of the Buddhist faith were expounded in Chinese texts and by a clergy and regiments of nuns and monks who performed minutely prescribed religious functions inside vast halls filled with the pungent smell of incense and with statues of the holy in human form. Buddhism channeled silent and spontaneous interaction with the spirits into an organized program of ritual observance and explained the mysteries of life in a set of laws.

The rise of Buddhism in Japan was accelerated during the life of Prince Umayado, better known by his Buddhist name of Prince Shotoku (Wise and Virtuous). He was an avid scholar and learned statesman whose cultural activities affected Japanese civilization substantively. Born into a court which had been receiving Buddhist images from Korea for twenty-one years and which was coming to terms with the new faith, Shotoku grew up in an atmosphere of cultural ferment. The pro-Buddhist Soga clan was actively upholding its beliefs, but not without opposition by adherents to the native religion called Shinto. Buddhist chapels were burned and the statues were damaged. Soga no Umako (died 626), head of the powerful family, placed his niece on the throne as Empress Suiko (reigned 592–628) and ordered Prince Shotoku, then only nineteen years old, to act as regent. Prince Shotoku attempted to centralize power and to unify the clan-chiefs, whose rivalries had previously dominated Japanese life. He used as a model the Chinese court and thereby played a leading role in the absorption of Chinese aristocratic culture in Japan. Shotoku built his palace at Ikaruga and next to it a Buddhist temple over a Korean model. By 614, or fifty years after the presentation of the first Buddhist statue to Japan, there were 46 temples and 1,385 ordained monks and nuns. After his death and during the struggle for power, both his palace and temple were destroyed. Shotoku's legacy, the primacy of learning and moral values, was so firmly implanted among the aristocracy and clergy, however, that the ruined temple was soon rebuilt and was called Horyu-ji.

Buddhist sculpture preceded Buddhist architecture outside of India, for images were brought in the luggage of missionaries, travelers, and pilgrims across the great trade routes of Central Asia. Such icons were set up in shrines built in the traditional Chinese style and grew until the monastery or temple became a kind of palace with courtyards, pavilions, galleries, and gardens. No attempt was made to imitate Indian temples, and the *stupa* was transformed into the *pagoda*, the multi-tiered tower which serves as a relic hall.

The main image in the *kondo* at Horyu-ji bears the date 623 and is the work of a caster of statues named Tori, a descendant of Chinese immigrants. The Mahayana Buddhists believe that there will be an infinite number of Buddhas, all of them manifestations of the One Absolute Buddha. He was thought to be beyond the limits of human vision, but practitioners began to believe that one manifestation was revealed to the living and could therefore be represented. These images were to be used as aids to enable the beholder to understand existence beyond form and substance. The Buddha is represented with a serene and remote aspect, larger than life (fig. 163). He wears a monk's robe and is seated in the position of meditation. His elongated ears, the mark on his forehead, and his hair recall his noble birth. His attendants, the smaller *bodhisattvas*, are dressed in worldly costumes with crowns and jewels indicating their dedication to assisting earthly beings in their suffering. Buddha's frontal, seated pose, his dress, and hand gestures (*mudras*) are all prescribed by tradition. This manner of presentation, so similar to prototypes from Korea, China, and even India, speaks of an ecumenical tradition fueled both by the assimilative nature of Mahayana Buddhism and the economic and political aspirations of the leaders who embraced the religion.

163. TORI BUSSHI
(Master Craftworker Tori)
Shaka Triad. 632 (Asuka period). Bronze with gilt, height of central figure 69 1/4". Golden Hall (*kondo*), Horyu-ji complex. The Buddha's hand gesture is the *abhaya mudra*, the gesture of reassurance that suggests "fear not."

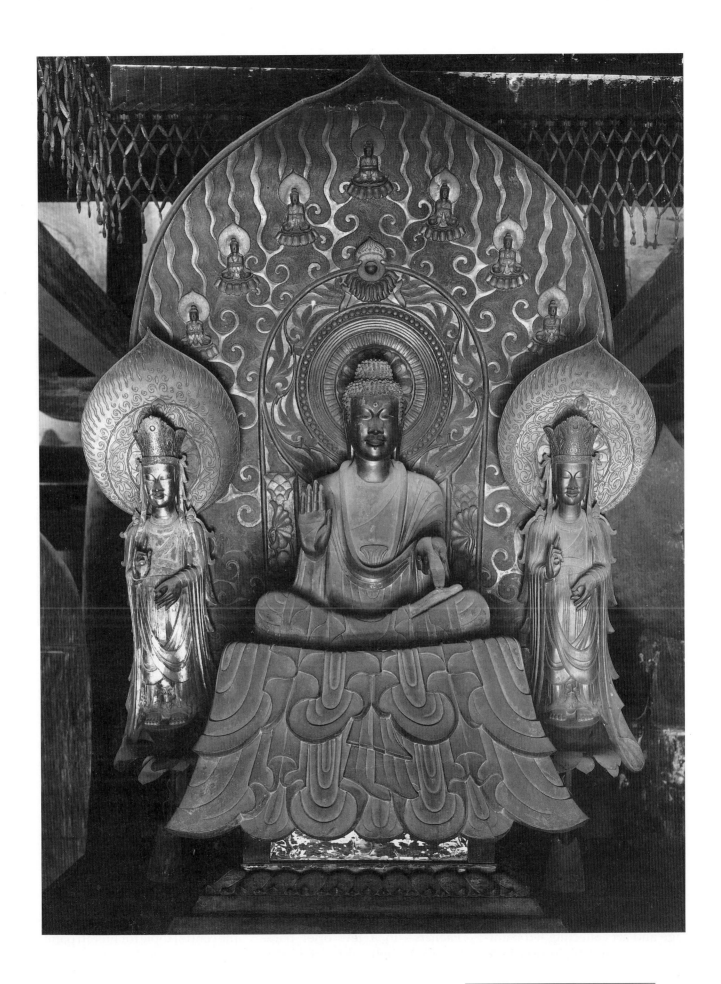

CHINESE ART: LANDSCAPE PAINTING

In 755 a provincial Chinese commander named An Lu-shan rebelled, marched on the capital, and forced the elderly emperor Ming Huang into exile in Shu. This much repeated subject in Chinese art (see fig. 164) celebrated the full flowering of the emperor's enlightened leadership (713–56) and his final downfall. In his liberal and extravagant court, for instance, there were eight orchestras, two from Central Asia, and four hundred horses trained to dance at banquets. His enthusiastic patronage and art collecting led painters, poets, and philosophers to

new ideas and subjects. The Tang period brought landscape painting and nature poetry to life. While human beings were believed to be earthbound, clouds, rocks, and streams exuded *qi*, or breath of life. This idea was examined by artists.

To the Chinese, a picture was a mysterious thing containing the essence of the world of nature. Standards for painting were set down in the mid-sixth century by an obscure portrait painter named Xie He in his *Gu hua pin lu (Classified Record of Ancient Painters)*. In a few brief paragraphs he defined the Six Laws

164. After LI ZHAODAO
Emperor Ming Huang's Journey to Shu. c. 755 (Tang dynasty). Hanging scroll, ink and color on silk, length 21 1/4". National Palace Museum, Taibei, Taiwan, R.O.C.

which became the cornerstone of all later Chinese aesthetics: spirit consonance and life movement; structural strength in the use of the brush; fidelity to object; correct color; proper placement and disposition; and transmission of ancient masters by copying with the example set by Tang artists. Landscape became the central topic for literati painters in the later dynasties.

After LI ZHAODAO, *Emperor Ming Huang's Journey to Shu: c.* **755**
751: Arabs lose Turkestan to China
787: Council of Nicaea temporarily rejects iconoclasm

166. *Buddhist Temple in the Hills After Rain* (detail)

165. LI CHENG (attributed)
Buddhist Temple in the Hills After Rain. c. 950 (Five
Dynasties/Northern Song). Hanging scroll, ink and
color on silk, length 42". Nelson-Atkins Museum of
Art, Kansas City, Missouri (Nelson Fund). The author-
ship of few tenth-century landscape paintings is
known with certainty. Descriptions of the work of
these masters by critics of their own time make attri-
butions such as this possible, however.

In the picture attributed to Li
Cheng (active from about 940 to
967), the autumn skies are clear-
ing, leaving only mist in the low
valleys and above the mountain
pathways (figs. 165, 166). In the
immediate foreground are a
group of huts and two pavilions
built over water. The buildings
and figures are painted with such
careful detail that we can distinguish both peasants and courti-
ers at their meals in the rustic inn
and scholars at the wine shops
gazing off into the landscape
from the pavilions. The temple
with its hexagonal tower occupies the very center of the painting and is parallel to the peaks
which dominate the far distance
and the top of the picture. Such
axially symmetrical monumental configurations of mountains
and water came to be associated
with the imperial government in
the tenth century—grand, ordered, realistic, and powerful.

Li Cheng as a person represented the ideal Chinese painter—an artist who claimed descent from the imperial clan of the Tang dynasty (618–907), was educated in the humanities through study of the *Classic Books* (ancient texts on history, philosophy, and literature), and was occupied with painting for his own delight without ambition for honors or advancement. He was a scholar and a gentleman who enjoyed a quiet life devoted to the philosophic study of Nature as opposed to merely copying forms in the out-of-doors (nature). Monochrome ink painting of landscape was the most preferred type produced by Li Cheng and his colleagues.

Like many other landscape painters of the tenth century, Li Cheng had a preference for autumnal or wintry scenes full of bleak, stony crags, gnarled trees with leafless crab-claw shaped branches, and looming distant peaks. *Buddhist Temple in the Hills After Rain* shares with other landscapes of the period a preference for monochrome ink laid on the silk in broad and jagged strokes which describe the essential outlines of forms (rocks, trees, buildings). These shapes were then broken up and modeled with washes of ink. On top of that were placed *cun*, small brushstrokes dabbed on quickly to create the sense of texture. Closely associated with calligraphy, the brush paintings of China were produced for and by the intelligentsia, who painted as an avocation.

The ideals of painting of the tenth century were written down by a contemporary of Li Cheng named Ching Hao. In his essay the *Record of Brush Methods*, or *Essay on Landscape Painting*, Ching Hao recorded his thoughts through a narrator, an old man whom he pretended to meet while wandering in the mountains. This wise man told him the six essentials of painting: first is spirit, second rhythm, third thought, fourth scenery, fifth brush, and sixth ink. This is a logical system (based on Xie He) which first lays down the concept of painting and then its expression, distinguishing further between resemblance, which reproduces the formal, outward aspects of what is depicted, and truth (or spirit), which involves knowing and representing inner reality. Correct balance between representing the visible forms of nature and expressing their deeper significance was the goal of these painters.

This doctrine of realism aims for truth to natural appearance but not at the expense of an examination of how Nature operates. In Li Cheng's painting, for instance, trees are bent and twisted but are organically constructed to expose their full skeletons—roots, trunk, and branches including, on their tips, the dormant buds ready for spring awakening. Moreover, this approach to realism explains the attitude behind shifting perspective in Chinese painting. In *Buddhist Temple* we are invited to enter the picture on the lower left and to explore as we move through the landscape. We can wander across the bridge, look down at rooftops, up at pavilions and the temple, and across to the towering peaks. One cannot take a panoramic view from a single position from outside or inside the painting, and the artist does not intend that we do so.

Rather, little by little, Nature is revealed as if we were actually walking in the out-of-doors. In this sense the painter combines the element of time in this art form in much the same way as in music. Shifting perspective allows for a journey and for a powerful personal impact on the individual viewer/participant. These paintings were meant to be visual exercises which allowed for examination of minute details as well as the structure of Nature or the Universe. The power of these great paintings is to take us out of ourselves and to provide spiritual solace and refreshment.

Guo Hsi, a pupil of Li Cheng and perhaps the best known of the eleventh-century landscapists, declared in his famous essay that "the virtuous man above all delights in landscapes." The virtuous (or Confucian) man accepts the fact that his civic responsibilities to society and state tie him to an urban life as an official, but he nourishes his spirit by taking imaginary trips into nature through viewing a landscape painting. Such paintings as *Buddhist Temple* and *Early Spring* (fig. 167) describe the potential of nature in landscape form and set a standard which was followed throughout Chinese history.

The impetus for the first of these painters was found in the Five Dynasties (907–960) and the Northern Song (960–1126). A most important occurrence of the period was the initial printing of the *Classical Books*, finished in 953. For the first time the supply of books became cheap and abundant. Scholars multiplied, and the knowledge of ancient literature was more widely spread throughout the nation. The con-

167. GUO HSI

Early Spring. 1072 (Northern Song dynasty). Hanging scroll, ink and slight color on silk, length 60". National Palace Museum, Taibei, Taiwan, R.O.C.

sequences of the expansion of the literate class were manifest in the Song, when Chinese lands were reunited into the third centralized empire in Chinese history. The unification of the empire was the work of policy rather than conquest, a powerful submission of an aristocracy weary of disunion and aware of its own cultural identity. The acknowledged, ancient civil-service examination system returned civilians to positions of prestige and power in government lost under previous military dictatorships. The prevailing pacifist policies and a series of enlightened sovereigns who were tolerant, humane, artistic, and intellectual provided substantial and consistent patronage for the arts. The collection of the Song emperor Hui Zong (1100–1126), for example, claimed 159 paintings by Li Cheng. The Song period produced the first important academy of painting in the Far East, and among its early members were landscapists.

The Song dynasty was an age of many-sided intellectual activities—poetry, history, and especially philosophy. Characteristic of Song thought was the return to older Chinese sources, a conscious archaism, and cultural introspection. The renaissance of classical literature branched off into the formation of a new system of philosophy called neo-Confucianism, enveloping traditional moral and ethical teachings with Daoist thinking about Nature and the cosmos, especially as presented in the *I-jing (Book of Changes)*. No distinction was made between the law of Nature and moral law. The world was thought to be inspired by the Supreme Ultimate (or what the Daoists called the Way), which the neo-Confucianists called *li* (law), a moral law identical to the ethical code upon which human conduct should be modeled. These Song thinkers were also interested in correspondences in Nature. The manifestation of *li* in painting included faithfulness to Nature as well as conventionalized symbols for the representation of rocks, foliage, bark, water, and so forth. *Li* also governed the way a picture was put together. Painters of the tenth and eleventh centuries were interpreters of *li*, and landscape became the principal subject for their consideration.

ISLAMIC ART: THE MOSQUE AT CÓRDOBA

In its present form, the interior of the Mosque at Córdoba is a vast space, 584 feet on the north-south axis and 410 feet on the east-west axis (fig. 168). It covers an area of 240,000 square feet, a space larger than any known church, including St. Peter's in Rome. This interior, unlike that of Christian churches, is viewed neither as a home of the gods nor as a place for liturgical worship. It is a place where the faithful gathered for prayer, all facing Mecca together to emphasize the unity of the faith.

Today Islam is the religion of more than four hundred million persons inhabiting large areas in Asia, Africa, and parts of Europe. Islam is a term which refers to the religion and to the whole body of believers (Muslims) and the countries in which they live. The youngest of the world's great religions, Islam developed in Arabia in the sixth century A.D. The area had been a frontier of the Roman Empire and was a land of independent nomadic tribes, a few trade outposts, and conflicting religious traditions.

The founder of Islam was Mohammed, who was born in Mecca in about 570 and believed himself to be a prophet of divine revelation. He was forced to flee in 622, but established himself in the rival city of Medina, where he gathered converts and condoned the *jihad* (holy war) as a means of collecting supplies to support his followers. In 630 he returned in triumph to Mecca. The Muslim calendar dates from his flight, or *hegira*. After his death in 632, the religion gained mo-

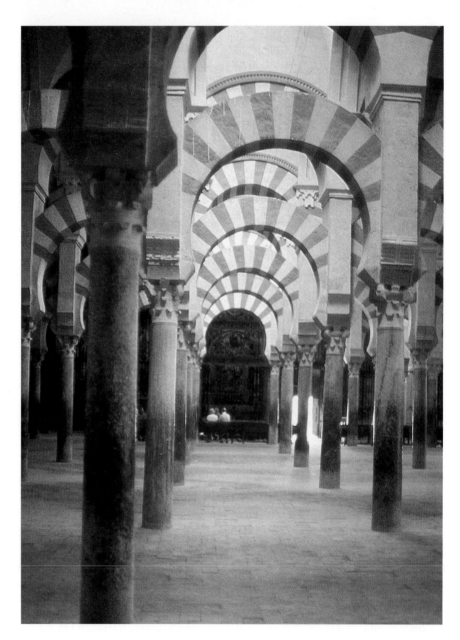

168. Interior, Mosque, Córdoba, Spain. Begun 786. This is a view across the hypostyle hall, looking west.

mentum and began to spread in Arabia and the Near East. Soon Islam became a powerful theocracy and a foe of institutions of the Western medieval world which derived their ecclesiastical support from Latin and Greek branches of Christendom.

Mohammed himself set up no priesthood and no organized church. However, the Koran, in which were collected the sayings of God as they were revealed to Mohammed in Arabic, became the guide for all life's endeavors. The "Five Pillars" of Islam set

Mosque, Córdoba: begun 786
777: Charlemagne fails in his attempt to invade Muslim Spain
781: Christian monasteries are built in China

169. One of the two small mosaiced domes, in the *madksourah*, flanking the main dome, before the *mihrab*. 961–76. Colored stucco, tile, and glass. Mosque, Córdoba

out duties for all believers. First, one must recite the creed, "There is no god but God; Mohammed is the Messenger of God." Second, there is the duty of worship and prayer after ritual washing and while facing the direction of Mecca, five times a day and in the mosque on Fridays. Third, one must completely abstain from food, drink, and sexual activity in the daylight hours during Ramadan, the month (ninth) when Mohammed first received revelations from God.

Fourth is the duty of almsgiving. Fifth is the duty of *hadj*, a pilgrimage to Mecca which every Muslim should undertake before death.

In point of time, Islam followed Judaism, Christianity, and Buddhism in its formulation. Islam acknowledges these great religions and believes itself to be the fulfillment of them. Indeed, Muslims believe that Abraham, Moses, and Christ all preached Islam, but that their followers changed their teaching into the

religions of today. In the Muslim view, only Mohammed's preaching preserved, unchanged, the message of God. Characteristic of Islam is the blending of ethnic and universal elements. It opens its ranks to all, stressing the brotherhood of the faithful before Allah (God), regardless of race or culture. It was, however, a national religion, firmly centered in Arabia and its political aspirations. The warriors who set out to conquer the earth for Allah did not expect to convert the unbelievers to Islam. Their aim was to rule, to enforce obedience to themselves as servants of the One True God. Those who wanted to share the privileged status could join Islam but had to become Arabs by adoption. They had to learn the Koran in Arabic and to adopt the social, legal, and political framework of the Muslim community. Unlike the Buddhists, the Arabs absorbed the conquered and their cultural heritage and adapted them to Islam.

Early in the history of the religion, no demands were made on the visual arts. Mohammed condemned idolatry, and the Koran placed statues among the handiwork of Satan. Painting and representation were not specifically mentioned and will figure in later art. During the fifty years following the death of the prophet, a Muslim place of prayer could be a Christian church or Persian columned hall taken over for the purpose, or even a rectangular field surrounded by a fence or ditch. These were the first mosques, or places for prayer.

Mosques of all periods have one element in common: the marking of the *qibla*, the direction to which Muslims must turn in prayer. That wall faces Mecca and was marked by a colonnade and by the entrance which was placed opposite it. By the end of the seventh century, Muslim rulers of conquered domains began to erect mosques and palaces on a large scale as visible symbols of power which were intended to outdo all pre-Islamic structures in size and splendor. They drew on craftworkers gathered from Egypt, Syria, Persia, and even Byzantium, whose designs and decoration echo their background and expansive spirit.

By the eighth century, within a hundred years of the death of Mohammed, the Muslims had conquered and converted most of the Near East and the African provinces of Byzantium as well as Spain, where they captured Toledo in 711. The Muslims entered Spain as a military force and lacked women, so nearly all took Spanish wives. Furthermore, during this time many Christians converted to Islam and retained their Romance language, giving Islamic culture in Spain a unique flavor soon reflected in architecture as well.

The greatest monument of the reign of the first Muslim ruler of Spain, Abdu'r-Rahman I (756–88), was the Mosque at Córdoba, which he built in one year, 786–87. The building was necessitated by the increased numbers of Muslims who needed a place of worship. Abdu'r-Rahman purchased part of the site from the Christians, saving only the Roman and Visigothic marble pillars which had been taken by the Christians from even earlier buildings. These pillars and the arches above were incorporated into this splendid mosque and became famous as an architectural invention. The superimposition of two tiers of arches gave added height and spaciousness. This feature was repeated by a succession of rulers as they enlarged the mosque in 832–48, 961, and 987, until it was converted back to Christian use after the reconquest of Córdoba in 1236.

The interior "forest of columns" in the mosque, with red-and-white Moorish (North African and Spanish style) horseshoe-shaped arches extending apparently endlessly in all directions, is unique, although the overall plan is a traditional Muslim one (see figs. 168, 170). It has a crenelated, rectangular perimeter enclosing a forecourt with a basin for ritual ablution, a covered colonnade, and a hall for prayer. The *qibla* is hollowed out in one place in the form of a sacred niche, or *mihrab*. Overlooking the courtyard is the *minaret*, the tower from which the *muezzin* (crier) calls the faithful to prayer five times a day.

In 961 the calif El Hakam II, mindful of his capital's prestige, bestowed upon the mosque its greatest jewel. At the end of the main aisle he built a superb, gleaming *mihrab*, preceded by a triple *madksourah*, or enclosure reserved only for the calif. The enclosure is roofed by three ribbed domes which rest on a most unusual series of interweaving multilayered arches (see fig. 169). All these interior areas are faced with mosaics against a background in gold.

Unlike Christianity or later Buddhism, the Islamic faith did not permit figurative representations of God or his prophets, and these mosaics, like most Islamic art, are stylized. No living creature is represented on Islamic religious structures, and the Koran is embellished with a luxurious, calligraphic version of Arabic lettering called Kufic (mistakenly named after the belief that the script originated in Kufa, Iraq). Kufic script, complemented by abstract ornamental designs, became the main decoration in the form of inscriptions on mosques, secular buildings, and even utilitarian objects in metal, clay, and weavings in wool (carpets). This Islamic preference for linear surface decoration was fully used in the interior decoration of mosques. At Córdoba, the dome before the *mihrab* is typical, for it includes a stylized gold inscription in Kufic script at its base and a web of ornament above and below made up of a variety of designs all disciplined by symmetry, repetition, and rhythmic order.

Following prayer in the mosque, the man who led the worship or his representative might speak on secular matters. This Arabic respect for learning contributed to advances in astronomy, mathematics, medicine, and optics through centuries of support of its scholars. Such secular and religious traditions continue in the modern world and predominate in Egypt and Syria, Saudi Arabia, Turkey, Albania, Iraq, Pakistan, Afghanistan, Iran, the Yemen, Indonesia, Malaysia, Morocco, Tunisia, and Libya.

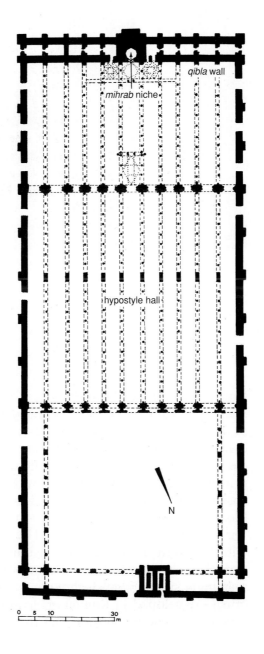

170. Plan, Mosque, Córdoba. This plan shows the enlargements of 832–48 and 961, but not the final expansion of 987.

Introduction to Carolingian Art

171. *St. Matthew,* from the *Coronation Gospel Book.* Produced at Aachen, Germany. Early 9th century. Manuscript painting on vellum, 12 3/4 x 10". Kunsthistorisches Museum, Vienna. This manuscript is said to have been found in the Tomb of Charlemagne when it was opened by Otto III in the year 1000. It is written on purple-stained vellum, which was reserved for the most important manuscripts.

172. *St. Matthew,* from the *Gospel Book of Archbishop Ebbo of Reims.* Produced in Reims, France. 816–35. Manuscript painting on vellum, 10 1/4 x 8 3/4". Bibliothèque Municipale, Épernay, France

During the reign of Charlemagne (Carolus, or Charles the Great), there was an interest in reviving the political unity and cultural ideals of the Roman world. Two images of St. Matthew (figs. 171, 172) demonstrate how the art of this era—known as Carolingian art— could revive aspects of classical style and yet remain true to medieval principles. The figure of Matthew in the *Coronation Gospel Book,* ancient in type, wears a toga and is seated naturalistically at work. Modeling creates a sense of three-dimensionality and illusionism. The artist has clearly been inspired by a model from a source imbued with the spirit of Hellenistic illusionism. In contrast, St. Matthew from the *Ebbo Gospels* shows the inspiration of Roman models in the seemingly spontaneous technique, but here the fluid strokes of the brush—developed in Roman art to suggest movement—express a frenzy of divine inspiration that threatens to subsume both figure

173. *Apocalyptic Vision of Christ in Majesty, with Four Old Testament Prophets and the Four Evangelists,* frontispiece to the Gospels from the *Vivian Bible.* Produced in Tours, France. 845–46. Manuscript painting on vellum, 19 1/2 x 13 5/8". Bibliothèque Nationale, Paris. This Bible, which has eight full-page illustrations and a number of other decorations, was dedicated and presented to King Charles the Bald by Abbot Vivian and the monks of St. Martin of Tours, probably in 846. It is also known as the *First Bible of Charles the Bald.*

and landscape. Shimmering gold highlights on the toga, hair, and landscape heighten the liveliness, for they appear and disappear with changes in the reflected light.

These two disparate styles merge in the dramatic image of the Apocalyptic Christ in Majesty from the *Vivian Bible* (fig. 173). The naturalism of classical style is evident in the modeling of the figures and the representation of movement, but the mystical and otherworldly quality of medieval art is present in the conceptual, geometric composition of a frontal, hypnotic Christ seated on a cosmic globe surrounded by Old Testament prophets and the Evangelists, the latter represented both as human figures and by their animal symbols. The prophets hold scrolls to indicate the Old Law, while the Evangelists have the books symbolic of the New Law. The abstract patterns that suggest spiritual excitement are ever-present in the impulsive movement of the drapery patterns, but none is so fantastic as Christ's, which offers a swirling whirlpool at the center of the composition.

HISTORY

The term Carolingian refers to the reigns of Charlemagne and his immediate successors, although in terms of art the particular qualities of Carolingian art did not endure long after his empire was divided by three grandsons in 843. Charlemagne, whose seal read *renovatio Romani imperii* (the revival of the Roman Empire), intended to create a Holy (that is, Christian) Roman Empire. He greatly expanded the Frankish kingdom he inherited, establishing a buffer between his kingdom and the Islamic threat in Spain and the East. On Christmas Day 800, Pope Leo III crowned Charlemagne emperor of Rome at St. Peter's Basilica.

Charlemagne's renewal included an interest in reform and education and a demand for order and efficiency. He codified law, issuing legal decrees from his capital at Aachen. He established a stable currency, ordered the creation of schools throughout his empire, reformed monastic life, corrected the calendar, established a large library, and encouraged the production of corrected copies of manuscripts, including the Bible. He required the use of a new, more easily readable style of lettering that is the basis of the typeface still used in most books. Literacy was a major goal, in part because it would enable people better to understand Christian doctrine and to participate in church services. Charlemagne could read, but Einhard, his biographer, tells how he wanted to learn to write, and that he kept notebooks under his pillow, so that "he could try his hand at forming letters during his leisure moments."

CAROLINGIAN ARCHITECTURE

Charlemagne's Palace at Aachen included a chapel (fig. 174), a centrally planned structure based on the most important church in the last Roman capital in the west, San Vitale in Ravenna. Charlemagne received permission from the pope to remove columns and capitals from structures in Rome and Ravenna to incorporate into his palace complex. To emphasize the Christian nature of his rule, Charlemagne modeled his throne on that of Solomon, described in the Old Testament, and placed it in the Palace Chapel opposite the altar.

The Carolingian ideal of a world that would combine the greatness of the ancient past with the Christian vision is revealed in a letter sent to Charlemagne in 799: "If many people became imbued with your ideas a new Athens would be established in France—nay, an Athens fairer than the Athens of old, for it would be ennobled by the teachings of Christ, and ours would surpass all the wisdom of the ancient academy. For this had only for its instruction the disciples of Plato; yet, molded by the seven liberal arts, it shone with constant splendor. But ours would be endowed with the sevenfold fullness of the Holy Spirit, and would surpass all secular wisdom in dignity."

174. Interior, Palace Chapel of Charlemagne, Aachen. 792–805

THE MEDIEVAL MONASTERY

175. St. Gall monastery plan. c. 819. Traced and drawn on five pieces of parchment sewn together, 44 x 30". Monastery Library, St. Gall, Switzerland. The St. Gall plan, traced from another plan now lost, represents an ideal formula to be adjusted for the particular site and needs. It even suggests the appropriate location of furnishings. Its logical and orderly design may be related to the reforms of the monastic system within the Carolingian empire, discussed at meetings in Aachen in 816 and 817. Not a document that normally would have been saved, it may have survived only because a life of St. Martin was written on the back.

The monastery was perhaps the single most important institution in Europe during the medieval period. The St. Gall plan reveals the complex and varied needs of a monastic community (fig. 175). The central structure is the church itself, which has a basilical form following Early Christian models; the nave and side aisles provide additional altars needed because each priest was required to say mass daily. At the western end of the church plan is a smaller apse with two towers forming a westwork. A Carolingian innovation in church design, it created an impressive entrance and was the source from which the traditional two-towered church facade would develop.

The subsidiary structures include a separate house for the abbot who ruled the monastery and for the monks, a complex attached to the church which included a dormitory, latrine, bathhouse, refectory (dining hall), and a cloister for walking and meditation. Outbuildings housed kitchen, mill, bakery, drying house, brew house, storerooms, barns, workrooms for artisans, and other facilities necessary for a self-sufficient community of approximately one hundred. There was also a separate chapel and housing for those who were preparing to become monks. A separate house, with its own kitchen, served special visitors. The services that the monastery provided the public included an infirmary, complete with herb garden, and its hospital for the poor. Usually there was a hospice to shelter travelers. In an area adjacent to the main altar were the library and the *scriptorium*, where manuscripts were copied and illustrated. The orchard served as the monastic cemetery. The complex seen here would have been surrounded by vast fields worked by the monks and hired laborers.

Monasticism has its roots in the early days of Christianity in the Middle East and Egypt, when many Christians retreated into the desert or lived in caves in order to spend their life praying, remote from the distractions and temptations of the world. Many chose to live a life of complete isolation, but some banded into communities that mark the beginnings of the monastic tradition. During the sixth century, St. Benedict gathered so many followers that he wrote a rule (c. 535–40) for their behavior. It became the basis for later medieval monastic organization, in part because Charlemagne imposed it on all monasteries in his empire; by the seventh century, a variant of the Benedictine rule was in use for women. Benedict required that the monks remain within the monastery for life and

St. Gall monastery plan: c. 819
782: Arab forces attack Constantinople
790: Irish monks reach Iceland
814: Death of Charlemagne
826: Crete is conquered by Muslim pirates from Spain

that they observe poverty, chastity, and obedience. A simple, humble garment and hairstyle were specified. The monks swore obedience to an elected abbot; daily life was a well-organized regimen of work, study, and prayer. There were at least eight daily services of psalms, hymns, and prayers. Work included all aspects of labor. Many monks and nuns became skilled in the arts, but Benedict's rule warns against the pride that could accompany artistic achievement: "Let such craftsmen as be in the monastery ply their trade in all lowliness of mind if the abbot allow it. But if any be puffed up by his skill in his craft . . . such a one shall be shifted from his handicraft, and not attempt it again until such time as he has learnt a low opinion of himself, and the abbot bids him resume."

Through an emphasis on literacy and education, which were required to participate fully in the Christian life, the monasteries played a vital role in continuing and preserving the Western heritage. A number of the greatest ancient works of literature, science, and philosophy survive only in copies handwritten by monks and nuns.

In the course of the Middle Ages there was a proliferation of monastic orders, but their rules were similar. Most were located in the country, away from the temptations of city life and far from other human beings. In the thirteenth century, two new orders, the Franciscans and

Dominicans, were approved by the pope. They emphasized public service in the urban environment, and their monasteries were established within the cities to serve the sick and the poor.

No monastery was built that exactly followed the design of the St. Gall plan, in part because any complex of such scale would evolve slowly over time and in relationship to the peculiarities of the particular setting. The Romanesque monastery at Cluny, however, can be studied as an example of a fully developed medieval monastery. Cluny, the mother church of a

reformed Benedictine order which played an important role in monastic renewal during the eleventh and twelfth centuries, became one of the most important centers for learning and patronage of art in Europe. It was famous for the splendor and beauty of its services, and its third church, begun about 1085 and consecrated in 1131–32, was, with a length of 555 feet, the largest church in all Europe (fig. 176). The monastic complex at Cluny has virtually all the same facilities as the St. Gall plan; especially impressive is the space given over to the huge infirmary.

176. Monastery, Cluny, France. Reconstruction of the Romanesque monastery and third church, as they looked c. 1157. The church and monastery were largely destroyed by Napoleonic edict in 1810.

Introduction to Romanesque Art

177. *Christ in Majesty with Angels, Symbols of the Evangelists, and Saints,* from San Clemente, Tahull, Spain. c. 1123. Apse fresco, diameter of apse approx. 13'. Museo de Arte de Cataluña, Barcelona

The term Romanesque (Romanlike) was first used in the nineteenth century to designate medieval art of the tenth to the mid-twelfth centuries, which is distinguished by a European-wide revival of monumental architecture, sculpture, and mural painting. In the Tahull apse painting, the enthroned *Christ in Majesty,* surrounded by a mandorla, is symmetrically flanked by angels and the symbols of the Evangelists (fig. 177). A row of standing saints below includes the Virgin Mary. The hierarchical presentation and the iconlike stare of the figures associate the painting with the Byzantine tradition (see fig. 157). But here the abstraction of earlier medieval art is intensified, for the drapery folds have a life of their own; instead of being used to reveal the body beneath the drapery, they flutter and fold in abstract patterns. And, rather than flowing together into an organic unity, each body part is treated independently, with heads and hands exaggerated in scale. Foreshortening is avoided, as is evident in the unnaturalistic rendering of Christ's book, with the inscription, "I am the light of the world." The simple and direct presentation, harsh modeling, unnatural but bold colors, and frontal stiffness combine to create a commanding composition.

HISTORY

During the tenth century, Europe stirred with revived economic, social, and cultural life. The wanderings and attacks of the barbarian tribes, a source of conflict and political unrest for centuries, abated, due in part to their conversion to Christianity. Following the 1054 split between the Roman and Byzantine churches, the Roman church consolidated its religious and political power in western Europe. England was united with much of France after the Norman conquest in 1066, and Norman victories in southern Italy and Sicily freed those areas from Byzantine control. The new political stability fostered an expanded economy.

The church gradually increased its influence in secular affairs, coming into conflict with the feudal nobility. The power and energy of the church were manifested in the enormous undertaking of the Crusades, which began in the 1090s in an attempt to free the Christian places of the Middle East from the Muslims. The *reconquistà*, the war waged against the Muslims in Spain, led to the capture of Córdoba by the Christians in 1236.

ROMANESQUE ART

The mainstays of earlier medieval workshop production—manuscript illumination, ivory carving, and metalwork—continued throughout the Romanesque period. More significant is the widespread revival of monumental architecture and art which distinguishes the eleventh century.

THE ROMANESQUE ARTIST

Artists, benefitting from the economic growth of the period, organized guilds to ensure quality and control in the production of art and the training of apprentices. Guilds offered protection for the artists as a group, encouraged a greater amount of self-regulation, and promoted an increased social prestige. Few works are signed and dated.

178. Above left: *Ste. Foi Reliquary.* Later 10th century. Gold with filigree and precious stones over wooden core, height 33 1/2". Cathedral Treasury, Conques. The masklike face of this reliquary, which enshrines the bones of the saint, is made from an ancient Roman gold face guard and parade helmet to which inlaid enameled eyes have been added. The forearms and hands date from a post-Romanesque restoration. For the church at Conques which enshrined her remains, see p. 188.

179. Above right: *St. Mark,* from a Gospel Book produced at Corbie. c. 1025–50. Manuscript painting on vellum, 10 3/4 x 7 7/8". Bibliothèque Municipale, Amiens

ART AND THE PILGRIM

The pilgrimage, which earlier in the Middle Ages had been prescribed for the atonement of sin, became a regular feature of Christian life during the Romanesque period. The pilgrim would travel over defined routes, known as the pilgrimage roads, either to Rome or to Santiago de Compostela in western Spain. At St. Peter's in Rome or the Church of St. James in Santiago, the pilgrim would invoke God's intercession. Along these routes, monasteries, which since the earlier medieval period had functioned as centers of learning and hospitality, sheltered the pilgrims. Developments in church architecture responded to the needs of both the clergy and the pilgrims.

To prepare spiritually for their destination at Santiago or Rome, pilgrims would visit churches along their routes, where they could pray before the relics of saints. These relics were usually encased in precious reliquaries such as that of Ste. Foi at Conques (fig. 178); many of the jewels that adorn her golden cloak were gifts from pilgrims.

MANUSCRIPT ILLUMINATION

The illumination of manuscripts continued to be a significant medium of painting during the Romanesque period. The figure of St. Mark in the Corbie Gospels (fig. 179), which displays the same intense color and bold outlines as the monumental apse painting from Tahull, is enlivened by an abstract curvilinear design. The saint, seated in his study, turns to grasp a scroll from his symbol, the lion. Framed within an arch, the scene is animated by the twisted body of the lion, whose contorted movement is echoed in the drapery around the arch and the diagonals of Mark's robe. The contrast between the stable framing of the scene and these lively patterns creates a dynamic interpretation of divine inspiration.

THE *BAYEUX TAPESTRY*

This unique embroidered narrative (fig. 180) depicts the events which led to the Norman invasion of England and the victory at Hastings in 1066. Our detail shows the English king Harold enthroned in his castle. A messenger informs the king that his rival William has ordered a fleet of ships to be built in order to cross the English Channel. In the sky to the left of the castle is Halley's comet, which was visible in England in late April 1066; here it signals impending disaster and should have been understood by Harold as a warning. The inscription reads: *Isti mirant[ur]stellam* (these men marvel at the star).

The sequence of historical events is narrated in a lively, engaging manner. The curving axes of the figures of King Harold and the messenger animate the scene, while the abstract tree to the right, with its undulating rhythm, demonstrates the continuation of Anglo-Saxon interlace motifs and asserts an organic vitality which permeates much of the work. The limited colors are used decoratively rather than descriptively, and the abstract rhythms of the composition enliven the historic narrative.

180. *King Harold Receiving a Messenger* (detail), from the *Bayeux Tapestry.* c. 1070–80. Embroidered wool on linen, height 20"; total length 231'. Musée de Peinture, Bayeux. Despite the fact that the technique is embroidery, this work is traditionally known as the *Bayeux Tapestry*. It was probably executed by a group of women artists, who specialized in the needle arts during this period of history. In more than seventy-five scenes accompanied by Latin inscriptions, it tells the story of the victory of William the Conqueror over King Harold during the Norman conquest of England. The embroidery, probably commissioned by Bishop Odo of Bayeux, half-brother of William, was intended for display in a great secular hall.

ROMANESQUE ARCHITECTURE: STE. FOI AT CONQUES

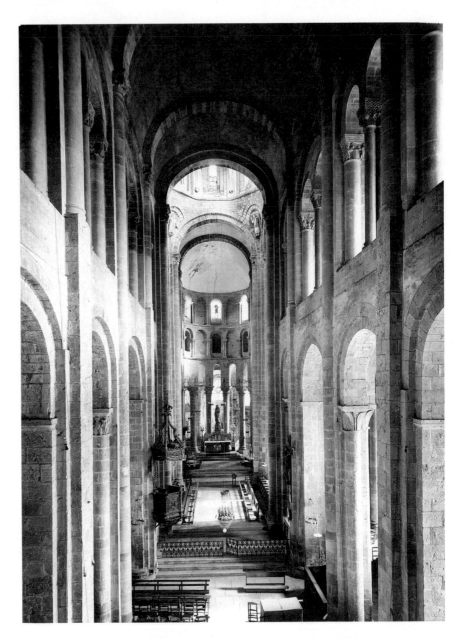

Viewing the crossing and the apse of Ste. Foi from the nave (fig. 181), we can immediately see why nineteenth-century historians coined the term Romanesque to describe this style of architecture. The use of round arches and stone vaults is reminiscent of ancient Roman building practice, and, like Roman architecture, the monumental scale establishes an austere, massive presence. The wooden truss roof common in Early Christian and Carolingian architecture has now given way to the favored construction feature of Roman architecture, the vault. At Ste. Foi, the barrel vault of the nave is reinforced with transverse arches (arches that traverse the nave). On the exterior, vertical buttresses make the interior rhythm of the bays readable from outside (fig. 182). On exterior and interior, then, the articulation of the individual bays creates an order and unity characteristic of Romanesque architecture. The transverse arches also make it possible to construct a thinner barrel vault, allowing for larger windows. Romanesque stone vaulting also served other purposes, for it helped prevent the

181. Nave, Ste. Foi, Conques, France. c. 1080–1120. The monastic church of Ste. Foi was located along one of the pilgrimage roads to Santiago de Compostela. The present Romanesque structure was built around an older church probably begun during the Carolingian period. Although located along the pilgrimage routes, Conques later remained isolated from the urban development that affected many other medieval towns and, with the exception of two nineteenth-century towers, the church has been spared the restoration activity that so often transformed medieval architecture. The church is dedicated to a third-century virgin martyr, Ste. Foi (known in English as St. Faith), whose relics were brought to Conques about 870 (fig. 178).

182. Aerial view, Ste. Foi, Conques

183. Plan, Ste. Foi, Conques

spread of fire, a prevalent threat with wooden truss-roof buildings, and it acoustically enhanced the liturgical chants of the monks.

Another feature of the Romanesque pilgrimage church was the use of a semicircular ambulatory (see fig. 183). Adapted from ancient Roman and Early Christian centrally planned buildings, it is here used to solve a particular problem. At churches with monastic foundations, it was necessary that the monks occupy the area around the high altar for numerous services. The ambulatory connecting the side aisles in one continuous passageway allowed masses of pilgrims to move through the church, stopping to pray and venerate relics in the apsidal chapels without disturbing the monks.

ROMANESQUE SCULPTURE

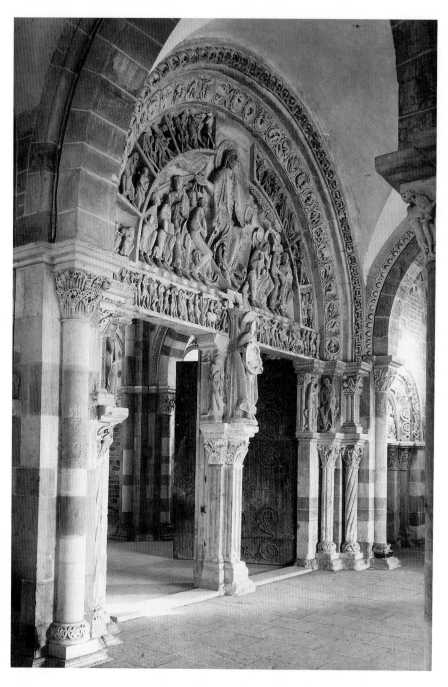

184. *Pentecost*, the *Peoples of the Earth*, and *St. John the Baptist*. Tympanum, lintel, and trumeau, central portal, Abbey Church of La Madeleine, Vézelay, France. 1120–32

In the central tympanum (lunette above the door) at Vézelay, Christ is on the axis, enthroned in a mandorla with his arms outstretched (fig. 184). Axiality and hierarchical scale convey Christ's significance, while the angularity of his legs and the swirling patterns of drapery, similar to those in contemporary manuscript illumination, animate his presence. Rays of illumination and inspiration flow from his hands (his left hand has been broken off) to the head of each apostle. Eight archivolts (arches of decorative and narrative motifs that enframe the tympanum) show the apostles preaching the Gospel and healing spiritual and physical ailments. In the outer archivolts, the zodiac symbols and representations of monthly labors signify that Christ is lord of all time and of everything in the world. On the sides of the doors (jambs) and on the central post (trumeau) are sculpted figures of saints and prophets.

The complex iconography of the Vézelay tympanum reveals the profound and inspired spirituality of the later Middle Ages. The mandorla around Christ, which lifts him above the groundline, refers to his ascension into heaven, while the rays symbolize the descent of the Holy Spirit to assist the apostles on their mission to carry the words of Christ to all humanity. Representations of the human race from all over the world—some based on medieval legends of exotic peoples and therefore fantastically conceived—are shown on the lintel, waiting to hear the Gospel. In the eight compartments the apostles fulfill their mission. John the Baptist, who predicted the coming of Christ, is placed on the trumeau in a position which visually and intellectually expresses his support of Christ.

Tympanum sculpture often spoke to the emotions of the people. The Last Judgment scenes at Conques and Autun emphasize the alternatives of eternal reward or everlasting punishment (figs. 185, 186). At Conques, Christ's judgment is reinforced by literary inscriptions. Axially positioned on the throne of justice, Christ announces to the saved: "Come, the blessed of my Father, take possession of the kingdom that has been readied for you." To the damned he proclaims: "Away from me, accursed ones."

At Autun the master sculptor Gislebertus signed his work just below Christ's feet. On the tympanum the events of the Last Judgment are dramatically portrayed. Across the lintel, humanity waits to be judged; the scales represent the weighing of souls to determine whether the evil a person has done outweighs the good. To Christ's right (our left), the blessed enjoy their reward in heaven, while to his left the damned begin an eternity of punishment at the hands of fantastic, demonic creatures. These horrific devils were visual proof of the punishment for sin, reinforcing the sermons preached inside the cathedral.

185. *Last Judgment.* Typanum and lintel, west portal, Ste. Foi, Conques, France. c. 1120. Stone, approx. 12 x 22'. Traces of paint remain on this tympanum, reminding us that color once played an important role in the total effect.

186. GISLEBERTUS
Last Judgment. Tympanum and lintel, west portal, Cathedral, Autun, France. c. 1125–35. Stone, approx. 12' 6" x 22'

LATER BYZANTINE ART

187. *Virgin of Vladimir.* 12th century. Tempera on wood, 31 x 21". State Historical Museum, Moscow. This icon, which was probably created in Constantinople, was taken to the Russian city of Vladimir and then to Moscow, where it was hoped it would ward off an attack by the Tartars. Only the faces date to the twelfth century for, like many icons, the drapery has been repainted in a style similar to the original, but stiffer and more abstract.

Only a few types of Madonna and Child compositions were permitted in Byzantine art, and each was dependent on an old and venerated tradition. Invention and variation were discouraged, and the figures gradually became more stylized and remote from visual reality. The *Virgin of Vladimir* (fig. 187) is the type known as the *Glykophilousa* or *Eleousa* (the affectionate, loving one), which features the Christ Child pressing his cheek to his mother's. Mary looks out at us, with a solemn expression and large eyes that seem to convey an intense melancholy. Her delicate features—long thin nose, tiny mouth, and sharply defined

188. *Pantocrator.* c. 1100. Dome mosaic. Daphni, Greece

eye sockets—remove her from the realm of the physical and sensuous. The shape of her veiled head, which is clearly drawn with a compass, is geometric and two-dimensional.

Mosaics continued to be the primary medium of decoration in church architecture. The Pantocrator (from the Greek for omnipotent) is an image of the triumphant Christ that was the usual theme for the dome or apse of a church (see fig. 188). This figure forcefully communicates the concept of God's watch over the universe.

Close trade and diplomatic relations between the republic of Venice in Italy and the Byzantine empire led to cultural and artistic influences as well. San Marco was rebuilt beginning in the eleventh century (fig. 189) on the model of a church which had been built by Justinian. Both churches combine the domed central plan with the Greek cross plan. The splendid decoration of San Marco's interior proceeds from patterned marble floors and lower walls covered with slabs of veined marble to culminate in barrel vaults and domes covered with thousands of square feet of Byzantine-style gold mosaics, a project so large it was not fully completed until the seventeenth century. In the central dome the story of Christ's ascension into heaven is represented (fig. 190), with Christ placed at the apex of the dome—the composition evolved in relationship to the shape and space of the dome. Nearby is a dome with the Pentecost, in which the Holy Spirit descends from heaven to inspire the apostles. In this dome the design emphasizes the opposite movement—from the apex

189. Nave, San Marco, Venice. Begun 1063. San Marco functions as the palace chapel of the elected ruler of Venice, the Doge, and is located next to the Doges' Palace. It enshrines the bones of the evangelist St. Mark, Venice's patron saint, which two Venetian merchants stole from the original tomb in Alexandria, Egypt, and brought to Venice in 828.

downward—as is fitting for a scene in which heavenly force descends to inspire the physical and intellectual world.

The exterior domes of San Marco are elevated high above the interior domes to create a festive and impressive design against the sky. Such picturesqueness, ultimately Byzantine in origin, is also seen in the later churches of eastern Europe, Greece, and Russia, as well as in the onion domes of Eastern rite churches all over America.

190. *Ascension.* Late 12th century. Dome mosaic. San Marco, Venice. Grouped below in a circular arrangement are the apostles, two angels, and the Virgin Mary, with palm trees to suggest a landscape setting. Between the windows are figures of virtues. In the pendentives are the Evangelists, with settings of cities and rivers to suggest the worldwide influence of their works.

Introduction to Gothic Art

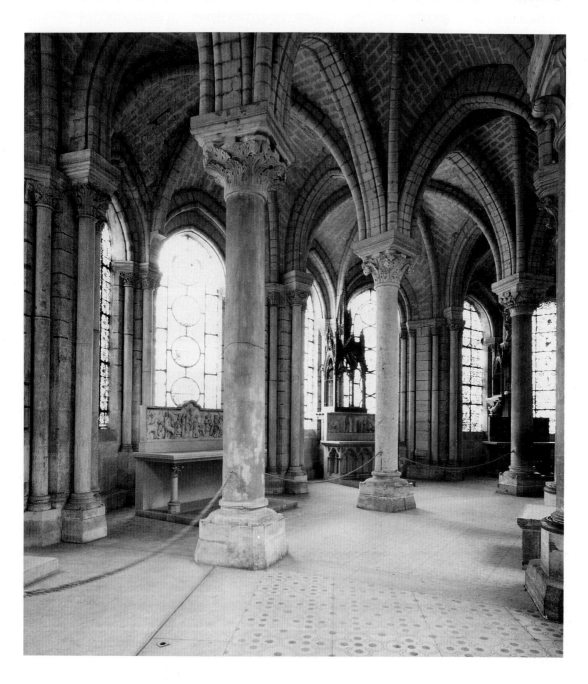

191. Interior, St. Denis, near Paris. Built under the direction of Abbot Suger. 1140–44. This view shows the ambulatory and radiating chapels. Here, where Gothic architecture was invented, we see the distinctive attributes of the style in the union of pointed arches, ribbed groin vaults, and large stained-glass windows.

The Gothic style was first defined in architecture, and architectural motifs appear throughout Gothic painting, sculpture, and the decorative arts. Gothic is easily identifiable because of its unique vocabulary: pointed arches, ribbed cross vaults, flying buttresses, cluster piers, and glowing stained-glass windows. Gothic architecture seems to have been invented by Abbot Suger, friend and adviser to the French kings Louis VI and VII, when he rebuilt the facade, ambulatory, and radiating chapels of the Royal Abbey Church of St. Denis (figs. 191, 192). The beauty of the Gothic style and the importance of St. Denis, the royal French church where the coronation regalia were stored and kings and queens were buried, helped to popularize the new style throughout France. The brilliant colors of the large stained-glass windows of chapels and ambulatory were designed to lead the sensitive observer to contemplate divine things and imagine the glories of the heavenly Jerusalem, the holy "City of God" in Paradise. In other words, the architecture was intended to help the worshipper rise from the physical, material world to an immaterial, spiritual realm. Light is a frequent metaphor for the divine in theological and mystical writings, and Suger wrote with mystical ecstasy about how his new architecture created a "crown of light" at St. Denis:

> For bright is that which is brightly coupled with the bright,
> And bright is the noble edifice which is pervaded by the new light;
> Which stands enlarged in our time,
> I, who was Suger, being the leader while it was being accomplished.

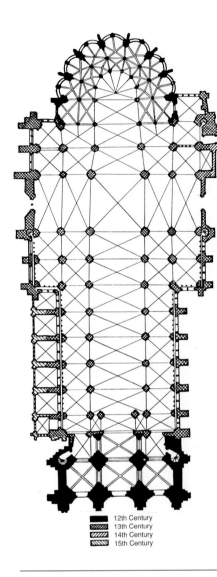

12th Century
13th Century
14th Century
15th Century

192. Plan, St. Denis, as it exists today, showing the various building campaigns. Abbot Suger rebuilt the facade (consecrated 1140) and the chapels and ambulatory (1140–44); from 1231 to 1281 the old Carolingian nave and upper choir were rebuilt in the mature Gothic style.

ABBOT SUGER

In an inscription over the west portal of the facade, Abbot Suger gives himself credit for the rebuilding of St. Denis; no artists' or architects' names are mentioned. His new vision of architecture is based on his belief that the material beauty and splendor of the church would lead worshippers to a new understanding of God and the spiritual realm, as is further clarified in an inscription on the golden doors of the west facade of the abbey:

> Marvel not at the gold and the expense but at the craftsmanship of the work.
> Bright is the noble work; but, being nobly bright, the work
> Should brighten the minds, so that they may travel, through the true lights,
> To the True Light where Christ is the true door.

Suger specifically compared the church at St. Denis to the Holy Jerusalem, the City of God: St. Denis and other, later Gothic cathedrals suggest the Paradise that awaits the pious Christian.

HISTORY

Growth during the Gothic period and financial and social developments meant that life changed dramatically for much of the population. The development of international banking was centered in

193. *Abbot Suger's Chalice.* c. 1140. Silver gilt and agate, with jewels, height 8". National Gallery of Art, Washington, D.C. (Widener Collection). The beauty of Suger's architecture is reflected in the costly vessels he had made for liturgical use. This chalice was created by adding a rim, foot, and handles to an ancient agate cup made in Alexandria in the second century B.C. It was originally inscribed *Suger Abbas* (Abbot Suger). For a view of equally rich objects on an altar at St. Denis, see fig. 138.

rapidly growing urban centers. Paris was the mercantile center of Europe, and its popular annual trade fairs brought together Europeans of many cultures. Among the merchandise bought and sold were works of art. The complex life in the cities led to better-educated administrators and bureaucrats.

That artistic preeminence in Europe should be centered in France during the later Middle Ages is not unexpected, for during the twelfth and thirteenth centuries Paris was the leading intellectual center in Europe and the capital of a strong monarchy (the Capetian line of French kings ruled from 987 to 1316). The University of Paris, the model for late medieval universities, including Oxford, Cambridge, and Padua, became the center for a new rational approach to philosophy and theology known as Scholasticism, which examined, questioned, clarified, and codified Christian dogma and practice. Thomas Aquinas, a professor at the University of Paris, wrote the *Summa Theologica,* an encyclopedia which set out to systematize and encompass all knowledge on theology and the world.

The Crusades, which had begun in the late eleventh century, continued into the Gothic era, but with little political or military success. They were a significant financial and manpower drain on western Europe, but they encouraged the development of banking, of new methods of taxation, and of a more complex money economy. In western Europe, many scientific and philosophical developments resulted from contact with the Islamic culture.

GOTHIC ART

Like so many other art-historical terms, Gothic originally had a pejorative connotation. It was coined during the Italian Renaissance to refer to the whole of medieval art, which, from the perspective of the Renaissance, seemed crude and without reason. Judged to be the work of barbarians, medieval art was called Gothic after the Visigoths, an early Germanic people who sacked Rome in 410. During the Gothic period itself, the new architecture was known as *opus modernum* (modern architecture), *opere francigena* (French architecture), or pointed architecture.

Gothic art is elegant, highly decorated, and characterized by the use of sumptuous, colorful materials. Architecture included churches, urban monastic complexes, and castles. Sculpture was focused on church portals and on elaborate tombs with architectural frames. Painting was largely limited to manuscript illuminations. The decorative arts—secular and liturgical—encompassed works in gold and other fine materials (see fig. 193), including ivory and precious gems. Increasing personal wealth meant that secular works—personal jewelry, tapestries, and ivory boxes and mirror backs—became more common.

The figural pose that characterizes Gothic art is revealed in the *Madonna of Jeanne d'Evreux* (fig. 194). The Madonna stands in the Gothic "hip-shot" position, in which one hip juts out to support the Christ Child; the effect is less naturalistic than elegant, giving the body a flowing *S*-curve shape. The small head of the Madonna is also a Late Gothic mannerism. In typical Gothic fashion, the body is completely covered by heavy drapery. The small scale of this statuette, its precious materials, and its delicate figure type and flowing drapery patterns reveal the sophistication and elegance of the fully developed Gothic style.

The *Annunciation* page from a Parisian book of hours (fig. 195) reveals the elaboration of decoration common in Gothic art. The Annunciation was traditionally one of the most ornate of all pages, for it is the moment of the Incarnation, when the seed of God was

194. *Madonna of Jeanne d'Evreux.* 1339. Silver-gilt with enamel, height 27". The Louvre, Paris. This work was presented to the Abbey of St. Denis by the French queen Jeanne d'Evreux. The stylized iris held by the Madonna is the symbol of French royalty, the fleur-de-lis.

195. *Annunciation*, from a book of hours created in Paris by an Italian artist. c. 1400–1410. Manuscript painting on vellum, 9 x 6". British Library, London. This book of hours was made for the Parisian market, for it features the particular devotions and saints common in Paris. The coat of arms at the bottom of each page was left blank in order to be painted later with the arms of the purchaser, revealing that the book was made for the art market and was not commissioned by a specific patron.

placed in the womb of the Virgin Mary and Christ was conceived and became flesh. In prayer books it is represented before the texts for Matins, the first service of the day, and therefore serves as a frontispiece not only to that important service, but to the whole of the book. Here the artist sets the scene in an elaborate churchlike structure, complete with altar and altarpiece; all the architectural motifs are Gothic. Although Gabriel holds a scroll bearing his message, Mary looks upward toward God, from whose figure emerges the dove of the Holy Spirit. Old Testament prophets, whose writings were held to predict the virgin birth and the coming of Christ, appear in the upper stories of the Gothic structure. Baby angels playing musical instruments populate the elaborate floral motifs of the borders. Typical of the growing interest in symbolism is the use of a number of complex symbols that elaborate on the content of the narrative. The caged bird behind Mary, which at first seems to be merely a household decoration, is a symbol for Christ's Incarnation, when his soul was "caged" within a physical body, while the mating birds in the border refer by contrast to the non-sexual manner by which God's seed was placed in Mary's womb. The spider and ladybug may refer to the devil, who was understood as ever-present.

THE GOTHIC ARTIST

During the Gothic period, the vast majority of works of art were not signed, but we begin to find references to specific artists in a few documents and inventories, where named artists are praised for their skill. A number of the architects/contractors who designed and constructed the cathedrals are known from inscriptions and documents. Some traveled widely: the Frenchman William of Sens was called to England to rebuild Canterbury Cathedral, and Villard de Honnecourt went to Hungary and Switzerland. Several artists are noted as active in more than one medium; Master André Beauneveu, who was working for King Charles V of France in 1364, was a painter, sculptor, designer of tapestries, and a consultant to architectural projects. Nevertheless, the majority of Gothic artists were anonymous. Later, during the Italian Renaissance, the art historian Giorgio Vasari would be puzzled by the Gothic artist's "indifference to fame."

THE FRANCISCANS AND THE DOMINICANS

The urbanization of Europe was accompanied by significant developments in monasticism that shifted the emphasis from rural retreats of work, prayer, and meditation to large complexes within the city where the monks could serve the poor and sick and preach the word of God in the language of the people. In the early thirteenth century, St. Francis of Assisi founded a popular new mendicant (begging) order, the Franciscans, which emphasized poverty and humility. The sermons and writings of his followers reveal a new emphasis on human emotion in interpreting the lives of Christ and the saints. Legend tells us that Francis developed the tradition of the Christmas pageant to make Christianity more immediate and meaningful for the populace. This is related to the contemporary widespread development of religious drama, the famous mystery plays. A Franciscan monk, writing in the late thirteenth century about the birth of Christ, urges a special kind of imaginary participation. He speaks directly to the reader, advising: "You too . . . kneel and adore your Lord God and then His mother, and reverently greet the saintly old Joseph . . . beg His mother to offer to let you hold [the baby Jesus] a while. Pick Him up and hold Him in your arms. Gaze on His face with devotion and reverently kiss Him and delight in Him" (*Meditations on the Life of Christ*).

THE GOTHIC CATHEDRAL: CHARTRES

Entering a great Gothic cathedral is a thrilling, emotional, and—many would say—spiritual experience. The emphatic verticality of a Gothic nave urges us upward, and it is easy to experience a sense of weightlessness and immateriality, a physical condition that can be related to spiritual enlightenment (see fig. 196). Space seems to expand not only upward, but outward to the sides as well, as we look both upward and through the nave arcade into the side aisles. Space, of course, is also a dominant experience in such earlier architecture as the ancient Roman Pantheon (fig. 127), whose simple and monumental union of dome and cylinder is in sharp contrast to the complex interrelationships and forms of varied sizes of the Chartres interior. In the Gothic structure the experience of space is much less lucid, and the ultimate effect, a combination of height, dark corners, and glowing stained-glass windows, is mystical and otherworldly.

From its foundations, sunk twenty-five feet or more into the earth, to the height of its vaults and roof (at Beauvais, the tallest of all cathedrals, the vaults peak at 157 feet over the floor and the roof reaches 223 feet above the street), the Gothic cathedral is a monument to the determination, engineering daring, and physical energies of patrons, architects, and builders. Despite construction campaigns that lasted over decades and even centuries, not one of the great French Gothic cathedrals was ever fully completed; the vision of patrons and

196. Nave, Cathedral of Notre Dame, Chartres, France. 1194–1220. Chartres Cathedral is the most memorable of French Gothic cathedrals not only for the superb quality of its architecture and sculpture, but because it alone preserves virtually all its original stained-glass windows. Begun again after a fire in 1194 destroyed the earlier cathedral (except for the west facade, with its sculpture, the crypt, and some of the stained glass, including *"Notre Dame de la Belle Verrière"*), the new construction was largely completed by 1220.

architects was too ambitious— too glorious—to be realized.

The high, narrow nave of the Gothic cathedral is the climax of a long tradition in Christian art in which architects tried to create a physical space that would express the spiritual goals of the Christian religion. The Gothic interest in ever increasing height, lightness, and slenderness of proportion is evidenced by these statistics, arranged chronologically:

197. Vaults of the nave, Chartres
Cathedral

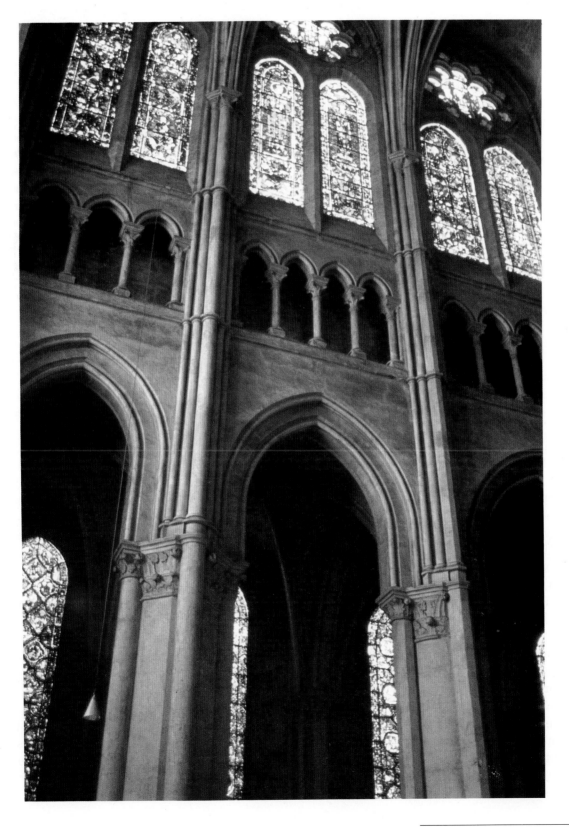

	approx. height of the nave vaults	approx. width of the nave	proportion of nave height to width
Laon, Cathedral 1160–1205	80'	37' 6"	2.13:1
Paris, Notre Dame 1163–96	115'	40'	2.88:1
Bourges, St. Étienne 1195–c. 1270/80	117'	44'	2.66:1
Chartres, Notre Dame 1194–1220	120'	45' 6"	2.64:1
Reims, Notre Dame designed 1210	125'	46'	2.72:1
Amiens, Notre Dame designed 1220	144'	48'	3:1
Beauvais, Cathedral (vaults before apse) designed 1230s	157'	47'	3.36:1

198. Plan, Chartres Cathedral

A taller church was thought to please God. In addition, it could fuel the rivalry between neighbors, for during the Middle Ages the local cathedral was the emblem not only of the sanctity of the town's population, but of their wealth, power, and pride as well.

The unique combination of pointed arch, ribbed groin vault, and flying buttress (see pp. 204–5) defines Gothic architecture. Although each of these elements had been used earlier elsewhere, it is their combination into a coherent and rational system that is new in the Gothic period. The pointed arch, seen everywhere in Chartres's interior (fig. 197), continuously directs our attention upward. The ribs of the vaults help define the parts of the architectural structure and also create a series of lines that keep the eye moving. The rational basis of Gothic architecture demands that each element be explicable and interrelated (as in the Gothic philosophical system known as Scholasticism), and each vault is related to and visually supported by a colonnette (a thin column) that begins at floor level. Groups of colonnettes turn the supporting piers into cluster piers. The interior elevation (fig. 200) is composed of a nave arcade, a triforium (a narrow gallery which opens the structure where normally there would be an expanse of wall), and an enormous, window-filled clerestory.

In most structures, we are aware of a continuous and relatively dense wall surface which is punctured and punctuated by doors and windows, but in the Gothic cathedral there is so little wall, and what remains is so dissolved or disguised by the linear patterns of ribs and colonnettes, that windows and wall are no longer alternatives. They are unified into an energetic skeleton with huge openings filled with vibrantly colored stained-glass windows. The flying buttress—hidden from an interior view by the stained-glass windows—is clearly visible on the exterior and adds lightness and visual energy to the exterior (see fig. 202).

The ideal Gothic church would have had seven spired towers—a twin-towered western facade (a development from the Carolingian westwork; see fig. 199), a tower at the crossing, and twin towers at both north and south transepts. Such a massing of vertical forms pointing upward suggests the dissolution of the mass of the structure and a denial of gravity consistent with the motivations and aspirations of the cathedral builders.

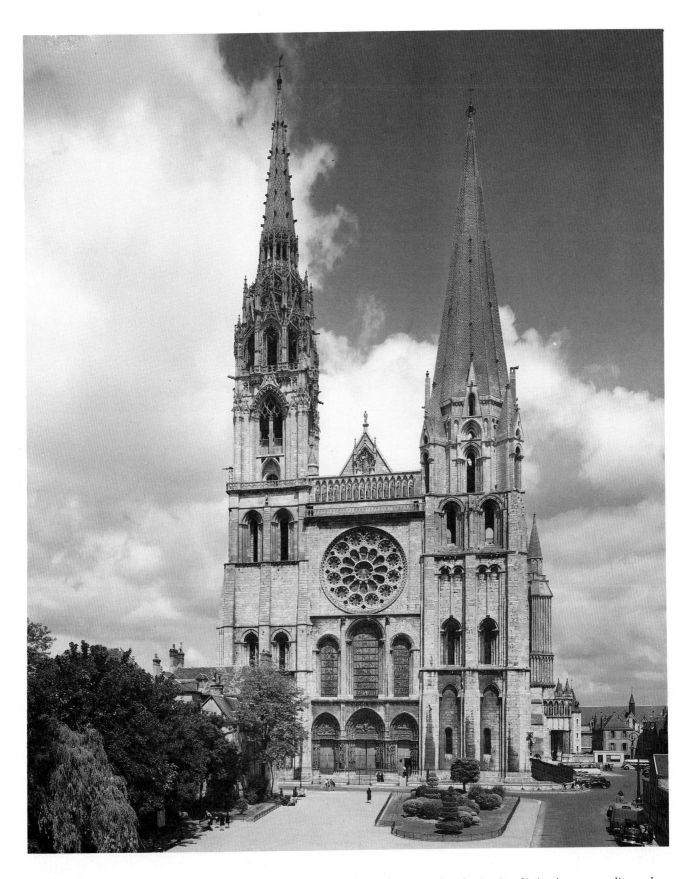

199. West facade, Chartres Cathedral. The mismatched towers of the Chartres facade give it a distinctive personality and reveal the changing nature of the Gothic style. The shorter, transitional Romanesque-Gothic tower was completed before the fire of 1194, while the elaborately decorated, fully Gothic example was not begun until 1507. For sculptures from the facade, see fig. 206.

GOTHIC ENGINEERING

200. Isometric projection and cross section showing the structure and parts of Chartres Cathedral

1. bay
2. nave
3. aisle
4. nave arcade
5. clerestory
6. cluster pier
7. triforium
8. buttress
9. flying buttress
10. wooden roof
11. colonnette

201. Plan and drawing of a Gothic rib vault. The pointed arches enable the openings on each side to reach a unified height. Compare this to the cross vault in fig. 124.

The Gothic cathedral is based on complex engineering principles (fig. 200). It is founded on the dynamic interaction/equilibrium between the outward thrust of the high cross vaults and the flying buttresses that contain this thrust. The desire for both height and maximum window surface led to the creation of a structure aptly described as "skeletal"; every element is manipulated to help meet these goals.

The Gothic cathedral is the result of the union of three distinct constructional elements:

The pointed arch: its very design gives a vertical emphasis, and the angle at which the sides meet at the apex focuses attention at the point of its greatest height. The pointed arch makes possible the unity of space characteristic of a Gothic structure. Since a pointed arch can rise to any height despite its width (unlike a round arch), it can vault a bay of virtually any shape—such as those of Abbot Suger's ambulatory. In addition, the outward thrust of a pointed arch is more vertical than that of a rounded arch, meaning that a lighter buttress is necessary and that larger areas of wall can be replaced with stained-glass windows.

The ribs of the vault: these not only make the vaults appear lighter; they allow for a physically lighter structure. The ribs were constructed first and, because of their weight-bearing potential, the surfaces of the vault can be composed of lighter materials. These surfaces, sometimes called the web, or infilling, seem stretched, like a fabric or skin, between the linear, skeletal supports of the ribs (see fig. 201).

The flying buttress: an invention which, by transferring the thrust and weight to an exterior support some distance from the wall, permits a lighter structure and a greater expanse of windows (fig. 202). In earlier architecture, heavy buttresses, greatly thickened parts of the wall surface, cut down on the amount of light which reached the windows and gave the structure a ponderous exterior appearance.

The structural dynamics of the Gothic cathedral—which today we can analyze with machinery and

202. Flying buttresses, Chartres Cathedral. Begun 1194

study through models—were explored by Gothic architects by building three-dimensional models of arches and buttresses. At times the Gothic desire for height and lightened structure led to difficulties. At Beauvais (fig. 203), the choir vaults peak at 157 feet above the floor, making the interior of the church as tall as a 15-story building; they collapsed due to inadequate foundations, piers, and buttressing and were rebuilt with additional supports and buttresses. A huge crossing tower—perhaps 500 feet tall—was then built, but when it collapsed, work stopped, and Beauvais today consists of little more than an apse.

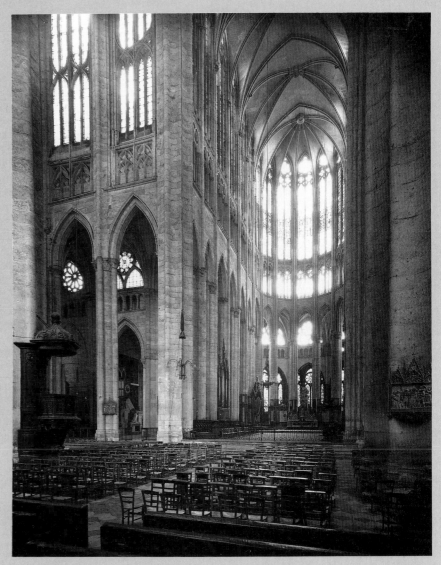

203. Interior, Cathedral, Beauvais, France. Begun 1247 on plans drawn in the 1230s

GOTHIC SCULPTURE

204. *Beau Dieu.* c. 1225–35. Stone. Trumeau figure, central portal, west facade, Cathedral of Notre Dame, Amiens, France. The popular name for this rather severe figure of the blessing Christ is the *Beau Dieu,* the Beautiful Lord. Like most Romanesque and Gothic portal sculpture, this figure was originally polychromed.

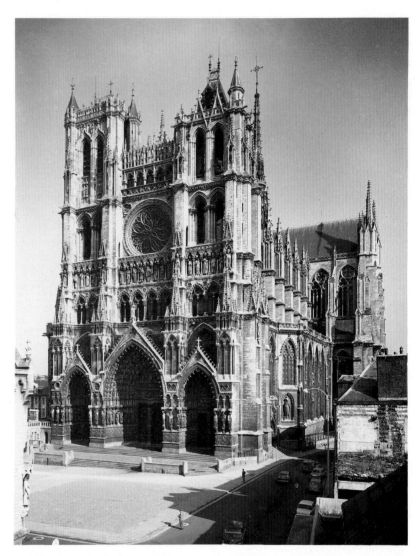

205. West facade, Amiens Cathedral. c. 1225–35

As they entered the main, western door of the Cathedral of Amiens, the faithful were greeted by the trumeau sculpture of Christ holding a book and mak-ing a gesture of blessing (fig. 204). The book, probably the Gospels, symbolizes Christ's words and deeds, but this image of the teaching Christ is also combined with the victorious Christ, as represented in the lion and the dragon trampled under his feet. In Christian tradition, the dragon symbolized the Devil, and in this context the lion was understood as a symbol of the Antichrist.

Unlike Romanesque trumeau figures, with their lively abstract patterns, the Amiens Christ is not only naturalistic, but quiet and stately. The simple verticality of the figure echoes the inherent architectonic role of the trumeau, the drapery falls in a naturalistic manner, and Christ's face has been given a human, solemn dignity.

As in Romanesque church

facades, sculpted figures populate the exterior of Gothic churches, not only on the three western portals, but on as many as six transept entrances as well. The west facade at Amiens reveals how figurative sculpture and applied decoration have increased (fig. 205). The deep porches contain rows of jamb and archivolt figures; narrative reliefs decorate many other areas. The sculptures represent figures and scenes from the Bible, including both the Old and New Testaments, as well as more secular themes, such as the signs of the zodiac and the labors of the months. The facade as a whole is intended to represent all God's creation. Its order, as commanded by the axial figure of Christ on the trumeau, reflects the divine order of the world.

The earliest Gothic portal sculptures, the *Ancestors of Christ* at Chartres, already display significant differences from their Romanesque predecessors (fig. 206). The elongated figures are columnar, for their restricted poses reflect the vertical columns behind them and of which they are a part. Drapery folds fall in abstract, linear patterns unrelated to underlying anatomical structure. These drapery patterns are unlike those of Romanesque figures, which are lively and expressive. The drapery at Chartres quietly reinforces the figures' verticality. The faces of the Chartres jamb figures, while still somewhat stylized, convey a softer and more naturalistic quality than, for example, the severe face of Christ in the tym-

206. *Ancestors of Christ.* c. 1145–55. Stone. Column figures, right jamb, central door (royal portal), west facade, Chartres Cathedral

207. *Vierge Dorée.* c. 1250. Stone. Trumeau figure, south portal, Amiens Cathedral. This sculpture is popularly known as the *Vierge Dorée* (The Gilded Virgin) because parts of the figure were originally decorated with applied gold leaf.

panum at Vézelay (fig. 184).

As portal sculpture developed through the Gothic period, especially into the thirteenth century, the figures began to be realized in higher and higher relief and began to lose their columnar orientation. The Amiens Christ exemplifies the increasing naturalism of early-thirteenth-century Gothic sculpture, while retaining the serious dignity which characterized the jamb figures at Chartres from about eighty years earlier. The *Vierge Dorée* at Amiens dates about twenty years later than the Amiens Christ (fig. 207). A new, relaxed elegance characterizes the sculpture. The figural proportions are elon-

gated, and Mary's body follows an exaggerated curve created by the tilt of the hip to support the arm holding the Christ Child. The drapery, falling in broad folds, contributes to the statue's elegance and emphasizes her sophisticated pose. A warm, affectionate smile plays across Mary's delicate face as she gazes at the child. The reverent dignity of the *Beau Dieu* and the human charm of the *Vierge Dorée* express the diverse vitality which occurs in the development of Gothic sculpture. The figures that decorate Gothic portals reintroduced monumental figural sculpture to western Europe.

GOTHIC STAINED GLASS

208. *"Notre Dame de la Belle Verrière."* 12th century (central portion); 13th century (surrounding angels). Stained glass, approx. 16' x 7' 6". Cathedral of Notre Dame, Chartres, France. This popular and venerated window is known as *"Notre Dame de la Belle Verrière"* (Our Lady of the Beautiful Window). The Enthroned Virgin and Child section which forms the central portion of this famous window was saved when the cathedral of Chartres burned in 1194. As the cathedral was being rebuilt in the new Gothic style of the thirteenth century, the earlier window was flanked by panels with angels in a more fully Gothic style.

The brilliant contrast between the blues and reds of *"La Belle Verrière"* establishes a dynamic equilibrium, and the other colors and the black paint used to define faces, drapery, and other details enrich and dramatize the window (fig. 208). The glowing, gemlike windows that decorate a Gothic structure help create the ideal of the church as a metaphor for the heavenly Jerusalem, which was described in the Bible as having foundations composed of precious stones (Revelation 21:19).

"La Belle Verrière" exemplifies two styles—the transitional style between Romanesque and Gothic and the fully mature Gothic style. The axiality of Mary and the Christ Child (whose faces have been restored) is eased by the slight tilt of Mary's head. In contrast, the angels in the side panels are more animated, and the pieces of colored glass used to form the image have bolder, more varied colors.

Like the exterior sculptural program of a Gothic church, the figurative imagery of a stained-glass window instructed the people through symbolic imagery and narratives from the Old and New Testaments. But with stained glass, this instructive purpose was uniquely joined with a spiritual, almost mystical, effect. When we enter the church, we leave an outside environment, in which the light level is approximately nine thousand lumens, for an interior space where the level is only a few lumens, even on a bright day. As our eyes adjust to the dark, cavernous space, a radiance of light seems to burst from the windows, where images executed in stained glass appear suspended in an aura of colored light. As light passes through these windows, it causes them to glow with a radiant richness and to cast beams and spots of color throughout the interior.

Abbot Suger wrote about how the sumptuous quality of Gothic objects brought him into the mystical presence of the divine: "Thus, when—out of my delight in the beauty of the house of God—the loveliness of the many-colored gems has called me away from external cares, and worthy meditation has induced me to reflect, transferring that which is material to that which is immaterial, on the diversity of the sacred virtues: then it seems to me that I see myself dwelling, as it were, in some strange region of the universe which neither exists entirely in the slime of the earth nor entirely in the purity of Heaven; and that, by the grace of God, I can be transported from this inferior to that higher world in an anagogical manner."

STAINED-GLASS TECHNIQUE

The origins of stained-glass windows, which are composed of pieces of colored glass joined by lead strips (fig. 209), are uncertain. Colored-glass windows and windows made of thin stone through which light could filter were already in use in Early Christian and Byzantine churches, and, although stained-glass windows became more common during the Romanesque period, it was only during the Gothic that they became a crucial and integral part of the architecture and a major means of artistic expression.

The colored glass is produced by adding metallic oxides to the molten glass (pot metal glass) or by fusing a layer of colored glass onto clear glass (flashed glass). During the Late Middle Ages, the design for a window would be drawn in chalk on a flat table. Pieces of glass were cut to fit each small shape or area of the design. The details of faces and drapery were added by painting in black enamel, which was then fused to the glass by firing. The fragments of glass were assembled, with lead strips bonding them in place, over the design. As these glass and lead designs were heavy, armatures of iron bands were used to strengthen and support the window when it was installed into the church. Stained glass is one of the most radiant and vibrant media in the history of human expression.

209. Photograph of a craftsperson making a stained-glass window. He is fitting the lead strips, which in section are shaped like a sideways H around the glass. The original design, used to determine the shapes of the glass pieces, is visible in the foreground.

GIOTTO, *MADONNA ENTHRONED*

210. GIOTTO
Madonna Enthroned with Angels and Saints. c. 1300. Tempera on wood, 10' 8" x 6' 8 1/4". Uffizi Gallery, Florence. Originally painted for the church of Ognissanti (All Saints) in Florence, this panel is sometimes called the *Ognissanti Madonna.*

contemporaries. A comparison between their compositions of the Madonna and Child reveals the significance of Giotto's innovations (figs. 210, 211). The scale and simple composition of Cimabue's painting create an impressive and severe effect consistent with the expressions of the faces. In his work, Giotto reestablishes the connection between the art of painting and the nature of objective reality, an attitude not evident in painting since ancient Roman illusionism. Giotto's figures are represented as massive, weighty forms that seem to exist within a spatial continuum in which gravity is an inescapable factor. These large, bulky figures have strongly modeled, naturalistic drapery, as seen in the flowing folds of the angels kneeling in the foreground (unfortunately, the darkening of the blue of the Madonna's robe and the repainting of her knees and lap have deprived the central figure of some of its original sense of weight and presence).

Once Cimabue thought that in painting
He commanded the field, and now Giotto has the acclaim.

As this quotation from Dante's *Divine Comedy* reveals, Cimabue was once the most important painter in Florence. His style represented the final statement of the Byzantine influence in Italy. Dante wrote that it was soon superseded by the revolutionary style of Giotto, an assessment that we share with Giotto's

211. CIMABUE

Madonna Enthroned with Angels and Prophets. c. 1285. Tempera on wood, 11' 7" x 7' 4". Uffizi Gallery, Florence. Tradition has it that Cimabue was the teacher of Giotto. The two Florentine painters are used by Dante to elucidate the fleeting nature of fame.

The heavy marble throne of Giotto's Madonna seems solidly fixed in space; Cimabue's wooden throne is lighter and less rational (there are no back legs). In both Cimabue's and Giotto's panels the figures to the sides overlap, but in Giotto's they seem to stand solidly on the ground; Cimabue's angels are placed in an abstract decorative pattern. The placement of Giotto's figures in space is clearly structured: the kneeling angels overlap the standing angels who, in turn, overlap the throne, and in the grouping of saints Giotto lets some of the haloes overlap shoulders and even faces. Giotto surrounds the Madonna and Child with figures placed to create a natural, believable effect, with no loss of dignity or emphasis.

Equally important for Giotto's revolution is the new responsiveness of the figures, which even in this hieratic subject is of such intensity that a dramatic effect is created. The angels respond to the impressive presence of the Madonna and Child with spontaneous expressions of awe. The Madonna and Child have neither the remoteness nor the insubstantiality seen in Byzantine art, and their parted lips and direct gazes convey a significant human presence.

Giotto's painting, with its recognition of both the physical and the psychological natures of human activity, is in direct contrast to the schematic composition and expressionless figures of Cimabue's panel. Giotto transformed the art of painting; by emphasizing the concept of the "painting as a window," he established an approach which would endure until the revolutionary experiments of Cézanne and the Cubists in the late-nineteenth and early-twentieth centuries.

TEMPERA TECHNIQUE

The use of tempera paint, which dates back to the Egyptians, was well-established by the later Middle Ages. The support used for tempera paint is usually wood. Large panels such as those of Giotto and Cimabue are composed of planks glued together with an integral frame constructed at the same time. This totality would be designed by the artist and produced by carpenters. To provide an appropriate surface for the paint, the wood panel was covered with a surface of linen or canvas and several layers of fine plaster. Onto this surface the painter would draw the preliminary designs, probably with charcoal. The final design would be scratched into the plaster surface, following the outlines of the forms to be painted.

Thin sheets of gold leaf would be applied, using red glue, to the background areas. The paint used was composed of ground pigments combined with egg and perhaps a little vinegar; the paint, which dried quickly, was applied methodically in numerous thin coats to prevent flaking. The finished paintings are characterized by rich colors against a luminous gold ground. Many later painters enhanced their work by elaborately decorating the gold background. Using carved tools, they impressed floral and Gothic decorative patterns into the surface of the gold to create borders and halo designs that caught the light and shimmered on the reflective surface.

GIOTTO, THE ARENA CHAPEL FRESCOES

212. GIOTTO
Lamentation. c. 1303–5. Fresco, approx. 72 x 78". Arena Chapel, Padua, Italy. The Arena Chapel was built and decorated for Enrico Scrovegni, a wealthy Paduan businessman. It was attached to the Scrovegni Palace, which had been built on the site of the ancient Roman arena of Padua, hence the name Arena Chapel.

213. GIOTTO
Last Judgment. Fresco, approx. 33' x 27' 6". Arena Chapel. Filling the inside of the entrance wall, and therefore the last thing the viewer sees as he leaves, is this panoramic representation of the *Last Judgment* at the end of time when, in Christian dogma, Christ will appear as the judge.

As in his *Madonna* (fig. 210), the figures in Giotto's *Lamentation* offer an illusion of weight and mass not seen in painting since antiquity. At the same time, they convey a convincing drama and expression of emotion (fig. 212). Through gesture and placement, the composition, with its simple friezelike arrangement and sloping hillside setting, focuses attention on the dramatic core of the narrative, the heads of the Virgin and Christ in the lower left corner. Two heavy figures seen from the back enframe this tender and private moment and communicate the tragic loss and mute pain appropriate to the agonized farewell of a mother to her son. The simple landscape of barren hill and dead tree supports the expressive figures. The Lamentation and the related theme of the Pietà, which are not mentioned in the Bible, are subjects that develop with the demand for a more emotional religious art in the late medieval period.

Giotto's *Lamentation* cannot be understood as an isolated composition and must be examined in relation to its context. In the Arena Chapel (fig. 214), Giotto painted a continuous cycle of thirty-eight scenes from the lives of the Virgin and Christ which starts at the top and, reading left to right, spirals around to culminate in six final scenes on the left wall. The cycle as a whole has a continuous left-to-right development, and this last section begins with an exceptionally strong left-to-right movement in a representation of Christ carrying the cross. This is halted by the centralized composition of the *Crucifixion,* but even it does not prepare us for the *Lamentation,* where Giotto forces our attention backward and downward to the conjunction of the heads of the Virgin and Christ. Giotto demands that we stop and concentrate on the *Lamentation.* The impact of the event is conveyed to us not only by the variety of human emotions expressed by Christ's

214. GIOTTO

Frescoes, Arena Chapel. The Arena Chapel has windows only on the right-hand wall, as seen in this view; the left is completely filled with the bands of narratives. Below are figures of the virtues and vices. High on the triumphal arch is a fresco of God sending Gabriel to earth and, to either side, the kneeling figures of Gabriel and the Virgin at the moment of the Annunciation and Incarnation. The vault above is decorated with blue sky, gold stars, and holy figures appearing in circular frames.

followers as they gather around his body, but by the reflection of these emotions in the angels who flood the sky with grief. Such a strong emphasis on experience and empathy is surely related to the preachings and writings of the followers of St. Francis.

In the *Last Judgment*, Christ appears in the center, flanked by saints and angels; below, on his right hand, are the blessed, while to our right are the damned (fig. 213). Near the center, to the left of the cross that marks the dividing line between Paradise and eternal damnation, is a representation of Enrico Scrovegni offering his chapel, represented as a model held by a monk, to the Virgin. Scrovegni's purpose in having the chapel erected and painted is thus clarified, for in making this offering he hoped to atone for the sins of his father, who had accumulated a huge fortune by charging exorbitant rates of interest, a sin called usury that the church condemned.

There are references to virtues and vices in other areas of the chapel. They appear as figures in *grisaille* (gray and white, simulating sculpture), which alternate with illusionistic marble panels.

The Renaissance artist Lorenzo Ghiberti said the Arena Chapel was "one of the glories of the earth," and the modern artist Henri Matisse announced that, on looking at a scene in the Arena Chapel, "I understood at once the feeling which radiates from it, and which is instinct in the line, the composition, the color."

15th–19th Centuries

V

FIFTEENTH-CENTURY ART

INTRODUCTION

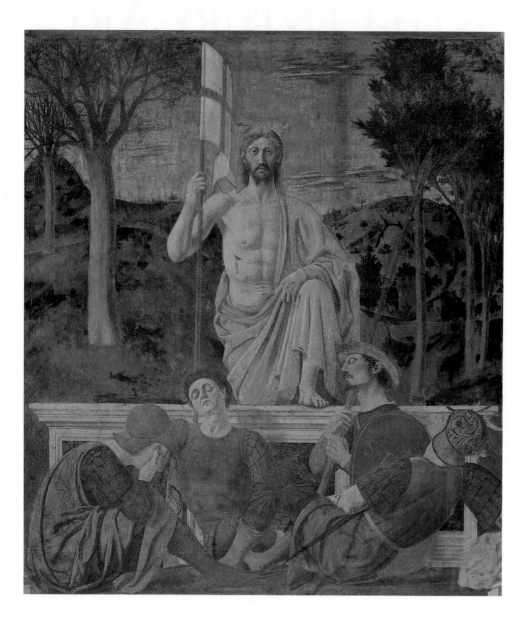

215. PIERO DELLA FRANCESCA
Resurrection. c. 1460. Fresco,
96 x 78"; the figures are approximately
lifesize. Town Hall, Borgo San
Sepolcro

These two paintings (figs. 215, 216) demonstrate some of the important artistic developments in fifteenth-century painting in Italy and Flanders. Both are large, with lifesize figures, and offer a naturalism not seen in painting since the time of the ancient Romans. The figures are realistically proportioned, seem to have weight and to occupy illusionistic space, and suggest the potential for movement; in addition, they are charged with emotional and psychological tensions that demand a response from the viewer. Piero's resurrected Christ fixes us with a compelling gaze, while in Rogier's painting waves of emotion sweep through the followers of Christ as they receive the body being lowered from the cross. They weep, convulse, and faint.

216. ROGIER VAN DER WEYDEN
Deposition. c. 1435–38. Oil on wood,
7' 2 5/8" x 8' 7 1/8". The Prado, Madrid

Yet significant differences between the two works suggest the artistic and cultural distinctions between Italy and Flanders in the fifteenth century. Piero's Christ is like a Greek god—his handsome musculature and dignified bearing can be compared to the *Apollo* from Olympia (fig. 60). Such an interest in classical motifs and types is seldom found in Flemish painting. Piero's forceful triangular composition, with Christ's head at the apex and the sleeping soldiers grouped below, reveals the Italian concern with harmony and order. Rogier's composition is much more visually complex, and its flowing forms weave a pattern of pathos and despair. This concentration is reinforced by Rogier's Flemish attention to precise detail, made possible by new developments in oil painting (see pp. 240–41).

FROM THE MIDDLE AGES TO THE RENAISSANCE: NAMING THE STYLES

The transition from the Late Middle Ages to the Renaissance in the cosmopolitan centers of Flanders and Italy was a gradual one, and many aspects of Renaissance society and art only evolved slowly from medieval traditions. Historians still debate if fifteenth-century

Flemish painting is best understood as a late manifestation of the Gothic or as a Northern version of the Renaissance. As neither Gothic nor Renaissance is a completely appropriate stylistic term for these Flemish works, they are here identified under an independent designation, fifteenth-century Flemish painting. In Italy, and especially in Florence, new Renaissance ideas dominate the production of art during most of the fifteenth century. This period is generally known as the Early Renaissance, to distinguish it from the late fifteenth and early sixteenth centuries, when the culmination of earlier ideas resulted in the period called the High Renaissance (see pp. 267–68).

HISTORY: FLANDERS IN THE FIFTEENTH CENTURY

In Flanders, an area roughly equivalent to present-day Belgium, a prosperous new merchant society based on the wool trade and banking was established during the fourteenth and fifteenth centuries. The flourishing city of Bruges was the most important center, and the presence of foreign bankers, especially the Medici from Florence, made it the banking capital of northern Europe. Other important centers included Ghent and Tournai. As in Italy, trade guilds controlled manufacturing, as well as the production of works of art.

Flanders was distinguished by a rich and diverse culture which included a revolutionary school of composers that dominated European musical developments throughout the century. Northern intellectuals, however, were not very interested in the revival of classical antiquity, so important to the Italians, and in Flanders some arts, especially architecture and the decorative arts, remained Gothic well into the sixteenth century.

HISTORY: FLORENCE IN THE FIFTEENTH CENTURY

Leonardo Bruni, a scholar versed in Latin and Greek and chancellor of Florence from 1427 until his death in 1444, praised Florence as "the new Athens on the Arno." He likened the civic values of his time to those fostered in democratic Athens and in Rome during the republic. But while Bruni praised Florentine republicanism, contrasting it to the despotic rule in other Italian city-states, in actuality Florence was led by an oligarchy of commercial interests. The Florentine democracy was eventually dominated by the rise of the Medici family, whose wealth was derived from banking and commerce. Beginning with Cosimo de' Medici, the family consolidated the reins of power behind a facade of republicanism. His descendants firmly tightened their political control, and Lorenzo, known as Lorenzo the Magnificent, ultimately ruled as a benevolent tyrant. Toward the end of the century, the domination of the Medici and the conspicuous wealth and humanist interests of the Florentine citizenry were challenged by the fiery sermons of the Dominican friar Girolamo Savonarola. Following the exile of the Medici in 1494, Savonarola assisted in restoring a representative form of government. But as Savonarola continued to act as the harsh conscience of Florence, the church and some of the citizenry turned against him, and he was executed for heresy in 1498. Florence maintained her republic until 1512, when the Medici again regained control.

THE IDEA OF A RENAISSANCE

Our use of the term Renaissance (French for rebirth) is drawn from a conception of history found in the writings of the sixteenth-century Italian painter, architect, and writer Giorgio Vasari, whose historical fame rests primarily on his *Lives of the Most Eminent Painters, Sculptors, and Architects*, a history of Italian art and artists. Vasari champions the works of ancient Greece and Rome, describing medieval art as a "disastrous decline," and argues that in Italy during the fifteenth and sixteenth centuries "art has been reborn and reached perfection in our own times." Vasari's concept influenced the French historian Jules Michelet, who in 1855 gave the title *La Renaissance* to a volume of his *Histoire de France* and thereby extended the idea of the Renaissance to embrace a cultural phenomenon which included northern Europe. Michelet's Renaissance was characterized by "the discovery of the world and the discovery of man."

For Italian Renaissance artists, the models of classical antiquity provided an impetus for artistic transformation, but it would be a mistake to view these artists as merely copying ancient works of art. They adapted the classical aesthetic to the attitudes of their own times, creating works of art distinctly different from those of antiquity. This "rebirth" of the antique encompassed not only works of art, but also the recovery of ancient texts and classical literary style. In addition, Leonardo Bruni's careful reading of antique texts and his application of ancient civic values to his own time led to a new historical consciousness fundamental to the growth of Renaissance humanism.

HUMANISM

The Renaissance concept of humanism (as distinct from modern concepts of humanitarianism and secular humanism) had a profound philosophical foundation. The title humanist was originally applied to a teacher of humanistic studies, a curriculum which included rhetoric, grammar, poetry, history, and moral philosophy. Humanism was integrated with Christianity; it sought to supplement faith by insisting on the dignity of the individual and the human potential for achievement. Although the development of humanism was centered in Florence, by mid-century most of the important courts in northern Italy had been significantly influenced by humanism.

Humanist values are visually exemplified on the *Tomb of Leonardo Bruni* (fig. 217), the Florentine statesman and champion of humanist education. An effigy of the deceased Bruni rests atop a bier supported by two eagles, standards of ancient Rome. Crowned with laurel, the ancient symbol of honor and victory, and with his hands embracing his *History of the Florentine People*, Bruni lies eternally in state. On the sarcophagus below is a Latin inscription in classical lettering: "At Leonardo's passing, history grieves, eloquence is mute, and it is said that the Muses, Greek and Latin alike, cannot hold back their tears." These antique literary references are reinforced by the classicizing architecture of the tomb. The Corinthian pilasters and round arch may refer to the ancient Roman triumphal arch (see fig. 111). Over the arch a heraldic lion symbolizes Florence. The relief of the Virgin and Child within the arch is the only reference to Christianity. Such a union of ancient traditions and Christian theology was one of the primary goals of humanism. It had an influence on many works of art, including Botticelli's *Birth of Venus* (fig. 263).

ART THEORY

Humanism also played an important role in the development of art theory. Leon Battista Alberti, well educated in humanistic studies, was attracted to the new work of such Florentine artists as Filippo Brunelleschi, Donatello, and Masaccio. He noted that these artists revived classical art, and using a literary approach that joined his knowledge of the principles of classical poetry and rhetoric, he wrote about the new art in *De pictura (On Painting)* in 1435. This cornerstone of Western art theory discusses the noble purpose of painting, the painter as an educated professional, and the use of mathematical principles, including scientific perspective (see pp. 232–33), in painting. *On Painting* gave art and artists a new dignity and opened the way for a new level of literary discussions on art.

THE UNION OF THE CLASSICAL AND THE NATURAL

The union of classical values with natural observation, a distinct feature of fifteenth-century art, was addressed by the late medieval artist Cennino Cennini in his practical manual for painters, *The Craftsman's Handbook*. He recommended learning to draw from the works of recognized masters: "Now you must forge ahead again, so that you may pursue the course of this theory. . . . Having first practiced drawing for a while . . . take pains and pleasure in constantly copying the best things which you can find done by the hand of the great masters." Having established the importance of studying masterpieces, Cennini turned to nature: "Mind you, the most perfect steersman that you can have, and the best helm, lie in . . . copying from nature. And this outdoes all other models; and always rely on this with a stout heart, especially as you begin to gain some judgment in draftsmanship." To the Renaissance artist, copying from nature led not only to the heightened perception gained from meticulous obser-

217. BERNARDO ROSSELLINO
Tomb of Leonardo Bruni. c. 1445. Marble with traces of paint and gilding, height to top of arch 20'. Santa Croce, Florence

218. PIERO DELLA FRANCESCA
Duchess of Urbino; Duke of Urbino. 1465. Oil and tempera on wood, each 18 1/2 x 13". Uffizi Gallery, Florence. Federigo da Montefeltro, the patron, ruled as the duke of Urbino from 1444 until 1482. His duchess, Battista Sforza, bore Federigo eight daughters and one son. Federigo was a soldier and a prolific patron of artists and architects.

vation, but also to an attempt to understand the principles that govern the order and processes of nature. This sympathy with the natural world was a decisive aspect of Renaissance art.

Donatello's equestrian monument of *"Gattamelata"* (fig. 219) combines naturalistic observation with a well-known antique type, as exemplified by the *Marcus Aurelius* (see fig. 110). An ambitious feat of bronze casting, it was the largest sculpture cast in bronze since antiquity. With the bronze *David* (fig. 247), Donatello revived the lifesize, freestanding, nude figure. The acceptance of nudity in art is related to the humanist insistence on the dignity of the individual and the view that the human figure is a microcosm of the macrocosm, a smaller, symbolic reflection of the larger universe.

INTELLECTUAL AND SCIENTIFIC ACTIVITY

The Gutenberg Bible—the first book to be printed using independent, movable type—was made between 1450 and 1456. By 1460 woodcuts were being used for illustrations in books and, as a relatively inexpensive method of producing illustrated books in large quantity, they contributed to the development of the sciences. Knowledge was more easily shared when a printed illustration could offer an exactly repeatable image, unchanged by the hand of a copyist. Through the medium of printing, knowledge would reach a level of dissemination only recently overcome by modern media, including the computer.

PATRONAGE

During the fifteenth century, artists and workshops received a variety of secular and religious commissions, and both rulers and the new mercantile class viewed patronage as an important activity of the responsible and enlightened citizen. Devotional images, portraits, mythological subjects, and secular decorations were commissioned by individuals to adorn their family chapels, private palaces, or town houses. In Flanders it became common for donors and family mem-

219. DONATELLO
Equestrian Monument of Erasmo da Narni, called *"Gattamelata."* c. 1445–53. Bronze, originally with gilded details, height 12'2". Piazza del Santo, Padua. Erasmo da Narni was a famous mercenary general who was employed by the Venetian government to raise and lead its armies; his nickname means honeyed cat.

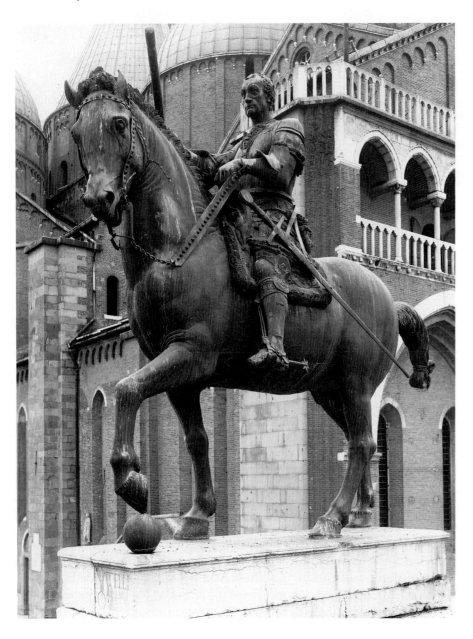

bers to be represented in the wings or at the sides of works they commissioned (see fig. 226).

In Florence, Cosimo de' Medici was generous in his support of libraries. He took an avid interest in the art of Donatello, and his patronage of scholars supported the formulation of Neoplatonism, a humanistic philosophy which sought to fuse Plato's ideals with Christian thinking. Cosimo's grandson, Lorenzo the Magnificent, collected antique works of art and encouraged commissions for Florentine artists; he was also a friend and supporter of the young Michelangelo. Such involvement with the arts was not solely altruistic, for support of humanist scholarship and the arts demonstrated benevolence and was useful in forming public opinion and securing fame. Moreover, given the political intrigue and conflict of the time, it was an advantage for rulers to surround themselves with intellectuals as advisers.

Rulers were often commemorated in portraits. Piero della Francesca gave his patrons, the duke and duchess of Urbino (fig. 218), an almost omnipotent presence. They seem elevated above everyday affairs, and the broad landscape backgrounds suggest the extent of ducal power. On the reverse they are shown on triumphal carts surrounded by virtues. The use of allegory is thus combined with the commitment to naturalism so apparent in the unidealized representation of Federigo's profile, which was disfigured in a tournament.

220. JAN VAN EYCK
Self-Portrait. 1433. Oil on wood, 10 1/4 x 7 1/2". National Gallery, London

THE FIFTEENTH-CENTURY ARTIST

The new self-consciousness that can be perceived in fifteenth-century society had an important influence on attitudes about artists. In contrast to the prevalent medieval attitude that the artist was a humble craftsperson serving God, the Renaissance artist was viewed as a trained intellectual, versed in the classics and geometry. Artists became famous; in 1481 Cristoforo Landino listed some Italian and Flemish artists, praising them for their skill and innovations, and suggested that Donatello could be "counted among" the ancient masters—the highest praise possible at the time. Artists began to sign their works with more frequency, and one artist, Lorenzo Ghiberti, wrote his autobiography.

During the first half of the fifteenth century, Flemish and Italian artists began to create self-portraits, a sure indication of their new status. In 1433 Jan van Eyck depicted himself wearing a fantastic turban—a tour de force of painting—and looking out at us with a penetrating gaze (fig. 220). On the frame are Van Eyck's motto (The best I can do) and the date. Artists even began to include self-portraits within their works. Lorenzo Ghiberti's *"Gates of Paradise"* (fig. 237) have both a self-portrait (fig. 221) and a Latin inscription that praises the "marvelous art" with which Ghiberti made the work. The new dignity accorded the artist in the fifteenth century is a foundation upon which the later conception of the artist as an inspired genius is based.

221. LORENZO GHIBERTI
Self-Portrait, from the *East Doors of the Baptistery* (see fig. 237). 1425–52. Gilded bronze, approx. height 3". Baptistery, Florence

EARLY RENAISSANCE SCULPTURE IN FLORENCE

222. DONATELLO
St. Mark. c. 1411–15. Marble, originally with limited polychromy and metal details, height 94". Formerly on Orsanmichele, Florence. This statue of the Evangelist was commissioned by the Guild of Linen Weavers and Peddlers, a trade guild, for their niche, one of fourteen niches assigned to the Florentine guilds on the civic shrine of Orsanmichele. The figure is shown in its original Gothic setting.

Donatello's *St. Mark* (fig. 222) overlooked a Florentine street, surveying the urban scene. His expression conveys a questioning intelligence. It is reported that when Michelangelo saw the work, he proclaimed "that he had never seen a figure which had more the air of a good man than this one, and that if St. Mark were such a man, one could believe what he had written." In other words, for Michelangelo the *St. Mark* expressed integrity. In medieval art the Evangelists had been depicted as figures receiving divine inspiration (see figs. 171, 172). Donatello's Renaissance interpretation emphasizes the more human attributes of wisdom and reason. In addition, Donatello's *St. Mark* attains the dignity we accord an individual, for in physiognomy and body type he suggests a specific, compelling personality. The revival of antiquity, so important for the Italian Renaissance, is readily apparent, for *St. Mark* is closer to ancient Greek and Roman figures than any figure created during the long interval of the Middle Ages. The emphatic *contrapposto* of the saint, which helps establish his naturalism,

DONATELLO, *St. Mark:* **c. 1411–15**
1394–97: Manuel Chrysoloras teaches Greek in Florence
1405: Florence buys Pisa
1410: Ptolemy's *Geography* is translated into Latin
1415: Jan Hus is burned at the stake for heresy

was influenced by ancient examples (see fig. 78).

The *Four Saints* by Nanni di Banco (fig. 223) on the same civic structure represent Christian stonecarvers who, during the late Roman Empire, were put to death when they refused to make a pagan idol. Their serious demeanor and the open mouth and oratorical gesture of the figure on the right suggest that Nanni has depicted the moment in their legend when they debate whether to compromise their religious beliefs or submit to death. Nanni's inspiration from ancient Roman models is obvious in the heads, one of which has a stubbly beard, and in the drapery folds of the togas. While such an interest is consistent with Renaissance attitudes, Nanni's antique references could also be viewed as part of his effort to establish historical veracity. What could be more appropriate than to emulate ancient Roman models when creating representations of figures who had lived in the late antique period? The new Renaissance respect for historical accuracy may have played a role in the conception of Nanni's group.

223. NANNI DI BANCO
Four Saints. c. 1410s. Marble, height 72". Orsanmichele, Florence. This grouping of four saints was commissioned by the Guild of Sculptors and Stone Masons for their niche at Orsanmichele.

THE LIMBOURG BROTHERS, *TRÈS RICHES HEURES DU DUC DE BERRY*

224. THE LIMBOURG BROTHERS *February*, calendar page from the *Très Riches Heures du Duc de Berry.* Before 1416. Manuscript painting on vellum, 11 3/8 x 8 1/4". Musée Condé, Chantilly, France. This manuscript is listed in an early inventory as "The Very Rich Hours of the Duke of Berry." The patron was John, duke of Berry (and brother of King Charles V of France), whose library included more than three hundred manuscripts. The artists were three brothers—Pol, Herman, and Jean Limbourg. The calendar pages, which traditionally accompany the listing of saints' feast days, include the labor of the month and zodiac signs with various astrological calculations.

The puff of frosty breath from the mouth of the figure hurrying across the farmyard and the smoke curling from the chimney are the kinds of subtle details that characterize the comprehensive realism developing in Flemish painting at the beginning of the fifteenth century (fig. 224). The traditional labor represented for February was a man cutting wood, but the Limbourg brothers' representation encompasses a modest farm, complete with dovecote, beehives, and sheepfold, set within a vast snowy landscape with a distant village. Several figures reveal the peasants' restricted winter activities. The sky is no longer merely

LIMBOURG BROTHERS, *February,* **from the** *Très Riches Heures:*
before 1416
1417: Movable type is used by printers at Antwerp

225. THE LIMBOURG BROTHERS
Crucifixion in the Darkness of the Eclipse, from the *Très Riches Heures.* Before 1416. Manuscript painting on vellum, 11 3/8 x 8 1/4". Musée Condé, Chantilly, France

a flat blue background, but offers atmospheric mid-winter effects that reveal the Limbourgs' study of natural phenomena.

The Limbourgs' attention to naturalistic effects also extends to biblical stories. Taking inspiration from the passage in Matthew's Gospel that, at the time of Christ's crucifixion, "there was darkness over all the land" (27:45), they created a panoramic crucifixion scene in tones of gray that suggest the naturalistic effects of an eclipse (fig. 225). In a blaze of gold, blue, and red, God the Father appears to bless his dying son. In the top right rondel, an astronomer surveys the heavens, searching for an explanation for this unexpected phenomenon.

The *Très Riches Heures* marks a final phase in the development of manuscript painting in the North. This sumptuous manuscript, with one hundred thirty illustrations, includes devotions for different periods of the day (a book of hours). The heightened interest in representing naturalistic lighting effects, panoramic landscapes, and precise details explains why this manuscript has been so admired and its compositions so often copied by later artists.

ROBERT CAMPIN, *THE ANNUNCIATION*

226. ROBERT CAMPIN

The Annunciation with Donors; St. Joseph in His Workshop. c. 1425–30. Oil on wood, 25 1/4 x 24 7/8" (center); 25 1/4 x 10 3/4" (each wing). The Metropolitan Museum of Art, New York (The Cloisters Collection). The patron who commissioned this work is represented kneeling in the left wing; his wife, beside him, has been painted over the green grass, suggesting that she was added after the picture was finished, probably at the time of their marriage. It was perhaps at this same time that Campin made the work even more realistic by painting over the gold leaf that had originally filled the central windows, substituting sky, clouds, and coats of arms in stained-glass windows that indicate the patron was a member of the Ingel-brechts family. This work is often referred to as the *Mérode Altarpiece* because it was owned by the Mérode family during the nineteenth century. Robert Campin is sometimes known as the Master of Flémalle.

This folding triptych (three-part altarpiece or devotional picture; fig. 226) represents a further development of the revolutionary new qualities evident in Flemish manuscript painting at the beginning of the fifteenth century (see figs. 224, 225). Perhaps most startling is the precision with which objects and figures are rendered. Naturally lit, they are modeled with subtle transitions from light to shadow that make them seem three-dimensional and weighty. This naturalism results from the union of the fine detail of oil paint with a revolu-tionary precision of observation on the part of the artist (see p. 240). It almost seems as if no artist had ever seen shadows with such clarity before—cer-tainly no artist had ever rendered them so precisely. Such natu-ralism demands intense concen-tration in both vision and tech-nique.

Accompanying this natural-ism of representation is the real-istic depiction of the subject, for a biblical event from the distant past is set in a fifteenth-century Flemish house. Gabriel enters to announce to a distinctly Flemish Mary that she will be the mother of the Son of God, while Mary's husband, Joseph, a carpenter, is shown in a fifteenth-century workshop in the right wing. Campin's depiction of this set-ting offers valuable evidence about woodworkers' shops and tools, including a folding shelf on which Joseph offers a mouse-trap for sale directly from his shop. As secular as this may seem, locating the Annunciation within a contemporary setting is intended to make the sacred events more comprehensible and meaningful. Such an approach to religious iconography is paralleled in popular devotional literature and is probably also related to the representation of such subjects in contemporary religious theater.

To understand Campin's interpretation, we must look beyond the dazzling surface realism, since a pervasive symbolism (sometimes called hidden symbolism) gives a religious content to virtually every object in the painting. The three lilies on a single stalk that decorate the Virgin's table, for example, refer to the Christian Trinity; the bud is Christ. An especially intriguing symbol is Joseph's mousetrap, for it expresses the late medieval notion that God married the Virgin to a devout older man to prevent the Devil from discovering that her child was the Son of God; in such an explanation Joseph became a "mousetrap" set by God.

The candle on the Virgin's table (fig. 227), just extinguished, releases a puff of smoke that suggests that the painting represents a precise moment in time. Light is a common metaphor for divinity, and the light of the Virgin's candle is extinguished because of the entry into the room (and into the world) of divine light in the person of Christ, who appears as a minuscule baby entering on rays of light through a round window on the left. The candle might also refer to the late medieval custom of the bridal candle, which was extinguished when the marriage was consummated. The blowing out of the candle and the presence of Christ within the Virgin's chamber would then express the moment of the Incarnation. Notice that this religious content is expressed by everyday objects and that, in

keeping with his naturalistic bias, Campin has not used haloes for his figures.

Robert Campin's style is known from a small number of paintings, all of which are similar in their use of ordinary people as models, their depiction of drapery with sharp, rather abstract folds, and their crowded compositions which avoid empty spaces (*horror vacui*). There was a revolution in 1423 in Tournai, where Campin lived, and a new democratic government, led by representatives of the craft guilds, was established. This democratic, mercantile culture certainly helps to explain the middle-class setting and virtues of Campin's *Annunciation* triptych, with its delight in a typical household and the inclusion of Joseph as a hardworking husband and father.

CAMPIN, *The Annunciation:* **c. 1425–30**
1422: England resumes war with France
1427: Thomas à Kempis, *The Imitation of Christ*

227. ROBERT CAMPIN
The Annunciation (detail)

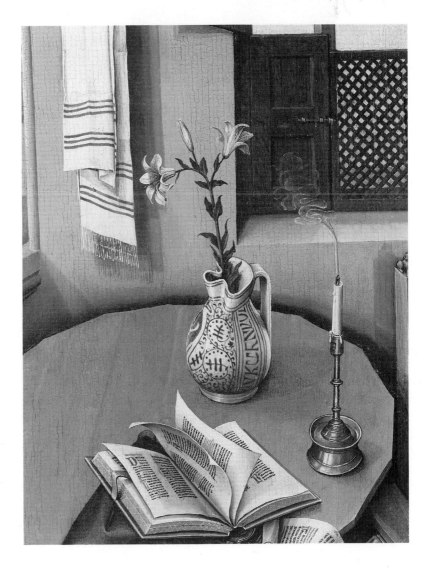

EARLY RENAISSANCE PAINTING: MASACCIO

The triangle, symbol of the Trinity, becomes the unifying compositional form in Masaccio's *Trinity*, with the head of God the Father forming the apex and the donors comprising the base (fig. 228). The triangular composition, popular in the Early Renaissance, is also visually clear and easy to read. This clarity is supported by the illusionary space created by the use of scientific perspective (see pp. 232–33). To the viewer positioned in front of the painting, the effect is of an actual chapel with real figures. The architectural forms are closely related to the Renaissance architecture being developed by Filippo Brunelleschi at this time (see p. 242). He may well have assisted Masaccio with this aspect of the painting. The clarity of the composition is combined with boldly three-dimensional figures recalling those painted by Giotto.

Masaccio here has advanced the innovations of Giotto by combining them with the coherent illusory space which distinguishes Renaissance painting.

A short time before he was commissioned to paint *The Trinity*, Masaccio was employed with another artist, Masolino, in decorating the Brancacci Chapel with scenes primarily from the life of St. Peter. In *The Tribute Money* (Matthew 17:24–27), Christ and

229, 230. MASACCIO

The Expulsion of Adam and Eve from Paradise; The Tribute Money. c. 1427. Fresco, height 96". Brancacci Chapel, Santa Maria del Carmine, Florence. These scenes are found in the middle register of the chapel. It is possible that the head of Christ in *The Tribute Money* was painted by Masaccio's collaborator, Masolino. The theme of the Tribute Money is rare in Christian art. Its appearance here may be related to a Florentine tax on wealth levied during the 1420s.

his apostles are confronted by a tax collector who requests that a temple tax be paid (fig. 230). Christ instructs Peter to go to the edge of Lake Galilee, to our left, where he finds the necessary coin of tribute in the mouth of a fish. To the right, Peter pays the tax collector, an act prophetic of Christ's words, "Pay to the emperor what belongs to him, and pay to God what belongs to God." Because three different episodes take place within the unified space of the composition, *The Tribute Money* exemplifies continuous narration, a thematic device which had been used in ancient Roman painting and sculpture (see fig. 113).

The perspective of *The Tribute Money* contributes to a unity of organization, while the boldly modeled figures reveal a light source that corresponds to the real light that falls into the chapel from its single window. The building at the right, which obeys the laws of scientific perspective, draws our attention to the head of Christ, while atmospheric perspective envelops the trees and hills of the background. Within the logic of this spatial illusionism, Masaccio's figures act out the story with simple, direct, and dignified movements.

Masaccio's sculpturesque modeling and bold figurative presentation are especially evident in *The Expulsion of Adam and Eve* (fig. 229). Having disobeyed God, Adam and Eve are driven by guilt and shame. In Masaccio's interpretation, Adam hides his face in his hands, leaving his genitals uncovered. Masaccio thus emphasizes the psychological rather than the physical nature of Adam's shame. The figure of Eve, which was inspired by an ancient sculpture of the Modest Venus, conceals her nakedness, but throws her head back in a moan as she bewails their fate.

Masaccio's figures, instilled with psychological presence, recall the human gravity of Donatello's sculpture, while the classicizing architecture and use of scientific perspective reveal his relationship with Brunelleschi. Although he died in his twenties, Masaccio translated into paint the Renaissance innovations of Donatello and Brunelleschi, and he influenced later generations of Renaissance artists, including Michelangelo. An epitaph, composed in the sixteenth century, recognized Masaccio's contribution: "I painted, and my picture was lifelike; I gave my figures movement, passion, soul: they breathed" (Annibale Caro, as cited in Vasari's *Life of Masaccio*).

SCIENTIFIC PERSPECTIVE

Uccello's *Perspective Drawing* is a virtuoso rendering of a geometricized chalice which is at least partially transparent (fig. 231). The geometricized rings at the top and base are derived from Uccello's studies of a wire- or wicker-frame construction (*mazzocchio*) that was wrapped with cloth to create a type of male headgear popular in the fifteenth century. Perhaps it was the faceting of the skeletal structure of this headdress which led Uccello to study the chalice with a similar geometric, linear emphasis.

The study of perspective, the rendering of figures or objects in illusory space, was an important innovation in Renaissance art. Perspective had been a conscious development in ancient Greek painting, and many examples of Roman art attest to the accomplished use of perspective in antiquity. During the Middle Ages, however, the pictorial reproduction of the physical world became less significant within a culture that emphasized spiritual and otherworldly values. Perspective gradually became valued in the later Middle Ages, but a coherent system allowing artists to determine the relative diminution of size of figures and objects was lacking.

That problem was solved by Filippo Brunelleschi, the Early Renaissance architect (see p. 242). Around 1415 Brunelleschi demonstrated a scientific perspective system (also called linear and vanishing-point perspective) in two lost panels. His new perspective system was incorporated in works by other artists, including Donatello's *Feast of Herod* (fig. 232).

Within the complex architectural

231. PAOLO UCCELLO

Perspective Drawing of a Geometricized Chalice with Mazzocchi. c. 1430–40. Pen and ink on paper, 13 3/8 x 9 1/2". Gabinetto dei Disegni, Uffizi Gallery, Florence. Vasari tells us that Uccello delighted in making such complex studies, and that he would often work late into the night, "seeking to solve the problems of perspective." When called to bed by his wife, Uccello would reply, "Oh, what a sweet thing is this perspective!"

232. DONATELLO

Feast of Herod, from the Siena baptismal font. c.1425. Gilded bronze, 23 1/2" square. Baptistery, Siena. Donatello uses continuous narration to depict the story of the beheading of John the Baptist. Within the distant arch in the left background, the just-severed head is given to a servant, while in the left foreground it is presented to Herod, who recoils in horror. In the right foreground, Salome still sways with the rhythms of her dance.

233. Diagram of the orthogonals of the perspective scheme of Donatello's *Feast of Herod*

structure of the *Feast of Herod*, Donatello narrates the dramatic events surrounding the beheading of St. John the Baptist. His use of scientific perspective assists in visually unifying these events. The diagonal lines created by the recession of architectural elements parallel to each other, such as those of the floor in the foreground, converge at a vanishing point. The convergence of these diagonal lines, which are called orthogonals, helps Donatello determine the exact diminution of figures and architecture (fig. 233).

Scientific perspective is based on the assumption that parallel lines receding from us seem to converge at a point on the horizon. This is the basis for the meeting of the orthogonals at the vanishing point. Scientific perspective also assumes that the diminution in size of objects is in direct proportion to their distance from us, and that space is, therefore, quantifiably measurable.

What Brunelleschi arrived at through empirical study, Alberti stated with theoretical reasoning in his book *On Painting*. By construct-

ing orthogonal lines crossed by transversals (lines which recede parallel to the picture plane) on the planar surface of a painting or relief, a receding modular grid pattern is created. This pattern establishes a coherent, mathematically measurable illusory space within which the artist can determine the proportional diminution of objects distant from the viewer. Brunelleschi's system was widely used by such Renaissance artists as Ghiberti, Perugino, and Leonardo (see figs. 236, 4, and 268).

HUBERT AND JAN VAN EYCK, *THE ALTARPIECE OF THE LAMB*

234. HUBERT AND JAN VAN EYCK

The Altarpiece of the Lamb (interior). Completed 1432. Oil on wood, 11' 5 3/4" x 15' 1 1/2". Cathedral of St. Bavo, Ghent. This work is also known as the *Ghent Altarpiece*. An inscription on the frame identifies the patron as Jodocus Vijd, the date of completion as 1432, and the painters as Hubert and Jan van Eyck. Hubert died before September 18, 1426, and the role each brother played in the conception and execution of the many panels has been much debated. Scholars today generally agree that the altarpiece includes a number of works by Hubert, some of which may have been left unfinished at his death, which Jan combined into a totality, adding works conceived by Jan (in particular, the figures of Adam and Eve) to complete the altarpiece. This would explain the juxtapositions in figural scale between the parts of the altarpiece. The luminous technique and fine detail are considered to be the work of Jan, who by the sixteenth century had been credited with the invention of oil painting.

The iconography is complex. The lower panels represent the Triumph of the Lamb of God, with crowds of saints pressing inward to worship the symbolic lamb on the altar. The upper panels include God the Father in the center flanked by the Virgin Mary and St. John the Baptist, musical angels, and Adam and Eve. Above Adam and Eve are small *grisaille* scenes of the story of Cain and Abel.

Adam and Eve were among the few subjects that permitted Northern artists to represent the nude, but Jan's virtually lifesize figures are unprecedented. Jan's commitment to realism here confronts traditional restrictions, for while the figure of Adam is clearly based on a nude model (notice the sunburned face, neck, and hands), Eve is an imaginative re-creation based on contemporary ideals rather than on observation of a live model. The small, high breasts and bulbous abdomen are Gothic stylizations. The emphasis on the large abdomen stresses the role of childbearer assigned to women in the fifteenth century.

In scale and wealth of detail, this large, hinged polyptych (multi-paneled altarpiece) is an overwhelming accomplishment—the work of years—and the most impressive of all early Flemish paintings (figs. 234, 235). The diverse scale and size of the panels and the variety of subjects represented allowed the Van Eycks to paint Flemish interiors, vast landscapes, illusionistic sculpture, portraits of living donors, the male and female nude, elaborate brocades, bejeweled and gold embroidered borders, and musical instruments. Jan van Eyck's ability to re-create the visual world in oil paint is staggering, but among the wealth of details offered by the *Ghent Altarpiece*, the most unforgettable may be the artist's self-portrait in the studio, which is reflected in one of the innumerable pearls in the papal crown worn by God the Father, the central figure of the interior. This tour de force of painting is one of several "reflected" self-portraits found in the work of Jan van Eyck (see also fig. 240). Jan's pride in his accomplishments is also evident in his *Self-Portrait* (fig. 220), one of the first independent self-portraits in the history of art.

Jan van Eyck's ability to represent textures as if they were real is based on his acute examination of light and how it reacts differently when it strikes and reflects from various surfaces. He composed his paintings to emphasize this, juxtaposing materials to contrast textures and heighten his illusion. Jan van Eyck's figures seldom express strong or dramatic emotions. The wonder that his paintings generate comes from his ability to observe reality and to convey in oil paints the excitement of vision.

235. HUBERT AND JAN VAN EYCK
The Altarpiece of the Lamb (exterior). Oil on wood, 11' 5 3/4" x 7' 6 3/4". The donors of the altarpiece, Jodocus Vijd and Isabel Borluut, are shown in the lower panels, kneeling before Sts. John the Baptist and John the Evangelist. In the upper register is a scene of the Annunciation; the topmost panels show representations of the Old Testament prophets Zachariah and Micah and two pagan sibyls.

LORENZO GHIBERTI, *EAST DOORS OF THE BAPTISTERY*

236. LORENZO GHIBERTI
The Story of Jacob and Esau, from the *East Doors of the Baptistery.* c. 1429–37. Gilded bronze, 31 1/4" square. Baptistery, Florence. The story of Jacob and Esau, from the Old Testament book of Genesis (25:19 through 28:5), tells how Jacob and his mother, Rebecca, contrived to steal the birthright of Jacob's twin brother, Esau, by deceiving the boys' father, the old and nearly blind Isaac. In Ghiberti's representation, the scene of the arranged blessing of Jacob is shown at the right, with Rebecca looking on, while the central figures represent the moment when Isaac and Esau discover the deception.

Ghiberti represents the story of Jacob and Esau with grand, classicizing architecture and graceful figures gathered into beautiful groupings (fig. 236). His ideal and orderly Renaissance world makes no reference to the treachery and emotional trauma inherent in the Old Testament narrative. Ghiberti chose to subordinate these unpleasant realities to his Renaissance interest in harmony. The fifteenth-century concern for fine detail and exquisite finish is obvious in every area of the relief, from the delicate Corinthian capitals of the loggia to the shaggy fur of Esau's dogs in the foreground. The regular recession of the Brunelleschian scientific perspective (see pp. 232–33) and the subtle diminution in the height of the relief, from the virtually three-dimensional figures of the left foreground to the low relief figure of Rebecca praying in the upper right corner, create a convincing and controlled illusion. The four female figures in the left foreground, who pose with such exquisite grace, play no role in advancing the narrative and have been added by Ghiberti to enhance the beauty of the work of art.

In his autobiography Ghiberti states that when he was offered the commission for the doors (fig. 237), "I was given a free hand to execute it in whatever way I thought would turn out most perfect and most ornate and richest." In this he seems to be following the precepts of the theorist Leon Battista Alberti, who, in *On Painting,* had defined the qualities of the perfect narrative painting (*istoria* or *historia*) in the following manner: "The first thing that gives pleasure in a '*historia*' is a plentiful variety. Just as with

237. LORENZO GHIBERTI

*East Doors of the Baptistery (*also known as the *"Gates of Paradise").* 1425–52. Bronze and gilded bronze, 18' 6" x 12'. Ghiberti's doors are the last of three sets of doors made for the portals of the Florentine Baptistery. His themes are drawn from the Old Testament. The doors were commissioned in 1425 and erected in 1452. The creation of wax models for the ten narratives has been dated 1429 to 1437, and the finishing of the details consumed most of the 1440s. Ghiberti employed a large workshop of assistants and apprentices to help him with the doors, which were by far the most expensive sculptural work produced in Florence during the fifteenth century. Most of the individual panels represent several scenes of a continuous narrative within a single architectural or landscape setting. For Ghiberti's self-portrait on the doors and a reference to the Latin inscription, see p. 223. The area between a baptistery and a cathedral was popularly known as the *paradiso,* which helps to explain the name attributed to Michelangelo, who supposedly said that Ghiberti's doors were worthy to serve as the "Gates of Paradise."

food and music, novel and extraordinary things delight us for various reasons but especially because they are different from the old ones we are used to, so with everything the mind takes great pleasure in variety and abundance.... I would say a picture was richly varied if it contained a properly arranged mixture of old men, youths, boys, matrons, maidens, children, domestic animals, dogs, birds, horses, sheep, buildings and provinces."

JAN VAN EYCK, *THE ARNOLFINI WEDDING PORTRAIT*

Giovanni and Giovanna, represented being married in a room in their home, are witnessed by the two required officials, seen reflected in the mirror on the back wall (figs. 238, 240). One of these is the great Flemish painter Jan van Eyck, as revealed by his florid Gothic signature above the mirror, "Jan van Eyck was here, 1434."

The single candle in the chandelier, which is lit despite the brightness of the day, is a symbol that expresses the divine presence of Christ, who oversees the sacrament of marriage. The bride and groom wear elegant and, to our eyes, exotic costumes. His huge hat and fur-trimmed cape reveal his wealth, as do the yards and yards of material in the bride's train, which she elegantly holds up in a pose which emphasizes her abdomen and stresses the idea that she will soon be ready to bear children. Her hair is forced into nets to create the fashionable "horns" of the period, and her headcovering is trimmed with elaborate ruffles of material. Both figures have covered their heads as a sign of respect and sanctity, for while the sacrament of marriage is taking place, their bedchamber has become a sacred place. For the same reason they have taken off their shoes, following the example of Moses, who removed his sandals when he met God in the burning bush on Mount Sinai (Exodus 3:1–10).

Jan van Eyck's composition is simple and symmetrical, stressing the individuality of the two figures and, in the joined hands on the central axis, their incipient union. Art-historical investigation has determined that the symbolism of the objects in the painting amplifies its meaning: the clear glass beads hanging on the wall and the fruit near the window refer to the bride's purity, while St. Margaret, represented in the statuette near the bed, is here as the patron saint of women in childbirth. The dog (fig. 241) offers mixed messages, for it can be interpreted as a symbol of marital fidelity or an emblem of erotic desire; that it is symbolic and not an actual possession is suggested by the fact that it is not reflected in the mirror.

There is no similar wedding portrait in all of Italian or Flemish fifteenth-century painting, and why the patrons commissioned the work is unknown. One theory proposes that since the groom is holding the bride's right hand in his left, this was a left-handed or morganatic marriage, in which the bride was of inferior social status. Van Eyck's panel certainly functions as a visual document, in the legal sense, of this particular contract. But Van Eyck might also be representing Arnolfini in the midst of saying the oath, ready to join his right hand to the bride's to seal a normal contract. Whatever the motivation, the desire of this couple to record their vows has given them immortality.

238. JAN VAN EYCK
Wedding Portrait of Giovanni Arnolfini and Giovanna Cenami. 1434. Oil on wood, 32 1/4 x 23 1/2". National Gallery, London. The figures are identified in an early inventory that also reveals that the frame, now lost, was decorated with verses from the writings of the ancient Roman poet Ovid. Giovanni Arnolfini was a wealthy Italian businessman who lived in Flanders.

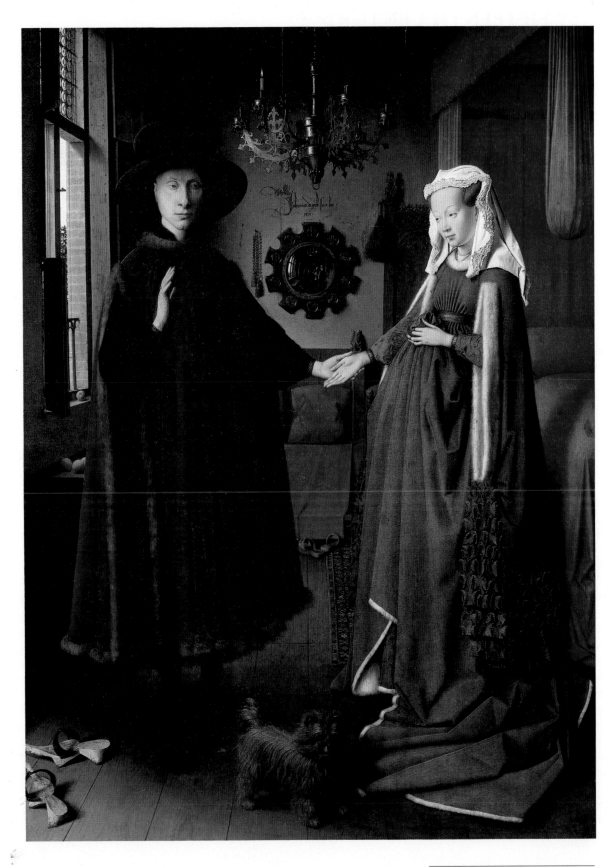

THE DEVELOPMENT OF THE OIL TECHNIQUE IN FLANDERS, EARLY FIFTEENTH CENTURY

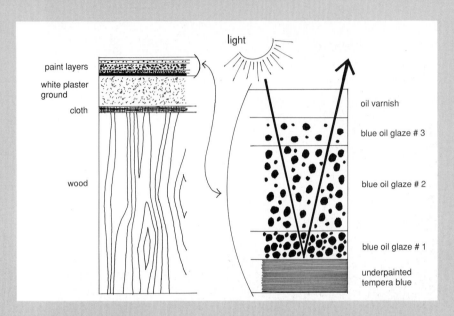

239. Schematic diagram of a section of a Flemish fifteenth-century oil painting, demonstrating the luminosity of the medium. The arrow suggests the manner in which light can penetrate the translucent oil glazes.

The details from Jan van Eyck's *Arnolfini Wedding* display impressive virtuosity (figs. 240, 241). The contrasting textures of the various materials are convincingly illusionistic. Such precise detail is made possible not only by the artist's acute perception, but by the development of oil paint as a primary vehicle, a step which revolutionized Flemish painting in the early years of the fifteenth century.

None of the materials used here are new. A traditional wooden panel covered with a layer of cloth and a fine layer of white plaster functioned as a support. Van Eyck probably explored compositional ideas by drawing on the plaster with charcoal and "erasing" unsuccessful designs with a feather. He would then have reinforced a satisfactory composition with fine lines created with a brush dipped into tempera paint. The pigments used to create the color are the same powdered materials used

by artists working in tempera (see p. 211). Oil as a drying vehicle had been known and used since ancient times. During the medieval period, oil was the final layer given a tempera painting to create a luminous surface finish. Here it is used as the primary vehicle.

Oil is a translucent vehicle; the suspension of the particles of powdered pigment in a translucent vehicle is shown in the diagram of a section of a Flemish panel painting (fig. 239). When it is applied in many thin layers (glazes), light will penetrate the layers and be reflected, creating a gemlike brilliance of color. This new resonant richness makes Flemish oil paintings such as those of Van Eyck and Campin distinctly different in appearance from their tempera antecedents.

Oil dries more slowly than tempera and its speed of drying can be further slowed by adding turpentine, permitting the artist to blend

colors to create the subtle tonal modulations that help suggest light falling on an object. Van Eyck's fine detail is accomplished by using oil and soft, fine brushes, and the resulting imperceptible transitions from color to color and the smooth surface finish offer virtually no hint of the artist's brushstrokes.

The greater resonance of color and the new realism of Flemish paintings are also due to the changed color palette. In tempera painting a particular hue, such as red, would be mixed with white to achieve the transitions from shadow (red) to highlight (white). In the oil technique, the same red would usually be mixed with black to accomplish the change from highlight (red) to shadow (black). In tempera paintings, then, colors are modeled upward toward white, while in oil paintings most colors are modeled downward toward black. The greatest intensity of a hue in tempera painting is in the shadows, while in oil it occurs between shadow and highlight. Most importantly, the scheme used in oil paintings is closer to what we observe in reality. Flemish painters learned this laborious craft as apprentices. Only years of watching and practice could prepare a young artist for a career working in such a painstaking and methodical technique. The results

of their fine and patient craftsmanship are evident in the superb condition of many of these paintings
today.

To learn how to paint like Campin
and Van Eyck took more than technical skill, however, for the artist
had to learn how to see—how to
distinguish the distinct patterns of
light and shadow observable on such
different surfaces as velvet, wood,
brass, and glass in various lighting
conditions. In the work of these two
artists, the precision of depiction is
intimately related to the fact that all
these objects are mirrors of religious
truths. A candle is not just a candle
and a triple lily is more than a floral
oddity. Like other techniques, the
development of the fine oil technique of the Flemish masters was a
response to a distinct need: they
created a technique which would
allow them to endow objects with a
magical potency—a dazzling realism—that could suggest the deeper
meanings that lie behind observation. Their new style is rooted in the
complexities of medieval symbolism and theology, but it contains a
seed of the new Renaissance concern with the individual and the
world. It is no surprise that the motto
of Jan van Eyck, painted on the frame
of his *Self-Portrait* (fig. 220), is "Als
ich can" (The best I can do).

240, 241. JAN VAN EYCK
The Arnolfini Wedding Portrait (details)

EARLY RENAISSANCE ARCHITECTURE BY FILIPPO BRUNELLESCHI

242. FILIPPO BRUNELLESCHI
Nave, Church of Santo Spirito, Florence. Begun 1436. In this view, we are looking toward the crossing and high altar; the elaborate canopy over the altar is a later, obtrusive addition.

243. FILIPPO BRUNELLESCHI
Plan, Church of Santo Spirito

The interior of Santo Spirito (fig. 242) provides a conspicuous contrast to Gothic architecture, which overwhelms us with its towering vertical emphasis (see fig. 196). In Brunelleschi's Renaissance church, on the other hand, we perceive a measured order and harmony. Here the human reason of the architect and faith in a rational God and universe create architecture that is an alternative to the spiritual striving of the Gothic.

The satisfying regularity of Santo Spirito is derived from the use of simple proportional schemes similar to those used in ancient Greek and Roman architecture. The plan (fig. 243) makes it clear that each of the square bays of the aisle or the ambulatory can be understood as a basic module. With this in mind, it can be demonstrated that the relationships which govern the interior design of Santo Spirito are few and simple: 1:1, 1:2, 1:4, and 1:8. The square crossing, under the dome, is four times as large in area as the basic module, as are the altar and transept areas that surround it (1:4). The nave is twice as wide as the module (1:2). An elevation or a view inside the church reveals how this proportional system continues in the three-dimensional structure. The bays of the aisles and ambulatory are four times as tall as they are wide (1:4), and the nave is twice as tall as the aisles and ambulatory (1:8). The nave is composed of an arcade (a series of arches supported by columns or piers) and of the clerestory above it. Each of these elements is as high as the nave is wide. This proportional approach is combined with the use of capitals based on ancient models and round arches. The result is an architecture which revives both the principles and the forms of classical antiquity. The regular placement of windows and the avoidance of both the stained-glass windows of the French Gothic and the frescoes of the Italian Gothic tradition mean that the rational order of Brunelleschi's church is well illuminated and clear, free of shadows and mysterious height.

Brunelleschi secured his fame as an architect and engineer by designing the enormous dome for the Cathedral in Florence and engineering its construction (fig. 244). The Cathedral of Florence, begun in 1296 to replace an earlier church, is a Gothic structure, but from its inception a dome over the crossing was intended. The difficulties of constructing such an immense dome, the largest in Europe since antiquity, were solved by Brunelleschi in the early fifteenth century by a design which was responsive to and harmonious with the original Gothic design. The pointed profile, with eight external ribs, is more Gothic than Renaissance, yet the eloquence of its grand

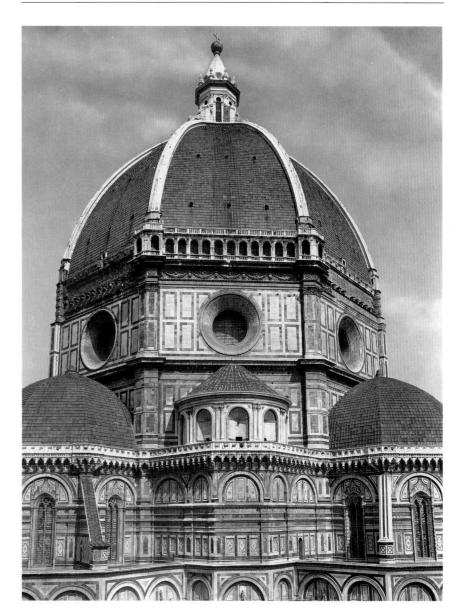

244. FILIPPO BRUNELLESCHI
Dome, Cathedral, Florence. 1420–36

scale and simple harmony express the clarity characteristic of the new Renaissance architecture. The cathedral dome was an architectural, engineering, and psychological feat. That so large a dome could be constructed without centering (see pp.126–27; Brunelleschi designed a self-supporting masonry system) was a technological achievement. In this joining of scale, design, and technology, the Florentine people found a source of civic as well as religious pride. Brunelleschi's dome continues to dominate the skyline of Florence, visual proof of a domineering spirit in the arts.

THE RENAISSANCE PALACE

245, 246. BRUNELLESCHI OR MICHELOZZO
Courtyard and exterior, Medici Palace, Florence. 1444–59. The illustration of the exterior shows the palace in an early print, before later extensions and changes. Unlike medieval castles, the Renaissance palazzo is found within the city, and its owner is less likely to be a hereditary noble than a self-made merchant or banker. Such palaces housed the entire family, including married children and grandchildren. The Medici, who were bankers, were among the richest families in Florence. In the course of the fifteenth century they gradually assumed control of the Florentine government.

The Medici Palace presents a departure in domestic architecture (figs. 245, 246). The centralized courtyard is decorated with a classical style arcade reminiscent of the atrium of an ancient Roman house (see fig. 103). In its references to antiquity and its lucid regularity, this courtyard reveals the new attitudes of the Renaissance. As a composition, the palace is a three-story masonry block, with regularly spaced windows and a large cornice which projects out from the roof. The rustication of the street-level story is gradually reduced on the upper two floors, and the heights of the floors are equally decreased. Lucid regularity is also demonstrated in the plan. It has been suggested that the regularity of the Medici Palace was inspired by the description of ancient Roman houses given by Vitruvius, the first century B.C. architect and theorist. The decoration of the palace included portrait busts of the Medici (see fig. 253), likewise based on ancient sculptural models.

Many of the paintings and sculptures in the Medici Palace had distinctive secular themes. The bedroom of Lorenzo de' Medici was decorated with panels by Uccello representing the Battle of San Romano, a victory credited to Niccolò da Tolentino, a friend and supporter of Cosimo de' Medici (see fig. 248). Tolentino died later in an accident perhaps arranged by Cosimo's enemies, and his victory at San Romano may have been commemorated at the palace in order to suggest that he was a Medici martyr.

Small bronze sculptures could be found throughout the palace. Pollaiuolo's powerful bronze statuette exemplifies an episode from the adventures of Hercules (fig. 249). Hercules was the mythological founder of Florence, and the use of the Hercules theme at the Medici Palace may have been a way of identifying the Medici with the city and its traditional founders and heroes. This also explains the presence of a statue of Donatello's *David* (fig. 247) in the Medici courtyard, for the youthful David was also a symbol of the city.

BRUNELLESCHI or MICHELOZZO, Courtyard, Medici Palace: 1444–59
1441: Africans are sold as slaves in the markets of Lisbon
1453: End of the Byzantine Empire

247. DONATELLO

Left: *David*. 1440s? Bronze with gilded details, height 62 1/4". Bargello, Florence. *David* is documented in the courtyard of the Medici Palace. Donatello's representation of the Old Testament hero is consistent with the biblical story (I Samuel 17:38–51). The broad shepherd's hat would have cast David's face into shadow, leaving his expression enigmatic. This is the first lifesize nude sculpture in the round since antiquity.

248. PAOLO UCCELLO

Below: *Niccolò da Tolentino Directing the Attack*, from a series of three paintings illustrating the Battle of San Romano. c. 1450s. Tempera and silver foil on wood, 5' 11 1/2" x 10' 6". National Gallery, London. Originally the three panels decorated the bedroom of Lorenzo the Magnificent. Their combined length was more than thirty-four feet.

249. ANTONIO DEL POLLAIUOLO

Above: *Hercules and Antaeus*. c. 1470s. Bronze, height 18". Bargello, Florence. Antaeus was the son of Mother Earth, and to defeat him, Hercules had to lift him, to separate him from his maternal source of power.

THE BEGINNINGS OF PORTRAITURE

250. ALESSO BALDOVINETTI
Portrait of a Young Woman. c. 1465.
Tempera on wood, 25 x 16".
National Gallery, London. The
elaborate hairstyle and high,
shaved forehead are typical of
Renaissance fashion. Among the
most expensive and elaborate parts
of a Renaissance woman's costume
were her detachable sleeves. In this
portrait the decoration on the
sleeves may be a reference to her
name or family.

**251. DOMENICO
GHIRLANDAIO**
Top right: *Portrait of a Man and a
Boy.* c. 1480. Tempera and oil on
wood, 24 3/8 x 18 1/8". The Louvre,
Paris. The artist has used the man's
disfiguring disease as an aesthetic
device, repeating similarly rounded
forms for the boy's curls and the
trees.

**252. DOMENICO
GHIRLANDAIO**
Above: *Portrait of a Man on His
Deathbed* c. 1480. Silverpoint and
point of the brush, heightened with
white on pink prepared paper,
11 5/8 x 12 5/8". Nationalmuseum,
Stockholm. This is a preparatory
drawing for fig. 251.

253. MINO DA FIESOLE

Portrait Bust of Piero de' Medici. 1453. Marble, height 18". Bargello, Florence. An inscription on the work identifies the artist, sitter, and date, as is common in male busts of this type.

BALDOVINETTI, *Portrait of a Young Woman:* **c. 1465**
1457: "Futeball" and "golfe" are forbidden by Scotland's Parliament
1464: Royal postal service is established in France

254. HANS MEMLINC

Madonna and Child (left wing); *Martin van Nieuwenhove* (right wing). 1487. Oil on wood, each 17 3/8 x 13". Hospital of St. John, Bruges. The inscriptions across the bottom date the work, identify the patron, and state that he was twenty-three years old. A merchant, Martin van Nieuwenhove later served as mayor of Bruges.

The silhouette or profile portrait (fig. 250) immediately reveals variations in individual physiognomy. Portraiture was revived in the fifteenth century, and Baldovinetti used the profile formula of the earliest Renaissance portraits. It was quickly superseded by three-quarter or full-view portraits and sculpted portraits. By the time of Leonardo da Vinci's *"Mona Lisa"* (see fig. 282), portraiture was a well-established subject, and it continued to provide an important means of support for artists until the advent of photography in the nineteenth century.

The precise function of the earliest portraits is not certain, and it is possible that Baldovinetti's sitter died young and the portrait was commissioned as a remembrance after her death. Such is certainly the case with the *Portrait of a Man and a Boy,* for Ghirlandaio's drawing made from the man's corpse survives (figs. 251, 252). The delicate and beautiful face of the child, unmarked by time, looks up with respect and love toward the old gentleman.

The sculpted, bust-length portrait became popular in the mid-fifteenth century in Florence, certainly partly in response to ancient Roman sculptural precedents. These were sometimes placed over the doorways of Renaissance palaces. The earliest surviving marble example represents a member of the Medici family, the richest and most politically important family in the city (fig. 253).

The simultaneous evolution of painted portraits in Flanders during the fifteenth century included a devotional type that represented an individual in an attitude of prayer with an image of the Madonna and Child (see fig. 254). These diptychs, which served as private devotional images, were hinged so they could travel easily and be self-supporting when opened. In Memlinc's example, the donor's natural three-quarter view contrasts with the frontal placement of the Madonna; the architectural setting suggests a Flemish room. The realistically depicted stained-glass window behind the donor represents St. Martin, the patron's name saint, and the donor's place in heaven seems assured by the inclusion of his coat of arms in the window behind the Madonna. The mirror, a symbol of virginity, reflects the foreground figures, confirming an intimate relationship between the real and sacred worlds.

ANDREA MANTEGNA, CAMERA PICTA, MANTUA

255. ANDREA MANTEGNA
Illusionistic balcony with women and *putti,* from the Camera Picta, Ducal Palace, Mantua. 1465–74. Fresco, diameter of balcony 60". This room is now popularly known by a later name, the Camera degli Sposi (Room of the Married Couple), in reference to the patron and his wife, who are shown seated in the fresco over the fireplace.

This dazzling and witty tour de force of illusionism proves the brilliance of both the artist, Andrea Mantegna, and his patron, Lodovico Gonzaga, duke of Mantua (figs. 255, 256). The magnificence of a Renaissance prince or princess was in part determined by the abilities of the artists at their humanist court. The painted illusion created by Mantegna and his workshop at the Ducal Palace in Mantua completely covers the vaulted ceiling and two walls. Most of the vault is painted with *grisaille* and gold decorative patterns in a classical style that simulate relief

decoration. This design emphasizes the ceiling's flat surface and serves as a foil for the central area, with its unexpected illusion of a circular opening with a balcony and a view up to the sky and clouds. The painted figures around the balustrade seem to interact with us and with each other, and a huge pot of plants,

256. ANDREA MANTEGNA
Camera Picta. Frescoes, wall with fireplace 19' 6" x 26' 6". The room is approximately 26' 6" square. The figures over the fireplace represent Mantegna's patron, Lodovico Gonzaga, duke of Mantua, with his family and retinue, and the scene to the left depicts a meeting between Cardinal Francesco Gonzaga and his father, Lodovico. The ceiling decoration has illusionistic insets with relief portraits of ancient Roman rulers. The side walls are painted with balustrades and pilasters.

precariously supported on a pole, threatens to fall into the room. This fictive space is populated with imaginary figures, baby angels derived from ancient Roman precedents and known in Italian art as *putti*. One is struggling, for he has caught his head in one of the round openings of the balustrade.

257. ANDREA MANTEGNA
A Foreshortened Christ. c. 1466. Tempera on canvas, 26 3/4 x 31 7/8". Brera Gallery, Milan. This painting, sometimes called *The Lamentation over the Dead Christ*, is almost certainly identical with the painting listed in Mantegna's house as *A Foreshortened Christ*. It may have been painted by the artist for his personal devotion.

FORESHORTENING

Mantegna's *putti* in the Camera Picta, represented as if seen from below, are rendered in a technique known as foreshortening. This involves representing a figure or object as if seen in sharp recession.

Mantegna's *Christ*, however, demonstrates how easily we accept an unrealistic representation (fig. 257). If we were to look at a corpse from this sharp angle, we would not see it as Mantegna painted it but with larger feet and a somewhat smaller head. Mantegna's treatment, however, serves to pull us into his composition and to fix our attention on Christ's wounds.

Dürer's woodcut (fig. 258) is less a demonstration of an actual technique used by artists than an illustration of the principles of foreshortening and how it can be studied (and illustrated in a book). The line of sight of the observer is represented by the cord fastened to the wall on the right. A piece of paper which can be swung aside has been placed in an upright frame. After the end of the cord is held on a place on the lute, the point where the cord passes through the frame is marked by the intersection of two movable threads. The paper is then swung back into place and the point transferred to the paper. The connect-the-dots diagram that results provides an accurate image of a lute seen in sharp foreshortening.

258. ALBRECHT DÜRER
Artist Drawing a Lute with the Help of a Mechanical Device. 1525. Woodcut, 5 1/8 x 7 1/4". This woodcut was designed as an illustration for Dürer's treatise *A Course in the Art of Measurement with Compass and Ruler*, published in Germany in 1525.

DRAWINGS BY LEONARDO DA VINCI

259. LEONARDO DA VINCI
Madonna and Child with Cat.
c. 1478–80. Pen and ink, 5 1/8 x
3 3/4". British Museum, London

260. LEONARDO DA VINCI
Drawing of a Flying Machine, from
the *Codex Atlanticus*. c. 1490. Pen
and ink. Biblioteca Ambrosiana,
Milan

Leonardo's pen-and-ink study of the *Madonna and Child* is a spontaneous, animated drawing in which Mary greets the Christ Child's attempt to embrace a struggling cat with tender approval (fig. 259). Quick and repetitive lines impart a pulsating energy to the theme. This rapidly executed design represents a revolutionary approach to the

use of preliminary compositional studies.

Previous to Leonardo, drawings by artists were often characterized by meticulous execution, not only because such precision was a part of the Early Renaissance aesthetic, but because they were done on such expensive surfaces as vellum. By the mid-fifteenth century, the availability

of cheap paper (a development in response to the demands of the new publishing industry) meant that drawing could become more common and more spontaneous. Leonardo was a decisive influence in developing the quick artist's sketch, which is so much a part of artists' work even today. He wrote: "You will first attempt in a drawing to give

LEONARDO DA VINCI, *Madonna and Child with Cat:* **c.1478–80**
1475: Dracula is killed in battle, near Bucharest
1475: First printed cookbook
1477: Turkish raiders approach Venice

261. LEONARDO DA VINCI
Study of the Spine. c. 1510. Pen, brown ink, and wash over traces of black chalk, 11 1/4 x 7 7/8". Royal Library, Windsor Castle

full-scale preparatory drawing known as a cartoon (from the Italian *cartone*, which refers to the thick paper used for this purpose). Leonardo's cartoon of the *Virgin and Child with St. Anne and Infant St. John* (fig. 265) displays the composition for a painting and indicates sculpturesque passages of modeling.

For Leonardo, drawing was not restricted to studies for works of art. "Art," he wrote, "truly is a science," and his remarkable examination of subjects ranging from engineering to the earth sciences found expression in more than 3,500 surviving pages of his notebooks. Numerous drawings, such as his projected flying machine (fig. 260), make visible Leonardo's powers of observation and imagination. Other investigations probed the physical sciences, including anatomy. His drawing of a spine from front, side, and back views—a didactic device still used in modern anatomy textbooks—demonstrates a knowledge of anatomical structures far in advance of that available to the medical profession at this time (fig. 261).

to the eye an indication of the intention and the invention which you first made in your imagination, then proceed to take away and add until you are satisfied."

After determining a basic composition, a Renaissance artist would make drawings studying the various elements within the composition. Leonardo's *Study for the Head of Judas* (see fig. 270) reveals the exacting interplay between his observing eye and talented hand. All these studies were then joined in a final,

ALESSANDRO BOTTICELLI, MYTHOLOGICAL PAINTINGS

262. ALESSANDRO BOTTICELLI
Realm of Venus (or *Primavera*). c. 1482. Tempera on wood with oil glazes, 6' 8" x 10' 4". Uffizi Gallery, Florence. This painting is first documented in 1498 in the Florentine palace of Lorenzo di Pierfrancesco de' Medici and Giovanni di Pierfrancesco de' Medici. The former, a cousin of Lorenzo the Magnificent who married in May of 1482, was most likely the patron.

Botticelli's *Realm of Venus* and *Birth of Venus* are among the first large-scale paintings to be devoted to mythological themes since antiquity. The *Realm of Venus* represents Venus reigning in a garden where it is always spring (fig. 262). The citrus fruit of the orchard was sacred to Venus. On the left, Mercury drives away clouds. Venus reigns as goddess of love and marriage, and Botticelli's painting may be a decoration made to celebrate a marriage. The unpredictable na-ture of love is suggested by the blindfolded Cupid, son of Venus, who shoots an arrow at the attendants of Venus. The physical nature of love is suggested by Zephyr, on the far right, who has the nymph Chloris in his arms. After seducing and marrying her, he returns her to the garden, where we witness her transmogrification into the goddess Flora, who strews flowers. She is also the goddess of spring (*primavera* in Italian). Her festival, Floralia, was celebrated in April and May. The astrological deities who rule these months are Venus and Mercury. The exquisite beauty of Botticelli's figures asserts their divine nature. They are other-worldly deities who do not belong to the realm of the real.

Botticelli's *Birth of Venus* cele-brates the legend that Venus was born full grown (fig. 263). Here she is blown ashore in a storm of roses by Zephyr and Chloris, to be received by one of her atten-dants. Her pose is based on an-cient sculptures, but she is hardly

263. ALESSANDRO BOTTICELLI
Birth of Venus. c. 1484–86. Tempera on canvas, 5' 9" x 9' 2". Uffizi Gallery, Florence. Who commissioned this secular, mythological painting is unknown, but most likely the patron chose the subject and suggested the particular interpretation. The most popular previous secular decorations for Florentine palaces had been Flemish tapestries, and the patterns, colors, and gold highlights of Botticelli's painting are an attempt to relate to and even rival tapestries.

sculptural. The elegance of the figure is set off by the intertwining patterns of Venus's hair. The enframing figures enhance the unexpectedly introspective quality of Venus.

The painting is strongly reminiscent of a passage in Alberti's *On Painting*: "Let [hair] wind itself into a coil as if desiring to knot itself and let it wave in the air like unto flames. . . . Let no part of the drapery be free from movement. . . . it will be well to put into the painting the face of the wind Zephyr or Auster blowing among the clouds, showing why the drapery flutters."

The dominant philosophy in Florence during the later fifteenth century was Neoplatonism, and Botticelli's paintings can be understood in the light of this complex movement. Neoplatonism emphasized a return to antiquity and a longing for an ideal removed from the earthly realm. In Neoplatonic terms, Venus personified beauty, and beauty equaled truth. The Neoplatonic philosopher Marsilio Ficino wrote in a letter that "Venus [is] Humanitas. . . . Her soul and mind are Love and Charity, her eyes Dignity and Magnanimity. . . . The whole, then, is Temperance and Honesty, Charm and Splendor. . . . How beautiful to behold!" The Neoplatonists went even further to equate Venus, source of divine love, with the Virgin Mary. Such an approach to ancient themes may explain why Botticelli's Venus is so meditative.

LEONARDO DA VINCI AND THE UNIFIED, HIGH RENAISSANCE COMPOSITION

In his *Lives of the Artists*, Vasari viewed the High Renaissance as the perfection and culmination of all the investigations and experimentation that had characterized Early Renaissance art, and he rightly understood that the transition to the High Renaissance occurred with the art of Leonardo da Vinci. One aspect of this transition took place when Leonardo developed a new unified composition in which he grouped figures to suggest a solid geometrical form, such as a pyramid or cone. In Leonardo's *Madonna of the Rocks*, the figures are related to each other to form a pyramid (fig. 264). Mary's head forms the apex; her right arm extends to grasp the infant St. John the Baptist, who is wor-

265. LEONARDO DA VINCI
Virgin and Child with St. Anne and Infant St. John. c. 1498–99. Charcoal on brown paper, heightened with white, 55 3/4 x 41". National Gallery, London

264. LEONARDO DA VINCI
Madonna of the Rocks. 1483–85. Oil on wood, transferred to canvas, 78 1/2 x 48". The Louvre, Paris. A second version of this painting is in the National Gallery, London. The interpretation of Leonardo's painting remains mysterious and elusive, with the holy group set within a darkened cave. Detailed foreground naturalism is combined with a background that seems to belong to a primitive world, where the forces of nature are still carving the mountainous landscape.

266. LEONARDO DA VINCI
Vitruvian Man. c. 1485–90. Pen and ink, 13 1/2 x 9 5/8". Accademia, Venice

LEONARDO DA VINCI, *Madonna of the Rocks:* **1483–85**
1484: Pope Innocent VII issues a proclamation against sorcery and witchcraft
1489: First epidemic of typhus in Europe

shipping the Christ Child. To our right, the angel's head and billowing red cloak define another side of the triangle, while the Christ Child, who blesses the Baptist, extends the triangle forward, anchoring the pyramid. In a splendid example of foreshortening, Mary extends her left hand out over the Christ Child, as if to offer protection and blessing. For Leonardo, the achievement of a unified composition did not mean a static presentation. The language of gesture in the *Madonna of the Rocks*, for example, is varied and complex.

Leonardo's use of the pyramidal composition has multiple meanings. As a compositional scheme, the pyramidal grouping offers visual unity and stability, while it also carries the religious association of the Christian Trinity. As a geometric form, the pyramid relates to the Renaissance macrocosmic/microcosmic tradition, based in antiquity, which held that everything in the universe is governed by

the order and precision of geometry. This tradition equated the human figure, or microcosm (small world), to the universe, the macrocosm. It found expression in a number of drawings known as the Vitruvian Man, the most familiar of which is by Leonardo (fig. 266). The image of a human figure with arms and legs outstretched to touch both a circle and a square is based on a passage from the ancient Roman writer Vitruvius, who suggested that there is a consonance between the human body and the perfection of geometry that related the body to the mathematical systems inherent in the universe. This fundamental belief in macrocosmic/microcosmic analogy influenced Italian artists to compose figures in geometric configurations, thus creating a visual harmony alluding to the ideal harmony of the universe.

Leonardo experimented with the unified composition in many studies, always seeking to incorporate a variety of poses to reflect the vitality of life. The cartoon for the *Virgin and Child with St. Anne and Infant St. John* (fig. 265) repeats the formula of the pyramidal grouping seen in the *Madonna of the Rocks*, but in this later work the composition is animated by the vigorous diagonal movement of the child.

In the 1480s Leonardo began to design a series of centrally planned churches (fig. 267). These drawings, which evolve from simple to more complex structures, were probably intended for a treatise on architec-

ture. None of Leonardo's designs were built. Leonardo's involvement with the central plan may have been in part inspired by Alberti's book *On Architecture*, which dates from about 1450. Alberti, citing the preference of circular forms in nature, recommended the central plan as an ideal one for church architecture. Theologically, the circle, without beginning or end, was considered symbolic of the perfection of God. Leonardo's conceptions of centrally planned churches as embodied in his drawings often combined exterior views with sections and/or plans. Drawn while Leonardo was working in Milan, they influenced Donato Bramante, who would later develop the centrally planned structure for St. Peter's in Rome (see pp. 278–79).

267. LEONARDO DA VINCI
View and Plan of a Centrally Planned Church. c. 1489. Pen and ink, 9 1/16 x 6 5/16". Institut de France, Paris

LEONARDO DA VINCI, *THE LAST SUPPER*

268. LEONARDO DA VINCI
The Last Supper. c. 1495–98. Oil, tempera, and varnish on wall, 14' x 28' 10 1/2"; the figures are over-lifesize. Refectory, Santa Maria delle Grazie, Milan. The Dominican monastery of Santa Maria delle Grazie was patronized by Lodovico Sforza, duke and ruler of Milan, who commissioned Leonardo to paint *The Last Supper*. This view shows the painting in the course of restoration.

269. LEONARDO DA VINCI
The Last Supper (detail). The recent restoration of Leonardo's painting has brought to light subtle details of facial expressions and radiant colors which had been covered by earlier restorers, who repainted rather than cleaned the surface.

According to Leonardo da Vinci, "Painted figures ought to be done in such a way that those who see them will be able to easily recognize from their attitudes the thoughts of their minds." Leonardo's *Last Supper*, painted in the dining hall of a monastery, exemplifies his maxim that figures should express emotional

LEONARDO DA VINCI, *The Last Supper:* **c. 1495–98**
1492: Christopher Columbus lands at San Salvador and Cuba
1492: Death of Lorenzo the Magnificent
1492: First known reference to smoking tobacco

and psychological realism (figs. 268, 269). The stable and calm figure of Christ, who is both on the axis and the focal point of the scientific perspective construction, forms a triangle which, while symbolic of the Trinity, also gives visual stability to the composition and contrasts with the activity of the apostles who flank him. Christ's followers are composed in four groups of three apostles each.

The agitated movement of the apostles reveals their psychological turmoil in reaction to Christ's declaration, "I say unto you, that one of you shall betray me" (Matthew 26:21). The impact of these words on the apostles is understandable when we realize that they had left their families, friends, and professions to follow Christ. Now, when celebrating a Passover meal, Christ announces that one of them will be a betrayer. The apostles' reactions are shown in different physical attitudes that reveal such psychological responses as surprise, piety, uncertainty, and faithfulness.

The powerful emotional drama that we perceive in the *Last Supper* is but one level of meaning in Leonardo's complex painting. In earlier Last Supper paintings, Judas had been shown on our side of the table, removed from the space occupied by Christ and his apostles. Leonardo, however, kept Judas with his fellow apostles. The fourth figure from the left, he is

shown recoiling from Christ. Judas is the only figure whose face is lost in shadow, a subtle indication that he is lost from the light of Christ.

Leonardo has joined the depiction of these two different, yet active, episodes with a third. The hands of Christ are directed toward the bread and wine on the table, suggesting the institution of the Eucharist.

The activity of these dramas is contained within a masterful organization. Light from the upper left (following the placement of windows in the hall) defines the figures. The grouping of the apostles on either side of Christ provides symmetry, while the positioning of the apostles in four groups discloses the numerical symbolism of the spiritual (three is the number of the Trinity) and material (four is the number of the elements) components of creation. This expression of universality, contained in number symbolism, is also apparent in the number twelve: in keeping Judas with the eleven faithful apostles, Leonardo retains the integrity of the number twelve, which refers not only to the apostles, but also to the months of the year and the hours of day and of night, extending the numerical symbolism to include the cycles of time.

It is now difficult to discern the subtle details which Leonardo intended, for in an attempt to achieve a new subtlety in mural painting, Leonardo,

always the inventor, mixed his pigments with a combination of oil, tempera, and varnish, producing a paint that proved disastrous almost from the start. Later attempts at restoration have even further dimmed our vision of this masterpiece. However, we can glean some sense of its intended effect from surviving preliminary drawings. The study for the head of Judas exhibits an acute understanding of anatomy and physiognomy (fig. 270). Such detailed, descriptive observation, found in numerous studies, was joined to a unified, yet complex narrative interpretation.

270. LEONARDO DA VINCI
Study for the Head of Judas. 1495–97. Preparatory drawing for *The Last Supper*. Red chalk on red prepared paper, 7 1/8 x 5 7/8". Royal Library, Windsor Castle

MICHELANGELO BUONARROTI, ST. PETER'S *PIETÀ*

271. MICHELANGELO BUONARROTI
Pietà. 1498–99. Marble, height 68 1/2"; the figures are over-lifesize. St. Peter's Basilica, Vatican, Rome. On August 27, 1498, a twenty-three-year-old sculptor from Florence, Michelangelo Buonarroti, signed a contract in Rome for a *Pietà*, intended as a tomb sculpture for a French cardinal. The contract was repeating rhetorical tradition when it stated that the completed group should be the "most beautiful work of marble in Rome," but the sublime work Michelangelo created within about a year and a half fulfilled the terms of the contract in a unique and unparalleled way.

MICHELANGELO, St. Peter's *Pietà*: 1498–99
1497: Vasco da Gama lands in Calcutta
1498: Savonarols is burned at the stake in Florence

Michelangelo's Rome *Pietà* demonstrates a mastery of concept and tragic expression, drawn with consummate skill from an inert block of marble (fig. 271). The Virgin Mary, seated on a rock, cradles the lifeless body of her son, which has just been taken down from the cross. With the open gesture of her left hand, she presents Christ's sacrifice to us. The design of the sculpture, with its sweeping passages of drapery and angular arrangement of limbs, is coherently resolved into a pyramidal composition.

The theme that we call the *Pietà* (Italian for pity and piety) is not found in the Bible, and the image first appears in northern European art during the Gothic period in sculptures where anatomical details are exaggerated to emphasize Christ's suffering and death. The German Gothic *Pietà* illustrated here demands an immediate and powerful devotional response from the viewer (fig. 272).

Michelangelo's biographer Ascanio Condivi, writing in 1553, recorded that with the St. Peter's *Pietà* the sculptor wanted to show "that the Son of God truly assumed human form," so that his physical suffering could be easily understood. But Michelangelo's conception of humanity is also rooted in the idealism of the Italian Renaissance, and he avoided the grotesque distortions of earlier *Pietà* images in favor of an interpretation that conveyed his views on the integ-

rity and beauty of the body. While still a young man in Florence, Michelangelo had studied human anatomy, and from early dissection practice he learned the structure of the human body. His mastery of anatomy is displayed here in the figure of Christ. In a more subtle way than with earlier *Pietàs*, we can identify with Christ's humanity and better understand his suffering and death. Unlike the wailing mother of the Gothic *Pietà*, Michelangelo's youthful and beautiful Mary bears her sorrowful burden with quiet, meditative resignation. Michelangelo here suggests an inner suffering restrained by dignity.

In describing the St. Peter's *Pietà*, Vasari, in his *Lives*, observed the beauty and technical achievement of the sculpture: "Among the lovely things to be seen in the work, to say nothing of the divinely beautiful draperies, is the body of Christ; nor let anyone think to see a greater beauty of members or more mastery of art in any body, or a nude with more detail in the muscles, veins and nerves over the framework of the bones, nor yet a corpse more similar than this to a real corpse. Here is perfect sweetness in the expression of the head, harmony in the joints and attachments of the arms, legs, and trunk, and the pulses and veins so wrought, that in truth Wonder herself must marvel that the hand of a craftsman should have been able to execute so

272. German. *Pietà*. Early 14th century. Polychromed wood, height 34 1/2". Provinzialmuseum, Bonn

divinely and so perfectly, in so short a time, a work so admirable; and it is certainly a miracle that a stone without any shape at the beginning should ever have been reduced to such perfection as Nature is scarcely able to create in the flesh."

The sculpture was an astounding success in Rome. Vasari goes on to report, however, that when the *Pietà* was newly finished, questions arose as to the identity of the artist. To end any doubts, Michelangelo carved his signature on the ribbon which crosses Mary's torso. The Rome *Pietà* is the only work Michelangelo ever signed.

ORTHOGRAPHIA·PARTIS·EXTERIORIS   TEMPLI·DIVI·PETRI

MICHAEL·ANGELVS·BONAROTA·INVENIT
STEPHANVS·DV PERAC·FECIT

Canne·10·

SIXTEENTH-CENTURY ART

VATICANO

INTRODUCTION

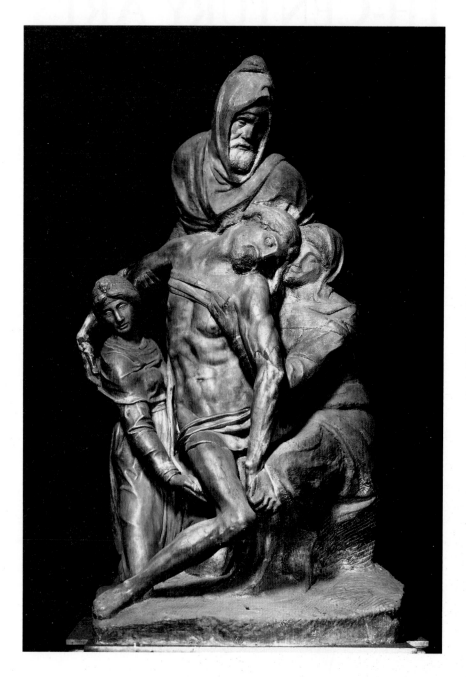

273. MICHELANGELO BUONARROTI

Pietà. c. 1547–55. Marble, height 92".
Museo dell'Opera del Duomo,
Florence. After working on this sculpture for almost a decade, Michelangelo smashed it in anger, leaving it seriously damaged. He presented the damaged work and broken fragments to a pupil, who repaired it and laboriously finished the figure of Mary Magdalene on our left. Although based on Michelangelo's design, she is now too small for the composition and no longer seems to be supporting Christ's right arm. Christ's left leg, which was once positioned over Mary's, is completely lost. Theories have been advanced as to why Michelangelo attacked the work. Giorgio Vasari, writing in 1568, stated that the artist discovered that the marble was flawed.

By the middle of the sixteenth century, when Michelangelo's Florence *Pietà* was created, the optimism that had characterized so much of fifteenth- and early-sixteenth-century Italian Renaissance art had evaporated. The new tragic, pessimistic mood is conveyed by Michelangelo's *Pietà* (fig. 273). We sense the dead weight of Christ's body in the angular arrangement of limbs, the head collapsed to one side, and the efforts needed to support the body. To our right, the Virgin tenderly presses her face against her son's head. Behind, the towering figure of Nicodemus, a follower of Christ, compassionately helps support his dead master.

Although the legacy of the High Renaissance is evident in the musculature of the body of Christ, the elongated figural proportions and angular, unstable composition break the norm of Renaissance harmony. Deep emotional grief has seized the participants. This emotional impact is reinforced when we realize that the face of Nicodemus is a self-portrait of Michelangelo, who intended this sculptural group to be placed over his tomb. Michelangelo was about seventy-two years old when he began carving the Florence *Pietà*. Its unsettling emotional content reflects his personal psychological condition and the tumultuous conflicts of sixteenth-century Europe.

274. LUCAS CRANACH THE ELDER
Portrait of Martin Luther. 1533. Oil on wood, 8 1/4 x 5 7/8". Germanisches Nationalmuseum, Nuremberg. This is one of some fifty portraits of Luther painted by Cranach and his workshop.

HISTORY

The main political protagonists of the sixteenth century, a period convulsed by shifting alliances, were the popes in Rome and the rulers of northern Europe. Pope Julius II succeeded in establishing the papacy as a major political power early in the century, but the newly strengthened church conflicted with the expansive plans of secular rulers in the North, where the strife between Emperor Charles V of the Hapsburg line and Francis I, king of France, affected many aspects of sixteenth-century life. In 1520 Charles V was crowned Holy Roman Emperor, a position which Francis I had also sought. The territories ruled by Charles V were vast; they encompassed Spain, the Netherlands, and parts of northern Italy, Germany, and central and northern Europe. France was effectively isolated, but even a brief imprisonment did not deter Francis from his conflict with the emperor. Charles was usually aligned with the pope, but a most significant break in this alliance occurred in 1527, after Pope Clement VII backed Francis I in an attempt to check the increasing power of the emperor. Charles V's troops entered and pillaged Rome and even imprisoned the pope. But the attention of Charles V was also directed toward the East, where he attempted to counter the expansion of the Ottoman Turks under Suleiman the Magnificent, who had extended his empire into eastern Europe and North Africa.

Throughout the century, expansion across the Atlantic continued. The Spanish were particularly active in colonizing. In 1513 Vasco Nuñez de Balboa crossed Panama to reach and name the Pacific

Ocean, while Juan Ponce de Leon established a settlement in Florida. In the late fifteenth and early sixteenth centuries, an Italian merchant and seafarer, Amerigo Vespucci, charted eastern coastline areas of the New World. In 1507 the mapmaker Martin Waldseemüller, drawing on Vespucci's information, demonstrated that the New World was formed of separate continents and suggested that they be named after Vespucci; hence they came to be called the Americas.

INTELLECTUAL AND SCIENTIFIC DEVELOPMENTS

Although the vast majority of Europeans still felt bound to the scientific beliefs and superstitions which had guided life for centuries, important discoveries in the sixteenth century laid the foundation for the modern development of science. These discoveries owed, in part, to the tremendously expanded publication rate of books. By 1600, about two thousand books per year were being produced, a rate double that of a century earlier.

In 1543 two publications appeared which began to overturn beliefs, many of which were based on ancient authors, about human anatomy and our universe. *De humani corporis fabrica (On the Fabric of the Human Body)*, written by Andreas Vesalius, a twenty-eight-year-old surgeon/anatomist, began to clear away traditional misconceptions about anatomy and provided a base for later advances in medicine. Also in 1543 the Polish astronomer Nicolaus Copernicus, in *De revolutionibus orbium coelestium (On the Revolution of the Celestial Spheres)*, asserted his theory of a heliocentric universe, in which the planets revolve around the sun. This "modern" view of the universe, which had been held by a minority of philosophers since antiquity, was later popularized by Galileo Galilei, whose teachings, challenged by the Catholic church, demonstrated the conflict between the new scientific reason and traditional religious authority.

THE REFORMATION

The most significant religious event of the sixteenth century, and one which would forever change the history of Christianity, was the Reformation. Over the centuries, the Catholic church had become increasingly materialistic. The rebuilding of St. Peter's (pp. 278–79) and the construction of a huge new papal palace led to such unscrupulous practices as the selling of indulgences. According to Catholic belief, before gaining access to heaven, souls had to enter purgatory to suffer in remorse for their earthly sins. An indulgence allowed a person to "buy" a soul out of purgatory by the payment of a "donation." The proceeds of this expedient were shared by the local Catholic hierarchy and the papacy. Indulgences were especially solicited in Germany, leading to disillusionment within the local clergy.

A German Augustinian monk, Martin Luther (see fig. 274), publicly questioned these practices, arguing that faith alone could "buy" salvation, in opposition to the church's position that faith needed to be combined with good works. Aiming at reform from within, Luther drafted ninety-five theses, which he nailed to the doors of Wittenberg Cathedral on October 31, 1517. Among his theses, he argued:

> 27. There is no divine authority for preaching that the soul flies out of purgatory as soon as the money clinks in the bottom of the chest.

> 50. Christians should be taught that, if the pope knew the exactions of the indulgence-preachers, he would rather the church of St. Peter were reduced to ashes than be built with the skin, flesh, and bones of his sheep.

Luther called on German rulers to assist in promoting reform within the church, but when he repudiated papal supremacy, the church excommunicated him.

The Reformation was soon bound to political realities. Most of the German princes were glad to restrict the power of the church, which was draining their territories of wealth. Luther was given protection by a German prince and by many Northern rulers, who were grasping the opportunity to counter church authority and seize church property. In 1529 Charles V ordered that measures be taken against those who dissented from the Catholic faith. The Lutheran princes who protested the emperor's order became known as Protestants. The open conflict that erupted in 1546 ended in 1555 with the Peace of Augsburg, which declared that the religion of a ruler determined the religion of that area. It was a victory for the Protestants.

Protestantism spread, with different groups developing in different areas of Europe. In England, King Henry VIII requested that Pope Clement VII annul his marriage. Papal refusal led to the 1534 Act of Supremacy, which made the English sovereign the head of the English (Anglican) church. In Switzerland another Protestant movement flourished under John Calvin. Calvinism stressed the supremacy of the Bible as a guide for moral conduct.

By the end of the century, approximately one-fourth of western Europe's population was Protestant. England, Scotland, Denmark, and Sweden had become Protestant nations, while Protestants in the Netherlands were fighting to obtain their independence from Catholic Spain. In Germany almost one-half of the population had become Protestant. The ramifications of these developments for art became obvious in the course of the seventeenth century and later.

275. ALBRECHT DÜRER
Praying Hands. 1508–9. Brush, heightened with white, on blue-grounded paper, 11 1/2 x 7 3/4". Albertina, Vienna. This is among a number of surviving drawings for one of Dürer's most famous works, the *Heller Altarpiece.*

THE COUNTER-REFORMATION

The response of the Roman Catholic church to the Reformation is usually known as the Counter-Reformation. Voices calling for reform had been heard within the Catholic church even before the Lutheran challenge, but the rapid growth of Protestantism led the church to call a major council at Trent, in north Italy. Between 1545 and 1563, the

276. RAPHAEL
Madonna and Child with St. John the Baptist (also known as *"La Belle Jardinière"*). 1508. Oil on wood, 48 x 31 1/2". The Louvre, Paris. The infant John the Baptist, kneeling in the foreground, holds a cross and wears an animal skin to refer to the time he will spend in the wilderness.

Council of Trent established policies for internal reform and planned a strategy to combat the spread of Protestantism, which was viewed as a heresy. The council affirmed the traditional belief that both faith and good works were the means to salvation, emphasizing the Bible and the "sacred tradition" as sources for doctrine (belief) and practice. It also enacted policies that would lead to a more educated priesthood. Enforcement of the church's beliefs and policies was given to the Inquisition, an ecclesiastical court established in the Late Middle Ages to punish heretics.

Calls for an educated priesthood were met by a new order of priests founded by Ignatius Loyola in 1534. Loyola, a Spaniard, had been a soldier in the armies of Charles V. While recovering from a leg wound, he read the lives of Christ and the saints and determined to devote his life to Christ and the defense of the church. He founded the Society of Jesus, commonly referred to as the Jesuits, which was distinguished by its missionary zeal, preaching, and scholarly interests. As teachers, Jesuits founded many influential schools. Jesuits were counted among the intellectual leaders of the time. Their achievements contributed greatly to a restored respect for the Catholic church.

At the final session of the Council of Trent, the church reaffirmed the value of art in promoting religious education. According to the

277. PARMIGIANINO
Left: *Madonna and Child with Angels*
(known as the *"Madonna with the Long
Neck"*). 1534–40. Oil on wood, 85 x 52".
Uffizi Gallery, Florence

278. LUDOVICO CARRACCI
Right: *Madonna and Child with Sts.
Jerome and Francis* (or *Madonna degli
Scalzi*). c. 1590. Oil on canvas, 84 x 60".
Pinacoteca, Bologna

council, religious art should appeal to the emotions, be morally
acceptable, and use clear compositions. Accuracy in theology was
required; failure to meet these requirements made the artist answer-
able to the Inquisition. The impact of this policy contributed to new
directions in art and was of significance for artistic and iconographic
developments in the seventeenth century.

SIXTEENTH-CENTURY ART

No single artistic style characterizes this century. With the patronage
of Pope Julius II, the High Renaissance style spread from Florence to
Rome. In Venice a group of artists developed a distinctively colorful
and richly luminous version of Renaissance painting, often with
complex philosophical and allegorical subjects. The ideality of Italian
High Renaissance art affected artists in northern Europe, especially
Albrecht Dürer. Much of Northern painting, however, retained a

strict naturalism which distinguished it from the idealizing, classicizing approach of Italian artists. Dürer's drawing of *Praying Hands* (fig. 275) is an example of the continuing commitment to naturalistic observation and fine detail by Northern artists.

Following the High Renaissance in Italy, Mannerism (see below) introduced new concepts and complexities to art. Late in the century, many Northern artists would adopt the affectations of Mannerism, while others, Pieter Bruegel in particular, would emphasize the Northern landscape and Northern traditions in paintings that laid the foundation for developments in the new republic of the Netherlands in the seventeenth century. By the end of the century, the climactic events of the Reformation and Counter-Reformation affect yet another direction in art.

279. PARMIGIANINO
Self-Portrait in a Convex Mirror. 1524.
Oil on wood, diameter 9 5/8".
Kunsthistorisches Museum, Vienna

THE STYLES OF SIXTEENTH-CENTURY ART

Three major styles dominate sixteenth-century Italian art: High Renaissance, Mannerism, and early Baroque. Three paintings with a similar theme demonstrate the visual characteristics of these styles.

Raphael's *Madonna and Child with St. John the Baptist* exemplifies the union of ideality and naturalism that characterizes the High Renaissance (fig. 276). Bathed in soft gold light, the seated Madonna tenderly embraces the Christ Child. The relaxed pose of the child lends a note of informality. The flowers and plants are painted with precise observation, and naturalism is also evident in the modeling of the figures and in the atmospheric perspective of the distant landscape. Such naturalistic details, however, are part of an idealized composition seen in the pyramidal grouping. In Raphael's painting the world as it is seen is joined to ideals of perfection.

Parmigianino's *Madonna and Child with Angels* was painted about thirty years after Raphael's *Madonna* (fig. 277). This Mannerist painting exhibits an aristocratic elegance: elongated figural proportions are evident (note especially the fingers of Mary's right hand), while the languid body of the Christ Child, the prominent leg of the angel, and the drapery clinging to Mary's torso create a distinctly sensual effect. The illusion of space is consciously disjointed, with columns (unfinished) in the background which rise to gigantic proportions. Derived from the Italian term *maniera*, meaning style in the sense of sophistication, elegance, and poise, Mannerist art moved away from the classical values of the High Renaissance. Mannerist artists sought to create an artificial and complex construction to demonstrate their intellectual and technical virtuosity and the sophistication of their patrons.

Ludovico Carracci's *Madonna degli Scalzi* might be seen as a reaction against the visual complexity of Mannerist painting (fig. 278). Dating from late in the century, it can be considered an early Baroque work, as the painting displays many of those features that will characterize Baroque art as it develops in the seventeenth century. The figures are rendered with an easily understood naturalism. Mary, raised on the axis on a crescent moon, holds a lively Christ Child.

Christ extends his hand to St. Francis, on our right, while St. Jerome, with his symbolic lion, looks attentively from the left. A halo of golden light surrounds Mary's head. The light reflects on a host of angels joyously playing musical instruments. Carracci's emphasis on religious expression, visualized in a direct, simple, yet forceful composition, has an emotional appeal well suited to communicate the aims of the Counter-Reformation church.

THE SIXTEENTH-CENTURY ARTIST

The new respect for the artist as an intellectual, which had developed in the fifteenth century (see p. 223), made impressive gains during the sixteenth century. In Italy, both Michelangelo and Raphael earned the nickname "il divino" (the divine one), surely a sign that the artist could now be viewed as an almost godlike creator. Artists continued to make self-portraits throughout the century. Parmigianino's unusual *Self-Portrait in a Convex Mirror* (fig. 279) reflects intellectual conceits associated with Mannerist art.

Art theory continued to evolve within an intellectual climate that nourished it, and other types of writings contributed to the elevated social status of the artist. Baldassare Castiglione, an Italian diplomat and literary figure, included witticisms and more serious discussions on art in his *Book of the Courtier*. Benvenuto Cellini's fame as an artist was buttressed by his theoretical writings and a roguish *Autobiography* that still enjoys great popularity.

Giorgio Vasari, an artist active at the Medici court in Florence, published his *Lives of the Most Eminent Painters, Sculptors, and Architects* in 1550 and revised it for a second edition in 1568. Vasari viewed Renaissance art as an evolutionary progression (see p. 219). Beginning with Giotto in the fourteenth century, he argued, Italian art had been rescued from the "dark ages" to be restored in the light of classical eloquence. Each generation of artists built upon the foundation set by the previous generation until perfection was reached with the High Renaissance. Throughout the *Lives*, Vasari noted the regard in which great rulers held artists, enjoying their friendship and advice.

When Vasari wrote the *Lives*, he had more in mind than just art history. He was promoting the establishment of an art academy. His efforts assisted in founding the Florentine Accademia del Disegno (Academy of Design) in 1563. In this academy, and in the many other academies that followed, artists were educated within a broad liberal-arts context. This enhanced education made it more possible for at least some artists to mingle with the higher social ranks. The artistic, intellectual, and social gains made by artists during the sixteenth century give us a new concept of the artist, that of an inspired genius.

One benefit of these social changes for the artist was that the profession began to open its ranks, however slowly at first, to women. During the Middle Ages, women artists had been active primarily as embroiderers and manuscript illuminators. By the sixteenth century, women were becoming established as painters as well. In Italy, Lavinia Fontana was a respected painter in Bologna (fig. 280).

280. LAVINIA FONTANA
Self-Portrait. c. 1577. Oil on copper, diameter 6". Uffizi Gallery, Florence. This *Self-Portrait*, which shows the artist in her studio, captures the confident elegance of Mannerist portraiture without the visual complexities which so engaged Florentine Mannerist painters.

MICHELANGELO'S *DAVID*

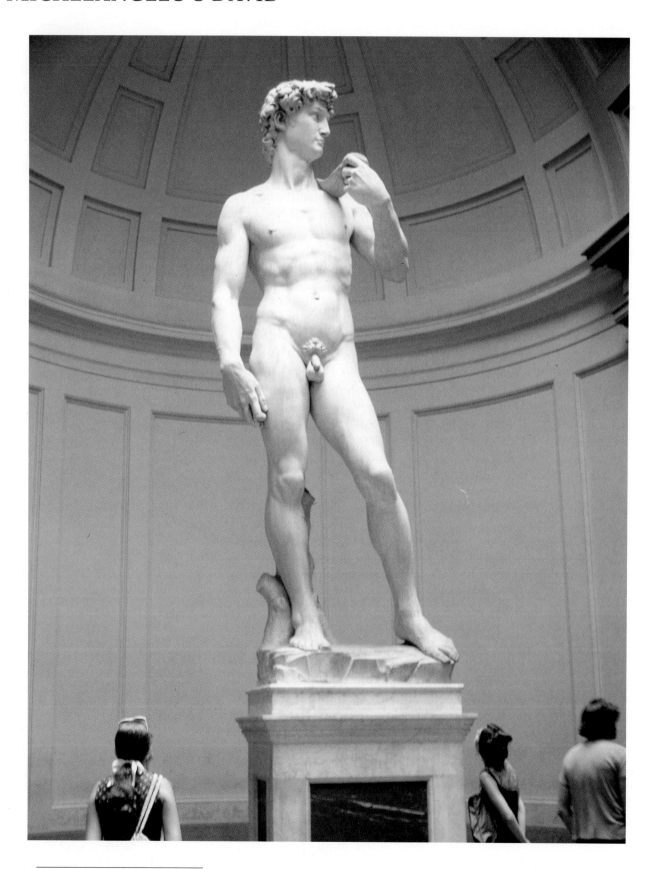

1494: Sebastian Brandt, *The Ship of Fools*
1495: *Everyman,* morality play, is performed
1501: Amerigo Vespucci's second voyage to the New World
1501: Africans are first brought as slaves to the New World

**281. MICHELANGELO
BUONARROTI**

David. 1501– 4. Marble, height
14' 3". Accademia, Florence. In 1873
the statue was moved from its
original location, at the entrance of
the Palazzo della Signoria, to the
Accademia, where a special setting
had been constructed for it. The
medium is white marble from
Carrara, near Pisa. These quarries
still produce vast quantities of fine
quality marble for artistic and
architectural use.

Michelangelo's colossal sculpture of the Old Testament hero
David is a stirring embodiment
of physical and psychological
strength (fig. 281). Michelangelo
chose an unusual moment to
represent, for he shows David
before the battle. The sling is over
his shoulder and the stone rests
in his right hand, but his muscles
are taut and a defiant scowl seizes
his face. The figure pulls powerfully to the left, away from the
implied enemy, and David's
apprehension is further indicated
in the swelling veins in the hand
and the sucking in of breath
revealed in the tensed muscles of
the abdomen. In Michelangelo's
interpretation, David has become
human. In his *Lives,* Vasari, referring to the huge block of white
marble from which Michelangelo
carved the *David,* said that the
sculptor had brought "to life a
thing that was dead."

In saying that Michelangelo
had given life to the stone, Vasari
alluded not only to his artistic

accomplishment, but to the history of the block of marble from
which the *David* was carved.
Quarried in 1464, before Michelangelo's birth, the enormous
block was brought to Florence to
be carved, perhaps under the
supervision of the aging Donatello, as a David, one of a series of
Old Testament prophets to be
placed high above street level on
the buttresses of the cathedral.
Earlier in the century a gigantic
terra-cotta figure modeled by
Donatello had been set into place,
but other attempts to add to the
prophet series had not been successful. The 1464 project was
abandoned in 1466, when Donatello died. The stone, partially
carved, languished in the courtyard of the cathedral workshop
for decades.

We do not know to what extent the stone had been carved
before Michelangelo received the
commission to finish the statue
in 1501 and cannot, therefore,
judge the difficulties he had to
overcome. We do know that it
was decided not to hoist the
completed sculpture into position on the cathedral buttress.
Perhaps there was fear that the
sculpture might be damaged, or
the work may have been too impressive to be removed from
close public attention. A committee which included Leonardo
da Vinci and Alessandro Botticelli decided to place the *David* at
the entrance to the Palazzo della
Signoria, the center of Florence's
civic government. That decision

was significant, for the meaning
of the *David* gained an enhanced
political impact.

Michelangelo's *David* was
carved after the expulsion of the
Medici, when the republic of
Florence had been reestablished.
The Medici tyrants would again
rule the city in 1512, but at the
time of the *David,* the democracy
and liberty of the old Florentine
republic reigned, and Michelangelo's sculpture was seen as a
manifestation of those civic virtues. Just as the biblical David
had triumphed against the physical power of Goliath, so too had
the Florentine people coura-
geously restored their republic.
The *David* symbolized the Flor-
entines' defiance of tyranny.

Fulfilling its new role as a
political symbol, the *David* par-
took of the Renaissance in yet
another way. While conforming
to the designation *statua,* as
public sculpture had been explained by the ancient writer
Pliny the Elder, Michelangelo's
David also elevated *statua* to a
grand and heroic scale. With the
David, Vasari proclaimed that
even the cherished art of antiquity had been surpassed: "Without any doubt this figure has put
in the shade every other statue,
ancient or modern, Greek or
Roman . . . such were the satisfying proportions and the beauty
of the finished work. . . . To be
sure, anyone who has seen
Michelangelo's *David* has no
need to see anything else by any
other sculptor, living or dead."

HIGH RENAISSANCE PORTRAITURE

The *"Mona Lisa,"* probably the most widely known portrait and perhaps even the best-known painting in the history of art, is difficult to appreciate today (fig. 282). Covered by layers of yellowing varnish and a protective sheet of thick glass, the painting seems to have none of the naturalistic effects reported by Vasari in the sixteenth century: "The nose, with its beautiful nostrils, rosy and tender, seemed to be alive. The opening of the mouth, united by the red of the lips to the flesh tones of the face, seemed not to be colored but to be living flesh." While the careful blending of tones which creates the incredible subtlety of Leonardo's modeling survives, the freshness of Leonardo's color and observation are obscured. What remains clear is Leonardo's composition, which became a model for many later Renaissance portraits. As in his earlier religious works (figs. 264, 265, 268), the basic form is a pyramidal shape. Leonardo successfully and naturally integrates the hands into his portrait, adding yet another vehicle for the expression of personality into the tradition of portraiture.

Even in the Renaissance, the mystery of the sitter must have excited the imagination of the viewer. The androgynous quality—neither fully female nor fully male—and the self-satisfied expression, created by the blurring of the corners of the mouth and eyes, are tantalizing. Our uneasiness is in part created by the unexpected appearance of a figure with shaved eyebrows and forehead, which were fashionable in the Renaissance. Also disturbing is the fantastic mountainous landscape setting. Note that the horizon lines of the landscapes are clearly on different levels. Whoever she is, the "Mona Lisa" continues to project and protect her mysterious secret.

In Raphael's *"Donna Velata"* (Veiled Lady), the natural beauty of the woman and the High Renaissance style are mutually compatible (fig. 283). The woman appears to be a specific individual. Her expression can be interpreted as conveying warmth, gentleness, and intelligence. The High Renaissance demand for unity is evident in the sweep of the veil, which unites a myriad of complex forms into the favored conical composition. The beautifully rounded forms of the head and eyes are repeated in the necklace and again in its individual stones, as well as in the curves of the neckline and bodice; the pearl set against the dark hair is a microcosm of the whole composition. The costume is a coloristic symphony in shades of gold and white, a scheme which emphasizes the flesh tones and draws attention to the compelling dark eyes and enframing hair. The elaborate sleeve, a painter's triumph, enhances the elegance of his sitter and confirms Raphael's technical skill.

LEONARDO DA VINCI, *Portrait of a Woman:* **c. 1503–5**
1506: Machiavelli establishes a citizen militia in Florence
1511: Pocket watch is first mentioned

283. RAPHAEL
Portrait of a Woman (now known as *"Donna Velata"*).
c. 1513. Oil on canvas, 33 1/2 x 23 1/2". Pitti Gallery,
Florence. It is suspected that the beautiful sitter for this
portrait was Raphael's beloved, the baker's daughter
(*la fornarina*), mentioned by Vasari.

282. LEONARDO DA VINCI
Portrait of a Woman (known as the *"Mona Lisa"*).
c. 1503–5. Oil on wood, 30 1/4" x 21" (cut down). The
Louvre, Paris. The sitter is unknown, despite the traditional title. Vasari said that she was the wife of Francesco
del Gioconda, which led to the popular name "La
Gioconda" for the painting. Vasari also tells the unforgettable tale that during sittings for the portrait, Leonardo employed musicians or jesters to keep her full of
merriment and to chase away any trace of melancholy
that might arise from the boredom of sitting quietly
posed, repeatedly, for long hours. Leonardo, who seems
to have worked on the painting over a number of years,
took it with him when he went to France, where he died
in 1519. After Leonardo's death the painting was owned
by King Francis I of France. In the early nineteenth
century, Napoleon kept the portrait in his bedroom. The
painting has been cut down. It was once wider, and the
figure was shown enframed by columns to either side.
Today only the column bases survive.

ALBRECHT DÜRER

The increasing contact between Italian and Northern artistic traditions is demonstrated in Dürer's *Adam and Eve* (fig. 284). The precise detail of the heavily wooded background reflects Northern tradition, while the use of antique models for the figures reveals Dürer's contact with Italian Renaissance art (Dürer went to Italy twice, in 1494–95 and again in 1505–7). Dürer's difficulty in blending these two distinct styles is evident, for the figures, which resemble sculptures rather than living beings, seem out of place in this dense forest setting. Dürer, who studied proportional systems for the human body from nature and from classical and Italian Renaissance sources, completed two volumes of a proposed four-volume *Treatise on Human Proportions*. The diverse animals in the background symbolize the various "humors," fluids within the body that were believed to control personality. The rabbit stands for the lust or lechery of humanity, which will become active as soon as Adam takes a bite of the apple held by Eve.

Dürer's prints brought him international fame, and during his lifetime he was recognized as the leading German artist and the greatest living printmaker. When Dürer was in Venice in 1505–7, the senate offered him a regular salary if he would become a Venetian citizen. He received many commissions and was employed by Maximilian I, the Holy Roman Emperor. In 1520–21 Dürer traveled to the Netherlands, where he saw a room full of Aztec gold treasures sent back by Cortes. He praised these exotic objects, writing, "I have seen nothing that rejoiced my heart so much as these things, for . . . I marveled at the subtle ingenuity of men in foreign lands." He had sympathies with the Protestant movement, and when he heard a rumor that Luther had been murdered, he wrote, "If Luther is dead, who will explain the Gospel to us now?"

In Dürer's *Knight, Death, and the Devil* (fig. 285), the central figure, dressed as a Renaissance knight, is an allegorical representation of the Christian soul. He is every human being, riding through life, which is shown as a landscape filled with terrors. The Devil is a hideous horned monster, and the skeleton of death, his crown entwined with serpents, brandishes an hourglass as a reminder of the inevitability of death. These imaginative creations belong to a Northern tradition, but the knight and his sturdy mount are inspired by classical

DÜRER, *Adam and Eve:* **1504**

1504: Columbus returns from his final voyage
1504: Erasmus, *Instructions for the Christian Soldier*

and Renaissance works Dürer had seen in Italy.

Dürer's impressive engravings were intended for a sophisticated audience of wealthy print collectors, but he also produced more reasonably priced and easily understood prints in series for a popular audience—the *"Small" Life of the Virgin Mary,* the *"Large"* and *"Small" Passions,* and the *Apocalypse.* These works, executed in the bolder and more direct medium of woodcut, were printed in large quantities to be sold at fairs and carnivals, as well as by Dürer and his agents. The subject matter is both more

traditional and more direct, as in the *Four Horsemen of the Apocalypse* (fig. 286), drawn from Revelation 6:1–8. Death ("on a pale horse") in the foreground and the other riders follow John's description: Famine has a pair of scales, War a sword, and "the conqueror" (Pestilence, or the Plague) carries a bow. Dürer's powerful patterns reinforce the relentless motion of the horsemen as they ravage humanity. The Apocalypse and Last Judgment were popular themes just before 1500, when it was feared time would end and Christ would appear to judge humanity.

285. ALBRECHT DÜRER

Above left: *Knight, Death, and the Devil.* 1513. Engraving, 9 5/8 x 7 1/2". Dürer called this print *The Rider,* but scholars have related the symbolism to Erasmus's handbook, *Instructions for the Christian Soldier,* published in 1504. The initials, with the *A* encompassing the *D,* create a unique monogram, an indication of Dürer's pride in his work.

286. ALBRECHT DÜRER

Above right: *Four Horsemen of the Apocalypse.* c. 1497–98. Woodcut, 15 1/2 x 11" (for a detail see fig. 288). The *Apocalypse* series, of which this is a part, was based on the Book of Revelation. It consisted of fifteen prints with relevant texts on the back in German or Latin.

PRINTMAKING: ENGRAVING AND WOODCUT

print media the surface of the print form can be re-inked and a number of additional prints (an edition) produced. The development of this relatively cheap means of mass-producing an image, which was related to improvements in the quality of paper and a tremendous decrease in its price, had a dramatic impact on western European culture. Now avidly collected by museums and connoisseurs, most of the earliest prints were simple book illustrations or modest, inexpensive religious images intended for popular consumption. In the hands of such skilled artists as Dürer, however, the techniques became sophisticated, their expression more subtle, and the iconography more complex. The resulting prints were produced for the connoisseur and the collector.

The woodcut was first developed in China in the late ninth century; the earliest European examples date from the late fourteenth century. Woodcut is called a relief process because the lines and surfaces to which the ink adheres are higher than the parts that are not to be printed. To create a woodcut, the artist draws the design on a piece of wood sawed lengthwise along the grain (see fig. 289). Using a knife or chisel, he or she then cuts away the background areas, leaving the raised design. When the woodblock is

These enlarged details from an engraving and a woodcut by Dürer reveal his acute vision and the technical accomplishment and expression he achieved in these two media (figs. 287, 288). They are especially impressive given the distinctive technique of these two major types of printmaking. In the engraved head, multiple fine lines, often placed parallel (hatching) and perpendicular (cross-hatching) to each other, create highlights, modeling, and subtle pockets of shadow. In addition, these lines suggest the illusion of specific textures. In the woodcut head, the effect is more linear, and the sharp distinctions between light and dark patterns add drama and movement to the work. In woodcuts the defining lines either follow the naturalistic shapes or are grouped parallel to each other.

The printmaking processes involve pressing a piece of paper (or, rarely, some other absorbent material, such as vellum or silk) against a surface to which ink has been applied (technically known as the print form). When the paper is removed, a reversed impression adheres to it; this is known as a print. In most

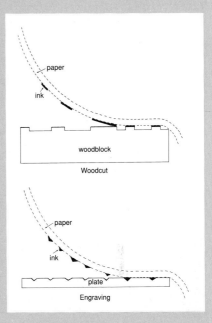

289. These diagrams of the woodcut and engraving techniques show schematically the moment when the paper is being lifted from the woodblock or the plate at the completion of the printing process. Note how the ink is transferred from the print form to the print.

288. ALBRECHT DÜRER
Four Horsemen of the Apocalypse (detail of fig. 286). Woodcut

inked, the ink adheres to the raised surfaces. Dampened paper is applied and the print can be made by hand or in a printing press. Approximately a thousand good prints can be made before the prints will reveal that the block is showing signs of wear. Our understanding of the woodcut technique makes Dürer's accomplishment even more impressive, for, unlike earlier harsh and simple images, his designs suggest the illusion of three-dimensional forms with light playing across them.

Engraving is known as an intaglio process (from the Italian *intagliare,* to carve or cut) because the lines that print are incised into the surface of the print form. In engraving, this print form is a thin metallic plate, usually of copper. With a sharply pointed steel instrument called a burin, the artist incises grooves in the surface of the plate (fig. 289). The plate is then inked with a heavy, viscous ink and wiped with a rag (or the palm of the hand), leaving the ink in the grooves. The paper used for printing an engraving is slightly moistened before being applied to the inked plate. Plate and paper are then run through a printing press which can apply the sufficient pressure (more than is needed to print a woodcut) to force the paper to pick up the ink in the grooves. The printed lines that result are sharply defined and slightly raised. Several hundred high-quality prints can be made before weak lines on the print reveal that the copper plate is wearing down.

NEW ST. PETER'S BASILICA

theon on top of the Basilica of
Constantine" (the diameter of the
dome of St. Peter's is 138 feet,
only about 6 feet smaller than
that of the Pantheon).

Before journeying to Rome,
Bramante had known Leonardo
in Milan in the 1480s and 1490s
and had experimented with
centrally planned church designs. For St. Peter's, Bramante
joined the central plan, symbolic
of God's perfection, with a Greek
cross pattern. The ancillary
spaces between the cross arms
enclose this central plan within a
square. Unlike the cruciform
basilica plan of Old St. Peter's,
where the cross shape emphasized salvation, Bramante's central plan expressed the universal
harmony of God's created world.

The new St. Peter's was not
consecrated until November 18,
1626, over one hundred and
twenty years after Bramante's
reconstruction was begun. The
work encompassed the reigns of
twenty popes and the efforts of
fourteen architects, including
Raphael and Michelangelo. Each
succeeding architect had to con-
tend with Bramante's original
plan, as well as the advancing
construction of the building
under successive architects.

On April 18, 1506, Pope Julius II,
who was aggressive in both religious and political matters, laid
the foundation stone for a new
St. Peter's. As part of a campaign
to restore Rome to be worthy of
its status as the capital of Christendom, he commissioned Bramante to rebuild the structure.
Since the late fourteenth century,
St. Peter's and the Vatican had
been home to the popes, and
although Old St. Peter's (fig. 145)
was one of the most revered
churches in Christendom, it had
fallen into disrepair and no
longer seemed grand enough to
serve as the church that marked
the burial spot of the first pope
and, now, the religious center for
the papacy.

Bramante's design (figs. 290,
291), never completed, would
have replaced the Early Christian basilica with a centrally

planned church, a plan appropriate to St. Peter's function as a
martyrium and consistent with
Renaissance philosophical ideals (see fig. 267). Four equal arms,
terminating in apses, radiate
from a central crossing crowned
with an immense dome sur-
rounded by smaller domes. The
underlying geometry of the design is simple, producing a
monumental effect not unlike the
unified compositions offered in
painting and sculpture by Leonardo, Raphael, and Michelangelo.

The boldest aspect of Bramante's conception is its colossal scale. Bramante set out to
surpass the monumental architectural remains of ancient Rome,
creating a structure that would
dominate all Rome. Bramante is
reported to have stated that he
was inspired to "place the Pan-

291. DONATO BRAMANTE
Plan, New St. Peter's. 1506

25 meters
— N →

292. MICHELANGELO BUONARROTI
Plan, New St. Peter's. 1546–64. Pope Paul III appointed Michelangelo chief architect of St. Peter's. The artist, burdened by his advancing age and numerous other artistic projects, took charge of the construction of St. Peter's without pay and for the "salvation of his soul," as he expressed it. Throughout the sixteenth century, an argument continued over whether the design of St. Peter's should be limited to Bramante's and Michelangelo's central plan or whether a nave should be added to create the more traditional basilica structure. In the early seventeenth century, the present cruciform basilica plan was finally carried through, by Carlo Maderna (see fig. 345).

more cohesive unity by simplifying it, giving a new lucidity to the exterior form and the interior spaces. This unity is further expressed in the use of the giant order (pilasters or columns that span more than one story of the structure) on both the exterior and the interior. On the exterior, Michelangelo's wall design is more varied than Bramante's, sheathing the building like muscle and flesh over bone and creating an external vitality enveloping the inner, structural core (figs. 293, 294).

The commanding dome of St. Peter's, also based on a design by Michelangelo, was erected by Giacomo della Porta between 1588 and 1591. Structural reasons dictated that it be slightly more pointed, to exert less thrust, than Michelangelo's original design. The dome retains Michelangelo's grand scale and articulation and is a worthy climax to Bramante's earlier vision.

Michelangelo took charge of construction in 1546, noting that "every architect who has departed from Bramante's plan . . . has departed from the right way." Michelangelo's plan (fig. 292) retains the integrity of Bramante's central plan, but it achieves a

293, 294. MICHELANGELO BUONARROTI. Longitudinal section and elevation of St. Peter's (engravings by Dupérac, 1569)

MICHELANGELO, SISTINE CHAPEL CEILING

295. MICHELANGELO BUONARROTI
The Creation of Adam (detail of the Sistine Chapel Ceiling). 1508–12. Fresco. Sistine Chapel, Vatican, Rome

He who made everything,
  made every part,
And then chose what was
  most beautiful,
To reveal on earth the
  excellence of His creation,
And the divine art with
  which He made it
(Michelangelo, *Sonnet*,
  c. 1510).

In the gap between Adam's list-less hand and God's command-ing gesture, the energy of crea-tion is concentrated (fig. 295). Seldom in the history of art has such a small segment of pictorial space been endowed with such powerful meaning. God the Fa-ther, his thrusting, forward movement intensified by his bil-lowing cloak, sweeps dramati-cally toward Adam. A host of *putti* accompany God, who with his left arm embraces a female figure who may represent Eve or the Virgin Mary. Adam re-clines in a barren landscape, his arm supported by his upraised knee. His figure is so powerfully muscled that even in repose we sense immediately the energy that will be released once God touches him and endows him with a soul, with life.

Following his triumph in Florence with the colossal *David* (fig. 281), Michelangelo was called to Rome in 1506 by Pope Julius II, nephew of Sixtus IV. At first Julius asked Michelangelo to design and execute a grand papal tomb for himself, but by 1508 he had commissioned him to paint the ceiling of the Sistine Chapel, where fifteenth-century artists had decorated the walls with frescoes (see fig. 4). Michel-angelo accepted the task grudg-ingly; as he describes in a sonnet (fig. 298), painting the ceiling was a demanding physical labor:

I've got myself a goiter
  from this strain . . .
My beard toward
  Heaven, I feel the back of
  my brain
Upon my neck, I grow the
  breast of a Harpy;
My brush, above my face
  continually,
Makes it a splendid floor
  by dripping down. . . .
Pointless the unseeing
  steps I go.
In front of me, my skin is
  being stretched
While it folds up behind
  and forms a knot,
And I am bending like a
  Syrian bow. . . .

Although the scheme is often discussed as if Michelangelo

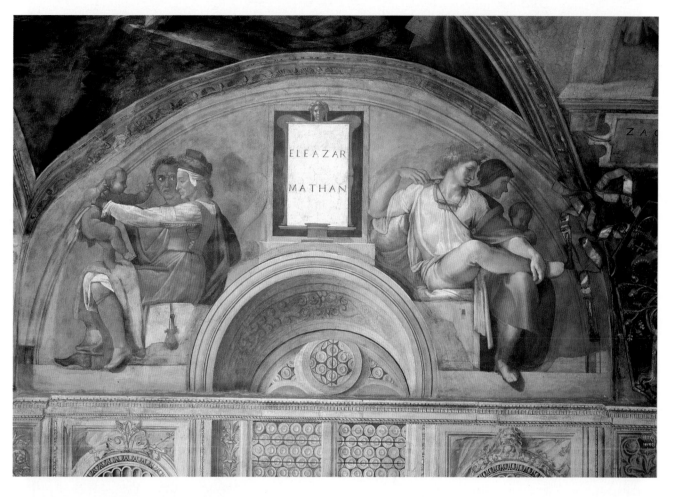

296. MICHELANGELO BUONARROTI

Eleazar and Matthan. 1508–12. Fresco (after cleaning). Lunette, Sistine Ceiling. The cleaning of the entire ceiling will be completed by the early 1990s.

were his own iconographer, the complexity of the cycle suggests that the ceiling's intricate iconography was developed in consultation with his patron, and one or more theologians. Our first impression of the ceiling is of a maze of complexly posed human figures that have to be seen from different viewpoints (fig. 297). Order, however, is created by the painted architectural framework. The central spine of the ceiling has a sequence of nine scenes, alternating in size from small to large, from passages in Genesis (1:1 through 9:27). To see the figures along the side walls, the viewer must turn ninety degrees to the left or right. The largest figures are the Old Testament prophets and ancient Sibyls who, possessed by the spirit of God, foretold the coming of Christ. In the window lunettes and spandrels, Michelangelo portrayed the ancestors of Christ (fig. 296).

Another level of figures, nude males called *ignudi* (nudes), are seated in poses that vary from the decorative to the energetic. They support painted bronze medallions decorated with scenes from the Old Testament that refer to wise and just rule. Garlands of oak leaves and acorns, emblems of Julius II's family, are held by some of the

ignudi, but their primary role is to embellish Michelangelo's cycle.

As our eyes ascend from the first level of ancestral figures toward the histories, the figures in each horizontal level are distinguished by an increasing freedom of movement. In Neoplatonic philosophy (see p. 223), unrestricted figural movement was symbolic of the freedom of the human soul to ascend to the divine, for as the soul ascended, it was believed to be less and less restricted by the bonds of earthly matter: the eloquent movement displayed by the *ignudi* is a metaphor for the freedom of the soul.

The symbolism of our aspiration to join God is conveyed by the central histories, which relate God's love in the acts of creation and in the story of Noah. The cycle runs backward in time, but it has an internal logic. Michelangelo begins with the sin and disobedience of Noah, the most righteous man God could find on earth, to stress the sinfulness of all humanity. What redeems this human sin is the love of God, with which the cycle concludes in the first moment of the Creation. God's initial act of love, dividing Light from Darkness, is painted directly over the altar.

RAPHAEL, STANZA DELLA SEGNATURA

299. RAPHAEL
Philosophy (popularly known as *The School of Athens*). 1509–11. Fresco, 19 x 27'. Stanza della Segnatura, Vatican, Rome

Raphael's *Philosophy* has long been viewed as the ideal of High Renaissance painting (fig. 299). Figures representing venerated ancient philosophers in a consummate variety of postures are composed within a classicizing architectural setting. The use of scientific perspective, within a lucid and impressive setting, directs our attention to the two main figures in the center. The coffered vaults and the niches with sculpture remind us of the decoration of the baths of ancient Rome (see fig. 130) and of Bramante's new church of St. Peter's (fig. 290), being erected nearby at that very moment by the same patron.

The philosophers in the center are the gray-haired Plato, holding his *Timaeus*, a book on the origin of the universe, and Aristotle, who holds his *Nicomachean Ethics*. Plato points heavenward to indicate his philosophical approach to the world of ideas, while Aristotle gestures over the earth to suggest that the universal can only be understood through examining the natural world. Other philosophers can be identified by their attributes. Euclid the geometrician, seen bending over a compass and board in the right foreground, has the features of Bramante, a close friend of Raphael who secured this commission for the

young painter from Pope Julius II. Vasari suggests that Bramante designed the architectural setting of this particular scene for his friend. Plato bears a resemblance to the elderly Leonardo, who was in Rome at this time. Raphael himself engages our attention, for in his self-portrait near the right border he looks out at us. By portraying the historical personalities from antiquity with the visages of contemporary people, Raphael gave personal meaning to the ideal of the Renaissance as a revival of classical values.

Another portrait is the brooding, melancholic figure in the left central foreground who, pen in hand, appears self-absorbed. His inclusion was an afterthought, for he was painted on a fresh patch of plaster. The figure represents the ancient philosopher Heraclitus, who expressed the solitary, pensive nature of the creative temperament. In pose the figure recalls the prophets from the Sistine Ceiling (fig. 297), while the face suggests that it is a portrait of Michelangelo. Raphael added the figure in homage to the older master, probably after the partially completed Sistine Ceiling was unveiled in August 1511.

In a beautiful semicircular composition, *Theology* presents groupings of saints in heaven and theologians on earth, all gathered around a central axis which descends from God the Father, Jesus, and the Holy Spirit

RAPHAEL, frescoes, Stanza della Segnatura: 1509–11
1514: Papal proclamation against slavery and the slave trade
1515: Thomas More, *Utopia*

to the bread of the Eucharist displayed on the altar (fig. 300). Raphael's composition forms an apse, and the fresco visually embodies the concept that it is persons—in heaven and on earth—who comprise the church. *Philosophy* and *Theology* face each other in the Stanza della Segnatura, expressing the union that the Renaissance forged between Christian theological values and the classical philosophical tradition.

300. RAPHAEL

Stanza della Segnatura. 1509–11. *Theology,* known as the *Disputà,* is on the wall opposite *Philosophy,* and in the lunette over the window is *Justice.* The room originally functioned as Julius II's study and personal library; only later did it receive the name by which it is known today. The themes chosen for the walls—Philosophy, Theology, Justice, and Poetry—relate to its use as a library. The ability of the High Renaissance to simplify and clarify is evident in this program, which encompasses the four basic realms of scholarship and literature. It has also been suggested that the four themes refer to the pope's interest in Truth (*Philosophy* and *Theology*), Goodness (*Justice*), and Beauty (*Poetry*). Early sources reveal that Pope Julius II himself designed this impressive program.

HIGH RENAISSANCE PAINTING IN VENICE

Giorgione's *Sleeping Venus* helped establish the reclining female nude as a standard type in the history of European art (fig. 301; for a later example, see fig. 436). This subject is obviously erotic, and Giorgione's composition accentuates the sensuous quality of the female body by contrasting the swelling forms of the upper contour—head, breast, abdomen, and wrist—with the long curve of the bottom edge of the figure. The elegant slenderness of Venus's body is emphasized by her pose, with the right arm raised and the right ankle and foot hidden behind the left. The shimmering white drapery and deep red pillow accentuate and enhance the warm flesh tones of the body, isolating the figure in a verdant green landscape with a luminous Venetian sky and clouds. Giorgione established a new oil paint-

301. GIORGIONE (completed by TITIAN)
Sleeping Venus. c. 1510. Oil on canvas, 42 3/4 x 69"; the figure is lifesize. Staatliche Gemäldegalerie, Dresden. The painting was apparently damaged at an early date and a kneeling cupid near the feet of the figure, the attribute which identified the figure as Venus, was painted over. An early source suggests that Titian completed both the cupid and the landscape. Giorgione, who died in the great plague of 1510, may have left the work unfinished. The face of Venus has been repainted, probably in the nineteenth century.

ing technique in which the forms are rendered without detail (see p. 293). In the *Sleeping Venus*, the

technique emphasizes the delicacy and softness of the body. The landscape setting removes the figure from the more erotic setting of a bed, and by representing Venus with her eyes closed, as if asleep, Giorgione encourages the male patron and

302. TITIAN
Venus of Urbino. 1538. Oil on canvas, 47 x 65". Uffizi Gallery, Florence. The work was painted for Guidobaldo II della Rovere of Urbino. Although a letter from Guidobaldo to his agent refers to the painting not as Venus, but as "la donna nuda" (the nude woman), the roses in her hand and the myrtle, symbol of Venus, growing in the pot in the background support an identification with Venus. The dog at her feet has been recognized as an emblem of marital fidelity.

GIORGIONE (and TITIAN), *Sleeping Venus:* **c. 1510**
1501: Venetian printers use movable type to print music
1504: Venetian monopoly on the spice trade is broken by Portugal
1508: The League of Cambrai is formed to attack Venice
1516: Jewish "ghetto" is established in Venice

his friends to observe her beauty without embarrassment. At the same time, such a pose establishes a certain distance and restraint, and the kneeling cupid may have served as a guardian figure. The ultimate effect is of a slender figure dreaming in a warm Italian landscape.

It is not surprising that the first great painting of the sensuous nude was painted in Renaissance Venice. Venice, "Queen of the Adriatic," was the most cosmopolitan city in Europe. It was famous for its exotic buildings, fine food, and beautiful courtesans.

Titian's painting (fig. 302) was modeled on Giorgione's, perhaps at the request of the patron. The same red, white, and green tones enhance the flesh of the painted figure, but now the setting is an interior, complete with a bed with rumpled sheets and bed curtains. Now the nude is awake: she looks directly at us, posing without embarrassment. Titian's ability to suggest texture is especially evident in the locks of wavy Titianesque red hair which flow onto her shoulders. The maids in the background are gathering her garments from a Renaissance chest.

Giorgione's *Tempestuous Landscape* is a difficult work, and scholars have long debated its specific iconographic meaning (fig. 303). A young man and a nude woman nursing a child occupy the foreground; their relationship is inexplicable, but the "soldier" seems to be watching

over the "gypsy." The landscape which dominates the composition offers both ruins and contemporary buildings. Lightning bolts cross the background, and the trees are dramatically silhouetted against the eerie light of the stormy sky. The main purpose of this painting may be to set a mood rather than tell a story, and perhaps we appreciate it best by surrendering logic to feeling. That an emotional sensation should be the main purpose of a

303. GIORGIONE
Tempestuous Landscape with a Gypsy and a Soldier (traditionally known as *The Tempest*). c. 1505–10. Oil on canvas, 30 1/4 x 28 3/4". Accademia, Venice. A reference to the painting in 1530 calls it "the little landscape on canvas with the tempest [and] gypsy and soldier."

work of art is a new idea in the history of art, but one which seems consistent with the Venetian interest in the suggestive and poetic.

HIERONYMUS BOSCH, *"GARDEN OF EARTHLY DELIGHTS"* TRIPTYCH

304. HIERONYMUS BOSCH
The Creation of Eve in the Garden of Eden; "Garden of Earthly Delights"; Hell (interior of the *"Garden of Earthly Delights"* triptych). c. 1510–15. Oil on wood, 86 5/8 x 76 3/4" (center); 86 5/8 x 38 1/4" (each wing); the figures in the foreground of the central panel are approximately ten to fourteen inches tall. The Prado, Madrid. The iconography of the work has been much debated, and there is no general agreement as to its meaning or exact purpose. The work may have been commissioned by Hendrik III for the palace of the House of Nassau in Brussels, where it was hanging in 1517. In this setting the painting must have been a novel secular decoration and a focus for intellectual discussions.

The left and right wings of the interior of Bosch's triptych represent traditional Christian subjects (see fig. 304). The left wing shows the Garden of Eden, with God the Father creating Eve as Adam looks on, while the right wing presents a vision of the devastation of hell after the Last Judgment. Placed between these views of humanity's past and future is the central panel, which has been interpreted as representing the present, when humanity indulges the sins, begun in the Garden of Eden, that will

lead to hell. Bosch's moral stance seems self-evident, and few of the hundreds of naked figures cavorting in the expansive garden of the central panel express even momentary delight. In the central section of the detail (fig. 305), a man looks up guiltily as he embraces a woman, while nearby figures greedily gather around a giant floating berry. A pearl seeps from between the legs of a couple lying within a giant shell carried by another man. Hundreds of unexpected episodes and surprising details

capture our admiration for the painter's imagination in expressing humanity's determined perversity. In the landscape are real and imaginary birds and beasts, including the owl, symbol of perverted wisdom (it can see only in the dark), and huge raspberries, strawberries, and other fruits, whose multiple seeds hint at rampant promiscuity. The work is executed in seductive pastels. It has been suggested that the theme here is humanity before the great flood, when God, grieving "that he had made man

BOSCH, *"Garden of Earthly Delights"* triptych: c. 1510–15
1509: Erasmus, *In Praise of Folly*
1517: Luther's Ninety-five Theses

on the earth," destroyed all but Noah and his family (Genesis 6:5–6; 6:11–13). Whatever the exact theme, seldom in the history of humanity has the role of evil in the world been more astonishingly and unexpectedly depicted.

In light of the iconography of the main panel, a reexamination of the wings reveals unusual details. The birds, beasts, and plants that inhabit the Garden of Eden include composite creatures that suggest that even in Eden unnatural cross-fertilization has taken place. Life in God's creation is violent: the animals and birds of Paradise already stalk and devour each other. The delighted expression on Adam's face as he ogles the newly created Eve suggests that, in Bosch's inter-

pretation, sexual pleasure is the first thought of the first man.

The devils that populate Bosch's *Hell* provide further evidence that he is the first great artist of the fantastic. The ponds in the left and center panels give way in *Hell* to a wasteland, above which rises an edifice created by a combination of a dead tree and a man that represents the "tavern of lost souls." The Devil is enthroned as a frog with a bird's head who endlessly devours sinners. They are excreted only to face further torment. Although the triptych as a whole is related to Last Judgment paintings, it offers no view of souls in Paradise. In this world, there is no redemption.

Details about Bosch's life help

little in clarifying his art. His grandfather and father were both painters. Bosch himself seems to have had a successful life. He was a member of the Brotherhood of Our Lady, a pious religious group, and through his wife he owned a large estate. Internationally known, he received commissions from the archduke of Austria, and his works were collected by important connoisseurs. It has been suggested that the tree-man in the center of *Hell* is a self-portrait. The face, which is in sharp contrast to the other, generalized figures, looks askance at the suffering around him. Bosch has been claimed by the twentieth-century Surrealists as their true ancestor (see p. 484).

MATTHIAS GRÜNEWALD, *ISENHEIM ALTARPIECE*

306. MATTHIAS GRÜNEWALD
St. Anthony; Crucifixion; St. Sebastian; with the *Lamentation* below (exterior of the *Isenheim Altarpiece*). c. 1512–15. Oil on wood, 9' 9 1/2" x 10' 9" (center); 8' 2 1/2" x 3' 1/2" (each wing); 2' 5 1/2" x 11' 2" (base). Musée d'Unterlinden, Colmar, France. The altarpiece was painted for the chapel of the monastic Hospital of St. Anthony at Isenheim, near Colmar. The hospital specialized in treating patients with skin diseases, including leprosy and syphilis, and the monastery chapel was a pilgrimage shrine for those suffering from such diseases. Given the mission of the hospital, the scars and sores on Christ's body are especially poignant and appropriate. In the late medieval period it was believed that all physical illness was a manifestation of spiritual illness, and the first step in treating patients at the Hospital of St. Anthony was to bring them before this crucifixion to pray. Grünewald's representation of Christ was created so that patients could identify with his sufferings.

Grünewald's monumental *Crucifixion* depicts the gruesome details of Christ's death with unsparing realism (fig. 306). Christ is dead; his head falls dramatically to the side, the blood pouring from the wound in his side begins to congeal, and his body is covered with wounds from the flagellation. The weight of his body pulls down on the crossbar, and the torture wrought by the nails in his hands and feet is painful to see. The lower abdomen is violently compressed, while the rib cage almost bursts through the skin as a result of the anguished death by suffocation brought about by crucifixion. As the Bible relates, darkness envelops the scene. The painting also

GRÜNEWALD, *Isenheim Altarpiece:* **c. 1512–15**
1513: Ponce de Leon plants orange and lemon trees in Florida
1513: Balboa discovers the Pacific Ocean
1513: First European ship lands in China
1519: Leonardo da Vinci dies in France
1520: Raphael dies in Rome

emphasizes the suffering of Christ's mother and Sts. John the Evangelist and Mary Magdalene. St. John the Baptist points to Christ, stating, "He must become more important, while I must become less important" (John 3:30). The dark sky and red garments add drama.

The choice of subjects and their interpretation can be directly related to the position and role of Grünewald's altarpiece within the monastic and hospital complex at Isenheim. Usually the wings would be closed to emphasize Christ's death and Sts. Sebastian, invoked by sufferers of the plague and other diseases, and Anthony, patron saint of the monastery. When the *Crucifixion* panel was opened (notice that Grünewald has painted Christ's body to the right of the opening),

the joyful scenes of the *Annunciation, Mystical Nativity,* and *Resurrection,* painted with vivid, luminous colors, became visible (fig. 307). Certainly these inner panels would have been shown on the feast days of the subjects celebrated here—the Annunciation, Christmas, and Easter. And since Christ's resurrection is celebrated every Sunday, they would most likely have been visible on a weekly basis as well. The innermost decoration, with sculpted figures and two scenes from the life of St. Anthony, would have been shown on Anthony's feast day.

The contrasts between the various layers of the altarpiece are explicit. In the *Resurrection,* an immediate contrast to the grisly *Crucifixion,* Christ's body is healed and his wounds have

become glowing, rubylike jewels. He rises weightless and triumphant while the soldiers guarding the grave fall helplessly in confusion below. The restored beauty of Christ's body would have encouraged hope on the part of the hospital's patients. Even in the joyful scenes, however, a sense of the crucifixion as Christ's destiny is found, for the cloth in which Mary holds the Christ Child in the *Mystical Nativity* is the same tattered fabric that serves as his loincloth when he is crucified.

307. MATTHIAS GRÜNEWALD
Annunciation; Mystical Nativity with Musical Angels; Resurrection (Isenheim Altarpiece with the first set of wings open). When these wings were opened, the innermost scenes, depicted in sculpture, were visible.

TITIAN

Titian's *Madonna* pioneered a new compositional mode (fig. 308). Nothing in earlier Renaissance art prepares us for this asymmetrical composition, with the Madonna set off to one side before grandiose columns seen in diagonal recession. The six members of the Pesaro family who gather below are introduced to the Madonna and Child by Sts. Peter and Francis. The movement inherent in the composition is also found in the twisting figure of St. Peter at the center and in the Madonna and Child, who direct their attention in opposing directions. The child kicks his foot and plays with his mother's veil with a liveliness unusual in religious art (fig. 310).

Titian's *Assumption and Coronation of the Virgin* (fig. 309) ac-complishes an effect of dynamic spontaneity through movement, strong color, and painterly brush-strokes. The standing figure of the Virgin Mary is placed within a circle created by the semicircular frame and a ring of clouds and *putti* below. Above, God the Father sweeps in with open arms to welcome her. God the Father and the Virgin wear garments of a brilliant red, and the Virgin's dominance is enhanced by her rich blue cloak. Titian's triad of primary colors is consistent with High Renaissance practices in Rome. Two apostles in red garments below create the base of Titian's compositional triangle. The combination of rich color with simple composition is perfect for the altarpiece's position, which demands that it be legible

308. TITIAN
Left: *Madonna of the Pesaro Family.* 1519–26. Oil on canvas, 16' x 8' 10"; the figures are approximately lifesize. Santa Maria Gloriosa dei Frari, Venice. The patron was Jacopo Pesaro, who led papal troops to victory over the Turks in 1502. The armored figure with the banner and the turbaned Turkish prisoner allude to Pesaro's victory.

309. TITIAN
Right: *Assumption and Coronation of the Virgin.* c. 1516–18. Oil on wood, 22' 6" x 11' 10"; the figures are over-lifesize. Santa Maria Gloriosa dei Frari, Venice. This huge altarpiece is in situ in its original Renaissance frame on the main altar of the Frari in Venice.

from the main entrance of the church, some three hundred feet away.

VENETIAN PAINTING TECHNIQUE

This detail from Titian's *Madonna* reveals the new painterly style begun in Venice during the early sixteenth century (fig. 310). The traditional Renaissance techniques of tempera and fresco were unsatisfactory in the humid Venetian climate; by about 1500 oil painting on canvas was becoming the accepted medium. The development of a new style and technique in oil painting began with Giorgione (see p. 286), who softened and blurred the edges of his forms, partly as a result of the influence of Leonardo, who visited Venice in 1500. Titian, Giorgione's pupil, went further to develop a style using bold, large, painterly brushstrokes that are consistent with his interest in movement and asymmetrical compositions.

In creating a painting, Titian would paint or stain the canvas a medium brownish-red and then outline his forms in dark paint and reinforce them by modeling them in monochrome, from white to black. After this underpainting dried, he would add layers of translucent oil glazes (varnish, often with a small amount of color), building up a rich color through their superimposition.

Later in Titian's life his brushstrokes became bolder, and he used large, thick strokes *(impasto)* to define form. In the *Rape of Europa* (fig. 311), one of a series of *poesie* (poetic mythological themes), *impasto* is evident in the scales of the fish in the foreground, the feathers of the cupids, the mountains, and the quickly sketched figures of Europa's friends, waving from the distant shore. The shape and direction of the brushstroke reinforce the figural movement and the directional patterns of the composition.

310. TITIAN
Madonna of the Pesaro Family (detail of fig. 308)

311. TITIAN
Rape of Europa. c. 1559–62. Oil on canvas, 73 x 81".
Isabella Stewart Gardner Museum, Boston. This painting, made for King Philip II of Spain, depicts the moment when Zeus, having disguised himself as a bull, abducts a princess. Titian was inspired by the story as it is told in Ovid's *Metamorphoses* (II, 870–75). The unexpected nature of the abduction is expressed in the position of Europa, who seems about to slip off the back of the bull/Zeus.

LATER MICHELANGELO AND THE DEVELOPMENT OF MANNERISM

312. MICHELANGELO BUONARROTI
Medici Chapel, including the *Tomb of Giuliano de' Medici* and the altar wall. 1524–34. Marble, size of entire bay 23 x 15';
length of reclining figures approx. 7'. Medici Chapel, San Lorenzo, Florence. The Giuliano de' Medici commemorated here
was the son of Lorenzo the Magnificent and brother of Pope Leo X, who, in part, sponsored Michelangelo's work at San
Lorenzo, the Medici family church in Florence. Michelangelo never saw the Medici Chapel sculptural and architectural
ensemble as we see it today; it was assembled by pupils following his designs and instructions. On the wall opposite the
Tomb of Giuliano, Michelangelo designed a similar tomb for Lorenzo, the grandson of Lorenzo the Magnificent. Lorenzo is
depicted as Contemplative Life, with allegories of *Dusk* and *Dawn* beneath his idealized portrait.

Michelangelo's Medici Chapel introduces a new organic vitality to the interrelationship between sculpture and architecture in sixteenth-century art (fig. 312). In the *Tomb of Giuliano de' Medici,* an idealized portrait of Giuliano as Active Life is seated, clad in ancient Roman armor. Resting atop the sarcophagus are allegories, the female *Night* and the male *Day.* Michelangelo's plan called for two allegories of rivers, to be placed on a platform below.

The allegories of the times of day symbolize the passage of time as it consumes mortal life, while the river allegories were perhaps intended to represent the Arno and Tiber to refer to Medici power in Florence and Rome. In his position above, Giuliano transcends both time and matter, fulfilling the spiritual ascent of Neoplatonism and the resurrection to eternal life celebrated in masses for the dead (a fresco of Christ's resurrection was intended for the altar wall).

The figures of *Night* and *Day* are twisted in a manner related to *contrapposto.* This type of posture became known later in the century as the *figura serpentinata* (serpentine figure). Although developed during the High Renaissance, this pose became a hallmark of Mannerist art.

In the Medici Chapel, the poses are further enlivened by the visual activity of the walls, where flat walls give way to planes which articulate different levels of surfaces. The cornice is segmented to extend forward into the space of the chapel. The "movement" of these architectural forms establishes a vibrant interplay between the architecture and sculpture.

The Medici Chapel expresses Michelangelo's genius and demonstrates his ability to create a new aesthetic within a given artistic vocabulary. Much of the visual energy and artistic license which develop in Mannerist art and architecture is derived from this freedom of expression.

In 1534 Michelangelo left Florence for Rome, never to return. Rome at mid-century was a changed city. The sack of Rome in 1527 by imperial troops had been brutal. The impact felt from the Reformation caused further turmoil. The psychological climate was leaden.

Michelangelo was commissioned to paint a *Last Judgment* in the Sistine Chapel, where he had painted the ceiling earlier. But while the ceiling expressed God's love and the promise of salvation (fig. 297), now pessimism broods (fig. 313). Christ, on the axis and surrounded by an aura of light, looks toward hell and raises his right hand against the wicked. Mary recoils next to him, "slightly timid in appearance and almost as if uncertain of the wrath and mystery of God" (Ascanio Condivi, 1553). Angels blow trumpets to announce the day and awaken the dead.

In the bottom register, to our left, the dead rise, some being pulled from their graves. To our right, the damned are being dragged down to eternal torment. Above, figures ascend to heaven, where the elect flank Christ. In the semicircular lunettes at the top of the fresco,

MICHELANGELO, Medici Chapel: 1524–34
1534: Henry VIII breaks with the Roman church
1534: St. Ignatius Loyola founds the Jesuits
1534: Sir Thomas More is beheaded

313. MICHELANGELO BUONARROTI
The Last Judgment. 1534–41. Fresco, 48 x 44'. Sistine Chapel, Vatican, Rome. Originally, many of the figures in the *Last Judgment* were nude, but in the climate of the Counter-Reformation, some observers found nudity offensive in a papal chapel. Between 1559 and 1565, drapery was added to many of the figures.

angels wrestle with the instruments of Christ's passion. Around Christ, martyrs brandish the weapons used to torture and kill them.

To the right of Christ, St. Bartholomew, who was flayed, looks to Christ. He holds a knife in his right hand, while his flayed skin hangs from his left hand. The face on the skin was identified as Michelangelo's self-portrait only in 1925. The anguished facial features, which reflect Michelangelo's tortured spirit, add a highly personal message to the painting.

Of Michelangelo's *Last Judgment*, Condivi, the artist's friend and biographer, wrote: "In this work Michelangelo expressed all that the art of painting can do with the human figure, leaving out no attitude or gesture."

MANNERISM

314. AGNOLO BRONZINO
Allegory of Time and Lust. c. 1545.
Oil on wood, 61 x 56 3/4". National
Gallery, London. Much about this
painting remains a mystery to us.
Although the circumstances of its
commission are unknown, it may
have been made for the Medici to
be given to King Francis I of France.

Bronzino's *Allegory of Time and Lust* is a visually and intellectively complex painting (fig. 314). At the top, allegories of Time and Fraud pull back a blue curtain, revealing the central figure of Venus, who, exposed by a cool, harsh light, is being caressed by her son, Cupid. Additional allegorical figures, including Deceit, to the right, behind the *putto*, and Jealousy (recently interpreted as representing Syphilis), demonstrate the results of lust. The precise iconography of the work is still debated; this difficulty of interpretation reveals the elevated intellectual themes of Mannerist art. The crowded figures and exceptionally varied poses address a new style of highly artificial composition and unusual spatial effects.

Mannerism often invited the knowledgeable viewer to appreciate the subtle and hidden conceits of the work. Mannerist art was not intended to appeal to a mass audience. The works of Michelangelo and Raphael provided a starting point for the Mannerists, who developed selected ideas and forms to achieve a stylized, artificial elegance.

Cellini's *Saltcellar* reveals the artist's delight in demonstrating both technical accomplishment and artistic invention (fig. 315). In its graceful refinement, the *Saltcellar* reflects the conspicuous wealth and manner of sixteenth-century European courts. In its decorative treatment of counterbalanced nude figures and complex iconographic details, it demonstrates the visual and thematic complexities which

BRONZINO, *Allegory of Time and Lust:* **c. 1545**
1536: Lower California is discovered by Cortes
1542: Pope Paul III establishes the universal Inquisition
1546: Death of Martin Luther
1554: Palestrina publishes his first book of music for the mass

315. BENVENUTO CELLINI

Saltcellar of Francis I. 1543. Gold and enamel, 10 1/4 x 13 1/8". Kunsthistorisches Museum, Vienna. Cellini's saltcellar (a receptacle for table salt) was made for the French king Francis I.

316. GIAMBOLOGNA

Rape of the Sabine Woman. Completed 1583. Marble, height 13' 6". Loggia dei Lanzi, Florence. The theme is drawn from an event which occurred in the early development of ancient Rome, when the Romans abducted Sabine women as wives.

occur in Mannerist art. The work was created to delight both the eye and the mind.

Giambologna's *Rape of the Sabine Woman,* with its twisting, spiraling, upward movement, was titled only after its completion (fig. 316). Contemporary sources reveal that the artist was initially inspired not by a subject, but by the challenge to compose a group of multiple interlocking figures in dynamic movement. Giambologna's solution, based on a continued use of the *figura serpentinata* (see p. 294), offers effective and varied visual expressions when viewed from different positions. The rhythmic interplay of the figurative forms, emphatically stressed along diagonals, contributes to the work's dynamism, while the spiraling movement compels us to walk around the sculpture to view its varied presentations. This complex and energetic spatial involvement is a characteristic of late-sixteenth-century sculpture; it continues the course set earlier by Michelangelo's exaggerated figural style. But whether the sculpture is monumental or more intimate, the dazzling display of the artist as virtuoso performer is apparent.

EARLY LANDSCAPE PAINTING

317. PIETER BRUEGEL THE ELDER
December Landscape (commonly known as *Hunters in the Snow*). 1565. Oil and tempera on wood, 46 1/8 x 63 3/4".
Kunsthistorisches Museum, Vienna. This landscape is part of a series of six that represented different times of the year;
five survive today. They probably were originally displayed in the home of a wealthy Antwerp banker.

Bruegel's *December Landscape* (fig. 317) emphasizes nature not only by the vast sweep of the terrain but also by the manner in which the season—as expressed in the landscape—dominates and controls the activities of the peasants. Trudging peasants with a pack of motley dogs lead us into a village scene with skaters in the middle ground. The landscape culminates with distant, atmospheric peaks reminiscent

of the Alps that Bruegel crossed on a trip to Italy. The leaden gray-green of the sky and its subtle transformation in the colors of the frozen ponds, in combination with the stark, silhouetted trees and birds, evoke the time of year, the kind of day, and even the temperature of the moment.

Our present-day enjoyment of landscape is not historical. In earlier periods, landscape was often viewed as an adversary, a

frightening and unpredictable element populated with thieves and the unknown. With the exception of some ancient Roman frescoes and mosaics, landscape as a theme developed only late in the history of art. These examples from the sixteenth century are some of the first paintings to convey appreciation for landscape.

One of the first artists to show an interest in the expressive

PIETER BRUEGEL THE ELDER, *December Landscape:* 1565
1558–1603: Queen Elizabeth reigns in Britain
1569: The Mercator projection map of the world is published in
Flanders

318. ALBRECHT ALTDORFER
Left: *Battle of Alexander and Darius.*
1529. Oil on wood, 62 1/4 x 47 1/4".
Alte Pinakothek, Munich. Altdorfer's panoramic landscape
combines natural observation with
historical fantasy. Its ostensible
subject is the famous ancient battle
at Issus, where Alexander the
Great defeated the Persian king
Darius in 333 B.C. The painting was
commissioned by the city of Re-
gensburg at the request of Duke
Wilhelm of Bavaria. This historical
theme almost certainly refers to the
sixteenth-century hope that German
troops would be able to stop the
advance of the Turks into Europe.

319. EL GRECO
Right: *Toledo.* c. 1600–1610. Oil on
canvas, 47 3/4 x 42 3/4". The Metropolitan Museum of Art, New York
(Bequest of Mrs. H.O. Havemeyer).
El Greco, who was born on the
island of Crete and who studied in
Venice, lived in Toledo, Spain, from
about 1575 until his death in 1614.

power of landscape was the German painter Altdorfer. His masterpiece is a landscape which is
also a history painting (fig. 318).
The global scope of the landscape is tied to Altdorfer's historical narrative, for he wants to
suggest that the battle at Issus
was a struggle for control of the
known world. This earthly conflict seems to take on an even
cosmic significance, for Altdorfer presents a struggle between
the setting sun and the rising
moon as they vie for superiority
in the background.

The configuration of hills,
valleys, and monuments in El
Greco's painting identifies the
city as Toledo (fig. 319), but both
the natural forms and the city's
structures have been stretched
and verticalized to create a nervous effect that is heightened by
the somber colors and stormy
sky. Along the banks of the river
and on the hillsides are tiny
human figures who are dominated and threatened by the
landscape. El Greco's vision of
the city where he lived is less a
portrait than a vehicle to convey
a mood of drama and, perhaps,
religious ecstasy.

BRUEGEL, *Peasant Wedding Feast:* c. 1566
1565: Tobacco is introduced into Britain
1578: China's population reaches 60 million

PIETER BRUEGEL THE ELDER

320. PIETER BRUEGEL THE ELDER
Peasant Wedding Feast. c. 1566. Oil on wood, 44 7/8 x 64 1/8". Kunsthistorisches Museum, Vienna. The bride is the smug woman seated in front of the suspended cloth with a crown above her head. To either side are the groom and the couple's parents. To the right a priest is in conversation with a distinguished-looking man who probably represents the landowner for whom these peasants worked.

In his *Peasant Wedding Feast*, Bruegel emphasizes the rustic nature of peasant life (fig. 320). In the huge, grain-filled barn of a prosperous landowner, a wedding feast is being celebrated. In the right foreground, two men carry food on a huge makeshift tray composed of a door balanced on two sticks. The guests reach eagerly to pass the plates. The composition is based on the strong right-to-left diagonal recession of the table, which is opposed by the movement of the figures carrying the food. The lower right corner offers a glimpse of a chair; the left has a figure pouring beer into a miscellany of jugs and a child licking its fingers. Bruegel's palette, with simple browns set off by white, red, and the abundant gold of the grain, suggests the rich simplicity of peasant life.

For the twentieth-century observer, Bruegel's paintings of peasant life provide a fascinating source of knowledge about lower-class life, but the function of these paintings for Bruegel and his contemporaries is uncertain. Details of the present picture suggest some criticism of peasant life: the smugness of the bride, the gluttony of the participants, the fact that the priest and the landowner have withdrawn from the rest of the crowd. In the absence of evidence to the contrary, however, it is reasonable to suggest that Bruegel was recording, not condescending. He may have decided to record the local traditions which enrich daily life specifically because they represent the actual and expected.

Bruegel was a friend of intel-lectuals and his works were collected by connoisseurs. He also designed prints, including copies after works by Bosch and works in Bosch's style. Bruegel traveled as far as Italy. He died, only in his late thirties or early forties, in 1569. During Bruegel's lifetime the Netherlands was engaged in a long battle for independence against foreign overlords. Some of his paintings representing the horrors of war refer to this conflict, and in some, specific details convey the dignity of the local populace and the oppression of the Spanish. In this light, it is tempting to question whether Bruegel's emphasis on local traditions in the peasant paintings could also have a patriotic connotation. The peasant pictures represent the vitality of Northern life, but without any obvious reference to the Spanish overlords who governed the subservient nation.

THE ARCHITECTURE OF ANDREA PALLADIO

321, 322. ANDREA PALLADIO
Facade and interior, San Giorgio Maggiore, Venice. Begun 1566. Andrea di Pietro della Gondola was given the nickname Palladio, an allusion to Pallas Athena, the Greek goddess of wisdom.

The imposing church of San Giorgio Maggiore, with its white marble facade radiant against the blue sky and water, is built on an island just across the lagoon from the main public square of Venice (fig. 321). Renaissance architects had long wrestled with one major problem of facade design for basilica churches: how to reconcile the different roof heights of the nave and side aisles within a visually coherent design. Palladio's novel solution was to superimpose one classical temple front, reaching the height of the nave, over another, broader temple front, which spans the width of the side aisles. The use of the giant order unifies the double-tiered arrangement, while the sequence of pediments creates a dynamic, axial accent. The facade is vigorous and simple. Its commanding scale and Renaissance harmony carry especially well from the public square near San Marco.

The articulation of the facade design is carried through the interior (fig. 322). Shorter pilasters, corresponding to those on the lower, broader temple front on the exterior, face the side aisles, while a giant order of pilasters and engaged columns face the nave, crossing, and apse.

Palladio's designs, whether for ecclesiastical or secular architecture, such as the Villa Rotonda (fig. 9), express visual harmony. Palladio's proportional systems were derived from musical scales, and they governed the interrelationship of all of the parts of a building as a totality.

Palladio had an incalcuable influence on later developments in Western architecture because his ideas were published in editions illustrated with ground plans, sections, and elevations of his buildings. Palladio's *Four Books on Architecture*, first published in 1570, found their way into many great European and American libraries, including those of Robert Adam and Thomas Jefferson (see pp. 350 and 362–63).

VERONESE AND THE IMPACT OF THE COUNTER-REFORMATION

323. PAOLO VERONESE
Last Supper/Feast in the House of Levi. 1573. Oil on canvas, 18' 3" x 42'. Accademia, Venice. Veronese continued to paint in the Venetian High Renaissance style.

At first glance, this huge and sumptuous painting by Veronese (fig. 323) seems to represent a secular banquet. The setting is a palatial loggia, and the figures at the table are surrounded by richly costumed servants. However, Veronese created this work in response to a commission to paint a Last Supper for a monastery refectory in Venice. His interpretation of the Last Supper was questioned by the patron, at which point Veronese was called before one of the Inquisition tribunals established by the Catholic church (see pp. 265–66). The transcript from his trial survives, giving us rare insight into a confrontation between the needs of the Counter-Reformation church and the nature of artistic freedom in the Renaissance.

Veronese is asked to describe the painting and to defend the inclusion of so many extra figures in the composition:

Inquisitioner: What is the significance of those armed men dressed as Germans, each with a halberd [battle weapon] in his hand?
Veronese: We painters take the same license the poets and jesters take. . . . They are placed here so that they might be of service because it seemed to me fitting that the master of the house, who was great and rich, should have such servants.
Inquisitioner: And that man dressed as a buffoon with a parrot on his wrist, for what purpose did you paint him on that canvas?
Veronese: For ornament, as is customary. . . .

Inquisitioner: Did anyone commission you to paint Germans, buffoons, and similar things in that picture?
Veronese: No, milords, but I received the commission to decorate the picture as I saw fit. It is large and, it seemed to me, it could hold many figures.
Inquisitioner: Are not the decorations which you painters are accustomed to add to paintings or pictures supposed to be suitable and proper to the subject . . . ? Does it seem fitting at the Last Supper of the Lord to paint buffoons, drunkards, Germans, dwarfs and similar vulgarities?
Veronese: No, milords.
Inquisitioner: Do you not know that in Germany and in other places infected with heresy [Protestantism] it is customary with various pictures . . . to mock

VERONESE, *Last Supper/Feast in the House of Levi:* **1573**
1572: Protestant Huguenots are massacred in France
1575: Thomas Tallis and William Byrd publish music

324. JACOPO TINTORETTO
Last Supper. 1592–94. Oil on canvas, 12' x 18' 8". San Giorgio Maggiore, Venice (see p. 301 for a discussion of San Giorgio Maggiore). Tintoretto's painting is stylistically related to Mannerist developments.

. . . and scorn the things of the Holy Catholic Church in order to teach bad doctrines to foolish and ignorant people? . . .
Veronese: Illustrious Lords, I do not want to defend it, but I thought I was doing right. I did not consider so many things and I did not intend to confuse anyone.

The tribunal contended that Veronese's *Last Supper* lacked decorum because the inclusion of so many extra figures was inappropriate to the subject. It was suggested that the secular elements could be viewed as an attempt to confuse and belittle the church's authority. Veronese's additional figures should be understood as a reflection of the extravagances of Venetian society rather than the

ideas of the Reformation, and the artist based his defense on artistic license. He argued that artists should have the right to adorn and decorate their work as they saw fit. Ultimately he satisfied the tribunal by changing the name of the painting to suggest that it represented another New Testament story, the feast in the house of Levi (Luke 5:29–39), in which Christ dined with tax collectors.

Tintoretto's *Last Supper* (fig. 324) shares elements with Veronese's painting, such as the inclusion of a number of servant figures and animals, but it offers an emphasis on the mystical content of this subject that is in keeping with the attitudes of the Counter-Reformation church. The strong diagonal of the table is a departure from the tradi-

tional Last Supper format, in which the table was placed parallel to the picture plane (see fig. 268). The powerful thrust of the table into space creates a visual tension which complements Tintoretto's dynamic treatment of the theme. Christ rises, his head surrounded by an intense glowing halo, to offer the bread, predicting the Eucharist, to the apostles. The space of the room is energized and spiritualized by ethereal angels, whose transparent, swirling forms emphasize the spirituality of Christ's act. The visual drama of the painting demands an emotional response from the viewer, while its didactic role promotes the Counter-Reformation ideal of the church as the path to salvation.

VII

SEVENTEENTH-CENTURY ART

INTRODUCTION

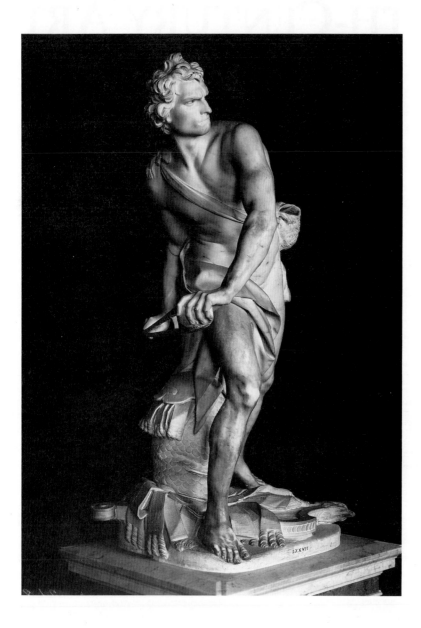

In their representation of vivacious movement and in the manner in which they engage our attention, Bernini's *David* and Hals's *Merry Drinker* (figs. 325, 326) are characteristic of much of the art produced during the seventeenth century. In his depiction of the Old Testament hero David, Bernini has caught the figure coiled in space like a taut spring, about to sling the stone at the giant Goliath. His bursting energy urges us to step aside. In Frans Hals's painting a man invites us to join him in a drink: we impulsively want to reach out and grab the glass he holds so precariously. The loose brushstrokes and warm, golden color enhance the movement and naturalism of the painting.

In creating his tour de force, Bernini, an Italian, was certainly aware that his work would be compared to the sculptures of David by his two great predecessors, Donatello and Michelangelo (figs. 247, 281). He rivals their accomplishments by representing a new moment in the David narrative. His choice of the moment of greatest action is consistent with much of seventeenth-century art. Frans Hals's painting is a work virtually without precedent, in part because it is the product of a new and unique society—the mercantile, bourgeois, Protestant nation established in the Netherlands in the seventeenth century. Despite significant differences in medium, size, and function, these works are similar in the artists' determination to involve us in the action they represent and in their emphasis on depicting arrested motion.

The art of the seventeenth century, however, is not this simple. The two qualities cited above, which are part of a movement within the century known as the Baroque (see below), are not shared by all seventeenth-century works, in part because of increasingly complex and diverse developments in history.

HISTORY

Europe had become steadily more prosperous in the course of the sixteenth century, partly as a result of the influx of wealth from the Americas and the development of new markets in the New World. European wealth continued to increase in the seventeenth century, especially in areas with stable governments and strong commercial and trading interests. The centers of European financial power gradually shifted northward, to the rapidly growing cities of Amsterdam, Paris, and London.

Much of the pluralism of seventeenth-century art can be related to historical developments, for it is during this century that many of the national identities recognized today were consolidated as the map of Europe assumed territorial divisions similar to those of the twentieth century. New, or newly powerful, national entities had a profound influence on artistic developments.

The establishment of the new republic of the Netherlands was perhaps the most dramatic historical development of the seventeenth century. By 1609 the rebels from the northern Netherlands won their independence after a decades-long war against Spanish Catholic overlords. The new nation was unlike any other in Europe, for it was a true republic, with no traditional hereditary aristocracy. It was governed by merchants, who quickly developed a sound commercial basis for the economy. By providing goods at more reasonable prices, they developed markets all over Europe and in the New World. Although the Netherlands became largely middle class, a number of successful businessmen achieved great wealth. Amsterdam became the fastest-growing city in Europe, and the Netherlands soon had a more highly urbanized population than any other European country. In addition, it became Europe's leading maritime power, establishing the East and West India companies and taking control of much of international commerce, including a monopoly on the spice and the slave trades. The Dutch were both Protestant and tolerant, and Jews who fled Poland, Spain, and Portugal during this period largely settled in the Netherlands. Amsterdam also became a lively intellectual community and the most important book-publishing center in Europe. It was in the Netherlands that the new philosophy of the Frenchman René Descartes, which was founded on the principle of universal doubt, was published. It should be no surprise that important new developments in art occurred here.

By the end of the seventeenth century, France, with a population of approximately nineteen million, was the largest nation in Europe and the strongest and wealthiest. Reunited by King Henry IV at the beginning of the century, the monarchy consolidated its power under a series of energetic and able administrators—Richelieu, Mazarin, and Colbert—during the reigns of Kings Louis XIII and XIV. Under Louis XIV, the Sun King, who ruled until 1715, the centralization of power and wealth under the monarchy was completed. The power of the traditional nobility in France was broken, and the king governed as a supreme and autocratic ruler. By the end of the century, France

327. ANNIBALE CARRACCI
Ceiling, Farnese Gallery. c. 1597–1604.
Fresco, 67 x 20'. Farnese Palace, Rome

had an army of 150,000 that was feared throughout Europe.

The decline of Spain as a European power, which had begun in the sixteenth century, continued. Spain's economy was stagnant, despite its important territories. It still controlled the southern Netherlands (or Flanders, roughly equivalent to today's Belgium) and all of Italy south of Rome, including the huge shipping port of Naples. But the conservative rigidity of the Spanish court restricted growth. The Spanish Netherlands remained Catholic and under the control of a traditional aristocracy, but it had been substantially weakened by its foreign overlords, and the country's outstanding Baroque artist, Peter Paul Rubens, found his most important commissions outside his homeland.

The central and northern portions of the Italian peninsula were still controlled by local city-states, the largest of which were Milan and Venice. Here, too, the economy stagnated, with Venice gradually losing its traditional maritime supremacy in the Mediterranean to English and Dutch shippers, whose prices were substantially lower. The most powerful political force in Italy was the papacy in Rome, which during the seventeenth century flourished under a series of dynamic and ambitious popes. They rebuilt Rome with glorious Baroque monuments, fought Protestantism, and reasserted the authority of the Catholic church.

Germany was devastated by the Thirty Years' War (1618–48), which destroyed the power of the Holy Roman Empire and killed at least one-third of its population. Political turmoil consumed energies in England, where the important collector and art patron King Charles I was overthrown and beheaded in 1648.

INTELLECTUAL AND SCIENTIFIC ACTIVITY

The explosion of printed information that followed the invention of movable type in the fifteenth century led to greatly increasing levels of literacy. By the end of the seventeenth century, almost half of the adult male population of Europe was literate. In addition, scientific questioning, more possible after the Reformation, led to important advances in medicine and the other sciences by such major figures in scientific theory and invention as Bacon, Galileo, Newton, Harvey, Hobbes, Kepler, Locke, Leeuwenhoek, Descartes, and Pascal. Many of the European capitals developed academies and learned institutions in science and in other areas, which began publishing scholarly periodicals. In literature, poetry and drama found a new, more vivid and emotional expressiveness in the works of Milton, Corneille, Molière, Racine, and Shakespeare. The caricature, a humorous or critical portrait based on exaggeration, had been invented earlier, but it was popularized and developed by Bernini and Annibale Carracci. In Florence a group interested in reviving ancient Greek drama offered musical presentations which gave the primary impetus to the development of opera. One of the first of these was Jacopo Peri's *Euridice*, which was performed at the marriage by proxy of Marie de' Medici to King Henry IV of France in 1600 (see p. 322). One of the guests was the artist Rubens.

THE STYLES OF SEVENTEENTH-CENTURY ART

Given the complexity of these historical and intellectual developments, it should not be a surprise to learn that seventeenth-century art encompasses a number of different styles. The most typical style is known as the Baroque, a term sometimes confusingly applied to all art produced in the seventeenth century. In painting, this style is characterized by asymmetrical compositions, powerful effects of movement, and strong lighting in combination with dramatic interpretations of subject matter. Similar effects in sculpture are accomplished, often with rich materials and surprising light sources from hidden windows. In Baroque architecture, the classical orders continue to be used as vocabulary, but they are arranged in new patterns that are dynamic and energetic. The Baroque is a style that is espe-

328. GIANLORENZO BERNINI
Fountain of the Four Rivers. 1648–51.
Marble and travertine, with Egyptian
obelisk. Piazza Navona, Rome

cially suited to the goals of autocratic rulers or the Counter-Reformation Catholic church. The exact origins of the word baroque are not clear, but it seems to have first been used to describe works of art in the eighteenth century, when it became a derogatory term for works that were considered strange, irregular, and irrational.

During the seventeenth century there is also interest in continuing the classicism of the High Renaissance, although with a greater complexity of composition and in a grander and more highly decorative manner. These stylistic qualities were usually reserved for subjects drawn from classical mythology or history. This style can be called Baroque Classicism. A typical example is Annibale Carracci's ceiling fresco decoration for the Farnese Palace in Rome (fig. 327). The theme is mythological (the loves of the ancient gods), and although his sources of inspiration include Michelangelo, Raphael, and classical sculpture, the effect is more complex and ornate. Examples of Ba-

329. GIOVANNI BATTISTA GAULLI (assisted by GIANLORENZO BERNINI)

Triumph of the Name of Jesus. 1672–85. Ceiling fresco with gilded stucco surround and white stucco angels by Antonio Raggi. Il Gesù, Rome. Gaulli is also known by the nickname Baciccio.

roque Classicism in architecture are Versailles (fig. 369) and Christopher Wren's St. Paul's Cathedral in London.

A third style that needs to be recognized is the Dutch Baroque, which is limited to painting. This style is represented by thousands of Dutch paintings of Dutch subjects, characterized by their realism and naturalism. Although some of these paintings can be shown to have certain elements in common with Baroque works elsewhere (as was demonstrated with Hals's *Merry Drinker,* above), Dutch Baroque paintings are noted for their relatively small scale, and their choice of everyday subject matter. Mythological and religious paintings were usually avoided. The exception is Rembrandt, who cannot be characterized as a Dutch Baroque artist (as the style has been defined above) and whose style at different times in his life has affinities with both the Baroque and with Baroque Classicism.

Some seventeenth-century works overlap categories, and some fall outside the three which have been defined here (as do those of the Spanish painter Velázquez). Our stylistic distinctions are merely an aid in understanding the complex art of this century. These distinctions will be refined and expanded in subsequent discussions of individual works, but one should resist the temptation to assume that seventeenth-century works of art can be easily categorized.

SEVENTEENTH-CENTURY ART

In Italy, Flanders, and Spain, countries that remained Catholic, the Counter-Reformation (see pp. 265–67) led to the production of dramatic Baroque religious images, especially of subjects that fostered and supported Catholic beliefs: the lives of Christ and the Virgin Mary, the miracles and martyrdoms of saints, and the lives of monks, nuns, and priests. Elaborate cycles of paintings of religious subjects and dramatic sculptural groupings were produced for churches throughout the Catholic world. Architecture in these areas generally followed the same enthusiastic Baroque style.

In the Netherlands, the prevailing religion of Calvinism, which forbade the representation of God or Christ, led to a virtual moratorium on the production of religious subjects (again, Rembrandt stands as a distinct exception). At the same time, the absence of aristocratic or civic patronage meant a decline in interest in mythological subjects. The lively artistic production in the Netherlands specialized in naturalistic paintings of Dutch subjects—landscapes, genre themes, still lifes, portraits—for the home. There was little interest in grand architectural or sculptural projects.

In the countries which had a strong court and aristocracy—France, Flanders, Spain—and in the Italian cities of Florence, Naples, Rome, and Venice, the production of portraits and history paintings continued to provide an important livelihood for painters. Royalty, such as King Charles I of England or Marie de' Medici, queen of France, the noble families of Rome, and members of the clergy, not to mention the papacy, provided lucrative commissions for artists. France offers the best example of art and architecture in the service of autocracy since the ancient Roman Empire.

Although fountains had played a role in urban planning and garden decoration since ancient Roman times, new possibilities in fountain design were explored by that inventive Baroque genius, Bernini. His most triumphal fountain, in the Piazza Navona in Rome (fig. 328), has an ancient Egyptian obelisk raised over a huge rocky landscape with four monumental figures—each as big as Michelangelo's *David*. They symbolize what at the time were considered to be the four main rivers of the world, the Danube, Nile, Rio della Plata, and Ganges. The theme of the fountain, a papal commission, is consistent with the Counter-Reformation, which suggests that all the peoples of the world will be converted to Catholicism through the efforts of an energetic papacy and the revived church of the Counter-Reformation. Bernini forces the water of the fountain to cascade in sheets to create the maximum noise and splash. The water, integral to his conception, is incorporated into both the design and the theme. He even incorporates the drain into his design, for a smiling, cavorting fish "swallows" the water, adding yet another sound to this lively complex. The fountain has a new excitement and energetic dynamism consistent with Baroque attitudes.

330. JUDITH LEYSTER
Self-Portrait at the Easel. c. 1635. Oil on canvas, 29 3/8 x 25 5/8". National Gallery of Art, Washington, D.C. (Gift of Mr. and Mrs. Robert Woods Bliss, 1949)

331. PETER PAUL RUBENS
Left: *Self-Portrait with Isabella Brandt*. 1609–10. Oil on canvas, 69 x 53 1/2". Alte Pinakothek, Munich. This double portrait was painted at the time of the couple's marriage, when the bride was seventeen years old.

332. ARTEMISIA GENTILESCHI
Right: *Self-Portrait as the Allegory of Painting*. 1630. Oil on canvas, 38 x 29". The Queen's Collection, Hampton Court

BAROQUE CEILING PAINTING

Baroque ceiling painting is one of the dramatic and powerful expressions of the Baroque aesthetic and Counter-Reformation ideals. The figures in Gaulli and Bernini's *Triumph of the Name of Jesus* (fig. 329), which is framed with a wide gilded frame held by angels in relief, seem to come to life. Struggling, suffering figures appear to fall down toward us, into the space of the church, while at a vast distance high in the sky, the monogram of Christ (IHS) glows with an unearthly intensity. The painting offers a view of heaven, with angels and ranks of the faithful adoring Christ's name, while the rays of light that flow downward propel disbelievers away from this mystic vision, into a realm of shadowy darkness. With a touch of wit Gaulli here heightens his illusion by interrelating the three-dimensional and painted forms: the foot of one of the angry stucco angels who surround the frame gives an extra push to one of the sinful figures being cast out of Paradise.

A great deal of the success of the illusion painted on the vault of the church of Il Gesù is due to the gilded stucco frame and ceiling coffering, which establish a point of reference for the spatial development. The progressive diminution of the figures is joined with gradually intensifying light to lead us past the frame, beyond the limits of the architecture, while the clouds and figures that overlap the frame emerge into our space. Their position within the church seems confirmed by the shadows they cast on the coffering. This ensemble seems to fulfill the tenets of the Council of Trent of more than a century earlier. With vigor and enthusiasm, it seduces and overwhelms us in an attempt to convince us of the truth of what we see.

THE SEVENTEENTH-CENTURY ARTIST

Seventeenth-century artists were willing to undertake huge projects, and the most successful were entrepreneurs like Rubens and Bernini, who managed large workshops of assistants and apprentices. Only with such help could they have carried out gargantuan projects like Rubens's Marie de' Medici cycle and Bernini's sequence of works for St. Peter's (see pp. 322 and 324). The Baroque is also the period of the virtuoso, in art no less than in drama and music. Artists enjoyed demonstrating their creative powers to enthusiastic patrons, and a typical Baroque work was an incredible tour de force. Perhaps the most breathtaking of all sculptures is Bernini's *Apollo and Daphne* (see fig. 3), in which marble has been transformed by Bernini's ability to suggest textures which convey the mythological miracle: hair becomes leaves and toes take root as bark encompasses the instantaneously frozen figure of Daphne.

Another important development, new in the history of art, took place in the Netherlands in the seventeenth century, where there was such a demand for paintings that a free market in works of art developed. Rather than waiting for a commission to work on a specific project for a specific patron, Dutch artists made more general works for a wide and popular audience. These works were bought not only by citizens, but by art dealers as well, who established shops selling art. For the first time, the relationship between the artist and the public began to approach the situation we know today. Speculation in works of art became a part of the commercial activity of the Netherlands. In fact, there was so much activity that artists could support themselves working as specialists in a single category, such as marine painting, flower painting, or genre painting.

In France, where the king and his ministers controlled all aspects of culture, artists were less free than elsewhere. An academy determined production and through lectures and publications enforced the state-favored style of Baroque Classicism. In most of Europe the Renaissance tradition of the artist as a respected intellectual continued to develop in the seventeenth century, aided by the explosion in art criticism and in writing about art that was a part of the enormous increase in publishing during the century.

The public's interest in the artist and the artist's new self-confidence are expressed in the increasing number of self-portraits. In the two preceding centuries, the self-portrait was unusual and exceptional, but a much larger percentage of seventeenth-century artists have left us self-portraits, and it was during this period that the Medici of Florence began a collection of self-portraits. Among the most impressive self-portraits of the period is Rubens's charming *Self-Portrait with His Wife* (fig. 331).

The interest in self-portraits by women artists that we noted in the sixteenth century continued in the seventeenth. Perhaps the most remarkable is Artemisia Gentileschi's *Self-Portrait as the Allegory of Painting* (fig. 332), a representation in which the painter says, in essence, "I *am* painting." The Dutch artist Judith Leyster represents herself informally at the easel, smiling out at us with ease and a typical Dutch familiarity (fig. 330).

CARAVAGGIO AND HIS INFLUENCE

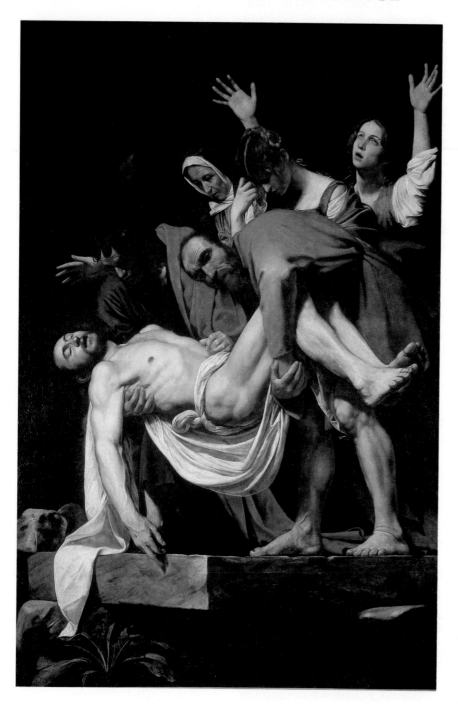

333. CARAVAGGIO
Entombment of Christ. 1603–4. Oil on canvas, 9' 10 1/4" x 6' 8"; the figures are over-lifesize. Vatican Museums, Rome. In 1642 this painting was listed as being Caravaggio's greatest work.

a troubled, weary expression. We seem to be below, in a dark and empty space. Caravaggio may be suggesting that we are standing in the tomb of Christ. The figural composition flows downward from the upper right, beginning with the dramatic gesture of one of the Marys, who raises her hands in supplication, and concludes with the descending dead weight of the body of Christ. The painting is clear, direct, and moving.

Two particular qualities characterize this powerful painting as the work of Caravaggio: the strong lighting and the inclusion of lower-class figure types. The light enters in a bold flash, creating strong highlights and deep pockets of shadow. It seems like a sudden illumination in a world full of darkness. The figures, modestly dressed, range in age from the youthful women to the old, tired figure of the Virgin Mary. Their wrinkles and bare feet are only two of the obvious means by which Caravaggio gives his figures a new actuality.

Our participation in a dramatic religious event is demanded by *Christ with the Doubting Thomas* (fig. 334). The lifesize figures are half-length, and our presence as spectators, standing before the picture, fulfills the semicircular grouping of Christ and the

Caravaggio's *Entombment* is an arresting painting (fig. 333), for it seems as if we are really there—the figures are naturalistic, the strong light gives them a sharp physical presence, and their actions and emotions are convincing. The figures stand on a great tomb slab which seems to jut out of the picture into our space. This command that we become part of the experience is supported by the gaze of Nicodemus, the old man who looks out at us with

CARAVAGGIO, *Entombment of Christ:* 1603–4
1599: Globe Theatre opens in London
1600: Italy's population is about 13 million
1600: North America's population is about 1 million
1602: Shakespeare, *Hamlet*
1611: University of Rome is founded

334. CARAVAGGIO
Christ with the Doubting Thomas.
c. 1602–3. Oil on canvas, 42 1/8 x
57 1/2". Neues Palast, Potsdam

apostles. The composition seems to need us to be complete. In the biblical story, Thomas doubts that the figure appearing to the apostles is Christ. Christ tells him that for proof he should stick his finger in the wound in his side. The text implies that Thomas did not do this, but Caravaggio has chosen to represent Christ forcing Thomas's finger into the wound. Such a shocking, physical emphasis is not uncommon in Caravaggio's works. While the Bible stresses the humble origins of the apostles, Caravaggio is one of the few artists who gives them a compelling reality and dignity.

Not everyone appreciated Caravaggio's vigorous realism. A seventeenth-century critic said that one of his paintings lacked "proper decorum, grace, and devotion." But Caravaggio's art was revolutionary precisely because it was not ennobled by a concept of beauty and because he did not adhere to the idealistic theories of art that had evolved during the Renaissance.

Caravaggio's mastery at depicting internal emotion is evi-

335. CARAVAGGIO
Conversion of St. Paul. c. 1601. Oil on canvas, 90 1/2 x 70". Santa Maria del Popolo, Rome

dent in his representation of the *Conversion of St. Paul* (fig. 335). In the biblical story (Acts 9:1-9), the Roman Saul was traveling toward Damascus to persecute Christians when "suddenly a light flashed from the sky all around him," and he fell to the ground. He heard a voice saying, "Saul, Saul, why do you persecute me?" When Saul asked, "Tell me, Lord, who you are," the reply was, "I am Jesus, whom you are persecuting." Saul, who was blinded by the "brilliance of the light" for three days, was converted to Christianity and baptized with the new name of Paul.

Divine revelations and mystical conversions were common themes in the art of the Counter-Reformation. In Caravaggio's painting, the powerful light comes from almost directly overhead, and Caravaggio suggests that the force of the light has thrust Paul to the ground. Paul reaches out to embrace the light in a natural gesture that is both supplicating and receptive.

Although Caravaggio seems to have had no direct pupils, his art had a potent impact on Italian art and on the many foreigners studying and working in Rome. His close followers were known as Caravaggisti. The Caravaggesque movement became international when French, German, Spanish, Flemish, and Dutch artists returned home to teach and work. Prints after works by Caravaggio and his followers also had an impact on these developments, and artists who never visited Rome and probably never saw an original painting by Caravaggio knew and were inspired by the great Italian painter's innovations.

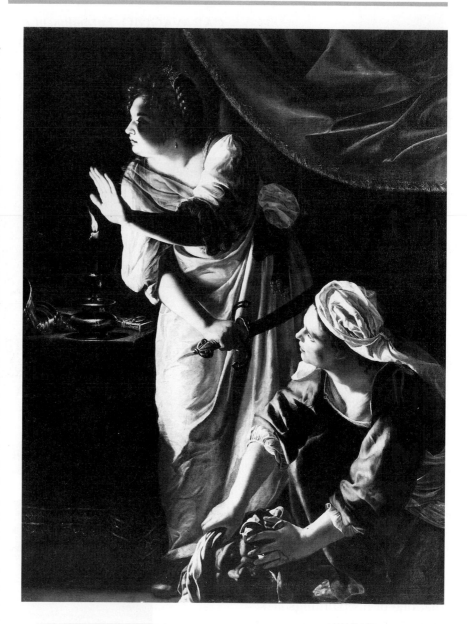

336. ARTEMISIA GENTILESCHI
Judith and Her Maidservant with the Head of Holofernes. c. 1625. Oil on canvas, 72 1/2 x 55 3/4"; the figures are over-lifesize. Detroit Institute of Arts (Gift of Leslie H. Green, 1952). The story of Judith and Holofernes is told in the biblical Old Testament Apocrypha. Judith was a virtuous Jewish widow who saved her people during a siege by sneaking into the Assyrian camp. She captured the attention of the enemy general Holofernes and, after he became intoxicated at a banquet, beheaded him. She is a symbol of Fortitude and, because she saved her people, is often seen as a prototype for the Virgin Mary.

In Artemisia Gentileschi's monumental *Judith and Her Maidservant* (fig. 336), we are intruders—walking in on an episode charged with excitement and fear. The Caravaggesque qualities are evident in the dramatic tension, powerful light, and realistic figures. Holofernes has been decapitated and the head is being wrapped for their escape when Judith hears an unexpected sound. The momentary effect achieved as the nerv-

337. GERRIT VAN HONTHORST
Merry Company (The Prodigal Son in the Brothel). 1620. Oil on canvas, 54 x 84". Uffizi Gallery, Florence. The Dutch painter Honthorst arrived in Rome in 1609 or 1610, too late to study with Caravaggio, but he was so successful at painting Caravaggesque night scenes like this one that he was nicknamed Gherardo delle Notte (Gerard of the Night Paintings). In 1620 he returned to Holland, where he painted and trained pupils in the Caravaggesque manner.

338. JUDITH LEYSTER
Gay Cavaliers. c. 1628–29. Oil on canvas, 35 1/8 x 29". Philadelphia Museum of Art (Johnson Collection). This painting is also known as *The Last Drop.* Leyster was a teacher (in 1635 she had three male students) and a successful, independent artist who painted genre pictures, portraits, and still lifes. Her production diminished after she married a fellow artist and had three children.

ous women look up is dramatized by the light. When Judith holds up her hand to shield her vision from the candle's glare, a strong shadow is cast on her face. The painting communicates a mood of tension and emotional drama that few of Caravaggio's followers could match. Artemisia, daughter of the painter Orazio Gentileschi, specialized in large-scale paintings of biblical or mythological subjects, often choosing themes that featured female heroes. She was proud of her accomplishments, and after finishing a painting for one patron declared: "This will show your Lordship what a woman can do."

Caravaggio never included a source for the strong light which illuminated his subjects, realizing the mystery and drama that an unknown light source can convey. But his followers often chose to introduce the light source into the painting, and in the Dutch painter Honthorst's *Merry Company* (fig. 337) there are two. Honthorst's composition, with half-length, lifesize figures around a table, follows patterns established by Caravaggio. One pair of lovers is completely absorbed in each other, while the other pair laughs at the drunken man to the right, who holds up a full glass and a bottle. The smiling young woman, feeding him and holding up a candle to illuminate the scene, is assisted by a haggard old woman, probably the procuress. The pairing of the couples, the introduction of music—the language of love—with the lute player, and the presence of the old woman (a madam?) suggest that Honthorst may be painting a scene set in a brothel. Although the subject at first seems to be a straightforward genre scene, there are suggestions that it represents Christ's parable of the prodigal son (Luke 15:11–32), and

specifically the theme of the son wasting his inheritance on "riotous living."

In Judith Leyster's *Gay Cavaliers* (fig. 338), the light once again emanates from a candle. The figures are posed to catch the light from different angles, enhancing the composition's lively, momentary effect. Their abandoned gestures of delight in the intoxication of alcohol and tobacco (a new vice in the seventeenth century) are naturalistic, but we are uncertain whether Leyster intended any critical comment.

BAROQUE GENRE PAINTING

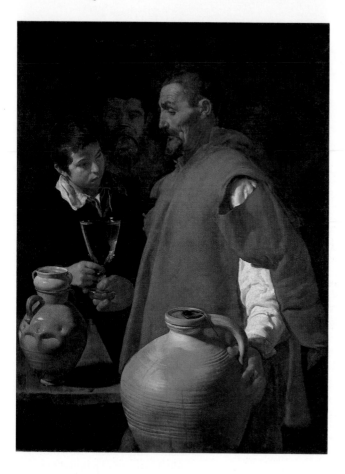

In Velázquez's painting (fig. 339), the simple act of offering, accepting, and consuming a glass of water gains dignity and import. The old water seller, who has brought a jug of fresh spring water from the mountains to the city, offers a youth a goblet of water sweetened with a fresh fig. In the shadowy background a man is drinking. Both the heat of the day and the coolness of the water are revealed in the rivulets of condensation that run down the earthenware jug in the immediate foreground.

The influence of Caravaggio is evident in the half-length, lifesize figures, dark background, and strong light, as well as in the impressive dignity with which these individuals are represented. The composition is simple and pyramidal, focusing attention on the expressions: the downcast, sober eyes of the old

339. DIEGO VELÁZQUEZ
The Water Carrier. c. 1619. Oil on canvas, 41 1/2 x 31 1/2". Wellington Museum, London. This is an early work by Velázquez, painted when he was only about twenty. He presented this genre painting to the king of Spain as a demonstration of his ability as a painter.

340. JAN VERMEER
A Maidservant Pouring Milk. c. 1660.
Oil on canvas, 17 7/8 x 16 1/8".
Rijksmuseum, Amsterdam

man, who is seen in profile; the hesitation in the three-quarter face of the boy; the meditation of the central figure, shown frontally. The somber mood suggests that this scene of everyday life has a deeper significance. The old man seems to be passing on the gift of life to the shy boy. The mood has been described as "sacramental."

Velázquez's profound interpretation of a genre subject is not unique in the seventeenth century, for there are many genre paintings by other European painters that communicate the dignity and seriousness of everyday life. At the same time that Caravaggio gave a new profundity to his religious subjects by infusing them with reality (see fig. 334), genre themes were being given a new seriousness as patrons and painters found the sacred and the holy in the everyday.

Louis Le Nain's *Peasant Family* has an equally serious quality (fig. 341). The somewhat awkward composition lends reality to this quiet gathering, while the figures display an impressive dignity. The drab colors of their home and clothing are relieved by the warm tones of the fire and by the deep ruby red of the glass of wine, held as if in preparation for a visitor. We find this and other similar paintings by Louis Le Nain and his brothers impressive, but we do not understand their function within the elegant, court-oriented culture of seventeenth-century France.

Genre had its greatest popularity in the Netherlands, where straightforward representations of Dutch home and tavern life were especially popular. In contrast to the works of Velázquez and Le Nain discussed here, most

341. LOUIS LE NAIN
Peasant Family. c. 1640. Oil on canvas, 44 1/2 x 62 1/2". The Louvre, Paris

Dutch genre paintings emphasize a pleasing and homey domesticity. The greatest of the Dutch genre painters was Jan Vermeer, who produced only about forty paintings in his lifetime. The *Maidservant* (fig. 340) is typical in its subject: a single woman is shown in the corner of a room, with light coming from a window in the left wall. The setting offers typical objects from a Dutch kitchen, including a footwarmer on the floor and a border of Dutch blue-and-white tiles. It is Vermeer's depiction of light that elevates this humble subject to the status of a masterpiece. Dots of paint make the objects sparkle and glow. It is as if we sense for the first time the beauty inherent in everyday things. Evidence in this and other paintings suggests that Vermeer studied his subjects through a *camera obscura*, an apparatus for projecting an image onto an interior screen of a darkened box, lit

only by a small hole, so that the image could be traced (see also p. 402). This explains the slight abstraction in the treatment of light in Vermeer's work, which heightens its impact. Like other Baroque painters, Vermeer owes a debt to Caravaggio, whose interest in and emphasis on light sensitized the artists of the entire century.

Vermeer most often used models in elegant contemporary clothing, and his focus on a humble subject here may have a specific iconographic meaning. The bread and milk provide the basic nourishment necessary for human life, and by portraying the clean kitchen and humble, hardworking maid, Vermeer may be making a statement about the virtues of domestic life.

PETER PAUL RUBENS

342. PETER PAUL RUBENS AND WORKSHOP
The Arrival and Reception of Marie de' Medici at Marseilles. 1621–25. Oil on canvas, 13 x 10'. The Louvre, Paris. This is one of a series of twenty-one huge paintings by Rubens celebrating her life that Marie commissioned from the artist for the newly completed Luxembourg Palace in Paris.

In Rubens's painting of *Marie de' Medici* (fig. 342) we are thrust into a world of fantasy, where jubilant mermaids and a barebreasted allegorical flying figure celebrate the arrival on French soil of the new wife of the king. The scene represents a historical event, but it has been transformed to express what the patron felt was the underlying meaning of the event. Marie, who had been married by proxy to King Henry IV of France, was not met by her husband, who, history reveals, was at a hunting lodge with his favorite mistress. Rubens has painted Marie being welcomed by the personification of France herself. Above, Fame trumpets Marie's arrival. Marie's crossing had been rough, and Neptune, mythological god of the seas, and his mermaids jubilantly celebrate her safe arrival. By allegory, vivid colors, and lively movement, Rubens has created a pageant to satisfy the aspirations of his royal client. In the other scenes of Marie's life, Rubens blended his knowledge of symbolism and allegory with an enthusiasm for lively movement and brilliant colors.

Rubens was one of the best educated and most intellectual artists of the seventeenth century. He was certainly the only artist of the period to receive an honorary degree from Cambridge University. He served as court painter and ambassador for the rulers of the Spanish Netherlands and was as active as a diplomat as he was as an artist. He counted many members of the royalty and nobility among his friends. He was widely traveled, and his influence helped to make the Baroque an international style.

As a diplomat, Rubens worked tirelessly to promote peace in Europe. One of his most profound allegorical paintings conveys his opinions on the meaning of war for humanity (fig. 343). Rubens himself explained the content in a letter: "The principal figure is Mars, who has left the temple of Janus open (which according to Roman custom remained closed in time of peace) and struts with his shield and his bloodstained sword, threatening all peoples with disaster; he pays little attention to Venus, his lady, who, surrounded by her little love-gods, tries in vain to hold him back with caresses and embraces. On the opposite side, Mars is pulled forward by the Fury Alecto with a torch in her hand. There are also monsters signifying plague and famine, the inseparable companions of war. Thrown to the ground is a woman with a broken lute, as a symbol that harmony cannot exist beside the discord of war; likewise a mother with a child in her arms indicates that fertility, procreation, and tenderness are opposed by war, which breaks into and destroys everything. There is furthermore an architect fallen backwards, with his tools in his hands, to express the idea that what is built in peace for the benefit and ornament of cities is laid in ruin and razed by the forces of arms . . . you will also find on the ground, beneath the feet of Mars, a book and a drawing on paper, to indicate that he tramples on literature and other refinements. . . . The sorrowing woman . . . clothed in black with a torn veil, and deprived of all her jewels and ornaments is unhappy Europe which for so many years has suffered pillage, degradation, and misery affecting all of us so deeply that it is useless to say more about them." This passage reveals the intellect of Rubens and his knowledge of traditional subject matter and history, as well as his humanity and the universal meaning of this seventeenth-century work of art.

343. PETER PAUL RUBENS AND WORKSHOP
Allegory of the Outbreak of War. 1638. Oil on canvas, 6' 9" x 11' 3 7/8". Pitti Palace, Florence. This work was painted for the grand duke of Tuscany.

GIANLORENZO BERNINI'S WORKS FOR ST. PETER'S

As a glowing dove of the Holy Spirit descends, angels and golden rays fill the apse of the church, and the columns of the canopy *(baldacchino)* over the high altar appear to writhe with excitement (fig. 344). We seem to be witnessing a miracle.

Bernini's *Baldacchino* solved some important problems. It provided a focal point for the vast interior by marking the burial spot of St. Peter and the high altar of the basilica, without blocking the view to the apse or overwhelming the interior. The dark bronze and gilded highlights stand out against the white marble of the basilica's architecture, as do the dynamic spiral columns and the beautiful angels, curving volutes, and scallops with tassels—all emulating temporary cloth *baldacchinos*—of the top. Later, Bernini's *Baldacchino* became a frame for the *Cathedra Petri*, a multi-media climax at the end of St. Peter's which enshrines, like a huge reliquary, a wooden and ivory chair thought to be the papal throne used by St. Peter. Four figures of early theologians—Sts. Ambrose, Athanasius, John Chrysostom, and Augustine—support the reliquary just as they had approved the primacy of St. Peter and the Roman church in their writings. One of Michelangelo's windows has been changed by the addition of a stained-glass, alabaster, and gilded stucco representation of the Holy Spirit surrounded by golden rays and *putti* which sweep out with Baroque splendor to dominate Michelangelo's Renaissance apse.

Bernini's colonnade, which

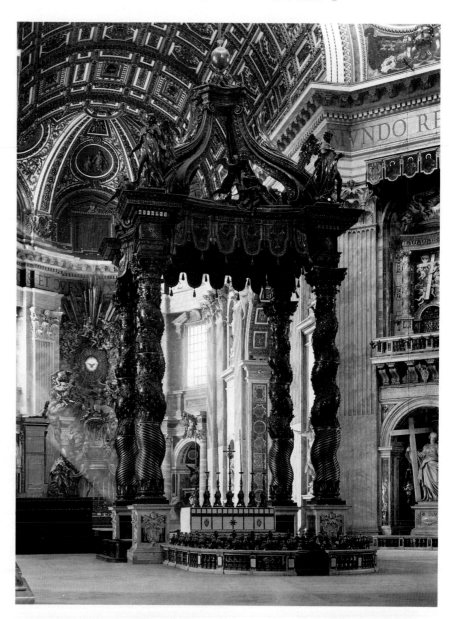

344. GIANLORENZO BERNINI
Baldacchino. 1624–33. Bronze with gilding, height 93' 6"; *Cathedra Petri*. 1656–66. Marble, bronze with gilding, stucco, alabaster, and stained glass. St. Peter's Basilica, Vatican, Rome. Bernini's use of twisted columns is based on the altar railing of Old St. Peter's, which had ancient twisted columns believed to have decorated the great Temple of Solomon in Jerusalem.

shapes the piazza in front of St. Peter's, is more than just an impressive entrance to the basilica, for it also serves to define the space where the faithful gather to receive the papal blessing (fig. 345). Bernini's design is based on an oval with a width of almost eight hundred feet. As we enter this huge and richly decorated space, the broad axis creates a dynamic effect, and space seems

BERNINI, *Baldacchino:* **1624–33**
1628: Harvey publishes on the circulation of the blood
1633: The Inquisition forces Galileo to retract his defense of the
Copernican system

345. GIANLORENZO BERNINI
Colonnade, St. Peter's, Rome. Begun 1656. Travertine, longitudinal axis approx. 800'. A drawing reveals that Bernini conceived of the sides of the colonnade as the arms of St. Peter's, and that the design is meant not only to define and contain but to embrace as well.

to expand to either side. When Bernini built the piazza, the area was surrounded by medieval houses and narrow, winding streets, an approach which would have rendered the spatial explosion of the piazza even more impressive. Huge travertine columns—284 placed in rows of 4—define the piazza without closing it off from the surrounding areas. As a result, it can be quickly emptied when a crowd wants to disperse.

Bernini, who was appointed main architect for St. Peter's in 1637, worked on the building and its decoration for forty-two years, until his death. Among his other works are two papal tombs, another tomb, the altar decoration of the Chapel of the Holy Sacrament, and the nave decorations. From the ancient Roman bridge that was the ceremonial entrance to the Vatican, which Bernini and his assistants adorned with statues of angels in the 1660s, to the dramatic *Cathedra Petri,* works by Bernini transformed St. Peter's from a Renaissance structure into a Baroque experience.

THE DUTCH BAROQUE GROUP PORTRAIT

346. FRANS HALS
Banquet of the Officers of the Civic Guard of St. George. 1627. Oil on canvas, 5' 10 1/2" x 8' 5 1/2". Frans Halsmuseum, Haarlem. The various civic militia groups of the first half of the seventeenth century descend from groups that played a crucial role in gaining the independence of the Netherlands. They continued to have important functions, including guarding the city and keeping order, and it became traditional that they have their portraits painted. Often, as here, they are shown at the annual banquet given them by the city.

The boisterous members of Frans Hals's militia seem to be inviting us to join their celebration (fig. 346). Just to the right of center, a man holds his glass upside down; he was a brewer, and the artist suggests that he is more than slightly inebriated. The vivacious activity of Hals's lifesize figures as they turn, converse, and gesture seems completely spontaneous. Hands are raised, mouths are open, and figures glance in various directions. The suggestion of movement is enhanced by the diagonals in the composition, by repeated strokes of strong color, and by the use of bold diagonal brushstrokes.

The group portrait had its first important development in the democratic, bourgeois Netherlands, and its first great master was Frans Hals, who overcame the inherent repetitiveness of this subject, in which an artist had to paint a group of individuals, all about the same age and all of whom wore the same or similar costumes. The democratic traditions of the Netherlands demanded that the individuals be shown as equals, and usually each paid the painter an identical amount to be included. Hals is able to capture the individuality of each member, as well as the exuberant union that joins the group into a whole.

Rembrandt's *"Night Watch"* is surely the most famous painting known by a completely misleading name. The scene is not represented taking place at night, and the correct title is *The Militia Company of Captain Frans Banning Cocq* (fig. 347). Rembrandt's dramatically composed and lit portrait of the members of this Amsterdam militia company offers a radical solution to the problems of the militia portrait.

Rembrandt subordinates the democratic ideal to pictorial drama and focus, creating a sense of unified action. The moment chosen is not the indulgent banquet, but the captain and lieutenant ordering the militia to march. The other members of the company, as well as certain additional figures—a young woman with a dressed bird hanging from her belt (the bird's claws were the emblem of the militia guild), a boy firing a rifle, and others—are gathered in seemingly spontaneous groupings. Bold light and lightly colored costumes emphasize the main figures and give focus to the composition. A number of subordinate figures are virtually lost in shadow. They were added by Rembrandt to create variety, not militia members who had paid to be included. The composition, rich and complex, is truly

HALS, *Banquet of the Officers of the Civic Guard of St. George:*
1627
1626: Purchase of Manhattan island
1630: Bubonic plague kills 500,000 Venetians
1636: "Haarlem" is founded by Dutch settlers on Manhattan island
1643: Death of Louis XIII

347. REMBRANDT
The Militia Company of Captain Frans Banning Cocq. 1642. Oil on canvas, 12' 2" x 14' 7". Rijksmuseum, Amsterdam. This group portrait, Rembrandt's largest surviving work, is usually known, inaccurately, as *"The Night Watch"* because layers of dirty varnish once made it seem like a night scene. The painting was part of a series of group portraits of militia companies that decorated a great hall in the headquarters of the Amsterdam civic guard. The patrons were members of Cocq's company, each of whom paid a sum consistent with his prominence in the painting. In the eighteenth century, the painting was cut down, and as a result, the composition was transformed. Rembrandt's group portrait was commissioned for a specific position. To reconstruct the angled view that a spectator would have had when approaching the work from the only doorway in the room, hold this book at an angle so that the painting is to your right and sharply receding. This clarifies a number of elements in Rembrandt's composition, including the glance and gesture of Captain Cocq, who, it can now be understood, was looking toward the spectator. Rembrandt adjusted his composition to gain maximum effectiveness given the intended location of his painting. The other civic militia portraits in the same hall included the artist's self-portrait, and Rembrandt, with wit, represented himself in the back of the crowd. All we see is an eye, part of his nose and forehead, and a painter's beret.

Baroque. The figural composition is set off by the off-center gateway—a reference to an ancient triumphal arch—in the background.

No documentary evidence supports the popular myth that the members of the company were unhappy with Rembrandt's brilliant and unexpected solution to the problem of the group portrait. The painting was praised in the seventeenth century, and one of Rembrandt's pupils wrote: "It will outlast all its competitors, being so artistic in conception, so ingenious in the varied placement of figures, and so powerful that, according to some, it makes all the other pieces there look like decks of playing cards."

Rembrandt was the most famous Dutch artist of the seventeenth century and virtually the only one with an international reputation. As a young man he hoped to be a history painter, but his earliest success came as a painter of group and individual portraits. In 1642, the year of this group portrait, his wife Saskia died, leaving him with an infant son to raise. His art had already shown signs of change, and after 1642 he sought subjects and techniques that would satisfy a personal need for profundity and emotional depth (see figs. 356–58).

BAROQUE ARCHITECTURE: FRANCESCO BORROMINI

This dome by Borromini almost appears to be a hallucination (fig. 348). The hovering oval form, with its elastic coffers, seems to bear no relation to the heavy, solid stuff of architecture. If we blink, will it disappear, descend, or snap back into a circular shape with regular coffering? Startling and unbelievable architecture is typical of the works of Borromini. His Baroque monuments tantalize us with their energy, complexity, and tension. The oval form used here is one which has an inherent dynamism, for an oval establishes an axial direction and presents a variation in curvature, but Borromini also exaggerates the diminution of the coffering to suggest that the dome is larger than reality and, by adding hidden windows at the base of the dome, he creates a floating, levitating sensation. The excitement generated by the dome at San Carlo is resolved by the circle in the middle of the lantern, which is decorated with a triangle, symbol of the Trinity and emblem of the Trinitarian order that commissioned the church.

The demand that we be involved, the effect of captured movement, and the dramatic lighting of this architecture are consistent with the Baroque innovations examined in the paintings of Caravaggio and his followers. This small church is only one example of Borromini's brilliant inventiveness in creating new and exciting experiences within the classical vocabulary of architecture.

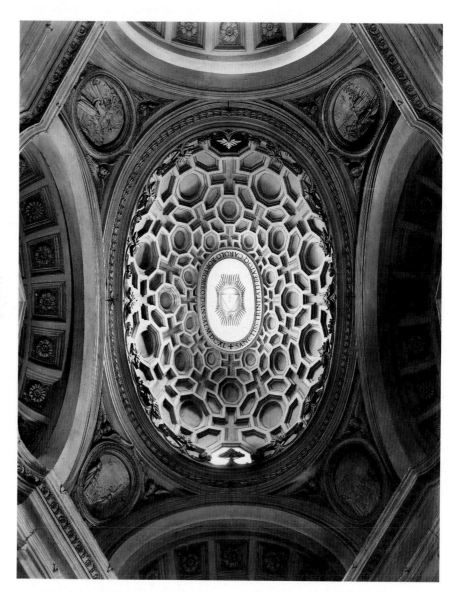

348. FRANCESCO BORROMINI
Dome, San Carlo alle Quattro Fontane, Rome. 1638–41. Dedicated to a recently canonized saint, Charles Borromeo, this church is also named after its location at an intersection with four fountains (*quattro fontane*).

The complexity that characterizes the interior of San Carlo (fig. 349) rivets our attention as we try to discern the logic and order we expect in a building based on the classical orders. The entablature is composed of contrasting flat and concave sections that surge around the small interior, while the patterns of columns and of triangular and semicircular pediments create two overlapping and interlocked systems. The design is both logical and brilliantly complex. Art historians have analyzed the mathematical formulas on which Borromini based his structures. In

BORROMINI, Dome, San Carlo alle Quattro Fontane: 1638–41
1635: Boston's public Latin School opens
1639: Smithfield hams from Virginia are sold in London

349. FRANCESCO BORROMINI
Plan, San Carlo alle Quattro
Fontane. 1638–41. Note the
irregular space available to
Borromini for the church and how,
because of the configuration of the
two streets, the facade of the church
could not be perpendicular to the
axis of the interior.

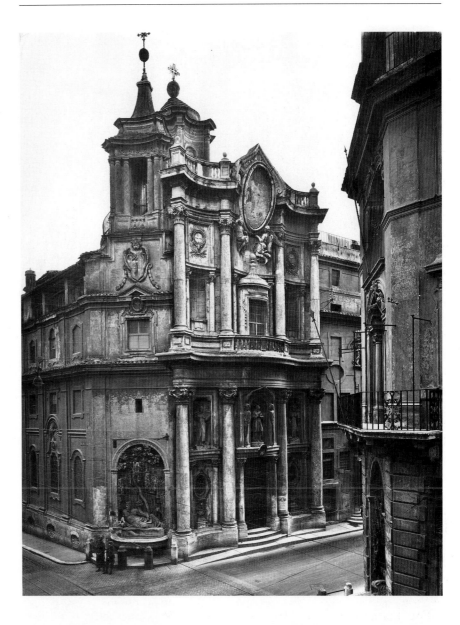

this case he evolved his design from the triangle, symbol of the Trinitarian order. At its most basic level, then, the shape of San Carlo alle Quattro Fontane has a form and an iconographic content that can be related to both a particular religious order and the Christian religion in general.

The facade predicts the interior in the grouping of four evenly spaced columns, in the undulation of the surging entablature, and in the scale of the lower story of columns (fig. 350). When one is standing in the narrow street before the church, however, the complex energies of contrasting concave and convex forms overwhelm any sense of logic. The upper row of columns completely masks the dome, making it a total surprise for the unsuspecting observer.

350. FRANCESCO BORROMINI
Facade, San Carlo alle Quattro
Fontane. 1665–67. Although the
facade was completed long after
the rest of the church, it is more
likely based on plans Borromini
had drawn earlier.

BERNINI, *ECSTASY OF ST. TERESA*

"It pleased the Lord that I should sometimes see the following vision. I would see beside me . . . an angel in bodily form. . . . He was . . . short and very beautiful, his face so aflame that he appeared to be . . . all afire. . . . In his hands I saw a long golden spear and at the end of the iron tip I seemed to see a point of fire. With this he seemed to pierce my heart several times . . . he left me completely afire with a great love for God. The pain was so sharp that it made me utter several moans; and so excessive was the sweetness caused me by this intense pain that one can never wish to lose it, nor will one's soul be content with anything less than God. It is not bodily pain, but spiritual, though the body has a share in it—indeed a great

351. GIANLORENZO BERNINI AND WORKSHOP
Ecstasy of St. Teresa. 1645–52. Marble and bronze, height approx. 11' 6"; the figures are over-lifesize. Cornaro Chapel, Santa Maria della Vittoria, Rome. Teresa, a sixteenth-century nun and a leading personality in the Counter-Reformation church in Spain, founded a new, stricter reformed group of Carmelite nuns known as the barefoot Carmelites. For this reason she is represented as barefoot in Bernini's sculpture. She wrote a number of works about the mystical life, including a popular and widely read *Autobiography* in which she detailed the visions and ecstasies she experienced.

BERNINI, *Ecstasy of St. Teresa:* **1645–52**
1648: Taj Mahal is completed in India
1650: World population is about 500 million

share" (St. Teresa, *Autobiography*).

Bernini has visualized Teresa's words and experience in his sculpted altarpiece (fig. 351), capturing in the saint's pose and facial expression the combination of "sweetness" and pain she describes so vividly and physically. Her abdomen seems to convulse, her arm is limp, and her head slumps back, her mouth open and her eyes half-closed. The figure of the angel smiles radiantly, and its drapery ripples with flamelike folds that evoke Teresa's words.

Bernini's interpretation, however, encompassed more than just Teresa's description of this single ecstasy. It relates this experience to other aspects and events of her life and to contemporary attitudes about ecstasies and saints. Teresa's miraculous death, as described by those who witnessed it, is evident here in the beauty Bernini gives the saint. Although her homeliness is documented, at the moment of her death, when she was in her sixties, witnesses testified that she became youthful and beautiful, and that she died while in a state of ecstatic love for God. The relationship between ecstasy, death, and fervent love of God, and the ideal of the marriage of the soul with the divine are revered parts of the mystical tradition which has its roots in the Old Testament love poetry of the Song of Songs. Teresa herself had written a commentary on the Song of Songs in which she related Christian death and ecstasy to the soul's desire to expire in the anguish of divine love.

Bernini shows the saint levitating, transported off the ground by heavenly clouds. Levitation is described by Teresa in the context of other ecstasies she experienced after attending mass. By levitating the figure, Bernini makes his sculptural group more impressive and its effect more momentary, while in the context of Teresa's life he also refers to her devotion to the Eucharist, an appropriate emphasis in an altarpiece.

Bernini's representation of the ecstasy of St. Teresa is itself a miraculous apparition, for the large white figures of the angel and the saint float above the altar. Originally they must have glowed in a gentle, mysterious light that flowed dimly down on golden rays from a window filled with stained glass. Today electric lights have been added, which make the lighting more dramatic than Bernini intended.

The vision of the miraculous ecstasy is enhanced by the enshrinement of the altarpiece group in a pedimented tabernacle of brilliant multicolored marble that is the centerpiece of a visually sumptuous chapel complex, every detail of which was originally designed by Bernini (see fig. 352). The back wall is covered with marble paneling which is broken by the surging pediment of the tabernacle that undulates outward and upward. The ceiling is frescoed with a burst of heavenly light, and angels seem to pour down into the chapel, accompanying the angel in Teresa's ecstasy. The altar frontal is a gilded

352. *The Cornaro Chapel.* 18th-century painting. Staatliches Museum, Schwerin

bronze and lapis-lazuli relief of the Last Supper, while the floor tombs are decorated with inlaid figures of gesticulating skeletons in foreshortening, as if those buried below were being resurrected by the saint's ecstasy.

Bernini unites painting, sculpture, and architecture in a beautiful totality, one which breaks down the barriers between the world in which we live and the work of art. The altarpiece and tabernacle invade our space, demanding that we become involved. A text on a banderole held by angels on the entrance arch offers words which, Teresa wrote, were spoken to her by Christ during one of her visions: "If I had not already created heaven I would create it for you alone."

THE ART OF DRAWING: DRAWINGS BY REMBRANDT

353. REMBRANDT
A Man Rowing a Boat on the Bullewyk. c. 1650. Quill pen and brown wash heightened with white, 5 1/4 x 7 7/8". Devonshire Collection, Chatsworth. The location is a tributary of the Amstel River, near Amsterdam, with the spire of the Ouderkerk (Old Church) in the background. The white used here is an opaque paint that allowed Rembrandt to suggest white highlights.

The freshness of nature is captured in Rembrandt's spontaneous drawing of this still tributary near Amsterdam (fig. 353). A few quick pen strokes capture the wind as it riffles the leaves of the trees around the cottage. Rembrandt applied wash (ink thinned with water) with a brush to achieve the darker shadows that give weight to the mass of the cottage and create the reflection of the trees and cottage on the surface of the water. A thin wash at the top suggests the sky, and a dark mass in the lower left corner establishes the *repoussoir.* Rembrandt's economy of means captures the flux of nature.

Throughout the centuries, artists have made and used drawings for a great variety of purposes (see p. 250). We normally think of drawings as being preparatory—studies made in the process of creating a larger, more finished work in another medium—and such is often the case. Although almost all drawings created before the Renaissance are lost, this does not mean that artists in earlier periods did not use preparatory drawings. Egyptian and Greek stonecarvers, for example, probably drew guidelines on the four sides of their blocks of stone before they began carving, and their contemporaries surely made some kind of sketch or drawing prior to beginning to paint or to build a building. Many later paintings are based on drawings on the plaster or canvas surface (known as underdrawings because of their position under the finished work). Artists have also made drawings as records of completed works, often as a means of documenting their production. Finely finished drawings were sometimes made to be presented to collectors and friends. These are known as presentation drawings. Drawings were first systematically collected during the Renaissance, when the artist was recognized as a genius whose every creative effort was worth preserving.

There are many media in which drawings have been executed: charcoal, lead pencil, pen and ink, chalk in various colors, metalpoint, and pastel. Wash, watercolor, and gouache (see p. 419) are also considered drawing techniques, even though they are liquid media applied with a brush. Although paper is the most widely accepted support for drawings, artists have also used vellum, parchment, and other materials.

354. REMBRANDT

Saskia in a Straw Hat. 1633. Silverpoint drawing on white prepared
vellum, 7 1/8 x 4 1/8". Kupferstich-
kabinett, Staatliche Museen, West
Berlin. The drawing is inscribed:
"This is drawn after my wife, when
she was 21 years old, the third day
after we were engaged—8 June
1633." Rembrandt and Saskia were
married in 1634.

Hundreds of drawings were executed by Rembrandt in virtually
every drawing medium that was
available to him. While some can be
identified as studies for paintings or
etchings, the majority are sketches
of genre scenes, landscapes, and
animals. All the evidence suggests
that Rembrandt made his drawing
of *A Man Rowing* for his own pleasure, for none of his landscape paintings are endowed with this kind of
naturalism. We know from an inventory of his possessions that

355. REMBRANDT

Two Women Teaching a Child to Walk. c. 1637. Red chalk drawing on rough
grayish paper, 4 1/8 x 5". British Museum, London

Rembrandt sorted his drawings and
stored them by subject. The implication is that when he began a new
painting or etching, he could look
through his drawings for inspiration drawn from life.

When Rembrandt made a romantic drawing of his fiancée, Saskia,
shortly after they became engaged,
he chose the difficult technique of
silverpoint on specially prepared
vellum (fig. 354). During the fifteenth
and sixteenth centuries, drawing
with sharpened points of silver (or
gold) on specially prepared paper
or vellum had been common, but by
the seventeenth century, this medium was rare. The virtue of this
particular technique is that it creates
a very fine line. It was especially
favored by artists interested in precision, such as Van Eyck, Dürer, and

Leonardo. Silver- and goldpoint
demand a special proficiency, for
the drawn lines cannot be erased or
changed. Before the silver oxidizes
and darkens, the shimmering lines
are precious and even sumptuous.
Rembrandt has chosen the perfect
medium to capture forever the face
of his fiancée.

In a drawing executed with soft
red chalk, Rembrandt has, with incredible economy, captured a hesitant child, wearing a padded hat for
protection, in the process of learning
to walk (fig. 355). The child is encouraged by two women, one of
whom, on our right, betrays her age
by her stiffness. There is no setting,
nor is there a single extraneous detail. It is a tiny drawing of the utmost
simplicity, but the moment of life
that it captures is precious.

REMBRANDT

356. REMBRANDT
Bathsheba with King David's Letter.
1654. Oil on canvas, 55 7/8 x
55 7/8". The Louvre, Paris. A
repeated motif in the Old and New
Testaments is the sinfulness of
humanity; the Old Testament king
David, slayer of Goliath and the
author of the Psalms, is no exception. After David had forced a
married woman, Bathsheba, into
his bed, he connived to have her
husband, Uriah, killed in battle so
he could marry her. In Rembrandt's
painting, Bathsheba holds the
message from David, who has
summoned her to the palace, while
her maid prepares her for this first
meeting with the king.

Rembrandt's later works are characterized by subjects of universal human significance, as in this example of the story of Bathsheba (fig. 356). The main subject here is the female nude, but the interpretation emphasizes her inner emotions and meditation. Rembrandt has overturned tradition by painting a nude figure that is more emotional than physical, more thoughtful than sensuous. In keeping with the Dutch interest in naturalism, his model is a mature and dignified woman, one who is capable of understanding the profound implications of the king's demands. Despite the secondary figure at her feet, Bathsheba is alone in her predicament.

Dutch artists in general avoided emotionally complex themes, but the restriction on religious subjects and the general disinterest in historical and mythological themes in the Netherlands were irrelevant to Rembrandt, who, perhaps in reaction to the unemotional art being created by his fellow countrymen, chose to probe deeply into human life for subject matter and to paint religious subjects if their emotional content interested him.

Rembrandt's works often have a direct and sympathetic correlation with the events of his life and the people whom he loved. The model for Bathsheba is probably Hendrickje Stoffels, Rembrandt's second, common-law wife, whom he was unable to marry because of financial restrictions in the will of his deceased wife, Saskia. In 1654, the same year that Rembrandt painted *Bathsheba*, Hendrickje was called before the council of the Reformed Church and barred from receiving communion because she was living with a man to whom she was not married. The connection between Hendrickje's difficulties and the Bathsheba story are indirect, but the human predicament is related.

The *Return of the Prodigal Son* is Rembrandt's largest history painting (fig. 357). The impressive figures are over-lifesize. The son, in rags and worn-out shoes, throws himself to his knees to indicate his repentance. The aged father bends over him, pulling the young man toward him with stiff hands. The son gently lays his head on his father's chest and closes his eyes. Time seems to stop. The richness of their inner experience is in part expressed abstractly by the textures of the *impasto* with which Rembrandt paints their garments and by the warm, sonorous colors. Christ's parable used the human story to illustrate a moral: God will forgive sinners who repent. Rembrandt uses the same story to emphasize a human experience—the forgiving love of a parent for a child.

Rembrandt's painting of a couple who face us and embrace each other is one of his final tes-

taments to the power and beauty of love (fig. 358). There has been lengthy scholarly debate about the iconography of this image, and whether it is based on a biblical story or perhaps a theatrical source is still not certain. It is probably not a commissioned portrait, given the historical costumes worn by the figures.

Nevertheless, the message Rembrandt intended is clear: the power of the love, spiritual and physical, between two human beings. The composition has a simplicity reminiscent of the High Renaissance, for the two figures are joined in an indissoluble pyramidal entity. The paint seems to have been applied as much with a palette knife as with a brush, and the surface is richly textured. The depth of Rembrandt's translucent glazes makes the red and gold of their garments seem to glow from within, a visual metaphor for the love that joins them.

REMBRANDT, *Bathsheba with King David's Letter:* **1654**
1648: End of the Thirty Years' War in Germany
1649: King Charles I of England is beheaded
1652: War is declared between England and Holland
---

357. REMBRANDT
Return of the Prodigal Son. c. 1662–68. Oil on canvas, 8' 8" x 6' 8". Hermitage Museum, Leningrad. We have seen in other examples how Christ's parable of the prodigal son (Luke 15:11–32) was popular with the followers of Caravaggio, and especially with the Dutch Caravaggisti (fig. 337). Here Rembrandt represents the most profound moment in the parable: the son, reduced to complete poverty, returns home to discover that his father, who still loves him, will forgive him.

358. REMBRANDT
"The Jewish Bride." c. 1662. Oil on canvas, 47 7/8 x 65 1/2". Rijksmuseum, Amsterdam. The traditional name is an eighteenth-century invention.

PRINTMAKING: ETCHING AND DRYPOINT

Rembrandt presents us not with a specific biblical subject, but with an interpretation of Christ as a humble and gentle teacher who stands within the crowd in a city street to preach (fig. 359). He is surrounded by people of all ages, rich and poor, and in Rembrandt's representation they react as individuals to Christ's words. Some ponder his meaning, others seem uninterested. A child busies himself drawing in the dust in the foreground.

Rembrandt's technique is etching, and this is one of a number of prints produced from the same plate for collectors of prints. It is the etching technique which permits the creation of blurred lines and a soft, atmospheric quality not possible in woodcut or engraving. Etching is not a new technique—Dürer and other printmakers had experimented with its possibilities—but it was Rembrandt who first realized its potential for expression.

Etching is an intaglio technique (see p. 277), and the same thin copper plate used for engraving functions as the print form (fig. 360). To create an etching, one must cover the plate with an etching ground, an acid-resistant, resinous mixture. The artist scratches through this ground with a steel etching needle, creating lines that expose the copper. When the design is completed (or when the artist wants to test the progress of the composition), diluted acid (nitric, iron chloride, or hydrochloric) is poured over the plate or it is dipped into an acid bath. The acid eats into the copper, creating grooves where the needle has scratched through the ground. The ground is then cleaned off and the plate is inked and printed, as in the process for printing an engraving. If the results are unsatisfactory or incom-

359. REMBRANDT

Christ Preaching. c. 1652. Etching with drypoint and burin, 6 1/8 x 8 1/8". Rembrandt was internationally famous as a printmaker during his own lifetime, and his prints regularly sold for high prices. Less than twenty years after Rembrandt's death, the Florentine art historian Filippo Baldinucci would write: "This artist truly distinguished himself . . . in a certain most bizarre manner which he invented for etching on copper plates. This manner too was entirely his own, neither used by others nor seen again; with certain scratches of varying strength and irregular and isolated strokes, he produced a deep chiaroscuro of great strength."

Etching

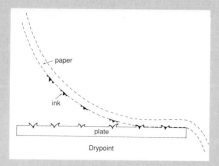

Drypoint

360. Diagrams of the etching and drypoint techniques. The more blurred lines of the drypoint technique are the result of the burr of the drypoint line.

plete, the ground can be reapplied, the design can be strengthened or completed with the needle, and the acid bath can be used again. Another alternative is to strengthen the lines by using the burin (as in engraving) and/or drypoint (see below). Only about fifty excellent and two hundred reasonably good prints can be made from an etched plate.

An eighteenth-century development in the etching process was the soft-ground etching, which uses a greater percentage of tallow or wax in the ground. A thin sheet of paper is laid over the ground, and a drawing is made on the paper. When the paper is lifted, a soft, grainy impression is left on the plate. The plate is then etched, using a weak acid bath (see fig. 488).

The etching technique encouraged freedom and spontaneity, for the etching needle moves easily through the ground to scratch the plate (unlike the concentrated pressure needed to push the burin through the resistant copper to create an engraving). While an etched line lacks the sharp and precise quality of an engraved line, its bluriness creates the atmospheric effect that we admire in Rembrandt's work. Rembrandt's earliest printed works were pure etchings, sometimes with the use of the burin for strengthening. Later, to achieve an even greater effect of atmosphere, he began to add lines in drypoint, as is the case in *Christ Preaching*.

Drypoint is the technique of scratching directly onto the copper plate with the etching needle (fig. 360). This creates grooves which have tiny raised ridges of copper, known as the burr, to either side, where the expelled material is forced by the needle. These drypoint ridges catch the ink and create rich areas of deep, soft shadow. The necessary pressure applied by the press during printing will wear down the burr rather quickly, and only about ten good and twenty reasonably good impressions can be made. In *Christ*

361. REMBRANDT
The Three Crosses. 1653. Drypoint and burin (first state), 15 1/4 x 17 3/4".
Rembrandt made successive changes to the plate in producing this print.

Preaching, drypoint lines are visible in the beard and hair of Christ and in the deep shadows of his drapery.

A few of Rembrandt's last prints are executed entirely in drypoint, with an additional use of the burin for certain sharp details. Rembrandt's last print was probably the large *Three Crosses* (fig. 361), which he worked on over a period of years. He created three successive stages, known as states, in 1653 by reworking the plate and a final, almost completely reworked state in the early 1660s. It is a profoundly moving personal interpretation of the crucifixion based on the text in Luke 23:44–47: "And it was about the sixth hour, and there was a darkness over all the earth until the ninth hour.

And the sun was darkened, and the veil of the temple was rent in the midst. And when Jesus had cried with a loud voice, he said, Father, into thy hands I commend my spirit: and having said thus, he gave up the ghost. Now when the centurion saw what was done, he glorified God, saying, 'Certainly this was a righteous man.' "

The centurion is kneeling, to suggest that Rembrandt is representing the very moment of the death of Christ. The powerful shaft of light is a momentary blaze, a heavenly response to Christ's words and his death. In this late work Rembrandt avoids painstaking detail to emphasize powerful emotional experiences.

DIEGO VELÁZQUEZ

363. DIEGO VELÁZQUEZ
Las Meninas (detail)

362. DIEGO VELÁZQUEZ
Las Meninas (The Maids of Honor). 1656. Oil on canvas, 10' 5" x 9'; the figures are
lifesize. The Prado, Madrid. The cross on Velázquez's chest indicates that he
has been made a Knight of the Order of Santiago. As Velázquez did not receive
this honor until 1659, three years after the painting was dated, the cross must
have been added later.

For just a moment Velázquez's painting convinces us that the little princess and her attendants—including dwarfs and a large dog—are posing just for us (figs. 362, 363). Although *Las Meninas* is a large picture, its subject seems intimate and even casual. We glimpse a view into a large dark room in the palace, where the painter is at work on a huge canvas. He looks out and leans back, raising his brush as he prepares to apply a stroke of paint. In the foreground the five-year-old infanta Margarita, daughter of King Philip IV, surrounded by her maids *(las meninas)* and the dwarfs and retarded persons who were a traditional part of life at the Spanish court. With the excep-tion of the princess, all these fig-ures are represented in the midst of movement, as is Velázquez. Note especially the figure to the right who, one hand raised, awakens the dog, which slowly raises its head. Velázquez's illu-sionism attempts to convince us that we are seeing reality.

But is the infanta posing for us? The shimmering surface on the back wall is a mirror which reflects the figures of King Philip and his queen. A real mirror, of course, would have reflected the whole room, but Velázquez, with

VELÁZQUEZ, *Las Meninas:* 1656
1656: Pendulum clock is invented
1657: London's first chocolate shop opens

364. DIEGO VELÁZQUEZ
Portrait of Juan de Pareja. 1650. Oil on canvas, 32 x 27 1/2". The Metropolitan Museum of Art, New York (Fletcher Fund, Rogers Fund, and Bequest of Miss Adelaide Milton de Groot, by exchange)

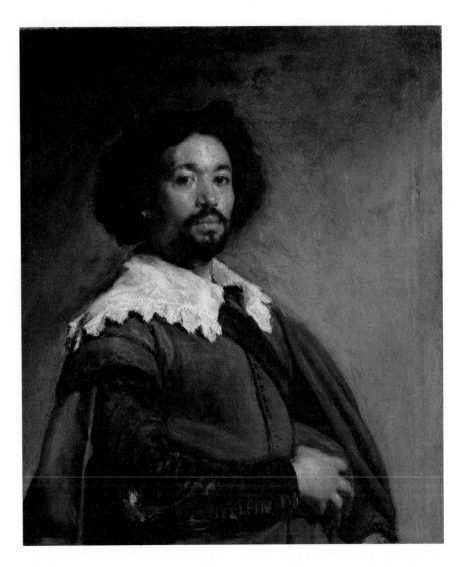

artistic license, includes this reference to his royal patrons as the sole element that reminds us that this is indeed a painting.

In Velázquez's *Portrait of Juan de Pareja* (fig. 364), the sitter looks out with calm and assured dignity. Velázquez's loose brushstroke and subtle light create an effect of immediacy and, again, reality. The painting is a coloristic triumph, for within a restricted palette of white, black, grays, and beiges, Velázquez creates an impressive variety of tones. The restriction of color is no accident,

for this portrait of one of Velázquez's assistants was a practice piece. Velázquez was in Rome, buying paintings and ancient sculptures for King Philip, when he received the commission to paint a portrait of Pope Innocent X. This particular portrait was a difficult task, for the pope, who had a ruddy complexion, had to be painted wearing red papal garments, seated in a red chair in a setting dominated by red hangings. To

prepare himself for this challenge, Velázquez posed a similar problem by painting Juan de Pareja, who was of Moorish descent, using a restricted color palette based on his flesh tones. The picture was a sensational success. After it was exhibited at the Pantheon, Velázquez was elected to the Rome Academy. One contemporary remarked that while all the other paintings in the exhibition were art, "this alone was truth."

NICOLAS POUSSIN

Poussin's idealized painting transports us to remote antiquity, where we stand with shepherds and a shepherdess by a monumental tomb (fig. 365). Arcadia is an idyllic region in Greece, where, during the ancient golden age, it was believed that humanity had lived peacefully and harmoniously with nature. To the shepherds who lived there, life seemed perfect until they discovered a tomb and realized that death is a reality that they will someday have to confront. Despite the dramatic implications of the subject, the mood of the painting is calm and contemplative. In Poussin's approach, even death becomes philosophical.

Poussin's style is consistent with his intellectual interpretation of the subject. The composition is lucid and the poses of the figures are clearly articulated and interrelated. To assure satisfying compositions, Poussin worked them out by arranging miniature wax figures on a stage in a small box until he was pleased with their disposition. The colors are cool and simple, the light regular and undramatic, and the brush-

365. NICOLAS POUSSIN
The Arcadian Shepherds. c. 1660.
Oil on canvas, 34 1/4 x 47 1/4".
The Louvre, Paris. The inscription on the tomb is *Et in Arcadia Ego*— Even in Arcadia I [Death] am to be found.

stroke controlled. The influence of the High Renaissance style of Raphael is evident, and the costumes and facial types reveal Poussin's careful study of ancient art. Poussin's paintings are among the finest examples of Baroque Classicism. The landscape is based on the area around Rome, which Poussin knew well.

Nicolas Poussin was probably the most classical, intellectual, and philosophical painter of the seventeenth century. Although born in France, he spent most of his mature life in Rome. A close circle of similarly minded French friends there and in Paris were the patrons for his well-studied, thoughtful compositions. He preferred heroic or stoic themes from antiquity.

Poussin's landscapes always include a narrative subject, usually one drawn from antiquity. In the *Body of Phocion Carried Out of Athens,* the landscape is clearly not taken from nature (fig. 366). Poussin has rearranged nature to provide the properly sober, clear, and balanced setting for his profound theme.

366. NICOLAS POUSSIN
Landscape with the Body of Phocion Carried Out of Athens. 1648. Oil on canvas, 47 x 70 1/2". The Louvre, Paris. Phocion was a loyal Athenian general whose character was in many ways like that of Poussin: he was stern, prized economy, and was dedicated to truth. His austerity and moral rectitude, however, made him hated by the popular faction in Athens, who, when they gained power, had Phocion executed on a false charge of treason and decreed that his body had to be carried outside the city for burial. This is the event shown in Poussin's painting. Later Phocion was given honorable burial in Athens.

DUTCH STILL-LIFE PAINTING

367. MARIA VAN OOSTERWYCK
Still Life with a Vanitas Theme. 1668. Oil on canvas, 29 x 35". Kunsthistorisches Museum, Vienna. Maria van Oosterwyck did not come from an artistic family, but tradition tells us that she was determined to become a still-life painter. She developed an international reputation and produced works for Louis XIV of France and the members of other European royal houses.

Realistic still-life painting is a democratic art—one needs no background in aesthetics or art theory to appreciate Maria van Oosterwyck's ability to render the butterfly that lights on the book or the mouse nibbling at the grain, not to mention the fresh flowers, skull, and globe (fig. 367). There is even a fly on a book to the right and a self-portrait of the artist reflected in the flask to the left. It was in the democratic Netherlands that such still lifes were most fully appreciated, and the market for pictures such as this one was so large that artists could become specialists in still-life painting and hone their skills

so as to produce increasingly more brilliant depictions of objects in ever more elaborate profusion.

Sixteenth- and seventeenth-century art theorists, however, largely ignored still-life painting, as they did also the painting of landscape, genre, and portraits. These types of art were considered unimportant because they were merely copies from nature. A painter's most significant accomplishment, they argued, was a history painting, the conception, design, and execution of which demanded intellectual prowess and academic training. The painter of histories also

needed an understanding of anatomy and experience in drawing the male nude. Still-life, landscape, portrait, and genre paintings were considered to be much less valuable than history paintings and generally sold at much lower prices.

During the seventeenth century a number of women artists excelled at still-life painting, in part, perhaps, because this was a category of art in which they could succeed without threatening the long-established dominance of male artists. Since at this time women were not admitted to the academies, they hardly had the option of receiving training in creating history paintings. The two artists examined here were both products of the more liberal Dutch culture, but during the sixteenth and seventeenth centuries there are documented French, Flemish, and Italian women still-life artists as well.

The theorists, of course, underestimated still-life painting. To select the forms of a still-life painting and arrange them into a satisfying composition, with coordinating and contrasting patterns of textures and colors, demands different skills from those required of the history painter. And still-life paintings are not always purely decorative displays, devoid of any deeper meaning. The title of Van Oosterwyck's painting reveals that it forms part of a distinguished tradition of seventeenth-century paintings on the theme of Vanity, one of the minor vices, that expressed the transience of the things of the world and the inevitability of death. Such paintings were especially popular in the Netherlands, where the tradition of complex symbolism goes back to Van Eyck (see p. 238). In the most impressive of these compositions, of which Van Oosterwyck's is an example, each element contributes its own special content to the meaning of the whole. The hourglass, for example, refers to the inexorable passage of time. The fly is a symbol of sin, ever present in the world, and the mouse symbolizes evil. The large book is labeled "Reckoning. We live in order to die. We die in order to live."

An early source tells us that Van Oosterwyck was very pious, and the underlying Christian hope of her *Vanitas* is expressed in these words and in the butterfly, symbol of the resurrection of Christ and the salvation of mankind. Although the skull is an obvious reference to death, when it is wreathed in ivy, as here, it refers to life after death. All these objects and symbols are united in a masterful composition which takes maximum advantage of contrasting forms, colors, and textures.

Rachel Ruysch's *Flower Still Life* (fig. 368) is arranged along a prominent diagonal which is enhanced by the curving stems of the blossoms at the upper right and lower left. The simple centrality of the vase and niche is enlivened by the diagonal recession of the table and by the contrast in light to either side. On the right, a light area silhouettes the forms and emphasizes their irregularity, while on the left a completely different effect is accomplished by setting off the complexity of many small blossoms against the dark background. Ruysch's father was an important professor of anatomy

VAN OOSTERWYCK, *Still Life with a Vanitas Theme:* **1668**
1669: Jan Swammerdam, *History of the Insects*
1670: Minute hands are first used on watches
1675: Anton van Leeuwenhoek invents the microscope

368. RACHEL RUYSCH
Flower Still Life. After 1700. Oil on canvas, 30 x 24". Toledo Museum of Art. Rachel Ruysch is ranked among the greatest still-life painters in the Netherlands, and her international reputation continued after her death. She was apprenticed to an important still-life painter at the age of fifteen and by eighteen was active as a painter in the same genre. From 1708 to 1716 she was court painter to the Elector Palatine in Düsseldorf.

and botany, and his collection of scientific specimens may have inspired her inclusion of the insects found so often in her paintings. She depicts them with impressive accuracy, a technical precision that reveals her participation in the new scientific interests and investigations of the seventeenth century.

THE PALACE AT VERSAILLES

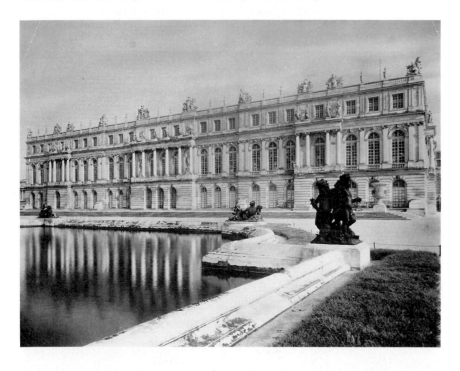

369. LOUIS LE VAU AND JULES HARDOUIN-MANSART
369. LOUIS LE VAU AND JULES HARDOUIN-MANSART
Garden facade, Palace of Versailles, France. 1669–85. Begun by King Louis XIV, who decided to enlarge a royal hunting lodge eleven miles southwest of Paris, Versailles officially became not only the main royal residence in 1682, but the governmental seat as well. The administrator, J.-B. Colbert, who also advised Louis on political, economic, and religious matters, and the painter Charles Lebrun were in charge of the artists and workmen—sometimes as many as thirty thousand at one time—who created the buildings and grounds. At its height, the palace served a court that totaled almost twenty thousand people, including nine thousand soldiers quartered in the town and about four thousand servants who lived within the palace itself.

The palace of the French kings at Versailles is the largest and most emulated royal residence in the world (fig. 369). It has hundreds of rooms, and its facade is almost a half-mile long; the garden encompasses two hundred and fifty acres. Its impressive scale actually made a political statement, for it was intended to assert for the French populace and nobility, as well as for foreigners, the power of the French monarch. In some ways the very creation of Versailles may have played a role in establishing and perpetuating that power.

The expansive length of the garden facade itself makes a powerful architectural statement, but the architects faced the problem of how to articulate such a long structure. They decided not to break the mass in any dramatic way and chose to emphasize the horizontal sweep by articulating the second floor with pilasters. They created punctuation points with columned pavilions that jut out only slightly from the mass of the structure, with sculpture decorating their cornices. The design and ornament are completely classical, in keeping with the French interest in drawing a relationship between the principles of order and control and the rule of the French monarchy.

The Salon de la Guerre offers a rich scheme of multi-media Baroque decoration (fig. 370). A huge oval stucco relief over the fireplace with a monumental equestrian figure of Louis XIV immediately draws our attention. Below, dark bronze reliefs represent prisoners in chains, while above, gilt stucco angels trumpet his fame and offer him the hero's crown. The relief in the fireplace shows the muse of history, Clio, recording Louis's triumphs. The combination of materials—stucco, bronze, gilded stucco, and marble—and the parquet floors, mirrors, paintings on the ceiling, and a crystal-and-gold chandelier testify to the wealth of the king, while the iconography emphasizes his imperialistic ambitions. Such a room was, of course, primarily a setting for court ritual and would be in use especially on those occasions when its particular iconography would be most effective.

In the great park, every pond and pathway seems infinite, and at each crossroads there are several choices of direction in which

LE VAU and HARDOUIN-MANSART, Versailles: begun 1669
1664: Heinrich Schütz, *Christmas Oratorio*
1666: Great Fire of London
1667: Brooklyn is chartered
1667: Milton, *Paradise Lost*
1670: Molière, *Le Bourgeois Gentilhomme*

to proceed (fig. 371). The vistas and paths offer surprises: fountains, basins, terraces, flights of steps, sculptural groups, flowerbeds, hedges, and even small architectural monuments. Nature on a vast scale has been tamed and ordered, to provide a place of pleasure for the king and his court. Although the most basic purpose of the park is the same as that of the palace—to reflect the glory of the French monarchy and the king's centralized authority—Le Nôtre has also been sensitive to the delights of nature that such a park can offer to the observer. The plan informs us of the general layout, but Le Nôtre's park was not designed to be seen from above, but by the human spectator, walking, choosing pathways and vistas.

370. JULES HARDOUIN-MANSART, CHARLES LEBRUN, AND ANTOINE COYSEVOX
Salon de la Guerre (Room of War), Palace of Versailles. Begun 1678. This room, at one end of the Hall of Mirrors, is a pendant to the Room of Peace at the opposite end; the decoration of these rooms celebrated recent French victories. The sculptor Coysevox is responsible for the huge stucco relief of *King Louis XIV on Horseback* over the fireplace. The painted ceiling, the theme of which is France at war, is by Lebrun. The Hall of Mirrors was named for the large mirrors opposite the arched garden windows. As decoration, this room had bejeweled trees and gold and silver furniture, but these were melted down in 1689 and 1709 to help pay for French wars.

371. ANDRÉ LE NÔTRE
Plan of the gardens and park, Versailles (17th-century engraving). Designed 1661–68; executed 1662–90. Note that the main streets of the town of Versailles, at the bottom of the map, converge on the palace to emphasize its significance. André Le Nôtre, son of a royal gardener, became the greatest designer of formal gardens and parks in seventeenth-century Europe. The layout of the garden uses radiating diagonals and dramatic long vistas.

Landscape Painting

372. JACOB VAN RUISDAEL
The Dutch Landscape from the Dunes at Overveen. c. 1670. Oil on canvas, 21 7/8 x 24 3/8". Mauritshuis, The Hague

During the seventeenth century, the flat expanses of the Netherlands, reclaimed from the sea and wrested from Spanish domination, were painted thousands of times by Dutch painters. These paintings were avidly collected by the proud and patriotic citizens of the new nation. Although there had been a sporadic interest in landscape among North-

ern painters during the sixteenth century, now, for the first time in the history of Western art, landscape became a truly popular theme. In the seventeenth century, the Netherlands was more highly urbanized than any other European nation, and the nostalgia felt by city dwellers for open countryside may have been an additional factor in explaining

VAN RUISDAEL, *The Dutch Landscape:* **c. 1670**

1669: Antonio Stradivari makes violins in Cremona, Italy
1670: André Le Nôtre lays out the Champs-Elysées in Paris
1675: Native American population drops to about 20,000

the popularity of landscape painting.

Despite its relatively small size, Ruisdael's painting captures the salient features of the Dutch countryside: land, sky, and a changing relationship between light and shade (fig. 372). More than two-thirds of the canvas is given over to the clouded sky, which is the dominant feature of the Dutch countryside. The sky becomes the mediator by which we perceive the land as well. As the clouds rush by, the earth is intermittently revealed by patches of bright light.

Ruisdael's landscape is precisely identifiable, for the great Gothic church that rises among red tile roofs in the background is St. Bavo in Haarlem. The ubiquitous Dutch windmills, so necessary to keep the land drained of excess water, dot the countryside, and in the foreground we see small figures stretching linen to be bleached, a proud reference to the prosper-

ous Haarlem linen industry. The function of this realistic image is clear: to represent and exalt the local countryside and its livelihood.

Although other seventeenth-century painters occasionally demonstrate an interest in landscape—Poussin with his classical landscapes (see fig. 366) and Rubens with his views of the Flemish countryside—these are exceptions, and only in the Netherlands did a truly national school of landscape painters develop. Although the Dutch seem to have preferred realistic views of local scenery, Dutch painters also produced a variety of other types of landscape painting, including seascapes with Dutch vessels and rather fantastic views of wild scenery. A number of Dutch artists settled in Rome, where they painted views of the sun-drenched Italian countryside which were popular back home.

The sixteenth-century Flem-

ish interest in landscape found a worthy successor in Rubens, whose landscapes have the same tumultuous vitality and visual excitement as his religious, mythological, and allegorical pictures. In his landscapes, he puts us in contact with the growth and energies of the world of nature. In his *Landscape with Het Steen* (fig. 373), the rising sun is a shimmering silver-yellow disk near the right edge of the painting. A hunter and his dog in the foreground draw our eyes to a stump, which in turn leads us to an undulating row of trees that surge into the landscape toward the fresh, glowing morning sky. Simultaneously, a peasant family going to market in the shadowy left foreground draws our attention to the opposite direction. Rubens's personal energies and his understanding of the dynamic and ever-changing nature of landscape are united in this splendid work.

373. PETER PAUL RUBENS
Landscape with Het Steen. c. 1636. Oil on panel, 51 5/8 x 90 1/4". National Gallery, London. Het Steen was Rubens's country estate, which he bought in 1635.

VIII

EIGHTEENTH-CENTURY ART

INTRODUCTION

Boffrand's interior design for the Princess's Salon (fig. 374) exemplifies the decorative exuberance of the Rococo style, which in the eighteenth century succeeded the Baroque. The decoration of the oval room is animated with carved and painted woodwork, stucco, and a series of integral paintings depicting the tale of the mythologi-

374. GERMAIN BOFFRAND
Salon de la Princesse, Hôtel de Soubise, Paris. 1736–39. The term *hôtel* in this context refers to the lavishly adorned town houses of the French aristocracy.

375. ROBERT ADAM
Fireplace niche, Entrance Hall, Osterley Park House, Middlesex, England. Begun 1761. Adam's adaptation of classical architectural forms was so successful that one phase of the English Neoclassical style is known as the Adamesque.

cal lovers Cupid and Psyche. The web of gold woodwork and stucco ornament creates a light, airy sensation that seems to transform the white walls into thin screens, while the undulating movement of the curving cornice joins the rhythm of the delicate arches to further enliven the interior. The effect is elegant and ebullient.

Just slightly more than twenty years later, the English architect Robert Adam began remodeling Osterley Park House. The fireplace niche in the entrance hall (fig. 375) demonstrates Adam's use of an alternate eighteenth-century style, Neoclassicism, in which the ornamentation is based on antique prototypes, from the pilasters and coffered half dome to the wall moldings. The axis is visually reinforced by the Neoclassical relief set over the fireplace, while the flanking niches with their antique sculptures balance the composition and add further references to the cultures of classical antiquity. In contrast to Boffrand's Rococo interior, Adam's Neoclassical design is disciplined and controlled. The antithesis between these designs confirms the enormous artistic contrasts of the eighteenth century.

HISTORY

"It was the best of times, it was the worst of times, it was the age of wisdom, it was the age of foolishness, it was the epoch of belief, it was the epoch of incredulity, it was the season of Light, it was the season of Darkness" (Charles Dickens, *A Tale of Two Cities,* first published 1859). The memorable opening lines from Dickens's novel about the French Revolution can describe the eighteenth century as a whole. It was a century of social, cultural, and artistic contrasts, prodigious scientific and technological advances, and sweeping political changes. Historians often refer to the close of this century as the period which marks the beginning of our modern world.

Politically, the century opened with the dominance of France under Louis XIV. Rigaud's Baroque portrait (fig. 376) conveys the solemn majesty of his authority and the opulence with which the French monarchs were surrounded. After Louis XIV's death in 1715, however, France's military and political influence began to abate. Frederick the Great, who came to the throne in Prussia in 1740, seized opportunities to expand and establish the German states as the premier military power on the Continent. To check Prussia's growing political and military strength, France and Austria entered an alliance. In the resulting conflict, known as the Seven Years' War (1756–63), Prussia was victorious. France's holdings and influence in the New World were diminished when Quebec surrendered to the English in 1759 (see fig. 395), effectively ending the French and Indian War in North America. Austria was defeated in the Seven Years' War but prospered in the latter part of the century, under Maria Theresa and her son, Joseph II, to become one of Europe's most distinguished cultural centers.

376. HYACINTHE RIGAUD
Portrait of Louis XIV. 1701. Oil on canvas, 9 x 6'. The Louvre, Paris

England's economic stability and political importance grew steadily through the century. By the 1750s England was established as an important maritime power, and the victory over the French in America made the English masters of much of North America. By the close of the century, England enjoyed the highest per-capita income in western Europe as the new industrial economy took root. London's population grew to over one million, the first modern city to reach that size. At the same time, King George III, who ruled from 1760 to 1820, saw the power of the monarchy wrested away by Parliament. Increased taxation led the American colonies to declare independence in 1776 and, with French assistance, the defeat of the British at Yorktown in 1781 won the Revolution for the colonies. A peace treaty was signed between England and the new American nation in 1783.

The growing desire for self-rule, one of the features of the philosophy of the Enlightenment (see below) in response to the authoritarian rule of Europe's traditional absolute monarchs, also affected developments in France. During the reign of Louis XVI and his wife, Marie Antoinette, lavish government expenditures led to economic depression. As relations between the French aristocracy and the people deteriorated, a National Assembly was formed in 1789 to compose a written constitution for France. During the French Revolution, a constitutional monarchy was established, but internal political factions and outside military pressure threatened the new government. Within France, hostility against the aristocracy rose to a fever pitch by 1792, and in the series of bloody executions which followed, even Louis XVI and his queen were guillotined. Within this context of domestic uncertainty and foreign wars, a young military commander, Napoleon Bonaparte, rose in power and, at the age of thirty in 1799, was made first consul of the French Republic.

INTELLECTUAL AND SCIENTIFIC ACTIVITY

The eighteenth century has been called the Age of Enlightenment. The influence of the Catholic church declined, and philosophical investigations were directed less to theological than to secular and scientific issues. Descartes's belief in the supremacy of human reason and the centrality of the natural sciences, which dates from the seventeenth century, was inherited and advanced by eighteenth-century philosophers. The Enlightenment meant faith in human reason, natural human rights, science, and progress toward a utopian society. This joining of the natural sciences with philosophical questioning strengthened the belief in empiricism, a view that human knowledge was pragmatically gained from experience and sensation. The foremost proponent of empiricism from the late seventeenth century was the English writer John Locke. Locke's treatises on government, based on his experience with the rise of parliamentary government in England, avowed that a nation's power derived from its people. The people entered in a social contract with their government and retained the right to dissent and withdraw support if their government proved no longer responsive to their will and needs. Locke's political philosophy guided the American Revolution and the drafting of the U.S. Constitution and, through Voltaire, assisted in fomenting the French Revolution.

Empiricism also fertilized the growth of the natural sciences. Building on Isaac Newton's observations and discoveries, advances continued in physics, mathematics, and astronomy. In 1759 Edmund Halley's name was given to the comet which returns every seventy-six years. Zoology, botany, and mineralogy were established as scientific disciplines. The chemist Antoine Lavoisier was the first to demonstrate correctly the process of combustion; he later named the reactive element, essential for life, oxygen. Constant improvements in such devices as the telescope, microscope, barometer, and thermometer allowed for greater accuracy in scientific observation.

Technology benefited from this increasing scientific knowledge. New processes in metallurgy contributed to the use of iron as a building material, and the perfection of the steam engine by James Watt in 1769 brought Europe closer to the momentous and far-reaching economic and social changes of the Industrial Revolution.

EIGHTEENTH-CENTURY ART

The Rococo and Neoclassical styles dominated the visual arts during the eighteenth century. The term Rococo, derived from the French *rocaille* (literally meaning rock-work or rubble), was first used to designate a style of French art associated with the reign of Louis XV. In early-eighteenth-century France, charm and finesse were the hallmarks of an artificial code of social behavior. The Rococo's light, ornamental elegance, as exemplified in Elizabeth Vigée-Lebrun's portrait (fig. 377), complemented the artificiality of aristocratic values and tastes.

The Neoclassical style, first named in the mid-nineteenth century, developed as an alternative to the Rococo. Fueling the Neoclassical style at mid-century was a reawakened interest in classical antiquity, spurred by the rediscovery of Herculaneum in 1738 and Pompeii in 1748 (see p. 108). The revival movement of Neoclassicism is sometimes understood as the first step in the development of Romanticism (see p. 374).

The most eloquent spokesperson for Neoclassical taste was the German art historian Johann Winckelmann, who had his portrait painted by Angelica Kauffmann, one of the most famous artists of the period. He viewed the rationality and ideality of classical art as the summit of artistic achievement. In his influential *Thoughts on the Imitation of Greek Art in Painting and Sculpture* of 1755, Winckelmann wrote: "Good taste, which is spreading more and more throughout the world, had its beginning under a Greek sky. . . . To take the ancients for models is our only way to become great, yes, unsurpassable if we can. As someone has said of Homer: he who learns to admire him, learns to understand him; the same is true of the art works of the ancients, especially the Greeks."

Neoclassical art was well suited to the changing political realities

377. ELIZABETH VIGÉE-LEBRUN
Portrait of Marie Gabrielle de Gramont, Duchesse de Caderousse. 1784. Oil on wood, 41 3/8 x 29 7/8". Nelson-Atkins Museum of Art, Kansas City, Missouri. Elizabeth Vigée-Lebrun was one of the foremost artists of Louis XVI's court.

of the late eighteenth century. Compared to the lighthearted and aristocratic elegance of Rococo art, the Neoclassical style offered a restrained, solemn design which was intended to convey a moral dignity. As ancient classical edifices first bore witness to the representative governments of Athens and Rome, what better style was there to emulate during the new age, which asserted that each individual had natural rights—or, in the words of the Declaration of Independence, "inalienable rights"—and that among these were a voice in government? To the Neoclassicists, the art and history of the classical world offered models to be used as guides for human behavior and achievement.

THE EIGHTEENTH-CENTURY ARTIST

The education of artists in academies (see p. 30) was now firmly established in Europe. The Royal Academy of Painting and Sculpture in Paris, founded in 1648, flourished, sending promising students to Rome to study classical art. Its primacy was gradually challenged by the Royal Academy of Arts, founded in London in 1768, which also championed Neoclassicism. The guiding spirit of England's Royal Academy was Sir Joshua Reynolds, a painter who had spent two years in Italy studying both ancient and Renaissance arts (see fig. 389). As the Royal Academy's first president, Reynolds delivered fifteen *Discourses*, which expressed his views on learning the "grand style" of art, and outlined an education based on imitating the perfection of nature as revealed through classical and High Renaissance art: "The moderns are not less convinced than the ancients of [the] superior power existing in art; nor less sensible of its effects. . . . The *gusto grande* of the Italians, the *beau ideal* of the French, and the *great style, genius,* and *taste* among the English, are but different appellations of the same thing. It is this intellectual dignity . . . that ennobles the painter's art . . . we must have recourse to the ancients as instructors . . . they will suggest many observations, which would probably escape you, if your study were confined to nature alone." Reynolds also recommended the study of the "great masters" of the Italian Renaissance: "I would chiefly recommend, that an implicit obedience to the Rules of Art, as established by the practice of the great masters, should be exacted from the young students. That those models, which have passed through the approbation of ages, should be considered by them as perfect and infallible guides; as subjects for their imitation, not their criticism."

Although the Royal Academy was founded to raise the status of both the arts and the artists, its conservative dogmatism, as revealed by Reynolds's preemptory language, began to be viewed by some as a constrictive environment. The tradition of the academy, which in the later sixteenth century had begun as part of a liberating ambience for the artist, was now becoming a conservative cloak, dictating proprieties in subject matter and form. One academic priority was history painting, which was promoted as the most noble of artistic expressions. History painting drew its iconography from the classical

379. ANGELICA KAUFFMANN
*Self-Portrait Hesitating Between the Arts
of Music and Painting.* 1794. Oil on
canvas, 58 x 86". Nostell Priory,
Yorkshire

378. ADÉLAIDE LABILLE-GUIARD
*Portrait of Madame Labille-Guiard and
Her Pupils.* 1785. Oil on canvas,
82 3/4 x 59 7/8". The Metropolitan
Museum of Art, New York (Gift of
Julia A. Berwind). Labille-Guiard was
instrumental in convincing the French
Academy to lift its quota on women
members, who had been limited to
four, and to allow women professors.

past and, less often, the more recent past. Themes were selected
which could be interpreted on several levels. Academic history
painters most often picked themes that exemplified an elevated code
of human behavior. Such themes were considered appropriate for
the "grand style" or the "grand manner" in art.

To truly understand the "grand style," every artist who aspired to
gain professional fame felt compelled to make a tour of the antiquities of Italy. We can understand the importance of viewing the actual
artistic remains of the classical and Renaissance past from the letters
of Benjamin West (see p. 365), an American painter who, en route to
London, traveled from 1760 to 1763 through Italy. West later wrote to
another American artist, John Singleton Copley, advising him on
what to see in Italy: "In regard to your studies in Italy my advice is as
follows: That you pursue the higher Excellences in the Art, and for the
obtaining of which I recommend to your attention the works of
Ancient Sculptors, Raphael, Michelangelo, Correggio, and Titian, as
the Source from which true taste in the arts have flowed. "

Eighteenth-century artists' self-portraits reflect the vitality of the
different art styles which characterized the Age of Enlightenment.
Adélaide Labille-Guiard's painting (fig. 378) continues the Rococo
style into the latter years of the century. Noted for her abilities as both
an artist and a teacher, she depicts herself, in elegant dress, at her easel
with two attentive students. An early self-portrait by Angelica
Kauffmann (fig. 379) shows the young artist between figures representing the classical allegories of Music and Art. Kauffmann, who
was an accomplished musician, here adapted the Neoclassical style
to demonstrate her dilemma at having to choose between a career in
music or in painting.

ROCOCO PAINTING

380. ANTOINE WATTEAU
A Pilgrimage to the Island of Cythera. 1717. Oil on canvas, 51 x 76 1/2".
The Louvre, Paris. As Watteau's reception piece for the French Royal Academy,
this painting was listed as "une fête galante," a new category of painting in
which elegant aristocratic men and women are represented partying in a landscape setting.

Watteau's *Pilgrimage to Cythera* combines reality and fantasy to express the transitory nature of romantic love (fig. 380). Delicately scaled couples in eighteenth-century dress move slowly toward a fanciful ship that will return them from the island of Cythera, mythical home of Venus, goddess of love. The statue of Venus at the right has been adorned with garlands by these pensive lovers, who came to worship at her shrine and engage in the rituals of her cult. Their reluctance to leave pleasure behind is expressed in their gestures and poses, while the muted colors and light brush-stroke express the transience of love. The composition moves from the statue of Venus to the vessel of departure, reversing our normal reading direction and heightening the bittersweet nature of the departure. Watteau simultaneously conveys the poetry of love and suggests how remote it is from everyday reality. Romantic love survives only in the world of the imagination.

Fragonard's painting, on the other hand, reaffirms the pleasures of lovers' games (fig. 381). The painting was commissioned by Baron de Saint-Julien, who specified the details of the subject. His mistress is in a swing pushed by a bishop, "so high that her slipper falls off the tip of her foot and her skirt shoots upward for the delight of the indiscreet eyes of a charming youth reclining among the flowers beneath her; happily there hovers above him a cupid whose

gesture enjoins him to keep the secret of what he has seen." The theme incorporates a pun, for the baron served as the government representative who collected the taxes paid by the church. His title was *Receveur général des biens du clergé* (receiver general of the "goods" offered by the clergy). Fragonard's pastel palette, which centers around the pink dress and the blue-green trees, and the delicate lightness of his brushstroke express the frivolity of the subject.

The qualities seen in these two works help to define Rococo painting. The colors are unusually light and the thin paint is delicately brushed onto the surface. The figures are generally small and delicate in proportion, and the composition creates a flowing, idyllic movement. Themes are superficial scenes from court life and especially romance.

Hogarth's series of paintings on *Marriage à la Mode* presents a satirical view of modern life (see fig. 382). It exposes the difficulties of a loveless "city" marriage of convenience. The serious nature of Hogarth's social criticism of both the *nouveau riche* and the nobility is evident throughout the series, which begins with the signing of the marriage contract between the daughter of a rich, social-climbing merchant and an impoverished nobleman (Count Squanderfield). In a sequence of six scenes, their debauchery progresses through adultery, the murder of the husband by the wife's lover (Silvertongue), and her death by suicide, leaving their only child an orphan. Our scene shows the husband returning at 1:20 P.M. with a hangover after a night on the town. The dog sniffs at a woman's cap hanging from his pocket. His pose is meant to suggest sexual exhaustion. The wife's pose and the overturned chair and scattered music suggest that her lover is the music teacher, who seems to have departed quickly. Extravagance is evident in the ugly mantelpiece, with its ostentatious display of bric-a-brac, and the stack of bills held by the clerk. The painting over the mantel features a figure of Cupid, Venus's assistant, blowing a bagpipe—an inharmonious phallic symbol—amid ruins. The venereal disease that will ultimately infect their child is already evident in the black spot on the husband's neck. In style, the looseness of Hogarth's brushstrokes in the original paintings is indebted to the example of contemporary French painting.

381. JEAN-HONORÉ FRAGONARD
Happy Accidents of the Swing. 1767. Oil on canvas, 31 7/8 x 25 3/8". Wallace Collection, London

WATTEAU, *A Pilgrimage to the Island of Cythera:* **1717**
1700: The population of London, Europe's largest city, reaches 550,000
1717: Handel's *Water Music* is performed on the Thames
1719: Defoe, *Robinson Crusoe*
1721: J. S. Bach, *Brandenburg Concertos*
1728: Gay, *The Beggar's Opera*
1748: Fielding, *Tom Jones*

382. WILLIAM HOGARTH
Marriage à la Mode, Scene II. 1743. Oil on canvas, 27 1/2 x 35 3/4". National Gallery, London. This is the second scene in a series of six. To Hogarth's contemporaries, "à la mode" implied something fashionable but cheap and short-lived. The series was subtitled *Modern Occurrences in High Life.* Hogarth's painted series on moral subjects were reproduced as popular engravings. The artist compared himself to dramatists and novelists, saying that he "considered subjects as writers do," adding, "My picture was my stage and men and women my actors." The inspiration of contemporary English theater (Gay) and literature (Fielding, Defoe) on Hogarth is well documented. In two earlier series Hogarth chronicled *A Harlot's Progress* (1728–30), which follows an attractive young girl from her arrival in London, where she is discovered by a procuress, to her death and *A Rake's Progress* (1735), in which a weak young man wastes the father's fortune, ending up in an asylum, probably the infamous English Bedlam.

Romantic love—its dreams and disappointments, pleasures and pains, realities and fantasies—becomes a central theme in Rococo art. The variety of interpretation, demonstrated in these three examples, and the probing character of the representations reveal important changes as the themes of art are broadened, revealing an expanded interest in the psychological and emotional states that affect people in their everyday lives.

ROCOCO ARCHITECTURE AND SCULPTURE

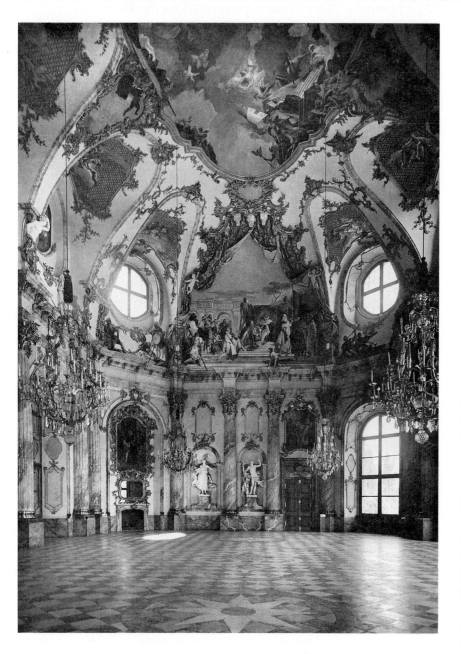

elaborate, gilded curtains. Painted figures and animals by Tiepolo wander out onto the entablature to chat, sit, and look down at us.

The Rococo style in architecture developed in France at Versailles about 1700 and flourished in southern Germany in part because of political connections. The palace at Würzburg was built by a family of local hereditary prince-bishops who set out to surpass Versailles (see fig. 369). The Rococo style is perhaps at its most exuberant here, where all restraint seems to evaporate in gilded decoration, fake marble columns, and an indissoluble union of painting and architecture. Although it owes its origins to the classical vocabulary of the Renaissance, the Rococo offers a new lightness of color and of movement and a new delicate scale of ornament, which are in contrast to the more ponderous forms and colors of Baroque architecture.

Equally exuberant is the church nicknamed Die Wies near Munich (fig. 384). Here Rococo architecture and decoration be-

The Kaisersaal documents the life of the aristocracy in the eighteenth century (fig. 383). One must imagine it filled with the elaborate furniture of the period, its crystal chandeliers lit with flickering candles. The shape of this elegant salon is too complicated to be either an oval or an octagon, but it is surmounted by a high oval dome pierced by windows. The columns seem to be a beautiful pink marble but, like most such columns in Rococo buildings, they are stucco painted and polished to give the illusion of marble. The lightness of the architecture is enhanced by the large irregular frescoed oval and by two scenes enframed by

NEUMANN, Kaisersaal: 1735–44
1732: Benjamin Franklin's *Poor Richard's Almanack* is issued
1739: John Wesley founds the Methodist movement
1741: Handel, *The Messiah*

come a visionary premonition of the heavenly Jerusalem. Die Wies is a pilgrimage center where devout Catholics of all classes worship at the shrine of a miraculous statue of Christ. Virtually every surface is decorated—this is architecture that does not let the eye rest and, like the French Gothic style (see fig. 197), its celestial metaphor is in part accomplished by an attempt to deny visually the weight of architectural forms. The white gilded stucco capitals have a flamelike movement, and irregularly shaped windows pierce the walls. The openness and lightness of the oval "nave" area contrast with the colors of the architectural climax at the altar, where the statue is enclosed

within a shrine of red and white columns. The vault is pierced with curving, Rococo openings that let light in from windows in the outer wall. This denial of the principles of vaulted architecture makes Die Wies seem like an apparition not dependent on normal structural systems. Nor is it subject to the force of gravity. The exuberance of Catholic Rococo architecture may be in part a reaction to the severity characteristic of contemporary Protestant architecture.

At Rohr (fig. 385), a light-filled white and gold nave directs attention to the richer colors of the columns behind the high altar that enframe a monumental sculptural group. While gesticulating apostles surround a

385. EGID QUIRIN ASAM
Assumption of the Virgin (detail). 1721–23. Painted and gilded stucco and stained glass. Monastery Church, Rohr, Germany

384. DOMINIKUS ZIMMERMAN
Interior, Die Wies, Germany. 1745–54. The frescoed vault and stucco decoration are probably by Johann Baptist Zimmerman, the architect's brother. The exterior of this structure is rather plain, and the contrast between exterior and interior is an important part of the architectural experience.

Rococo sarcophagus, we gasp as we seem to witness the Virgin being carried to heaven by angels. The architecture seems to open and a golden stained-glass window offers a portal to heaven. Since the Renaissance, religious drama had used special effects of lighting (candles, torches, fireworks) and theatrical machinery to make transcendent miraculous events seem more realistic and more dramatic, and one of the most successful Counter-Reformation tools employed by the Jesuits in southern Germany was the use of sacred theater as a teaching device. Asam's *Assumption* is a permanent version of one of these theatrical representations.

EIGHTEENTH-CENTURY PORTRAITURE

Copley's honest and informal portrait of the Boston silversmith and engraver Paul Revere represents both the New England work ethic and Copley's artistic joy in rendering exact visual detail (fig. 386). The darkened background focuses our attention on Revere and the tools and products of his trade in the foreground. He wears the simple work clothes of an artisan. Such a straightforward approach, which dignifies labor and craftsmanship, was in keeping with Puritan values. Copley convincingly portrays a sense of immediacy between Revere and ourselves. It is as though we have discovered Revere deep in thought, almost as if he has forgotten the engraving of the teapot and is now engrossed in the contemplation of more difficult issues. Revere's eyes meet ours, and his raised right eyebrow seems to signify an acknowledgment of our presence. It is clear that Copley delighted in the naturalistic representation of figures and objects. Note how the sharp, detailed reflection of Revere's fingers in the silver teapot contrasts with the diffused reflection of his shirt on the polished wooden worktop.

Copley and Benjamin West (see fig. 395) are acknowledged as America's first significant artists. Copley's fame in the colonies was established primarily on his ability as a portraitist. His sensitive observation and carefully developed talent earned him a distinguished reputation and a significant financial income, both in the colonies and in

386. JOHN SINGLETON COPLEY
Right: *Portrait of Paul Revere.* c. 1768–70. Oil on canvas, 34 7/8 x 28 1/2". Museum of Fine Arts, Boston (Gift of Joseph W., William B., and Edward H. R. Revere). Paul Revere was a political activist in Boston. His famous night ride to warn Bostonians of the advance of the British army occurred on April 18, 1775. Copley's family was sympathetic to the British, and the artist left the colonies forever on the eve of the Revolution.

387. ROSALBA CARRIERA
Below right: *Portrait of Louis XV as a Young Man.* 1720–21. Pastel on paper, 18 1/2 x 14 ". Museum of Fine Arts, Boston (The Forsyth Wickes Collection)

his later career in Britain. Although portrait painting ranked behind history and religious painting in the academic classification of subject matter, it was an economic mainstay for many artists.

Rosalba Carriera's painting of France's young King Louis XV demonstrates the elegant grace of Rococo portraiture (fig. 387). The soft, delicate effect is achieved not only by the blending of high valued colors, but also by the use of pastel as a medium. Carriera, a Venetian artist, was a master of pastel portraits. Her influence in France and Italy popularized the medium in the eighteenth century.

In England two competing artists excelled in portraiture: Sir Joshua Reynolds, president of London's Royal Academy (see p. 354), and Thomas Gainsborough. Our two portraits, which

display the abilities and different approaches of these two artists, both represent Sarah Kemble Siddons, a popular and accomplished actress of the period (figs. 388, 389).

True to his philosophy that painting should aspire to the "grand style," Reynolds chose to depict Siddons as a classical alle-

COPLEY, *Portrait of Paul Revere:* c. 1768–70

1750: World population is about 750 million
1760: Population of American colonies is about 1.6 million
1762: Catherine the Great becomes czarina of Russia
1764: Mozart, age eight, writes his first symphony
1770: Boston "Massacre"
1778: Death of Voltaire

388. THOMAS GAINSBOROUGH
Below: *Portrait of Mrs. Siddons.* 1783–85. Oil on canvas, 49 3/4 x 39 1/4". National Gallery, London

389. SIR JOSHUA REYNOLDS
Below right: *Allegorical Portrait of Mrs. Siddons as the Tragic Muse.* 1784. Oil on canvas, 93 x 57 1/2". Henry E. Huntington Library and Art Gallery, San Marino, California

gorical figure, the muse of tragic drama. She sits on a throne, head and eyes raised as if in response to divine, creative inspiration. Behind her are figures symbolizing Pity and Terror, the attributes of tragic drama. Reynolds's composition directly recalls Michelangelo's figures of prophets and sibyls on the Sistine Chapel Ceiling (see fig. 297), demonstrating his adaptation of Renaissance masters.

When Gainsborough painted the same celebrated actress, he chose to portray her as an elegantly dressed, confident woman. The painting, which recalls the rich tradition of Venetian and Baroque portraiture, is a sumptuous treat for our eyes. The blues and whites of her dress enhance the warm, golden tones of her shawl and muff, while the magnificent black hat is silhouetted against a deep red curtain. Gainsborough's painterly technique and luxurious colors create an impressive portrait of a dynamic woman.

THOMAS JEFFERSON AND NEOCLASSICAL ARCHITECTURE IN THE UNITED STATES

"You see I am an enthusiast in the subject of the arts. But it is an enthusiasm of which I am not ashamed, as its object is to improve the taste of my countrymen, to increase their reputation, to reconcile them to the respect of the world, and procure them its praise" (Thomas Jefferson, in a letter to James Madison, 1785). Jefferson's Virginia State Capitol (fig. 390) must have surprised many Richmond residents, for it was the first public building in the youthful American republic to be modeled on the classical temple form. Jefferson designed the building while he was serving as U. S. minister to France, where he was inspired by both French architects already working in the Neoclassical style and the ruins of the ancient Roman civilization in Gaul. He was especially influenced by a Roman temple at Nîmes, in southern France, which is similar to

391. THOMAS JEFFERSON
University of Virginia, Charlottesville. 1817–26

390. THOMAS JEFFERSON
State Capitol, Richmond, Virginia. 1785–89. The side wing seen here and a pendant on the other side are later additions.

the Temple of Portunus (see fig. 100) in Rome. Jefferson wrote in a letter that he had gazed at the temple for hours, "like a lover at his mistress." While maintaining its basic design, he greatly enlarged it for the Virginia State Capitol. The resulting structure, with its Ionic portico, pediment, and classical proportions, confers a solemn, dignified appearance, appropriate, as Jefferson himself believed, to the ideals of a young democratic nation.

Although the Neoclassical architectural style flourished throughout the Western world, it was particularly meaningful in the United States, as the nation adopted a democratic form of government following the Revolution. The emulation of Roman buildings was viewed as an appropriate vehicle to express architectural dignity and command public respect. For Jefferson, public architecture demanded a moral content. The nobility of the Neoclassical edifice would serve as a guide to the behavior and aspirations of the young Republic. The Neoclassical architectural style in the United States is also known as the Federal Style because of its prominent use for government buildings.

In 1817 Jefferson, now a former president, began planning the first state university in America. His design for the University of Virginia harmonizes the stateliness of the Federal Style with the practical needs of an educational community (fig. 391). The mall is dominated by the Rotunda, an adaptation of the ancient Pantheon in Rome (see fig. 129). The Rotunda contained the library, while the individual

JEFFERSON, State Capitol: 1785–89
1783: First successful hot-air balloon flight
1784: Steam is first used to power textile machinery
1786: Mozart, *Marriage of Figaro*
1787: U. S. Constitution is signed
1790: Washington, D.C., is founded
1790: U.S. population is almost 4 million

pavilions along the mall each housed a different academic discipline, including living quarters for the faculty and classrooms.

Jefferson's design for his country home, Monticello, demonstrates the adaptability of Neoclassical architectural features to domestic buildings (fig. 392). The use of antique architectural elements is evident, but Jefferson's sources for the composition here are also drawn from the Renaissance, particularly the villas of Andrea Palladio. The Villa Rotonda (see fig. 9) and others inspired the main block, with its domed ballroom, while other Palladian villas in the countryside around Venice were the source for the wings that reach out to embrace the landscape and unify the house with the farms and countryside which support the estate. Soon houses throughout America would sport Doric, Ionic, and Corinthian porticoes as an indication of America's democratic ideals.

392. THOMAS JEFFERSON
Monticello, Charlottesville, Virginia. 1768–82; remodeled 1796–1809. The Italian name Monticello (little mountain) was adopted by Jefferson because of the hilltop setting of his home.

NEOCLASSICAL PAINTING

393. JACQUES-LOUIS DAVID
Death of Socrates. 1787. Oil on canvas, 59 x 78". The Metropolitan Museum of Art, New York (Wolfe Fund, 1931). The liberal philosophy of Socrates, the fifth-century B.C. Athenian philosopher, stressed the worth of the individual over that of the state in a manner which upset Athenian officials. Because he could not be brought to trial for his philosophical beliefs, he was tried for "impiety," found guilty, and ultimately sentenced to death. It was clear that he could have gone free if he had renounced his teachings, but Socrates himself pointed out that death had been the verdict of a legitimate court. Following Athenian practice, he drank hemlock. The painting was commissioned by a lawyer at the French Parliament.

Heroic suicide may seem to be a contradiction in terms, but the purpose of David's theme (fig. 393), painted in the unsettled years in France before the Revolution, was to demonstrate the need to live by principles and the heroism of the stoic virtue of absolute self-sacrifice. David depicts a heroic, muscular Socrates reaching for the cup of poisonous hemlock held by a distraught disciple. With an exclamatory gesture, Socrates points upward, insisting on the truth of his ideals. On viewing the painting, one contemporary observer remarked, "This is the triumph of virtue which is raised higher than all other things by a heroic courage and an inspired soul."

While the theme of the death of Socrates is taken from the classical past, David's choice and interpretation of subject are strictly contemporary, and within the cultural context of late-eighteenth-century France would have been easily understood. In 1758 the philosopher and writer Denis Diderot had detailed a proposed drama on Socrates' death that popularized the theme with artists and writers. Socrates' unwavering devotion to his ide-

als provides the theme for this history painting. Both the lesson and David's representation were acclaimed by critics and the public. The work offered a guide for moral behavior in the troubled social climate of France. David became a supporter of the French Revolution, and the *Death of Socrates* illustrates his belief that paintings "of heroism and civic virtue offered the eyes of the people [will] electrify its soul, and plant the seed of glory and devotion to the fatherland." The crisp modeling of the figures creates precise, linear, sculptural forms, revealing David's academic training and approach, while the planar space of the painting suggests that ancient relief sculpture may have been one of David's inspirations.

The Swiss painter Angelica Kauffmann also championed the virtues of history painting. The theme of Kauffmann's *Cornelia* (fig. 394) is drawn from Roman antiquity. Cornelia was renowned as a devoted mother. After a friend, who had just displayed her own jewelry, asked to see Cornelia's gems, Cornelia presented her two sons. The personal and emotional implications of the theme are clear, and it should perhaps be pointed out that Kauffmann selected and successfully represented a subject that would be recognized as revealing a particular feminine insight. Kauffmann's elegant, yet disciplined Neoclassical compo-

1787: Dollar currency is introduced in the U.S.
1788: The *Times* of London begins publication
1791: Mozart, *The Magic Flute*

394. ANGELICA KAUFFMANN
Cornelia, Mother of the Gracchi. 1785. Oil on canvas, 40 x
50". Virginia Museum of Fine Arts, Richmond (Williams
Fund, 1975)

395. BENJAMIN WEST
The Death of General Wolfe. 1770. Oil on canvas, 59 1/2 x
84". National Gallery of Canada, Ottawa (Gift of the
Duke of Westminster). The story of the death of the
British commander James Wolfe on the battlefield at
Quebec in 1759 was inspirational. After three months of
stalemate, Wolfe had led his troops to victory over a
much larger French force but, mortally wounded, he
died in the arms of his officers at the moment of victory.

sitions gained her an international reputation.

Benjamin West's *Death of General Wolfe* (fig. 395) popularized a new concept within the category of history painting, for West represented the figures in contemporary costume, avoiding the antique clothing and setting which, traditional academic rules held, could elevate a subject to its universal significance. West's earliest biographer tells that Sir Joshua Reynolds, president of the Royal Academy, had advised West to "adopt the classic costume of antiquity, as much more becoming the inherent greatness of . . . [the] subject than the modern garb of war," and that West had replied: "The event intended to be commemorated took place on the 13th of September, 175[9], in a region of the world unknown to the Greeks and Romans, and at a period of time when no such nations, nor heroes in their costume, any longer existed. The subject I have to represent is the conquest of a great province of America by the British troops. . . . If, instead of the facts of the transaction, I represent classical fictions, how shall I be understood by posterity! . . . I want to mark the date, the place, and the parties engaged in the event; and if I am not able to dispose of the circumstances in a picturesque manner, no academical distribution of Greek or Roman costume will enable me to do justice to the subject."

Earlier masterpieces inspired the work's impressive composition, which was stimulated by a serious study of classical sculpture and of the works of Renaissance and Baroque artists. West's painting, a popular success, pioneered an important change in the representation of contemporary history. Although he avoids classical costume, West does refer to tradition in including the Indian as a personification of America. The painting successfully communicates the tragedy of the death of Wolfe, an event which inherently demonstrated the universal values of self-sacrifice, courage, and patriotism. King George III commissioned a copy of West's painting and made him the official history painter at the court.

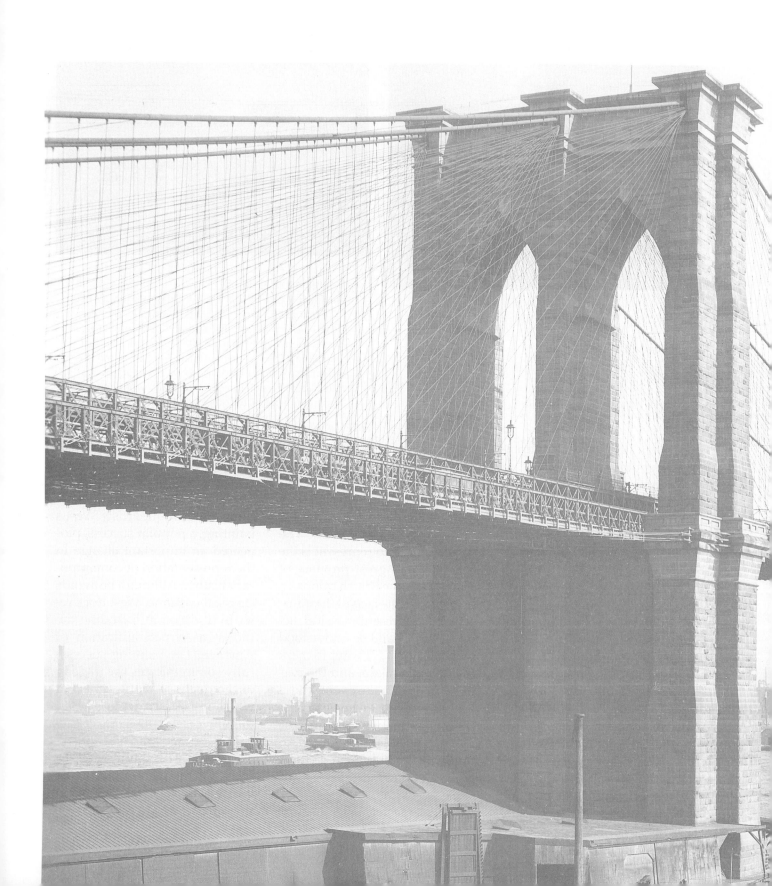

IX

NINETEENTH-CENTURY ART

INTRODUCTION

396. EUGÈNE DELACROIX
Liberty Leading the People. 1830. Oil on canvas, 8' 6 3/8" x 10' 8". The Louvre, Paris

The ideal of revolution, so important for the development of the modern world and so central to the history, ideology, and art of the nineteenth century, is expressed in two paintings by Delacroix and Monet (figs. 396, 397). Delacroix's subject celebrates the July Revolution of 1830, when an uprising of Parisians mounted a revolutionary red, white, and blue flag—the tricolor—on the spires of Notre Dame and forced the abdication of King Charles X and the adoption of a new charter that doubled the number of citizens who elected the legislative chamber. This was a modest but important triumph for the liberals, lower bourgeoisie, and skilled workers who had led the revolt. In Delacroix's painting, the personification of Liberty, holding the tricolor, leads an army of Parisian rebels over the bodies of their dead comrades toward victory. Delacroix's technique is likewise revolutionary, for in reaction to the sharp linearity of the prevailing Neoclassical style (see p. 364), he introduces blurred edges, strong colors, and loose brushstrokes in an active style appropriate to his modern subject. Of Delacroix's significance, the later painter Paul Cézanne would say, "We all paint differently because of him."

From later in the century, Monet's revolutionary painting expresses new Impressionist ideals. In defiance of the attitudes that had endured since the Renaissance, the Impressionists asserted that subject matter in a work of art was not more important than the work's purely visual qualities. Monet chose this particular cityscape not in response to patriotic fervor, for example, but because he was challenged by the problem of how to represent the visual effect of the brilliant colors and the ever-changing movement offered by the flags. Monet's goal was to capture a visual "impression" of what the eye sees, regardless of subject. Traditional critics were as upset by this attitude about subject matter as they were by his loose brushstrokes.

HISTORY

Economic, technological, and political revolutions dominate the history of the nineteenth century in Europe and America. The Industrial Revolution, with its mechanization of production in factories, transformed life for a large percentage of the population. The rapidly expanding lower and middle classes, concentrated in the cities near their factory jobs, organized to demand democracy and more humane treatment. The institutions, life-styles, and class structures that resulted had an important impact on art. The spirit of reform that began in the nineteenth century extended into the twentieth, eventually leading to universal suffrage.

During the nineteenth century the world seemed to become a smaller place as steam-powered trains and ships led to increased world trade. The expansion of communications with the establishment of cheap newspapers and periodicals, printed on high-speed printing presses, and the development of the telegraph and telephone led to international awareness. A world culture gradually evolved, prompted by world trade and centered around the great international fairs held in the second half of the century. More and more artists traveled from America to Europe to be trained, and soon even painters from Pittsburgh were trying to exhibit at the Salon in Paris and the Royal Academy in London. Inexpensive reproductions of works of art were widely disseminated. The importation of Oriental works of art into Europe and America had a significant impact not only on the development of art, but on popular taste and collecting as well (see fig. 398).

Napoleon dominated European history in the first decade of the nineteenth century, leading French armies to victory until he controlled all of Europe. Only Britain, which defeated Napoleon's navy at Trafalgar, was able to repel the French. Napoleon was proclaimed

397. CLAUDE MONET
Rue Saint-Denis Festivities on June 30, 1878. 1878. Oil on canvas, 29 7/8 x 20 1/2". Musée des Beaux-Arts, Rouen

emperor of France in 1804 and king of Italy in 1805. Determined to break the traditional and historic power of the Catholic church and its clergy, Napoleon closed monasteries and destroyed symbols of ecclesiastical and monastic power. To enlarge his own private collections and those of the French state, he appropriated many works of art. He attacked Russia in 1812 but failed to take Moscow; in retreat his army was virtually annihilated. Napoleon abdicated in 1814, returned briefly to power in 1815, and was defeated by the English at Waterloo. The new European borders set at the Congress of Vienna in 1815, after Napoleon's defeat, established a balance of power that endured until World War I.

The French Revolution and later revolutionary uprisings in France in 1830 and 1848, as well as the success of the new democracy in America, gave impetus to other revolutionary movements. Through-

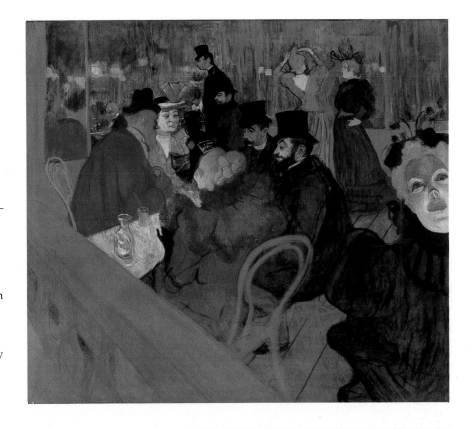

398. KUNISADA

A Woman Frightened by Thunder. 1849-53. Woodblock print. This print was part of a large collection of more than 200 Japanese prints owned by the Post-Impressionist painter Vincent van Gogh; the artist owned 165 prints by Kunisada alone. Japanese prints were a formative influence on many French nineteenth-century painters, especially Manet, Monet, Degas, Toulouse-Lautrec, and Van Gogh. The bold silhouetting and complex patterning of their designs (especially evident here in the pattern of the mosquito netting over the designs of the woman's costume), the truncation of the forms (note the flying reed shade in the upper right corner and the lightning bolt that flashes into the room), the unusual, high viewpoint, and the diagonal recession of the architectural settings all had a distinctive effect on the development of modern French painting.

399. HENRI DE TOULOUSE-LAUTREC

At the Moulin Rouge. 1892. Oil on canvas, 48 3/8 x 55 1/4". The Art Institute of Chicago (Helen Birch Bartlett Memorial Collection). The dramatic lighting of the face in the foreground, which reflects the strong color of the cabaret's gas lighting, reveals the Impressionist interest in the realistic rendering of light.

out Europe there was an increased demand for "liberty, equality, and fraternity (nationalism)." There were eleven revolutionary uprisings in major European cities in 1848–49. The nineteenth-century demands for revolution, however, would reach their most significant outcome with the Russian Revolution of 1917. Great Britain remained stable and the British Empire underwent tremendous expansion accompanied by an astonishing financial development—the result of peace, industrialization (see below), and the world market provided by the empire. The power of the British naval and merchant marine was unrivaled. In America, rapid expansion and industrialization led to prosperity and optimism, but this mood was dissipated by the divisive Civil War (1861–65), and after the war America became increasingly dependent on European culture. By the end of the nineteenth century, nationalistic desires for unification in Italy and in Germany had succeeded.

THE INDUSTRIAL REVOLUTION

By the mid-nineteenth century, Britain led the world in the mechanized production of inexpensive goods for mass public consumption.

400. FRÉDÉRIC-AUGUSTE BARTHOLDI
Liberty Enlightening the World (now known as *The Statue of Liberty*). 1870–86. Hammered copper over wrought-iron pylon designed by Gustave Eiffel; height from base to top of torch 111' 6". New York Harbor

Such production became the financial base for England's expansion during the century. Simultaneously the Industrial Revolution spread through much of Europe and into America. When power-driven machinery revolutionized the production of textiles, entrepreneurs established huge mills in which hundreds of workers manufactured vast amounts of cheap fabric. Factory-made nails and milled lumber, produced by the power-driven sawmill, revolutionized the housing industry in America. The rapid spread of the railroads transformed transportation, the delivery of merchandise, and communications.

The new industrial production was celebrated in a series of great international exhibitions, beginning with the Great Exhibition of the Works of Industry of All Nations at the Crystal Palace in London in 1851 (see fig. 427). This exhibition emphasized England's role as the world's greatest manufacturing center. It also brought together handicrafts and manufactured goods from all over the world.

The Industrial Revolution raised standards of living for large groups of people, but it also contributed to problems of unemployment. The terrible working conditions and life in the cities are documented in contemporary novels by Victor Hugo *(Les Misérables)* and Charles Dickens *(Oliver Twist)*. The Industrial Revolution also transformed art, for the mass production of cheap prints developed a new audience for art. Reproductions of paintings were available virtually everywhere. Illustration flourished, led by such entrepreneurs as Currier & Ives in America. The mass production of furniture and other household goods led to a reaction in the second half of the century, when the finely finished works of the individual craftsperson were exalted in the Arts and Crafts and Art Nouveau movements.

INTELLECTUAL AND SCIENTIFIC ACTIVITIES

The social and financial inequities that resulted from industrialism led to a number of responses—socialism, anarchism, utopian movements, and revolutionary communism. The latter was explicitly defined by Karl Marx and Friedrich Engels in the *Communist Manifesto*, published in 1848.

Intimately connected with industrialization were advances in science, engineering, and technology. Science replaced philosophy as the most influential university discipline. New scientific theories, especially Charles Darwin's controversial *The Origin of Species* (1859), with its message of the "survival of the fittest," deeply affected attitudes about religion and the meaning of life.

The explosion of activity in the fields of literature and music makes it impossible to mention all the important figures at work during the nineteenth century. Some of the artistic movements had parallel developments in literature and music. Romanticism in literature was expressed in poetry, historical novels, fantasy and horror tales, and romance and adventure stories. Among its titanic figures are Lord Byron in England, Johann Goethe in Germany, Victor Hugo in France, and Aleksander Pushkin in Russia. Romanticism and Realism are united in the works of Dickens. The Romantic movement in music includes Frédéric Chopin (who even wrote a "revolutionary étude"), Johannes Brahms, Richard Wagner, and Pëtr Tchaikovsky. Impressionism is paralleled in music in the compositions of Claude Debussy. Art criticism flourished, and partisans of both conservative and "modern" art developed.

NINETEENTH-CENTURY ART

The subjects of nineteenth-century painters ranged from historical, mythological, and religious themes to scenes of the everyday life of the working classes. By the end of the century, even the vulgar characters and activities of a popular dance hall had become acceptable as a theme for art (see fig. 399). The development of exhibitions, such as those at the Parisian Salon and London's Royal Academy, and of art galleries in every major city in Europe and America meant that more and more painters and sculptors were producing works for exhibition and for the general art market. As the percentage of commissioned works declined, there was a growing division between artist and public, and the gulf between conservative and revolutionary artists, who assumed the title of avant-garde, gradually became wider. Although the development of photography robbed the painter of a traditional means of support, the elite continued to commission painted portraits. Landscape became a particularly popular subject, perhaps because it was such a good vehicle for expressing aesthetic theories (see p. 382). Despite the significance of the Industrial Revolution, scenes of industry were relatively rare.

The popular print developed with the growth of newspapers and periodicals to become a prominent vehicle for social protest (see p. 384). The photograph, invented in the nineteenth century, was used both as a journalistic and as a documentary tool. In sculpture, the heroic monument dominated the century and was considered to be the primary challenge of the sculptor (see figs. 400, 401), but the diversity of the century is seen in examples of traditional architectural sculpture and works that demonstrate revolutionary attitudes about sculpture (see fig. 443). In architecture, new forms were demanded by the dramatically increasing pressure of population and business crowded in great urban centers. Impressive technological and engineering advances made possible the skyscraper, the railroad station, and the great bridges (see fig. 428) and monuments of the later nineteenth century.

401. **GUSTAVE EIFFEL**
Diagram of the construction of *The Statue of Liberty*

THE PRIMACY OF FRANCE

Not all the great works of art produced during the nineteenth century were made by French artists, but it was developments in France that gave names to most new movements, and much of the art created elsewhere reflected French styles. There was a sequence of movements and great artists in France that the rest of the world watched

402. FRANCISCO GOYA
*Self-Portrait Being Attended by
Dr. Arrieta.* 1820. Oil on canvas, 45 1/2
x 31 1/8". The Minneapolis Institute of
Arts (The Ethel M. Van Derlip Fund,
1952). The inscription at the bottom of
this painting reads: "Goya, in gratitude, to his friend Arrieta, for the skill
and care with which he saved his life
in his acute and dangerous illness,
suffered at the end of 1819 at the age
of 73. Painted in 1820."

with interest, enthusiasm, and dismay. The annual art exhibitions of
the French Salon were the most famous in the world and the ones in
which virtually all serious artists desired to be included. To be
represented in a Salon could make one's reputation.

Conservative interests dominated the Salon exhibitions, however,
and when the Salon jury of 1863 rejected a number of works which we
would consider modern, there was such an outcry that a special
exhibition of the rejected works, known as the Salon des Refusés, was
established: "Numerous complaints have reached the Emperor on
the subject of works of art which have been refused by the jury of the
exhibition. His Majesty, wishing to let the public judge the legitimacy
of these complaints, has decided that the rejected works of art are to
be exhibited in another part of the Palace of Industry. This exhibition
will be voluntary, and artists who may not wish to participate need
only inform the administration, which will hasten to return their
works to them. This exhibition will open on May 15. Artists have until
May 7 to withdraw their works. After this date their pictures will be
considered not withdrawn and will be placed in the galleries"
(*Proclamation of the Salon des Refusés, 1863*).

THE STYLES OF NINETEENTH-CENTURY ART

The basic styles defined in this century receive their names from
terms applied to paintings—to French paintings in particular. The
new style at the end of the eighteenth century, Neoclassicism, continued in popularity well into the nineteenth century, especially in the
arts of architecture and sculpture (see p. 376). It received a special
impetus from Napoleon's enthusiastic support for a variation of
Neoclassicism known as Empire, which supported his new status as
emperor. Soon, however, the rational and lucid order of the Neoclassical style and its belief that art should express universal truths were
challenged by a style that might be considered its opposite, Romanticism. This style, with its expression of spontaneous, strong, and
even violent individual feelings, is in part based on a new distrust of
rationalism. In architecture, Romanticism, in combination with a new
interest in history and historical precedent, helps explain the interest
in reviving earlier styles, especially the Gothic Revival (see p. 386), so
important in American and European architecture. Some critics
would even include the Neoclassical style within the general category of Romanticism.

In France, Romanticism was challenged by two styles: Academic
Art and Realism. Academic Art is the term applied to the conservative and even reactionary art—heroic, moral themes rendered in
exact verisimilitude—that prevailed in the French Salon exhibitions
and in the French academies. Realism encompasses everyday subjects rendered with emphatic boldness. By denying to art the exalted
mission preached in the academies, Realism was considered to be
revolutionary. Realist attitudes about subject matter and technique
influenced the Impressionists, who set out to represent a momentary
impression of light, color, and atmosphere in paintings of contempo-

rary subjects. A number of painters who went through an Impressionist phase but later moved on to other styles are known as Post-Impressionists. The end of the century saw the beginnings of Expressionism. There were styles in architecture and the decorative arts which can be subsumed in the general category of Victorian, which implies a heavy, often fussy, elaborately decorated style of rich materials, complex silhouette, and varied textures and colors. A reaction to the Victorian style and to the industrialization of the arts appeared in the Utopian style of the Arts and Crafts Movement as invented by William Morris and in the effulgent Art Nouveau style.

THE NINETEENTH-CENTURY ARTIST

The nineteenth century saw an increased sense of the individuality of the artist as a creative and expressive personality. The logical outcome of this was more personalized and revealing self-portraits, as in Goya's portrait of himself on the verge of death (fig. 402). By the end of the century, the revealing personal drama evident in Van Gogh's self-portraits (fig. 403) is not unexpected, although his particularly dramatic evolution from Impressionism could not have been predicted. The modern conception of the artist as a political and social liberal and a revolutionary is largely a product of such nineteenth-century personalities as Théodore Géricault, Gustave Courbet, and James McNeill Whistler. In the Renaissance, artists had worked hard to convince people that they were individuals worthy of recognition and status by their upper-class and noble patrons. In the nineteenth century, artists began to emphasize their bonds to the middle and lower classes. Georges Seurat planned to write a book about his principles and techniques which would enable anyone to paint a masterpiece.

403. VINCENT VAN GOGH
Self-Portrait with Bandaged Ear and Pipe.
1889. Oil on canvas, 20 1/8 x 17 3/4".
Private collection

THE CONTINUATION OF NEOCLASSICISM

404. ANTONIO CANOVA
Left: *Napoleon.* 1806. Marble with gilded bronze staff and figure of victory, height 11'. Wellington Museum, London. This work was commissioned by Napoleon, who wanted to be immortalized by Canova, then considered Europe's greatest artist. The sculpture was bought by the British government and presented to the victorious duke of Wellington, who defeated Napoleon at Waterloo.

405. JEAN-FRANÇOIS-THÉRÈSE CHALGRIN AND OTHERS
Above: Arc de Triomphe, Paris. 1806–36. Height 164' without staff. Inspired by ancient Roman triumphal arches, Napoleon decided to commemorate his military victories with the largest arch ever built. It was not completed until long after his downfall. For one of the sculptures on the arch, see fig. 411.

How well sculpture conveys political concepts, and how quickly the political situation changes, are revealed in Canova's monumental representation of Napoleon, commissioned by the emperor himself in 1802 (fig. 404). Napoleon is represented nude in the guise of Mars, ancient Roman god of war. By the time the sculpture was delivered, in 1811, Napoleon's position had become less secure. The heroic concept no longer seemed completely relevant, and Napoleon decided not to put the

work on public display. After Wellington defeated Napoleon, he acquired the statue as a trophy of victory, as well as a reminder of how quickly the powerful can fall. It is still displayed in Wellington's home in London.

Throughout the nineteenth century, Neoclassical architecture was popular, especially for public buildings and monuments. The Arc de Triomphe (fig. 405) is Napoleon's inflated and grandiose version of the ancient Roman arches, which honored

victorious emperors, and its function is exactly the same. Unfinished at his death, the sculptures added after it was completed honor instead the heroic people of the French Revolution.

The style of Ingres's *Jupiter and Thetis* demonstrates the continuing impact of the Neoclassical mode in painting (fig. 406). The sculpturesque modeling of the heroically posed Jupiter and the crisp drapery folds of Thetis's garment reveal Ingres's academic training. Painted while Ingres was working at the French Acad-

1800: Volta invents the electric battery
1800: World population reaches 870 million
1800: U.S. population is 5.3 million; China's population is 295 million
1803: Louisiana Purchase greatly enlarges U.S.
1804: Napoleon crowned emperor of France
1804: Beethoven, Third Symphony *(Eroica)*

406. JEAN-AUGUSTE-DOMINIQUE INGRES
Jupiter and Thetis. 1811. Oil on canvas, 11' 4 5/8" x 8' 5 1/4". Musée Granet, Aix-en-Provence. This painting, based on an episode from the Trojan War delineated in the *Iliad*, depicts Thetis, a sea nymph and mother of Achilles, pleading with Jupiter to look favorably upon a request she has delivered from Achilles.

407. HORATIO GREENOUGH
George Washington. 1832–41. Marble, height 12'. National Museum of American History, Washington, D.C. Commissioned by Congress in 1832, this colossal work was intended for the Capitol Rotunda. Greenough, America's first famous sculptor, was an expatriate who worked in Italy, where his designs were carved by native stonecarvers. The *George Washington* was only completed and delivered in 1841, by which time the enthusiasm for Neoclassical sculpture in America had passed.

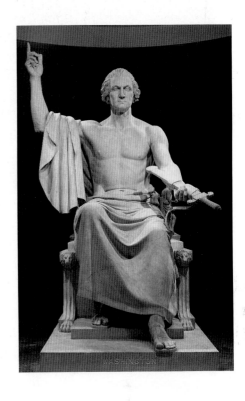

emy in Rome, *Jupiter and Thetis* was sent back to the academy in Paris. The references to antiquity go beyond the theme, for the pose of Jupiter, the Roman equivalent of the Greek Zeus, king of the gods, was derived from the lost ancient cult statue of Zeus from his temple at Olympia. Created by Phidias, this was a magnificent sculpture of ivory and gold considered one of the finest artistic accomplishments of classical civilization.

This lost statue of Zeus was also the inspiration for Greenough's monumental sculpture of George Washington (fig. 407). In a typical Neoclassical effort to aggrandize and immortalize Washington—to clarify his significance for later generations—Greenough posed the great founder as the most powerful Olympian god. With rhetorical gestures, Washington offers us a sword and points upward in a declaratory manner, much like David's determined Socrates (see fig. 393). Most nineteenth-century Americans would not have known Greenough's source, and without this reference, the statue seemed at best ridiculous. The abrupt juxtaposition of Washington's face set on an idealized semi-nude body led to a disappointed reaction from the statue's patrons and the public. Blaming the harsh interior light of the Rotunda of the U.S. Capitol, Greenough had the sculpture moved outdoors, where it proved to be even less appreciated. The history of Greenough's *George Washington* reveals the increasingly rapid manner in which style and attitude can change—an important characteristic of the modern world. This impressive sculpture, with its monumental scale and commanding composition, continues to convey the heroic and even godlike characteristics often ascribed to Washington during the period of the early Republic.

FRANCISCO GOYA

408. FRANCISCO GOYA

The Execution of Madrileños on the Third of May, 1808. 1814–15. Oil on canvas, 8' 9" x 13' 4"; the figures are lifesize. The Prado, Madrid. Madrileños is the name given to the residents of Madrid. Napoleonic troops occupied Spain from 1808 to 1814, and this painting is one of a pair by Goya representing an uprising against the French in Madrid on May 2, 1808, and the execution of rebels and a number of innocent victims during the night of May 2–3. This was a decisive act in the consolidation of French power in Spain, and the French commander, Napoleon's brother-in-law Murat, announced that "yesterday's events have given Spain to the emperor." But the riots of May 2 also marked the beginning of Spanish resistance to the French occupation throughout the country (underground warfare is still called guerrilla warfare, from the Spanish term for little war). In 1814, after Napoleon had been defeated, Goya petitioned the new Spanish government for support to "perpetuate with his brush the most notable and heroic actions or events of our glorious insurrection against the tyrant of Europe." The two paintings were commissioned in 1814.

Despite Goya's commission to perpetuate the "most . . . heroic actions of our glorious insurrection," *The Execution of Madrileños on the Third of May, 1808,* is a brutal and unsettling painting (fig. 408). It emphasizes a confrontation between helpless individuals and the inhuman power of an anonymous authority. The universality of Goya's interpretation overwhelms the specific event of the title. These Spaniards are not heroes, but victims—perhaps even innocent victims—rounded up to be murdered by French troops. Goya represents the terror and helplessness they feel as they confront death from a faceless firing squad. More victims come slowly up the hill, testifying to the extent of the French brutality. Goya simultaneously commemorates history and condemns war and its effect on the individual.

The simple composition and focused light concentrate our attention on the terror and desperate helplessness of the central figure. The night setting, dramatic *chiaroscuro* contrast, and right-to-left composition heighten the drama, and Goya's loose brushstroke emphasizes the writhing movement of the victims. The color scheme is dull, with the exception of the red for blood splashed on the left foreground.

Goya published several series of prints, including a large group now known as *The Disasters of War.* Begun during the Napoleonic occupation and continued

409. FRANCISCO GOYA
Great courage! Against corpses! c. 1810–15. Etching, 4 x 6" (no. 39 from *The Disasters of War* series). Goya's title for this series was *The Fatal Consequences of Spain's Bloody War with Bonaparte and Other Striking Caprichos.* The titles of the etchings in this series evoke Goya's intent: *With reason or without it; One cannot bear to see this; No one can know why; They cry in vain; And there is no remedy; This is worse, Even worse, Barbarians!; Cartloads to the cemetery; Bury and shut up; I saw this; Why?*

in the repressive political period after the French withdrawal, they were not published until 1863, after Goya's death. In some of these prints the nationalities of the French and Spanish soldiers are clear, but which are the torturers and which the tortured alternates. Other scenes, like the one reproduced here (fig. 409), are less specific; they provide Goya's comments on the terrible inhumanity created by war. Even the title condemns the futility and terrible cruelty of this act.

Many of the prints represent atrocities Goya witnessed during the occupation, and his cry of "Enough!" resonates across the centuries. The creation of these prints may have helped the artist deal with his emotions of helplessness, frustration, and sorrow, but the demons he expelled remain to haunt us. The etching medium, with its rough, scratchy lines, here serves as a most appropriate vehicle for Goya's expression.

ROMANTICISM

Géricault's momentous *Raft of the Medusa* signals a new departure in the development of history painting, for its subject is not a heroic event but a needless modern tragedy (fig. 410). When the French frigate *Medusa* sank off the African coast, the captain and senior officers commandeered the lifeboats, abandoning one hundred fifty other survivors to a makeshift raft. After floating for thirteen days, the fifteen who were still left alive were rescued. Géricault represents the moment when they first sight the ship that will rescue them on the horizon. The inex-

perienced captain of the *Medusa* owed his position to his noble birth and his connections with the French government. Géricault's painting is intended both as a dramatic record of the event and a condemnation of a government that would allow such a thing to happen. Whereas in the past most works of art that made a political statement were designed to sustain the government in power, Géricault's social and political consciousness demanded that he create a work which was critical.

The precise modeling of the figures, as well as their dramatic

gestures and varied poses, reflect Géricault's study of the art of Michelangelo and Rubens, while the strong *chiaroscuro*, diagonal composition, and agitated figurative poses remind us of Baroque painting. But here these visual devices have been adapted to a theme of continuing and uncertain conflict. As the survivors

410. THÉODORE GÉRICAULT
The Raft of the Medusa. 1818–19.
Oil on canvas, 16' 1" x 23' 6".
The Louvre, Paris. In preparing for this enormous painting, Géricault read published accounts of the event, interviewed survivors, and visited hospitals and morgues to study dying and dead people.

GÉRICAULT, *The Raft of the Medusa:* **1818–19**
1818: Byron, *Don Juan*
1829: Greece wins its independence from Turkey
1830: Berlioz, *Symphonie fantastique*
1831: Hugo, *Notre Dame de Paris*

excitedly catch sight of a ship on the horizon, they are in constant danger of being engulfed by the turbulent sea. Géricault's painting creates a frightful, emotional drama.

The Raft of the Medusa introduces us to Romanticism, a new style which challenged the dominance of Neoclassicism in the early nineteenth century. Later in the century, Émile Zola, the French novelist and critic (see p. 401), would help define Romanticism when he wrote, "A work of art is part of the universe as seen through a temperament." Romanticism stressed the subjective view of the artist, which meant that it was not dominated by a single, unified style. Romantic artists freely looked to a variety of past art styles, as well as to nature around them, to express their temperament. Opposing the rational and restrained aesthetic of Neoclassicism, Romanticism championed the unbridled spirit of human imagination. The expression of the artist's feelings and convictions became paramount.

The powerful and contagious emotional surge of Romanticism is evident in Rude's enormous high-relief sculpture which decorates one of the piers of the Arc de Triomphe (fig. 411). An angry and determined allegory of the Genius of Liberty urges the people forward with a vigorous right-to-left movement. Despite the specific title, Rude depicts the soldiers in classical nudity or wearing ancient armor to express a universal theme—humanity's fight for liberty.

411. FRANÇOIS RUDE
The Departure of the Volunteers of 1792 (popularly known as *"La Marseillaise"*). 1833–36. Limestone, height about 42'. Arc de Triomphe, Paris (see fig. 405).
So stirring was Rude's sculpture that it soon received the nickname *"La Marseillaise,"* after the French national anthem, which was written in 1792 and first gained popularity when it was sung in the streets of Paris by troops from Marseilles.

ROMANTIC LANDSCAPE PAINTING

Constable's painting of English scenery (fig. 412) is affectionate, with its simple cart, humble cottage, and a dog standing at the river's edge. The composition is unaffected and natural, as if we had accidentally come upon this quintessential scene. But Constable's painting is unified by the cloudy English atmosphere and by flecks of light and color—surprisingly loosely applied—that re-create the sparkling luminosity of the English countryside after the rain. Despite its naturalistic basis, the work can also be termed Romantic. Constable said that "painting is for me but another word for feel-

ing." Here the rush of feeling lies in Constable's love for and exaltation of his native countryside.

In the nineteenth century, landscape painting became a vehicle by which Romantic artists expressed their personal thoughts and emotions. One of the earliest was the German painter Caspar David Friedrich, who wrote: "The painter should depict not only what he sees before him, but also what he sees inside himself. . . . Close your physical eyes so that you see your picture first with your spiritual eye. Then bring forth what you saw inside you so that it works on others from the exterior to

412. JOHN CONSTABLE
The Hay Wain. 1821. Oil on canvas, 51 1/4 x 73". National Gallery, London

their spirit." Friedrich often encourages a quiet meditation before nature, as in his *Abbey in an Oak Forest* (fig. 413), an evocative painting in which a funeral procession of monks is moving slowly past the ruins of a Gothic structure. The barren, skeletal branches of the towering oak trees, their linear patterns echoing the window tracery of the Gothic ruins, are set against the somber, leaden sky, suggesting the void of death. Friedrich has

CONSTABLE, *The Hay Wain:* 1821
1821: Egyptian hieroglyphics on Rosetta stone are deciphered
1823: Monroe Doctrine ends European colonialism on American continent
1824: Beginning of rugby football, at Rugby School, England

413. CASPAR DAVID FRIEDRICH
Abbey in an Oak Forest. 1809–10. Oil on canvas, 44 x 68 1/2". Schloss Charlottenburg, West Berlin

captured one of the moods of nature, filling it with melancholy by the addition of the procession. Winter and time have consumed nature and the product of human endeavors. Friedrich and other nineteenth-century landscape artists (see fig. 421) sought to communicate the grandeur of nature, which inspires an almost religious reverence.

The concept of struggle was also an important theme of Romanticism. The human struggle against the seemingly overwhelming forces of nature is expressed in Turner's *Slave Ship* (fig. 414). This painting, ablaze with a fiery red sunset which almost consumes the activity of the theme, depicts a slave ship heading into a typhoon. Turner's evocative use of color and broad brushstrokes create an urgent, anxious feeling. To lighten the ship's load, the captain inhumanly has thrown overboard his cargo—the slaves. We witness their death struggle in the water, yet the final outcome of the brutal slavers and their ship will be determined by nature, as the ship itself faces the fury of the impending storm.

414. JOSEPH MALLORD WILLIAM TURNER
The Slave Ship. 1840. Oil on canvas, 35 3/4 x 48 1/4". Museum of Fine Arts, Boston (Henry Lillie Pierce Fund)

HONORÉ DAUMIER AND THE POLITICAL PRINT

415. HONORÉ DAUMIER
Rue Transnonain, April 15, 1834. 1834. Lithograph, 11 1/2 x 17 5/8". This print was published in *L'Association mensuelle*, July 1834.

The dying baby lying under its dead father is the most moving detail in Daumier's powerful condemnation of the brutality of French governmental policy in dealing with the working classes (fig. 415). The specificity of the title was chosen so that there could be no doubt about the subject. In April of 1834, workers in Lyon and Paris, led by the secret Society of the Rights of Man, rioted to demonstrate against harsh working conditions and the passage of a new law forbidding unionization. On the night of April 14–15 a sniper in Paris killed an officer. A number of innocent residents of the sniper's building were then murdered by the police in retaliation, including a woman and a child.

Daumier's printer, Charles Philipon, wrote of this print: "This is not caricature . . . it is a blood-stained page in the history of our days, traced by a vigorous hand and inspired by noble indignation . . . he has created a picture which will never lose its worth or duration, even if it consists of only black lines on a sheet of paper." Daumier's print was publicly displayed and was sold in mass quantities in a journal in which Daumier's other political and humorous prints often appeared. Already in 1832, at the age of twenty-four, Daumier had served five months in prison because he had caricatured King Louis Philippe as Gargantua, but this did not weaken

his determination to make statements through his prints about the moral and political problems and issues of his day.

Daumier made thousands of prints in a long career, and no one was safe from his attacks: radical artists, bored and quarrelsome married couples, naughty children, amateur artists, arrogant connoisseurs, corrupt politicians, and even figures from classical antiquity and mythology were lampooned. One of the popular political periodicals which published Daumier's work was called *La Caricature*. Its name helped popularize the term we use today for exaggerated and humorous representations.

Daumier's heroes most often came from the working classes. In *Freedom of the Press* (fig. 416), a

youthful typographer, fists clenched at his sides, stands ready to defend free speech and the liberty of writers, artists, and publishers to comment on contemporary affairs. The vignette in the right background shows the defeated French king Charles X, who had been driven from power in 1830 in part as a result of criticism leveled by the press. Other European monarchs come to his aid as he is exiled. The sturdy hero, who looks toward the arrival of the current king, Louis Philippe, who is caricatured as a pearlike form, is ready again to do battle to protect his rights.

The specific opinions and criticism revealed in such popular prints by Daumier and others, however, became too much for the government to bear. In 1835

1830: U.S. population reaches 12.9 million, including 3.5 million black slaves
1830: First passenger steam railways open
1833: Factory act in England forbids employment of children under nine
1834: Britain's Consolidated Trades Union is dissolved
1834: Troops are used for the first time in a U.S. labor conflict

416. HONORÉ DAUMIER
Freedom of the Press: Don't Meddle with It. 1834. Lithograph, 11 1/2 x 17 5/8". This print appeared in *La Caricature,* March 1834.

laws were passed which proclaimed that "Frenchmen have the right to circulate their opinions in published form," but that "drawings" were such an "incitement to action" that complete liberty in this realm was no longer permitted. At this point Daumier's prints became more humorous and less political.

LITHOGRAPHY TECHNIQUE

Lithography (stone-drawing), invented in France in 1798, became the most popular print medium of the nineteenth century, as lithographs came into use to illustrate newspapers and books (see fig. 417). Lithography is based on the affinity of grease for grease and the antipathy of water to grease. The print form is usually a very smooth slab of limestone on which the artist creates a composition using either a greasy crayon or lithographic ink applied with a pen or a brush. The resulting design is adhered chemically to the surface of the stone. The stone is moistened with water, which stays only in the non-greasy areas. When greasy ink is subsequently applied with a roller, it adheres only to the composition. A dampened paper is applied, stone and paper are put through a press, and a lithograph is created. The technique, spontaneous and relatively cheap, is especially appropriate for the mass media because the design can be mechanically transferred from the original print form to additional stones, allowing a large and rapid print edition.

417. Diagram of the lithography technique

ROMANTIC REVIVAL ARCHITECTURE

418. SIR CHARLES BARRY AND AUGUSTUS W. N. PUGIN
Houses of Parliament, London. Begun 1836; opened 1852; completed 1870. Barry, who won the 1835–36 competition to design the new Houses of Parliament, hired Pugin to help with the detailing. The resulting Gothic Revival complex even has Gothic Revival inkwells and coatracks.

The decision to rebuild the Houses of Parliament in the Gothic Revival style (fig. 418) was not based solely on aesthetic grounds. A more profound cultural and moral basis declared that the Gothic style was historically appropriate, for it had flourished in England during the late medieval period. And, more important for the nineteenth century, the Gothic was understood as a style that expressed spiritual goodness, truth, and the properly reverent relationship between humanity and God.

And, of course, the Gothic was understood as the quintessential Christian style. One critic in 1836 described it as "a style of architecture which belongs peculiarly to Christianity . . . whose very ornaments remind one of the joys of life beyond the grave; whose lofty vaults and arches are crowded with the forms of prophets and martyrs and beatified spirits, and seem to resound with the choral hymns of angels and archangels . . . the architecture of Christianity, the sublime, the glorious Gothic."

The Romantic architects of the nineteenth century revived a multitude of historical styles, but each was understood within a specific cultural, moral, and historical context that encompassed both the nineteenth century and the period when the style originated. The Greek Revival in America, for example, as witnessed in a house in Demopolis (City of the People), Alabama (fig. 419), and in hundreds of banks, courthouses, churches, and homes throughout America, was a response to a movement to

BARRY and PUGIN, Houses of Parliament: begun 1836
1837–1901: Reign of Queen Victoria
1840: Penny post is established in England

419. Unknown architect
Gaineswood, Demopolis, Alabama.
1842– c. 1860. The heritage of the
early-nineteenth-century American
enthusiasm for things Greek
survives in structures in the Greek
Revival style in stone, wood, and
stucco, in coordinating furniture
and decorative arts, and in such
place names as Demopolis; Troy,
New York; Olympia, Washington;
and Sparta and Athens, Michigan.

**420. ALEXANDER JACKSON
DAVIS**
William Rotch House, New
Bedford, Massachusetts. 1845

find an architectural style appropriate for the political ideals of
the young nation. Thomas Jefferson had championed the
Neoclassical style (see p. 362),
but the early nineteenth century
turned more directly to the
monuments of ancient Athens,
history's first documented democracy, for inspiration. American architects and publishers
produced how-to books with
plans and elevations for Greek-
style houses and churches, and
all across America buildings with
handsome Doric porticoes—
some in stone but many in wood,
like this one—were erected.

In America the Greek style was
gradually supplanted in popularity by the Gothic Revival style.
A.J. Davis's home in New Bedford, Massachusetts (fig. 420), is
decorated with the architectural
vocabulary invented in the later
Middle Ages for the great French
Gothic cathedrals. The cusping
along the eaves and the lacy
patterns of the porch posts— cut
from wood—are an American
version of the gilded ornamentation on a medieval Gothic reliquary. The widespread popularity of this "carpenter" Gothic
movement and other revival
styles can be explained in part by
the cheap pattern books produced by architects and publishers that brought such fantasy
within the range of every pioneer with a saw.

ROMANTIC LANDSCAPE PAINTING IN AMERICA

"A landscape is great in its proportion as it declares the glory of God, not the works of man" (Asher B. Durand, *Letters on Landscape Painting*). Enthusiasm for the God-given beauty and richness of the American landscape is the subject of Cole's painting (fig. 421). A dramatic natural confrontation is emphasized as the sweeping peak soars victorious above the clouds. The season is autumn, when the American landscape offers a special coloristic splendor not found in the landscapes of Europe. Schroon Mountain is located near the source of the Hudson River in New York State, and after visiting there in 1837, Cole wrote: "The scenery . . . has

a wild sort of beauty . . . quietness—solitude—the world untamed . . . an aspect which the scene has worn thousands of years. . . . I do not remember to have seen in Italy a composition of mountains so beautiful or pictorial as this."

Cole's emphasis on the uniqueness of American scenery is significant, for in his paintings nationalistic spirit was joined to the ideal of the American landscape as a new Garden of Eden—a God-given paradise which would guarantee America's future greatness. Cole himself was to write: "Those scenes of solitude from which the hand of nature has never been lifted affect the mind with more deep-

421. THOMAS COLE
Schroon Mountain, Adirondacks. 1838. Oil on canvas, 39 3/8 x 63". Cleveland Museum of Art (Hinman B. Hurlbut Collection). The mayor of New York City wrote, "I think every American is proud to prove his love of country by admiring Cole."

toned emotion than aught which the hand of man has touched. Amid them the consequent associations are of God, the Creator. They are his undefiled works, and the mind is cast into the contemplation of eternal things." Later the landscape painter Asher B. Durand would write that every American family should own a painting of the American landscape, counseling

422. GEORGE CALEB BINGHAM
Fur Traders Descending the Missouri. 1845. Oil on canvas, 29 x 36". The Metropolitan Museum of Art, New York (Morris K. Jessup Fund, 1933). Bingham's original title for this work was *French Trader and Half-Breed Son.* There is still debate about the identification of the tethered animal. In a later version of this same theme, however, it is clearly a bear cub.

American landscape. Landscape seemed an especially democratic art, for its meaning was immediately accessible to the public, without scholarly reference.

In Bingham's painting (fig. 422) our romantic, atmospheric view of the wide American river is momentarily disrupted as a dugout canoe moves downstream, close to us and in sharp focus. The trailing smoke from the trader's pipe reveals the speed of the current. The old trader and his son look at us with contrasting expressions—the boy seems bemused, the father serious.

Bingham's composition places the canoe parallel to the picture plane to emphasize both the horizontal vastness of the mighty river and its right-to-left movement. A surprising percentage of the painting is given over to the sky, where the sudden luminosity of dawn highlights the wispy clouds. The subdued colors and blurred forms of the atmospheric setting give emphasis to the foreground forms, which are richer in color and pattern and more precisely executed. These are in turn blurred themselves in the splendidly painted reflection. Bingham's painting of life on the frontier, an evocation and exaltation of the American west, was intended for an audience in the urbanized cities of the east.

that it should hang in the parlor, over the table where the family Bible was kept.

America's first painters had concentrated on portrait painting (see p. 360), an art which flourishes in democratic, mercantile societies. In the late-eighteenth and early-nineteenth centuries, however, a number of painters went to Europe to study, returning home full of enthusiasm for Neoclassical history painting (see p. 364). They soon discovered that the intellectual subjects of history painting held little appeal for the American public or patrons. Beginning in the 1820s American scenery was identified as the ideal subject for American artists, and it was Thomas Cole who was recognized by his contemporaries as the first great painter of the

FRENCH REALISM: GUSTAVE COURBET

423. GUSTAVE COURBET
The Stone Breakers. 1849. Oil on canvas, 5' 3" x 8' 6". Formerly Gemäldegalerie, Dresden (destroyed in 1945)

"The art of painting can consist only in the representation of objects visible and tangible to the painter. An epoch can be reproduced only by its own artists. I mean by the artists who have lived in it. I hold that the artists of one century are fundamentally incompetent to represent the things of a past or future century . . . It is in this sense that I deny the existence of an historical art applied to the past" (Gustave Courbet, 1861).

To our eyes, there is nothing offensive about Courbet's *Stone Breakers* (fig. 423), for the scene of a youth assisting an older man in breaking stones for a roadbed is a genre subject, an objective view of life in the mid-nineteenth century. When it was first exhibited, however, *The Stone Breakers* shocked and angered critics and public alike. During the Neoclassical and Romantic eras, the significance of a painting was judged by the didactic virtue of its theme and by the painter's adherence to academic rules of composition and execution. Courbet broke these rules, insisting that the only goal of the artist was to reproduce "objects visible and tangible to the painter." To those schooled in the traditional attitudes about art, however, truly commonplace figures and subjects seemed trite, even vulgar.

Courbet's words were given an even fuller expression in *A Burial at Ornans* (fig. 424). We stand at the side of a grave during a funeral in Courbet's hometown, outside Paris. Virtually without comment, Courbet records the visual facts: a priest and attendants reciting prayers, the mourners and a gravedigger, a dog, and a hole in the ground in the immediate foreground. No spiritual promises of an "eternal reward" are apparent here. The emotional pulse of Romantic

COURBET, *The Stone Breakers:* **1849**
1846: Potato famine in Ireland
1848: Marx and Engels, *Communist Manifesto*
1848: First convention of women's rights, New York
1848-49: Revolutions in France and elsewhere

424. GUSTAVE COURBET
A Burial at Ornans. 1849. Oil on canvas, 10' 3 1/2" x 21' 9". Musée d'Orsay, Paris

painting has given way to simple, direct observation.

When Courbet's *Burial at Ornans* and another large painting were rejected by the jury of the Universal Exposition of 1855, an infuriated Courbet withdrew the eleven pictures they had accepted and had his own exhibition building constructed, where, with customary bravado, he held a one-man show in competition with the official exhibition. The so-called Realist Manifesto, which may have been written in part by the Realist writer and critic Champfleury, was actually the introduction to the catalogue of Courbet's private exhibition: "The title of 'realist' has been imposed upon me, as the men of 1830 had imposed upon them the title of 'romantics.' Titles have never given a just idea of things; were it otherwise, the work

would be superfluous. Without trying to clear up the degree of correctness of a qualification which no one, one must hope, will be asked to understand exactly, I will limit myself to a few words of explanation to cut short any misunderstanding.

"I have studied the art of the masters and the art of the moderns, avoiding any preconceived system and without prejudice. I have no more wanted to imitate the former than to copy the latter; nor have I thought of achieving the idle aim of *art for art's sake*. No! I have simply wanted to draw from a thorough knowledge of tradition the reasoned and free sense of my own individuality.

"To know in order to do: such has been my thought. To be able to translate the customs, ideas, and appearance of my time as I

see them—in a word, to create a living art—this has been my aim."

In a letter, Courbet wrote to a patron that Realism was "a holy and sacred cause, which is the cause of Liberty and Independence." Throughout the 1850s Courbet's paintings gained greater public acceptance, although critics also became more vociferous, accusing him of being a propagandist for leftist or socialist causes. Courbet's redirection of subject matter toward the realism of the commonplace was an important influence on younger French artists, especially Édouard Manet and the Impressionists (see pp. 400 and 406).

ACADEMIC ART

425. EMANUEL LEUTZE
Washington Crossing the Delaware. 1851. Oil on canvas, 12' 5" x 21' 3". The Metropolitan Museum of Art, New York (Gift of John S. Kennedy, 1897). When this painting was exhibited in New York in 1852, fifty thousand people paid to see it, and the wide sale of a reproductive engraving made this one of the most famous images in America. Leutze worked hard to make his painting authentic, but history buffs will note a number of errors.

Washington Crossing the Delaware (fig. 425) reveals the Academic approach to history painting, with its blend of a serious subject, historical fact (or what passes for historical fact), artistic manipulation, precise detail, and a carefully digested blend of elements studied from the High Renaissance and Baroque masters. Although he had grown up in America, Leutze returned to his native Germany to spend many years teaching and studying at the influential academy at

Düsseldorf. Many American painters studied there, returning to America to advocate the strict and precisely painted realistic style for which the Düsseldorf academy and Leutze were famous.

The highest goal of Academic painters was to create history paintings of significant moral import, paintings which would document the past and provide inspiration and guidance for the future. In his painting, Leutze set out to express the significance

of Washington's crossing of the Delaware. His success can be judged by the manner in which his treatment continues to capture the public's enthusiasm. It is through this painting that generations of schoolchildren have come to understand a famous national event; rather than representing history, Leutze's painting has formed it. The success of the picture is based on its precise and studied realism, a style which makes its historical theme convincing. Even more

LEUTZE, *Washington Crossing the Delaware:* **1851**
1845: Wagner, *Tannhäuser*
1850–59: U.S. receives 2.5 million immigrants
1851: First submarine cable, under the English Channel
1861: Most of Italy is united as one kingdom

426. ROSA BONHEUR
The Horse Fair. 1853; retouched 1855. Oil on canvas, 8' x 16 ' 7 1/2". The Metropolitan Museum of Art, New York (Gift of Cornelius Vanderbilt, 1887). Like many women artists in the period before 1900, Rosa Bonheur was the daughter of an artist. She and her sister and two brothers all began receiving art lessons while young; Rosa, the eldest and most successful, began to study at the Louvre at the age of fourteen and by nineteen was exhibiting in the Paris Salons. Her works received great critical and popular success. In 1865 the empress of France awarded her the Cross of the French Legion of Honor, declaring "genius has no sex."

important is the striking composition, with a valiant Washington shown standing heroically against the wind.

Rosa Bonheur's *Horse Fair* (fig. 426) was one of the most famous paintings of the nineteenth century. After creating a sensation at the Salon of 1853, it toured to crowds in America for three years. The painting's success can be attributed to its academic realism, which extends from an expert understanding of animal anatomy (Bonheur went often to horse fairs, disguised as a boy, to draw from the living animals) to the precise rendition of the pebbles in the foreground. The effective composition is the result of numerous studies of details and of the whole design. Most impressive is the powerful movement of the horses and men that surges, almost uncontrolled, across the breadth of this huge painting. Bonheur here modified her usually fine brushstroke for a bolder stroke to enhance the effect of rippling energy, and the natural colors of the horses are heightened by contrast with the brilliant colors worn by the grooms. Paintings and sculptures of animals were popular in the nineteenth century, in part because they functioned as metaphors for the more human content that painters were reluctant to represent. The combination of grace and power in Bonheur's beautiful horses communicates an ideal of energy and vitality.

NEW MATERIALS AND ENGINEERING IN ARCHITECTURE

The Crystal Palace (fig. 427) demonstrates two new developments that transformed architecture during the second half of the nineteenth century: the importance of new, artificial materials and the advantages of prefabrication. This huge structure of prefabricated cast-iron membering and glass was made and erected in nine months, proving the speed and economy of such a procedure. The basic module used in the design of the building was not based on aesthetic principles but on a practical fact: the maximum size of the glass which could be manufactured was approximately four feet. The cast-iron components were based on the larger module of twenty-four feet, and no single prefabricated part was allowed to weigh more than a ton. Because it was intended to be a temporary, utilitarian structure (the exhibits of machinery and other works of art and industry were the focus), the references to earlier architectural styles demanded in nineteenth-century building were not required. One perceptive critic pointed out that "here the standards by which architecture had hitherto been judged no longer held good,"but the fact remains that the Crystal Palace was not

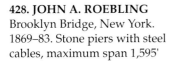

428. JOHN A. ROEBLING
Brooklyn Bridge, New York.
1869–83. Stone piers with steel
cables, maximum span 1,595'

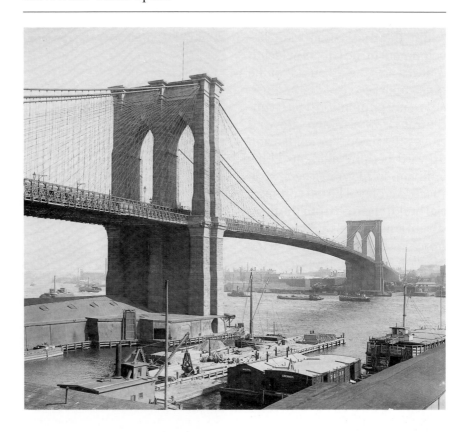

considered to be architecture with a capital *A*. There was no re-evaluation here, as there was with virtually all other nineteenth-century structures of significance, which were endowed with references to traditional architectural styles (see p. 386).

The new technological investigations and accomplishments of the nineteenth century were widely published in books and technical journals and thus their impact could be immediate and universal. Metal and glass were at first held to be fireproof, but iron proved to be susceptible to melting and collapse in a conflagration. Ironically, the Crystal Palace itself was ultimately destroyed by fire, but only in 1936.

The Brooklyn Bridge pio-neered another new material—steel (fig. 428). The advantages of using metal for bridges were first realized in a cast-iron bridge erected in England in 1779. In bridge-building, cast iron was subsequently replaced by wrought iron, and wrought iron by steel plates. The Brooklyn Bridge is more than half again as long as any earlier bridge, and its four huge cables are formed from parallel galvanized cast steel wires that were spun in place to create an ultimate strength of 71.5 tons per square inch. But despite the modern technology that made this huge span possible, the dramatic masonry supporting piers were given Gothic arches.

Before he won the competi-tion to build a temporary structure for the Universal Exposition of 1889, Gustave Eiffel had established an international reputation as an engineer and designer of bridges, locks, and the skeleton for *The Statue of Liberty* (see fig. 400). The purpose of his tower (fig. 429) was to provide a dramatic and unforgettable symbol for the exposition and, by elevators, to make it possible for fairgoers to have fabulous views of Paris. But Eiffel also set out to design a pleasing structure, and he disguised the underlying modern grid frame on which the work is engineered with sweeping curves and dramatic proportions. Even so the design was criticized as a monstrosity, and the architect Charles Garnier (see

p. 398) circulated a petition demanding that it be demolished.

But the most significant development in the later nineteenth century was the invention of the skyscraper (see p. 428). As business and population were concentrated in rapidly growing cities, the need for expansion upward became evident. Louis Sullivan, in his *Autobiography of an Idea*, wrote: "The tall commercial building arose from the pressure of land prices, the land prices from pressure of population, the pressure of population from external pressure." In 1852 Elisha G. Otis invented the Otis safety elevator, which he demonstrated at a New York industrial fair in 1854. By 1857 the first commercial passenger elevator had been installed in a New York building, and in 1861 Otis made a significant improvement by patenting a steam-powered elevator. Before Otis's invention, the height of a building had been limited by how many flights of steps the owner was willing to make his clients climb. With an elevator the height was limited only by the potentials of the material available and the economics of high construction.

Most urban structures were of heavy masonry (that is, stone or brick) construction, and the taller the building, the heavier the lower stories had to be to support the tremendous weight of the increased height. All this changed with the development of the load-bearing steel cage, based on the new lower price of steel due to the invention of the Bessemer process (1855), and of reinforced concrete.

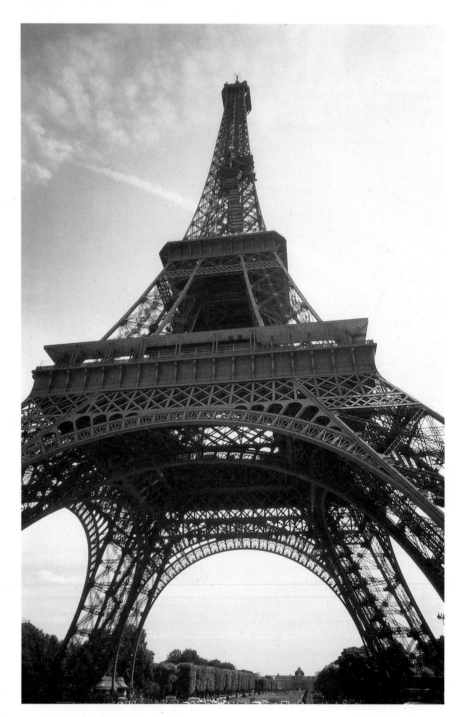

429. GUSTAVE EIFFEL
Eiffel Tower, Paris. 1887–89. Wrought-iron superstructure on a reinforced concrete base, original height 984'; current height 1,052'. Eiffel's design was the winning entry from seven hundred submissions in a competition to design a temporary structure for the Paris Universal Exposition of 1889, which celebrated the one-hundredth anniversary of the French Revolution. Until the erection of the Empire State Building in 1930–32, the Eiffel Tower was the tallest structure in the world.

NEW STRUCTURAL PRINCIPLES IN ARCHITECTURE: LOAD-BEARING STEEL-FRAME CONSTRUCTION AND REINFORCED CONCRETE

steel reinforcing bars

430. WILLIAM LE BARON JENNEY
Detail of steel-frame construction, as used in the Fair Store, Chicago. 1890–91

431. FRANÇOIS HENNEBIQUE
Diagram of monolithic reinforced-concrete joint; patented 1892

Load-bearing steel-frame construction (fig. 430) is based on an earlier development in wood, the balloon frame, in which wood joists are joined horizontally and vertically to create grids which become a skeletal structure for the building. Both outer "skin" and inner walls are attached to and hang from this skeleton. Load-bearing steel-frame construction employs the same method, but the load-bearing members are prefabricated steel I-beams. In constructing tall buildings, the steel frame offers several significant advantages. The high tensile strength of steel, for example, makes possible a substantial reduction in both the amount of material needed and the thickness of the walls. In a brick or stone walled structure, each story that is added to the height means a significant increase in the thickness of the walls at the base: "It was inherent in the nature of masonry construction to fix a new limit of height; as its ever-thickening walls ate

up ground and floor space of ever-increasing price, as the pressure of population rapidly increased" (Louis Sullivan, *The Autobiography of an Idea*, 1926). Steel is much stronger, and its tensile strength means that the finished building will have the elasticity necessary to allow it to move and respond to the pressure from high winds, a problem in a masonry building, which will topple because it cannot sway.

Reinforced concrete (fig. 431), in which concrete is strengthened by embedded wire rods or mesh, was developed in France in the second half of the nineteenth century. The steel gives the concrete an impressive tensile strength. It is a remarkably flexible material and can be formed at the site, during construction, or prefabricated. As is typical of the nineteenth century, this economical new construction method was first used only for utilitarian structures such as mills.

REVIVAL ARCHITECTURE, LATE NINETEENTH CENTURY

432. CHARLES GARNIER
The Opera, Paris. 1861–75

Many mid- to late-nineteenth-century buildings impress us by their scale, richness of materials, and inventive abundance of historical references. The style of Charles Garnier's design for the Paris Opera (fig. 432) can be termed Second Empire Italianate Neo-Renaissance/Baroque, which reveals the eclecticism of this building which, in its visual effect, seems so unprecedented. More sumptuous than any Baroque structure, it established a standard of extravagant decoration for cultural institutions which would have a wide impact, affecting even the development of the motion picture "palace" in twentieth-century America. The opulence of the exterior, with its sculptures (see fig. 441), mosaics, and gilded details, is continued in the interior with a magnificent grand staircase, foyer, and auditorium. Garnier stated his philosophy in pointing out that a "staircase crowded with people was a spectacle of pomp and elegance" and that "by arranging fabrics and wall hangings, candelabra . . . and chandeliers, as well as marble and flowers, color everywhere, one makes of this ensemble a brilliant and sumptuous composition." This is the kind of architecture that is popularly termed Victorian, whether it was built within the empire of Queen Victoria or not.

Richardson's courthouse and jail (fig. 433), erected for one of the world's great industrial centers, uses a modern version of the Romanesque style which avoids decoration to emphasize mass, weight, and solidity. The heavily rusticated walls, corner pavilions, and tall, centralized tower of the courthouse express the enduring authority of law and government. In contrast, the jail offers irregular masses, a lively silhouette, and unexpected placement of openings, effects which may refer to lawlessness and a lack of order. This "iconography" is not accidental, for the building specifications from the Allegheny County commissioners indicated that "the buildings should suggest the purpose for which they were intended." A low bridge, copying examples in Venice, allows a secure transfer of the accused to trial in the courthouse. Richardson's particular, personal use of the Romanesque style (see p. 188) had a widespread popularity in the 1880s. Perhaps its sheer weight and architectural presence were reassuring after the disruptive trauma of the Civil War. Richardson's first biographer wrote of the courthouse: "It is as new as the needs it meets, as

In the closing decades of the nineteenth century, a monumental classical style was re-created in the works of America's most popular architectural firm, McKim, Mead, & White. Their white granite Boston Public Library (fig. 434) seems like a grandiose Renaissance palace. A row of impressive rounded arched windows emphasizes the second floor. The inspiration from Renaissance palaces is perhaps not purely aesthetic, for the trustees' commission was for a "palace for the people." A dignified inscription across the facade expresses the building's public purpose and patrons: "The Public Library of the City of Boston Built by the People and Dedicated to the Advancement of Learning." This is the most important building of a movement sometimes known as the American Renaissance.

434. MCKIM, MEAD, & WHITE
Public Library, Boston. 1887–95

American as the community for which it was built. Yet it might stand without loss of prestige in any city in the world." Richardson himself was most pleased with its massive scale: "If they honor me for the pigmy things I have already done, what will they say when they see Pittsburgh finished?"

ÉDOUARD MANET

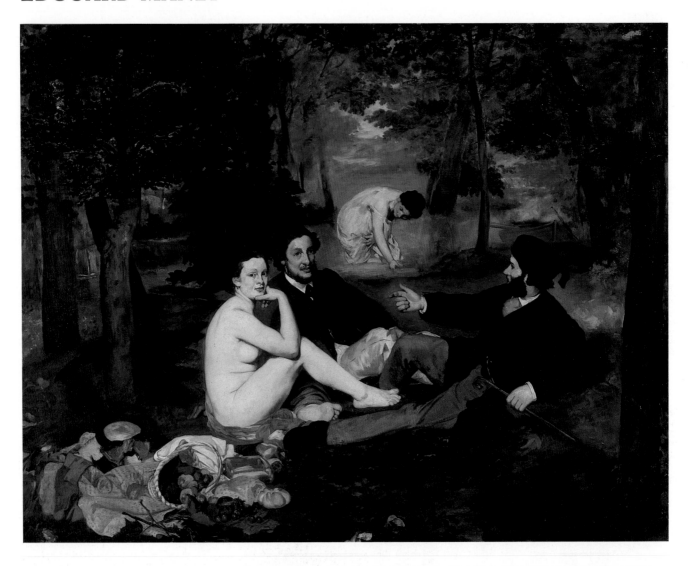

"A commonplace woman of the demimonde, as naked as can be, shamelessly lolls between two dandies dressed to the teeth. These latter look like schoolboys on a holiday, perpetrating an outrage to play the man, and I search in vain for the meaning of this unbecoming rebus.... This is a young man's practical joke, a shameful open sore not worth exhibiting this way.... The landscape is well handled ... but the figures are slipshod" (a critique of *Le Déjeuner sur l'herbe*, 1863).

Manet's *Déjeuner sur l'herbe* of 1863 (fig. 435) created a scandal, even at the Salon des Refusés (see p. 374). Its iconography is perplexing. We are unashamedly confronted by a female nude, her dress and undergarments thrown down near a basket of luscious fruit in the foreground. She is accompanied by two fully clothed men, while in the middle ground a second woman bathes in a small lake. The visual impact of Manet's style is equally powerful and unexpected, for the star-

435. ÉDOUARD MANET
Le Déjeuner sur l'herbe (The Picnic).
1863. Oil on canvas, 7' x 8' 10".
Musée d'Orsay, Paris

tling lack of modeling in the female nude and the large strokes of thick, rich paint had not been seen in earlier French painting. The abstract passages of paint that create the fruit are especially beautiful. In iconography and composition *Le Déjeuner sur l'herbe* was in part inspired by Renaissance works by Titian and Raphael, but does Manet's updating of earlier artistic sources have a deeper social meaning, representing the polarity of French society, with the natural world confronting the artificial, or does the painting simply represent artists with their models? We shall probably never know the exact meaning or meanings, but we do know that from Manet onward, a new course was set for avant-garde painting of the late nineteenth century, as artists would begin to turn further and further away from prescribed academic rules in painting.

Two years after the French critics and public were shocked by *Le Déjeuner sur l'herbe*, they were sent reeling by Manet's entry in the 1865 Salon. The scandal revolved around both Manet's methods of painting, with loose brushstrokes and flat areas of color, and his disrespect for proper subject matter. Here (fig. 436), in the pose usually reserved for the idealized female nude, Manet has realistically painted a model, with a dubious reputation, named Victorine. One of Manet's sources for his *Olympia* was Titian's *Venus of Urbino* (see fig. 302), a painting which had helped establish the theme of the reclining nude female figure as a subject. The tiny, sleeping dog, a symbol of fidelity in Titian's painting, has become a lively black cat, a traditional symbol of lust. Titian's servants attend to their work, but Olympia's maid brings a bouquet of flowers, a gift from a client. Again Manet provoked the public and critics, who argued that not only was Manet painting mundane subjects, as had Courbet, but that he did not even paint these with the proper technique.

Manet did have his champions, however, and one was the noted author and critic Émile Zola. In writing a defense of Manet, Zola pointed out that Manet's paintings are responsive to life, rather than to academic traditions of art: "M. Manet's temperament is dry, trenchant. He catches his figures vividly, is not afraid of the brusqueness of nature and renders in all their vigour the different objects which stand out against each other. His whole being causes him to see things in splotches, in simple and forceful pieces. . . . Don't bother looking at the neighboring pictures. Look at the living persons in the room. Study the way their bodies look against the floors and walls. Then look at M. Manet's paintings: you will see that there lies truth and strength."

Manet's devotion to painting form as he saw it, irrespective of its meaning, is summarized in Zola's comments as one of Manet's subjects: "I remember posing for hours on end. . . . Now and again, half dozing as I sat there, I looked at the artist standing at his easel, his features taut, his eyes bright, absorbed in his work. He had forgotten me; he no longer realized that I was there." When Manet died in 1883, Zola, Degas, and Monet all served as pallbearers. Renoir and Pissarro paid their respects, and even the reclusive Cézanne came to Paris from Provence.

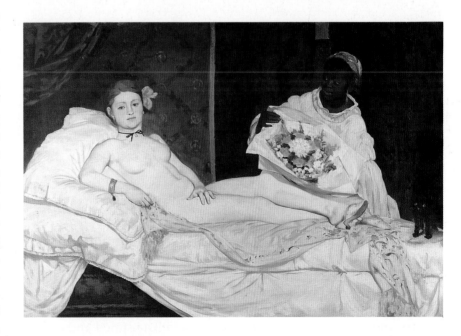

436. ÉDOUARD MANET
Olympia. 1863. Oil on canvas, 51 x 74 3/4". Musée d'Orsay, Paris. Of Manet's *Olympia,* the later painter Cézanne would say, "Our Renaissance dates from it." The source and exact meaning of Manet's title are obscure.

Early Photography; Photographic Technique

437. NADAR (GASPARD-FÉLIX TOURNACHON)
George Sand. 1864. Albumen print. George Eastman House, Rochester, New York. George Sand was the pen name of Aurore Dupin, an important French novelist and feminist.

Nadar's portrait of George Sand (fig. 437), with its controlled lighting and careful attention to pose and detail, was part of a series which included the major French literary and artistic figures of the mid-nineteenth century. That such a series should be produced is not novel, but that it was produced using the relatively new photographic medium greatly assisted the legitimization of photography. Nadar pioneered the use of interior studio lighting, and even today his portraits communicate the dignity of his sitters with a refined and articulate image.

One of the components of photography (from the Greek *photo*, light, and *graphis*, to write or describe) dates back centu-ries. The *camera obscura* (from the Latin, meaning dark room) was an enclosed box with an opening at one end. Rays of light passing through the opening projected an inverted image on the opposite wall. The *camera obscura* had been in use since the Renaissance and was primarily an aid in understanding perspective. Artists traced the projected image inside the "camera." What was lacking, however, was a method to "fix" that image, a process whereby it could be made permanent. In the early eighteenth century it was discovered that silver salts were light sensitive, and, building on this and other, more recent advances, Joseph-Nicéphore Niépce in 1826 created the first photograph using a *camera obscura* and a pewter plate coated with bitumen, a light-sensitive substance. Niépce's first photograph required an eight-hour exposure time.

In 1829 the elderly Niépce formed a partnership with Louis Daguerre, who, in 1837, success-fully produced the first da-guerreotype, which used a chemically treated silver-plated sheet of copper to retain the image. The result was a far clearer image than Niépce's, with a greatly reduced exposure time. Improvements over the next decade made the daguerreotype practical, with an exposure time of thirty to sixty seconds. Da-guerre's excited claim, "I have seized the light, I have arrested its flight," announced the begin-ning of modern photography.

Developments in photogra-phy quickened. In 1839 William

438. Diagram of a camera

439. OSCAR REJLANDER
The Two Paths of Life. 1857. Combination albumen print, 16 x 31". George Eastman House, Rochester, New York. To achieve this tableau-like effect, Rejlander photographed a model of the set and each of the figures separately. These thirty negatives were then printed on one photographic paper.

Henry Fox Talbot, a British scientist, invented the photographic negative, allowing multiple prints to be made from the same exposed plate, and by mid-century glass-plate negatives were being used to produce remarkably sharp images. Our illustration (fig. 438) shows a modern version of a camera.

The early relationship between photography and art was, at best, a difficult one. Some photographers, such as Oscar Rejlander, sought to make photography an art by copying the traditional themes found in contemporary academic painting. *The Two Paths of Life* (fig. 439) represents an allegorical subject. As a photograph it is impressive for its size and technical achievement, for it was a combination print which consisted of thirty negatives individually printed on a single sheet of paper. The young men on either side of the elderly father must choose between a life of virtue, displayed on our right, or a life of vice. Such an overtly theatrical composition was related to the publicly accepted values of Academic Art

(see p. 392). Here photography tried to "copy" painting to win public acceptance.

It was, however, in portraiture that photography found its most immediate and popular use. The reduced exposure time and affordable price made photographic portraits available to almost everyone. Julia Margaret Cameron developed a distinctive style which emphasized the face of the sitter (see fig. 440). Cameron was fully aware that photography is not just a medium which reproduces reality. Speaking of her portraits, she wrote, "When I have such men before my camera, my whole soul has endeavoured to do its duty toward them in recording faithfully the greatness of the inner man as well as the features of the outer man. The photograph thus taken has been almost the embodiment of a prayer."

440. JULIA MARGARET CAMERON
Alfred Lord Tennyson. 1865. Silver print, 10 x 8". Royal Photographic Society, London. Cameron, who began photography only in her late forties, after she had received a camera as a gift, was primarily self-taught. The poet Tennyson was a friend and neighbor.

LATE-NINETEENTH-CENTURY SCULPTURE

As architectural sculpture, Carpeaux's *Dance* (fig. 441) is part of a tradition that includes the Parthenon and Gothic cathedrals (see figs. 84, 205). Charles Garnier designed his Opera (fig. 432) with large reliefs by the main entrances representing the various arts. Carpeaux went beyond Garnier's intention, making his figures virtually freestanding, an effect further enhanced by their energetic movement. The exuberant, winged male allegory of dance leaps upward and outward, while the smiling female

442. MARCELLO (ADÈLE D'AFFRY, DUCHESS CASTIGLIONE-COLONNA)
Pythia. 1870. Bronze, height 9' 6". Opera, Paris. Marcello was the pseudonym used by a talented and highly successful female sculptor who exhibited at the Paris Salons beginning in 1863. This work was shown at the 1870 Salon, where it was purchased by Charles Garnier to decorate the Grand Foyer of the Paris Opera (see fig. 432).

nudes encircle him, moving outward into our space in a dance. Carpeaux's allegory communicates the joy of dancing, but originally its nudity shocked contemporary Parisians, who demanded its removal.

Movement conveys a different emotional state in Marcello's *Pythia*, oracle at the sanctuary of Apollo at Delphi and the most important prophetess of the ancient Greek world (fig. 442). After breathing fumes emanat-

441. JEAN-BAPTISTE CARPEAUX
The Dance. 1867–68. Plaster model, height 15'. Musée de l'Opéra, Paris

1867: Karl Marx, *Das Kapital*
1867: New York establishes a free public school system
1867: Strauss, "The Blue Danube Waltz"
1867: Baseball's curve ball pitch is invented
1870: Rome becomes the capital of Italy
1873–75: Daniel Chester French, *Minuteman*

ing from the earth, the Pythia, who was believed to be possessed by Apollo, would answer queries and predict future events, employing dramatic gestures and language that were often incomprehensible. Marcello's beautiful young woman is given a pose that conveys her convulsed state. As she jerks forward, her breasts swing out to either side. The smoothness of the flesh is sharply contrasted with the multiple drapery folds and with the unruly, flying hair. The snakes hidden in her hair, attributes of Apollo, startle the viewer. *Pythia* is a thoroughly convincing representation of pagan religious ecstasy as it was understood during the nineteenth century.

Degas's *Little Dancer* (fig. 443), the only sculpture he ever exhibited, is now one of his most popular works, and a number of later bronze casts, with real cloth tutus and satin ribbons, are visible in museums. But the version illustrated, now in a private collection, is of wax, a material used for popular sculptures which were meant to be intensely realistic, and real fabric and hair (the technique is still in use in wax museums around the world). Degas followed the popular tradition by coloring the wax to resemble flesh, and he heightened the illusionistic reality of the figure by using a silk faille bodice, a tutu of tulle and gauze, fabric ballet slippers, and a satin ribbon to tie back a wig of real hair. Degas's appropriation of a multi-media technique that so accurately mimics the world of reality is consistent with the attitudes of the French Realist and Impressionist painters. He cre-

ated art that is virtually identical to reality. And, therefore, like the Impressionists, he questioned the relationship between nature, vision, and art.

When Degas's sculpture was shown at the Sixth Independent Exhibition in 1881, the critics recognized its novelty but received it with hostility because the model was not attractive:

"He chooses her from among the most odiously ugly; . . . she is sturdy and carefully studied, but what is the use of these things in the art of sculpture? Put them in a museum of zoology, anthropology, or physiology, fine; but, in a museum of art, forget it!"

"I do not always ask that art be graceful, but I do not believe that its role is to represent only ugliness."

". . . a dancer in wax of a strangely attractive, disturbing, and unique Naturalism . . . The vicious muzzle of this young, scarcely adolescent girl, this little flower of the gutter, is unforgettable."

The modernity of Degas's work did not go unnoticed, however:

"The terrible realism of this statuette makes the public distinctly uneasy, all its ideas about sculpture, about cold,

lifeless whiteness, about those memorable formulas copied again and again for centuries, are demolished. The fact is that on the first blow, M. Degas has knocked over the traditions of sculpture, just as he has for a long time been shaking up the conventions of painting."

443. EDGAR DEGAS
Little Fourteen-Year-Old Dancer.
c. 1881. Wax, silk, satin ribbon, and hair, height 39". Collection Mr. and Mrs. Paul Mellon, Upperville, Virginia. Degas's model was a Belgian girl studying at the Opera in Paris.

IMPRESSIONISM

444. CLAUDE MONET

Impression-Sunrise. 1872. Oil on canvas, 19 1/2 x 25 1/2". Musée Marmottan, Paris. When their paintings were rejected for the Salon exhibitions, a group of painters, some of whom we today classify as Impressionists, decided to hold independent exhibitions. The first of a series of eight such exhibitions was held in Paris in 1874; it included this painting. It was sponsored by a group which called itself the Anonymous Society of Painters, Sculptors, Engravers, etc., a title which indicates the diverse nature of this group, who had banded together to create independent exhibitions. Monet's painting of the *Rue Saint-Denis, Festivities of June 30, 1878* (fig. 397) was included in the Fourth Independent Exhibition, in 1879.

Impressionist paintings such as Monet's *Impression-Sunrise* engage us immediately by their ravishing depictions of nature (fig. 444). Here Monet's representation of the interaction of light, atmosphere, and color heightens our awareness of the beauty in the seascape. But it is important to realize that Monet did not set out to paint a beautiful picture. His goal was to create a painting that recorded reality as he saw it. As an Impressionist, he wanted to capture in paint the visual effect of reality as it appeared to him at that moment. Monet was especially sensitive to transitory effects of color—how color changes in response to shifting light and varying atmospheric conditions. In *Impression-Sunrise* the combination of the moving surface of the water and the red/orange rays of the sun provided a perfect vehicle for his demonstration.

Impressionism had a strong scientific basis, although this is not immediately obvious in looking at Impressionist paintings. A critic of the First Independent Exhibition said that Monet, Renoir, Degas, and Morisot should be called by the "new term impressionists. They are impressionists in the sense that they render not the landscape, but the sensation produced by the landscape." The use of the term Impression by Monet in his title and the painters' adoption of the term Impressionism suggest the influence of new theories about the physiology of perception. The new color theory emphasized the presence of color within shadows and, in asserting that there was no black in nature, inspired the Impressionists to ban black from their palette. In addition, Impressionism is based on an understanding of the interrelated mechanisms of the camera and the eye: just as a photograph is created by light as it passes through a lens to make an impression on light-sensitive paper, so is our vision the result of the light and

445. CLAUDE MONET
Gare St. Lazare, Paris. 1877. Oil on canvas, 32 1/2 x 39 3/4". Fogg Art Museum, Harvard University, Cambridge, Massachusetts (Maurice Wertheim Collection). This painting was exhibited at the Third Independent Exhibition, in 1877.

446. AUGUSTE RENOIR
A Luncheon at Bougival (now known as *The Luncheon of the Boating Party).* 1881. Oil on canvas, 51 x 68". The Phillips Collection, Washington, D.C. This work was included in the Seventh Independent Exhibition, in 1882.

color which create an "impression" on the back surface of the eyeball. By embracing the principle that subject matter is less important, and in determining that painting should represent as closely as possible what the individual eye sees, the Impressionist painters are clearly related to the realism of Courbet and the innovations of Manet (see pp. 390 and 400). Their works look so different from Courbet's and Manet's because of their scientific interest in how the eye sees, and because of their determination to capture quickly the vivid color that exists in nature, whether in light or in shadow.

Monet's emphasis on paint-

ing visual reality means that his subjects are scenes or views of the world around him, but it is probably not accidental that he was one of the first painters of the modern urban cityscape. By painting the city streets and the railroad station, as in the *Gare St. Lazare* (fig. 445), he emphasized the actuality of modern life. In the railroad station, the open air in the background interacts with the light that filters down through the glass roof and the billowing smoke of the engines to provide another appropriate vehicle for Monet's investigation of the ever-changing patterns of light, color, and atmosphere. An Academic painter would never have chosen such a subject, of course, and if required to paint it, would have rendered the clouds of smoke in tonalities of gray. Monet sees not merely gray, but shades of blue and lavender as well.

Although he embraced the ideas and employed the techniques of the Impressionists, Renoir was interested in human life and relationships, which led him to favor compositions with human figures rather than landscapes. His masterpiece is certainly *A Luncheon at Bougival*, with its everyday subject, casual composition, strong strokes of arbitrary color, and bold *impasto*—the latter is especially evident in the beautiful shimmering glasses and bottles of wine on the table (figs. 446, 447). *A Luncheon at Bougival* was singled out for praise by critics when it was exhibited in the Seventh Independent Exhibition in 1882, and one critic captured the contemporary, momentary quality of Renoir's subject in writing that the painting is "a charming work, full of gaiety and spirit, its wild youth caught in the act, radiant and lively, frolicking at high noon in the sun, laughing at everything, seeing only today and mocking tomorrow. For them eternity is in their glass, in their boat, and in their songs." It was this emphasis on the momentary that made paintings such as this one unacceptable to the Salon juries, who favored history painting with controlled academic technique.

447. AUGUSTE RENOIR
A Luncheon at Bougival (detail)

IMPRESSIONIST TECHNIQUE

To capture the subtle effects of ever-changing light, Monet and the other Impressionists painted outside, on the spot, working quickly with loose, bold strokes of color to create a representation of the impression of color in nature before the light changed. The increased brightness of Impressionist paintings (one critic complained that they made his eyes hurt!) was in part made possible by the use of a canvas covered with white underpainting rather than the beige, tan-reddish, or even darker ground that had been traditional since the Renaissance. In addition, an invention of the Industrial Revolution—the collapsible, sealable tube—made it possible for the Impressionists to paint outside, while the development of synthetic pigments meant that the intense colors they needed were no longer prohibitively expensive. Monet applied paint in rich, thick strokes of virtually pure color, without black. The bold physical presence of these strokes and the heightened color emphasize the surface of the painting. Monet also used a painting stroke which maximized accidental effects of color. By dipping a relatively wide brush into two or more pigments, he allows the colors to blur and blend as the brush strokes the canvas.

EDGAR DEGAS, BERTHE MORISOT, AND MARY CASSATT

Edgar Degas disliked being referred to as an Impressionist and preferred to call himself a realist or an independent. His work nevertheless demonstrates many similarities to Impressionist works, and he exhibited in numerous Independent Exhibitions. Degas's realism is in part revealed by his subject matter, for, no matter how romantic we may find his representations of ballerinas today, they were considered neither an appropriate nor a beautiful theme for art in his own day. He was often criticized for picking unattractive dancers by critics who did not realize that, like the other Impressionists, he was depicting modern life (see p. 409). He also shared with the Impressionists a taste for strong and even arbitrary color, despite the fact that most of his work represents figures in rather subdued interiors. The subtlety of natural light in an interior space provided him with a distinct challenge.

In addition to his concern with light and color, Degas had a special interest in the interaction between movement and composition. One contemporary critic wrote that "Degas continues to be passionately devoted to movement, pursuing it even in violent and awkwardly contorted forms." He found that movement, especially the repeated, choreographed movement of dancers onstage or in rehearsal, had a greater intensity when seen from an unexpected viewpoint. In *The Rehearsal* (fig. 448), the strong diagonal recession of the dancers' parallel arms

448. EDGAR DEGAS
The Rehearsal. c. 1873–74. Oil on canvas, 18 x 24". Fogg Art Museum, Harvard University, Cambridge, Massachusetts (Bequest of Maurice Wertheim, 1951)

and legs and of the windows in the room creates a thrusting perspective, which is counteracted only by the empty space in the right foreground. The broad brushstrokes reemphasize the pictorial surface. The influence of Japanese prototypes (see fig. 398) for Degas's work is evident in the diagonal recession and in the cutting off of the forms by the edges. Degas's peculiarly realistic viewpoint was discussed by one of his friends, Edmond Duranty, who published a pamphlet on *The New Painting* in 1876 in which he pointed out how our visual field is limited by "the frame that endlessly accompanies us . . . cutting off the external view in the most unexpected ways, achieving that endless variety and surprise that is one

of reality's greatest pleasures."

We can see the same unusual viewpoint and the compositional motif of the strong diagonal thrust cut off by the edges in Berthe Morisot's *Marine* (fig. 449). When this work was shown in the First Independent Exhibition, a critic remarked, "What a lovely vagueness [there is] in the distance at sea where the tiny points of masts tilt!" Morisot, who once wrote, "My ambition is limited to the desire to capture something transient," remains true to Impressionist principles in striving to capture the strong visual qualities of an actual view. The parasol shields the face of the woman—Morisot's sister Edma, also a painter—and as a result her features are left a blur; her identity is less important than

DEGAS, *The Rehearsal:* **c. 1873–74**
1873: Jules Verne, *Around the World in Eighty Days*
1874: Women's Christian Temperance Union is founded

449. BERTHE MORISOT
Marine (The Harbor at Lorient). 1869. Oil on canvas, 17 1/8 x 28 3/4". National Gallery of Art, Washington, D.C. (Ailsa Mellon Bruce Collection). Berthe Morisot, one of the founders of the Impressionist movement, exhibited in seven of the eight Independent Exhibitions, and her works were also accepted at many of the Salon exhibitions. The artist presented this work to Manet after he admired it. After her death in 1895, a large exhibition of her work was arranged by Monet, Renoir, Degas, and the poet Stéphane Mallarmé.

her significance as a colored form within the composition. Light reflects from the warm brown of the stone railing to create a pink shadow on her white dress.

Mary Cassatt, an American who trained in France and spent most of her life working there, exhibited in several of the Independent Exhibitions. In writing about works by Cassatt at the Sixth Independent Exhibition in 1881, a critic defined Impressionist practice: "Like her brothers in independence, Manet and Degas, Cassatt works relentlessly to bring her eyes to a state of sensitivity, nervous excitement, even irritation, so she can seize the smallest flicker of light, the smallest atom of color, and the slightest tint of shadow." Another critic, however, voiced the frequent complaint that Impressionist paintings were unfinished, lamenting that Cassatt had changed her style and was now "aspiring to the partially completed image."

Cassatt's *Boating Party* (fig. 450) reveals the inspiration of both Degas and of Japanese prints in the unexpected but realistic viewpoint it enforces. We are behind the rower, and his dark, bold silhouetted form sets off the pastels of the rest of the composition. Cassatt maximizes realism in the partial profile of the rower and the foreshortening of the child's head. Neither is an attractive view, but both are realistic and skillfully executed.

Large areas of unmodeled color and the potent compositional shapes of the yellow interior of the boat and the partial view of the sail emphasize the two-dimensional quality of her composition. In the use of black and in the greater solidity with which she endows her figures, Cassatt reveals her independence within the Impressionist movement.

450. MARY CASSATT
The Boating Party. 1893–94. Oil on canvas, 35 1/2 x 46 1/8". National Gallery of Art, Washington, D.C. (Chester Dale Collection)

JAMES MCNEILL WHISTLER

451. JAMES MCNEILL WHISTLER
Nocturne in Black and Gold (The Falling Rocket). c. 1874. Oil on canvas, 23 3/4 x
18 3/8". The Detroit Institute of Arts (Gift of Dexter M. Ferry, Jr.). Born in
America but largely raised abroad, Whistler moved to Paris in 1855 to study
painting; after 1860 he resided in London and Paris.

"For Mr. Whistler's sake, no less than for the protection of the purchaser, they [the Grosvenor Gallery] ought not to have admitted works into the gallery in which the ill-educated conceit of the artist so nearly approached the aspect of wilful imposture. I have seen and heard much of cockney impudence before now, but never expected to hear a coxcomb [Whistler] ask 200 guineas for flinging a pot of paint in the public's face" (the art critic John Ruskin, in a review of Whistler's exhibition at the Grosvenor Gallery in London in 1877; his reference seems to be to *Nocturne in Black and Gold*, which was priced at two hundred guineas).

Ruskin's condemnation of Whistler's *Nocturne in Black and Gold* (fig. 451) brought a swift response from the painter, who sued the critic for libel. The testimony in the trial that resulted illuminates the controversy that swirled around avant-garde art in the later years of the nineteenth century. Ruskin was perhaps the most widely read art critic and commentator of the period, and his books *Modern Painters* and *Mornings in Florence* were in thousands of libraries in England and America. In addition, he lectured widely, further disseminating his views. Ruskin championed the importance of truth, beauty, and sincerity in art and stressed that artists should use subject matter of profound moral content. Whistler, on the other hand, was well known as a champion of the avant-garde and of the concept of art for art's sake.

Whistler's *Nocturne in Black and Gold* was certainly singled out by Ruskin because it is one of the most abstract of his works. Using scattered dots and blobs of paint against a deep blue background, Whistler suggested falling fireworks against a London setting. In Whistler's mind, however, the abstract composition of colors and forms on the surface was more important than any suggestion of reality. During the trial, the painter argued that *Nocturne* was first and foremost "an arrangement of line, form, and color." To emphasize the significance of abstract qualities, Whistler chose names commonly used for musical compositions—"symphonies" and "nocturnes." In describing his purpose in discussing another *Nocturne*, he said, "My whole scheme was to bring about a certain harmony of color." When he was asked at the trial to explain the "beauty" of the painting, he responded: "It is impossible for me to explain to you the beauty of that picture—as it would be for a musician to explain to you the beauty of harmony in a particular piece of music, if you had no ear for music."

Whistler's highly personal and subjective style is also evident in his *Arrangement in Black and Gray (Portrait of the Painter's Mother)*. Here (fig. 452) the sophisticated compositional structure, which balances the figure against a grid of verticals and horizontals, is matched by an equally subtle color palette. Every element in the composition is balanced by an alternative form. Notice how the design loses strength if any single element is covered, even the tiny edge of a framed work of art in the upper right corner. This abstract composition reveals the influence of Japanese woodcuts. As is often the case with Whistler's pictures, the work is so thinly painted that it is almost translucent; this sometimes led to accusations that a work was unfinished. At the Ruskin trial, Whistler said that it took him about two days to paint a *Nocturne*. When the judge said, "And that was the labor for which you asked 200 guineas?" the artist replied, "No, it was for the knowledge gained through a lifetime."

When Whistler submitted his portrait of his mother for the annual exhibition at the Royal Academy in 1872, it was at first

1874: Hardy, *Far from the Madding Crowd*
1874: Strauss, *Die Fledermaus*
1876: Gen. George Custer is killed at the Battle of Little Big Horn

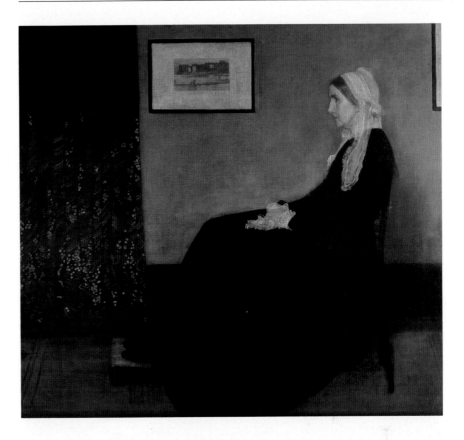

452. JAMES MCNEILL WHISTLER
Arrangement in Black and Gray (Portrait of the Painter's Mother). 1871. Oil on canvas, 57 x 64 1/2". Musée d'Orsay, Paris. The simple, restrained furnishings of the room reflect Whistler's belief that one's environment should be plain, without the Victorian clutter common at the time. In this he was partly influenced by Oriental models; he collected Oriental pottery, fans, and woodcuts, and the fabric that hangs to the left is Oriental in origin. The framed print on the wall is Whistler's etching *Black Lion Wharf.*

rejected. Only pressure from an important academy member led to its acceptance. The work is, of course, more than an "arrangement" of a particular color scheme. Whistler not only captured the facial features of his mother but, in his characterization of a simple, stern, and dignified woman, he also conveyed her personality. Although it is these qualities which explain the work's enduring popularity, the message that the painting offers to artists about the virtues of simple, clear composition and restrained color had an impressive impact on modern art.

Whistler sued Ruskin for a thousand pounds. Although he won the suit, the jury, following a recommendation by the judge, awarded him only a farthing. Ruskin lost the case, but the judge split the court costs between Ruskin and Whistler. As a result, Whistler was forced to declare bankruptcy.

AMERICAN REALISM: THOMAS EAKINS AND HENRY TANNER

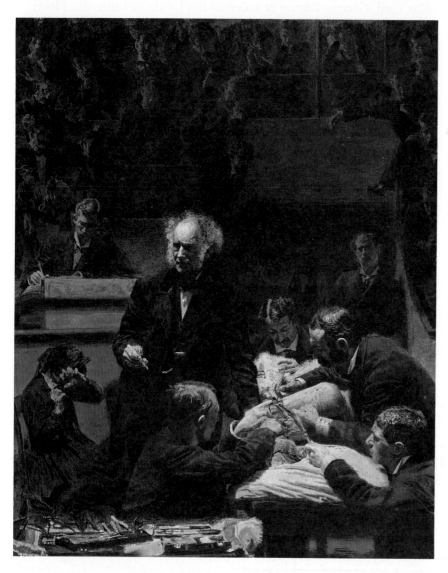

453. THOMAS EAKINS
Copy after *Portrait of Dr. Samuel Gross.* 1876. India ink wash on cardboard, 23 5/8 x 19 1/8". The Metropolitan Museum of Art, New York (Rogers Fund, 1923). We here reproduce a monochrome copy made by Eakins after the painting for reproduction purposes. Eakins's realistic portrayal of surgery at Jefferson Medical College reveals how medical practice has changed. In Eakins's day surgeons operated in their street clothes, and operations were scheduled between 11:00 A.M. and 3:00 P.M. to take advantage of the bright sunlight in the college's amphitheater.

vey to aspiring doctors the significance of his life's work. He holds a bloody scalpel, the sudden sight of which makes the patient's mother, in the left middle ground, cringe.

Eakins's light is focused and concentrated, and the powerful *chiaroscuro* contrast makes Dr. Gross, teacher and surgeon, a dramatic figure. The sharp overhead light directs our attention to Dr. Gross's head, silhouetting it against the dark background. The craggy features of the face are emphatically three-dimensional, emphasizing the serious line of the mouth and throwing the eyes into meditative shadow. Eakins emphasizes the light as it catches Dr. Gross's bushy gray hair and vigorous sideburns. This visually electrifying effect suggests that Eakins is searching for a concrete metaphor for the intensity of Dr. Gross's thoughts. The original painting has an overall warm harmony, the result of red underpainting which unifies and heightens the limited pal-

To Thomas Eakins, the Philadelphia physician Samuel Gross was a heroic figure. Gross was a respected surgeon and professor at Jefferson Medical College and a physician with an international reputation. A pioneer in using new techniques in surgery, he was an inspiring educator, teaching medical students both surgical procedures and the human purpose that stood behind the medical profession. Dr. Gross specifically emphasized the sig-

nificance of clinical instruction, and Eakins represents him in the operating amphitheater at work (fig. 453). He is performing an operation in which he specialized, a new, lifesaving treatment for osteomyelitis (infection of the bone), when the diseased bone is cut away. At the same time he is also teaching, and Dr. Gross looks up from the incision in the thigh of the patient, an expression of intense concentration on his face as he searches for words to conette, with its strong blacks, flesh tones, and areas of white. Punctuation marks of red draw our attention to the pen of the clinical recorder, the incision, and, most importantly, the bloody hand and scalpel of Dr. Gross. In contrast to the abstract treatment of the surgeon's head, his hand and scalpel jump out because they seem to be exactly in focus. Eakins, himself a photographer, seems to have thrown the other parts of his composition out of focus (note especially the loose painting of the instruments in the immediate foreground) to draw attention to the skilled hand and its tool, making them the focal point in his composition. The contrast in treatment between the head and hand is not accidental: while the physical aspect of Dr. Gross's accomplishment is completely comprehensible, the workings of his intellect cannot be discerned.

Eakins painted his *Portrait of Dr. Samuel Gross* specifically to submit to the arts section at the Centennial Exposition, to be held in Philadelphia in 1876. It was rejected, apparently because the subject was not considered appropriate; other, less significant works by Eakins were accepted. Through the influence of Dr. Gross, the painting was exhibited in the medical department of the exposition.

Henry O. Tanner studied with Eakins at the Pennsylvania Academy in 1880–84, but his mature style merged Eakins's realism with some stylistic effects learned from the French Impressionists. Tanner moved permanently to Paris in 1891; in 1896 he received an honorable mention at the Salon; and in 1897 his work was awarded a gold medal. In *The Banjo Lesson* (fig. 454) the choice

EAKINS, *Portrait of Dr. Samuel Gross:* **1875**
1875: Electric dental drill is patented
1875: Bizet, *Carmen*
1876: Bell patents the telephone
1879: Pavlov uses dogs to study the conditioned reflex
1885: First successful appendectomy

and interpretation of the theme grow from Eakins's example, but the lighter palette, softer light, and delicacy of brushstroke reveal the influence of the new French style of Impressionism.

454. HENRY O. TANNER
The Banjo Lesson. c. 1893. Oil on canvas, 48 x 35". Hampton University Museum, Hampton, Virginia. Tanner was the first American black artist to achieve an international reputation.

AUGUSTE RODIN

455. AUGUSTE RODIN
The Burghers of Calais. 1884–86. Bronze, height 82 1/2". Hirshhorn Museum and Sculpture Garden, Smithsonian Institution, Washington, D.C. In 1884 the city of Calais in northern France commissioned Rodin to fashion a public monument that would honor six leading citizens (burghers) who, in 1347, had offered themselves as hostages to the English king Edward III, who had laid siege to the city. The burghers were ready to sacrifice their lives if their city would be spared. Edward III was so impressed with their courage that he spared both the burghers and Calais.

Rodin's *Burghers of Calais* (fig. 455), commissioned as a public monument to display the courage and civic virtue of the Calais burghers, disappointed many at first, for it lacked the overtly heroic antique references which then dominated public sculpture. Rodin's re-creation of the six hostages, with its realism and psychological honesty, assisted in bringing a fresh vision of the human figure to late-nineteenth-century sculpture. From his

study of the works of such sculptors as Donatello and Michelangelo, Rodin understood how gesture and expression could reveal an inner psychological state. Here the burghers betray philosophical questioning, acceptance, defiance, and sorrow. Through Rodin's sculpture, the burghers are revealed to us as human beings like ourselves, not idealized superheroes.

To understand better the impact of Rodin's work, we must

keep in mind that Neoclassical and Romantic attitudes still dominated public sculpture. Rodin's physical and psychological naturalism seemed to run counter to critical and public taste, and the psychological depth of Rodin's work was missed by many critics.

Rodin's *Monument to Balzac* (fig. 456) is an audacious sculpture in both theme and execution. The great novelist is shown wrapped in the heavy robe in

RODIN, *The Burghers of Calais:* **1884–86**
1883: Metropolitan Opera House opens in New York
1883: Brooklyn Bridge opens to traffic
1884: Brahms, Third Symphony
1885: Pasteur introduces rabies vaccine
1886: Eighth and last Independent Exhibition in Paris
1886: *Statue of Liberty* is dedicated
1886: American Federation of Labor is founded

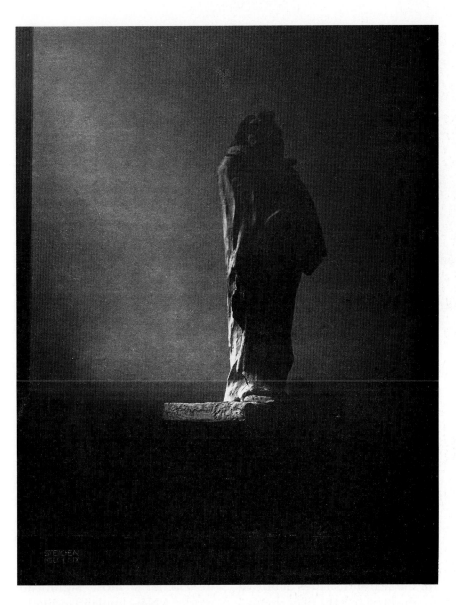

456. AUGUSTE RODIN
Monument to Balzac. 1893–97. Plaster, height 9' 10 1/8". This historic 1908 photograph of the plaster model is by Edward Steichen, one of America's foremost photographers. Steichen so successfully captured the creative ambience of *Balzac* that, on seeing Steichen's photographs, Rodin remarked, "You will make the world understand my *Balzac* through these pictures. They are like Christ walking in the desert."

which he worked late at night. His dramatic posture and penetrating facial features vividly communicate the fury of creative inspiration. Balzac's face and massive robe seem to be emerging from the plaster, from the raw material from which the sculpture was first formed. This unfinished quality contributes to our perception of a transformation; Rodin, in displaying the process of bringing form from the raw material, has visually expressed the creative energy which has seized Balzac.

Stating his philosophy on the relationship of art and the artist to nature, Rodin wrote: "I grant you that the artist does not see Nature as she appears to the vulgar, because his emotion reveals to him the hidden truths beneath appearances. But, after all, the only principle in art is to copy what you see. . . . There is no recipe for improving nature. The only thing is to see. Oh, doubtless a mediocre man copying nature will never produce a work of art, because he really looks without seeing, and though he may have noted each detail minutely, the result will be flat and without character. . . . The artist, on the contrary, sees; that is to say, his eye, grafted on his heart, reads deeply into the bosom of nature."

WINSLOW HOMER

457. WINSLOW HOMER
The Fog Warning. 1885. Oil on canvas, 30 x 48". Museum of Fine Arts, Boston (Otis Norcross Fund)

The unusual cloud bank rolling in in the background of Homer's *Fog Warning* (fig. 457) warns the fisherman that his life is suddenly in danger, for it signals the arrival of a particularly fast-moving and dangerous fog. The hunter, preying on nature, suddenly becomes the hunted. Homer's composition heightens the mood of instability and uncertainty by representing the small rowboat being heaved upward by a large swell. The right-to-left thrust of the row-

boat is counter to the movement of the fisherman's home vessel in the background, which is about to sail out of the range of vision. The realistic colors—yellowish-white for the sky, green for the sea, and shades of brown for the boat and the fisherman—are somber and appropriate for this theme. The bold and simple silhouetted composition, the diagonal thrust of the boat, and the truncated oar reveal the influence of Japanese woodcuts. Homer's brushstrokes are broad

and simple; note especially the rough strokes in the foreground that represent the foamy waves.

The power of natural forces and their challenge to humanity are universal themes that reoccur in Homer's most significant works. A New England individualist, Homer spent many winters living in isolation along a particularly dramatic and treacherous stretch of the Maine coastline, where he had many opportunities to observe the power of a turbulent sea.

HOMER, *The Fog Warning:* **1885**
1884: Mark Twain, *Huckleberry Finn*
1885: The modern bicycle is invented
1890: Yosemite National Park is created

458. WINSLOW HOMER
The Blue Boat. 1892. Watercolor over graphite, 15 1/8 x 21 1/2". Museum of Fine Arts, Boston (Bequest of William Sturgis Bigelow, 1926)

WATERCOLOR AND GOUACHE TECHNIQUE

Watercolor is aptly named, for it is a medium in which ground pigments are mixed with water and, as an adhesive binder, a little gum arabic. It is usually applied to paper. The brilliance possible in watercolor is evident in this example by Homer (fig. 458). The liquidity of the medium is apparent in the broad strokes that so convincingly render sky and water. Watercolor is transparent, and in some areas Homer has laid one color over another, creating veils of transparent color. The natural color of the paper shows through in the clouds and water, and Homer commonly added a few touches of gouache (an opaque watercolor) to strengthen certain areas. As early as the 1780s English artists had begun to work with watercolor. Homer was one of the founders of the American Watercolor Society, an organization which helped popularize watercolor as a medium for serious artists in the United States. Previously it had been used largely by amateurs.

THE POST-IMPRESSIONISM OF PAUL GAUGUIN AND GEORGES SEURAT

459. PAUL GAUGUIN
The Vision After the Sermon. 1888. Oil on canvas, 28 3/4 x 36 1/2". National
Gallery of Scotland, Edinburgh

Gauguin's *Vision After the Sermon* was painted in the rural area of Brittany, in northern France, which the artist visited in 1888 to divert his mind and art away from what he felt were the restrictive artistic and social pressures of Paris (fig. 459). The painting depicts Breton women, deep in prayer, experiencing a vision. Our viewpoint is from behind the group of women, in native dress, and a priest in the right foreground. A tree limb creates a strong diagonal across the composition, separating the left middle ground from the "vision" to the right, which represents the Old Testament figure Jacob wrestling with an angel, a story in which God tested Jacob's enduring love. The flat red ground creates a strong planarity that contrasts with the perspective indicated by the diminution of size. This causes a visual tension. The heavy outlines of the figures combine with the patternlike configuration of the Breton headdresses to create a simple, direct, and forceful composition. While the red ground may have been inspired by a religious festival that included the blessing of horned animals and a night with bonfires that cast a red glow over the fields, Gauguin's choice of color also carries a symbolic content. The red ground symbolizes the theme of struggle, and in choosing it Gauguin has freed himself from the traditional use of color to describe nature. Here it is used in an abstract, expressive way.

Gauguin had left his wife and family, as well as a successful brokerage career in Paris, to seek a more natural, unindustrialized environment, first in Martinique, then in Brittany and later Arles in southern France, and finally in Tahiti, in the South Seas. In attempting to remove himself from Western centers of civilization,

460. PAUL GAUGUIN
Where do we come from? What are we? Where are we going? 1897. Oil on burlap,
4' 6 3/4" x 12' 3 1/2". Museum of Fine Arts, Boston (Tompkins Collection)

GAUGUIN, *The Vision After the Sermon:* **1888**
1887: A. Conan Doyle, first Sherlock Holmes tale is published
1887: Edison and Swan produce electric lamps
1888: J. B. Dunlop invents the pneumatic tire

Gauguin sought an unbridled artistic and psychological response to nature.

During his second Tahitian period, Gauguin, in poor health, nearly broke, severely depressed, and planning suicide, painted what he envisioned as his final masterpiece (fig. 460). His suicide attempt failed and he later detailed the meaning of the painting in a letter. The woman, child, and dog in the right foreground symbolize birth and the innocence of life. The figure near the center tries to pick a fruit from the tree of knowledge in an attempt to understand the meaning of life, while in the left foreground "an old woman approaching death . . . reconciled and resigned to her thoughts" is joined by "a strange white bird [that] represents the futility of life." In the right middle ground, two standing clothed figures betray the sorrow that life's knowledge can bring; the idol to our left expresses the forces which rule our primitive passions. Gauguin's abstract visual language of colors and forms helps communicate his content.

By the time of the last Independent Exhibition in 1886, Impressionism, which a decade earlier had been considered revolutionary, had gained critical and public acceptance. New avantgarde styles were now being explored by Post-Impressionist artists, such as Gauguin, who had moved from Impressionism to more individualized styles. Post-Impressionism is the generic title that covers the diversity of these individual styles—styles which laid the foundation for modern art.

Georges Seurat was the youngest of the Post-Impressionist painters. His monumental painting *A Sunday Afternoon on the Island of La Grande Jatte* (fig. 461), which was two years in preparation and execution, exemplifies his theories of Divisionism, which was also called Neo-Impressionism. The still and transfixed quality of the scene reminds us of works of the Renaissance master Piero della Francesca (see fig. 215), whose work Seurat admired. But the classicism of Renaissance art has been updated, joined with the modern revelation of light and color begun by the Impressionists. Seurat systematized contemporary scientific advances in color theory to create what he termed optical painting. Colored paint is methodically applied in a series of small dots (now popularly known as Pointillism, a term not used by Seurat), usually in complementary colors. The resulting surface, covered with thousands upon thousands of controlled spots of color, is both vibrant and luminous, at once relating to the surface of the picture plane and to forms in an illusory depth bathed in natural light.

461. GEORGES SEURAT
A Sunday Afternoon on the Island of La Grande Jatte. 1884–86. Oil on canvas, 6' 9 1/2" x 10' 1 1/4". The Art Institute of Chicago (Helen Birch Bartlett Memorial Collection)

THE POST-IMPRESSIONISM OF VINCENT VAN GOGH

"Today I am probably going to begin the interior of the Cafe where I eat, by gas light, in the evening.

"It is what they call here a *Cafe de Nuit* (they are fairly frequent here), staying open all night. 'Night prowlers' can take refuge there when they have no money to pay for a lodging, or are too tight to be taken in. All those

462. VINCENT VAN GOGH
The Night Cafe. September 1888. Oil on canvas, 27 1/2 x 35". Yale University Art Gallery, New Haven, Connecticut (Bequest of Stephen C. Clark). Van Gogh painted *The Night Cafe* in Arles, in the south of France, where he lived in 1888–89. Vincent wrote that when he painted this picture he stayed up three consecutive nights, sleeping only during the day. On September 17, 1888, he wrote to his brother Theo that "the problem of painting night scenes and effects on the spot and actually by night, interests me enormously."

VAN GOGH, *The Night Cafe:* **1888**
1888: *National Geographic* begins publication
1889: Electric lights are installed in the White House
1889: *Wall Street Journal* begins publication
1895: Oscar Wilde, *The Importance of Being Earnest*

things—family, native land—are perhaps more attractive in the imaginations of such people as us . . . than they are in reality. I always feel I am a traveller, going somewhere and to some destination.

"If I tell myself that the somewhere and the destination do not exist, that seems to me very reasonable and likely enough. . . .

463. VINCENT VAN GOGH
Starry Night. June 1889. Oil on canvas, 28 3/4 x 36 1/4". Collection, The Museum of Modern Art, New York (Lillie P. Bliss Bequest). Van Gogh can be classified as a Post- or Counter-Impressionist because after painting in the Impressionist style (he saw the Eighth, last Independent Exhibition in 1886 in Paris), he developed his own personal style. Van Gogh eloquently revealed his understanding of his own intense personality and his loneliness by writing, "One may have a blazing hearth in one's soul and yet no one ever comes to sit by it. Passersby see only a wisp of smoke rising from the chimney and continue on their way."

"The room is blood red and dark yellow with a green billiard table in the middle; there are four citron-yellow lamps with a glow of orange and green. Everywhere there is a clash and contrast of the most disparate reds and greens in the figures of little sleeping hooligans, in the empty, dreary room, in violet and blue. The blood-red and the yellow-green of the billiard table, for instance, contrast with the soft tender . . . green of the counter, on which there is a pink nosegay. The white coat of the landlord, awake in a corner of that furnace, turns citron-yellow, or pale luminous green" (Vincent van Gogh, letter to his brother Theo from Arles, September 8, 1888).

The Night Cafe is one of the most powerfully emotional paintings in a series of dramatic works created during Van Gogh's stay in Arles (fig. 462). Van Gogh later referred to Arles as the place where he "attain[ed] the high yellow note," suggesting that this was a particularly strong point in his career. Here he adopted the Japanese belief that the color yellow is symbolic of hope. However, Arles was also a place of

intense despair for Van Gogh, which may help explain the heightened intensity of the Arles works. He said that this painting, given to his landlord in exchange for rent, was "one of the ugliest pictures I have done."

The ugliness of which he writes is intentional, for in this painting color is used arbitrarily, allowing him to express personal meanings and emotions through the "clash and contrast" of glaring yellow, bright green, and "blood" red. In a letter to his brother Theo, who was living in Paris, he explained the psychological impact which he wanted the painting to have: "I have tried to express the terrible passions of humanity by means of red and green . . . the cafe is a place where one can ruin oneself, run mad, or commit a crime." Van Gogh's goal is in part conveyed to us by the claustrophobia of the tense and threatening atmosphere. Drunks slump over tables within a tilted and close perspective space that is unnerving for the viewer. Van Gogh is here experimenting with the relationship between color, space, theme, and emotions. His efforts make him

one of the forerunners of Expressionism (see p. 446). He tries to express the mood he senses at the cafe, and in doing so, he reveals some of his feelings about his own alienation.

In the early 1880s, Van Gogh had been involved briefly in the rapidly changing styles of art. Like many other artists, he began to collect Japanese prints (see fig. 398), and in *The Night Cafe* we sense their influence in the bold delineation of the forms, the intricate patterning of horizontal and vertical lines, the unusual viewpoint, and the vivid, arbitrary colors. The oddly exaggerated perspective of the painting may also be attributed to other influences. Evidence suggests that Van Gogh may have suffered from temporal lobe epilepsy and that some aspects of his art may have been influenced by the visions he experienced during the beginning of a seizure. We also know that Van Gogh often spent his limited money on alcohol, rather than food, and absinthe, one of the artist's common indulgences, is known to affect the occipital lobe, which controls vision.

In the *Starry Night* (fig. 463), painted in 1889, Van Gogh displays his fascination with the earth and sky, and his philosophies of life and death and their connection to nature: "For my own part, I declare I know nothing whatever about it, but to look at the stars always makes me dream, *as simply* as I dream over the black dots of a map representing towns and villages. Why, I ask myself, should the shining dots of the sky not be as accessible as the black dots on the map of France? If we take the train to get to Tarascon or Rouen, we take death to reach a star. One thing undoubtedly true in this reasoning is this, that while we are *alive* we *cannot* get to a star, any more than when we are dead we can take the train" (letter to Theo, mid-July 1888). This depiction of night "in situ," as Van Gogh described it, reveals his continuing interest in a favorite subject, the flamelike cypress tree used in France and Italy to mark graves. Almost black, the tree dominates the foreground. The night sky overwhelms the little town of Saint-Rémy, but the expansiveness of space and the solidity of the earth are formally linked: the tip of the cypress tree crosses the nebula, and the steeple of the church enters the area of the sky.

In a letter to his brother, Van Gogh wrote that he felt that nighttime was more colorful than the day—as is suggested here by the vividness and luminosity of the celestial bodies. Deeply saturated colors—purple and violent green—clash, and a thickly painted "glow" surrounds each star, planet, and the moon. These qualities seem to express Van Gogh's testament that there are lives and colors on other planets, and perhaps even better conditions. Here the artist projects his own destiny: death represents not an ending but a metamorphosis.

The significance of nature for Van Gogh is apparent in the following quotation, from a letter which he wrote to Theo in September 1889, right after Theo was married: "Well, do you know what I hope for, once I let myself begin to hope? It is that a family will be for you what nature, the clods of earth, the grass, the yellow corn, the peasant, are for me, that is to say, that you may find in your love for people something *not only to work for,* but to comfort and restore you, when there is need for it."

The *Self-Portrait* of 1889 (see fig. 403) was probably painted shortly after Van Gogh left the hospital in Saint-Rémy in early January 1889. His ear is still bandaged from the self-mutilation he had inflicted in December, when he cut off part of his ear, probably to punish himself because of a quarrel he had had with Paul Gauguin. The placement of the green coat against the red background and the blue cap against orange demonstrates his interest in using complementary colors to achieve rich coloristic and dramatic effects. The violent juxtaposition of the red and orange draws attention to Van Gogh's solemn eyes. As he wrote, "[I find myself filled with] a certain undercurrent of vague sadness, difficult to define. . . . My God, those anxieties—who can live in the modern world without catching his share of them?"

THE POST-IMPRESSIONISM OF PAUL CÉZANNE

"I want to make of Impressionism something solid and durable, like the art of the museums" (Cézanne). In his paintings Cézanne set himself an impossible task: he wanted to establish an equilibrium between the vivacious color and solid form of three-dimensional objects and the two-dimensional surface of the picture plane. He sought to achieve illusionistic solidity and a strong compositional structure in two dimensions. His frustration with Impressionism was twofold: Impressionist painters did not create paintings that were compositionally strong, and they were not interested in endowing painted objects with three-dimensional solidity. Cézanne wrote: "In art, everything is theory, developed and applied in contact with nature." It is the union of nature with the philosophical truth of the flatness of a painting's surface that absorbed Cézanne's attention.

Cézanne's *Still Life with Basket of Apples* (fig. 464) demonstrates his ability to render objects with solidity—note the white napkin, with its deep angular folds and pockets of shadow. The pieces of fruit have a physical presence that is in part the result of an unexpected richness of color, exemplifying Cézanne's dictum that "when color is richest, form is fullest." He modeled the fruit with pure, unmixed colors, juxtaposing, for example, yellow with green and red. He thereby created a richer effect than that produced by the typical acade-

464. PAUL CÉZANNE
Still Life with Basket of Apples. 1890–94. Oil on canvas, 24 3/8 x 31". The Art Institute of Chicago (Helen Birch Bartlett Memorial Collection)

mic practice of rendering modeling by reducing coloristic intensity with the addition of white or black. Cézanne does not outline his forms to distinguish them one from another. They have rather loosely painted edges, and it is the internal color that creates their solidity. Cézanne once said, "The secret of drawing and modeling resides in the contrasts and relationships of tone."

If we analyze Cézanne's *Still Life with Basket of Apples* as an illusion or as an exercise in accurate drawing, it is a failure: neither the front nor the back edges of the table, for example, are continuous; the wine bottle, itself tilted, offers a distinctive contour on each side; and the pastries stacked on the plate seem

tilted upward. But these observations are based on the wrong questions. In Cézanne's work these visual "inaccuracies" reveal the moving viewpoint of the artist relative to the objects being painted. Renaissance scientific perspective insisted that the artist's (and therefore the viewer's) eye be at a fixed point. Cézanne, on the other hand, expresses a basic fact of vision: our understanding of an object or space is based on our movement relative to that object or space. The difference in the edges of the table, for example, results because the table edge is seen from lower or higher, closer or farther viewpoints. The issues Cézanne has selected to investigate are difficult ones to resolve.

CÉZANNE, *Still Life with Basket of Apples:* **1890–94**
1890: Emily Dickinson poems are published
1890: Oscar Wilde, *The Picture of Dorian Gray*
1895: First professional football game

465. PAUL CÉZANNE
Mont Ste.-Victoire. 1904–6. Oil on canvas, 25 5/8 x 31 7/8". Private collection. Mont Ste.-Victoire in Provence, a symbol of Cézanne's local area, is one of his most common subjects. In 1901–2 he built a study in the countryside with a large window facing the mountain.

Later Picasso would praise Cézanne for his "restless striving."

The structured pictorial surface Cézanne accomplished is best expressed in his later works (fig. 465). While the most significant monument in the landscape is the powerful, thrusting mountain, Cézanne has constructed his painting out of blocks of color and no one area or object is less strong than another. Cézanne urged painters to "see in nature the cylinder, the sphere, the cone," and this painting demonstrates his approach. Surface strength is also accomplished by intermingling blocks of limited color—in this case violet, green, ocher, and blue: the violet of the atmospheric perspective reappears in the foreground, and the green of the middle ground is also found in the sky. When the work is compared to an Impressionist painting, such as *Impression-Sunrise* (fig. 444), two completely different effects can be noted. Cézanne has sacrificed the ravishing, momentary subtlety of color that forms the foundation of Monet's accomplishment in his attempt to create a landscape that has an enduring strength and power. In ancient times Mont Ste.-Victoire was believed to be a holy mountain, a home of the gods, and in Cézanne's painting it is once again endowed with a mysterious presence. Cézanne's paintings had an important impact on developments in the twentieth century: Matisse called him the "father of us all."

THE BEGINNINGS OF THE SKYSCRAPER

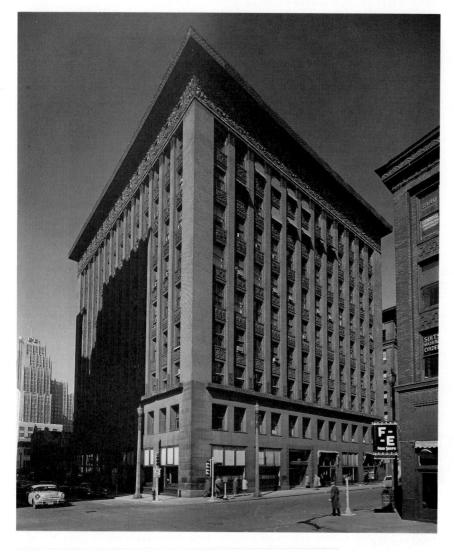

"What is the chief characteristic of the tall office building? And at once we answer, it is lofty. . . . The force and power of altitude must be in it. . . . It must be every inch a proud and soaring thing, rising in sheer exultation that from bottom to top it is a unit without a single dissenting line" (Louis Sullivan, *The Tall Office Building Artistically Considered*, 1896). To accomplish his lofty exaltation, Sullivan based his Wainwright Building on a design concept analogous to that of a column (fig. 466). The first two stories act

as a base which supports the unimpeded vertical members, rising like the flutes on the shaft of a column, to support a cornice, decorated with foliage ornament, that crowns the structure like a capital. This intelligible design hides the load-bearing steel-frame construction, which other early skyscraper architects had emphasized by creating a grid of balanced horizontals and verticals (see p. 397). Sullivan chose instead to stress the vertical articulation. Only every other vertical corresponds

to the interior steel cage. In addition, the vertical elements dominate because the windows are recessed between them, and the horizontal membering, hidden behind recessed panels of decorated terra-cotta, is reduced in importance.

The integrity of the design depends on the proportional relationships between the parts and the whole, which Sullivan has carefully calibrated. The wide corners balance and set off the elegant, narrow verticals between the windows, while the effulgent decorative terra-cotta at the cornice level, a full story high, unites with the narrow uppermost cornice to provide an elegant final closure which defines the mass of the structure. The decorated panels below each window provide a typically Sullivanesque touch, offering a pleasant decoration for office workers in adjacent buildings. The total effect is of a finely articulated mass, elegant and substantial at the same time.

The most impressive developments in skyscraper architecture occurred in Chicago, where a devastating fire in 1871 leveled much of the city. During the clos-

1890: One-third of U.S. population now resides in cities and towns
1890: Los Angeles population is 50,000
1893: Dvorák, *New World Symphony*
1893: Henry Ford builds his first car
1895: H. G. Wells, *The Time Machine*
1900: Half of all U.S. working women are farmhands or domestic servants

467. LOUIS SULLIVAN
Carson-Pirie-Scott Store (formerly Schlesinger and Meyer Department Store), Chicago. 1899; enlarged 1903–4 and 1906

ing decades of the century, the city's rapidly increasing population spurred a building boom. Sullivan's last major commission was the design for the Schlesinger and Meyer Department Store (fig. 467). The idea of a huge urban store carrying luxury items for middle- and upper-class patrons was novel, and Sullivan emphasized elegant public entrances and huge plate-glass windows on the lower floor by fantastic cast-iron ornamentation of his own design. The upper floors, with their huge "Chicago" windows and very plain terracotta decoration, refer in a streamlined fashion to the concealed steel cage, but note that the horizontal members are emphatically wider and therefore dominant. Sullivan's sensitivity to the shape and placement of the building as a whole is evident in the cylindrical tower at the corner, an unexpected element adding a vertical punctuation mark that makes the horizontal sides even more forceful. Here Sullivan completely avoids any historical references, creating a building that is one of the first works of modern architecture.

EDVARD MUNCH

468. EDVARD MUNCH
The Scream. 1893. Oil, pastel, and casein on cardboard, 35 3/4 x 29". National Gallery, Oslo. Munch originally titled this work *Despair.*

"I was walking along the road with two friends. The sun set. I felt a tinge of melancholy. Suddenly the sky became a bloody red.

"I stopped, leaned against the railing, dead tired, and I looked at the flaming clouds that hung like blood and a sword over the blue-black fjord of the city.

"My friends walked on. I stood there, trembling with fright. And I felt a loud, unending scream piercing nature" (Edvard Munch, *Diary*, 1892).

The composition of *The Scream* (fig. 468) effectively expresses Munch's personal anxiety, creating a formal tension which reinforces the psychological tension that is the theme. As in Munch's description, the sky is a blood red. Its undulating rhythms melt into the blue-black waters of the fjord. The perspective of the bridge is unnatural. Its sharp angle creates a visual tension, for it is caught between the flatness of the picture plane, which is emphasized by the shapes of clouds and water, and the illusory space established by the diminution of Munch's companions and the ships on the fjord. The curving rhythm of Munch's body, transformed into an existential symbol, incorporates itself into the rhythms of the environment. He is becoming one with nature, realizing his worst agoraphobic nightmare. As the figure screams, its face is distorted to resemble a skull, with the iconographic association of death. These visual manipulations communicate an emotional impact not as a representational image, but as a symbol of a schizophrenic psychological state.

The terrifying tension Munch felt that evening was in part the result of his alcoholism and a dread of open spaces. In this condition, Munch experienced himself being pulled into his environment, losing his identity. He heard a scream within him, the scream of nature "dying" in flaming bursts at sunset. The inner scream became so intense that Munch, looking at us, screams to relieve the pain within.

The Scream was one of a series of twenty-two paintings and prints that Munch exhibited as a coordinated group in the opening years of the twentieth cen-

469. EDVARD MUNCH
The Frieze of Life exhibition.
Photograph of the installation
at Leipzig, 1903

tury. The exhibition was titled *Motifs from the Life of a Modern Soul*, yet it more often carried the simpler title *The Frieze of Life* (fig. 469), which better suggests the universal content, intended by Munch, of the flowering and passing of love, life's anxieties, and death. As a young person growing up in Norway, Munch had led a bohemian life, and the ideas for the paintings began with his personal, subjective experiences, which were then transformed into more universally symbolic themes.

For Munch, the emotionally expressive abstraction of forms was a way of creating art which possessed what he termed a "deeper meaning," one which conveyed the content of the human soul. The impact of his art would exert a profound influence on the development of early modern painting

TWENTIETH-CENTURY ART

INTRODUCTION

470. GIACOMO BALLA
Speeding Automobile–Study of Velocity.
1913. Oil on cardboard, 26 x 37 7/8".
Municipal Gallery of Modern Art,
Milan

"A roaring motorcar which seems to run on machine-gun fire is more beautiful than the *Victory of Samothrace*" (fig. 90), wrote Filippo Marinetti, an Italian poet of the Futurist movement, in 1908–9. The works we have chosen to introduce the twentieth century relate the dynamism of modern art to the vigor of modern life. *Speeding Automobile —Study of Velocity* by the Futurist artist Giacomo Balla (fig. 470) is an abstract representation that can be related to a 1910 *Futurist Manifesto* which declared that "the gesture . . . we would reproduce on canvas shall no longer be a fixed *moment* in universal dynamism. It shall simply be the dynamic sensation itself." Balla's painting represents the propulsive energy of a speeding car; the sequential placement of diagonal lines communicates dynamic force. Balla, an associate of Marinetti's, has visualized the poet's remarks on the new aesthetic of beauty as exemplified by the speed of a "roaring motorcar."

The sleek, aerodynamic design of Pinin Farina's *Cisitalia "202" GT* (fig. 471) is both superbly functional—it cuts the wind resistance— and aesthetically elegant. Even standing still, the car gives the impression of movement. In function and appearance, both Balla's painting and Farina's automobile are uniquely modern. They represent one aspect of the complex developments which characterize twentieth-century art.

HISTORY

The poet Marinetti's and the painter Balla's glorification of speed was symbolic of the impact of the technological revolution on the arts. The decades which opened the twentieth century were characterized by a population boom and unprecedented improvements in living conditions in the Western world. By the 1890s, electric lighting and motors were common, and the radio, invented by Guglielmo Marconi in 1895, greatly facilitated communication over vast geographic areas. Television was introduced in the 1920s, computers in the 1940s. But perhaps no more dramatic example can be used to demonstrate the astounding pace of modern technology than air and space flight. The 1903 flight of the Wright brothers at Kitty Hawk, North Carolina, was followed by rapid advances; Charles Lindbergh soloed across the Atlantic in 1927, and in 1969 Neil Armstrong became the first human to set foot on the moon.

Advances in technology were often set against a backdrop of political conflict, war, and violent revolution. By the end of the first decade of the twentieth century, the European nations and Great Britain had built up enormous armed forces. Germany, Austria-Hungary, and Italy were allied against Great Britain, France, and Russia. War became inevitable after Archduke Ferdinand, heir to the throne of Austria-Hungary, was assassinated in 1914. The Great War, now known as World War I, erupted within months. Although all parties hoped it would be of short duration, it lasted, stagnated in trench warfare, until 1918. America committed her armies in 1917.

471. PININ FARINA
Cisitalia "202" GT. 1946. Aluminum body, length 13'. Collection, The Museum of Modern Art, New York (Gift of the manufacturer)

472. VLADIMIR TATLIN
Historic photograph of the model of
the Monument to the Third International Communist Conference.
1919–20. The model, height 16', was of
wood and netting; the final building,
of iron (painted red) and glass, was to
have been more than 1300' high.

The Treaty of Versailles ended World War I, but the harsh restrictions imposed on Germany set the foundation for yet another conflict.

Before the war had ended, events in Russia had brought a new political force to the world scene. A populist revolution of 1917 overthrew Czar Nicholas II, and a "dictatorship of the proletariat" was established by a well-organized party of Bolshevik Communists headed by Nikolai Lenin. Lenin withdrew Russia from the war in 1918, but internal civil war only ended in 1921. In 1923 the Union of Soviet Socialist Republics was formed. Communist parties outside of the U.S.S.R. were federated with Soviet Communism in 1919 to form the Third International. In proposing a structure that would provide a center for world communism, Vladimir Tatlin, a Russian artist who had visited the avant-garde art centers of Berlin and Paris in 1913, offered an ambitious spiraling architectural form (fig. 472). The dynamic energy of the Communist party was to be expressed by the glass-enclosed meeting rooms that would revolve around the building's axis. The lowest—a cube—would turn once per year, the pyramid in the center once per month, and the upper, cylindrical chamber once per day.

Following World War I, economic instability arose as nations returned to peacetime industrial production. Prosperity seemed assured by the late twenties, but an economic collapse in 1929 plunged the West into the Great Depression, which, in America, would leave about one in four workers without a job. Compounding the economic ruin in America, a drought in the southwestern states devastated farming.

During the 1930s, as the West struggled to regain economic stability, the Nazi government of Adolf Hitler took control in Germany, and the Fascist dictators Benito Mussolini in Italy and Francisco Franco in Spain seized power. In 1939 a second world war broke out in Europe. World War II reached global involvement following Japan's attack on the American naval base at Pearl Harbor, Hawaii, in 1941. This war ended with the defeat of Germany and Japan, but the explosion of the atomic bomb over Hiroshima, Japan, on August 6, 1945, ushered in our current era, with its constant threat of atomic and nuclear weapons.

Max Beckmann's *Departure* (fig. 473) is a potent image of frustration and inhumanity born from the scars left on Europe from the savage first world war and the growing totalitarian regime of Nazi Germany. The two wings represent scenes of torture and mutilation, while in the center panel the precious realization of freedom is symbolically rendered with the departing queen holding a child. The figurative exaggerations, harsh brushstrokes, and severe colors contribute to the expression of brutality. Beckmann wrote of the painting: "On the right wing you can see yourself trying to find your way in the darkness, lighting the hall and staircase with a miserable lamp dragging along tied to you as part of yourself, the corpse of your memories, of your wrongs, of your failures, the murder everyone commits at some time of his life—you can never free yourself of your past, you have to carry the corpse while Life plays the drum. The Queen carries the greatest treasure—Freedom—as a child in her

473. MAX BECKMANN
Departure. 1932–33. Oil on canvas,
84 3/4 x 45 3/8" (center); 84 3/4 x 39 1/4"
(each wing). Collection, The Museum
of Modern Art, New York (Given
anonymously)

lap. Freedom is the one thing that matters—it is the departure, the new start."

In America, both foreign and domestic conflicts have marked the years since 1945. Between 1950 and 1953 America sent the largest contingent of troops to a United Nations force, which fought in Korea to stop the aggression of Communist North Korea. The 1950s also witnessed an intensification of the civil rights movement. Led by Martin Luther King, Jr., a Baptist minister who would receive the Nobel Peace Prize in 1964, black Americans were in the forefront of the struggle to achieve equality and dignity in human and legal rights. By the early 1960s, American combat troops were becoming more deeply involved in a civil war in Vietnam, while at home, efforts to sustain American involvement were met with bitter divisiveness. By 1975 U.S. forces were withdrawn. In Washington, the *Vietnam Veterans Memorial* (fig. 474) offers the more than 58,000 names, etched into black granite, of Americans who lost their lives in that conflict. It is an unprecedented public monument. Simple and direct in design, it creates an almost solemn environment. The polished surface of the granite reflects the transient life before it, while the names immutably impose themselves, constantly reminding us of the human suffering and loss that are the ultimate costs of conflict.

474. MAYA LIN
Vietnam Veterans Memorial. 1982.
Black granite, length 500'. The Mall,
Washington, D.C. Commenting on her
conception for the memorial, Lin
wrote, "I didn't want a static object
that people would just look at, but
something they could relate to as on a
journey, or passage, that would bring
each to his own conclusion."

INTELLECTUAL AND SCIENTIFIC ACTIVITY

Scientific advancements during the twentieth century have been revolutionary in many areas. In physics, Albert Einstein's general theory of relativity demonstrated the relationship of geometry to

475. EDWARD HOPPER
Nighthawks. 1942. Oil on canvas,
30 x 60". The Art Institute of Chicago
(Friends of American Art Collection)

gravity and radically modified our concept of space and time. Our understanding of the very essence of matter itself has been altered, as the atom has been reduced to its subatomic components.

Twentieth-century developments in psychology have greatly influenced the course of art, especially in the movements of Surrealism and Abstract Expressionism (see pp. 484 and 492). Utilizing therapeutic approaches which included free association and the interpretation of dreams in treating his patients, Sigmund Freud established the active and even dynamic role of the human unconscious in guiding behavior. To Freud, unmasking the subconscious was the key to understanding the human mind. Carl Jung extended, modified, and at times countered Freud's theories to develop additional psychological insight into human behavior. Jung advanced the notion of a "collective unconscious," a layer of unconscious underlying the personal unconscious that carries the inherited disposition of our species. The "collective unconscious" was revealed by the common use of archetypal images, such as the circle, across diverse cultural traditions.

Radical changes were introduced in twentieth-century music. Igor Stravinsky's ballet music for *The Rite of Spring*, with its driving, primal rhythms and fragmented melodies, nearly caused the audience to riot at its first performance. In Germany the composer Arnold Schönberg devised a new system of musical tonality; Schönberg's pantonality (which is commonly referred to as being atonal) is a free but not unstructured use of musical tones without traditional chord progressions or resolutions. At mid-century, the American composer John Cage began to incorporate elements of chance into his work. One composition from 1952, titled *4'–33*, has a performer come on stage and sit at a piano for four minutes and thirty-three seconds. During this time, the unpredictable sounds from the audience and other accidental noises "create" the musical experience. Cage's avant-garde concept of music has been influential for contemporary poets, painters, and performance artists (see p. 506).

TWENTIETH-CENTURY ART

Twentieth-century art is often referred to as modern art, although the terms are not exactly synonymous. The concept of modernism is relative within the context of history. It expresses an attitude which distinguishes a current time from the immediate past. Renaissance artists, for example, felt themselves to be working in a "modern style." In the history of art, developments in the nineteenth century countered well-established traditions in art, laying the foundation for the radical and rapid changes which have occurred in this century. These changes in twentieth-century art have been so distinctive that the term modern is applied in both a chronological and a descriptive sense.

The present century has brought a variety of artistic experiences unparalleled in the history of art. Throughout the century, the avant-garde has rapidly been transformed; these new movements and styles can often be related to dramatic historical, cultural, and scientific changes. More traditional currents in art, including realism and illusionism, have also been sustained throughout the century. Edward Hopper developed a personal style and iconography devoted to the theme of the loneliness and isolation of the individual. Hopper's settings could be anywhere in America, and his people are ordinary, nameless figures from the middle class: He aims for an art that is not local and specific but universal. We have to be careful not to infuse these images with the nostalgia that their settings and costumes now evoke. Hopper intended his paintings to represent the here and now. In *Nighthawks* (fig. 475) we are cut off from the quiet individuals inside the diner, and the harsh interior light exposes the lack of communication that Hopper so often emphasizes in his images of modern urban life. At times, representational art achieved avant-garde status, as in Andy Warhol's *Green Coca-Cola Bottles* (fig. 476), which focused visual attention on consumer commercialism.

It is, however, abstraction and non-objectivity which have become the hallmarks of twentieth-century art. Continuing formal developments advanced by the Post-Impressionist artists, twentieth-century artists expanded the new vocabulary of visual expression. Georgia O'Keeffe's *Evening Star III* (fig. 477) is from a series of watercolors inspired by viewing the evening star at sunset, but representational associations have here been abstracted to express the rhythmic pulsations of the star over the landscape. O'Keeffe's painting communicates a sensation rather than the appearance of a scene. Constantin Brancusi's *Kiss* (fig. 479), with its compact, rectangular masses joining two abstract figures, conveys the essence of unity. For Brancusi, the expression of a concept, which in this sculpture is the wholeness of two individuals as symbolized by the kiss, overrode concerns of naturalism.

Some artists totally denied any representational aspects in their work. Helen Frankenthaler's *Tobacco Landscape* (fig. 478), for example, is a non-objective painting belonging to a style from the sixties called Post-Painterly Abstraction. Using a water-soluble, plastic-based paint known as acrylic, which is flexible and quick-drying, Frankenthaler

476. ANDY WARHOL
Green Coca-Cola Bottles. 1962. Oil on canvas, 82 1/4 x 57". Whitney Museum of American Art, New York (Purchase, with funds from the Friends of the Whitney Museum of American Art)

poured thin washes of this paint onto the raw canvas, creating an expressively fluid and textural composition.

In viewing twentieth-century art, we shall witness a tremendous expansion of the materials used by artists. Traditional mediums, such as marble, bronze, and wood for sculpture, will be joined by commonplace, found objects, and even discarded junk in creating assemblage works. Even the raw earth will become a significant medium of artistic expression (see fig. 556).

After mid-century, the fashioning of an art object became less important to some artists. In the Happenings of the 1950s and 1960s (see fig. 481), artists, usually without a preconceived script, performed and directed the activity of the audience during a quasi-theatrical event, often outside the confines of a museum or gallery. Happenings and Performance Art have countered traditional definitions of the work of art as a tangible object. The same is true of Installation Art, which fashions a temporary environment within a gallery space. Judy Pfaff's installations (see fig. 480) are each distinctive and thought-provoking; the exuberance of the overlapping, contrasting patterns, shapes, and colors of *N.Y.C.—B.Q.E.*, for example, created a scintillating experience but one that also seemed bittersweet and fleeting because of its temporary nature.

One uniquely modern international medium of artistic expression is cinema. In the late nineteenth century, experimental photographers succeeded in presenting a "moving picture" by projecting a sequential series of photographs taken at exposures as quick as 1/2000 of a second. The forerunner of our motion-picture projector, however, was the Vitascope, invented by Thomas Armat and manufactured by Thomas Edison in 1895. These projectors achieved the illusion of movement by rapidly projecting a series of still photographic images in sequence. The persistence of our vision, from the image retained on the retina of the eye, lets our minds interpret the rapidly shown still frames as continuous movement. By 1895 the Lumière brothers had opened the first public movie theater in France and soon their *cinématographie* were being shown throughout Europe.

Like those traditional art forms with which we have already

477. GEORGIA O'KEEFFE
Evening Star III. 1917. Watercolor, 9 x 11 7/8". Collection, The Museum of Modern Art, New York (Mr. and Mrs. Donald B. Straus Fund)

become familiar, cinema is primarily a visual experience. Techniques of shooting can effectively manipulate our perspective as we remain stationary. But special to film is the depiction of movement over a course of time. The expression of a continued time has been an important element in many works of art, but with cinema time is not only actual, but our perception of it may be altered by various methods of editing, the "cutting and pasting" of sequences of film together. Sergei Eisenstein's montage editing in *Potemkin* (figs. 482, 483), rapidly shifting us from scenes of Cossacks firing into the crowd to scenes expressing the anguish of the people, conveys the tragedy of the event. The efficacy of the modern medium of cinema was vividly expressed by the noted Swedish director Ingmar Bergman when he stated: "I can transport my audience from a given feeling to

481. ALLAN KAPROW
From *Household*, a Happening commissioned by Yale University, 1964

the feeling that is diametrically opposed to it, as if each spectator were on a pendulum. I can make an audience laugh, scream with terror, smile, believe in legends, become indignant, take offense, become enthusiastic, lower itself, or yawn with boredom. . . . I am able to mystify, and I have at my disposal the most astounding device [the motion-picture camera] that has ever, since history began, been put into the hands of the juggler."

As we shall see, the twentieth century will bring us to the position where the artist becomes the work of art, in Performance Art, and the work of art as an object itself will be deemed less important than the concept or idea to create it. Joseph Kosuth's *One and Three Chairs* (fig. 553) only refers to the potential of an art object rather than being one in itself.

THE TWENTIETH-CENTURY ARTIST

"The thing that interests me today is that painters do not have to go to a subject matter outside themselves. Modern painters work in a different way. They work from within" (Jackson Pollock, 1951). Pollock's statement, made at mid-century, summarizes the unique experience of the artist in this century. The rapidity of social changes, the impact of technology, and new artistic freedoms have altered many traditional notions of the role and identity of the artist. The twentieth-century artist has forged a new independence with diverse materials, and often works of art are imbued with a highly introspective content. This aspect of self-gratification in art leads us to experience many works as a revelation of the artist's inner self. It is almost as if this disclosure of the inner self, which in the past was usually restricted to self-portraits, is the main content of many twentieth-century works of art. But the diversity and subjectivity of this new freedom have also posed problems in the critical evaluation of art and even in the identity of the artist. Having broadened the definition of art, customary notions concerning the education of artists and the

482, 483. SERGEI EISENSTEIN
Details of film stills from *Potemkin*. 1925. Eisenstein's film dealt with the 1905 mutiny aboard the Russian ship *Potemkin* and the failed anti-czarist uprising.

parameters of a work of art have been opened to a flood of conjectural questions concerning quality, value, and meaning.

Our self-portraits demonstrate that the twentieth-century artist has maintained a continuing integrity, while countering tradition with complex symbolic and psychological insight. *The Two Fridas*, a double self-portrait by the Mexican artist Frida Kahlo (fig. 484), is a complex image filled with symbolism. Although the two figures hold hands and are joined by a common blood system, the duality Kahlo feels is revealed by the contrasting costumes, Mexican and European. Her dual heritage is likewise expressed in the two hearts, for the figure in the European dress has her chest ripped open in a reference to Aztec sacrificial practices, while the other figure's heart resembles Catholic representations of the Sacred Heart of Jesus. This revealing, if enigmatic, work was painted as Kahlo was being divorced, and the open artery on her lap may refer to her suffering at this time. Such personal self-revelation is not unusual in twentieth-century art.

From later in the century, Alice Neel's *Nude Self-Portrait*, although realistic, does not communicate a faithful naturalism (fig. 485). The adjusted figural proportions, stern modeling, and austere pose portray a psychological presence within a probing, unashamed honesty. Such introspective and deliberate honesty, revealed within a wide variety of visual means, can be one of the keys to understanding the modern artist.

484. FRIDA KAHLO
Left: *The Two Fridas*. 1939. Oil on canvas, 69 x 69". Museo de Arte Moderno, Mexico City

485. ALICE NEEL
Right: *Nude Self-Portrait*. 1980. Oil on canvas, 54 x 40". National Portrait Gallery, Washington, D. C.

FAUVISM

"I cannot copy nature in a servile way, I must interpret nature and submit it to the spirit of the picture—when I have found the relationship of all the tones the result must be a living harmony of tones, a harmony not unlike that of a musical composition....

"The chief aim of color should be to serve expression as well as possible.... What I dream of is an art of balance, of purity and serenity devoid of troubling or depressing subject-matter, an art ... like an appeasing influence, like a mental soother, something like a good armchair in which to

rest from physical fatigue" (Henri Matisse, *Notes of a Painter*, 1908).

In Matisse's representation of the mythical land of Arcadia (fig. 486), lovers embrace and dance to the strains of music. The sinuous nudes who inhabit this verdant pasture of pleasure are defined by the same curving, rhythmic lines that describe trees and foliage. This sensuous landscape suggests harmony between humanity and the natural order. As we can judge from the preparatory study, the colors are intense and vibrant (fig. 487).

486. HENRI MATISSE
The Joy of Life. 1905–6. Oil on canvas, 68 1/2 x 93 3/4". The Barnes Foundation, Merion, Pennsylvania. When it was exhibited in 1906, *The Joy of Life* was singled out for criticism. The painter Paul Signac complained that Matisse had "gone to the dogs."

Matisse's monumental painting descends from a tradition of pastoral images that began in antiquity and was revived during the Renaissance and Baroque periods. In this twentieth-century interpretation, the diminution of the figures indicates spatial recession, but the broad areas of unmodulated bold color and the powerful flowing linear rhythms create a patterned, flat composition that adheres to the picture plane.

In the opening years of the present century, Matisse, who during the 1890s had painted with an Impressionist palette, assimilated artistic influences from the Post-Impressionists and began to make paintings in which color, independent of descriptive reality, was exalted for its expressive and sensuous self. Matisse worked in Paris with a group of painters who were exploring this liberation of color, and at a Parisian exhibition in 1905 their works were displayed in a room with a classicizing sculpture, causing the critic Louis Vauxcelles to remark: "Donatello au milieu des fauves!" (Donatello among the wild beasts). This witty denunciation gave the name Fauvism to this new style. Fauvism was short-lived, but its revelling in the freedom of color, as seen in *The Joy of Life*, had an impact still being felt in twentieth-century art.

MATISSE, *The Joy of Life:* **1905–6**
1904: Henry James, *The Golden Bowl*
1904: Puccini, *Madame Butterfly* premieres, Milan
1904: Rolls-Royce Company founded

487. HENRI MATISSE
Study for *The Joy of Life*. 1905. Oil on canvas, 18 x 22". Statens Museum for Kunst, Copenhagen. As the Barnes Foundation does not permit color reproductions of *The Joy of Life*, this sketch has been included to indicate the approximate colors of the final painting.

KÄTHE KOLLWITZ AND GERMAN EXPRESSIONISM
(DIE BRÜCKE)

488. KÄTHE KOLLWITZ
Whetting the Scythe. 1905. Soft-
ground etching, 11 11/16 x 11 11/16".
Käthe Kollwitz was the first
woman artist elected to the
Prussian Academy of Art. Her
prints, often published in a series,
are striking images of the social and
political struggles of the poorer
classes.

Whetting the Scythe (fig. 488)
strikes us with a direct visual
and psychological impact. The
composition is cogent and compact; the peasant, sharpening her
scythe, occupies almost the entire area of the print's surface.
Attention is drawn to the rough
hands and the timeworn face
pressed against the scythe's
blade. We begin to sense an
ominous force, for the scythe,
used in reaping and harvesting
grain, is also a traditional symbol of the grim reaper, Death.
The deep shadows, particularly
effective with Kollwitz's choice

of the etching medium, seem to
prophesize a brooding, uncertain future.

Kollwitz's etching was the
third in a series of seven prints
published in 1908 on the theme
of the Peasants' War, a sixteenth-
century rebellion in Germany.
Kollwitz's series describes more
than just the history of the revolt,
for the faces and gestures of the
peasants express the social and
economic conditions which led
them to revolt. Although she
remained independent of any
formal expressionist art movement in Germany, the communicative and emotional impact of
her work shares aspects with
German Expressionism.

The seeds of the modern
movement known as German
Expressionism were planted in
work of the late nineteenth century by Van Gogh and Munch.
Expressionist tendencies, such as
distortion of form and intensification of color, had surfaced earlier in the history of German art.
Now, in the opening years of the
twentieth century, artists looked
to these artistic precedents to find
forms that would express the
intensity of feeling which they
believed was a part of the Northern cultural tradition.

In 1905 a group of young architectural students formed an as-

1901: London's population is 6.6 million; New York City's is 3.44 million
1903: First flight in a heavier-than-air machine
1904: Helen Keller graduates from Radcliffe College
1905: "Bloody Sunday," Russia; police brutally crush demonstration in St. Petersburg
1905: General strike in Russia; first Workers' Soviet (council) formed

sociation that they called *Künstler-Gruppe Brücke* (The Artists Group of The Bridge). As an association, *Die Brücke* was based on the medieval guilds; the artists lived and worked together as a community. The symbol of the bridge, adopted from Nietzsche's writings, indicated their role as a transitionary force by which "all the revolutionary and surging elements" of modernism could bring German art to a new and fulfilling future. The artists of *Die Brücke* turned away from academicism, looking instead for inspiration to the stylizations and spirituality that they sensed in medieval, African, and Oceanic art.

The leading artist of *Die Brücke* was Ernst Ludwig Kirchner, who often painted the vitality of the urban street: "The modern light of the cities, the movement in the streets—there are my stimuli. . . . Observing movement excites my pulse of life, the source of creation." For Kirchner, the dynamic interaction of color and movement on a city street was the paragon of modernity. In *Street, Berlin* (fig. 489), arbitrary, intense colors are joined with sharply stylized figures and a distorted perspective to communicate the animation of twentieth-century urban life.

489. ERNST LUDWIG KIRCHNER
Street, Berlin. 1913. Oil on canvas, 47 1/2 x 35 7/8". Collection, The Museum of Modern Art, New York (Purchase)

THE ORIGINS OF CUBISM

490. PABLO PICASSO
Les Demoiselles d'Avignon. 1907. Oil on canvas, 96 x 92". Collection, The Museum of Modern Art, New York (Acquired through the Lillie P. Bliss Bequest). The Avignon to which the title refers is a street in Barcelona's red-light district.

Picasso's *Les Demoiselles d'Avignon* (fig. 490) is a harsh and aggressive painting. Inside a brothel we confront five naked prostitutes with abstract anatomies. Three figures conceal their faces behind vividly painted African masks that both hide their identity and communicate a frightening ferocity. Picasso considered these masks "magic things" that added a mysterious potency to the work. Compounding the psychological anxiety communicated by these masked figures is a composition which sets formal elements in violent visual combat: warm flesh tones and shades of pink and rust are set against icy blues, while spatial illusionism seems denied by the flat, abstract shapes, despite the manner in which the nude entering from behind parted drapes and the *repoussoir* table and still life suggest perspectival recession. The nude figures are discordantly composed of geometric, angular facets and organic, curving passages. *Les Demoiselles d'Avignon*, a paradox of formal and psychological tensions, threatened the tradition of illusionism that had characterized painting since the Renaissance.

The painting began, however, in a less anguished, more traditional spirit. In the spring of 1907 Picasso, a young Spaniard working in Paris, took up the challenge of painting a monumental modern composition of female nudes. After seeing a 1906 Paris retrospective of Cézanne's paintings, Picasso began to apply the planar, geometric simplifications of Cézanne's forms to the study of the human figure. In a preliminary study for the painting, two clothed male figures were surrounded by five female prostitutes. This confrontation, as well as the still-life arrangement on the table, suggests a traditional *memento mori* theme—all physical pleasure is passing.

Les Demoiselles d'Avignon seemed a brutal and ugly painting to many of Picasso's friends, including the French painter Georges Braque, but Braque was inspired by the manner in which Picasso was wrestling with the question of pictorial structure and the issues raised by Cézanne. In the summer of 1908, Braque was in southern France, the landscape which had earlier been transformed by Cézanne (see fig. 465). Braque's *Houses at L'Estaque* (fig. 491) develops the planar simplification and faceted surface structure of Cézanne's paintings but, in contrast to Cézanne's intention, now the houses seem to lack solidity and weight. Braque's eccentric use of model-

1906: Upton Sinclair, *The Jungle*
1907: Louis Lumière invents a process for color photography
1907: Mother's Day established in Philadelphia
1908: Ford Motor Company produces the first Model T

491. GEORGES BRAQUE
Houses at L'Estaque. 1908. Oil on canvas, 28 3/4 x 23 5/8". Hermann and Margit Rupf Foundation, Kunstmuseum, Bern

ing highlights different areas of the landscape simultaneously and reinforces the planarity of the pictorial surface.

Reviewing a 1908 exhibition of Braque's paintings in Paris, which included *Houses at L'Estaque,* the French art critic Louis Vauxcelles (who had earlier given us the name Fauvism;

see p. 445) wrote that Braque "despises form, reduces everything . . . to cubes. Let us not make fun of him, since he is honest. And let us wait." Cubism, the style that would result from these experiments of Picasso and Braque, would become one of the most significant movements of early-twentieth-century art.

AFRICAN ART: BOBO MASKS

These Bobo masked figures (fig. 492) are about to take part in purification rites, which are believed to be indispensable to the cycle of renewal and rebirth. As with all mask-using societies in Africa, the Bobo have a developed ritual life which has to do with their environment and conduct in daily life. The name Bobo is applied to those people living in an area bounded by Mali and the Niger River on the north and west and by Ghana to the east. They live in one part of a broad zone of open, rather arid savannah which extends across the continent from the Atlantic Ocean to the Red Sea to the south of the Sahara Desert.

The visual arts of sub-Saharan African traditional societies include an ensemble of objects, activities, and performances:

492. Bobo masked dancers at annual purification rites, Upper Volta. 20th century

BOBO Masked Dancers: 20th century
1905: Russian sailors mutiny aboard *Potemkin*
1908: Congo Free State becomes the Belgian Congo
1910: Union of South Africa achieves dominion status within British Empire
1911: Italy occupies Tripoli

493. Leaf Mask. 20th century. Leaves of the *karité* tree, fiber, straw, and colored string. Bobo, Upper Volta

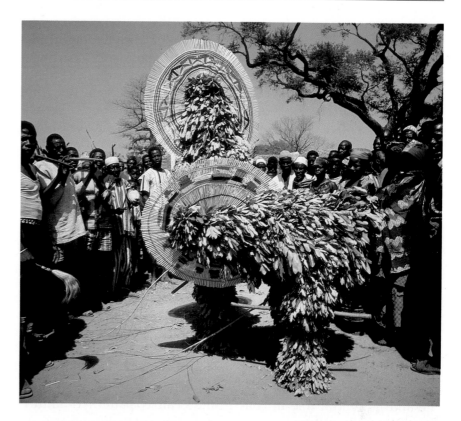

494. *Bird of the Night* (Butterfly) Mask. 20th century. Wood, paint, and raffia. Bobo, Upper Volta

masks and sculptured figures; body paint and scarification; costumes of all sorts; dance, music, and musical instruments; and the recitation of myths. Every element, from costumes to choreography, from choral to solo singing, has a place in an overall belief system, and every tiny detail of the code carries specific meaning. This strict code links events that are believed to have occurred at creation with their repetition, in symbolic form, in the world of today. The symbolic performances are neither anecdotal nor narrative. The painter or sculptor is not representing an act that has been or will be staged in a transient or fixed period of time. On the contrary, these African arts are meant to ensure the permanence of ceremony in daily life and its central role in continuation of the culture.

Such arts are documents of African thought and action and contribute to the sense of well-being in the parent culture. They are part of the normal experience of the average member of the culture. In most instances the "meaning" of the arts is broadly known to the community to which they belong. In this public sense, one meaning of a work is generally known and refers to present and future security of the individual, the family, the village, or the nation. From this level of commonly held knowledge there arises a pyramid of more detailed and often more sacred meanings. Political and priestly elites are usually the

keepers of such esoteric knowledge. This knowledge can be speculative or mythological, historical or aphoristic (asserting a general truth), of applied science (the medicine givers) or from free association. Such knowledge is the basis of cultural beliefs and the justification for social acts. A higher value is placed on the good of the group than on the needs of the individual. African art exists at the intersection between the human and spirit worlds. It is vital to survival.

Outside the major political centers, the village is the dominant political unit. The Bobo people are divided into as many autonomous political units as there are villages. While not isolated from their neighbors, they maintain a number of distinct and localized patterns of culture, including language and arts. All these groups, however, share the same concept about the relationship of human life to nature and perform a series of ritual activities which are similarly outfitted with costume, dance, and music.

In the Bobo region, agriculture is the predominant source of wealth. The fear of drought or even delay in the arrival of the rainy season is a source of great mental stress, which is eased for the farmers of the dry savannah by a highly developed and elaborate scheme of institutions and rites which preserve the relationship between nature, the source of all life, and survival. The Bobo differ from other African societies (Dogon and Yoruba, for example) in that they do not represent nature as an ambivalent force either generous or dangerous, but see nature as essentially benevolent. The needs, mistakes, and offenses of people upset her, so the function of the ritual performances is to chase away evil, which is bound to occur in human communities. Such rites are necessary at times of transition—at creation, birth, upon entering adult life, death, planting, and harvest.

Wuro, the Supreme Being of the Bobo, installed harmonious order among the sun, rain, and the earth at creation. Human beings, given their lifeways and weaknesses, threaten that equilibrium. The techniques of agriculture involve violation of the soil. This outrages Soxo, the divinity of the bush, and through him, Wuro the Creator. Moreover, if one transgresses the laws (taboos) of society, a sequence of calamities will occur: drought leads to starvation, sickness, sterility, and sometimes death. Wuro gave some of his bounty to Dwo, who acts as mediator between God and human life to restore balance. Dwo is incarnated in the leaf masks of the Bobo.

These leaf masks cover the entire body of the dancer (see fig. 493) and are made in the bush after the millet crop is safely stored. The leaves are those of a local tree, the *karité* (a type of mahogany), and are tied together with vegetable fiber. Feathers or a straw crest indicate that the mask is male. The leaf masks enter the village at dusk and roam the alleys, lightly brushing against storehouses, huts, and the people of the village. The rustling leaves collect all the dust particles, which represent the offenses of human beings. They cleanse that which they touch of all their impurities and thus absorb the evil that has accumulated throughout the year. They purify the village. The masks themselves are perishable, and their potency is spent in this activity. They, too, are part of the life cycle and are regenerated at the end of the next agricultural season.

The human community also is regenerated by participation in renewal rites of nature which take place at the end of the dry season, before the first rain falls and planting begins. These rites signify the end of the period of mourning. They also constitute purification and appeal to the spirits of the underworld. They require the presence of leaf masks and also of fiber and sculpted masks.

The fiber masks are plaited and dyed by the blacksmiths, and their natural materials are associated with substances of the bush. They are decorated with clan emblems linked to veneration of human lineage. The wooden, sculpted masks are usually rendered in animal form and represent the protective genii of the village. They include the male flat-horned buffalo, the female buffalo with circularly

sectioned horns, the warthog, the cock with its crest, the toucan, the fish, the antelope, and the serpent, which is sometimes as much as ten feet long. The *Bird of the Night,* or butterfly, mask appears after the first rains of the season (fig. 494). The fluttering movements of the butterfly are imitated by the dancer. Clearly a record of the essence of the animal is what is sought by the carver and dancer and not an exact visual representation.

Another important type of mask is the *dodo* or *nwo.* These have round faces and eyes in concentric circles and are topped with a polychrome blade. They combine the face of an owl, a ca-loo beak, and sometimes a snake skeleton with geometric patterns such as lozenges, checks, triangles, and chevrons. As messengers, the bird connects human life to the realm of the spirits. Such masks are only one part of the whole image, which includes a mask, costume, human bearer, and performance in motion.

Whether made of leaf, fiber, or wood, whether representational or abstract, these images embody the benevolent force of Dwo and thereby the concept of fertility, fecundity, and growth. As with many African arts, masks were collected by Western artists, anthropologists, and collectors in the late nineteenth century because they were moved by their direct and powerful formal expression. Only recently have they begun to be understood in their own context by outsiders.

495. HOPI Tribe
Opposite: *Kachina* dolls. Late 1800s to present. Cottonwood roots adorned with mineral paints and other natural materials. The Heard Museum, Phoenix, Arizona (Fred Harvey and Barry Goldwater Collections)

HOPI *kachina* dolls: 20th century
1906: San Francisco earthquake
1907: Oklahoma is admitted as forty-sixth state
1908: Founding of the Boy Scouts
1909: Indian Councils Act increases elected members on Indian councils
1911: Revolution in Mexico

These wooden figurines (fig. 495) are called *kachin-tihus* (or *kachina* dolls) and were carved by Hopi tribesmen. The elaborate head-dresses, some of them fitted with birds' feathers, are thought to assist in transmitting messages to and from the spirits. Another *kachina* represented here (fig. 496) is a human figure wearing a costume and headdress not unlike those on the wooden figurines. As with most Native American art, these examples must be seen as functional, that is, they were not produced solely for their own sake as decorative objects, but were meant to serve social and

496. HEMIS (JEMEZ) Tribe
Kachina. 20th century. Costume of feathers, yarn, buckskin, and grass. The figure holds cattails.

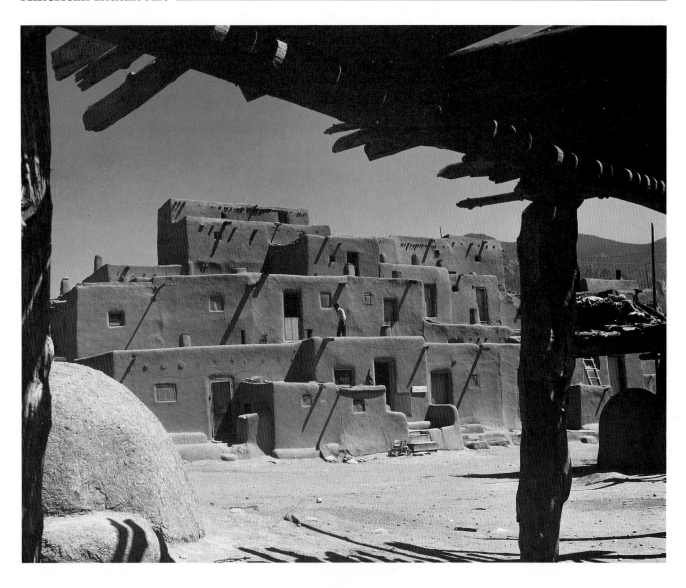

497. Pueblo, Taos. Carson National Forest, New Mexico

religious purposes. Each example is invested with sacred symbolism.

Kachina are supernatural beings who act as links between the gods and human beings. The spirits (gods) are thought to live in the San Francisco Mountains of California and are believed to visit the Hopis at their current home in northeast Arizona during the first half of the year, when the planting of new crops is being prepared. Among their many powers, these important spirits are thought to exercise control over weather. The Hopi were and

still are farmers who grow corn, beans, and squash. Because of their dependence on agriculture in this arid region, the Hopi have developed a complex religious life centered around rain-making and crop fertility.

In the Hopi religion, there are three manifestations of the *kachinas:* the spirit, a human acting as a spirit, and a carved figurine. The spirit, which, of course, cannot be seen, is impersonated by members of the Hopi tribe. By placing masks over their heads and wearing elaborate costumes and headdresses, these men and women are regarded as having taken on the supernatural character of the *kachina* spirit. Through special masks, costumes, paint, and actions of the impersonators, the otherworldly spirits are given power, substance, and personality. *Kachina* dolls *(kachin-tihu)* are miniature representations (eight to ten inches in height) of the masked impersonators. There are about two hundred and fifty *kachina* personalities, though a limited number are favored. They personify a variety of natural elements, including clouds, rain, crops, animals, or even abstract concepts such as growth. From archaeological evidence, we know that they have been in use since the Hopi first inhabited the southwestern United States about two thousand years ago.

The Hopi culture was not much disturbed by European influence until the later nineteenth century, and the Hopi claim that they, more than any other North American tribe, live "in the old way." Since 1882 the Hopi have been officially confined to government reservations in northeast Arizona. This is the traditional homeland of the Navajo and the Zuñi as well and is typified by steep-walled canyons and isolated mesas formed by the steady down-cutting of rivers. Hopi communities are based on cooperation, as their survival in such a difficult environment depends on shared responsibility. They count on ceremonies to give them unity and cohesiveness. Group rituals depend on cooperation and are important models for the whole community to witness.

Viewing a Hopi village, one can see that the buildings seem to grow directly out of the mesa top, and their materials and shapes give them continuity with the living rock on which they are built (see fig. 497). This is often called an organic mode of building, for there is little conscious separation between what is made by human hands and what is natural environment.

Village life is organized around the plaza, a central space left open for the performance of ritual dances. Preparation for such rituals takes place in underground chambers called *kiva*. These *kiva* represent the underworld from which the Hopi believe their people emerged in primordial times. Among other beliefs, the *kiva* is where the ritual of growing new food plants for the coming season takes place. Those rituals are performed by men. Upward movement from the dark *kiva* to the open daylight symbolically enacts the Hopi "origin myth," in which they emerged from the chaos of the underworld to begin settled agricultural life on the mesas.

Ceremonies take place over a seven-month period beginning in December. In the winter, when the earth's vegetation is dormant and covered with snow, the *kachina* rituals are held at night in the *kivas*. These dances include warriors and hunters, emphasizing combat and death. Spring and summer rituals take place in the outdoor plaza in daylight and are associated with fertility, themes of growth, and regeneration. These are happy and boisterous occasions involving both men and women in costume who sing and dance in an ordered and stately fashion. Some other *kachina* dancers are ogres whose role is to admonish everyone, especially children, to obey the rules of the Hopi society. In a society based on cooperation rather than authoritarian control, such *kachinas* are important for social stability. The *kachina* figurines serve a didactic purpose: to remind Hopi children of religious and social mores. They are not toys; these art forms are clearly an integral part of life and are thought to ensure Hopi survival.

FRANK LLOYD WRIGHT

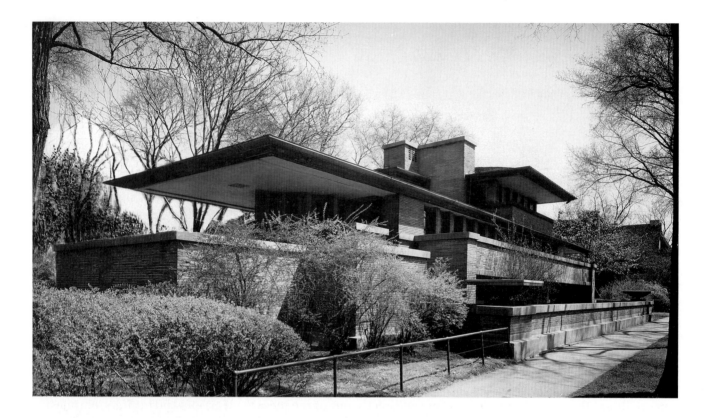

Wright's Robie House (fig. 498) is distinguished by an emphatic horizontal design, with rooms and porches extending out from a central core defined by the chimney mass. It is astonishing to realize that the Robie House, with its contemporary appearance, was actually constructed in the first decade of the twentieth century. The house was designed by Frank Lloyd Wright, an architect who had worked as an assistant to Louis Sullivan from 1888 to 1893. By 1900 Wright had developed a new and personal style, and in the opening years of this century, he designed a series of private homes in the Chicago area that shared similar compositional qualities, one of which was an emphasis on the horizontal features of the design.

Wright's style, which was inspired by the flatness of the terrain where the homes were built, is known as the Prairie style.

In the Prairie style, Wright developed what he termed his organic theory of architecture. The organic concept governs both the design of the structure and its relationship to the site. The cantilevered projections (see below) from the core of the house lessen the distinction between inside and outside, while the abstract, geometric massing of the architectural forms creates a distinctly modern effect.

The interior design of the rooms continues the geometric organization apparent from the outside. Wright's use of furniture, much of which he created particularly for each house, is

498. FRANK LLOYD WRIGHT
Exterior, Robie House, Chicago. 1909. Wright's Prairie Style designs, including this house, were published in Europe in 1910. They influenced later developments in modern European architecture, including De Stijl and the Bauhaus.

distinctive for its severely geometric design and its hand-crafted elegance (fig. 500). It reiterates and complements the architectural forms and, in its rich use of wood and modern decorative elements, enhances the intimate scale of the rooms.

Viewing the plan, one becomes aware of another feature of the organic theory (fig. 499). The interior spatial flow from room to room, around the central core of the fireplace and stairway, is free and unobstructed; rooms are not

WRIGHT, Robie House: 1909
1909: Freud lectures in America
1909: Admiral Peary reaches the North Pole

499, 500. FRANK LLOYD WRIGHT
Robie House, Plan and dining room, with original furniture designed by Wright

UPPER FLOOR

boxed off. Interior spaces merge one with another. A new continuity of interior spatial design is established.

The decorative features of the house's exterior are minimal. Instead of applied ornamentation, Wright utilizes the color and texture of the materials themselves. On the exterior, red brick contrasts with powerful horizontal accents in stone. The unadorned planarity of the exterior walls will become one of the distinguishing features of modern architecture.

Certain features of Wright's organic theory are antithetical. For example, the desire to merge the house with the environment is countered by the severely geometric and planar design, but it was precisely the harmony of the balancing of antithetical design features which distinguished Wright's achievements.

THE CANTILEVER

The cantilever, an architectural support system utilized by Wright in both the Robie House and Fallingwater (see fig. 11), horizontally projects an architectural member out into space without external support. It is counterbalanced by a weight on the interior end. The materials used in the construction of a large cantilever must possess a high tensile strength; usually steel beams and reinforced concrete are used. For this reason, the cantilever as a method of construction reached its fullest expression in modern architecture.

ANALYTICAL CUBISM

The theme of Georges Braque's *Violin and Palette* (fig. 501) is traditional—a still-life arrangement of a violin, a music stand with sheet music, a painter's palette hung on a *trompe l'oeil* nail at the top, and green folds of drapery as a backdrop. Each of these common elements, however, is broken up into disengaged fragments. The violin, for example, is composed of a series of planes or facets which represent parts of the violin as seen from different points of view. These have been reassembled to form a highly abstract composition on the picture plane of the painting.

Braque's fragmented violin is in part the result of influences stemming from Cézanne, who introduced planar modeling and multiple viewpoints in his paintings from the late nineteenth century (see fig. 464). From 1907 onward, Picasso and Braque, working together in Paris, experimented with this analytical abstraction, applying it to figural and landscape representations. By the fall and winter of 1909–10, they had developed Cubism.

Since the Renaissance, naturalistic illusionism had been a primary concern of painting. Cubism confronted that tradition by asserting a new independence for the painted image. Given the visual clues that Braque offers us in *Violin and Palette*, we conceptually understand, for example, that one of the images refers to a violin. The image does not represent a particular violin as seen from a specific viewpoint.

501. GEORGES BRAQUE
Violin and Palette. 1909–10. Oil on canvas, 36 1/8 x 16 7/8".
The Solomon R. Guggenheim Museum, New York

Rather, the simultaneous viewpoints suggest the *essence* of a violin—those shapes, forms, and colors which define a violin as a distinct object, different from the music stand, sheet music, palette, or drapery. In this process of analysis, seeing becomes both visual and conceptual.

The initial phase of Cubism, which analyzes objects from different viewpoints, to re-create them as planar facets on the picture plane, is known as Analytical Cubism. The process of abstraction inherent in this visual and conceptual analysis led to ambiguities of interpretation, but Cubism never became non-objective.

In 1911 a new element—lettered, stenciled shapes—was introduced onto the surfaces of Analytical Cubist paintings. Picasso's *Ma Jolie* (fig. 502) contains both letters and musical notations. While the shapes of the letters reinforce the planarity of the painting's surface, they also act as a clue, for they were taken from a current popular song. The words also become a reference for the viewer, for above them we can glimpse shapes that suggest a figure holding a stringed instrument. The color has been reduced because Picasso's primary examination in this work is of form; color, which depends on light, is deemed extraneous to form. However abstract, the painting offers the persistent observer a representation of a posed model. The network of planar shapes has given a new reality to painting, one which asserts its two-dimensional surface while still maintaining references to the objective, three-dimensional world.

1910: Stravinsky's *Firebird* is performed in Paris
1910: Halley's comet returns
1910: U.S. population reaches 92 million; 13.5 million are foreign-born

502. PABLO PICASSO
Ma Jolie (Woman with Guitar). 1911–12. Oil on canvas, 39 3/8 x 25 3/4". Collection, The Museum of Modern Art, New York (Acquired through the Lillie P. Bliss Bequest). *Ma Jolie* (French for my pretty one) has a double meaning here. It refers both to the words in a popular song and to the name Picasso used for his new lover, Eva, who probably posed for this painting.

SYNTHETIC CUBISM

The upper portion of Picasso's *Still Life with Chair Caning* (fig. 503) bears the familiar fragmentation of Analytical Cubism (see p. 460). This arrangement of objects includes an oyster shell, lemon slices, a knife, pipe, and wineglass, while the stenciled *JOU,* for *Journal,* indicates the presence of a newspaper. These objects have been painted over chair caning. But this chair caning, which seems to be the most realistic aspect of the work, is itself an illusion, for it is in actu-

ality cheap printed oilcloth pasted onto the canvas. Even the frame dares us to consider new expectations of painting, for it is common, ordinary rope instead of a traditional frame.

Picasso's use of the collage medium (see below) is an extension of the questions first posed by Analytical Cubism. Now the issues are compounded, for the conceptualized transcription of reality into art demonstrated in the abstract still-life arrangement is joined to printed oilcloth that

503. PABLO PICASSO
Still Life with Chair Caning. 1911–12. Collage of oil and pasted oilcloth, simulating chair caning, on canvas, oval 10 5/8 x 13 3/4". Musée Picasso, Paris

504. PABLO PICASSO
Three Musicians. 1921. Oil on canvas, 79 x 87 3/4". Collection, The Museum of Modern Art, New York (Mrs. Simon Guggenheim Fund)

looks like yet another reality: chair caning. With Picasso's Cubist collage, we are exposed to the paradoxical realities of life and art; while we easily recognize the artificial composition of the still-life objects, the oilcloth disguises its reality behind the illusion of chair caning.

Still Life with Chair Caning ushers in a new phase of Cubism in which painted elements are combined with commonplace materials. The resulting works join traditional artistic media with materials previously considered outside the realm of art. This second phase of Cubism is known as Synthetic Cubism.

Soon the effects of the Synthetic Cubist collage were translated wholly into painting, as seen in Picasso's *Three Musicians* (fig. 504). Although some of the flat, patterned areas of this work appear to be collage materials, they are in actuality all painted. The abstract figures retain an objectivity which is clearly recognizable, while the reality of the picture plane is also emphasized. The tradition of the picture plane as an element through which we view an illusion of space has been overturned. Painting now asserts itself as a completely flat surface.

COLLAGE AND ASSEMBLAGE

Collage, from the French word *coller* (to glue), is used to designate works of art which incorporate such materials as pieces of newspaper, cloth, colored paper, and the like. With their Synthetic Cubist collages and assemblage sculptures, Picasso and Braque extended the range of materials accepted in art, while influencing later avant-garde movements, including Futurism, Dada, and Surrealism.

Assemblage has broader connotations than collage, although historically the term has been used to include collage. Assemblage usually involves a combination of actual three-dimensional objects, some of which are "found" objects from the household or the junkyard, into a coherent composition. Examples of assemblage include Duchamp's "ready-mades" (see p. 472).

THE INFLUENCE OF CUBISM

506. UMBERTO BOCCIONI
Unique Forms of Continuity in Space.
1913 (cast 1931). Bronze, height
43 7/8". Collection, The Museum of
Modern Art, New York (Acquired
through the Lillie P. Bliss Bequest)

Cubism was tremendously influential on developments in
early-twentieth-century art from
Paris to New York and Moscow.
The techniques of planar fragmentation, used in Cubism to
portray a conceptual vision, were
adapted to express different artistic philosophies. Marcel
Duchamp, for example, utilized
a complex sequence of fragmented planes to describe the
dynamic movement of a figure

descending a staircase (fig. 505).

In Italy the portrayal of the
dynamism of modern life was
the aim of a group of avant-garde
artists who called themselves
Futurists. Their task, as expressed
in a 1910 *Manifesto*, was to free
Italy from its past artistic traditions and thrust it forward into
the twentieth century. The Futurist artists also embraced political anarchy. Among other
defiant statements, the *Manifesto*

507. KASIMIR MALEVICH
Suprematist Composition: White on White. c. 1918. Oil on canvas, 31 1/4 x 31 1/4".
Collection, The Museum of Modern Art, New York

declared "THAT ALL SUBJECTS PREVIOUSLY USED MUST BE SWEPT ASIDE IN ORDER TO EXPRESS OUR WHIRLING LIFE OF STEEL, OF PRIDE, OF FEVER AND OF SPEED.

"THAT THE NAME OF 'MADMAN' WITH WHICH IT IS ATTEMPTED TO GAG ALL INNOVATORS SHOULD BE LOOKED UPON AS A TITLE OF HONOR.

"THAT UNIVERSAL DYNAMISM MUST BE RENDERED IN PAINTING AS A DYNAMIC SENSATION."

Futurist works in painting and sculpture were a response to the challenge established in their *Manifesto.* The intensity of speed suggested in Balla's *Speeding Automobile* (see fig. 470) meets the demand for "dynamic sensation," as does the implied stride of Boccioni's innovative *Unique Forms of Continuity in Space* (fig. 506). Forms that suggest both working, moving muscles and sweeping drapery folds are thrust outward into space in order to convey the determined energy of a quickly striding figure. The sculpture is dramatically different when seen from varied viewpoints. Boccioni wrote: "No one can any longer believe that an object ends where another begins. . . . We therefore . . . proclaim . . . the complete abolition of definite lines and closed sculpture. We break open the figure and enclose it in environment."

Included among the avant-garde in Russia was Kasimir Malevich, who developed a series of non-objective paintings. *Suprematist Composition: White on White* (fig. 507) reduces the formal elements of the painting to two squares of white that are separated only by the slightest value contrast. In the geometric and color purity of these works, Malevich set out to communicate pure uncorrupted emotion. He titled this new style Suprematism, writing: "The Suprematists have deliberately given up the objective representation of their surroundings in order to reach the summit of the true 'unmasked' art and from this vantage point to view life through the prism of pure artistic feeling" (*The Non-Objective World*).

GERMAN EXPRESSIONISM *(DER BLAUE REITER)*

508. WASSILY KANDINSKY
First Abstract Watercolor. c. 1913.
Watercolor and ink, 19 1/4 x 25".
Collection Mme Nina Kandinsky.
Kandinsky identified this as his
first non-objective watercolor,
dating this experiment to 1910, but
later scholars have suggested that
the work more probably dates to
c. 1913.

Vibrant passages of color and
line burst on the surface of Wassily Kandinsky's abstract watercolor (fig. 508). This ebullient
composition of colored shapes
and lines does not correspond to
any reality in nature; the painting can therefore be termed non-
objective. This important break-
through, which led to many later
developments in twentieth-century art, was accomplished by a
number of artists during the
second decade of the century.

Kandinsky had begun a ca-

reer as a law professor when, in
1896, he left Russia to study painting in Germany. His education
had included studies in art and
music, but the decision to become a professional artist was
made in 1895, when he viewed a
Moscow exhibition of Impressionist paintings. Particularly
impressed by the intense color of
one of Monet's *Haystack* paintings, Kandinsky wrote, "I had
the impression that here painting itself comes into the foreground; I wondered if it would

not be possible to go further in this direction." As Kandinsky traveled throughout Europe, he studied German Expressionism and Fauvism and, returning to Munich in 1908, he painted a series of landscapes which pulsate with color.

A chance occurrence assisted in clarifying Kandinsky's thoughts about non-objective painting: "It was the hour of approaching dusk. I was coming home with my box of paints after sketching, still dreaming and caught up in my thoughts about the work I had done, when suddenly I found myself face to face with an indescribably beautiful picture drenched with an inner glow. At first I hesitated, then I rushed toward this mysterious picture in which I could discern no visible subject, but which appeared to be completely made up of bright patches of color. Only then did I discover the key to the puzzle. It was one of my own paintings, standing on its side against the wall. . . . I knew for certain now that the depiction of objects in my paintings was not only unnecessary but indeed harmful."

The realization that painting could communicate an emotional content without recognizable subject matter was a catalyst in Kandinsky's thoughts about art and the expressive values of color. These issues occupied not just his paintings, but also his writings. In late 1911

Kandinsky published *Concerning the Spiritual in Art,* in which he asserted that the function of art was to release us from a "nightmare of materialism" by revealing an "internal truth" which awakens the human spirit. The key to this awakening was the "psychic effect" which colors could evoke: "Color is a power which directly influences the soul. Color is the keyboard, the eyes are the hammers, the soul is the piano with many strings. The artist is the hand which plays, touching one key or another, to cause vibrations in the soul."

In writing *Concerning the Spiritual in Art,* Kandinsky drew from many varied and rich sources, including Expressionism, Fauvism, and African and Oceanic art. Expressing a kinship with non-Western artists, Kandinsky wrote, "Like ourselves, these artists sought to express in their work only internal truths, renouncing in consequence all consideration of external form." The musical innovations of Arnold Schönberg added further inspiration. "[Schönberg's] music leads us into a realm where musical experience is a matter not of the ear but of the soul alone—and from this point begins the music of the future." Kandinsky believed that the emotional power of music could be paralleled by abstraction in painting.

In 1911 Kandinsky and other Expressionist artists working in Munich formed an artists group which they called *Der Blau Reiter (The Blue Rider;* the title was derived from a work by Kandinsky which depicted an abstract rider and horse unified by a single value of blue). *Der Blaue Reiter* was an association of artists who sought to communicate the spiritual values that lie behind the facade of appearances.

FANTASY

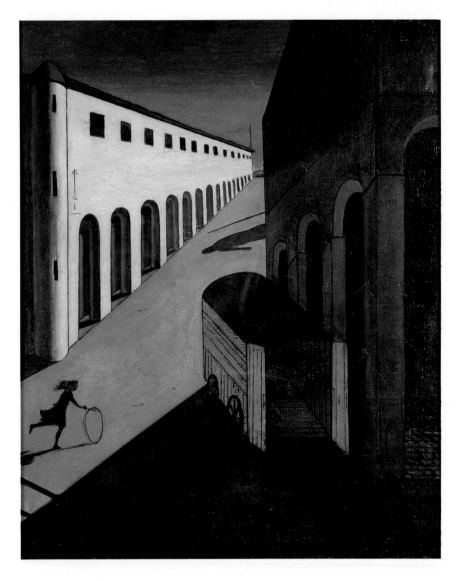

509. GIORGIO DE CHIRICO
The Melancholy and Mystery of a Street. 1914. Oil on canvas, 34 1/4 x 28 1/2". Private collection

are representational. The arcaded buildings, the wagon, and even the intense light are features that can be found in many an Italian piazza. In De Chirico's painting, however, stark *chiaroscuro* is joined with an exaggerated perspective to create an unexpectedly dramatic spatial illusion. The anxiety created by the convergence of diagonals is heightened by the iconography. The setting is void of life except for a young girl who innocently plays with a hoop. Her path will take her into the menacing emptiness of the piazza, where the shadow of a large statue falls, almost threateningly, across her path. De Chirico's manipulation of representational forms opens the world of the subconscious, the frightening exaggeration we often sense in dreams. De Chirico considered his paintings to be metaphysical, that is, they offered encounters with mysterious truths beyond our understanding. The juxtaposition of disassociated objects is intended to awaken the unconscious within us.

The Swiss artist Paul Klee usually worked on a small scale, but *Ad Parnassum* is one of his larger and most ambitious works (fig. 510). Klee set out to discover elemental symbols: here the pyramid suggests not only the

"Formerly we used to represent things visible on earth, things we either liked to look at or would have liked to see. Today we reveal the reality that is behind visible things, thus expressing the belief that the visible world is merely an isolated case in relation to the universe and that there are many more other, latent realities" (Paul Klee, 1920). The attempt to express visually a reality which supersedes that of the objective, physical world distin-

guishes the early-twentieth-century avant-garde movements of Fauvism, German Expressionism, and Cubism. Another approach to this problem is found with the artists of fantasy, painters who, questioning rationalist views, explored the expression of their personal, inner visions.

As its title hints, Giorgio de Chirico's *Melancholy and Mystery of a Street* opens to us a world that is disturbing and possibly even forbidding (fig. 509). The forms

510. PAUL KLEE
Ad Parnassum. 1932. Oil on canvas,
39 x 42". Kunstmuseum, Bern.
Klee's wife was a piano teacher,
and the title of this work may
derive from *Gradus ad Parnassum*
(*Steps to Parnassus*), a series of
piano exercises based on scales for
the beginning piano pupil.

DE CHIRICO, *The Melancholy and Mystery of a Street:* **1914**
1914: Panama Canal opens
1915: W. Somerset Maugham, *Of Human Bondage*
1915: D. W. Griffith film, *The Birth of a Nation*
1917: Carl Jung, *Psychology of the Unconscious*
1917: Bolshevik Revolution in Russia

mysteries of ancient Egypt but also, because of the title, Mount Parnassus near Delphi, which was sacred to the ancient Greeks as the home of the Muses, who inspired creative activities. The red circle that suggests the sun may refer to the role of the sun in world religions, as well as to the concept of gradual enlighten-ment. The division of the surface into thousands of tiny squares of pure color creates a precious and beautiful effect that suggests the shimmering nature of light as it illuminates a form. From a multi-tude of smaller forms, monumen-tal constructions can be created: from stone blocks come pyra-mids; from scales, symphonies. But ultimately the full expres-sive content of Klee's work be-comes a matter of individual perception and understanding. Klee believed that there were visual equivalents for spiritual states and, as so often in his work, the few simple forms of *Ad Par-nassum* suggest deep and elemen-tal mysteries.

CONSTANTIN BRANCUSI AND ALEXANDER ARCHIPENKO

"They are imbeciles who call my work abstract; that which they call abstract is the most realist, because what is real is not the exterior form but the idea, the essence of things" (Brancusi). Brancusi's concern with portraying the "essence of things," an artistic philosophy that he shared with other members of the European avant-garde, led to the abstraction evident in *The Newborn* (fig. 511). The particulars of a baby's head and facial features have been reduced to a primordial egg form with sweeping arcs uniting the forehead with the nose and gaping mouth.

Brancusi was a Romanian artist who took up residence in Paris at the age of twenty-eight, in 1904. By 1907 his talent and reputation had so developed that Rodin (see p. 416), who dominated French sculpture, invited Brancusi to work with him. Brancusi, who learned from Rodin's sculptural innovations, refused the aging master's offer with the observation, "Nothing grows under the shade of great trees." Working in a variety of traditional sculptural media, and often guided by a subjective synthesis of diverse traditions, including the simplified, abstract features of Romanian folk and African tribal sculpture, Brancusi reduced representational images to elemental forms.

We can follow Brancusi's pioneering journey through abstraction in a series of sculpted heads from 1908 through 1915. *Sleep*, from 1908 (fig. 512), displays representational facial features. Rodin's influence is felt in the

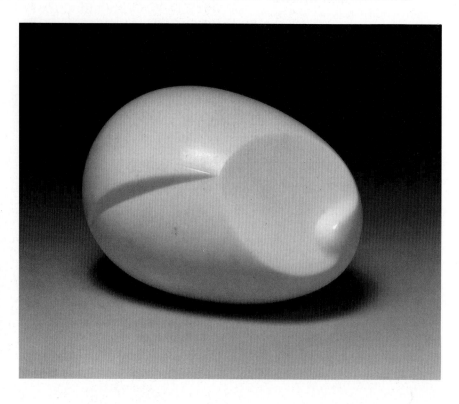

consciously unfinished forms of the work and in the manner in which the form of the head seems to evolve from the enveloping marble. Within two years the reduction away from representation had become apparent. The head of the *Sleeping Muse* (fig. 513) has been transformed by a union between the head and the primordial form of an egg. The particulars of the face have become geometric abstractions. By 1915 this transformation, aimed at uncovering an essence, was complete. *The Newborn*, with which we opened this discussion, communicates the essence of the cry of a new life.

Brancusi's evolution in abstract sculpture paralleled in time the explorations of Picasso and Braque in Cubism. Cubism in-

fluenced developments in sculpture as well as in painting. Archipenko's *Walking Woman* (fig. 514) displays the simplified planar abstraction which we associate with Cubism. Note how the dissected lower left leg resembles the forms of Duchamp's *Nude Descending a Staircase* (see fig. 505). What is novel, however, is Archipenko's transformation of the interpretation of mass in space. Archipenko has opened voids in the head and torso areas, where previous figural sculptures had always asserted the strongest concentrations of mass. In the innovative spirit of early-twentieth-century art, traditional interpretations of mass and space in sculpture were constantly and vigorously challenged.

BRANCUSI, *The Newborn:* **1915**

1912: Brancusi, *The Kiss*
1915: Albert Einstein develops the general theory of relativity
1915: First U.S. transcontinental telephone call
1916: John Dewey, *Democracy and Education*

511. CONSTANTIN BRANCUSI
Opposite: *The Newborn.* 1915.
Marble, height 5 5/8". Philadelphia
Museum of Art (Louise and Walter
Arensberg Collection)

512. CONSTANTIN BRANCUSI
Right: *Sleep.* 1908. Marble, height
10". National Gallery, Bucharest

513. CONSTANTIN BRANCUSI
Above: *Sleeping Muse.* 1909–10. Marble, height 11 1/2".
Hirschhorn Museum and Sculpture Garden,
Smithsonian Institution, Washington, D.C.

514. ALEXANDER ARCHIPENKO
Right: *Walking Woman.* 1912. Bronze, height 26 3/8".
Collection Mme Alexander Archipenko

DADA

Marcel Duchamp was an artist of unprecedented and unsettling works which still seem shocking to us today, although they were done over seventy years ago (see fig. 515). On the pedestals in the gallery, where we expect to find sculpture, we see a manufactured *Bottle Rack*, a common object used at the time for drying bottles. In 1914 Duchamp felt that he could confer an artistic dignity on a bottle rack by designating it a work of art. Another pedestal supports an upended porcelain urinal, officially titled *Fountain*. Duchamp signed the urinal "R. Mutt," a pun on the name of the company which manufactured it, the Mott Works Company. On the wall behind is a reproduction of Leonardo's *"Mona Lisa"* (see fig. 282), which Duchamp

defaced by adding a moustache, goatee, and, at the bottom, the letters L.H.O.O.Q., which suggest the French phrase, "She has a hot ass." If all of this appears absurd to you, and it certainly did to critics and the public in the early twentieth century, then you are beginning to understand the function of these objects as works of art. Marcel Duchamp, a Parisian avant-garde artist who came to New York in 1915, asserted that "found objects" or "ready-mades" could be works of art. Although these were simply mass-produced objects, Duchamp felt that by his saying they were art and by exhibiting them within a gallery, they had entered into the realm of art.

Duchamp never officially declared himself a Dadaist (see

515. MARCEL DUCHAMP
Bottle Rack, Fountain, and other works; reproductions of works originally created between 1914 and 1919. Installation, Moderna Museet, Stockholm

below), but his works from 1913 onward, especially the "ready-mades," are formally and spiritually akin to those produced by Dada artists. As an artistic, musical, and literary movement, Dada was officially consecrated in 1916 at the Cabaret Voltaire in Zurich. Dada bred confusion, and even the origin of the title remains, appropriately, a matter of uncertainty: two of Dada's founders, writers Richard Huelsenbeck and Hugo Ball, state that the word, which is French for hobby-horse, was discovered by chance

DUCHAMP, *Fountain:* 1917
1917: U.S. enters World War I
1917: Sigmund Freud, *Introduction to Psychoanalysis*
1918: World War I ends; about 8.5 million have been killed;
21 million wounded
1920: In U.S., urban population first exceeds rural population
1921: U.S. population reaches 107 million

in a German-French dictionary, but another founder, the German painter Hans Richter, holds that it was simply the Slavonic word for "yes," and that "da, da" meant only "yes, yes."

Other theories as to the origin of the term are also advanced, but what defined Dada was a nihilistic mocking of traditional values in the arts and, by extension, Western society as a whole. This artistic anarchy grew from a profound psychological disgust. Dada glorified the irrational. The Swiss artist Jean Arp, for example, created collages by dropping torn pieces of paper randomly onto a paper surface and then gluing them into place (fig. 516). These works were composed according to chance. In the words of Arp: "Dada aimed to destroy the reasonable deceptions of man and recover the natural and unreasonable order. Dada wanted to replace the logical nonsense of men of today by the illogically senseless. That is why we pounded with all our might on the big drum of Dada and trumpeted the praises of unreason. . . . Dada is senseless like nature."

The senselessness and nihilism of Dada, however absurd, were born from an even greater absurdity, World War I. Dada was an art of social protest, a protest against the senseless slaughter and destruction of life and meaning. "We searched for an elemen-

tary art that would, we thought, save mankind from the furious madness of these times" (Jean Arp).

516. JEAN (HANS) ARP
Collage with Squares Arranged According to the Laws of Chance. 1916–17. Torn and pasted paper, 19 1/8 x 13 5/8". Collection, The Museum of Modern Art, New York (Purchase)

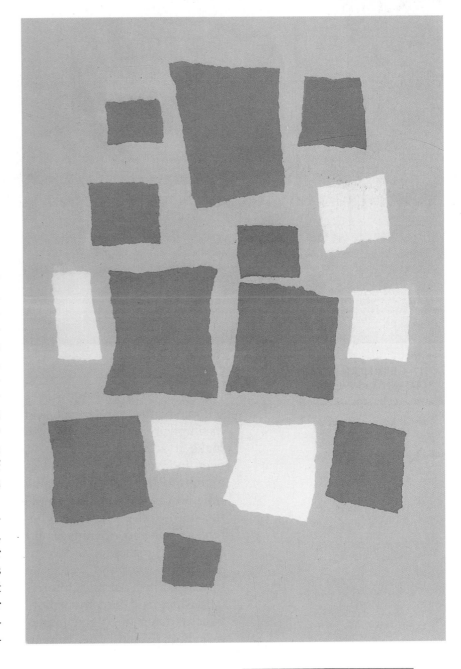

DE STIJL AND THE BAUHAUS

517. GERRIT RIETVELD
Schröder House, Utrecht,
The Netherlands. 1923–24

Rietveld's Schröder House is without historical reference, and its simplicity and severity of form make it seem absolutely new, even today: it offers a timeless modernity (fig. 517). At the same time, however, it is neither simple nor simplistic. The contrasts between wall and opening, solid and void, horizontal and vertical, aggressive and recessive forms establish complex interrelationships, and the composition, which is determinedly asymmetric in both two and three dimen-

sions, is sharpened and enhanced by the precision with which the forms are defined. On both exterior and interior, openness integrates the forms of the house with the surrounding space. The Schröder House is a powerful and convincing example of the "equilibrium of equivalent relationships" that was one of the aesthetic goals of the De Stijl movement.

The De Stijl (The Style) movement was founded in 1917 in Amsterdam by several Dutch

RIETVELD, Schröder House: 1923–24

1922: Oswald Spengler, *The Decline of the West*
1922: James Joyce, *Ulysses*
1924: Lenin dies
1924: George Gershwin, *Rhapsody in Blue*
1924: Gandhi fasts for 21 days, protesting the violent conflict between Hindus and Moslems in India
1925: Hitler publishes *Mein Kampf*
1925: F. Scott Fitzgerald, *The Great Gatsby*
1927: Charles Lindbergh becomes the first person to fly the Atlantic alone

518. WALTER GROPIUS
Workshop wing, Bauhaus, Dessau, East Germany. 1925–26. The Bauhaus was an influential modern school of architecture and design.

artists who felt a mission to carry abstraction to what they termed "its ultimate goal." The group was motivated in part by the tragic events of World War I and was inspired by such modern philosophical movements as Theosophical Mysticism and Neopositivism. Their utopian aspirations are revealed in the name, which suggests that this is the ultimate style, the perfect style that, mass-produced, could satisfy all humanity for the rest of the world's history. This search to find a visual equivalent for spiritual and philosophical purity led to the development of a completely new and abstract style in architecture, painting, sculpture, and the decorative arts. Their motivation was ethical, for they felt that their perfectly balanced and serene art could carry the qualities of harmony and purity into the very soul and being of the viewer.

519. WALTER GROPIUS
Student dormitory room, Bauhaus

Their ultimate goal was to bring about world understanding, unity, and peace. They avoided individualism and subjectivity, arguing that these concepts had led the world into war: "The old tends to the individual. The new tends to the universal. The struggle between the individual and the universal is revealed in both the world war and contemporary art." They wanted to create an art that was universal and comprehendible to all humanity, regardless of nationality or creed. "Man adheres only to what is universal," wrote Piet Mondrian, one of the movement's founders, in 1919.

These profound goals reached fulfillment in a series of works produced by Mondrian between the two world wars (see fig. 5). In these simple abstractions, which are characterized by a studied balance between forms and colors, Mondrian hoped to accomplish, in his words, an "equilibrium of opposites." The universality of this goal, with its search for worldwide peace, should be related to other modern philosophies and artistic philosophies—such as the Bauhaus (see below)—as well as to the contemporary founding of the World Court and the League of Nations, which led eventually to the establishment of the first worldwide governmental body, the United Nations, after World War II.

Walter Gropius's philosophy on the unity of the arts guided his design for the new home for the Bauhaus at Dessau (fig. 518). The structure at Dessau exemplified the modernist aesthetic.

A complex of classrooms, library, and offices is externally unified by planes of reinforced concrete walls and vast expanses of windows. A rectilinear design, with verticals and horizontals meeting at right angles, governs the plan and determines the exterior articulation. The plain, unornamented surfaces used throughout the building contribute to its modern, clean appearance. The interior design of the classrooms and even the desks and chairs respond to the design aesthetic which governs the entire structure. Gropius's own office had furniture of his design and a rug, wall hanging, and lighting created in the Bauhaus workshops. The student dormitory room illustrated here reveals how strictly the Bauhaus aesthetic could govern an environment (fig. 519). This is what Gropius meant by the "complete building" when, in 1919, he wrote: "The ultimate aim of all visual arts is the complete building! . . . Today the arts exist in isolation, from which they can be rescued only through the conscious, cooperative effort of all craftsmen. . . . Architects, sculptors, painters, we must all return to the crafts! For art is not a 'profession.' There is no essential difference between the artist and the craftsman."

Gropius, a German architect and industrial designer, played a leading role in founding the Bauhaus in 1919 at Weimar. The name Bauhaus, chosen by Gropius, is derived from the *bauhütte*, the medieval German builders' lodge, which housed the masters and craftspeople who built

the great cathedrals of the Late Middle Ages. The recent Arts and Crafts Movement and Art Nouveau's unity of design had reinforced Gropius's belief in the total integration of the arts. Unlike those late-nineteenth-century movements, however, the Bauhaus philosophy of design was guided by the technology and materials of industrial production.

The design of the building at Dessau, where the Bauhaus relocated in 1924, was itself inspired by the rectilinear massing of Frank Lloyd Wright's Prairie style designs (see p. 458) and by the geometric planarity of De Stijl architecture. The resulting building, with its clean, precise, and almost mechanistically tuned appearance, does not display a regional or national identity. The Bauhaus style has reduced the essence of design to a visual common denominator. It promised, with the assistance of modern technology, a future in which a total design aesthetic would not be restricted by cultural or national boundaries. Reacting to the horror of World War I, the Bauhaus offered a utopian vision where art and architecture would assist in the realization of our common human heritage.

In 1933 Adolf Hitler, then chancellor of Germany, manifesting the intolerance which totalitarian regimes commonly share toward the avant-garde, ordered the Bauhaus closed. Like apostles to foreign lands, those who had worked at the Bauhaus carried its philosophy throughout Europe and to America.

DIEGO RIVERA AND MEXICAN MURAL PAINTING

"Only the work of art itself can raise the standard of taste. Art has always been employed by the different social classes who hold the balance of power as one instrument of domination— hence, as a political instrument. One can analyze epoch after epoch—from the stone age to our own day—and see that there is no form of art which does not also play an essential political role. . . . What is it then that we really need? An art extremely pure, precise, profoundly human, and clarified as to its purpose" (Diego Rivera, 1929).

These mural paintings by Diego Rivera (figs. 520, 521) are on the third floor of an open courtyard in the Ministry of Education building in Mexico City. They are but two of one hundred twenty-four which the artist painted throughout the decade of the 1920s. The scenes present a direct and didactic contrast between the debauchery of the rich, which includes excessive drinking and hoarding money, and the quiet, peaceful sleep of the poor peasants after an honest day's work. A few of the peasants remain awake into the night, educating themselves by lamplight. In the left background of *Night of the Poor*, the Marxist content of the mural is reinforced as bourgeois onlookers disdainfully watch, while in *Night of the Rich* revolutionary soldiers observe the decadent behavior of the wealthy ruling class.

These scenes, and indeed the entire cycle of paintings, are unyielding expressions of class struggle. They communicate the purposes and promises of the Mexican Revolution, which began in 1910 with a dramatic demand for economic and social reform. A decade of internal civil strife and bloodshed followed, and only during the twenties and

520. DIEGO RIVERA
Night of the Rich. 1923–28. Fresco.
Ministry of Education, Mexico City

521. DIEGO RIVERA

Night of the Poor. 1923–28. Fresco. Ministry of Education, Mexico City. These frescoes are from the final cycle of paintings, begun by Rivera in 1927, for the Ministry of Education. The images in this cycle are loosely related to the words of two revolutionary songs (*corridos*), which appear on the painted festoons. In part, one of the *corridos* reads: "The clock strikes one, two, and the rich keep awake thinking what to do with their money so that it keeps multiplying. It's only seven o'clock at night and the poor have gone to rest. They sleep very peacefully because they are tired. Blessed the tree that yields fruit, but very ripe fruit. Yes, gentlemen, it is worth more than all the hard dollars."

thirties would some of the aims of the 1910 revolution be realized. Rivera's paintings propagandize the causes and goals of the continuing revolution.

The impact of Rivera's murals is direct and immediately comprehendible, for here the artist has eschewed modernist abstraction in favor of an easily understood representational form and content. Rivera, who had traveled in Europe, returned home in 1921 to join with other Mexican artists in creating a unique and forceful style which, while borrowing elements from Expressionism and Cubism, was also rooted in the bold, severe forms of native Indian art. In the hands of the Mexican muralists, art became a vehicle to promote social awareness; in Rivera's words, "Mural painting must help in man's struggle to become a human being, and for that purpose it must live wherever it can; no place is bad for it, so long as it is permitted to fulfill its primary functions of nutrition and enlightenment."

RIVERA, *Night of the Rich*: 1923–28
1925: Alan Locke, *The New Negro*
1926: A. A. Milne, *Winnie the Pooh*
1929: The word apartheid is first used

EARLY MODERN PAINTING IN AMERICA

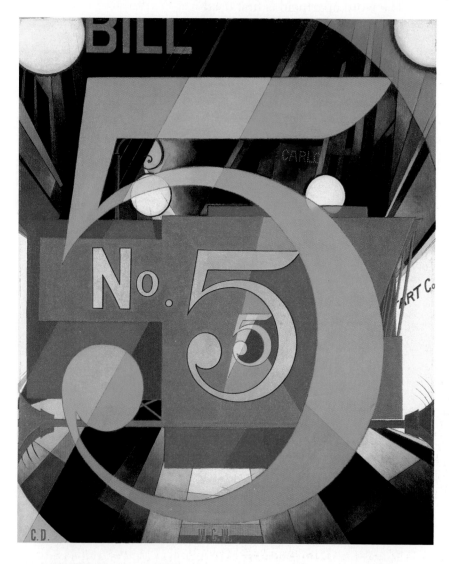

522. CHARLES DEMUTH
I Saw the Figure 5 in Gold. 1928. Oil on composition board, 36 x 29 3/4". The Metropolitan Museum of Art, New York (The Alfred Stieglitz Collection, 1949)

Among the rain
and lights
I saw the figure 5
in gold
on a red
fire truck
moving
tense
unheeded
to gong clangs
siren howls
and wheels rumbling
through the dark city
(William Carlos Williams,
The Great Figure).

Demuth's painting (fig. 522), inspired by this poem by the distinguished American poet William Carlos Williams, is intended as a modern portrait of the poet; "W.C.W.," "Carlos," and the nickname "Bill" appear in the painting. This is one of Demuth's "poster portraits," a series inspired by the stark forms and lettering of advertising billboards. The vibrant 5 is repeated, just as the accompanying "gong clangs" and "siren howls" would have echoed off the hard surfaces of the city streets. The blocky red forms refer to the fire truck, the white circles suggest the streetlights, and the quickly pulsating forms of the composition as a whole visually suggest the jerky rhythm of the poem. The style, with its sharp edges and flat, unmodeled forms, developed in the 1920s in America and is known as Precisionism.

In the first four decades of the twentieth century, the influence of modern European art played a significant role in the development of modernism in America, aided by exhibitions organized by Alfred Steiglitz at Gallery "291" (see p. 482). At the same time, however, the Americans maintained an independent stance and were less willing to give up subject matter than were their European counterparts. Instead, they searched for contemporary American subjects and evolved styles adapted from one or more twentieth-century European styles. Until 1940 American modernism was conservative by European standards.

The expressive potential of flat, unmodeled forms in a narrative context was explored by Jacob Lawrence, who gained national prominence in the 1940s. Lawrence's *Migration of the Negro* series joined historical research with intensely personal memories of the stories he had heard as a youth in Harlem (see

DEMUTH, *I Saw the Figure 5 in Gold:* **1928**
1927: *The Jazz Singer,* first successful full-length motion picture
1928: Penicillin is discovered to have antibacterial properties
1928: Joseph Stalin's first five-year plan
1928: D. H. Lawrence's *Lady Chatterley's Lover* denied publication in England
1929: Stock market crash in America; beginning of the Great Depression

fig. 523). As black people migrated North in search of dignity and opportunity, they were frequently met with cruel suspicion and violence. The sharp, piercing forms and harsh colors of Lawrence's painting give this representation of a race riot a terrifying and threatening immediacy. During the 1930s and 1940s in America, a number of artists used their work as a vehicle for protest, demonstrating the often brutal reality of social conditions. Lawrence's painting is aimed at our social conscience.

523. JACOB LAWRENCE
One of the Largest Race Riots Occurred in East St. Louis (panel 52 from *The Migration of the Negro*). 1940–41. Tempera on composition board, 12 x 18". Collection, The Museum of Modern Art, New York (Gift of Mrs. David M. Levy). The sixty panels of Lawrence's *Migration of the Negro* series tell how Southern blacks migrated to Northern cities in the early twentieth century because of violent discrimination and lynchings in the South.

PHOTOGRAPHY

524. ALFRED STIEGLITZ
Equivalent. 1930. Chloride print. The Art Institute of Chicago (The Alfred Stieglitz Collection)

Equivalent by Alfred Stieglitz (fig. 524) is an evocative image; the moon and its light are diffused through clouds in the upper right, while below, separated by the diagonal thrust of a cloud, an impenetrable darkness enters the composition. The photograph was produced without staging or significant darkroom manipulation, but the emphasis is less on the representational quality of the image than on abstract patterns of light and dark to create a somber, pensive mood.

When Stieglitz began his *Equivalent* series in 1922, he was already established as one of the most significant artists of the

early twentieth century. In 1902 he had broken away from the conservative posture of traditional photography to form the Photo-Secession Group. One year later he founded *Camera Work*, a quarterly publication which stressed, with numerous illustrations, an ever-widening range of photographic innovation.

In 1905 Stieglitz founded an art gallery at 291 Fifth Avenue in New York City. "291," as the gallery was known, brought the art of the European avant-garde to the United States. Exhibitions included works by Cézanne, Brancusi, and Picasso and such American artists as Charles

Demuth and Georgia O'Keeffe. In 1917 Stieglitz began to decrease his gallery and publication involvements to devote fuller attention to photography. Stieglitz's work and vision assisted in establishing photography as an independent artistic medium.

An important advance in photography in the 1920s was the development of the hand-held, lightweight, 35 mm roll-film camera. No longer burdened by bulky equipment, the photographer now had a new freedom of mobility. One artist who took full advantage of this freedom was André Kertész. In 1933

1930: Sinclair Lewis wins Nobel Prize for literature for *Babbitt*
1930: First analog computer is placed in operation
1930: World population nears 2 billion

525. ANDRÉ KERTÉSZ
Distortion No. 4. 1933. Gelatin silver print. Estate of Kertész. Kertész's *Distortion* photographs, commissioned by a French magazine in 1933, were not published until 1976.

527. HENRI CARTIER-BRESSON
Sunday on the Banks of the Marne. l938. Gelatin silver print

526. MARGARET BOURKE-WHITE
Fort Peck Dam, photograph for the cover of the first issue of *Life* magazine, November 23, 1936. Bourke-White was one of the original staff photographers for *Life* magazine. During World War II she became the first woman photographer to work with the U. S. armed forces.

Kertész, a leading Hungarian photojournalist working in France, created a series of photographs with figurative distortion reminiscent of expressionist tendencies (see fig. 525) and Surrealism. Kertész achieved these effects by photographing models reflected in "fun house" mirrors with varied surfaces.

Margaret Bourke-White's cover story for the first issue of *Life* magazine was a photo essay about a dam being constructed at Fort Peck, Montana. Her photographs revealed both the strength and promise of industrial development, as is evident in her powerfully abstract compositions of the steel-and-concrete structure, and the dynamics of the lives of the men and women who were bringing the dam into existence (see fig. 526).

The French photographer Henri Cartier-Bresson sought to communicate in his work what he termed "the decisive moment" in an image where overt activity uncovered a deeper psychological understanding. In *Sunday on the Banks of the Marne* (fig. 527), Cartier-Bresson has captured, in a summary manner, the activity of a picnic—wine is being poured and food eaten. From our viewpoint we have joined the picnickers for lunch, but we can also observe, with some wit, how their corpulent bodies contrast with the sleek design of the boat. Cartier-Bresson believed that a photograph should seize both the scene in front of the eye and that which the eye sees as it looks inward, into the self of the photographer.

SURREALISM

In the hallucinatory world before our eyes (fig. 528), watches—sturdy, metallic timekeepers—grow limp and decay like organic refuse; one attracts a fly, ants converge on another. One watch has melted over a biomorphic form that bears a fantastically conceived profile of the artist. A smooth, satiny beach gives on to a limitless expanse of mirror-smooth water abutted by cliffs. Within this landscape of stillness, the limp watches suggest the inevitable decay of the passing of time.

Dali's painting succeeds in conveying its subconscious, dreamlike vision by the uncanny juxtaposition and fantastic manipulation of representational objects. This communication of the subconscious realm introduces us to Surrealism, a literary and artistic avant-garde movement which began in Europe in the early 1920s. The roots of Surrealism grew from the metaphysical paintings of De Chirico and the found-object constructions and collages of Dada (see pp. 468 and 472). Although it

eludes an exact interpretation, Dali's fantasy conveys a frightening psychological oppression.

Surrealism was inexorably bound with the psychoanalytic theories of Sigmund Freud. André Breton, the French writer who authored the first *Surrealist*

528. SALVADOR DALI
The Persistence of Memory. 1931. Oil on canvas, 9 1/2 x 13". Collection, The Museum of Modern Art, New York (Given anonymously)

DALI, *The Persistence of Memory:* **1931**
1931: U.S. population reaches 124 million
1931: Pearl S. Buck, *The Good Earth*
1931: Al "Scarface" Capone jailed for tax evasion
1932: Amelia Earhart becomes the first woman to fly solo across the Atlantic Ocean
1933: Hitler becomes chancellor of Germany
1933: Franklin D. Roosevelt is inaugurated as president

Manifesto in 1924, acknowledged Freud's revolutionary discoveries when, in defining Surrealism, he wrote: "SURREALISM, n. Pure psychic automatism, by which it is intended to express verbally, in writing, or by any other means the real process of thought. Thought's dictation, in the absence of all control exercised by the reason and outside all aesthetic or moral preoccupations." The Surrealist translation of the unconscious into visual form was realized, in one style, in the figurative works of Dali and René Magritte, where representational or fantastically conceived forms are juxtaposed within a spatial illusion.

The abstraction of André Masson's *Battle of Fishes* (fig. 529) is the result of automatism, a concept which relates to Freud's use of "free association" to divulge the subconscious. Breton used the word automatism in his definition of Surrealism, and in describing the process for writing an automatist Surrealist composition, Breton suggested that you should "write quickly without any previously chosen subject, quickly enough not to dwell on, and not to be tempted to read over, what you have written." This process of "automatic" writing was viewed as a revelation of the subconscious. In art, lines or colors were quick-

529. ANDRÉ MASSON
Battle of Fishes. 1926. Sand, gesso, oil, pencil, and charcoal on canvas, 14 1/4 x 28 3/4". Collection, The Museum of Modern Art, New York (Purchase)

ly set down on a surface, without reference to a preconceived theme. The conscious mind would then associate these nonobjective marks with objective forms. In Masson's work, a ferocious battle among fishes has evolved, exhibiting his intense anxieties about the brutality of nature, feelings which were born of the severe physical and mental wounds he received in World War I.

PABLO PICASSO, *GUERNICA*

Despite the perplexity of highly abstract shapes, which owe a formal debt to Synthetic Cubism, the *Guernica* mural, inspired by the bombing of an innocent Spanish town during the civil war, achieves an immediate impact (fig. 530). An architectonically stable composition underlies the surface tumult, for the verticality of the two side figures, the woman with upraised arms to the right and the woman cradling the dead child on the left, acts to secure the central group, which is resolved in the shape of a triangle. This simplified geometric order imparts an underlying strength to the composition.

The restriction of the color palette to black, white, and values of gray, and the newsprint-like lines across the body of the horse, remind us of the reporting of disastrous events in newspapers. It was by reading such reports that Picasso learned of the disaster at Guernica. Writing

later, the American painter Ad Reinhardt considered the *Guernica* a "design that diagrams our whole present dark age," and of the limited color range Picasso used, Reinhardt stated, "The dead have no color."

The artist refused to elaborate on the particular intentions he invested in each figure, preferring to encourage the viewer to understand the work on an emotional and intuitive level. On the right and left sides of the composition two women, shrieking in anguish with eyes transformed to the shape of tears, look toward the heavens, source of their pain and death. The left figure holding a dead child adapts the *Pietà* theme to this nightmare (see p. 259) while the woman to the right cries from the flames which have engulfed her house. Below her, another woman drags her mangled leg and, with arms outstretched, pleads for help and understanding. Above, an oil lamp, reminis-

530. PABLO PICASSO
Guernica. May 1–June 4, 1937. Oil on canvas, 11' 6" x 25' 8". The Prado, Madrid. Picasso placed the painting on extended loan to the Museum of Modern Art in New York for many years, stipulating that it be given to Spain and her people only when democracy was restored. The painting was returned to Spain in 1981.

cent of the light held by allegorical figures of Truth and Liberty, is thrust into the chaos. This light, however, is overwhelmed by the harsh radiance from the bare electric bulb, added to the composition only in the final stages of painting (see fig. 531). Previously this area had represented the sun or an eye. The change to the electric light is most likely an allusion to technology, which, during the bombing of Guernica, was unleashed as a malevolent and destructive force.

In the central group, a horse has been lanced; its head is twisted back and the pointed tongue becomes a silent scream of pain and accusation. While the horse may symbolize the suffering of Spain, it also expresses the totality of a conflict that involves all of nature. The bull suggests brute power, perhaps in reference to Franco and Fascism (see below). Below the horse are the dismembered remains of a fallen soldier. His hand, while still clutching a broken sword, also clings to a delicate flower, the only promise of hope in this image of suffering and death.

The brutal Spanish Civil War (1936–39) was the result of conflicting political ideologies and of internal tensions that were centuries old. In 1931 the Bourbon monarchy that had ruled Spain since 1700 was replaced by a republican government that promised social and economic reform, including the redistribution of land and the secularization of certain governmental functions controlled by the church. Such reforms, which were aimed at countering the political power of wealthy landowners and the clergy, provoked the formation of conservative alliances. During the increasing civil disorder after the elections of 1936 (won by the republicans), General Francisco Franco, claiming allegiance to his nation rather than to any political group, led an insurrection which immersed Spain in civil war. Nazi Germany and Fascist Italy aided Franco, while the U.S.S.R. assisted the leftist coalition, which included the Communists. The major Western democracies maintained an official position of neutrality, but many individuals supported the republican cause as the cruel reality of Franco's oppression became apparent.

PICASSO, *Guernica:* 1937

1937: Jean-Paul Sartre, *La Nausée*
1939: John Steinbeck, *The Grapes of Wrath*
1940: World population reaches 2.3 billion, with 500 million in China

531. PABLO PICASSO

Guernica. Photograph of the painting on May 11, 1937, by Dora Maar. This is the first of seven photographs made of the work in progress. Many of the main themes are already established, but virtually all will be dramatically reworked. Note that at this early point defiance on the part of the dead warrior is expressed by his upraised arm and fist.

After three years and the loss of hundreds of thousands of lives, Franco established an authoritarian rule which continued until his death in 1975.

In January 1937, in the midst of the civil war, the republican government commissioned Picasso, who was living and working in France, to paint a mural for the Spanish Pavilion at the World's Fair scheduled to open in Paris that year. Picasso had yet to settle upon an exact theme when news of the events of April 26 reached him. On that day, Franco had used his Nazi allies to conduct the first "total" air raid. In what seems to have been an experiment in saturation bombing, the historic city of Guernica, a town of no military significance, was bombarded for more than three hours. When Picasso learned of the bombing, he started to paint a work which would be an invective against both the particular event and the senseless brutality of conflict. Picasso, whose republican sympathies had already been manifested in satirical etchings called the *Dream and Lie of Franco,* wrote: "In the panel on which I am working which I shall call *Guernica,* and in all my recent works of art, I clearly express my abhorrence of the military caste which has sunk Spain into an ocean of pain and death." The story is told that while viewing a photograph of *Guernica,* a Nazi official queried Picasso, "So it was you who did this?" The reply came sharply, "No, you did!"

SCULPTURE TO 1945

Moore's *Recumbent Figure* is immediately recognizable as a reclining female figure—one of the great traditional themes that have inspired Western artists (fig. 532). Like its distinguished antecedents, it suggests the voluptuous forms of the female figure. While the positions of the head and breasts are evident and the figure seems propped up on one elbow, the torso below the breasts is an open cavity, and the other forms suggest only hips, a knee, and legs, without informing us of the exact pose. The rugged and simple forms also suggest the hills and gullies of a landscape. The sculpture interrelates with its environment through the powerful masses and unexpected openings that surround and mold space. Moore has written that "sculpture in air is possible, where the stone contains only the hole, which is the intended and considered form."

The abstract forms, however, are interrelated in a manner that suggests the organic qualities of a living, breathing figure with a

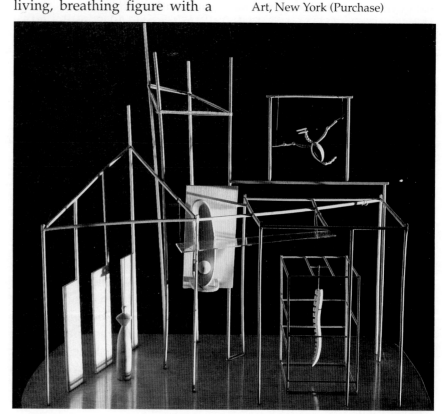

1937: First photocopies made
1938: Hindemith, *Mathis der Maler*
1939: Pocket Books publishes first paperback books in America
1939: Scientists split the atom
1939: War in Europe again
1941: Japanese bombing of Pearl Harbor

potential for movement. Moore never denies the dignity and beauty of the human body, and many of his figures are heroic in scale and in content.

During the 1930s and 1940s sculptors' interest in abstraction took a number of forms. The possibility of sculpture composed of thin, almost weightless forms, for example, is demonstrated by Giacometti in *The Palace at 4 A.M.* (fig. 533), an example of Surrealist sculpture. The palace enclosure is defined by slender forms that outline the shape and space. In haunting isolation within this airy structure are a number of evocative forms: an armless woman in a long gown, a skeleton-like bird, a spinal column enclosed within a box, three repeated rectangular forms, and a highly abstract form against a vertical slab that represents, according to the sculptor himself, a self-portrait. The standing woman was identified by Giacometti as his own mother, "just as she appears in my earliest memories." The spinal column stands for a woman with whom Giacometti had a relationship and the pterodactylian skeleton represents the bird which sang at 4 A.M. on "the very night before the morning in which our life together collapsed." Such personal revelations become more and more common in modern art. While they elucidate the origins of Giacometti's work, the enigma which the sculpture expresses is

more universal. The thinness of his forms and the fragility of the materials create a mood of secretive mystery and hesitant uncertainty that is heightened by the juxtaposition of objects. The artist has both revealed and hidden his feelings. This loneliness and isolation later became a constant motif in Giacometti's art.

Mobile is the term, invented by the artist Marcel Duchamp, for a new type of sculpture shown at an exhibition in 1932 by the American artist Alexander Calder. Calder's earliest mobiles were moved by hand cranks or motors, but by 1932 he had evolved the lightweight, delicately balanced, suspended sculptures, moved by air currents, that have spawned so many popular variations. While

534. ALEXANDER CALDER
Lobster Trap and Fish Tail. 1939. Mobile of steel wire and sheet aluminum, 8' 6" x 9' 6". Collection The Museum of Modern Art, New York (Commissioned by the Advisory Committee for the stairwell of the Museum). Calder received his earliest training as an engineer.

most of Calder's mobiles are completely abstract, the title of the present example suggests that the graceful movements of the curvilinear forms are a reference to swimming fish (fig. 534). In Calder's mobiles the intimate relationship between form and space seen in earlier sculpture attains a new complexity as air currents move the forms slowly through space to create ever new compositions.

INTERNATIONAL-STYLE ARCHITECTURE

535. PHILIP JOHNSON
Glass House, New Canaan, Connecticut. 1949. The Glass House, the architect's own home, is secluded on a large estate, and privacy is not a problem. A brick cylinder placed asymmetrically provides the fireplace and the enclosure necessary for the bathroom and mechanical equipment. A counter forms the kitchen area, and a freestanding block of closets provides storage space and gives the bedroom privacy.

Philip Johnson's Glass House (fig. 535), a satisfying combination of pure geometric form, subtle proportional relationships, and elegant materials, is an outstanding example of the modern architectural movement known as the International Style. This style, named by Philip Johnson in 1932 in the context of an architectural exhibition held at the Museum of Modern Art in New York, is based on the refined glass box. It was expressed as early as the 1920s in works by the German architect Mies van der Rohe, who later became the director of the Bauhaus (see p.

477). Mies emigrated to America in 1937, becoming a citizen in 1944. The International Style only came to full fruition after World War II, when Mies was commissioned to create a number of works, including skyscrapers in Chicago and New York and an entire campus for the Illinois Institute of Technology in Chicago. These popularized the style and led to its adaptation throughout the Western world. By the 1960s virtually every Western capital had many metal and glass skyscrapers.

Even while it was under construction, the Seagram Building

was recognized as an especially elegant and impressive modern structure (fig. 536). Mies's choice of materials reveals his goals of harmony and elegance, for the exposed structural I-beams are composed of bronze which exactly matches the amber-tinted glass. The building is tall and wide when seen from the front, but its relative thinness gives it a soaring refinement. The proportions of the design are based on a simple modular system much like the satisfying Early Renaissance architecture of Brunelleschi. The open lower stories, where there is a bank of eleva-

JOHNSON, Glass House: 1949
1945: World War II ends; almost 55 million people have died
1949: U.S. minimum wage raised from 40 to 75 cents an hour
1949: George Orwell, *1984*
1950: World population exceeds 2.5 billion

tors and a small glassed lobby, lighten the structure and help establish the proportional integrity of the whole. The building in every way reflects Mies's personal motto, "Less is more." Because it occupies less than one-half of the site, the building does not have to conform to the restrictions of the set-back law, which explains the staggered rooflines of so many Manhattan buildings. The structure is placed on a large plaza that sets it off as a gigantic sculptural form.

The glass box represents a pure ideological statement without historical precedent or references, but in its materials it is a product of the machine culture. Its origins lie in mass production, prefabrication, and the glorification of the precision of the machine. Even more importantly, it shares in the utopian ideals that had inspired De Stijl (see p. 474), one of its sources; as pure architecture, expressing the Platonic ideal with thoroughly modern materials, it shares in the idealism of much twentieth-century thought.

Despite the purist, reductive beauty of Johnson's Glass House and Mies's Seagram Building, the International Style quickly reached a dead end. The glass box is an impersonal object, and as cities all over the world became crowded with such buildings, many people felt that their environment had become a cold and sterile place in which to live and work. Because the emphasis is on purity of design at the expense of function, such buildings, all of which look similar, demonstrate little interest in the needs of the client or of the people who work in them. In their modern purity they ignore the subtle relationships to site, climate, or local architectural tradition that were crucial for earlier masterpieces of architecture.

536. MIES VAN DER ROHE
Seagram Building, New York. 1956–58. The International Style glass-box skyscraper became popular with corporate America because it projected a modern, up-to-date image for the business it housed. Few buildings in this style, however, have the sophisticated elegance of the Seagram Building, Mies's masterpiece. Philip Johnson, who assisted Mies in the design of the building, was largely responsible for the creation of the interior spaces.

ABSTRACT EXPRESSIONISM

"My painting does not come from the easel. I hardly ever stretch my canvas before painting. I prefer to tack the unstretched canvas to the hard wall or the floor. I need the resistance of a hard surface. On the floor I am more at ease. I feel nearer, more a part of the painting, since this way I can walk around it, work from the four sides and literally be in the painting. . . .

"I continue to get further away from the usual painter's tools . . . I prefer sticks, trowels, knives and dripping fluid paint or a heavy impasto with sand, broken glass, and other foreign matter added.

"When I am in my painting, I'm not aware of what I'm doing. It is only after a sort of 'get ac-quainted' period that I see what I have been about. I have no fears about making changes, destroying the image, etc., because the painting has a life of its own. I try to let it come through. It is only when I lose contact with the painting that the result is a mess. Otherwise there is pure harmony, an easy give and take, and the painting comes out well" (Jackson Pollock, 1947).

Convergence bursts forth with the dynamism of exuberant colors and interpenetrating layers of undulating paint (fig. 537). This weblike mass of colors and rhythms offers a new and provocative approach to painting; it records the process by which the artist's unconscious has been laid bare. Pollock's method of paint-ing is derived from Surrealist automatism, and while creating these innovative works, Pollock, often described as being in a trancelike state and moving with the grace of a dancer, aggressively flung paint onto the canvas, the action of his arm being guided by his unconscious (see fig. 539). But unlike Surrealist automatism, Pollock has not consciously completed the image to bring it within the realm of objectivity. The painting, totally abstract, communicates a raw, expressive energy.

But what are we to make of all this? What does it mean for us to

1950: Korean War begins
1951: J.D. Salinger, *The Catcher in the Rye*
1951: Rodgers and Hammerstein, *The King and I* musical opens in New York
1951: Color TV is introduced in America
1952: Ernest Hemingway, *The Old Man and the Sea*
1953: Eisenhower is inaugurated as president of the U.S.
1953: Simone de Beauvoir, *The Second Sex*
1953: Korean armistice is signed

538. MARK ROTHKO
White and Greens in Blue. 1957. Oil on canvas, 8' 6" x 7'. Private collection, New York

confront this painterly record of an artist's unconscious? Surrealism, one of the roots of Abstract Expressionism (defined below), was bound to the psychoanalytical investigations of Freud, but Carl Jung's concept of a "collective unconscious" is equally significant here. As Pollock has exposed his human unconscious, we should be able to draw meaning intuitively from the painting, as its large scale, abstract rhythms, and intense colors meet an unconscious response in us.

Pollock's drip paintings exemplify one style within Abstract Expressionism, a movement that, beginning in New York after World War II, thrust America into the avant-garde of Western art. As we have seen, the roots of Abstract Expressionism were grounded in the psychoanalytical theories of Freud and Jung and in Surrealism. During the 1930s, with the rise of Nazi Germany casting an increasingly foreboding shadow over Europe, many leading European artists came to America. The impact of their work and their presence was felt in a major 1936 exhibition of Dada and Surrealism at New York's Museum of Modern Art. European artists, some of whom opened their studios as teachers, found a particularly responsive audience among a younger generation of American artists who, bound with a collective American identity resulting from the common hardships of the Depression, were searching for new avenues of expression. With Surrealism illuminating one

of the avenues, these American artists assumed control of the avant-garde in the late 1940s.

The term Abstract Expressionism had been used earlier in the century to designate the non-objective paintings of Kandinsky, but it was resurrected in 1946 to describe the works of a group of American painters centered in New York (these artists are also sometimes referred to as the New York School). What joined these artists was not a unified style, but a common attitude that stressed the unique individuality of the creative act.

Within the stylistic differences of the Abstract Expressionist painters, we can discern two fundamental approaches; one, termed Action Painting by the critic Harold Rosenberg in 1952, was a free, gestural expression of paint on the canvas, as demonstrated by the paintings of Jackson Pollock. Another mode, exemplified by the work of Mark Rothko, is referred to as Color Field Painting. It displayed limited areas of color within simple and controlled, non-objective compositions, leaving the shapes and colors to communicate an aesthetic and/or emotional experience.

Rothko, who arrived at this mode of expression after experimenting with the human form and with Surrealist biomorphic compositions, always insisted that paintings must be about something, that they must have a strong content: "It is a widely accepted notion among painters that it does not matter what one

paints as long as it is well painted. This is the essence of academicism. There is no such thing as a good painting about nothing. We assert that subject matter is crucial and only that subject matter is valid which is tragic and timeless."

In Rothko's *White and Greens in Blue* (fig. 538), horizontal planes stacked vertically carry associations of nature, such as landscape and sky, while also establishing a hierarchical order. The interplay of these elements is joined to an emotive use of color. We draw a melancholic sensation from the sobriety of the colors. The densely darkened green rectangles which weigh down the bottom rectangle of white seem to convey unconsciously the suppression of hope.

Rothko, believing in the evocative nature of his paintings, became increasingly sensitive to charges that his work lacked content, that it was only an exercise in color relationships. An interviewer once posed the question of content to Rothko, who replied: "I'm interested in expressing only basic human emotions—tragedy, ecstasy, doom, and so on—and the fact that lots of people break down and cry when confronted with my pictures shows that I communicate these basic human emotions. . . . The people who weep before my pictures are having the same religious experience I had when I painted them, and if you, as you say, are moved only by their color relationships, then you miss the point."

539. Photograph of Jackson Pollock painting

LE CORBUSIER

540. LE CORBUSIER
Exterior, Notre-Dame-du-Haut, Ronchamp, near Belfort, France. 1950–54. Le Corbusier, "the crowlike one," is the nickname of the French architect Charles-Edouard Jeanneret. Notre-Dame-du-Haut is built in the foothills of the Alps, on the edge of a high promontory overlooking the town of Ronchamp. It marks the site of an earlier chapel, destroyed in World War II, that had displayed a miracle-working statue of the Madonna, now incorporated into the new structure. In ancient times this area had been sanctified by a pagan shrine. An outside altar and pulpit are used when pilgrimage crowds become too large to be accommodated within the chapel. The building is constructed of reinforced concrete.

In its highly personal, non-repeating forms, Le Corbusier's chapel at Ronchamp offers a dramatic, individualized alternative to the geometric purity of the contemporary International Style in architecture (figs. 540, 542). Like the great French Gothic cathedrals, this structure sets out to astonish and move us by its unexpected and mysterious form and structure. The sweeping roof seems thin and billowing, like an air-filled sail. Although the roof is made of natural brown-gray cement, its detachment from the thick, curving walls below gives it a particular lightness. The sail-like roof of Notre-Dame-du-Haut creates a relationship with nature, for it seems to respond to the winds that sweep the promontory site. The structural system is based on nature, for Le Corbusier was inspired by a crab shell he picked up on a beach.

On the interior (fig. 541), the darkness and the thick, roughly textured walls suggest a mysterious cave, while a slit of light

LE CORBUSIER, Notre-Dame-du-Haut: 1950–54
1951: U.S. population reaches 153 million
1952: First hydrogen device is exploded
1952: First pocket-sized transistor radios

541. LE CORBUSIER
Interior, Notre-Dame-du-Haut. The interior, approximately 43 x 82', has pews for only about fifty worshippers.

542. LE CORBUSIER
Axonometric projection,
Notre-Dame-du-Haut

between wall and ceiling and the sagging shape of the ceiling itself reinforce the billowing sail effect of the exterior. The thick wall is pierced by irregularly sized and spaced windows filled with stained glass on which traditional religious symbols (a dove, the sun) and phrases ("Marie," "Blessed among Women") have been painted. Like sculpture in the round, the building forces us to move to understand it, and as we explore the structure, three chapels, mysteriously lit by hidden windows in towers, are discovered. The building becomes an adventure and, for some, a journey of personal religious discovery. In discussing the building, Le Corbusier called it "totally free architecture," describing it as "sculpture 'of an acoustical nature,' that is to say projecting afar the effect of its forms and, in return, receiving the pressure of the surrounding spaces. The key is light and light illuminates shapes and shapes have emotional power."

THE RETURN TO THE OBJECT: JASPER JOHNS AND ROBERT RAUSCHENBERG

Jasper Johns's *Flag* (fig. 543) strikes us as a blatantly representational image, even more so when we consider that it was created in the mid-1950s, when various modes of non-objectivity ruled the avant-garde in painting. The composition is clearly and intentionally recognizable, but in place of the solid colored shapes of red, white, and blue that we expect in a flag, Johns has substituted a painterly texture whose thinness in places reveals collage elements underneath. Johns's painting is not a flag of the United States. The

artist has carefully manipulated the surface to emphasize the reality of the painting as a mixed media work of paint and collage. This artistic transformation is intended to drain the image of its immediate symbolic content. Johns thus forces us to realize that the painting itself is first and foremost a composition of shapes and colors—an object.

During the early 1950s, a group of artists reacted to the non-objective aesthetic that had dominated the American avant-garde with Abstract Expressionism and Hard-Edge Painting. Artists such

as Johns and Robert Rauschenberg began to incorporate, in the most literal of ways at times, representational imagery and recognizable objects in their work. This served at least two purposes: It avoided the sometimes uncomfortable defensiveness viewers felt with non-objective art, while simultaneously offering the image, or its combination with actual "found objects," as a given

543. JASPER JOHNS
Flag. 1954. Encaustic and collage on canvas, 42 1/4 x 60 5/8". Collection Philip Johnson, New York

544. ROBERT RAUSCHENBERG
Monogram. 1959. Construction,
42 x 72 x 72". Moderna Museet,
Stockholm

JOHNS, *Flag:* 1954

1954: *Brown vs. Board of Education,* U.S. Supreme Court rules
against school segration
1954: Tennessee Williams, *Cat on a Hot Tin Roof*

fact of our experience, without reference to symbolic comment. There is no precise name for this artistic activity of Johns and Rauschenberg in the mid-fifties. It is sometimes referred to as Neo-Dada, but although there is a similarity to Dada in the use of "found objects," the artistic transformation of common images and objects and the different philosophical context of the fifties make these works distinct from earlier Dada.

In *Monogram* (fig. 544), Robert Rauschenberg attached a stuffed Angora goat that had a used tire around its midsection to a base which joined collage elements with broad, gestural strokes of paint. Rauschenberg referred to these works as "combines," for they associated elements of life with those of art in a "matter of fact" manner which was inspired by the avant-garde musical compositions of John Cage (see p. 438). In the words of Rauschenberg:

"Any incentive to paint is as good as any other. There is no poor subject.

"Painting is always strongest when in spite of composition, color, etc., it appears as a fact, or an inevitability, as opposed to a souvenir or arrangement.

"Painting relates to both art and life. Neither can be made. (I try to act in the gap between the two.)

"A pair of socks is no less suitable to make a painting with than wood, nails, turpentine, oil, and fabric.

"A canvas is never empty."

Amid the abstraction of the American avant-garde, these works of Johns and Rauschenberg emphasized the literal role of the object in the work of art.

HARD-EDGE AND OP ART

"The colors in my paintings are juxtaposed for various and changing effects. They are to challenge or to echo each other, to support or oppose one another. The contrasts, respectively boundaries, between them may vary from soft to hard touches, may mean pull and push besides clashes, but also embracing, intersecting, penetrating.

"Despite an even and mostly opaque application, the colors will appear above or below each other, in front or behind, or side by side on the same level" (Josef Albers, c. 1964).

Albers's *Affectionate* (fig. 545) is one of a series of paintings of virtually identical composition.

In all these works square planes of color are set within larger square planes. Differences of color lead to varying perceptions of spatial illusion created without reference to representational forms. In our painting, the red square of the center appears suspended in advance of the darker, burgundy-colored square behind. This spatial configuration, however, is confounded by the lighter colors of the outer two squares, creating a complicated spatial illusion.

Albers, who studied and then taught at the Bauhaus, moved to America in 1933. His preference for controlled, geometric compositions derives from the

Bauhaus design aesthetic. Early in his career, Albers studied the process of how we perceive and understand illusionism in painting, beginning to work on a series of paintings that created spatial illusions with non-representational, geometric elements. Albers's studies continued throughout his distinguished career, culminating in a series of paintings in the 1950s titled *Homage to the Square*. In America, generations of artists were influenced by both his teaching and his works.

Within the realm of Hard-Edge Abstraction in the 1960s (the term was coined in 1958 to indicate a type of abstract painting whose shapes met in clearly defined edges), Frank Stella began to work with a series of shaped canvases that broke the rectangular format traditional for paintings. In *Empress of India* (fig. 546), the angular outward movement of the lines seems to have determined the boundaries, or shape, of the canvas. To Stella, the destruction of the traditional pictorial format opened to the viewer a greater understanding of the painting as a physical object—a support with colors attached. As Stella said in 1966: "I always get into arguments with people who want to retain the old values in painting—the humanistic values

546. FRANK STELLA
Empress of India. 1965. Metallic powder on shaped canvas, 6' 5" x 20' 4". Collection, The Museum of Modern Art, New York (fractional gift of S. I. Newhouse, Jr.)

ALBERS, *Homage to the Square: Affectionate:* **1954**
1954: J. R. Tolkein, *The Lord of the Rings*
1955: A.F.L. and C.I.O. merge

they always find on the canvas. My painting is based on the fact that only what can be seen is there. It is really an object. . . . All I want anyone to get out of my paintings, and all I ever get out of them is the fact that you can see the whole idea without any confusion. What you see is what you see."

Bridget Riley's *Drift 2* (fig. 547) exemplifies another movement from the 1960s known as Op Art, short for Optical Art. It was a descendant of Albers's non-objective illusory compositions and Hard-Edge Abstraction. Its medium is emulsion, a liquid mixture in which one of the elements does not mix with the others but remains suspended in minute droplets. Although *Drift 2* is a flat canvas, its pattern is composed so that it seems to surge and undulate before our eyes. This illusion of movement, however, is dependent on our

perception of the optical effects of pattern. Op Art questions the very process by which we see and understand.

547. BRIDGET RILEY
Drift 2. 1966. Emulsion on canvas, 91 1/2 x 89 1/2". Albright-Knox Art Gallery, Buffalo, New York

SCULPTURE SINCE 1945

The concept of Assemblage sculpture reaches back to the earlier part of the twentieth century (see p. 472). In composing *Sky Cathedral* (fig. 548), Nevelson assembled cut and scrap pieces of wood—parts of furniture, architectural decoration, and the like—in each box. The individual boxes were then arranged to form a wall-like construction. The overall black paint unites the piece, integrating the multiple, diverse forms. Shadows within and among the boxes increase a sense of mystery. In Nevelson's assemblage sculptures, the commonplace has been transfigured.

Nevelson's *Sky Cathedral* confirms the variety and inventiveness which have characterized developments in sculpture following World War II. An impetus for expansion and change, influenced by both the evolution of earlier modern sculpture and current concepts in painting,

548. LOUISE NEVELSON
Sky Cathedral. 1958. Wood painted black, height 9' 7". Albright-Knox Art Gallery, Buffalo, New York (George B. and Jenny R. Mathews Fund, 1970)

especially the geometric compositions of Hard-Edge and Minimal Art (see below), led artists to realize vitally creative approaches to sculpture. The geometric, non-objective constructed sculptures of David

1957: Leonard Bernstein's musical *West Side Story* opens in New York
1958: European Common Market is formed
1958: National Aeronautics and Space Administration (NASA) is established
1959: Hawaii is admitted as fiftieth state
1959: Richard Rodgers, *The Sound of Music*
1959: Fidel Castro becomes premier of Cuba
1960: World population exceeds 3 billion
1961: Population of New York City is 14.2 million

549. ISAMU NOGUCHI
Cube. 1968. Steel subframe with aluminum panels, height 28'. Marine Midland Building, New York

550. PETER VOULKOS
Plate A. 1978. Glazed stoneware, diameter 23". Courtesy Braunstein/Quay Gallery, San Francisco

Smith (see fig. 8) at mid-century are powerful yet visually economical stainless-steel configurations. Their wire-brushed surface treatment imparts an impulsive energy while the empathetic composition vigorously asserts a dynamic relationship between sculptural mass and space.

Smith's *Cubi* sculptures, along with the impact of Hard-Edge Abstraction, influenced developments in Minimal and Primary sculpture during the 1960s. Minimal Art (which also embraced painting) presented the work of art as an elemental form with the least amount of visual components, divorced from either symbolic or personal expression. Primary Structures is a specific term used for sculpture on an architectural scale; often Primary Structures exhibit the geometric purity of Minimal Art.

Noguchi's *Cube* is a bold, direct sculptural form (fig. 549). Its elemental composition refers to Minimal Art while its enormous size simultaneously lets us understand the impact of Primary Structures. Noguchi's unique interpretation, however, contrasts the visually massive weight of the form with a precarious, teetering balance.

Another revolution of post-World War II sculpture affected the medium of clay. Traditionally, clay had served primarily for the fashioning of utilitarian vessels and the construction of sculptors' models. In the 1950s, Peter Voulkos, a ceramic artist, began deliberately distorting functional clay works. The scars and slashes on *Plate A* (fig. 550) remind us of the gestural record of Abstract Expressionism. In using clay as an intimately expressive medium, Voulkos contributed greatly to the expansion of ceramic art that we have witnessed recently.

POP ART

551. ROY LICHTENSTEIN
As I Opened Fire. 1964. Magna on canvas, each panel 68 x 56". Stedelijk Museum, Amsterdam

Lichtenstein's *As I Opened Fire* (fig. 551) is fashioned after a drawing in an out-of-date adventure comic book that the artist has blown up to an enormous size. The expression of the thoughts of the pilot across the top and the emblazoned BRAT! are a natural and expected adjunct to the bold and simple style of the planes and blazing guns. The broad areas of flat color, contained by heavy black outlines, are in places created by enlarged patterns of dots inspired by the process used to print color illustrations in comic books and newspapers. Lichtenstein thus draws our attention not only to the overtly melodramatic imagery of the comic book, itself a representative subject of post-World War II culture, but also to the processes by which images are created for mass consumption.

Lichtenstein's painting exemplifies Pop Art, a movement which began in England in the mid-1950s and whose initial impact was felt in America in the early 1960s. The inspiration for Pop Art was found in the commercialism which developed following World War II. Named in England by the art critic Lawrence Alloway, Pop Art emerged with a 1956 exhibition *This is Tomorrow*. According to Richard Hamilton, one of the leaders of the movement, Pop Art was to be "Popular (designed for a mass audience), Transient (short-term solution), Low-cost, Mass-produced, Young (aimed at youth), Witty, Sexy, Gimmicky, Glamorous, Big Business."

In America, the literal objectivity of artists like Johns and Rauschenberg assisted in the development of Pop Art. Pop Art celebrated objects and ideas

which were not only familiar, but banal in their content. Nowhere was the habitual repetition of commercialization felt more fully than in the works of Andy Warhol, who, in 1956, wrote in referring to his paintings of repetitive images: "The reason I'm painting this way is that I want to be a machine, and I feel that whatever I do and do machine-like is what I want to do." Many of Warhol's images were silkscreened by assistants in a studio, which from the mid-1960s he called "The Factory," suggesting an equation between the process of art and consumer production. But if Warhol's rows upon rows of Coke bottles (see fig. 476), Campbell's soup cans, images of Marilyn Monroe, or accident scenes are born from an aesthetic numbness produced by the commercial environment, they also begin to communicate

1961: Berlin Wall is built
1962: World population reaches 3.1 billion
1962: Cuban missile crisis
1962: Rachel Carson, *Silent Spring*
1963: Massive civil rights demonstration in Washington, D.C.
1963: President John F. Kennedy is assassinated

552. CLAES OLDENBURG
Standing Trowel. 1971. Painted steel,
height approx. 40'. Kröller-Müller
Museum, Otterlo, The Netherlands

how we are in danger of becoming unfeeling "products" within an industrialized environment.

Pop Art also left its distinctive mark on sculpture. In the realm of public sculpture, Pop Art overturned many traditional values which had been associated with monumental sculpture in public spaces. Claes Oldenburg achieved notoriety for altering the scale or texture of commonplace, manufactured objects. His monumental *Standing Trowel* (fig. 552) literally elevates the status of a household object. But, as is true of other forms of Pop Art, there is more than wit involved here. Oldenburg once remarked, "The important thing about humor is that it opens people. They relax their guard and you can get your serious intention across."

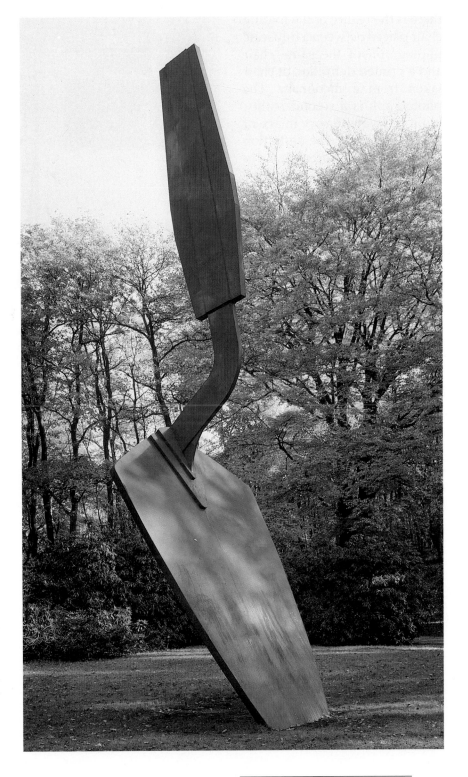

CONCEPTUAL, PERFORMANCE, AND VIDEO ART

Joseph Kosuth's *One and Three Chairs* (fig. 553) informs us of three different realities. First, there is the reality of the folding chair placed between a full-scale photograph of the same chair and a printed definition of chair taken from a dictionary. The photograph is a second reality, but it bears an illusory image of the chair. Finally, the definition communicates a verbal description of a chair. The idea that we form from the definition exists in our minds and might therefore be termed a "conceptual reality." *One and Three Chairs* presents the actuality, the image, and the idea of a chair, thus demonstrating the relationship between an object and communicative methods of signifying that object.

Kosuth's emphasis on the creative idea and the process of expressing that idea are characteristic of Conceptual Art. This term was first used in the early 1960s to designate an artistic philosophy which held the supremacy of the artist's concept and the process intended to achieve it over the actual execution of the work. This modern tradition of stressing the intellectual creative act begins with Dada, and especially the "readymades" of Marcel Duchamp.

Conceptual Art requires that the concept for a work of art be documented, but that documentation need not take the form of a finished, crafted work. It might, for example, be expressed verbally or in another visual medium. In 1967 another conceptual artist, Sol Lewitt, wrote, "In

553. JOSEPH KOSUTH
One and Three Chairs. 1965. Wooden folding chair, height 32 3/8"; photograph of chair, 36 x 24"; photographic enlargement of dictionary definition of chair, 24 x 25". Collection, The Museum of Modern Art, New York (Larry Aldrich Foundation Fund)

Conceptual Art the Idea or concept is the most important aspect of the work . . . all planning and decision are made beforehand and the execution is a perfunctory affair. The idea becomes the machine that makes the art."

Another contribution from the 1960s which continues to expand the definitions of art is Performance Art. Historically, such art is related to the Happenings of the fifties. Performance Art, which celebrates a temporal experience for an audience, was not geared toward the making of an object; rather, the artist became the work of art, freely acting within a theatrical environment. Performance artists often utilize a multi-

media approach. Joseph Beuys, a German artist who was a major practitioner of Performance Art, incorporated a wide variety of "props" in his "actions" (as he termed his performances), from found objects to live animals. Beuys, a pilot shot down in a barren frozen area of the Crimea during World War II, used Performance Art as a means to communicate autobiographical experiences in a symbolic manner, causing us to question the deeper values in our lives. For Beuys, Performance Art was to lead to a rebirth of the human mind and soul (see fig. 554).

With Video Art, television becomes a medium of artistic

KOSUTH, *One and Three Chairs:* **1965**
1964: Vietnam War escalates
1965: World population reaches 3.3 billion
1965: *Help,* a Beatles film, is released
1967: First human heart transplant
1967: U.S. population exceeds 200 million

554. JOSEPH BEUYS
Photograph of Beuys with cymbal from *Iphigenie/Titus Andronicus.* May 1969. This work premiered during an avant-garde theater festival in Frankfurt in 1969. The performance consisted of selected simultaneous readings of Goethe's *Iphigenie* and Shakespeare's *Titus Andronicus* while Beuys, who designed the "set," acted on stage. Beuys's actions included spreading margarine on the stage floor and occasionally clashing cymbals.

555. NAM JUNE PAIK
Photograph from performance of *Bra for Living Sculpture* (worn by Charlotte Moorman). 1969. Television sets and cello. Photograph © 1969 Peter Moore. Collection Charlotte Moorman

enterprise. Nam June Paik, a Korean artist, once remarked, "As collage technique replaced oil paint the cathode ray tube will replace the canvas." In one of his Performance/Video works from 1969, Paik devised a garment for cellist Charlotte Moorman that included two miniature TV sets (fig. 555). As Moorman played the cello, the mechanized bulk of the TV sets and the banal image carried on their screens, which changed in response to musical vibrations produced by the cellist, brought a jarring juxtaposition to the intimate, sensual association between the human figure and the music that was being performed. Conceptual, Performance, and Video Art have broadened the boundaries of art beyond any traditional definitions, raising intriguing questions about the nature of art as we approach the end of the twentieth century.

EARTH AND LAND ART

556. ROBERT SMITHSON
Spiral Jetty. 1969–70. Black rock, salt crystals, earth, and red water (algae), diameter 160'; coil length 1500'; width 15'. Great Salt Lake, Utah. This photograph shows the jetty soon after it was first completed. Smithson died in 1973 in an airplane crash while working on a later project.

Robert Smithson's *Spiral Jetty* in the Great Salt Lake is an aggressive and dramatic gesture in the natural landscape (fig. 556). The artist used assistants and huge earth-moving equipment to create the work. The top of the jetty functioned as the roadbed as the rock was moved into place in the lake. The jetty was meant to be walked on and to be seen from the shore and the sky. The resulting form, which is both regular and open, transformed the quality and color of the water within the jetty, for the encircled areas of water heated to a higher temperature, changing the amount and color of the local algae. But Smithson's mark on the landscape was not meant to be permanent. He knew it was a temporary structure that would eventually be transformed, if not obliterated, by the forces of nature. Recently it has been hidden by an unexpected rise in the water level of the lake. Although the geometric purity of the spiral form can be related to formalism and Minimalist Art, it also has a historical and iconographic content. Smithson learned that early Mormon settlers believed that the Great Salt Lake was bottomless and connected to the Pacific Ocean by an underground canal and that from time to time Pacific currents would cause huge whirlpools to form on the lake's surface. His choice of design was based on this legend.

Beginning in the 1960s, a number of American artists became interested in producing large-scale works of art in the natural environment. This type of art became known as Earth Art, Land Art, or Environmental Art. Some artists moved large amounts of earth, creating a personal statement and transforming the land in a manner offensive to environmentally minded citizens. Others were determined to reassert and even recreate the natural quality of nature. Some projects took advantage of the natural forces in nature: ice, flowing water, wind, even animals and birds. All redirected attention to nature, mak-

SMITHSON, *Spiral Jetty:* **1969–70**
1968: Assassination of Martin Luther King, Jr.
1968: First successful heart transplant operation
1969: Human beings land on the moon
1969: *Sesame Street* program is introduced on P.B.S.
1969: Woodstock music festival

557. CHRISTO
Running Fence. 1976 (now dismantled). 2,050 steel poles set 62' apart; 65,000 yards of white woven synthetic fabric, height 18'; total length 24 1/2 miles. Sonoma and Marin Counties, California. © Christo and Running Fence Corporation. The planning stages of this work began in 1972. This project, which was completed in fourteen days, cost more than two million dollars and used sixty-five skilled workers and more than three hundred and fifty volunteers.

ing us see it with new eyes and a new awareness, and raising the issue of the importance of nature in modern, industrialized society.

Christo's *Running Fence* (fig. 557) crossed the hills of California to run into the sea, highlighting by its existence not only the forms of the landscape but also, as it caught the changing effects of light and the shifting winds, the constant movement inherent in nature. Perhaps its best vantage point was from an airplane, for only thus could the enormous scope of the project be encompassed in a single view. Part of

the creative act for Christo is not just conceiving and executing the project, but raising the funds (through lecturing and the sale of books, films, preparatory drawings, and prints), acquiring the legal permissions required, and finding volunteers who will help with the intensive, large-scale labor of the project, and creating a reasonable timetable so that the project can be completed on schedule. Christo's early works included projects in which objects were stacked (a project to create a great mastaba form by stacking two million oil barrels was never completed) or

the wrapping of objects or buildings in fabric that was then bound with ropes, including the wrapping of more than one million square feet of the cliffs of the coast of Australia. In 1971–72 he closed off a canyon in Colorado with an orange nylon curtain 365 feet high and 1,368 feet long (documented in a film, *Valley Curtain*), and in 1983 he surrounded eleven small islands in Biscayne Bay off Miami with six million square feet of bright pink polypropylene fabric, exaggerating their natural shapes and turning them into a sequence of enormous pink flowers.

ARCHITECTURE SINCE 1970

558. RENZO PIANO AND RICHARD ROGERS
Georges Pompidou National Arts and Cultural Center, Paris. 1971–78. The center incorporates not only museum spaces for permanent and temporary exhibitions, but a public library and an audiovisual center. One critic, Charles Jencks, categorized the Pompidou Center as "Bizarre Architecture."

At first glance the architecture of the Pompidou Center in Paris seems to be completely honest (fig. 558). Not only are the structural elements completely exposed—without and within—but air-circulation ducting, escalators, and other mechanical equipment are brought into public view and even emphasized. Bright colors are used to designate each different mechanical function, so that we are constantly aware of the operating systems needed to keep the building functioning; in such a program, the mechanical systems also function as decoration. Inside, all the walls are movable, and each space can be redesigned as needed. It is not only an adventure in architecture, but a demonstration in understanding the complex workings of the advanced technology of a huge contemporary building. Leaving the mechanicals on the exterior allows for their easy replacement when they wear out or new technology is available. Rogers recently wrote, "I believe in the rich potential of a modern industrial society. Aesthetically one can do what one likes with technology for it is a tool, not an end in itself, but we ignore it at our peril. To our practice its natural functionalism has an intrinsic beauty." Architects have been inspired

PIANO and ROGERS, Georges Pompidou National Arts and
Cultural Center: 1971–78
1972: Nixon visits China and U.S.S.R.
1973: Picasso dies

by the direct bluntness of industrial "architecture," such as oil refineries and grain elevators, where function forms the design.

In the recent style known as Post-Modern (a term that equates the earlier abstract glass box of the International Style with modernity), architects have revived historical architectural vocabulary and references in a creative and even playful non-traditional manner. In Charles Moore's Piazza d'Italia (fig. 559), columns and capitals representing numerous orders (see p. 81), arches, including a triumphal arch, and inscriptions from the classical tradition are transformed by the bright and unexpected colors, neon outlining, stainless steel, and varied scale. Some of the "columns" are composed of flowing water, with the streams of water wittily suggesting fluting, and two human masks that spout water into the fountain from a Roman arch are versions of Moore's self-portrait. When viewed from above, the center of the composition is the island of Sicily, the area from which most New Orleans Italians have come. At night, dramatic lighting gives the piazza a dazzling, commercial quality.

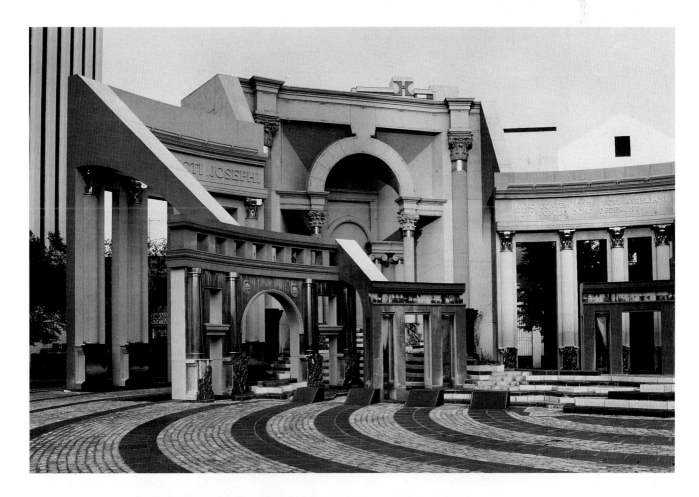

559. CHARLES MOORE (in collaboration with U.I.G. and Perez Associates, Inc.)
Piazza d'Italia, New Orleans. 1975–80. The piazza was designed to provide the Italo-American population of New Orleans with a piazza where the annual festival of St. Joseph could be celebrated. The central fountain is in the shape of the map of Italy, with the water from the fountain flowing down courses shaped like the major Italian rivers.

THE NEW ILLUSIONISM

ESTES, *Double Self-Portrait:* 1976
1974: Watergate scandal in U.S.
1975: U.S. and U.S.S.R. spacecrafts and their crews are joined in space, 140 miles above the earth

560. RICHARD ESTES
Opposite above: *Double Self-Portrait.* 1976. Oil on canvas, 24 x 36". Collection, The Museum of Modern Art, New York (Mr. and Mrs. Stuart M. Speiser Fund)

561. AUDREY FLACK
Opposite below: *Queen.* 1975–76. Oil and acrylic on canvas, 80 x 80". Private collection

The complex and highly illusionistic details of *Double Self-Portrait* immediately command our attention (fig. 560). We seem to be standing on an urban sidewalk, facing the large glass windows and doors of a diner. In these panes of glass a myriad of forms—cars, buildings, and street signs—are reflected. It is as if we "see" in two directions at the same time. Reflected in the lower right area of the central pane of glass is the artist, Richard Estes, with his camera on a tripod. The inclusion of the reflected camera in *Double Self-Portrait* alerts us that this painting, with its vivid *trompe l'oeil* realism, is not a direct painting of a scene, but a painting made using a photograph. In preparing for each painting, Estes takes a series of photographs to examine the different elements of a scene. In the final composition these images are combined with a sharp-focus realism, leaving us to explore the transformation of photographic information into paint.

Estes's painting belongs to a movement in the 1970s which was known as the New Illusionism. The avant-garde movements of the mid-twentieth century had emphasized non-objectivity; the New Illusionism countered with *trompe l'oeil* representations of the world around us.

Audrey Flack invests a psychological and emotional content in her paintings. Using a process different from Estes's, Flack first arranges a still-life composition combining objects to suggest both personal and universal meaning. One series of paintings in the mid-1970s, including *Queen* (fig. 561), can be related to traditional *Vanitas* iconography (see fig. 367). The inclusion of the watch and the transient beauty of the flower and fruit stress the passage of time, while more personal objects—makeup, photographs, a key chain, the card, and the chess piece—tantalize the viewer by suggesting additional layers of meaning. When she is pleased with the arrangement of objects, Flack photographs her composition with color-slide film. She then projects the slide onto the canvas and paints following the guidelines offered by the projected image. Her use of an airbrush (a small, high-quality paint sprayer) softens the contours of the objects, giving the painting a suggestive, evocative effect. This soft focus combines with the iconography of the objects to appeal to our emotions in a way that is quite different from the sharp focus and detached objectivity of Estes's urban scene. The fact that Flack's huge and dazzling objects leap out toward us by overlapping the gray border gives them a compelling presence. Like the *trompe l'oeil* artists of ancient Rome, the current New Illusionists both delight and intrigue us.

THE 1980s: PATTERN AND DECORATION; NEO-EXPRESSIONISM

562. JOYCE KOZLOFF
Mural for *Harvard Square Subway Station: New England Decorative Arts.* 1984. Painted and glazed tiles, 8 x 83' overall. Public Transport Station, Cambridge, Massachusetts

Joyce Kozloff's tile mural for the Harvard Square subway station is a delightfully encyclopedic and joyfully colorful composition of representational images and abstract patterns (fig. 562). The mural details the cultural, social, ecological, and economic life of New England. Its representational images of homes, factories, and plants are rendered with a naive realism reminiscent of early American painting, while the decorative areas remind us of the patterned patchwork of a quilt.

Kozloff's vibrant mural belongs to a contemporary style often referred to as P+D, an abbreviation for Pattern and Decoration. P+D utilizes nonobjective shapes inherent in decorative motifs, some of which, as here, have been derived from traditional sources. Unlike the severe, impersonal abstraction of

Hard-Edge or Minimal Art, P+D revels in bold colors and less-constrained compositions.

Countering the impersonal traits of recent abstraction, Neo-Expressionism, which is especially strong in Europe, reinvests an emotional and empathetic content in painting. *Midgard,* by the German artist Anselm Kiefer, expresses dread and desolation in the vast scorched earth that stretches before us (fig. 563). It is as if our worst nightmares of nuclear holocaust have become manifest. Waves froth at the top of the painting, and the somber colors of destruction are everywhere. The only sign of life is the snake in the central foreground, which is moving slowly but inexorably toward a labyrinth-like circular area of land that also represents an artist's palette. We are overwhelmed by a sense of loss and doom.

KOZLOFF, Mural, *New England Decorative Arts:* **1984**
1984: Bishop Desmond Tutu of South Africa is awarded the Nobel
Peace Prize
1986: Halley's comet returns
1986: Nuclear disaster at Chernobyl
1987: Missile treaty between U.S. and U.S.S.R. is signed

Kiefer's painting visualizes an event from Nordic mythology. Its title means middle garden, a name traditionally given to the earth by the ancient Norse gods. In Norse mythology, the destruction of the earth comes after three years of winter, when the Midgard serpent and other demons destroy all life. In the enormous scale, desolate composition, and barren colors (the artist used a blowtorch to achieve the scorched effect), Kiefer explores and expands one of the invigorating currents of twentieth-century art, Expressionism. *Midgard* is a dramatic painting of a traditional mythological subject which, in Kiefer's reinterpretation, still has the power to grip the human imagination.

563. ANSELM KIEFER
Midgard. 1980–85. Oil and emulsion on canvas, 11' 10" x 19' 9 3/4". The Carnegie Museum of Art, Pittsburgh

RECENT DEVELOPMENTS IN SCULPTURE

564. SUSANA SOLANO
Què Duda Cabe #3. 1987. Iron, steel, and lead, 32 1/2 x 32 1/2". Collection Mera and Donald Rubell. The title of this work is a colloquial phrase that might be translated as "Is there room for doubt?" or "Can doubt be contained?" Solano once described space by saying, "Space doesn't exist for me, it is something so ambiguous that I feel the need to delimit it. . . . Space [is also] where we are, or what is around me . . . when I am with my daughter in her room and I can hear her breathe. These are spaces that are delimited, defined and, above all, experienced. The void is like closing your eyes, like darkness." The object she has created out of some of the heaviest and coldest of materials defines a physical space but does not enclose it. It offers the evocative and mysterious qualities so often sensed in an empty space. As in other works by Solano, the reference to a cage seems intentional, and this and other works suggest that the distinctions between confinement and freedom are subtle.

565. MARTIN PURYEAR
Verge. 1987. Pine and red cedar and paint, 67 1/2 x 81 1/2 x 34 1/2". Collection Edward R. Broida Trust, Los Angeles, California. The single word of the artist's title is a literal equivalent for the intersecting forms of *Verge*. The two shapes Puryear uses are simple and similar, but their interaction is carefully studied. This work is monumental in scale and, like other works by the artist, brings to mind the elemental forms of tribal totems.

The tempo of artistic innovation and change seems to have accelerated even further in our Post-Modern era, and we have chosen to conclude our text with a visual sampling of recent and diverse works of art. One of the strengths of recent sculpture is its ability to draw our attention to subtle and intuitive relationships of form and space. Sculptural forms, whether composed of traditional media, modern metals, or found objects, often suggest correspondences without objectively stating them. We are thus free to explore the physical and psychological effects proposed by these works.

RECENT DEVELOPMENTS IN PAINTING

566. ELIZABETH MURRAY
Untitled. December 1987–January 1988. Oil on canvas, 52 x 49 1/2 x 15 1/2". Collection Mr. and Mrs. David Gersh, Beverly Hills, California. The dynamic forms of Murray's shaped canvases interact with strong colors to create a dramatic and even emotional impact. In their complex, vital spatiality and surging, often aggressive forms, they suggest the tensions that are a part of everyday life—tensions that lead us to break from old bonds or ideas to search for new relationships and meaning. Murray has asserted the deeper and more personal content of her work, for when she was asked if her paintings are political, she replied: "I want my work to reflect my feelings about the society we live in; [they're] political in that sense."

In painting, many new works draw inspiration from earlier movements of modern art, returning to further explore concepts whose impact was first felt earlier in our century. Geometric abstraction, Assemblage, Expressionism, shaped three-dimensional canvases, and Conceptualism are among the currents of modernism which continue to provide a wellspring of fresh experiences for younger artists.

567. VLADIMIR MIRONENKO

Part V: The Final Struggle (from the series *Completely Secret Plan for World Transformation*). 1988. Oil and acrylic on canvas, 78 3/4 x 45 3/4". Collection the artist. Mironenko, a leader of the Soviet avant-garde since the late 1970s, believes in the ethical and moral responsibility of art to "remake the world." The C.C.C.P. stenciled (or painted as if stenciled) on the canvas is the equivalent of U.S.S.R. in the Cyrillic alphabet. The use of words and emblems is common in contemporary Soviet art, and the critic John Bowlt recently emphasized how Soviet and Russian culture "is, or has been until very recently, a culture of the word." In addition to specific references to the government and to the identity of the Soviet Union in the painting itself, the title of the work enhances its content. The "plan for world transformation" most likely refers to the Leninist determination to convert the world to Communism. Whether the "completely secret" refers to the approach or to the status of the revolution is unclear and perhaps ironic. The bold, flat forms of the canvas are a reaction to the illusionism of the official Soviet style of Socialist Realism and may also refer to the experiments of such Russian painters as Kasimir Malevich (see fig. 507).

568. LOTHAR BAUMGARTEN

The Tongue of the Cherokee (detail). 1985–88. Painted, laminated, and sandblasted glass, 100 x 43'. Permanently installed at the Carnegie Museum of Art, Pittsburgh. The letters which Baumgarten has used in this installation are the eighty-five letters of the Cherokee alphabet as it was invented by Sequoyah between 1809 and 1821. Sequoyah seems to have been the only person in history to have developed his own alphabet; he did not understand English, but he used English letters, without a knowledge of their relationship to sound, as a basis. In the nineteenth century, Sequoyah's alphabet was widely used by the Cherokees, and between 1828 and 1834 the *Cherokee Phoenix* was published in two languages—Cherokee and English. The Sequoyah language largely died out with the suppression of the Native American population, and this monumental work, which scatters the letters and their accents like random decoration, comments on its demise. Baumgarten has a long-standing interest in the effects of "civilization" on vital native cultures.

RECENT DEVELOPMENTS IN ARCHITECTURE

569. MICHAEL GRAVES
Dolphin and Swan Hotels, Walt Disney World, Orlando, Florida. Site model. 1988–90. These two hotels will have a total of 2300 rooms and, with the convention center (the vaulted hall in the background), will be the largest convention/resort hotel complex in the Southeast. The Swan Hotel in the foreground will be painted with a pattern of waves and decorated with 47-foot-tall swans. The Dolphin Hotel, with its 55-foot-high dolphins, will be painted with a pattern of banana leaves in blue-green and coral and will have huge lighted fountains on top of the four pavilions. The fantasy quality of Graves's work seems especially appropriate for Walt Disney World. In January 1989, this project won one of the prestigious *Progressive Architecture* awards.

The inventive vocabulary of Post-Modernism continues to provide an engaging and often witty architectural environment. Bold colors, no longer the sole domain of painting, have become integral to the experience of much recent architecture. Technological and material developments continue to have a direct impact on architecture, whether they are exposed as structure or hidden within the design.

570. NORMAN FOSTER ASSOCIATES
Century Tower Project for the Obunsha Publishing Company, Tokyo, Japan. Model of early version. 1988–90. The gigantic braced trusses that provide the basic support are also intended to help the building resist earthquakes. In addition, by moving virtually all the supporting technology to the outside of the building, Foster has been able to keep the interior spaces very open and flexible. The sides of the building house lavatories, elevators, and escape stairs so that these elements can be easily replaced when they become outmoded or are in need of repair. The differing heights of the two towers are the direct result of zoning requirements in the neighborhood. The tall pointed form will function as a radio mast to receive messages from a telecommunications center.

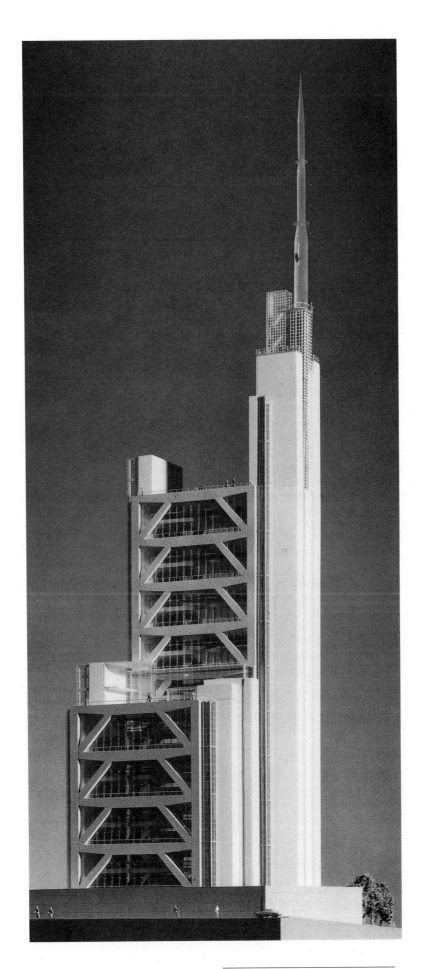

GLOSSARY

Definitions in the glossary are intentionally short; for further information and illustrations consult the references listed. Words in capital letters within an entry are defined in the glossary. An abbreviation used here is e.g., meaning for example.

ABACUS: on a DORIC capital, the flat slab between the rounded ECHINUS and the ENTABLATURE; see fig. 71 and p. 81.

ACID BATH: a shallow tray of acid used in the ETCHING technique; see pp. 336–37.

ACRYLIC PAINT: a fast-drying synthetic paint MEDIUM developed about 1960; see fig. 478.

AERIAL PERSPECTIVE: a device, used in painting to suggest PERSPECTIVE, in which forms nearer the horizon are blurred and their color is less intense and higher in VALUE, while the sky gradually shades from blue toward white above the horizon, as in Perugino's *Christ Giving the Keys* (fig. 4). Also known as atmospheric perspective.

AISLES: corridors flanking a large central area; Old St. Peter's Basilica has two aisles on either side of its central NAVE (figs. 145–46). Also known as side aisles.

ALTARPIECE: A painted and/or sculpted work of art that stands as a religious image upon and at the back of an altar; see the Van Eycks' *Altarpiece of the Lamb* (figs. 234–35).

AMBULATORY: a circular or semicircular vaulted passage, as at Chartres (fig. 198).

AMPHITHEATER: a circular or oval building with tiered seats for sports and entertainment, developed by the ancient Romans; e.g., the Colosseum or Flavian Amphitheater (figs. 121–23).

AMPHORA: an ancient Greek vase used to store olive oil, honey, or wine; see fig. 66.

ANICONIC: the representation of a deity by symbols rather than by figural form, as at Sanchi (fig. 96).

ANNULAR VAULT: a structural system composed of a series of vaults arranged in a curving or circular configuration; for examples see the ancient Roman Colosseum (figs. 121–23) and the AMBULATORY at Chartres (fig. 198).

APSE: in architecture, an area composed of a half cylinder or semipolygonal form surmounted by a half dome or vaulting, as at Old St. Peter's (fig. 146) and Chartres (fig. 198).

AQUEDUCT: a structure used to transport water in ancient Roman times; e.g., the Pont du Gard (fig. 125).

ARCADE: a series of ARCHES with their supporting COLUMNS or PIERS, as in the nave arcades at Chartres (fig. 196) and Santo Spirito (fig. 242).

ARCH: a means of construction in which an opening, usually semicircular, is spanned by a series of wedge-shaped elements (VOUSSOIRS and a KEYSTONE); see fig. 124 and p. 126.

ARCHITECTURE: a structure, usually functional, that encloses and defines space.

ARCHITRAVE: in architecture, the lowest part of an ENTABLATURE; see fig. 71 and p. 81.

ARCHIVOLTS: the moldings that enframe the TYMPANUM in a Romanesque or Gothic church; often decorated with sculptures, as at Vézelay (fig. 184).

ART: traditionally, defined as an object made by a person or persons that communicated a message, concept, or belief. Today art includes so many different kinds of products (including ephemeral performances, for example) that an all-encompassing definition is no longer possible.

ART THEORY: the discussion and establishment of philosophical ideals concerning the goals of art.

ASSEMBLAGE: a work of art which combines actual three-dimensional objects, some of which may be "found" objects from the household or the junkyard; see fig. 544.

ATMOSPHERIC PERSPECTIVE: see AERIAL PERSPECTIVE.

ATRIUM: an open courtyard, sometimes surrounded by a COLONNADE, found at the entrance to a Roman house (figs. 102–3) or a Christian church (fig. 146).

AXIAL COMPOSITION or ORGANIZATION: a compositional pattern with a central AXIS and bilateral symmetry, giving an impression of balance; see Botticelli's *Birth of Venus* (fig. 263).

AXIS: the imaginary straight line that passes through the center of figures or forms, or through an architectural composition. An analysis of the axes of a work helps establish its COMPOSITION.

AXONOMETRIC PROJECTION: a geometrical drawing that depicts a building in three dimensions; see the ancient Roman sanctuary at Praeneste (fig. 101).

BALDACCHINO: a canopy over an altar or throne; e.g., Bernini's at St. Peter's (fig. 344).

BALLOON FRAME: an architectural structure in which wooden beams are joined horizontally and vertically to create a gridlike structural system; e.g., Davis's wooden house (fig. 420).

BARREL VAULT: a deep arch that normally requires continuous BUTTRESSING; see fig. 124 and pp. 126–27. Also known as a tunnel vault.

BASILICA: to the ancient Romans, a large building used for public administration, as in the Basilica Ulpia in Rome (fig. 132). In Christian times, a specific type of structure, with a central NAVE, CLERESTORY, flanking AISLES, and APSE, as at Old St. Peter's (figs. 145–46).

BAS-RELIEF: relief sculpture in which flattened figures or forms project only very slightly from the background; e.g., the *Palette of Narmer* (figs. 35–36). Also known as low relief.

BATTERED WALL: a wall that slopes or slants inward, as in ancient Egyptian MASTABAS (fig. 43) and PYLONS (fig. 47).

BAYS: individual units of space defined by the PIERS and VAULTS in a vaulted structural system; the plan of the Gothic cathedral of Chartres (fig. 198), for example, reveals that the NAVE is seven bays long. Bays also refer to the vertical divisions of the exterior or interior surfaces of a building, as marked by such elements as windows, BUTTRESSES, COLUMNS, etc.

BOOK OF HOURS: a book of private devotions with prayers for the seven canonical hours of the Roman Catholic church. Sometimes contains a calendar and is illustrated with illuminations (figs. 224–25).

BUON FRESCO: see FRESCO.

BURIN: a tool with a sharp metal point used in the decoration of Greek vases (fig. 65) and in making ETCHINGS (see pp. 336–37).

BURR: the tiny raised masses of copper on either side of the groove created in the DRYPOINT technique; the burr catches the ink and creates rich areas of deep, soft shadow; see pp. 336–37.

BUTTRESS, BUTTRESSING: the projecting support that counteracts the outward thrust of an ARCH or wall; see figs. 124, 200, 202 and pp. 204–5.

CALLIGRAPHY: fine penmanship or beautiful writing (figs. 160, 195).

CALYX KRATER: an ancient Greek bowl with handles used for mixing wine with water; see fig. 66.

CAMERA OBSCURA: an enclosed box with an opening that allows an image to be projected inside the box; sometimes used by artists, including Vermeer (fig. 340), as a tool for understanding PERSPECTIVE recession.

CANTILEVER: a support system in which an architectural member projects horizontally into space, beyond its supports, as in Wright's Fallingwater (fig. 11).

CAPITAL: the decorated top of a COLUMN, PIER, or PILASTER; often helps effect an aesthetic transition from the vertical COLUMN to the horizontal ENTABLATURE; for examples from the Greek and Roman ORDERS, see fig. 71.

CARITYA: a sacred Buddhist site, complete with a shrine, MONASTERY, lecture hall, and other structures, as at Nara (figs. 161–62).

CARPET PAGE: a manuscript page with complex, abstract, decorative patterns, usually Hiberno-Saxon, as in the page from the *Lindisfarne Gospels* (fig. 159).

CARTOON: a full-size drawing for a painting, as in Leonardo's cartoon (fig. 265).

CARYATIDS: supports in POST-AND-LINTEL construction that are carved to represent female figures; their rarer male counterparts are sometimes also called caryatids, but more correctly are known as atlantes or telemones.

CASEIN: a technique of painting in which PIGMENTS are mixed with a milk protein; see fig. 468.

CAST SHADOWS: the shadows cast by an object onto surrounding surfaces and objects. In a painting, these shadows help increase the ILLUSIONISM, as in the ancient Roman still life (fig. 120).

CASTING: a method of producing a copy of a three-dimensional object by pouring a hardening material into a mold; see fig. 77 and p. 85.

CATACOMB: an underground complex of tunnels and rooms, used in ancient Roman times by Romans, Jews, and Christians for burial purposes; for a painting from a catacomb, see fig. 142.

CATHEDRAL: in western Christianity, a church which marks the residence of a bishop; for example, Chartres (figs. 196–99).

CENTERING: the temporary wooden support upon which an ARCH or VAULT is constructed; see fig. 124 and p. 126.

CENTRALLY PLANNED: denotes an architectural design in which regularized units radiate, usually at 90° angles, from a central area, often surmounted by a dome, as in the original High Renaissance design for St. Peter's in Rome (fig. 291).

CHIAROSCURO: in painting, the use of a contrast of VALUES to create effects of MODELING; see the Roman still life (fig. 120).

CHOIR: in a Christian church, an enclosed area near the altar where the monks or nuns chant the services, as at Chartres (fig. 198).

CHUMON: the entrance gate to a Japanese Buddhist temple area, as at Horyu-ji (figs. 161, 162).

CLERESTORY: in architecture, an area elevated above adjacent rooftops, usually along a central AXIS. Its purpose is to allow light into the interior, and it has windows on the sides, as in the Egyptian HYPOSTYLE hall (fig. 46), Old St. Peter's (fig. 145), Chartres (figs. 196–97), Santo Spirito (fig. 242), and elsewhere.

CLOISTER: an open court within a monastery, usually with an open ARCADE or COLONNADE; see figs. 175–76.

CLUSTER PIER: in the Gothic structural system (fig. 200), a pier with groups of COLONNETTES, as at Chartres (fig. 197). Also known as compound pier.

COFFERING, COFFERS: in architecture, recessed geometrical panels—often square—that decorate the interior surface of a VAULT; see the coffers of the DOME of the ancient Roman Pantheon (fig. 127) and elsewhere (fig. 348).

COLLAGE: a composition in which pieces of materials such as newspaper, cloth, or colored paper are glued to a canvas, paper, or other surface, as in Picasso's *Still Life with Chair Caning* (fig. 503).

COLLOCATION: the idea that an artist created a specific work for a specific location and that it is adjusted for that location and the spectator's viewpoint, as in Caravaggio's *Conversion of St. Paul* (fig. 335), Rembrandt's *Militia Company of Captain Cocq* (fig. 347), and Bartlett's *Sea Wall* (fig. 1).

COLONNADE: a continuous row of columns supporting an ENTABLATURE or ARCHES; see the Parthenon (figs. 80, 82).

COLONNETTE: a slender, columnar decorative motif, common in Gothic architecture, as at Chartres (fig. 197), where groups of colonnettes create COMPOUND PIERS that support the NAVE ARCADE.

COLOR PALETTE: the selection of colors used by an artist; for an example of a restricted color palette, see Mondrian's *Diamond Painting* (fig. 5).

COLOSSAL ORDER: see GIANT ORDER.

COLUMN: a freestanding cylindrical support, often FLUTED and with a CAPITAL, used in POST-AND-LINTEL construction, as at the Parthenon (fig. 82).

COMPOSITION: the arrangement or organization of the various elements of a work of art; e.g., the balanced symmetry of Perugino's *Christ Giving the Keys to St. Peter* (fig. 4).

COMPOUND PIER: see CLUSTER PIER.

CONCRETE: as developed by the ancient Romans, fast-drying hardening volcanic sand used in architectural construction; see pp. 126–27.

CONTRAPPOSTO: a term describing the position assumed by the human body when the weight is borne on one leg while the other is relaxed; e.g., the *Doryphorus* (fig. 78). Contrapposto creates a figure that seems to be relaxed and yet suggests the potential for movement.

CORINTHIAN ORDER: one of the ancient Greek architectural ORDERS; see fig. 71 and p. 81.

CORNICE: a projecting MOLDING surmounting and emphasizing a WALL or ARCH. Note the prominent interior cornices of the Pantheon (fig. 127) and the heavy cornice capping the Medici Palace (fig. 246).

CROSS-HATCHING: in drawings and PRINTS, superimposed layers of parallel lines (HATCHING) at an angle to one another, used to create shadows and MODELING, as in fig. 287.

CROSS SECTION: an architectural diagram that shows how a building would look from the inside if it were cut by a vertical plane from side to side; for a cross section of the Parthenon, see fig. 83. See also LONGITUDINAL SECTION.

CROSS VAULT: a structural system formed by two TUNNEL VAULTS intersecting at right angles; see fig. 124 and pp. 126–27.

CROSSING: in a Christian church, the area where the NAVE intersects the TRANSEPTS; for diagrams see figs. 146, 198.

CRUCIFORM BASILICA: a BASILICA with TRANSEPTS, forming a Latin cross plan, as at Old St. Peter's (fig. 146).

CUN: in Chinese painting, small brushstrokes dabbed on quickly to create the sense of a particular texture, as in Li Cheng's painting (fig. 166).

DAGUERREOTYPE: the earliest practical photographic process; see pp. 402–3.

DIMINUTION: a device used in drawing and painting to help suggest PERSPECTIVE. Forms are represented as progressively smaller to suggest their distance from the viewer; see Perugino's *Christ Giving the Keys to St. Peter* (fig. 4).

DOME: an architectural structural system that can be understood as an ARCH rotated 180° on a central axis; see fig. 124 and p. 127.

DORIC ORDER: the most vigorous and austere of the ancient Greek architectural ORDERS; see fig. 71 and p. 81.

DRESSED STONE: blocks of stone used for construction, each of which is carefully cut and trimmed for its specific place and purpose, as at the ancient Roman Pont du Gard (fig. 125).

DRUMS: the individual cylindrical units that are combined to create the SHAFT of a COLUMN; due to the ravages of time, the drums of the columns of the Parthenon are clearly visible today (fig. 82).

DRYPOINT: a printmaking process; see fig. 360 and pp. 336–37.

ECHINUS: on a DORIC CAPITAL, the rounded, cushion-shaped MOLDING below the ABACUS; see fig. 71 and p. 81.

EDITION: a group of prints made from a single PRINT FORM in one of the printmaking processes; see figs. 289, 360, 417. In current practice, artists sign and number each print in an edition.

ELEVATION: an architectural diagram that shows the exterior or interior surfaces of a building and their decoration diagramatically, without the recession and distortion that would result from a single viewpoint; see figs. 293–94. Elevation can also refer to one exterior side of a building.

EMULSION TECHNIQUE: a painting technique using a liquid mixture in which one of the elements is suspended as minute droplets, as in fig. 547.

ENCAUSTIC: a technique of painting using PIGMENTS dissolved in hot wax; see fig. 151.

ENGAGED COLUMN: see HALF COLUMN.

ENGRAVING: a printmaking process; see fig. 289 and pp. 276–77.

ENTABLATURE: the upper part of an architectural ORDER, usually includes ARCHITRAVE, FRIEZE, and CORNICE; see fig. 71.

ENTASIS: the bulging of a DORIC column about one-third of the way up from the base, creating an effect of muscular elasticity; for a subtle example of entasis see the columns of the Parthenon (fig. 82).

ETCHING: a printmaking process; see fig. 360 and pp. 336–37.

ETCHING GROUND: the acid-resistant, resinous mixture used to coat the PRINT FORM (a metal plate) in the ETCHING process; see pp. 336–37.

ETCHING NEEDLE: the sharp steel instrument used in the ETCHING technique; see pp. 336–37.

EXPRESSIVE CONTENT: the emotions and feelings communicated by a work of art.

FACADE: the front or principal face of a building, as in Palladio's San Giorgio Maggiore (fig. 321).

FERROCONCRETE: see REINFORCED CONCRETE.

FIGURE-GROUND RELATIONSHIP: the contrast between form (or positive elements) and background (or negative ground) in a work of art; see Piero's *Duke of Urbino* (fig. 218).

FLUTES, FLUTING: shallow vertical grooves on the SHAFT of a COLUMN that accentuate the column's cylindrical quality; see fig. 71.

FLYING BUTTRESS: a structural element in the form of an open half arch that counteracts the outward thrust of an arch or vault; see figs. 200, 202.

FORESHORTENING: the technique used in a painting or RELIEF SCULPTURE to suggest that figures, parts of the body, or other forms are shown in sharp recession, as in Mantegna's *Foreshortened Christ* (fig. 257).

FORMAL ANALYSIS: a visual examination and analysis of a work of art that studies how the integral parts of a work of art are united to produce its historical and/or individual style. Introductory formal analyses of works of art are offered for figs. 1, 3–5, 7–13.

FORUM: the official center of an ancient Roman town, with temple, marketplace, and governmental buildings; see the forum in Rome (fig. 109).

FREESTANDING: see SCULPTURE IN THE ROUND.

FRESCO: a technique of painting directly on a plaster wall or ceiling, usually when the plaster is still wet, as in Giotto's Arena Chapel (fig. 214) and Michelangelo's Sistine Chapel ceiling (fig. 297); see p. 123. Also known as buon fresco. See also FRESCO SECCO.

FRESCO SECCO: a technique of FRESCO painting in which the paint is applied to dry plaster.

FRIEZE: the middle section of the horizontal ENTABLATURE in the ancient Greek and Roman ORDERS; see fig. 71 and p. 81.

FUNCTION: the purpose for which a work of art was created; e.g., the function of the Egyptian sculpture of *Menkure and His Queen* (fig. 2) was to provide a home for the souls of the pharaoh and his queen throughout eternity.

GABLE ROOF: the most common type of roof, formed by two planes which slope downward from a central beam, as on the Parthenon (fig. 80). Also known as a pitched roof.

GENRE PAINTING or SCULPTURE: a representation of everyday life, as in Leyster's *Gay Cavaliers* (fig. 338).

GIANT ORDER: PILASTERS or COLUMNS that span more than one story of a structure; e.g., the pilasters on the exterior and interior of Michelangelo's design for New St. Peter's in Rome (figs. 293–94). Also known as colossal order.

GILDING: the covering of a work of art or part of a work of art with gold leaf or some other gold-colored substance; the background of Giotto's *Madonna* is gilded (fig. 210).

GLAZES: in the art of oil painting, thin layers of superimposed translucent varnish, often with a small amount of pigment added, to modify color and to build up a rich, sonorous color effect; used by Jan van Eyck (figs. 240–41), Titian (figs. 308–11), and others. In pottery, the glaze is a thin layer of a colored material that fuses with the surface when heated; the glaze provides the hard and colorful surface of a pottery vessel.

GOLDEN RECTANGLE: see GOLDEN SECTION.

GOLDEN SECTION: the proportional relationship of approximately 5:8, used by the ancient Greeks as the key to visual harmony; see fig. 79 and p. 87.

GOUACHE: opaque WATERCOLOR paint.

GREEK CROSS PLAN: a central plan with four arms of equal dimension placed at 90° angles, usually surrounding a DOME, as in Bramante's and Michelangelo's design for New St. Peter's (figs. 291–92).

GRISAILLE: the monochromatic painting of objects, often to simulate stone sculpture; see fig. 235.

GROIN VAULT: see CROSS VAULT.

GROUND PLAN: an architectural diagram that shows how a building would look from above if it were truncated by a horizontal plane approximately one meter above floor level; see figs. 198, 349.

GUILDS: legal organizations of merchants, craftspeople, and artists, rather like trade unions, that flourished in the later Middle Ages and the Renaissance. Guilds established standards for training and production and commissioned works of art; see the niches at Orsanmichele in Florence (figs. 222–23).

HALF COLUMN: a half-round decorative column attached to a supporting wall. Also known as engaged column.

HALF-HIPPED ROOF: a type of roof construction in which the ends are vertical and partly HIPPED, or they are hipped using two different angles, as at Nara (fig. 161).

HALO: a radiance of light, visually represented as a golden circle or disc, surrounding the head of a holy figure, as in the Byzantine mosaic at Mount Sinai (fig. 149).

HAPPENING: a quasi-theatrical event, common in the 1950s and 1960s, in which artists, usually without a preconceived script, performed and encouraged the spontaneous participation of the audience; see fig. 481.

HATCHING: in drawings and prints, closely spaced series of parallel lines that create effects of MODELING, as in fig. 287.

HIERARCHICAL SCALE: the representation of figures who are more important politically (or socially) as larger than less important figures, as in the Egyptian *Hunting Scene* (fig. 52).

HIGH RELIEF: RELIEF SCULPTURE in which the forms project substantially from the background; e.g., the altar of Zeus at Pergamon (fig. 94).

HIGH VALUE: a relatively light color, as in the high value of the yellow trousers in Goya's *Execution of Madrilenos on the Third of May* (fig. 408).

HIGHLIGHTS: in painting, areas of HIGH VALUE color which suggest light hitting the form to create MODELING; see the highlights on the metal pitcher in the Roman still life (fig. 120).

HIPPED ROOF: a type of roof construction in which the ends are sloped instead of being vertical.

HISTORICAL CONTEXT: the ideas, beliefs, or attitudes current in the period when a work of art was created. Historical context also encompasses how the work of art was perceived by its audience.

HISTORICAL SIGNIFICANCE: an understanding of how a work of art reveals the ideas, beliefs, or attitudes current in the period when that work of art was created.

HISTORICAL STYLE: a clearly recognizable artistic tradition (see FORMAL ANALYSIS) characteristic of a particular historical or artistic period.

HUE: the property of a color that distinguishes it from others; also the name of a color; see fig. 6.

HYPOSTYLE: a type of architectural construction in which the interior space is crowded with continuous rows of COLUMNS or posts, as in the Egyptian hypostyle hall (fig. 46) and the Mosque at Córdoba (fig. 168).

ICON: a special term used in Orthodox Christianity to refer to a painting of a religious subject, as in fig. 151.

ICONOGRAPHY: the art-historical study of the subject matter of a work of art, including the investigation of the symbolism and the meaning of the subject in the culture which produced it.

ICONOLOGY: the investigation of how the iconography of a work is related to the HISTORICAL CONTEXT.

IDEALIZATION, IDEALIZED: the improvement and abstraction of forms to conform to contemporary cultural standards of perfection and beauty; e.g., *Menkure and His Queen* (fig. 2).

ILLUMINATED MANUSCRIPT: a hand-written book with painted decoration, common in medieval and Renaissance Europe; see figs. 150, 159–60, 171–73, 179, 195, 224–25.

ILLUSIONISM, ILLUSIONISTIC: when the objects represented in a work of art (usually a painting) seem to be tangible and weighty, existing within actual space; e.g., Perugino's *Christ Giving the Keys* (fig. 4); see pp. 120–23.

IMPASTO: raised brushstrokes of thick paint, usually oil, as in Titian's *Rape of Europa* (fig. 311).

INCISED RELIEF: see SUNKEN RELIEF.

INDIVIDUAL STYLE: the particular formal qualities (see FORMAL ANALYSIS) used by an individual artist; e.g., the bold colors, thick paint, and heavy brushstrokes characteristic of the works of Van Gogh (figs. 403, 462–63).

INFILLING: see WEB.

INSTALLATION: a work of art that consists of an ensemble of objects, often three-dimensional, that are especially arranged by the artist for a particular location or site (see fig. 1).

INTAGLIO PROCESS: a printmaking process in which the lines to be printed are incised into the surface of the PRINT FORM, such as in the engraving, etching, and drypoint processes; see figs. 289, 360.

INTENSITY: the level of richness or saturation of a color; note the very intense red used in Van Gogh's *Night Cafe* (fig. 462).

IONIC ORDER: one of the ancient Greek architectural ORDERS; see fig. 71 and p. 81.

ISOCEPHALY: a COMPOSITION, usually relatively unnaturalistic, in which the heads of the figures form a horizontal line; see the mosaic of *Theodora and Attendants* at Ravenna (fig. 157).

ISOMETRIC PROJECTION: an architectural diagram that includes both a ground plan and a view of the exterior and/or interior from a specific point of view below or above the structure; for an isometric projection of a temple at Karnak, see fig. 50.

JAMBS: the areas flanking an ARCH, doorway, or window; in Romanesque and Gothic churches, the jambs are often decorated with sculpted figures, as at Amiens (fig. 205).

KACHIN-TIHU: a small wooden figure or doll (also known as a kachina doll) made by members of the Hopi tribe (fig. 495).
KEYSTONE: the central VOUSSOIR of an arch, rib, or vault; see fig. 124.
KONDO: the main hall at a Japanese Buddhist temple-MONASTERY complex, as at Horyu-ji (figs. 161–62).
KUFIC: a style of Arabic calligraphy, sometimes used as virtually pure ornament.
KYLIX: an ancient Greek drinking cup; see fig. 66.

LAY ARTIST: during periods when much artistic production was controlled by monks and nuns, a lay artist was one who lived and worked in the city, outside of the MONASTERY, and was often a member of a GUILD.
LEKYTHOS: an ancient Greek container to hold olive oil; see fig. 66.
LINEAR: the technique in painting, drawing, or printmaking of creating sharply defined forms or precisely delineated contours, as in Leonardo da Vinci's *Vitruvian Man* (fig. 266).
LINTEL: the horizontal beam spanning an opening, as in the POST-AND-LINTEL SYSTEM (fig. 48).
LITHOGRAPHY: a printmaking process; see fig. 417 and p. 385.
LONGITUDINAL SECTION: an architectural diagram that shows how a building would look from the inside if it were sliced by a vertical plane from front to back; see the Pantheon (fig. 128) and New St. Peter's (fig. 293).
LOST-WAX BRONZE CASTING: a technique of casting bronze and other metals; see fig. 77 and p. 85.
LOW RELIEF: relief sculpture in which flattened figures or forms project only

very slightly from the background, as in the *Palette of Narmer* (figs. 35–36). Also known as bas-relief.
LOW VALUE: a relatively dark color, as in the low value of the background in Goya's *Execution of Madrilenos on the Third of May* (fig. 408).
LUNETTE: a semicircular area enclosed by an ARCH, as at the Byzantine church of San Vitale (fig. 155).

MADKSOURAH: a special enclosure in a MOSQUE, reserved for the calif (ruler), as at Córdoba (figs. 169–70).
MANDALA: a diagram of the Buddhist cosmos, used as a basic design motif in Buddhist art, as at Sanchi (fig. 97).
MANDORLA: an oval or almond-shaped HALO that surrounds the body of a holy figure, as in the Byzantine mosaic at Mount Sinai (fig. 149).
MANUSCRIPT: a hand-written book produced in medieval and Renaissance Europe. If it has painted decoration, it is known as an ILLUMINATED MANUSCRIPT; see figs. 159–60 and 224–25.
MASTABA: a rectangular Egyptian burial monument, with BATTERED WALLS and a flat roof; see fig. 43.
MEDIUM/MEDIA: the material or materials of which a work of art is composed, or the technique used to create it; e.g., oil paint on canvas (fig. 463), bronze (fig. 249), and etching (fig. 359).
MEGALITH: a very large stone of irregular shape (not DRESSED) used in prehistoric monuments; see Stonehenge (fig. 54).
METOPES: the square areas between the TRIGLYPHS in the FRIEZE area of the ENTABLATURE of the DORIC ORDER; sometimes decorated with sculpture, as at the Parthenon (fig. 80); see fig. 71 and p. 81.
MIHRAB: in a MOSQUE, the ARCH or niche on the QIBLA wall that indicates the direction of Mecca, to which Muslims must turn in prayer, as at Córdoba (figs. 168–70).
MINARET: the tower in a MOSQUE complex, usually tall and slender, from which the Muslim faithful are called to prayer five times a day.
MIXED-MEDIA: a term used to describe a work composed of a variety of different materials, usually encompassing elements of painting, sculpture, and even architecture (see figs. 1, 544).
MOBILE: a sculpture that moves, usually a lightweight, delicately balanced suspended work; see the example by Calder

(fig. 534).
MODELING/TO MODEL: in painting, drawing, or printmaking, the creation of an effect of weight and mass in an object by the manipulation of VALUE to create HIGHLIGHTS and SHADING, as in fig. 265.
MOLDING: an ornamental band, depressed or projecting, that gives definition to an architectural surface.
MONASTERY: a religious establishment which houses a community of persons who have withdrawn from the world to pursue the religious life; see examples from St. Gall and Cluny (figs. 175–76).
MONOCHROMATIC: term used to describe a painting or drawing created by shades of black and white or values of a single color, as in Picasso's *Guernica* (fig. 530).
MOSAIC: a pattern made of small pieces (TESSERAE) of stone, tile, or glass, used on floors, walls, or ceilings; see Roman floor mosaics (figs. 92, 104) and the wall and ceiling mosaics at San Vitale (figs. 155–57).
MOSQUE: a place of worship in the Islamic religion, as at Córdoba (figs. 168–70).
MOUND ARCHITECTURE: an early type of architectural construction characterized by the creation of a solid mass, as in the Sumerian ziggurat (fig. 39) and the Egyptian pyramids (fig. 40).
MUDRAH: a hand gesture of Buddha, as in fig. 163. Each traditional gesture conveys its own meaning.
MURAL PAINTING: large wall decorations; e.g., those at the Villa of the Mysteries (fig. 117) and Giotto's Arena Chapel (fig. 214).

NAOS: the walled inner sanctuary of a Greek temple, where the cult statue is housed (fig. 83).
NARTHEX: an entrance hall or vestibule, often found in Christian churches, as at Old St. Peter's Basilica (fig. 146).
NATURALISM, NATURALISTIC: when the elements or forms within a work of art closely resemble the appearance of those forms in nature; e.g., Bernini's *Apollo and Daphne* (fig. 3).
NAVE: the large central hall, usually AXIAL and often with a CLERESTORY, that characterizes the BASILICA plan (see Old St. Peter's, fig. 146, and many Christian churches).
NAVE ARCADE: the series of ARCHES that divide the NAVE from the AISLES; see fig. 200.

NON-OBJECTIVE: when the forms in a work of art do not resemble forms in the visual world; e.g., Mondrian's *Diamond Painting* (fig. 5). Also known as non-representational.

NON-REPRESENTATIONAL: see NON-OBJECTIVE.

NUNNERY: a religious establishment which houses a community of women who have withdrawn from the world to pursue the religious life.

OCULUS: a circular opening in a wall or at the apex of a dome, as in the ancient Roman Pantheon (fig. 127).

OIL PAINT TECHNIQUE: a technique developed in the fifteenth century in which the pigments are mixed with the slow-drying and flexible medium of oil; see figs. 239, 241 and pp. 240–41.

ORDERS: a series of Greek and Roman architectural systems that give aesthetic definition and decoration to the POST-AND-LINTEL system; see fig. 71.

ORTHOGONALS: the converging diagonal lines that meet at the vanishing point in the SCIENTIFIC PERSPECTIVE system, as in Donatello's *Feast of Herod* (fig. 232). In reality these lines would be parallel; see fig. 233 and p. 233.

OVERLAPPING: a device used in painting and relief sculpture to help suggest perspective. Forms are placed in front of other forms to suggest their relative placement within the illusion of space.

PAGODA: the European name for a tall tower, often with a series of roofs in successive layers, that marks sacred Buddhist sites in China and Japan, as at the Horyu-ji complex (figs. 161–62).

PAINTERLY: in painting, the technique of using large brushstrokes and flecks of paint to define form; see figs. 310, 346.

PANATHENAIC AMPHORA: an ancient Greek vase awarded as a prize at the Olympic Games; see fig. 66.

PARCHMENT: the skin on a calf, sheep, or other animal which is scraped, stretched, and dried to be used as a surface for writing. Used in the medieval period for MANUSCRIPTS.

PASTEL: a drawing medium made of ground pigments mixed with gum water.

PATRON: the person, persons, or organization that asks an artist or artists to create a work of art. Usually they also pay for the work.

PATTERN BOOK: a book of images, prepared as an artist's tool, that preserves a tradition of images that can be copied; see fig. 140.

PEDIMENT: the triangular end of a GABLE ROOF; in a Greek temple this area is often decorated with sculpture; see figs. 60, 84–86.

PENDENTIVES: in a domed structure, the curved triangular segments that provide a transition from the four supporting piers to the circular base of the dome, as at the Byzantine church of Hagia Sophia (fig. 152). For a diagram see fig. 124.

PERIPTERAL: a term that describes a building with an exterior PERISTYLE; e.g., the Parthenon (fig. 80).

PERISTYLE: a continuous row of columns that completely surrounds the exterior of a structure; e.g., the ancient Greek Parthenon (fig. 80), or an inner courtyard, as at fig. 102.

PERSPECTIVE: depth. An illusion of perspective is suggested in many paintings; e.g., Perugino's *Christ Giving the Keys to St. Peter* (fig. 4). Devices that help suggest the illusion of perspective include SCIENTIFIC PERSPECTIVE, AERIAL PERSPECTIVE, DIMINUTION, and OVERLAPPING.

PICTORIAL RELIEF: relief sculpture that conveys an illusion of depth by using a subtle transition from high to progressively lower relief. See Donatello's *Feast of Herod* (fig. 232) and Ghiberti's *Story of Jacob and Esau* (fig. 236).

PICTURE PLANE: the flat surface of a picture. The picture plane, denied in such illusionistic works as Perugino's *Christ Giving the Keys to St. Peter* (fig. 4), is emphasized as a positive element in many nineteenth- and twentieth-century paintings, such as Mondrian's *Diamond Painting* (fig. 5).

PIER: the vertical supports used in an arched or vaulted structural system; see the supports of the ancient Roman Pont du Gard (fig. 125) and the nave piers of the Gothic cathedral at Chartres (figs. 196–200).

PIETÀ: an iconographic theme in which the dead Christ is shown being held by his mother, as in Michelangelo's *Pietà* (fig. 271).

PIGMENT: the substance, usually ground, that is used to give color in the TEMPERA, FRESCO, and early OIL painting techniques.

PILASTER: a shallow, virtually flat version of the columns of the Greek and Roman ORDERS; pilasters are usually decorative, not structural. See fig. 375.

PITCHED ROOF: see GABLE ROOF.

PLAN: see GROUND PLAN.

PLATE: the thin metallic plate used as a PRINT FORM in ENGRAVING and ETCHING; see figs. 289, 360.

POESIE: the Venetian name for a theme from mythology treated in a nostalgic and romantic manner; see Titian's *Rape of Europa* (fig. 311).

POINTED ARCH: an ARCH in which the sides rise to a point at the apex, as in Gothic architecture (figs. 196, 200–202).

POST-AND-LINTEL SYSTEM: a simple system of architectural construction in which horizontal architectural members (lintels) are supported by vertical supports (posts); see fig. 48 and p. 62.

POTTER'S WHEEL: a revolving platform on which clay vessels of regular and often graceful shape are formed. Examples of wheel-produced vessels include the ancient Greek pots shown in fig. 66.

PRESENTATION DRAWING: a finely finished drawing made to be given to a collector or friend.

PRIMARY COLORS: red, yellow, and blue. These are HUES that in theory are pure and not the combination of any other hues. On the color wheel (fig. 6), all other colors are understood as mixtures of these three hues.

PRINT: a work of art produced by one of the printmaking processes, including WOODCUT, ENGRAVING, ETCHING, DRYPOINT, LITHOGRAPHY, and silkscreen.

PRINT FORM: the surface—wood, copper, steel, glass, stone, etc. —to which ink is applied in any of the PRINTMAKING processes; see figs. 289, 360, 417.

PRINTMAKING: a series of techniques (WOODCUT, ENGRAVING, ETCHING, DRYPOINT, LITHOGRAPHY, silkscreen, and others) by which prints are produced.

PSALTER: a manuscript of the Psalms of David, as in the *Paris Psalter* (fig. 150).

PSEUDO-PERIPTERAL: a building that seems to have a PERISTYLE, but many of the COLUMNS are HALF COLUMNS or PILASTERS; e.g., the Roman Temple of Portunus (fig. 100).

PURE COLOR: a color at maximum or full intensity; a HUE without the addition of white, black, or other colors that would reduce the INTENSITY of the color; e.g., the colors used by Mondrian in his *Diamond Painting* (fig. 5).

PUTTI: figures of male babies, sometimes male baby angels, popular in

Renaissance art, as in Mantegna's Camera Picta (fig. 255–56).

PYLON: the entrance gate to an Egyptian temple complex, with broad BATTERED towers and flagpoles; see fig. 47.

QIBLA: in a MOSQUE, the wall that indicates the direction of Mecca, toward which Muslims must turn in prayer; see Córdoba (figs. 169–70).

QUADRIGA: a sculptural monument that consists of a figure in a chariot with four horses; the *Charioteer* (fig. 76) was part of a quadriga.

REALISM, REALISTIC: the use of subject matter drawn from actual life and experience; e.g., fig. 337. Not to be confused with the nineteenth-century movement known as Realism (figs. 423–24, 453).

REFECTORY: the dining hall in a MONASTERY or NUNNERY; the location for Leonardo da Vinci's painting of the *Last Supper* (fig. 268).

REINFORCED CONCRETE: concrete strengthened with embedded wire rods or mesh; see fig. 431. Also known as ferroconcrete.

RELIEF PROCESS: a PRINTMAKING process in which the lines and surfaces to which the ink adheres are higher than the parts that are not to be printed; e.g., the WOODCUT process; see fig. 289 and pp. 276–77.

RELIEF SCULPTURE: sculpture in which the figures or forms are united with a background; examples of relief sculpture types include LOW or BAS-RELIEF (figs. 35–36), HIGH RELIEF (fig. 94), SUNKEN RELIEF (fig. 31), and PICTORIAL RELIEF (fig. 232).

RELIQUARY: a container for a sacred relic, as in fig. 137.

REPOUSSOIR: an object in the immediate foreground of a painting that establishes the frontal plane of the illusionistic space; e.g., the low fence in the FRESCOED room known as Livia's *Garden* (fig. 119).

REPRESENTATIONAL: when a work of art reproduces the appearance of forms in nature; see Bernini's *Apollo and Daphne* (fig. 3).

RIBS: raised structural elements that outline and help support a ribbed VAULT, as at the Gothic cathedral of Chartres (figs. 196–97); see fig. 201 and p. 204.

SARCOPHAGUS: a stone coffin, sometimes decorated with sculpture; see fig. 144.

SCIENTIFIC PERSPECTIVE: a mathematical system used to create illusionistic depth in Renaissance paintings (see figs. 4, 268) and RELIEF SCULPTURE (figs. 232, 236). Lines that in reality would be parallel to each other become ORTHOGONALS that converge toward a VANISHING POINT when projected onto a two-dimensional surface.

SCREEN WALL: a non-supporting wall, usually with broad expanses of windows, that fills the opening under an ARCH or VAULT, as at the Byzantine church of Hagia Sophia (fig. 152). It is screen walls that sheathe the exterior of a modern steel-frame skyscraper.

SCRIPTORIUM: the room or rooms in a MONASTERY where MANUSCRIPTS are copied and illustrated, as in the St. Gall plan (fig. 175).

SCULPTURE IN THE ROUND: sculpture that is fully three-dimensional and finished on all sides; e.g., French's *Minuteman* (fig. 7). Also known as freestanding.

SHADING: in painting, drawing, and printmaking, progressive decreases in the VALUE and INTENSITY of colors to suggest the changes that result when light hits a form; note the progressive darkening on the face of the *Mona Lisa* (fig. 282).

SHAFT: in architecture, the vertical cylindrical form that supports the entablature; for example, Doric columns are shafts (fig. 82).

SHIFTING PERSPECTIVE: the use of multiple viewpoints in a painting or drawing, as in Li Cheng's and Cézanne's paintings (figs. 165, 464) or in Cubism (figs. 501–2).

SIDE AISLE: see AISLE.

SILVERPOINT: a drawing technique using a sharpened point of silver on specially prepared paper or parchment; e.g., Rembrandt's drawing of his fiancée Saskia (fig. 354).

SITE: the specific setting or location for which a work of art or architecture was designed; e.g., the location of Wright's Fallingwater over a waterfall (fig. 11).

SLIP: clay particles and water, sometimes used to decorate a pottery vessel, as in figs 65, 67.

SPOLIA: materials taken from an earlier structure and reused, as in the columns and capitals at Old St. Peter's (fig. 145) and the Mosque in Córdoba (fig. 168).

SPRINGING: the level at which an ARCH or VAULT begins to curve inward and upward; see fig. 124 and pp. 126–27.

SQUINCH: ARCHES, LINTELS, and/or corbels that jut across the corners of a square space to support a dome and to make the transition from the square space to a polygonal or round one; see the squinches that support the dome at Córdoba (fig. 169).

STAINED-GLASS WINDOWS: windows composed of pieces of colored glass joined by lead strips; see fig. 209 and p. 209.

STATES: the successive printed stages of a print, especially common in Rembrandt's ETCHINGS and DRYPOINTS (figs. 359, 361).

STEEL-FRAME CONSTRUCTION: an architectural structure in which steel beams are joined horizontally and vertically to create a gridlike structural system; see fig. 430.

STUPA: a large hemispherical Buddhist shrine, erected to hold a relic or mark a holy site, as in the Great Stupa at Sanchi (fig. 95); the form evolved from earlier burial mounds.

STYLE: a complex concept with several meanings, including HISTORICAL STYLE and INDIVIDUAL STYLE.

STYLOBATE: the stepped platform that forms the base for a Greek temple; see fig. 71.

SUBJECT MATTER: see ICONOGRAPHY.

SUNKEN RELIEF: an Egyptian style of RELIEF SCULPTURE in which the figures are recessed into the surface (fig. 31). Also known as incised relief.

TABLERO: in Mesoamerican architecture, a heavy, projecting, rectangular MOLDING outlined by a thick frame, as in the Pyramid of Quetzalcóatl at Teotihuacán (fig. 134).

TAOTIE: the stylized monster mask that decorates early Chinese bronzes (figs. 25, 27).

TECHNIQUE: how the artist or artists used the materials (the MEDIUM or MEDIA) to create the work of art; e.g., the vigorous, heavy OIL brushstrokes of Van Gogh (figs. 462–63) or the highly polished finish of Michelangelo's *Pietà* (fig. 271).

TEMPERA PAINT TECHNIQUE: a painting technique in which the pigments are combined with egg. The support is usually plaster-coated wood and the background is often decorated with gold leaf, as in Giotto's *Madonna* (fig. 210).

TENEBRISM: a dramatic contrast of light and dark used by Caravaggio and his followers; see pp. 316–19.

TENSILE STRENGTH: the internal longitudinal strength in a stone, steel, or wood beam which enables it to support itself without breaking.

TERRA-COTTA: a hard earthenware, glazed or unglazed.

TESSERAE: the individual cut pieces of stone, glass or other materials used in the MOSAIC technique (see fig. 157). One piece is a tessera.

THRUST: the outward force created by an ARCH or VAULT; this must be counterbalanced by BUTTRESSING; see fig. 124 and pp. 126–27.

TOU-KUNG BRACKET: in Chinese and Japanese architecture, CANTILEVERED brackets, often multiple and complex, that support the beams and roof of a structure, as at Horyu-ji (fig. 161).

TRANSEPT: in a cross-shaped Christian church, cross arms placed parallel to the NAVE; see fig. 146 and p. 150.

TRANSVERSALS: lines that are parallel to each other in reality that recede parallel to the picture frame in the SCIENTIFIC PERSPECTIVE system; see fig. 233 and pp. 232–33.

TRIFORIUM: in Gothic construction, an arcaded passageway above the NAVE ARCADE (fig. 200) and below the CLERESTORY, as in the cathedral at Chartres (figs. 196–97).

TRIGLYPH: in the Doric FRIEZE, the area between the METOPES, decorated with vertical grooves; see fig. 71 and p. 81.

TRIPTYCH: a three-part altarpiece or work of art.

TROMPE L'OEIL: illusionistic painting which emphasizes realistic effects to convince the viewer that the painted scene or object is actually real or not painted, as in Mantegna's Camera Picta frescoes (figs. 255–56).

TRUMEAU: the central supporting post between the two sides of a double door, which in Renaissance and Gothic churches is often decorated with sculpture, as at Amiens (figs. 204, 207).

TUFA: a soft, porous rock that hardens with exposure to air; used in construction.

TUNNEL VAULT: see BARREL VAULT.

TYMPANUM: the LUNETTE over the doorway of a church, which is often decorated with sculpture, as in Romanesque (figs. 184–86) and Gothic (fig. 205) structures.

UNDERDRAWING: a preparatory drawing done directly on the plaster or canvas and over which the artist paints the finished work.

VALUE: the relative darkness (LOW VALUE) or lightness (HIGH VALUE) of a HUE.

VANISHING POINT: in a work created using the SCIENTIFIC PERSPECTIVE system, the vanishing point is the place where the converging ORTHOGONALS would converge if continued, as in Donatello's *Feast of Herod* (fig. 233).

VAULT, VAULTING: a structural system based on the ARCH, including the TUNNEL (or BARREL) VAULT, the CROSS (or GROIN) VAULT, and the DOME; see fig. 124 and pp. 126–27.

VEHICLE: the drying liquid in which painting pigments are suspended; as it dries, it adheres the color to the surface.

VELLUM: fine PARCHMENT prepared from calf skin used for the pages in MANUSCRIPTS.

VILLA: a country house, as in the Villa Rotonda by Palladio (fig. 9).

VOLUTE: the spiral scroll motif that characterizes the capital of the IONIC ORDER; see fig. 71.

VOLUTE KRATER: an ancient Greek vase used for the mixing of wine with water; see fig. 66.

VOUSSOIRS: the individual blocks of stone (or bricks) which compose an ARCH; see fig. 124 and pp. 126–27.

WASH: ink thinned with water, applied with a brush to add effects of shadow, as in Rembrandt's *A Man Rowing* (fig. 353).

WATERCOLOR: pigments mixed with water (and gum arabic as a drying agent); used in Homer's watercolor *The Blue Boat* (fig. 458).

WEB: the surfaces of a Gothic RIB VAULT; see fig. 201. Also known as infilling.

WESTWORK: a church entrance with a centralized APSE enclosing a chapel on the second story and two flanking towers, typical of Carolingian churches, as in the St. Gall monastery plan (fig. 175).

WOODCUT: a relief printmaking process; for a diagram see fig. 289 and pp. 276–77.

YAKSHA, YAKSHI: ancient Indian nature spirits which became gods and goddesses of fertility, as at Sanchi (fig. 96).

ZIGGURAT: a stepped pyramid of mud brick, used by the Sumerians and the Assyrians as a sacred site.

BIBLIOGRAPHY

This is a general, broad bibliography intended to lead the reader to more specific books on individual sites, monuments, artists, and movements. As a rule, it includes only the most important sources, and only those in English.

GENERAL

Broude, Norma, and Mary D. Garrard. *Feminism and Art History: Questioning the Litany.* New York: Harper & Row, 1982.

de la Croix, Horst, and Richard G. Tansey. *Gardner's Art Through the Ages.* New York: Harcourt Brace Jovanovich, 1986.

Elsen, Albert E. *Purposes of Art.* New York: Holt, Rinehart and Winston, 1972.

Encyclopedia of World Art. 15 vols. New York: McGraw-Hill, 1959–68.

Fleming, John, Hugh Honour, and Nikolaus Pevsner. *The Penguin Dictionary of Architecture.* Harmondsworth: Penguin, 1980.

Goldwater, Robert J., and Marco Treves. *Artists on Art.* New York: Pantheon, 1974.

Gombrich, E.H. *Art and Illusion.* New York: Pantheon, 1972.

——————. *The Story of Art.* Oxford: Phaidon, 1984.

Hartt, Frederick. *Art: A History of Painting, Sculpture, Architecture.* New York: Abrams, 1985.

Holt, Elizabeth G. *A Documentary History of Art.* 2 vols. Garden City, N.Y.: Doubleday, 1981.

Honour, Hugh, and John Fleming. *The Visual Arts: A History.* Englewood Cliffs, N.J.: Prentice-Hall, 1986.

Janson, H.W. *History of Art.* New York: Abrams, 1986.

Kostof, Spiro. *The Architect: Chapters in the History of the Profession.* New York: Oxford University Press, 1977.

——————. *A History of Architecture: Settings and Rituals.* New York: Oxford University Press, 1985.

Lee, Sherman. *A History of Far Eastern Art.* New York: Abrams, 1982.

Nochlin, Linda. *Women, Art, and Power and Other Essays.* New York: Harper & Row, 1988.

——————, and Ann S. Harris. *Women Artists: 1550–1950.* Los Angeles: Los Angeles County Museum of Art; New York: distributed by Random House, 1976.

Roberts, Laurence P. *A Dictionary of Japanese Artists: Painting, Sculpture, Ceramics, Prints, Lacquer.* New York: Weatherhill, 1976.

Sayre, Henry M. *Writing About Art.* Englewood Cliffs, N.J.: Prentice-Hall, 1989.

Sullivan, Michael. *The Arts of China.* Berkeley: University of California Press, 1984.

Trachtenberg, Marvin, and Isabelle Hyman. *Architecture from Prehistory to Post-Modernism.* New York: Abrams, 1986.

Wittkower, Rudolf and Margot. *Born Under Saturn.* New York: Norton, 1969.

PREHISTORIC AND ANCIENT

Adams, Richard E.W. *Prehistoric Mesoamerica.* Boston: Little, Brown, 1977.

Aldred, Cyril. *Egyptian Art in the Days of the Pharaohs 3100–320 B.C.* New York: Oxford University Press, 1980.

Amiet, Pierre. *The Ancient Art of the Near East.* New York: Abrams, 1980.

Boardman, John. *Greek Art.* London: Thames and Hudson, 1985.

——————. *The Parthenon and Its Sculptures.* Austin: University of Texas Press, 1985.

Boëthius, Alexander. *Etruscan and Early Roman Architecture.* Harmondsworth: Penguin, 1978.

Brendel, Otto. *Etruscan Art.* Harmondsworth: Penguin, 1978.

Brilliant, Richard. *Arts of the Ancient Greeks.* New York: McGraw-Hill, 1973.

——————. *Roman Art form the Republic to Constantine.* London: Phaidon; New York: distributed by Praeger, 1974.

Grand, Paule M. *Prehistoric Art: Paleolithic Painting and Sculpture.* Greenwich, Conn.: New York Graphic Society, 1967.

Groenewegen-Frankfort, H.A., and Bernard Ashmole. *Art of the Ancient World.* Englewood Cliffs, N.J.: Prentice-Hall, 1972.

Kubler, George. *Art and Architecture of Ancient America.* Harmondsworth: Penguin, 1975.

MacDonald, William L. *The Architecture of the Roman Empire.* 2 vols. New Haven: Yale University Press, 1982.

Pollitt, J.J. *The Art of Greece 1400–31 B.C.* (Sources and Documents). Englewood Cliffs, N.J.: Prentice-Hall, 1965.

——————. *Art and Experience in Classical Greece.* Cambridge, Eng.: Cambridge University Press, 1972.

——————. *The Ancient View of Greek Art.* New Haven: Yale University Press, 1974.

——————. *The Art of Rome c. 753 B.C.–A.D. 337* (Sources and Documents). New York: Cambridge University Press, 1983.

——————. *Art in the Hellenistic Age.* Cambridge, Eng.: Cambridge University Press, 1986.

Strong, Donald. *Roman Art.* Harmondsworth: Penguin, 1988.

Ward-Perkins. J.B. *Roman Architecture.* New York: Abrams, 1977.

——————. *Roman Imperial Architecture.* Harmondsworth: Penguin, 1981.

MEDIEVAL

Conant, Kenneth J. *Carolingian and Romanesque Architecture.* Harmondsworth: Penguin, 1978.

Davis-Weyer, C. *Early Medieval Art 300–1150* (Sources and Documents). Englewood Cliffs, N.J.: Prentice-Hall, 1971.

Ettinghausen, Richard, and Oleg Grabar. *The Art and Architecture of Islam, 650–1250.* New York: Viking Penguin, 1987.

Frisch, T.G. *Gothic Art 1140–ca. 1450* (Sources and Documents). Toronto: University of Toronto Press, 1987.

Grodecki, Louis. *Gothic Architecture.* New York: Abrams, 1977.

Hearn, M.F. *Romanesque Sculpture.* Ithaca: Cornell University Press, 1981.

Huntington, Susan. *Art of Ancient India: Buddhist, Hindu, Jain.* New York: Weatherhill, 1985.

Krautheimer, Richard. *Early Christian and Byzantine Architecture.* Harmondsworth: Penguin, 1986.

Mango, Cyril. *The Art of the Byzantine Empire 312–1453* (Sources and Documents). Englewood Cliffs, N.J.: Prentice-Hall, 1972.

——————. *Byzantium.* London: Weidenfeld and Nicolson, 1980.

——————. *Byzantine Architecture.* New York: Rizzoli, 1985.

Snyder, James. *Medieval Art: Painting Sculpture Architecture 4th–14th Century.* New York: Abrams, 1989.

Stokstad, Marilyn. *Medieval Art.* New York: Harper & Row, 1986.

Swaan, Wim. *The Gothic Cathedral.* New York: Park Lane, 1981.

White, John. *Art and Architecture in Italy, 1250–1400.* Harmondsworth: Penguin, 1987.

Wilson, David M. *Anglo-Saxon Art from the Seventh Century to the Norman Conquest.* Woodstock, N.Y.: Overlook Press, 1984.

FIFTEENTH AND SIXTEENTH CENTURIES

Cole, Bruce. *The Renaissance Artist at Work.* New York: Harper & Row, 1983.

Gilbert, Creighton. *Italian Art 1400–1500* (Sources and Documents). Englewood Cliffs, N.J.: Prentice-Hall, 1980.

Hartt, Frederick. *History of Italian Renaissance Art*. New York: Abrams, 1987.

Heydenreich, Ludwig, and W. Lotz. *Architecture in Italy 1400–1600*. Baltimore: Penguin, 1974.

Klein, Robert, and Henri Zerner. *Italian Art, 1500–1600* (Sources and Documents). Englewood Cliffs. N.J.: Prentice-Hall, 1966.

Rosand, David. *Painting in Cinquecento Venice: Titian, Veronese, Tintoretto*. New Haven: Yale University Press, 1986.

Snyder, James. *Northern Renaissance Art*. New York: Abrams, 1985.

Stechow, Wolfgang. *Northern Renaissance Art 1400–1600* (Sources and Documents). Englewood Cliffs, N.J.: Prentice-Hall, 1966.

Wittkower, Rudolf. *Architectural Principles in the Age of Humanism*. New York: St. Martin, 1988.

SEVENTEENTH AND EIGHTEENTH CENTURIES

Blunt, Anthony. *Art and Architecture in France 1500–1700*. Harmondsworth: Penguin, 1973.

Crow, Thomas E. *Painters and Public Life in Eighteenth-Century Paris*. New Haven: Yale University Press, 1985.

Enggass, Robert, and Jonathan Brown. *Italy and Spain 1600–1750* (Sources and Documents). Englewood Cliffs, N.J.: Prentice-Hall, 1970.

Gerson, H., and E.H. ter Kuile. *Art and Architecture in Belgium 1600–1800*. Baltimore: Penguin, 1978.

Haskell, Francis. *Patrons and Painters: A Study in the Relations Between Italian Art and Society in the Age of the Baroque*. New Haven: Yale University Press, 1980.

Held, Julius, and Donald Posner. *Seventeenth and Eighteenth Century Art: Baroque Painting, Sculpture, Architecture*. New York: Abrams, 1971.

Rosenberg, Jakob, Seymour Slive, and E.H. ter Kuile. *Dutch Art and Architecture 1600–1800*. Harmondsworth: Penguin, 1977.

Schama, Simon. *The Embarrassment of Riches: An Interpretation of Dutch Culture in the Golden Age*. New York: Knopf, 1987.

Varriano, John. *Italian Baroque and Rococo Architecture*. New York: Oxford University Press, 1986.

Wittkower, Rudolf. *Art and Architecture in Italy 1600 to 1750*. Harmondsworth: Penguin, 1973.

NINETEENTH AND TWENTIETH CENTURIES

Arnason, H.H. *History of Modern Art*. New York: Abrams, 1986.

Baigell, Matthew. *A Concise History of American Painting and Sculpture*. New York: Harper & Row, 1984.

Boimé, Albert. *A Social History of Modern Art*. Chicago: University of Chicago Press, 1987.

Clark, T.J. *Image of the People: Gustave Courbet and the 1848 Revolution*. Princeton: Princeton University Press, 1982.

——————. *The Painting of Modern Life: Paris in the Art of Manet and His Followers*. Princeton: Princeton University Press, 1986.

Curtis, William J.R. *Modern Architecture Since 1900*. Englewood Cliffs, N.J.: Prentice-Hall, 1983.

Daval, Jean-Luc. *Photography: History of an Art*. New York: Rizzoli, 1982.

Eitner, Lorenz. *Neoclassicism and Romanticism 1750–1850* (Sources and Documents). Englewood Cliffs, N.J.: Prentice-Hall, 1970.

——————. *An Outline of 19th Century European Painting: From David Through Cézanne*. New York: Harper & Row, 1987.

Fry, Edward. *Cubism*. London: Thames and Hudson, 1966.

Gaggi, Silvio. *Modern-Postmodern: A Study in Twentieth-Century Arts and Ideas*. Philadelphia: University of Pennsylvania Press, 1989.

Hamilton, George H. *Nineteenth and Twentieth Century Art*. Englewood Cliffs, N.J.: Prentice-Hall, 1971.

——————. *Painting and Sculpture in Europe 1880–1940*. Baltimore: Penguin, 1981.

Herbert, Robert L. *Modern Artists on Art*. Englewood Cliffs, N.J.: Prentice-Hall, 1964

——————. *Impressionism*. New Haven: Yale University Press, 1988.

Holt, Elizabeth G. *From the Classicists to the Impressionists*. Garden City, N.Y.: Doubleday, 1966.

Hopi Kachina, Spirit of Life. The California Academy of Sciences. Seattle: distributed by University of Washington Press, 1980.

Hughes, Robert. *The Shock of the New*. New York: Knopf, 1981.

Hunter, Sam, and John Jacobus. *Modern Art: Painting, Sculpture, Architecture*. New York: Abrams, 1985.

Janson, H.W. *19th-Century Sculpture*. New York: Abrams, 1985.

Levin, Kim. *Beyond Modernism: Essays on Art from the '70s to '80s*. New York: Harper & Row, 1988.

Lucie-Smith, Edward. *Movements in Art Since 1945*. New York: Thames and Hudson, 1984.

——————. *American Art Now*. New York: Morrow, 1985.

McCoubrey, John. *American Art 1700–1960*. (Sources and Documents). Englewood Cliffs, N.J.: Prentice-Hall, 1965.

Newhall, Beaumont. *The History of Photography, from 1839 to the Present Day*. New York: Museum of Modern Art, 1982.

Nochlin, Linda. *Impressionism and Post-Impressionism* (Sources and Documents). Englewood Cliffs, N.J.: Prentice-Hall, 1966.

——————. *Realism and Tradition in Art 1848–1900* (Sources and Documents). Englewood Cliffs, N.J.: Prentice-Hall, 1966

Rewald, John. *Post-Impressionism: From Van Gogh to Gauguin*. New York: Museum of Modern Art; Boston: distributed by New York Graphic Society, 1978.

——————. *The History of Impressionism*. New York: Museum of Modern Art; Boston: distributed by New York Graphic Society, 1980.

——————. *Studies in Impressionism*. New York: Abrams, 1986.

——————. *Studies in Post-Impressionism*. New York: Abrams, 1986.

Rosenblum, Robert, and H.W. Janson. *Nineteenth-Century Art*. New York: Abrams, 1984.

Selz, Peter. *Art in Our Times*. New York: Abrams, 1981.

Smagula, Howard. *Currents, Contemporary Directions in the Visual Arts*. Englewood Cliffs, N.J.: Prentice-Hall, 1983.

Thompson, Robert Farris. *African Art in Motion: Icon and Act*. Los Angeles: University of California Press, 1974.

Wheeler, Daniel. *Art Since Mid-Century*. Englewood Cliffs, N.J.: Prentice-Hall, 1988.

Wilmerding, John. *American Art*. Harmondsworth: Penguin, 1976.

INDEX

Page numbers are in roman type. Figure numbers appear in *italics*. Names of artists and architects whose works are reproduced in this book are in CAPITALS and their nationalities indicated.

Aachen, Germany: Palace Chapel 180; *174*
Abbey in an Oak Forest (FRIEDRICH) 382–83; *413*
Abbot Suger's Chalice (Gothic) 197; *193*
Abdu'r-Rahman (Muslim ruler) 176
Abstract Expressionism 438, 492, 494, 498, 503; *537–39*
Abu Simbel, Egypt: Temple of Ramesses II 52; *32*
Academic Art 30, 354–55, 374, 390, 392–93, 403, 408, 426; *425, 426*
Accademia del Disegno, Florence 269
Achilles and Ajax Playing Draughts (EXEKIAS) 76; *65*
Acropolis, Athens 72, 88; *64*. *See also* Parthenon
Action Painting 494; *537, 539*
Ad Parnassum (KLEE) 468–69; *510*
ADAM, ROBERT (English) 301; Osterley Park House 351; *375*
Adam and Eve (DÜRER) 274; *284, 288*
African art 452; artists 31, 452; Bobo masks 450, 452–53; *492–94*; influence of 447, 448, 453, 467, 470, 488
Akhenaten (pharaoh) 51, 53; *31*
Akhenaten with Nefertiti (Egyptian relief) 51; *31*
ALBERS, JOSEF (American) 500, 501; *Homage to the Square: Affectionate* 500; *545*
Alberti, Leon Battista: *On Architecture* 255; *On Painting* 220, 233, 236–37, 253; *On Sculpture* 35–36
Alexander the Great 52, 73, 75, 95, 97, 299; portrait bust of 96; *91*
Alexandria, Egypt 95, 130, 196
Alfred Lord Tennyson (CAMERON) 403; *440*
Allegheny County Courthouse, Pittsburgh (RICHARDSON) 398–99; *433*
Allegorical Portrait of Mrs. Siddons (REYNOLDS) 360–61; *389*
Allegory of the Outbreak of War (RUBENS) 322–23; *343*
Allegory of Time and Lust (BRONZINO) 296; *341*
Alloway, Lawrence 504
Altamira, Spain 35
Altar of Peace (Ara Pacis), Rome 112; *107*
Altar of Zeus and Athena, Pergamon 99; *94*
Altarpiece of the Lamb (Ghent Altarpiece) (VAN EYCK) 235; *234–35*
ALTDORFER, ALBRECHT (German): *Battle of Alexander* 299; *318*
Amarna period, Egypt 51–52, 53
Amenhotep III (pharaoh) 60, 61
American Indians (*see also* Pre-Columbian art) 455–57, 519; *495–97*
Amiens, France: Cathedral 202; *205;* sculpture 206, 207; *204, 207*
amphitheaters, Roman 112–13, 124–25; *121–23*
Amsterdam 307, 308, 326, 327, 474–75
Amun (Egyptian god) 60; Temple of, Karnak 60–61; *46*
Amun-Mut-Khonsu, Temple of, Luxor 60; *45, 49*
Analytical Cubism 460–61; *501–2*
anatomy 251, 259, 264; *15, 261*
Ancestors of Christ (Gothic sculpture) 207; *206*
ancient civilizations 42–135; art 45–65; *68–135*; artists 46–47; history 44–45. *See also* Egypt; Etruscans; Greece; Hellenistic art; Pre-Columbian art; Roman Republic and Empire; Sumer, Sumerians
Andokides Painter 76
Anglo-Saxon art 163, 187; *158*
Animal Hunt (Çatal Hüyük) 37; *20*
Ankhaf (Egyptian official) 53; *34*

Annunciation (CAMPIN) 228–29; *226–27*
Annunciation (GRÜNEWALD) 291; *307*
Annunciation (manuscript painting) 197–99; *195*
ANTHEMIUS OF TRALLES (Byzantine): Hagia Sophia, Constantinople 156–57; *152–54*
Anubis (Egyptian god) 52
apartment houses, Ostia 112; *108*
Apelles (Greek painter) 75
Aphrodite (Greek goddess) 117
Aphrodite of Knidos (copy) (PRAXITELES) 92–93; *89*
Apocalyptic Vision of Christ (manuscript painting) 179; *173*
Apollo (Greek god) 70, 404, 405
Apollo and Daphne (BERNINI) 19–21, 315; *3*
Apollo and the Battle of the Lapiths and Centaurs (Greek sculpture) 70–71, 217; *60*
Aquinas, Thomas: *Summa Theologica* 197
Ara Pacis, Rome 112; *107*
Arabia 153, 174, 175, 177
Arc de Triomphe, Paris (CHALGRIN, et al.) 376, 381; *405, 411*
Arcadian Shepherds (POUSSIN) 340–41; *365*
Archaic period, in Greece 71, 75, 76, 78; *61, 65, 68, 69*
ARCHIPENKO, ALEXANDER (Russian): *Walking Woman* 470; *514*
architectural sculpture 90–91, 190–91, 206–7, 224–25, 381, 404; *84–87, 134, 184–86, 204–7, 222–23, 411, 441*
architecture 26–27, 29–30; American Indian 457; *497;* Assyrian 68–69; Baroque 310–11, 312, 313, 325, 328–29, 344–45; *345, 348–50, 369;* Buddhist 101–2, 166–67, 168; *95, 97, 161–62;* Byzantine 156–58, 161, 193, 209; *152–57, 189;* Carolingian 180, 182, 188; *174, 175;* Chinese 166, 167; classical orders, 81; *71;* Early Christian 150–51, 188, 209; *145–48;* Early Renaissance 230, 242–44, 255, 490; *242–46, 267;* Egyptian 51, 58–62; *40, 42–47, 49–50;* Flemish 218; Gothic 63, 194–95, 197, 199, 200, 242, 243; *191–96–205;* Greek 71–72, 75, 81–83, 88–89; *63–64, 71–74, 80–83;* Hellenistic 99; *94;* High Renaissance 278–79, 301; *290–92, 321–22;* Islamic 156, 176–77; *153, 168–70;* Japanese 166–67, 168; *161–62;* Mannerist 294–95; *312;* Neoclassical 362–63, 374, 376, 387; *390–92, 405;* 19th-century 373, 386–87, 394–99, 428–29; *418–20, 427–34, 466–67;* Persian 68, 69; *58;* prehistoric 36; *54, 55;* Rococo 358–59; *383–84;* Roman 81, 107–9, 113, 124–31, 244; *100–102, 108–9, 111, 121–32;* Romanesque 183, 188–89, 209; *176, 181–83;* Romantic 374, 386–87, 388; *418–20;* Sumerian 57; *39;* 20th-century 458–59, 474–77, 490–91, 496–97, 510–11, 520–21; *498–500, 517–19, 535–36, 540–41, 558–59, 569–70;* Victorian 375, 398; *432*
Arch of Titus, Rome 114; *111, 112*
Arena Chapel frescoes (GIOTTO) 212–13; *212–14*
Aristotle 74, 95, 96–97, 284
Arles, France 420, 422, 424
Armat, Thomas 440
Armory Show, N.Y.C. (1913) 464
Arnolfini Wedding Portrait (VAN EYCK) 238, 240; *238, 240–41*
ARP, JEAN (HANS) (Swiss): *Collage with Squares Arranged According to the Laws of Chance* 473; *516*
Arrangement in Black and Gray (WHISTLER) 413; *452*
Arrival of Marie de' Medici (RUBENS) 322; *342*
art: analysis of 18–21; in ancient civilizations 45–46; prehistoric origins of 35–36
art academies (*see also* Academic Art) 30, 115, 173, 269, 315, 342, 354–55, 374
art exhibitions (*see also* Independent Exhibitions; salons) 369, 373, 405, 415
Artist Drawing a Lute (DÜRER) 249; *258*

artists (*see also* avant-garde artists; women artists) 28–30; African 31, 452; in ancient societies 46; Anglo-Saxon 163, 164; Baroque 315, 342–43; Byzantine 154; Chinese 30–31, 46, 142, 172–73; Early Christian 148; Egyptian 53; 18th-century 354–55; Gothic 199; Greek 28, 46, 75, 113; medieval 29, 141–42, 183, 269; 19th-century 373, 375, 417; Pre-Columbian 135; prehistoric 38–39; Renaissance 30, 223, 240–41, 269, 302–3, 375, 439; Roman 113, 116–17; Romanesque 185, 187; 20th-century 442–43
art market 198, 315, 342, 373
Art Nouveau style 372, 375, 477
art theory 30, 220–21, 269, 342
Arts and Crafts Movement 372, 375, 477
As I Opened Fire (LICHTENSTEIN) 504; *551*
ASAM, EGID (German): *Assumption of the Virgin* 359; *385*
Asoka (king of India) 103, 167
Assemblage works 440, 463, 472, 502, 518; *480, 515, 548*
Assumption and Coronation of the Virgin (TITIAN) 292; *309*
Assumption of the Virgin (ASAM) 359; *385*
Assyrians 56; art 68–69; *56–57*
astronomy 66–68, 134, 135, 139, 177, 264, 353
At the Moulin Rouge (TOULOUSE-LAUTREC) 373; *399*
Athena (Greek goddess) 72; Altar of, Pergamon 99; *94;* cult statue of (PHIDIAS) 88, 90; *83;* on Parthenon pediment sculptures (PHIDIAS) 90–91; *85–86;* Temple of, Paestum 72
ATHENODOROS (Greek): *Laocoön* 115–16; *114*
Athens, Greece 72–73, 88, 218, 354, 387. *See also* Acropolis
Attalus I (king of Pergamon) 98–99
Augustine of Canterbury 163
Augustus (emperor of Rome) 107, 110–12, 114; *Res Gestae* 112; statue of 110–11; *106*
Augustus Prima Porta (Roman sculpture) 110–11; *106*
Austria 351, 435
Autobiography (Cellini) 269
Autobiography (St. Teresa) 330, 331
Autobiography of an Idea (Sullivan) 396, 397
automatism 485, 492; *539*
Autun, France: Cathedral 191; *186*
avant-garde artists: in the 19th century 30, 373, 412, 421; in the 20th century 436, 438, 439, 463, 464, 468, 470, 477, 482, 494, 498, 513, 519. *See also* Bauhaus; Dada artists; De Stijl
Avenue of the Dead, Teotihuacán 132, 134
Aztec culture 139, 274, 443

Bacchic Mysteries (Roman fresco) 121–22; *117, 118*
Bacchus (Roman god), 117, 121, 122. *See also* Dionysus
Bacon, Francis 310
Balboa, Vasco Nuñez de 263–64
Baldacchino (BERNINI) 324; *344*
Baldinucci, Filippo 336
BALDOVINETTI, ALESSO (Italian): *Portrait of a Young Woman* 247; *250*
Ball, Hugo 472–73
BALLA, GIACOMO (Italian): *Speeding Automobile* 434, 435, 465; *470*
balloon-frame construction 397
Balzac, Honoré de: monument to (RODIN) 416–17; *456*
Banjo Lesson (TANNER) 415; *454*
Banquet of Officers (HALS) 326; *346*
barbarians 74, 90, 118, 185, 197
Baroque art (*see also* Baroque Classicism) 310–11, 313–14; architecture 310–11, 312, 313, 315,

LIST OF CREDITS

The authors and publishers wish to thank the museums, galleries, libraries, and churches for permitting the reproduction of works of art in their collections. Photographs have been supplied by the owners or custodians of the works of art, except for the following, whose courtesy is gratefully acknowledged. Numbers refer to the illustrations.

Peter Aaron/ESTO: 474; Harry N. Abrams, Inc., archives, N.Y.: 10, 18, 117, 161, 162, 234, 235, 271, 303; Agence TOP, Paris, Michel Desjardins: 256; Alinari, Florence: 3, 59, 60, 78, 93, 104, 106, 112, 144, 189, 219, 221–23, 229, 236, 242, 244, 245, 255, 257, 273, 283, 295, 312, 313, 316, 328, 337, 344, 348, 350; Ancient Art and Architecture Collection, London: 118; Fred Anderegg (by permission of Princeton University Press): 140, 141; Wayne Andrews/ESTO: 374, 375, 420; Annan, Glasgow: 459; Ferdinand Anton, Munich: 134; James Austin: 186; Dirk Baaker: 479; Bauhaus Archiv, Berlin © 1969: 519; Peter Becker: 559; Bibliothèque Nationale, Paris: 415, 416; Hedrich Blessing, Chicago: 11, 12, 466, 498; Victor Boswell © National Geographic Society: 268, 269; British Museum, London: 15; British Tourist Authority, N.Y.: 54, 418; F. Bruckmann, Munich: 279; Busch-Reisinger Museum, Harvard University, Cambridge, Mass.: 488; Caisse Nationale des Monuments Historiques et des Sites, Paris: 181, 183–85, 199, 207, 441; Ludovico Canali, Rome: 4, 98, 109, 110, 119, 122, 210, 211, 213, 217, 228, 300, 324, 333, 335, 351; Eugenio Cassin, Florence: 237; Chicago Architectural Photo Co.: 500; Chicago Historical Society: 430; Geoffrey Clements, N.Y.: 476; Piero Codato, Cameraphoto, Venice: 214, 308, 309, 323; Michael D. Coe, Mexico © 1962, 1966: 135; Kenneth J. Conant, Cluny © 1968: 176; A.C. Cooper, Ltd., London: 332; Jeffrey Crespi: 495; Deutsche Fotothek, Dresden: 423; Deutschen Archäologischen Institut, Rome: 99, 103, 107, 148; Deutscher Kunstverlag, Munich: 383; Doesser Fotos, Laren, Neth.: 517; Edmund B. Feldman, Thinking About Art © 1985: 84, 200; Fotocielo, Rome: 345; Fotostudio C.N.B., Bologna: 215, 278; Fototeca Unione, Rome: 100, 108, 116, 129–31; Framton and Futugawa, Modern Architecture 1851–1945 © 1931, 1983: 431; Alfred Frazer and Henry A. Millon, Key Monuments of Architecture © 1965: 73, 115; French Tourist Board, N.Y.: 55, 432; Gabinetto Fotografico, Florence: 298; Gabinetto Fotografico Nazionale, Rome: 325; Ewing Galloway, N.Y.: 41; GEMS, N.Y.: 153; Giraudon, Paris: 205, 206, 225, 264, 341, 376; Barbara Gladstone Gallery, N.Y.: 562; Gianfranco Gorgoni, N.Y.: 556; Guernica/Pablo Picasso © 1947: 531; Susan Harder Gallery, N.Y.: 525; Cyril M. Harris, History of Architecture Sourcebook © 1977: 123; Frederick Hartt, Art: A History of Painting, Sculpture, and Architecture © 1989: 43, 44, 49; Biff Heinrich: 537; Greg Heinz: 311; Color Photo Hinz, Alschwil-Basel, Switz.: 17, 22; Hirmer Verlag Munchen: 29, 35, 39, 40, 45, 62, 68–70, 75, 76, 82, 88, 91, 142, 155; Hirschl & Adler Modern, N.Y.: 554; HOA-QUA, Paris: 492–94; Stephen Huyler: 96; Irish Historical Series © 1977: 209; Italian State Tourist Office, N.Y.: 121; H.W. Janson, History of Art © 1986: 128; Thomas Jefferson Memorial Foundation, Inc.: 392; S.W. Kenyon, Wellington, Eng.: 19; Kurt Lange: 36; E. Levy, Paris: 405; Library of Congress, Washington, D.C.: 419, 428; Life Picture Service, N.Y.: 526; MAGNUM Photos, N.Y.: 527; Bildarchiv Foto Marburg, Marburg, Ger.: 32, 174, 202, 385; Gene Markowski: 95; Matar Studio, N.Y.: 549; Robert Mates: 1, 501; MAS, Barcelona: 216, 304; Photo Mayer, Vienna: 315, 317; Louis K. Meisel Gallery, N.Y.: 561; James Mellart, Çatal Hüyük, 1967: 20; The Metropolitan Museum of Art, N.Y.: 284, 286, 294; Michigan-Princeton-Alexandria Expedition to Mt. Sinai © 1969: 151; Robert Miller Gallery, N.Y.: 485; Allan Mitchell, New Canaan, Conn.: 509; Collection, The Museum of Modern Art, N.Y.: 456; The Pierpont Morgan Library, N.Y.: 359; Hans Namuth, N.Y.: 539; National Gallery of Art, Washington, D.C.: 190, 416; Prints Division, New York Public Library, Astor, Lenox and Tilden Foundations: 285; Hans Petersen, Hornbaek, Den.: 487; Eric Pollitzer: 293; Mario Quattrone, Florence: 218, 263, 277, 280, 302, 343; Lois Fichner Rathus, Understanding Art © 1989: 145, 146, 201; Gerhard Reinhold, Leipzig-Molkan: 301; Rijksmuseum, Amsterdam: 361; Roget-Viollet, Paris: 397; Jean Roubier: 125; Routhier, Paris: 444; Scala, Rome: 92, 156, 157, 262, 281, 299, 327; Service Photographiques Reunion des Musées Nationaux, Paris: 56, 90, 194, 251, 276, 282, 342, 356, 365, 366, 380, 396, 410, 424, 435, 436, 452; Smithsonian Institution, Washington, D.C.: 496; Society for the Preservation of New England Antiquities, Boston: 7; Holly Solomon Gallery, N.Y.: 480; Ezra Stoller/ESTO: 536; Wim Swaan, N.Y.: 204, 208; C.Z. Swiechowski: 182; Marvin Trachtenberg, N.Y.: 9, 63, 72, 111, 113, 152, 168, 169, 191, 197, 321, 429, 540; U.S. Department of Agriculture: 497; Jean Vertut, Paris: 33; Vincent van Gogh Foundation/National Museum Vincent van Gogh, Amsterdam: 398; Virginia Chamber of Commerce: 390; Vizzavona, Paris: 369, 370; Leonard von Matt, Buochs, Switz.: 178; Achille Weider, Zurich: 23; Etienne Weill, Israel: 478, 558; Kurt Weitzmann, Department of Art and Archaeology, Princeton University: 149; David G. Wilkins: 247, 249, 253; Howard Wise Gallery, N.Y.: 555; ZEFA, Dusseldorf: 133.

Diagrams 13, 47, 66, 71, 74, 77, 79, 86, 239, 289, 360, 417, and 438 by Marlene Boyle.

Maps by Paul J. Pugliese.

The authors and publishers wish to acknowledge the following publications, from which quotations were taken: p. 20: Ovid, Metamorphoses, trans. by R. Humphries, Bloomington: Indiana University Press, 1969; p. 72: Susan Woodford, The Parthenon, Cambridge, Eng.: Cambridge University Press, 1981; p. 259: Giorgio Vasari, Lives of the Most Eminent Painters, Sculptors and Architects, trans. by Gaston Du C. de Vere, New York: Harry N. Abrams, Inc., 1979. All rights reserved; p. 271: Giorgio Vasari, The Lives of the Artists, vol. 1, trans. by George Bull, Harmondsworth: Penguin Classics, 1987. © George Bull, 1965; p. 354: Sir Joshua Reynolds, Fifteen Discourses Delivered in the Royal Academy, New York: E.P. Dutton, 1911; pp. 364, 390, 391, 417, 444, 478: Robert Goldwater and Marco Treves, Artists on Art: From the XIV—XX Century, New York: Pantheon Books. © 1945 by Pantheon Books, Inc. Renewed 1973 by Goldwater and Treves. By permission of Pantheon books, a division of Random House, Inc.; pp. 405, 409, 410, 411: Translation from Charles S. Moffett et al., The New Painting: Impressionism 1874–1886. © 1986 by The Fine Arts Museums of San Francisco. Reprinted with permission; p. 280: Translation by Creighton Gilbert, from Complete Poems and Selected Letters of Michelangelo, Princeton: Princeton University Press, 1980.